Gascony & the Pyrenees

a photo essay

1 Pine forest, Les Landes

2
3
4

2 Mountains, Bagnères-de-Luchon
3 Woodland, Girons
4 Dune du Pilat, Arcachon
5 Cinque at Bourns-du-Port, Bagnères-de-Luchon

6 La Bastide-Clairence
7 Gascon village

8
9

8 Air-drying maize
9 Les Landes
10 Geese, Gascony
12 Pottok ponies

12 Cirque de Lescun

13
14
COIFFURE

13 Lourdes
14 Pelote players, St-Etienne-de-Baïgorry
15 Harbour, St-Jean-de-Luz

16

16 Biarritz
17 Sauveterre-de-Béarn

18

18 St-Jean-Pied-de-Port

Dana Facaros and
Michael Pauls

GASCONY & THE PYRENEES

'When King Henri IV was born,
his grandfather rubbed the baby's lips
with a little garlic and some
Jurançon wine, just to make sure he
started out in life as a proper Gascon.'

CADOGANguides

Contents

Maps

About the authors

Dana Facaros and Michael Pauls live in an old presbytère in southwest France, overlooking a cemetery.

About the updater

Kate Read and her husband left the pressures of London for the peace of a farmhouse in southwest France, and have lived there for the past 12 years with their two sons. Kate is involved with "La Troupe d'Acteurs de Quercy" and she is currently working on her first book.

Acknowledgements

Kate would like to thank her husband, Victor, for his typing skills and patient support, to all the lovely ladies in remote tourist offices who were a mine of local information, to Isabelle and Simon Browne for their kind hospitality and to the authors, for being true friends.

Cadogan Guides
Highlands House, 165 The Broadway, Wimbledon, SW19 1NE
info@cadoganguides.co.uk
www.cadoganguides.com

The Globe Pequot Press
246 Goose Lane, PO Box 480, Guilford, Connecticut 06437–0480

Updated by Kate Read
Photo credits: Cover: front © Jon Arnold Images, back © John Ferro Sims. Photo essay: 1, 6, 7, 10, 17, 18 © John Miller; 2, 3, 9, 15 © John Ferro Sims; 4 © Travel Ink/Jeremy Philips; 5, 12 © Travel Ink/Marc Dublin; 8 © ICCE/H. Reece; 11 © Travel Ink/David Martyn Hughes; 13 © Travel Ink/Mike Politt; 14, 16 © ICCE/Archie Groom.
Maps © Cadogan Guides, drawn by Map Creation Ltd
Managing Editor: Antonia Cunningham
Editor: Matthew Tanner
Proofreading: Sheilagh Wilson
Indexing: Isobel McLean
Production: Navigator Guides
Printed in Italy by Legoprint
A catalogue record for this book is available from the British Library
ISBN 1-86011-154-8

Please help us to keep this guide up to date. We have done our best to ensure that the information in this guide is correct at the time of going to press. But places and facilities are constantly changing, and standards and prices in hotels and restaurants fluctuate. We would be delighted to receive any comments concerning existing entries or omissions. Authors of the best letters will receive a copy of the Cadogan Guide of their choice.

Introduction

For proof that France's southwestern corner is an exceptional place, one need look no further than the cartoon pictures in our children's old atlas: a graceful Basque pelote player dressed all in white, arching his long chistera at the ball, an izard perched atop a Pyrenean peak looking down at a mountain-climber, a mustachioed musketeer in a costume from the time of Louis XIII. For the Landes, there's an old-time shepherd on stilts, next to a stocky Gascon farmer in a beret with his geese. In short, this corner of France has character. And in a beautiful region that the disfiguring stresses of history and economics have passed over lightly, such character can be explored at leisure. Gascony is the perfect place for lazy touring, a place where nearly all the roads seem to be back roads, and where every village has its welcoming *auberge*; more likely than not this will include a restaurant where *madame* cooks up duck and game and other hearty dishes Parisians would die for. Besides the famous scenery and its multitude of other attractions, Gascony and the Basque lands, including the vibrant city of Toulouse, are home to some of France's finest *cuisine du terroir*, not to mention the seafood of the Bay of Biscay, and truly excellent wines.

The presiding angel of Gascony is Good King Henri – Henri IV – the Gascon, who three centuries ago saved the country from its religious squabbling and taught Frenchmen, with a joke and a smile, to take it easy and enjoy life rather than slaughter each other over abstractions. The basis of Henri's policy is expressed in a quote that everyone still remembers: he wished every Frenchman to have a chicken in the pot on Sundays. The stories say he liked to sneak down to the palace kitchens to see how his own *poule au pot* was cooking, and didn't mind helping chop up the vegetables. Thanks to Henri, perhaps, that part of the Gascon mystique is still very present: the sense of contentment simple pleasures can bring.

Fashions in holiday playgrounds come and go. Nobody now remembers that France's southwestern corner was, a century ago, the most popular holiday destination in the land, that Queen Victoria came to Biarritz or that the English laid out the continent's first golf course at Pau. The relics of the joys the Second Empire and the Belle Epoque knew can still be seen on every side: gracefully ageing '*grands hôtels*' and gardens, and the fantastical architecture of the old casinos and bath establishments, along with mountain refuges that recall the memory of the great Pyrenean explorers such as Henry Russell. For a long time, the region was eclipsed by flashier upstarts, notably Provence and the Côte d'Azur. But the long hiatus gave the far southwest some breathing space, allowing it to perfect its charm while sparing it the overbuilding and overpopulation of so many other holiday centres. The time for rediscovery is at hand; few parts of France have so much to offer.

40 km
40 miles
N
Bay of Biscay
GIRONDE
Arcachon
06 THE LANDES
LANDES
Mont-de-Marsan
Dax
BIARRITZ
DORDOGNE
LOT-ET-GARONNE
LOT
CANTAL
LOZÈRE
AVEYRON
TARN-ET-GARONNE
TARN
HÉRAULT
07 THE GERS
GERS
Auch
11 TOULOUSE
08 THE PAYS BASQUE
PYRÉNÉES ATLANTIQUES
09 BÉARN
Tarbes
Lourdes
10 THE HIGH PYRENEES
HAUTES-PYRÉNEES
HAUTE-GARONNE
AUDE
Foix
ARIÈGE
12 ARIÈGE, ANDORRA AND THE EASTERN PYRENEES
PERPIGNAN
ANDORRA
PYRÉNÉES ORIENTALES
SPAIN

A Guide to the Guide

For an area scarcely larger than Belgium, Gascony offers an amazing range of landscapes and climates. In the late spring, they'll be surfing in Biarritz while in the Pyrenees climbers will still be picking their way around patches of ice.

Gascony below the mountains divides neatly into the separate worlds of the Landes and the Gers. The **Landes** is a distinctive and thoroughly peculiar place. What was once a sandy wasteland has become Europe's biggest forest — a man-made one, a vast flat carpet of pines planted in the time of Napoleon III. The face it turns to the sea is a solid line of beaches, backing up into heaps like the massive Dune du Pilat, 300ft tall and still growing; beach resorts such as Arcachon and Hossegor-Capbreton provide welcome breaks among the lonely expanses of sea, sand and pines. The neighbouring department of the **Gers** is the picture of southwest France most people carry around: rich lands and sweet rivers, a country of geese and foie gras and vineyards destined to provide fine armagnac. The Gers is the homeland of D'Artagnan and the Musketeers, and its landmarks have changed little since the Middle Ages: rugged castles, abbeys and bastides, as well as the Renaissance art of Auch's great cathedral.

Looking over the Pyrenees, from west to east, we begin with the **Basque Lands**, a world in itself. Biarritz, St-Jean-de-Luz and Hendaye make up France's biggest and best-known Atlantic resort strip, but behind this glittering façade stretches the timeless preserve of Europe's oldest nation, with its unique language and folklore. The Basques hold on to their culture with remarkable tenacity, and as you drive through the lovely, neat-as-a-pin villages of the green Labourdin or Soule, you'll see them performing their dances and peculiar sports on any summer weekend.

The Basque country shares the department of Pyrénées-Atlantiques with an equally distinctive land: **Béarn**. For centuries, Béarn was a proudly independent state, and it retains memories of the good old days at King Henri's castle at Pau and in medieval towns like Salies-de-Béarn. In southern Béarn begins the long stretch of parallel Pyrenean valleys, each of which will easily take you to a distinctive part of the mountains. The Vallée d'Aspe and Vallée d'Ossau come first, where Pyrenean bears and eagles live on in the shadow of the majestic Pic du Midi.

The mountains have always played a dominating role in the life of the Gascons, so much so that the Gascon words for north and south are *dessous* and *dessus* – down and up. The array of mountain valleys continues into the heart of the chain, in the *département* of **Hautes-Pyrénées**. Lourdes is here, along with famous sights like the Cirque de Gavarnie and the gracious old spa resorts: Bagnères, Luchon, Cauterets.

Then, lest anyone should forget, there is **Toulouse**. If there's one thing that keeps southwest France from nodding off in its vats of goose fat and wine it is this big pink dynamo on the cutting edge of the 21st century.

There is another *département* in the centre of the chain, one not familiar to many. The sparsely populated **Ariège**, though, can show you surprises such as the wonderful palaeolithic cave art at Niaux and the cloud-castle of Montségur, mystical last refuge of the medieval heretic Cathars. The individual little mountain principality of Andorra may be irresistible as a trip out from Ariège, or you may prefer to continue to the eastern edge of the Pyrenees, and visit the historic Catalan city of Perpignan.

History

450,000–4000 BC

The dawn of history arrives in the Pyrenees, at a time when the rest of us are still snoring away

The Basques, the oldest nation of Europe, like to joke that when God created the first man, he got the bones from a Basque graveyard. No one knows for sure just how far back they go – only that someone, incredibly, must have been around even before them. For the areas around the Pyrenees are one of the oldest inhabited places on earth, and one of the cradles of human culture. The first European yet discovered, 'Tautavel Man', parked his carcass in a cave at the western end of the chain some 450,000 years ago. His possible successor, Neanderthal Man, was here too, as well as Cro-Magnon Man, who takes his name from the village in nearby Périgord where his remains were first discovered. The next and most spectacular human record begins with Mr Cro-Magnon's Palaeolithic era, *c.* 35,000 BC, and the first art in history. The most famous painted caves are in Périgord and northern Spain, but Gascony too has its share, at Niaux in the Ariège, Ustaritz in the Basque country, and several others. 'The infancy of art, not an art of infancy', as has been noted, Palaeolithic paintings combine masterful figurative drawing with a sophisticated turn of mind that often seems to share the aims and approaches of the art of our times.

Among the distinctions of the ancient artists in this area are the first known portrait, in the cave of Brassempouy in the Landes (Perigordian era, *c.* 35–30,000 BC), and the oldest work of sculpture ever found, a figurine of a goddess from Lespugue in the Haute-Garonne (Aurignacian era, *c.* 30–20,000 BC). This second period of Palaeolithic art was named after a Pyrenean village, Aurignac, where some of the first important finds were made. After a hiatus in the Solutrian era (*c.* 20–15,000 BC), when people concentrated more on perfecting stone tools and weapons, art made a great comeback in the fourth Palaeolithic period, the Magdalenian (*c.* 15–10,000 BC), represented in numerous Pyrenean caves (though few of them are open to visitors). The peoples responsible for this precocious art were probably largely nomadic, and as the last ice age slowly ended, they may well have gradually migrated northwards following the herds.

From then it's a long, dull wait until the next flowering of culture and Europe's first great civilization, in the Neolithic era. The result of a revolution in technology and culture that radiated outwards from the Middle East, the Neolithic world introduced agriculture, the domestication of animals, astronomy and building – their lasting monuments include dolmens, tumuli and menhirs. Neolithic peoples were great traders and liked to live near the sea or important rivers, and finds in the area of this book are limited to the Basque country in the far western Pyrenees. Their culture kept a remarkable unity across western Europe for some 3,000 years from 4000 to about 1000 BC. The metal-working cultures that replaced them often copied Neolithic forms, as in the small cromlechs (stone circles) found around the region, or the impressive burial tumuli in the Baronnies or near Bartrès, north of Lourdes. Both these sets of monuments lie close to one of Europe's oldest known roads, the 'Salt Road' that since

Neolithic times connected the Atlantic with the Mediterranean, passing by way of Salies-de-Béarn, Pau, Lourdes and St-Bertrand. Other important roads crossed the easiest passes of the Pyrenees: the 'Ténarèze', running from the Comminges up through the part of the Armagnac called by that name today, and another one passing through St-Jean-Pied-de-Port and up into the Landes.

4000 BC–AD 407

An agreeable people moves in to stay; the Romans muscle in and try to make serfs of them, with considerable success

Vascones, Gascons, Basques: the ways in which this simple name has been twisted about over the centuries provides a mirror for the obscure and often confusing history of this corner of France. It also provides a lesson in tenacity, with the intriguing suggestion by some French ethnologists that this region's history may have been unfolding with roughly the same cast of characters since the time of cave-painters.

'The Basques are like good women; they have no history.' So runs the old saying, but traces of habitation in the Basque lands go back at least 100,000 years, and somebody was painting on the walls of caves such as Ustaritz as early as 35,000 BC. Where did the Basques come in? The theories that they are related to the Palaeolithic people seem far-fetched; a more likely premise would be that they are the descendants of the Neolithic culture that arrived in these parts *c.* 4000 BC. Practically every word for common tools in Basque, Europe's oldest native language, comes from the ancient root *haiz*, meaning stone, even *haiztur*, scissors. The possibility of an identity between the Basques and the Iberians, the most ancient known inhabitants of Spain, is an open question.

About 800 BC, Celtic peoples started moving through the region, variously conquering or coexisting and intermarrying with the original peoples. When the Romans came, they found a nation they called *Ouasconum* or *Vascones* occupying much of the land between the rivers Ebro and Garonne, including almost all of the Pyrenees. Some of the names of the mixed Vascone-Celtic tribes are remembered in place names today: the *Bigerriones* (the Bigorre), the *Auscii* (Auch), *Tarbii* (Tarbes) and the *Garunni* (the Garonne River). Many of the outlandish names which so many Pyrenean villages have may also be of Basque origin, as far eastwards as the Mediterranean. If the *gaztelulak* are any evidence, the various tribes didn't always get along; the remains of these hilltop earthen forts are still a feature of the Basque country, which counts 242 of them.

The Roman conquest of Celts and Vascones did not happen all at once. Roman influence in southern Gaul was already felt in the 2nd century BC, following the Carthaginians, who probably stopped at Biarritz and other Atlantic harbours on their way up the important sea-trading route to Cornwall and its tin mines. In 71 BC, Roman control extended into the Comminges. Pompey passed through on a campaign against rebels in Spain that year and founded the city of Lugdunum Convenarum (St-Bertrand-de-Comminges), which was to be the metropolis of the northern flank of the mountains for centuries to come. For the final conquest, while Julius Caesar busied himself with stronger tribes to the north, his partner Crassus (a fantastically wealthy real-estate speculator who had gone into politics the Roman way, by purchasing a command, just as Caesar himself had done) was left with the job of subduing the southwest, which his legions managed without much fuss in 56, at a battle near Tartas in the Landes. Many of the Vascones escaped over the Pyrenees into the rugged country of northern Spain, where there was little the Romans could do about them.

For the next five centuries, the region made its way into classical civilization as Novempopulania, the 'land of nine tribes', organized as part of the Roman province of Aquitania. The old Salt Road became an even busier trading route, carrying the wine the Celts loved into the region, and then shipping it back the other way when Aquitanians found they could grow it themselves and undersell Provence and Italy. Most of the land fell into the hands of Roman speculators, or was parcelled out among the veterans of the legions, the usual Roman manner of pacifying and Romanizing new provinces in the west. Though Aquitania never became a prosperous, urbanized region like Italy or Provence, towns did appear and new technologies were introduced. The Romans, with their eternal obsession with taking the waters, developed nearly every thermal spring in Gaul, including Dax, Bagnerès, Luchon and a score of others. While most of the Celts seem to have easily assimilated into the new dispensation, the Vascones carried on in the Pyrenees, where the lack of roads made Roman control tenuous at the best of times, and so were able to resist Romanization and preserve their language and culture.

The average Aquitanian native might be excused for not appreciating Rome's contributions, for right from the beginning the Romans degraded most of their new subjects to the level of serfs. Rome's history, through Republic and Empire, is a story of the rich getting inexorably richer and everyone else losing what little they had, along with every last vestige of freedom and human dignity. By the 4th century AD, this process had reached its illogical extreme: nearly all the land in the province was owned by a handful of great families, who were able to build magnificent new villas for themselves, as at Montréal in the Gers and Montmaurin in the Haute-Garonne, even while the Empire was in permanent economic crisis and the towns were rotting away. When the end came for Rome, much of the Gaulish countryside was already in the hands of the *bagaudae*, outlaw bands who waged guerrilla war against the system; these were especially strong in Aquitania.

407–1000

In which the Vascones move back to the old homestead, and take in a pair of ill-mannered boarders named Frank and Norman

The fatal invasions came after 407. Both Vandals and Visigoths passed through the region, the former especially welcome among the common people for their policy of gaining support by smashing up the great villas and burning the tax rolls. After 420

Aquitania found itself part of the new Visigothic kingdom, with its capital at Toulouse, but this was not to last. The Franks whipped the Visigoths at the Battle of Vouillé in 507, and gained, if not control of Aquitania, at least the right to try to collect a little tribute from it. The new bosses distinguished themselves mainly by the destruction of Lugdunum Convenarum, after a revolt in 586, while the Visigoths retreated into Spain, where their kingdom was to last until the Arab conquest.

Now, this is where all the linguistic confusion comes in. Those Vascones who had fled the Romans and settled in Spain so long before now came into conflict with the Visigoths, and either were pushed back over the Pyrenees, or decided on their own to retake their old homeland, by then largely a wasteland. They reappeared on the northern side in the 580s, and people began calling the area as far north as the Garonne *Wasconia*, which somehow later got turned into Gascony. Those Vascones who lived in the western Pyrenees had already lapsed into complete independence. There was little incentive for any of the barbarian kingdoms to trouble them, and they were fierce enough to put up a good fight whenever it was necessary, specialists in guerrilla warfare and the mountain ambush. They have been there ever since, and are the people we call the Basques today.

In 602, the king of the Franks appointed a 'Duke of Aquitaine' and 'Duke of Wasconie', military overlords charged with bringing the entire area under closer control. The chronicles of the next two centuries tell a tale of continuous and spirited resistance on the part of the Vascones. A big surprise for both parties came when the Arabs roared through the mountains in the early 700s after their rapid conquest of Spain. Charles Martel, the Frankish mayor of the place, beat them decisively at Poitiers in 732, but they continued to hold parts of the Pyrenees, including the castle of Lourdes, for a long time after. After that, the Franks under their new Carolingian dynasty – headed by Charles' son Pepin the Short – came south in strength. The rebellious Duchy of Aquitaine, along the Atlantic coast, was brought into line in 774 after a bloody war of three decades, while the Vascones of the plains were finally and completely defeated in 781.

For Pepin's son Charlemagne, who harboured imperial ambitions that looked beyond the Pyrenees, the Vascones, or Basques, who held out in the mountains were a mere nuisance. The minor episode of Roland's ambush and death at Roncevalles in 778, later to inspire one of the most popular romances of the Middle Ages, was merely a chance for the Basques to get a little revenge on their hated enemy. Charlemagne was still warm in his grave when his overextended empire started to disintegrate. The troubles of the Franks gave the Vascones south of the Pyrenees a chance to regain their independence, and they founded a little state that would grow into the Kingdom of Navarre. Though the people of Navarre gradually traded their Basque language and culture for Spanish, the Kingdom would remain a major actor in the region's history for centuries to come.

North of the mountains, they weren't so lucky. Aquitaine and Gascony suffered the visitations of the most destructive barbarians of them all, the Vikings, or Normans. From the 840s they came raiding nearly every year, wrecking Bayonne in 862 and Eauze a decade later. Not until 982 did Duke Guilhem of Gascony finally convince them they weren't wanted, by destroying a big Norman force near Dax. By this time, the feudal pattern was set. The king of the Franks was just a bad dream somewhere up north, and besides Aquitaine and Gascony, the lesser vassals the Carolingians had created – the counts of Bigorre and Armagnac and Foix, and the viscounts of Béarn, among others – drifted into near-total independence. The arrangement makes history messy and complex, but it gave the southwest stability and some breathing space. After almost six centuries of terror, towns were growing again and churches began to spring up everywhere. By the magic year 1000, which everyone expected to bring the end of the world, medieval civilization was in fact well on its way.

1000–1259

Finally left in peace for a bit, Basques and Gascons tidy up the place and grow wealthy and happy in it

The dizzyingly rapid economic and cultural advances that created the medieval world are reflected even in this out-of-the-way corner of Europe. In the 12th century, new towns and villages were growing up everywhere around the castles (such places are called *castelnaux*; the Gers alone has over 200 of them), while monastic orders such as the Cistercians created new foundations and reclaimed land that had long lain waste. In the 1200s, expansion continued at an even faster rate. All over the south, forests were cleared and planned new towns, or *bastides*, were founded to house a burgeoning population that included many settlers from other regions, severely diluting the Basque element in Gascony north of the mountains and in the central Pyrenees. These areas joined the mainstream of the distinct, Occitan-speaking cultural world of the south. The busy traffic along the pilgrimage routes to Compostela gave an impetus to trade and cultural exchange, and the region benefited from proximity to culturally advanced Muslim Spain; influences from that direction ranged from the rediscovery of philosophy and learning to styles and methods in architecture. Most importantly, following the example of Spain, the troubadours of Provence and the southwest created modern Europe's first poetry.

Politically, the most important trend was the rise of the Duchy of Aquitaine. Under a long line of warlike dukes, all named Guilhem, Aquitaine grew to cover a fourth of what is now France, its dukes at most times more wealthy and powerful than the kings who were their nominal overlords. Guilhem VIII succeeded in adding the Duchy of Gascony to his dominions in 1058; Guilhem IX (1086–1127), who presided over Aquitaine at the height of its fortunes, was also one of the first troubadour poets. This Guilhem had a granddaughter, a beautiful and wilful woman whose life would be the stuff of romances, and whose career would change history: Eleanor of Aquitaine. Sole heir to the duchy, she married the French King Louis VII in 1137. The French thought they had picked the biggest feudal plum imaginable, but Eleanor's discontent with the cold, pious Louis led to a divorce and a more convivial marriage with Louis's mortal enemy: Henry Plantagenet, Duke of Anjou and soon to be Henry II, King of England. Along with Eleanor came the land, and for the next three centuries

Aquitaine would be a possession of the English crown. Despite high taxes to pay for their incessant wars, the English proved capable rulers; usually sympathetic to local concerns, they won a high degree of loyalty from the people of Aquitaine while they battled the French on every front for more lands.

Béarn, another durable and well-organized feudal state, provides a good example of how history worked in this period. Like Armagnac, destined later to be its mortal enemy, Béarn first appears in history with its conquest by Charlemagne and the appointment of a Frankish viscount. The position became hereditary, and the viscounts gradually grew accustomed to doing as they pleased, acknowledging the suzerainty of France (or Navarre) only when it suited them, and keeping in shape with endless trivial wars against the counts of Armagnac to the north. Throughout the Middle Ages, Béarn changed dynasties as often as it changed capitals (Lescar, Morlaas, Orthez and Pau all held that honour). Viscounts tended to be named Gaston – they were numbered by dynasties, so there are a few Gaston IIs and Gaston IIIs. One of them once remarked that he was in the position of 'a flea between two monkeys' – Béarn in those days never seemed too intimidated by its powerful neighbours; maybe he was thinking he could always bite whichever one he chose. On the other hand, the viscounts often had trouble asserting their authority within their own borders. The long tradition of mountaineer independence found its expression in the *For de Morlaas*, a charter of rights that Viscount Gaston IV was forced to proclaim in the early 11th century, typical of the sophisticated, liberal constitutional arrangements that governed Pyrenean life at the time.

As for the Basques, the Middle Ages meant a degree of freedom, but also an inexorable decline. As the medieval states that claimed Basque property – Navarre and the other Spanish kingdoms, England, Béarn and France – grew in wealth and power, there was increasingly little chance that an event like Roncevaux could be repeated. This was a world dominated by a feudal aristocracy, one made up of foreigners, the descendants of Germanic invaders and Roman landowners, and it is not surprising that the Basques never coalesced into a nation. In this period the Basques are practically invisible, their language merely the patois of countrymen, and nobody paid much mind to them. All through the Middle Ages, in fact, the Basque boundaries shrunk gradually, as the natives were either pushed out or assimilated by Spaniards, Gascons and Catalans. By the 1300s the Basque lands had contracted roughly to the boundaries they retain today.

1259–1530

In which the Gascons have fun and prosper through the Hundred Years' War, and then find they have to pay a price

After the 1259 Treaty of Paris, which stabilized the borders between English- and French-controlled lands, the two sides dug in for an uneasy peace. In an age when national consciousness and nation-states were dawning, feudal logic could not last: as dukes of Guyenne (from the English mispronunciation of Aquitaine), the English kings owed homage to the kings of France, a fine situation to be in whenever the two nations' interests were in conflict. The inevitable showdown came in 1337, and went into the books as the Hundred Years' War.

With England's early military successes, and Béarn's neutrality, the southwest was largely spared the terrors the war brought to France. By no means, though, did the Gascons care to keep out of the conflict. In his famous chronicles, Froissart echoed the prevailing opinion on the Gascons: '*Ils ne sont point estables*' – not a very stable lot, perhaps, but tremendous fighters when they were in the mood for it. With their own land relatively peaceful, Gascons picked up the habit of hiring themselves out as mercenaries for the English, the French or anybody else who could pay them, or who looked like a good bet for sacking towns and grabbing some swag. Gascons made up a majority in many of the *routier* bands that began terrorizing France in the 1350s – freebooters who went into business for themselves whenever the English and French had the effrontery to make a truce. Some of the Gascon captains were famous, such as Captal de Buch of the Landes.

Gascon mischief against the French was hardly limited to the *routiers*. In the early 1400s, just as it seemed that the long wars were finally dying down, France split up into factional conflicts, between the followers of the dukes of Burgundy and Orléans. Upon Orléans's assassination, leadership of his side fell to Count Bernard of Armagnac. 'Armagnacs' and 'Burgundians' spattered fresh blood all over France; by 1413 Count Bernard, allied with another Gascon, Constable of France Charles d'Albret, was in control of Paris and most of the country. A year later, Albret lay dead on the field of Agincourt; even after that climactic battle, though, the two factions continued to hate each other more than the English, permitting the occupation of Paris and the conquest of most of France by 1420. In the final phase of the war, however, the Gascons also contributed most of the troops that Joan of Arc inspired to victory – the English are recorded as calling her 'Jeanne l'Armagnacaise' in derision.

The departure of the English in the 1450s allowed France to extend its control over all of the southwest except Béarn. Only, this time, the French kings were not content with being mere feudal overlords. A typical example of the new policy was the destruction of the County of Armagnac in 1473. After unsuccessfully besieging the count at Lectoure, King Louis XI made an honorable peace with him – but when the gates were open, the French sacked the town and slaughtered the count along with his family; soon after, Armagnac became part of the royal domain.

French rule proved a disaster for Gascony, as in the rest of the south. Travelling over most of the region today, you will see villages and towns that have barely grown or changed since the Middle Ages. Far from a glorious process of national unification, as French historians today portray it, the new possessions were treated as conquests to be exploited. In Gascony, as in the rest of the Midi, the heavy-handed authoritarianism of Paris brought with it economic stagnation that was to last for centuries, and the enforced death of a culture that had been one of the first and most promising of medieval times. The 1539 Decree of Villars-Cotterets mandated the use of the French language in all matters of law and government, the first step along the road to the eradication of the *langue d'oc*, a policy pursued with vigour until our own time.

1530–1815

As Protestant and Catholic gods smile down from separate heavens, the Gascons turn their military talents on each other and speed their country on its long decline

French control was solid, and with political opposition impossible the first wave of southwestern rebelliousness came in the form of religious dissent. Protestantism found its way into the southwest from Calvin's Geneva, and found a warm welcome among the small middle classes. The first Protestant communities appeared in Béarn around 1532, notably at Oloron-Ste-Marie. At about the same time, the Béarnais dynasty was dying out, and its possessions eventually fell into the hands of Henri d'Albret and his wife Marguerite d'Angoulême. This ancient Gascon family had often been closely allied with the French kings. Henry II had given them the title of dukes over their lands in the Landes and Gers, and French assistance had been vital in allowing the Albrets to take over the throne of Navarre in 1481. Not that the title was worth much; at the time King Ferdinand of Aragon (soon to marry Isabella of Castile for the unification of Spain) had grabbed most of Navarre south of the Pyrenees by force, leaving a throne without much of a kingdom behind it. Henri and Marguerite presided over a refined Renaissance court, at Pau or at Nérac in the Agenais, where both Catholic and Protestant men of letters were welcome, but their daughter and heir, Jeanne d'Albret, turned out to be a grim Protestant bigot who forced all Béarn to accept her faith.

The southwest, along with the rest of France, was dividing into hostile camps. Even more than Jeanne, the kings and the *Parlement* of Bordeaux had started the fashion for intolerance by persecuting dissenters and occasionally massacring them wholesale. By 1560, it was outright civil war. Paris sent down Blaise de Montluc, a distinguished Gascon soldier, with the mission of ridding Gascony of Protestants. Montluc did the best he could, often stuffing village wells with all he could find of them. The Protestants, led by Jeanne and her captain, Montgomery, responded in kind. Montgomery's army roamed the southwest in the late 1560s, sacking monasteries and Catholic towns with a brutality to rival Montluc's.

As fate would have it, Jeanne's marriage to Antoine de Bourbon unexpectedly made her son the heir not only to Béarn and Navarre, but eventually to the throne of France. Henri of Navarre grew up to be a fierce and capable warrior in the Protestant cause, campaigning for two decades from one end of France to the other. When Henri III was assassinated in 1589, the Valois branch of the Capetian dynasty became extinct; next in line came the Bourbon branch, of which the senior member was Henri of Navarre – Henri IV. Hardline Catholics could never accept a Protestant king, and Henri had to fight on for a few years before deciding that Paris was worth a Mass. The historic compromise put an end to the wars, sealed by the 1598 Edict of Nantes decreeing religious tolerance, and the good Gascon soldier – *lou nouste Henric*, or 'our Henry' to the people of the southwest – became one of France's greatest and best-loved kings, under whose reign, as Gascons like to express it, 'France was annexed by Béarn'. Henri always had a special place in his heart for Béarn and especially Pau, his birthplace. He kept his royal titles of France and Navarre separate, and Béarn continued to be governed by its Sovereign Council, under its own system of laws.

Unfortunately, there were still plenty of fanatics loose in France. In 1610, one of them murdered Henri while his carriage was stuck in a Paris traffic jam. The religious peace held, though Henri's son, Louis XIII, and his minister Cardinal Richelieu had some very different ideas on how to treat the provinces. Louis marched down south with a big army in 1620 to put an end to Béarn's independence forever. Richelieu, ever concerned with limiting the ability of the nobility to defy the king, determinedly set about demolishing castles not necessary for the national defence – a policy that has robbed Gascony of a good number of tourist attractions.

The early 17th century witnessed a series of conflicts between France and Spain; the Pyrenees saw a number of battles, and raids from both sides. The Treaty of the Pyrenees in 1659 put an end to these troubles, followed by the marriage of Louis XIV and the Spanish infanta, Maria Teresa, the following year at St-Jean-de-Luz. The *roi soleil*'s long reign was a miserable period for the southwest, as for the rest of France, combining oppressive absolutism and economic mismanagement with crushing taxes for Versailles and for endless aggressive wars. Worst of all, Louis's religious bigotry led him to revoke the Edict of Nantes. It was open season on Protestants once again, and the persecutions were especially severe in the southwest. Dissenters who escaped death or imprisonment emigrated in large numbers to the Americas or Germany; often these were the most progressive and industrious members of the towns and villages they fled.

By the 1700s the southwest was confirmed in its role as a forgotten, impoverished backwater, overseen by *intendants* appointed by the king. Good ones, such as Baron d'Etigny, *intendant* of Auch in the 1750s, often contributed important improvements: good roads (often lined with avenues of plane trees, as can be seen around France today), bridges, and new parks and public buildings in the towns. D'Etigny also built the spa at Luchon in the Pyrenees, in an age when 'taking the waters' first became fashionable among Europe's aristocrats.

All through this era, the Basques had adapted well to French rule. Unlike Gascony, French-controlled Euzkadi (the Basques' name for their own land) retained a substantial degree of self-government up until the Revolution. In the Labourd, a kind of parliament called the *biltzar*, with elected representatives (but no nobles or clergy), met regularly to set tax rates and look after local business, and each small region or town possessed its *for*, its charter of rights and privileges, which the French usually respected. In return, the Basques remained stalwartly loyal to the French crown, and performed important services for it in time of war, especially on the seas, with the feared privateers of Bayonne. The Revolution marked a turning point, and brought with it the irony of this most democratic of peoples ranging themselves solidly on the side of reaction. It wasn't their fault. The Jacobins up in Paris abolished their self-government and traditional liberties, but even more resented than the Revolution's push for centralization and Frenchification, made worse under Napoleon, were the attacks on the church. The people who gave the church St Ignatius Loyola and St Francis Xavier were among the most devout Catholics you'll find (they still are).

1815–Present

The modern world dawns, bright with promise for every place except southern France

The only real result of the revolution for the southwest was a lasting economic depression, helped along by the British blockade and Napoleon's wars, the end of which found Wellington marching over the Pyrenees and besieging Bayonne on his way north. When the excitement was over, Paris-appointed prefects replaced Paris-appointed *intendants*, but few of the ephemeral governments in the 19th-century Gallic banana republic/monarchy/empire ever stirred themselves much to help the southwest. Nor did the region ever show much energy of its own. The railroad arrived at Bayonne and Tarbes in the 1850s, but this served mainly to help make it easier for young people to leave, and for imported goods to flow in and ruin the region's already hard-pressed farmers and manufacturers.

The southwest suffered more than any other part of France from rural poverty and depopulation. Young Gascons still went off to join the army, as they always had done; more simply emigrated to Paris or the colonies just to find a job. The Basque lands were as hard hit. Basques from the mountain uplands found their way in great numbers to the Americas, especially to Argentina and the United States, where the Basque connection goes back to the 1,500 sailors, many of them veterans of the privateers, who came to join Lafayette and fight for American independence. Simón Bolívar, liberator of Venezuela and Colombia, was of Basque descent. In the bayous of Louisiana and east Texas, as well as on the Argentine pampas, Basques became some of the New World's first cowboys in the 1840s, setting the model and contributing much to the image (*lariat*, among other cowboy terms, is a Basque word). There are still large Basque communities in Idaho, Utah, California and other states.

The only 19th-century regime that contributed much to the region, surprisingly, was the otherwise useless empire of Napoleon III. The Emperor himself had been conceived in a Pyrenean hotel (possibly with the help of a local shepherd), and he spent most of his frequent vacations in the region, helping to popularize both Biarritz and the mountains as holiday destinations. He also oversaw the reclamation of the empty Landes, transforming it into Europe's largest forest. Between the Pyrenees and the Basque coast, France's southwest corner developed into one of Europe's first holiday playgrounds. Thermal resorts such as Bagnerès-de-Bigorre and Salies-de-Béarn sprouted ornate grand hotels and casinos, while the English descended on Pau for its climate and gave the continent its first golf course.

In rural regions, though, the big story – the only story – was still abandonment and depopulation. The First World War contributed mightily to this trend; many villages lost a third or even half of their young men, and everywhere you will see pathetic war memorials to remind you of France's greatest tragedy since the Black Death of 1348. Between the war and natural decline, the southwest lost over a quarter of its population between 1850 and 1950. In parts of the Gers the figure was almost two-thirds. Though the Second World War was less costly and destructive for France, it was still a miserable and dangerous time for the people of the southwest. From the beginning, the Germans seized a strip along the entire Atlantic coast as part of the occupied zone. The 'border' with Vichy-controlled territory was heavily guarded, and locals needed special papers to cross it. The Resistance was not particularly strong in Gascony, though the Basques and other mountain men did good work smuggling escapees over into Spain, and helping Allied agents coming the other way.

Many members of the Resistance in the area were Spaniards, part of the tens of thousands of republican soldiers and civilians who had escaped into France when Franco's troops conquered the Spanish Basque country in 1937–8. Most of these people remained in France after the war, and added some new blood and new energy to many towns and villages. More new arrivals came in the sixties: *pieds-noirs*, French settlers in Algeria forced to leave after Algerian independence; you'll meet them everywhere you go in the southwest. Politically, the only big change since the war has been the creation of regional governments under the Socialists' decentralization programme in 1981. So far it isn't much, but as the first reversal in five centuries of Parisian centralism, it at least gives provinces a start in reclaiming some control over their own destinies. The Basques, jealous of the complete autonomy their countrymen have won over the border in Spain, continue to be quietly assertive in trying to push decentralization even further. An informal council of mayors, heir to the old *biltzar*, meets regularly.

Culture

Dread and Delight: Romanticism in the Pyrenees

The Pyrenees may not be the highest mountains in Europe, but to many people they are the most beautiful. Until the end of the 18th century, however, few people imagined that mountains of any kind could be of any aesthetic interest whatsoever; the Pyrenees, a secretive, solitary world blasted by snow and storms, haunted by savage wolves and bears, were looked upon with horror, the *Monts Affreux*, a distant menace. No one in their right mind would have anything to do with them. Louis XIV, in fact, claimed to abolish the Pyrenees altogether.

These attitudes about altitudes only began to change when opinion-makers came into first-hand contact with the Monts Affreux in the 16th and 17th centuries. France's Classical Age was in full bloom and Greek and Roman models and mythologies were the chief references of the academies and salons, which controlled French culture with the same sense of authority to which the *ancien régime* pretended over every other aspect of life. Beauty was an ideal agreed upon by an academy, far removed from the individual. Society was highly organized and art and literature had to follow rules too. What brought Louis XIV's morganatic wife, Madame de Maintenon, down to Barèges in the Pyrenees was not the views, but something of which an ancient Roman would have approved: the curative waters. Enough fashionable people followed in Madame de Maintenon's footsteps, and even went on little expeditions into the Pyrenees, to discover they weren't as evil as their reputation.

By the mid-18th century, Louis Ramond de Carbonnières became the first man to climb and scientifically study the Pyrenees, publishing in 1759 his *Observations Faites dans les Pyrénées*. At the same time, Jean-Jacques Rousseau, the great dropout from the salons and Encyclopaedist circle, wrote *La Nouvelle Héloïse* (1761), introducing the idea of communing with nature, while Voltaire helped initiate a French fad for foreign authors (Shakespeare, Richardson and, later, Byron and Scott from Britain, and Goethe, Schiller and Lessing from Germany), writers not bound by the same academic rules as the French intelligentsia.The birth of French Romanticism, however, had to wait for the tightly controlled structures of the Classical Age to crumble like a house of cards in the Revolution. And when it did spring into bloom, French Romanticism proved essentially different from the earlier romantic movements in Britain and Germany, both of which were a return to national traditions; in France romanticism was a revolt against the rules. With the old system destroyed, the individual had become the only reality; opinions were free; careful classical symmetry, order and balance and rationalism were replaced by flights of fancy and the imagination; sincerity, emotion and inspiration were all that counted. Overbred French classicism was replaced by fiery, emotional novels by the likes of Victor Hugo.

The Romantic movement revealed the Pyrenees to the French nation; here nature, in the form of majestic snow-crowned peaks, misty abysses, mysterious caves, deep blue lakes, rushing streams and waterfalls, seemed to mirror the passion in each individual; awe and enchantment replaced fear and loathing. Old Pyrenean legends, tales of witches and sorcerers and travellers' accounts and picturesque albums were published throughout the 1860s and 1870s, partly in response to a new interest in folk tales, again inspired by the Germans; Gustave Doré's dramatic fairytale engravings of the *Voyage aux Pyrénées*, stories collected by an out-of-work mountain guide named Taine, fired the imagination and remains one of the classics of the region. It was the age of the first big-game hunts; as bears, izards (chamois) and wild boar fell to the Paris sportsman's bullet, high society filled the spas and went on jaunts with their mountain guides, dressed in soft hats, woollen stockings, breeches and braces, hobnobbing with royalty and the literati – not only Hugo but all the great names of French Romanticism: Chateaubriand, Vigny, Flaubert, Sand, Lamartine, Mérimée and Delacroix.

Even then, the great Romantic of the French Pyrenees was not altogether French. The legendary Count Henry Russell Killough (1834–1909) was born in Toulouse of an Irish father and Gascon mother, a volatile combination that resulted in the most enthusiastic and ardent of all the lovers of the Pyrenees. After spending his youth on adventures in the Rockies, the Andes, the Himalayas, the Gobi and Sahara, New Zealand and Siberia, Russell returned to Toulouse and decided to devote the rest of his life to exploring his own back yard. He was utterly fearless, the first to scale 16 peaks in the Pyrenees. His special passion was Mount Vignemale above Barèges, which he climbed 33 times; in 1869 he did it in the middle of winter, earning himself another first in Europe. His passion for Vignemale was so great that in 1882 he began excavating caves to live in near its peak; when his Villa Russell was devoured by a glacier, he excavated two others, including, lastly, one he called Villa Paradis just under the summit at 10,660ft. When living on his own in his mountain 'villas', Russell was happy with a lamb's skin to sleep in; but when he entertained, no one did it with more style: Persian rugs, fine wines and food, candles and white tablecloths were spread on the glaciers. He wanted his guests to share his love for the mountains and would wake them at dawn to see the sunrise. Down in Pau, where he spent most of the winter with English expat society, he was famous for his love of mauve scarves. Author of the delightful *Souvenirs d'un Montagnard* (1908) and frequent contributor to the *Revue des Pyrénées*, he wrote of his beloved mountains with Romantic fire. 'My whole life has been a kind of challenge to civilization,' he once said, and wondered why people thought him eccentric.

Gascon Country Remedies

In 1881 Charles Lavielle, a Gascon country doctor, faithfully recorded all the 'alternative' cures he confronted in his practice and published them in his *Essai sur les erreurs populaires relatives à la médecine*. If nothing else, the remedies he found showed that a good deal of imagination over the centuries had accumulated on top of some fairly universal ancient beliefs. Among the errors the good doctor decried was a highly risky cure for eye diseases: touching the pupils nine times with the wedding ring of a new bride. This was sure to work, but only on the condition that the ring belonged to a woman of irreproachable virtue; apparently only purity in something invisible could counteract the blemish to make the world visible again.

Fortunately for the brides of Gascony, the main illness in the region, especially in the Landes, wasn't eye disease, but fever. One sure remedy for this was to cut the fingernails and toenails of the patient, gather up all the 20 clippings, stick them in a meatball and feed it to a dog. If that didn't work, it was necessary to take the membrane that encloses the white of a hen's egg and tie it tight with a silken thread around the left pinkie finger of the fever victim. The disease would thus be passed on to another object. Dogs, perhaps because they are the most susceptible to their owners' feelings, were likely targets; gouty people, for instance, could cure themselves by sleeping with a puppy. A branch of hawthorn, the most sacred tree of the indigenous Aquitaine peoples, was also good at absorbing fevers, but only if it was given an offering of bread and salt. It also warded off lightning.

From the night of time, when Neolithic shepherds blazed the 'salt route' in search of the mineral so essential for the health of their herds and flocks, salt has been a charmed substance; Dr Lavielle found that inflammations in the face, teeth and extremities were popularly attributed to the failure to carry a bit of salt on one's person when crossing water. A common preventative measure was always to carry three horse chestnuts in a trouser pocket (with reason: the substance between the outer shell of the conker and the kernel is essential for treating rheumatism). If the inflammation had already happened, it was necessary to fill a pot of water and drop in a handful of hay and nine pebbles; other people were to add dice, a comb and a pair of scissors. The pot was put on the boil, then the contents emptied into a vase while the inflamed part of the anatomy was exposed to the steam. The pain was supposed to be cut and combed away with the rising of the vapour. The nine pebbles may have in some way been related to the *esne harria* or 'milk stones' that many families in the Pyrenees used to heat up and drop in their hot milk every evening for the taste. The curious custom was preserved in 19th-century Toulouse café society, when *lait ferrat* was the rage: boiled milk with a stick of red-hot iron dropped in.

Giving birth in 19th-century Gascony had very little to do with the Lamaze and Leboyer techniques young mothers learn today. For an easy birth, the essential thing was to tie the mother's belt or girdle to the church bell and give it three good yanks; in some places, Dr Lavielle wrote, they tied the husband's knickers to the bell rope. Many Pyrenean valleys were far too remote for a doctor or midwife to assist the birth; mothers-to-be relied on old women who had proved their mettle by successfully bearing as many children as possible in the most trying circumstances. At the beginning of labour, it was important to eat a bowl of onion soup; throughout labour the old woman would ply the mother with wine and coffee. When the baby was about to be born, the mother would be helped to stand up and her assistant would catch the baby in a sieve. The umbilical cord would be cut as long as possible, to give the child a chance to have a beautiful voice, and it was important to wash the newborn in tepid, not hot, water, to keep the baby from turning brown. If the placenta was not expelled naturally, the old woman would put the husband's beret backwards on the mother's head. Some of this harks back to the ancient custom of *couvade*, noted by anthropologists in many cultures: immediately after birth the father takes the mother's place in bed with the child at his side, an old rite in the duel between matriarchy and patriarchy (i.e. the male desire to challenge the female even in her powers of reproduction) and one practised not so very long ago in Béarn and the Basque country. To this day fathers there seem to get most of the attention at birth celebrations.

If few of the remedies practised by Dr Lavielle's patients had any therapeutic value beyond that of trust and belief, the ancient treatment of shingles in the western Pyrenees is so effective that modern country doctors often refer their patients to village healers. *Lou cindré*, or the 'belt' as shingles is known, is an extremely painful viral disease. To be a healer, a person must already have had the 'belt' and been healed. This guarantees the necessary immunity, for what the healer does is 'take the belt' and 'return it to the earth' by hoisting the sufferer on his or her back and making ritual steps in two directions, tracing the form of a cross. The proper formulas are recited during this exercise, and the patient is asked the ritual questions: 'What are you wearing?' 'A belt.' 'I too had one, but Jesus took it away, and he'll take yours from you too.' If the healer is too old or frail to bear the weight, the patient has only to lay hands on his or her shoulders and follow the prescribed steps. The average doctor with all the products of modern medicine takes weeks and weeks to treat a shingles patient, but a healer in Béarn removes the symptoms in less than three days.

Mari, Mary

The apparition of the Virgin Mary to Bernadette at Lourdes may have been promoted into a global spectacle, but it was hardly the first. The Pyrenees are beyond doubt the most popular spot on the globe for Marian appearances; from the Atlantic to the Mediterranean over a hundred separate epiphanies have been recorded in as many different places since medieval times. Wherever you see a lone chapel in the mountains, the odds will be better than even it was built to commemorate a similar apparition, and usually the people of the nearest village will honour it with an annual pilgrimage procession.

Why does Our Lady choose to spend so much time in these mountains? Reaching back for the bits and shards of evidence that can be found on the beliefs of the earliest days, one finds that all mountains seem to be holy places – but the Pyrenees more so. There is no element of its landscapes, no chapter of its history and legend, that is not suffused with the otherworldly and the divine. One of the possible origins of the name Pyrenees is 'mountains of fire', for the ritual bonfires that shone from their peaks on the great holidays of the year (even today, the Catalans of the western Pyrenees surround their holy mountain, Canigou, with a ring of fires every Midsummer Day). Every Basque mountain had its attendant deity; some of these live on in folklore, such as Jauna Gorri, the 'Red Lord', who lives atop the Pic d'Anie (*Ahunamendi* in Basque) and sends the storms down to the valleys. Jauna Gorri tends a garden on the mountain top where the flowers of immortality grow, and he keeps his treasures there, guarded by hairy black giants called *pelutlak*. Beneath the mountains are the caves, sites of worship from the Palaeolithic era to the initiatory rituals of the Cathars.

Even more important than these are the region's many springs and *sources*. The Pyrenees are laced with them from end to end, including one of the world's largest concentrations of *sources* of medicinal value. The religion of Neolithic times seems to have been closely connected to the life-giving water that comes forth out of the earth, and here again, the tales of the Basques give ample evidence of a similar veneration. Nearly every *source* is associated with some spirit, inevitably female. In different localities they might be called *incantadas*, *senyoretas blancas*, or *daunas d'aygua* ('ladies of the waters'), and there are some charming stories attatched to them. (If you ever see a thread floating up to the top of a fountain, be sure to pull it out to the end even if it seems there is no end. The thread is the life of an *incantada*, imprisoned in the water by a spell, and only if someone gathers up all the thread can she regain her human form.)

All the Pyrenees' wealth of folk and fairy tales give only teasing hints of the ancient rites and beliefs from which they are descended. Without much in the way of written records, trying to reconstruct the details of the old religions is difficult indeed. A large number of inscribed votive altars from Roman times have been dug up around the Pyrenees, and, just to vex the archaeologists, nearly each one bears the name of a different god: Baicorrix, Aereda, Aherbelste, Exprecenn, Vaxus, Harauso, Abelio, and so on. As with the Celts, religion for the proto-Basques was a local affair; the same deities, more or less, might go under a different name and carry different attributes in every valley or even every village.

But concerning the most important deity in the Basque pantheon, there is no confusion. Her name is Mari, of all things, and she is the Pyrenees' version of the transcendent Great Goddess that ruled the old religion throughout Europe before the coming of the Indo-European peoples. At once the queen of heaven and of the underworld, she sends thunder and storms down from the mountain tops, the places where her rites were always observed; all the other goddesses, spirits and fairies created by the pantheistic mind are just aspects of her. This Mari is no virgin; her consort, shocking as it must have seemed to the ears of the Christian proselytizers, was a great serpent, named Sugaar or Maju – the prototype for all the Pyrenees' many dragons, and according to legend the founding father of many of the oldest Basque families.

The Pyrenees, like many mountain regions, has always been fantastically conservative in terms of religion – meaning a few centuries behind everyone else. Today the Basque country is the last corner of the world that will ever keep the Pope up at night worrying. Back in 1280, at the height of the 'Age of Faith' (to cite just one example), clerics in the Ariège were issuing furious decrees against ladies who insisted on staying out on the summits all night, enjoying the festivals of the goddess. Mari and Mary may bear the same name only by coincidence, but 1,400 years ago, when Christian missionaries began to expropriate the sacred sites, holidays and processions of the old religion to wean people gradually away from it, they probably did not realize they were helping maintain a religious continuity that goes back to the beginnings of time.

The Non-Violent Bullfight: the *Course Landaise*

The very first civilization on European soil, that of the Minoans of Crete, was only rediscovered in the early 1900s. Ever since then, the archaeological evidence coming out of Crete has bewitched the world; the Early Minoan period, beginning in 2500 BC, not only offers a link between the great Neolithic cultures of Europe and historical times but seems to add substance to many Greek myths. The Minoans lived during the great age of the bull: the sun was in the constellation Taurus; myths tell of the Minotaur; Minoan palaces and temples are decorated with 'horns of consecration'. Most curious of all are the frescoes and ivory statuettes found at Knossos that show young men and women leaping over bulls. When Minoan archaeologists showed these bull-leaping frescoes to Spanish bullfighters, the toreadors replied that it looked, if not impossible, certainly fatal. The archaeologists have duly theorized that bull-leaping was an elaborate kind of human sacrifice.

Not in Gascony. Or at least the only difference is that the leaping, while formerly done over bulls, is now mostly limited to the bull's slightly less dangerous wife – a black, long-horned Spanish breed, called the *vache landaise*. Bull sports in Gascony may not go back to Minoan times, but they're certainly nothing new. The first written records of bull running in the streets of St-Sever go back to 1457, but as in Spain the attachment is deeply ingrained and probably goes back at least to the Roman gladiators, who fought bulls as well as each other and every other beast imaginable.

In 1802 laws were passed that took the bulls off the streets and into the first wooden arenas. Now confined, rules for the game quickly evolved and achieved their final form in the Second Empire. This coincided with the introduction of the Spanish *corrida* in the south of France, hence much of the Spanish terminology in the *course landaise*: the team of *écarteurs* (the dodgers) is called a *cuadrilla* and all the cows, raised on *ganaderias*, or ranches in the Landes, are named Favorita, Paloma or Voluntaria. Each *ganaderia* fields a *cuadrilla* of six or seven *écarteurs* along with the 'men in white' – trainers, a lithe jumper or *sauteur*, and a rope man or *cordier*, whose existence often surprises many people attending their first *course landaise*. But there's reason: unlike the Spanish *corrida*, where the bull is killed, all the Favoritas and Palomas go back to the ranch after the show and over the years become cadgy old veterans in the ring. The job of the *cordier* is to let the cow get as close as possible to the *écarteur* without letting her actually touch him, and to prevent dangerous, vindictive turns of the head (the cows also wear rubber caps on their horns). The match is decided by points awarded by a jury, rather like figure skating; riskiness, as well as grace and art, are important factors in the scoring.

The *écarteurs* know each cow, and each cow knows all the tricks. The idea is to provoke her into charging, wait until the last minute, and like a dancer move just inches out of the way, or boldly leap over her – in a running jump, or with feet together, or 'dangerously'. For spectators this is the most thrilling (and most Minoan) part of the show. There are two levels, the *courses formelles* where the individual or *écarteur* or *cuadrilla* is judged, and the less serious *courses mixtes* that include a classic programme followed by clowning around (the *charlottade*). The most challenging *courses landaises* of the many that take place in the summer in the Landes (and also in Armagnac and the northern Pyrénées Atlantiques) pit three to six *ganaderias* and their various *cuadrillas* against one another, so that each team faces unfamiliar, unpredictable cows.

The Pariahs of the Pyrenees

Everywhere you go in this corner of France, you will see reminders of the Cagots. At the back end of a village, or set outside it, there will be a quarter that the locals call the *ancien Cagotérie*. Or a parish priest will show you the special door in the side of the church, the *porte des Cagots*, the only one they were allowed to use, or the *bénitier des Cagots*, the holy-water stoup reserved for them alone. Most of them were carpenters by trade, and wherever you see a really old market *halles*, or a wooden church steeple or a half-timbered house, chances are it was the Cagots who built it. The last full-blooded Cagot in Gascony died in the 1800s, though small communities of them were reported in obscure corners of the Basque country as late as 1902. But even as this mysterious people was fading away, French, Spanish and Basque writers and scientists were becoming interested in the strange story of these Gascon outcasts and who they really were.

The Cagots were peculiar to the territory covered in this book, along with Spanish Navarre. Under a number of different names, they are mentioned in documents dating back to the 11th century: Cagots, Crestias, Capots, Agots (in the Basque country), Ladres (Gascon for lepers), Gafets, Gézitains. People believed them to be lepers, and forced a stringent code of apartheid on them: Cagots could not farm, or enter a mill or a tavern, or drink out of public fountains save the ones reserved for them; they were kept at the back of the church, and served communion separately. Often they had their own church, and they were always buried in separate cemeteries. Though what remains of Cagot houses does not differ much from other dwellings, they were constrained to live apart, either in closed-off quarters of towns or in separate hamlets on the outskirts. In some localities they were forced to wear distinctive clothing, such as a goose's foot pinned to their tunics. There was an elaborate etiquette in everyday life to stop them coming into close contact with anyone else, and Cagots by law always married amongst their own kind. Although exceptions are recorded, almost all Cagots worked with wood; besides the master carpenters, they chopped trees for firewood, and made furniture, wooden plates and utensils. Back then it was believed that wood did not transmit diseases (a notion oddly born out by scientific tests in recent times; bacteria survive much longer on plastic, for example).

One thing is certain; lepers they were not. Leprosy, though a continuing scourge in the Middle Ages, is not a hereditary disease, and the Cagots made up a sort of caste that lived its separate life for centuries, without any evidence of chronic ill health – though country people believed that even the touch of one would burn your skin.

Plenty of imaginative guesses have been put forward as to their origins. Some held them to be descendants of Visigoths, caught behind after the Frankish conquests and reduced to servitude. Others claimed the first Cagots were Moorish slaves, brought back by the many Gascon lords who went to Spain to hire themselves out in the battles of the Reconquista. Miscellaneous conjectures include refugee Cathar heretics after the Albigensian crusade, Jews, religious excommunicates, or even gypsies.

The most reliable contemporary accounts of Cagots suggest they really didn't look much different from anyone else. And as for their origin, the correct answer might be 'all of the above, among others'. The most plausible hypotheses have the children of lepers still living apart, by habit or by force, in the old leper colonies that were once found all over the region. Over the centuries, they were possibly joined by any and every sort of vagabond and refugee. All the main pilgrimage routes to Compostela passed through Gascony – the last stop before the difficult crossing over the mountains – and a huge number of people made the trip each year (many of them forced to do it as penance or punishment for crimes); more than a few would be likely to stay. To these, add the people attracted by the huge land-clearing and *bastide*-building programmes of the 13th century (most of which welcomed criminals and anyone else willing to work) and it is easy to imagine all the loose ends of Europe piling up here on the Pyrenees' northern slopes. Neighbouring French-controlled Languedoc had no Cagots, but it did know several massacres of Jews and vagabonds in the 1300s (in medieval times, the lands of the king of France were never a very healthy place for minorities of any sort). Perhaps the stigma of a Cagot was a worthwhile trade for a peaceable life for some people. Still, the mystery of the Cagots will probably never be solved. Why, for example, were they called Crestias (Christians), and why, in the Middle Ages, were they exempt from civil law and taxes, subject only to Church laws and Church courts?

The end of the story is as remarkable as the beginning. The Cagots themselves seem to have undertaken an epic civil rights struggle, and incredibly enough, in the context of *ancien régime* France, they eventually won. In 1425, they complained about harassment by the consuls of the town of Lectoure, and won their case in the Count of Armagnac's courts. After losing another court battle in 1479, they appealed to the Parlement of Toulouse and obtained a medical inquest that concluded that they were not diseased in any way. Even so, it took until 1627 to get the Parlement to publish an ordinance prohibiting local officials from persecuting the *maîtres charpentiers* (as they evidently preferred to be known) – the Parlement also enjoined anyone from calling them 'Cagots'. From 1680 onwards, they are recorded fighting in Biarritz for the right to be buried in common ground; they won this too, with the Bishop of Bayonne interceding in their favour. Also in Biarritz, the decades that followed saw the first recorded incidents of men marrying Cagot women, and finally a prototypical Rosa Parks, a Cagot named Michel Legaret, got fed up one Sunday and stepped right up to the front of the church. He got a hundred days in the local jail for that, an outrage that finally moved the Bordeaux Parlement to outlaw all segregation.

Winning in court proved much easier than raising the consciousness of their fellow men. That last decision caused riots in Biarritz, and Bordeaux responded with a decree written by Montesquieu himself demanding that order be restored, and that the new laws be enforced. Throughout the 18th century, Parlements and church officials had to intervene often in remote villages, where peasants resisted the new laws and sometimes resorted to violence. By then the Cagots' numbers were on the decrease, as men found they could take their skill and make a living in another part of France or the colonies where no one had ever heard of a Cagot, let alone knew how to discriminate against one. The definitive end of Gascon Jim Crow came with 1789 and the Declaration of the Rights of Man; in return, grateful Cagots signed up for the army in large numbers to defend the Revolution. After that, there were no more Cagots, only Frenchmen.

Our Good Henry

If the stories of kings and queens of yore, passed around the hearth on a winter's night, were to be the sole posthumous judge of character, some cads would get off pretty easy (Richard the Lion-Heart, who burned and slaughtered his way across his own duchy of Aquitaine, is one who springs to mind). Others, like those of the 7th-century Caliph Harun al-Rashid in the Arabian Nights, portray so many distinctive virtues and faults that one can't help thinking that they must contain some kernel of historical truth about the man's character. In France, no king can approach Henri IV for attracting good stories. The fact that he is a well-documented and a fairly recent historical character hasn't stifled storytellers in Gascony in the least. In some of the tales he plays the same benign role as Harun al-Rashid, as in one of the best, collected by Jean-François Bladé in 1886, called 'The Blacksmith from Fumel':

Henry IV was staying in his château at Nérac, on the northern edge of the Armagnac country, with his daughter Princess Sad Face, who never smiled, and his favourite white horse, which was far too high-spirited to let itself be shod. Fed up with both of them, Henry issued a decree: whoever could shoe his horse and make his daughter laugh could marry the princess and inherit his kingdom. A blacksmith from Fumel decided to try his luck, and took all the gold and silver he owned and melted them down to make horseshoes of gold and nails of silver, then set off for Nérac. When he stopped to rest he met a cricket, who offered to come along and help, and it rode along on the blacksmith's chin. He next met a rat munching its way through a field of tobacco, its favourite food; the rat offered to come along and rode on the young man's beret. On his last rest, the young man met the Mother of all Fleas; she offered to come along too, and sat on his nose. The blacksmith had scarcely arrived in Nérac when he met King Henry strolling with Princess Sad Face; she took one look at the man wearing a cricket, rat and flea and burst out laughing.

'Now I would try the second task,' said the blacksmith, and showed King Henry and his daughter the golden horseshoes and silver nails. 'Why, I've never seen the like!' exclaimed the king, and the blacksmith nonchalantly lied through his teeth, 'Oh, this is nothing. I've plenty of gold and silver back home.' Off he went into the stable where the wild white horse pranced and whinnied. 'Cricket, do your job!' he said, and the cricket jumped in the horse's ear and sang 'Cri Cri Cri!' so loudly that the horse was made deaf, and stood still. 'Rat, do your job!' the blacksmith then said, and the rat hopped under the horse's nose and, 'Pan Pan Pan Ft Ft Ft!', gassed him to sleep with smelly tobacco farts. The blacksmith then easily shod the horse, and Henry IV, who always kept his promises, married him straight away to his daughter.

But rather than make merry at the wedding feast, the blacksmith sat there, glum and worried, because he had lied about his wealth and knew he would soon be caught out. Just then a rich young man of the court took him aside: 'Blacksmith,' he confided, 'I have loved Princess Sad Face for years, but she would never have me. If you swear on your soul not to touch your bride in bed tonight, I will give you a big bag of gold doubloons.' The blacksmith agreed, and when he went to the bridal chamber, all he did was pace back and forth all night long and ask the princess every hour: 'Wife, do you realize how many gold doubloons fit in a big sack?' The next morning, King Henry went to his daughter and inquired about her first night of wedded bless. 'It was terrible! I slept alone, while my husband marched around the room asking me how many gold doubloons fit in a big sack.' 'Your husband has deeply offended you,' said the king. 'But I'm sure things will go better tonight.' But the rich young lord had another bag of gold doubloons to offer, and the same thing happened the next night. Then he had a third bag of doubloons, and the same thing happened the third night. By then the blacksmith figured he was wealthy enough. But it was too late, for after enquiring about his daughter's third night of marriage, and hearing an earful of the same, King Henry was furious. 'He will not offend you again! You don't want a capon for a husband, and I certainly don't want one for my son-in-law.' And he annulled the marriage, and remarried Princess Sad Face to the rich young man who had paid the blacksmith the three bags of gold.

The blacksmith was heartbroken, but the cricket, rat and Mother of Fleas offered to come to his aid one more time. When the newly married couple went to bed, the cricket and Mother of Fleas jumped on and bit the rich young man until he bled and hopped about as if he were possessed. When he finally collapsed in exhaustion, up popped the rat full of tobacco farts, and, 'Pan Pan Pan Ft Ft Ft!', knocked him out until the morning, when King Henry came in to ask his daughter how it went. 'Even worse! Just look at him,' she said. 'Give me back my blacksmith.' And the next night the blacksmith proved he was hardly a capon.

Another little story from Béarn about Henry IV, affectionately known as the *Vert Galant* or 'Gay Old Spark' for his many loves, tells how he once fell for a beautiful Cagote. 'You are a Cagote,' he said as he took her in his arms. '*Eh bien*, I'm going to tell you a secret: I'm one, too. But you mustn't tell.'

Pilgrims of the Milky Way

The bare facts of the story hardly account for the millions upon millions of pilgrims who have made the journey over the last thousand years to Compostela to pay homage at the tomb of St James the Greater. James, or St Jacques, or Santiago, the brother of St John the Evangelist, was one of the first disciples selected by Jesus, who nicknamed him Boanerges, the 'son of thunder'. In the year 44, he became the first of the twelve Apostles to be martyred when King Herod Agrippa had his head chopped off in Caesarea. In faraway Spain, however, an apocryphal tradition stated that James had visited Zaragoza and converted the first Spaniards to the new faith. On the basis of that tradition, it seemed at least plausible that his followers just might have brought his body back to Spain after his death and buried it in the extreme northwest, in Galicia, a mystical land long sacred to the Celts and their Druid priests.

And that was the end of the story until the 9th century, when the Christian princes of Spain, chased by the triumphant Moors into remote pockets of northern Iberia, were desperately in need of divine aid to rally their forces. In 812, Pelayo, a monk of Galicia, duly saw a shower of stars and under it 'rediscovered' the tomb of St James, a find quickly authenticated by the Visigothic bishop Theodimir. By 844 Santiago had made his début as a ghostly knight, helping Ramiro I of Asturias defeat the Moors at the legendary Battle of Clavijo – the first victory of the Reconquista. By 950 the first French pilgrims, encouraged by the monks at Cluny, had blazed a trial to his tomb at the 'field of stars', or Compostela. Pilgrimages to Jerusalem or Rome were already something of a vogue; after the long centuries of the Dark Ages, the Church was keen on re-establishing the contacts across the old Roman empire it was determined to inherit for Christianity.

A vast network of major and minor pilgrims' routes descended through France like the veins on a maple leaf; pilgrims from Britain would sail down as far as the English port of Bordeaux, and nearly all converged on the Pyrenees passes at Roncevaux in the Pays Basque or the Col du Somport (linking Béarn to Zaragoza), although other passes further east were used as well, usually marked by a hospice, hostel or hospital founded by the Knights of St John; many survive at least in name. Crossing the Pyrenees was the most dangerous part of the whole journey; the famous 12th-century travel guide, the *Codex Calixtinus*, written by French monk Aymeric Picaud, warned of wolves and bears, of 'false pilgrims' (bandits) and rather unfairly, of the Basques ('a barbarous people...strangers to any good sentiment, but raised to vice and iniquity'); better, wrote Aymeric, to avoid Roncevaux and take the Col du Somport. The main route that joined up in Spanish Navarre was known as the Camino Frances, for the majority were French pilgrims.

In the Middle Ages, an estimated two million pilgrims a year walked to Compostela. The flood was gradually reduced to a ripple from the 16th to the 19th century; the pilgrimage seemed a bit old-fashioned in the newly hatching world of the Renaissance and Reformation. The urge to travel and see new things had always been a part of the journey, and now there were whole new continents to visit. Symptomatic of this loss of interest, the monks in Compostela even misplaced Santiago's body; warned of an imminent attack by Sir Francis Drake, they hid the precious relic, and by some extraordinary attack of amnesia, forgot where they put it; in 1879, by chance, it turned up during restoration work on the cathedral.

Although the pilgrims' hospice at Roncevaux still served 30,000 meals a year to pilgrims in the 18th century, by the 1970s it looked as if the pilgrimage to Compostela had dried up for good – just when it was about to undergo an extraordinary revival. In 1985, UNESCO designated the pilgrimage route as part of the World Patrimony of Humanity, helping to initiate the restoration of the superb Romanesque churches that punctuate the route (those at St-Sever, Aire-sur-Adour, and St-Bertrand-de-Comminges in this book offer a taste). The numbers have risen ever since: there were 4,918 pilgrims in 1990 and 9,734 in 1992, and at least triple that in 1993, a holy year (whenever 25 July, St James' day, falls on Sunday). The year 2000 saw an even greater increase as people made the pilgrimage to celebrate the millennium.

The renewal of Compostela is only part of the movement towards pilgrimages across Europe as conventional church attendance falls off, as the brave new world of the Renaissance and Reformation seems tired and old, and there are no new places to go but within one's self. Pilgrims today speak of spiritual rather than religious reasons for making the arduous trek to Compostela, seeking not indulgences or penitence, but the absolute and inner awareness, an alternative, something beyond what organized day-to-day life and church attendance can offer. Medieval pilgrims, who lived in the days of the totalitarian church, were no different, and were certainly better equipped than we are today to interpret the meaning behind the remarkable, unorthodox art in the medieval churches that lie along the way of initiation. The western quest appeals to something deep in the human soul, that resounds with poetic resonance. After all, it was a primordial Indo-European belief that a star appears in the Milky Way whenever a mortal is born, and 'shoots' towards the west when they die, towards the realm of the dead, towards Compostela (*campus stelae in finis terrae*), 'the field of stars at the world's end'.

Duck and Other Delicacies

Gascon Cuisine

'*C'est le pays du bien vivre et du bon manger,*' say the Gascons of their fertile, generous country, and with good reason. In the face of modern dietary theory, it sticks to its age-old traditions, based heavily on meat; a proper Gascon expects to see meat or poultry in the soup, as a main course, and in the gravy. The Gers and the Landes rival one another in their annual production of foie gras, the enlarged liver of either a goose (*oie*) or duck (*canard*). The Gers produces much of France's foie gras d'oie, generally said to be finer, while the Landes produces 60 per cent of the duck. Foie gras comes raw (*nature*) or half-cooked (*mi-cuit*) in a frying pan, with a bit of lemon or *verjus* (the tart juice of underripe grapes), salt and pepper and white grapes, and served with slices of toasted *pain de campagne*; a favourite Gascon way of serving it is mi-cuit, with grapes lightly sautéed in Armagnac, or with apples fried in the fat. The remaining parts of the goose or duck hardly go to waste: thighs, legs or wings are preserved as *confits* (traditional potted meats), cooked and then put up in their own fat, and reheated in the oven – absolutely delicious. *Magrets* (that's a Gascon word; the French spell it *maigrets*) are halves of duck or goose breast, best simply grilled and served with a very light cream sauce with parsley and garlic, or in the autumn, with fresh *cèpes*. First popularized in the 1950s, a grilled *magret* is like a steak, and if you order one you'll be asked how want it cooked; the French as usual tend to eat them quite rare (*bleu* – practically still alive, or *sanglant*, bloody; *à point* is what the French consider medium – it's still pink; *bien cuit* is well done; if you want it well done like they mean down in Texas, you'd better say something like *complètement brûlé* – really burned, although it may break a French chef's heart). The neck (*cou*) of the duck or goose is a delicacy, stuffed with truffle, minced pork and foie gras. Any meat that's left over is made into sausages, pâtés, terrines and meaty *rillons*, mixed with a bit of fat to make a smooth paste. *Gésiers* (gizzards) go into a *salade landaise*, along with slices of dried *magret* and foie gras. The fat is equally precious, and is used in a wide range of dishes instead of butter or olive oil. Even the fat-coated carcasses don't go to waste, but take the form of *demoiselles*, grilled on a wood fire, a traditional peasant favourite that occasionally makes it onto pricey restaurant menus. If you find all this distressingly rich, take courage from recent studies showing that the basic southwestern diet, with all its duck and goose fat and red wine, is actually good for you. Heart disease is half the rate it is in the United States, and many natives live well into their nineties. Perhaps a sign of things to come is the huge success of FR3 Aquitaine's cookery programme, *La Cuisine des Mousquetaires*, where Maïté and Micheline from the Landes show how it's done with traditional Gascon flair, amazing viewers from as far away as Toronto.

Other poultry gets less of the limelight and fewer billings on the restaurant menus. Gascony raises free-range chickens by the million; poulet de Loué from the Sarthe in the Gers is France's biggest producer, and the poulet de St-Sever in the Landes is second. Locally, much of it goes into soups. *Alicuit* is a traditional Gascon ragout of poultry giblets (even testicles), wings, potatoes, carrots and onions. Guinea fowl, capon, pheasant and partridge are often simply roasted in their own juice.

Game birds, 'gifts from heaven', are a veritable mania; quail, thrush, wild ducks, pheasants, and woodcock (*bécassier*) appear on autumn menus, but the real favourite is wood pigeon, or *palombe*, although few would countenance the way many are caught – netted a flock at a time as they migrate in October. All of the above birds are served roasted and flambéed in armagnac, or cooked *en salmis*: roasted and flambéed and served in a rich sauce made from the giblets that takes hours to prepare. But the greatest delicacy of all, the little *ortolan* (a kind of bunting), has been hunted almost to extinction and is protected by law, forcing ortolan hunters and eaters to go underground as well as under their napkins. Ortolans have been consumed in sacred gastronomic rites ever since the decadent Romans showed the Gascons how. The birds, who migrate to France in April, are captured alive in traps and force-fed a rich grain diet for three to six weeks before the *coup de grâce*: a glass of old armagnac forced down their beaks. They are then plucked but not gutted, tied up and cooked slowly in their own fat on a wood fire. They have such a heavenly aroma that the only way to eat them is with a great cloth napkin over the head to completely capture the aroma. Real effetes used to prepare them with an olive wedged in their beaks, inhale the aroma, eat the olive and throw the rest out.

Red meat – beef from the Chalosse – lamb and pork are certainly present, usually stewed or roasted (a *gasconnade* is a leg of lamb with anchovies and garlic); their sweetbreads, kidneys, brains, tongues and hearts star in a lot of dishes you'll never see back home. From the rivers, especially the Adour, come trout, pike (*brochet*) and crayfish (*écrevisses*), pike-perch (*sandre*), shad (*alose*) and salmon. Shad is one of the stars of local menus in the springtime: marinated in white wine and oil perfumed with bay leaves, then cooked on the grill over vine cuttings and served with diced ham and grapes; often it is stuffed with sorrel, which helps dissolve its many fine bones. Despite the Landes' long stretch of Atlantic coast, it only has one port, Capbreton, and seafood plays a correspondingly minor role in Gascon cuisine. Oysters are the most important single item, and most of them come from Arcachon, just over the border, served preferably raw with little grilled sausages called *crépinettes*.

A good deal of passion is reserved for *cèpes*, and hunting them in the autumn, especially on someone else's property, leads to huge rows, slit tyres, dog bites and gunshots. There are two kinds: the true *cèpe bordelais* (*cèpe de chêne*) and the less tasty *cèpe de pins*. They go into scores of dishes, from omelettes to *daubes*, or stews (usually pork in Gascony) cooked for hours in red wine, or grilled with garlic and served with ham. There are few strictly vegetarian dishes. Asparagus, both green and white, thrives in the sandy soil of the Landes and is often served as a starter; *soupe à l'oseille* (sorrel soup) is tasty, although it often has a dollop of goose fat in it. Fresh tomatoes are the main ingredient of *saupiquet*, stewed with white wine and onions.

Traditional Gascon desserts are somewhat rarer and invariably feature a generous nip of Armagnac. Prunes are marinated in armagnac and orange blossom water and topped with paper-thin pastry called *pastis*, of one part butter to four parts flour, in a *tourtière*; sometimes apples replace the plums and it's called a *croustade*. Unique to Gascony, the slightly heavy cake *millasson* is made from cornflour and comes in a range of variations, often with apples and armagnac. Crêpes are flambéed in armagnac. Melons from Lectoure, apricots or cherries are served in armagnac and followed by a little glass of the same potion to close out a meal in style. Although they are not as numerous in Gascony as further north, keep your eyes peeled for *ferme-auberges*, or farm restaurants, where most of what you eat has been raised on the spot and prepared according to age-old traditions in the farm kitchen.

Béarnais and Pyrenean Cuisine

Like Gascony, this is a region of geese (Henri IV loved them young and roasted) and goose and duck confits. But there are a number of specific dishes that originated in the Béarn kitchen, among them *garbure*, a hotpot made from a quarter of a goose carcass, green cabbage, beans, sausage and salt pork, with thick slices of country bread in the broth. It's traditional, at the end of the bowl, to add a dash of red wine, a custom called *chabrot* (or *goulade*). Closely associated with Henri IV, who wanted every French family to have some once a week, the *poule au pot* is another classic; the chicken must first be stuffed with ham and breadcrumbs, then boiled with vegetables. A favourite Béarnais soup, *tourin* (amongst many spellings), made with lots of garlic, onions, tomato paste, a pat of duck fat and slices of country bread, is popular throughout the southwest. Most of the *jambon de Bayonne* – a raw ham similar to prosciutto – is actually made, salted and dried in Béarn. To receive the coveted label of authenticity (Marque Deposée Jambon de Bayonne), the pigs must have been raised in Béarn, the Basque country or Armagnac, and the salt must come from Salies-de-Béarn. Frogs' legs (*cuisses de grenouilles*) are popular in a variety of forms, as is *truit au Jurançon*, trout baked with mushrooms and crème fraîche. Unlike Gascony, Béarn is an important cheese producer, and most of it comes from sheep's milk (*fromages de brebis*): best known are Iraty, a mix of cow's and sheep's milk, and the pure sheep's milk cheeses from Sost and Laruns.

East of Béarn in the Pyrenees, you'll find much the same. Tarbes, however, is proudest of its beans, *haricots tarbais*, introduced in the 17th century and planted among the maize, which acts as poles to support the bean stalks; you'll often find them served in salads. This is also a good place to look for cakes and sweets: the conical layer cake *gâteau à la Broche*, chocolate-covered creamed chestnuts (*châtaignes*), *haricot tarbais* (a sweet that resembles the famous bean, made of nougat and fine chocolate), red and yellow *bigourdettes* (a variety of chocolates) and *hussardes* (chocolate-covered almonds).

Farther east, the Ariège has a few fairly rustic specialities of its own and a rather Gertrude Stein-ish motto to go with them: *Per fe uno bouno mouleto, y cal bouta so que cal* ('to make a good omelette, you have to put in what you have to put in'). Cabbage is one of the favourite things local chefs feel compelled to put in: if a dish is prepared *à la ariégeoise*, it will have cabbage, salt pork, potatoes and kidney beans with it. *Azinat*, perhaps the most famous Ariège dish, is a hearty cabbage soup cooked in an earthenware pot. Main courses often feature lamb (the leg, or breast, or on a spit, or en croûte, shepherds' style); other items you'll also see on the menus are frogs' legs, trout with ham, *cassoulet ariégeois* (with a ragout of mutton), *civet de sanglier* (boar stewed in a sauce of red wine, mushrooms, bacon, and onions), or the *tripes du Comte de Foix* which aren't as nasty as they sound. Meat dishes or even azinat may come with *rouzoule*, a kind of stuffing of ham, garlic and breadcrumbs. Like the other Pyrenean departments, the Ariège produces plenty of cheese: Moulis, Bethmale, Bamalou, Rogalais and Broussette are all strong and delicious, as well as tomme and cabécou – goat's milk cheeses. Honey made from rhododendron, heather, chestnut, raspberry, or mixed wild flowers from the high mountains is especially good and widely available, direct from the producer. Although the wine produced in the northern Ariège is insignificant, there has recently been a revival of the medieval elixir Hypocras, the favourite tonic of Compostela pilgrims and Gaston Fébus alike, now made in Tarascon-sur-Ariège and sold as an aperitif.

Basque Cuisine

Basque cuisine is one of the spiciest in France, making liberal use of tasty dried red peppers called *piments d'Espelette*. They are a main ingredient in the essential Basque condiment piperade, made from red peppers, green peppers, tomatoes, garlic and whipped eggs, lightly fried and served with jambon de Bayonne; prepared minus the eggs, it is used as a relish. Seafood holds an important place in the diet: tuna, bonito tuna, and cod are caught on the high seas; special favourites are scallops (*coquilles St-Jacques*), lobster, small cuttlefish (*chiperones*, served stuffed or in a casserole in their own ink), big eels (served with parsley and garlic) and *pibales* (or *civelles*), baby eels that arrive in spring on the Basque coast straight from the Sargasso Sea, only to be drawn by the lights of night fishermen and tossed in the frying pan. At least once try the Basque fish soup *ttoro*, based on conger eel, gurnet and angler-fish, but with a hundred variations. In a land of shepherds, lamb is not surprisingly the favourite meat, especially lamb chops, sweetbreads and roast leg of lamb (*gigot*). The Basques are also known for their charcuterie, such as *tripotcha*, a kind of pudding (*boudin*) made from sheep's tripe, and *loukinkos* (also spelled *lukenques*), little garlic sausages. *Poulet basquaise*, stewed in a pot with peppers, tomatoes, mushrooms and wine, is universal, as is sheep's cheese (Etorki is sold everywhere in France). Finish a meal in grand style with an almondy *gâteau basque* topped with cherry sauce or some exquisite chocolate confection from Bayonne.

Catalan Cuisine

The Catalans in Andorra, Roussillon and the Eastern Pyrenees have many sterling qualities, but display only the most modest ones in their restaurants. The totem fish of the *département* is the little anchovy of Collioure, which hardy souls from Spain to Marseille pulverize with garlic, onion, basil and oil to make *anchoïade*, a favourite apéritif spread on raw celery or toast. A popular starter is *gambas à la planxa*, prawns grilled and served on a 'plank', or anchovies with strips of red pepper, which is better than it sounds. Main courses include *roussillonnade*, a dish of bolet mushrooms and sausages grilled over a pine-cone fire, and *boles de Picolat*, Catalan meatballs with mushrooms cooked in sauce. The classic dessert is *crème catalane*, a caramel-covered trifle flavoured with anise and cinnamon.

The Wines of Gascony and the Pyrenees

Because of its gentle climate (few people realize that Pau is south of Nice), the region between the Atlantic and the Pyrenees has been making wine at least since Roman times. The mountains, rivers and valleys form a complex variety of microclimates that protect the vines from frosts into November, allowing the grapes as much as an extra six weeks to ripen – hence the noble rot (*pourriture noble*) of the rich Jurançons, Vic-Bilhs and Pacherencs. Following the Dark Age invasions by Vascones, Visigoths, Franks and so on, the vineyards were re-established by the monasteries in the 11th and 12th centuries, most notably at Madiran. Bayonne was the main port for exporting the wines to England and the north, especially after the 1450s, when the River Adour, then the main highway into the interior, was forced to stop changing and use Bayonne permanently as its last stop before the ocean. After the Hundred Years' War trade slowed down dramatically; the wines of Béarn, which lacked even river access to the sea, were in danger of disappearing altogether until the Baron of Lahontan (near Bellocq) opened a waterway at his own expense between St-Pé-de-Bigorre and Bayonne (1630–58). Ironically, what ensured the success of the vineyards was the Revocation of the Edict of Nantes in 1695, which sent many Béarnese into exile to England and the Netherlands, where they craved wines from back home and reopened export markets. After the Second World War the wines of Gascony and the Pyrenees began their current revival, thanks to their strong individual characteristics and the high quality of the chief vintages: the ruby red, highly tannic Madiran (perfect with confits, game bird dishes, red meat and Pyrenean cheeses), the reds and rosés of Irouléguy (good with chicken dishes, or grilled or roast lamb), tangy sweet or dry Jurançon (the sweet is the traditional accompaniment for foie gras, while golden dry Jurançon and dry Pacherenc go well with both fresh-water fish and seafood) and the fruity whites and rosés of Béarn (ideal with mushroom dishes, omelettes, *garbure* and Bayonne ham).

The Basques distil their own digestive liqueur, Izarra, which comes in a potent green, a mix of Pyrenean herbs with exotic spices that is sold in every bar in the land. Gascony, for its part, is practically synonymous with its mellow amber brandy, armagnac, made from a low-alcohol white wine fortified with *eau-de-vie*, distilled in a process that approaches alchemy before being aged in special oak barrels for at least two or three years (*see* pp.120–22). Another high-octane Gascon speciality is *floc*, the 'Flower of Gascony', made by adding armagnac to stop the fermentation of the red or white wine, resulting in an apéritif ranging between 16° and 18° that is best when moderately chilled.

Travel

04

Before You Go

A little preparation will help you get much more out of your holiday. Check the list of events (*see* pp.46–8) to help you decide where you want to be and when, and book accommodation early; if you are planning to base yourself in one area, write ahead to the local **tourist offices** listed in the text for complete lists of self-catering accommodation, hotels and campgrounds in their areas (many of these have their own websites). Alternatively, contact one of the many agencies in the UK or USA. For more general information about your holiday, get in touch with a **French Government Tourist Office**:

UK: French Government Tourist Office, 178 Piccadilly, London W1V 0AL, **t** 09068 244 123, **f** (020) 7493 6594, *piccadilly@mdlf.demon.co.uk*, *www.franceguide.com*.

France: Maison de la France, 20 Av de l'Opéra, 75001 Paris, **t** 01 42 96 70 00, **f** 01 42 96 70 11.

USA: 16th Floor, 444 Madison Av, New York, NY 10020, **t** (410) 286 8310, **f** (212) 838 7855; Suite 715, 9454 Wilshire Bd, Beverly Hills, Los Angeles, CA 90212–2967, **t** (310) 271 2693, **f** (310) 276 2835

Canada: 1981 Av McGill College, No.490, Montreal, Quebec H3A 2W9, **t** (514) 876 9881, **f** (514) 845 4868

Getting There

By Air

The big international airports in the region are at Bordeaux and Toulouse. There are smaller ones at Lourdes/Tarbes, Agen, Pau, Biarritz and Carcassonne. Lourdes/Tarbes is the second biggest charter airport in France, and 80 per cent of passengers are pilgrims; travel organizations and Catholic organizations can fill you in on pilgrim charters.

Air France, UK **t** 0845 0845 111, flies daily to Toulouse from Heathrow and Birmingham. From Paris Orly, Air France flies daily to Biarritz, Bordeaux, Toulouse, Pau and Agen and Lourdes/Tarbes.

British Airways, UK **t** 0345 222 111, France **t** 08 02 80 29 02, *www.british-airways.com*, flies direct to Bordeaux and Toulouse.

Air Liberté, **t** 0803 805 805, *www.airliberte.fr*, has daily flights between Paris Orly-Sud and Toulouse.

Some new low-cost airlines have provided several options for reaching the region:

Ryanair, **t** 08701 569 569, in France **t** 05 59 43 83 93, *www.ryanair.com*, has daily no-frills cheap flights to Biarritz and Carcassonne.

Flybe, *www.flybe.com*, the internet-only wing of British Airways, has daily budget flights from the UK to Toulouse and Bergerac.

By Train

Air prices and the sheer brain-mushing awfulness of airports make travelling by high-speed train an attractive alternative. **Eurostar** trains, **t** (0870) 186 186, *www.eurostar.com*, leave from London Waterloo or Ashford International in Kent, and there are direct connections to Paris (Gare du Nord; 3 hours) and Lille (2 hours). Fares are cheaper if booked at least 7 days in advance and you include a Saturday night away. You must check in at least 20 minutes before departure, or you will not be allowed on to the train.

France's high-speed **TGVs** (*trains à grande vitesse*) shoot along at an average of 180mph when they're not breaking world records. The journey from Paris' Gare de Montparnasse on the TGV Atlantique to Bordeaux takes 2hrs 58mins, and continues on to Toulouse in slightly under 5hrs; branches race to Tarbes in about 6hrs, and to Dax, Bayonne and Biarritz. Travel costs are only minimally higher on a TGV than on slower trains; some weekday departures require a supplement and all require seat reservations, which you can make when you buy your ticket or at the station before departure.

Another pleasant way of getting there is by overnight **sleeper** (the slower trains for the southwest all depart from the Gare d'Austerlitz in Paris).

People aged under 26 are eligible for a 30% **discount** on fares (*see* the travel agencies listed above) and there are other discounts if you're aged over 65 available from major travel agents.

You can book tickets for through-journeys from outside France. In the UK tickets can be

Charters, Discounts and Special Deals

UK and Ireland

Trailfinders, 194 Kensington High St, London W8 7RG, **t** (020) 7937 1234, *www.trailfinders.com*.

Travel Cuts, 295a Regent St, London W1R 7YA, **t** (020) 7255 1944, *www.travelcuts.co.uk*.

Budget Travel, 134 Lower Baggot St, Dublin 2, **t** (01) 661 1866, *www.budgettravel.ie*.

United Travel, Stillorgan Bowl, Stillorgan, County Dublin, **t** (01) 288 4346/7.

Try websites such as *www.cheapflights.co.uk* and *www.lastminute.com*.

USA and Canada

New Frontiers, USA **t** 800 677 0720; Canada, in Montréal, **t** (514) 871 3060,*www.newfrontiers.com*.

Travel Avenue, USA **t** 800 333 3335, *www.travelavenue.com*.

Air Brokers International, USA **t** (800) 883 3273.

Last Minute Travel Club, USA **t** (877) 970 3500; Canada **t** (877) 970 3500, *www.lastminuteclub.com*. Payment of an annual membership fee gets you cheap standby deals; there are also special rates for the major car rental companies in Europe, and on train tickets.

www.traveldiscounts.com. Members get special rates on flights, hotels and tours.

Student Discounts

Students equipped with relevant ID cards are eligible for considerable reductions, not only on flights, but on trains and on admission fees to museums, concerts and more. Agencies specializing in student and youth travel can help you in applying for the cards, as well as filling you in on the best deals.

USIT Campus, *www.usitcampus.co.uk*, 52 Grosvenor Gardens SW1, London, **t** (0870) 240 1010. Also branches at most UK universities: Bristol **t** (0117) 929 2494; Birmingham **t** (0121) 359 5955; Cambridge **t** (01223) 360 201; Edinburgh **t** (0131) 225 6111; Manchester **t** (0161) 274 3105; Oxford **t** (01865) 242067.

STA Travel, 86 Old Brompton Rd, London, SW7 3LH, **t** (0870) 160 6070, *www.sta-travel.com*; for insurance, overland travel and hotels call **t** (020) 7361 6150.

Many other branches in the UK, including: 117 Euston Rd, London, NW1 2SX, **t** (020) 7581 4132; Bristol **t** (0870) 167 6777; Leeds **t** (0870) 168 6878; Manchester **t** (0161) 839 7838; Oxford **t** 0870 163 6373; Cambridge **t** (01223) 366 966.

In the USA, New York City **t** (212) 627 3111.

In Australia, Sydney **t** (02) 9361 4966.

Europe Student Travel, 6 Campden St, London W8, **t** (020) 7727 764; non-students as well.

USIT, *www.usitnow-ie*, Aston Quay, Dublin 2 **t** (01) 602 1600; Cork **t** (021) 270 900; Belfast **t** (028) 90324 073; Galway **t** (091) 524 601; Limerick **t** (061) 332 079; Waterford **t** (051) 872 601.

Council Travel, 205 E 42nd St, New York, NY 10017, **t** (212) 822 2700. Specialist in student and charter flights; branches across the USA.

Travel Cuts, 187 College St, Toronto, Ontario M5T 1P7, **t** (416) 979 2406, *www.travelcuts.com*. Canada's largest student travel specialists; branches in most provinces.

For help in France contact:

CIDJ (*Centre d'Information et de la Documentation Jeunesse*), 101 Quai Branly, 75740 Paris, Cedex 15, **t** (01) 44 49 12 25, **f** 01 40 65 02 61.

UFCV (*Union Française des Centres de Vacances et de Loisirs*), 10 Quai Charente, 75019 Paris, **t** (01) 44 72 14 14, **f** (01) 40 34 53 49; organises cultural, sporting and leisure holidays for young people aged 4 to 18.

USIT Voyages, 4 Rue Vivienne, 75002 Paris, **t** (01) 42 44 14 00, **f** (01) 42 44 14 01

booked from any British Rail station or travel centre, or from the **International Rail Centre**, Victoria Station, **t** (020) 7834 2345. You can also visit the **Rail Europe Travel Shop**, 179 Piccadilly, **t** 08705 848 848, or book on-line at *www.raileurope.co.uk*. or *www.sncf.fr*.

SNCF central reservations and information is available on **t** 08 36 35 35 35, 7am–10pm daily. If you reserve by phone or Minitel (3615 SNCF), you must pick up and pay for your ticket within 48 hours.

If you plan on making several long train journeys, look into the variety of **rail passes**. A **Eurodomino** pass allows unlimited journeys on France's rail network for three to eight days' travel within one month, but this must be bought before travelling to France. Discounted rates are available to children aged 4 to 11, and young people aged 12 to 25. Visitors from North America have a wide choice of passes, including **Eurailpass**, **Flexipass** and **Saver Pass**, which can all be purchased in the USA; call **t** (212) 308 3103 for information, **t** 1 800 223 636 for reservations. A variety of passes and discounts are available once you are within France (*see* 'Getting Around', opposite).

You must always '***composter votre billet***' (date-stamp your ticket in the orange *composteur* machine at the station) before starting your journey.

For long-distance train travel, **bicycles** need to be transported separately, and must be registered and insured. They can be delivered to your destination, though this may take several days. On Eurostar you need to check in your bike at least 24 hours before you travel, or wait 24 hours at the other end.

By Ferry

Two ferry companies make the journey from Britain to northern Spain, from where it's a short car journey to the Pyrenees.

Brittany Ferries, **t** (08705) 561 600, *www.brittanyferries.com*, sail from Plymouth to Santander, and offer excellent standards including air-conditioned en suite cabins, a choice of restaurants, cinemas, swimming pool and sauna.

P&O Ferries, **t** (0870) 129 6002, *www.mycruiseferries.com*, sail from Portsmouth to Bilbao; their *Pride of Bilbao* is the UK's largest ferry, with accommodation for 2,500 passengers and 600 cars; it offers several restaurants, a cinema, sauna, swimming pool, and has cabins for all passengers.

If you prefer to cross the Channel, **Brittany Ferries** sail from Portsmouth to Caen and St-Malo, Poole to Cherbourg and St-Malo, and Plymouth to Roscoff; **P&O** can transport you from Dover to Calais and from Portsmouth to Le Havre and Cherbourg; **Sally Line**, **t** (020) 7409 2240, leave Ramsgate for Dunkirk; **P&O Stena**, **t** (0870) 242 4999, *www.posl.com*, sail from Dover to Calais, Southampton to Cherbourg and Newhaven to Dieppe.

Hoverspeed Fast Ferries, **t** (08705) 240 241, have a new Superseacat that goes from Newhaven to Dieppe in 2hrs.

By Coach

The cheapest way to get from London to southwest France is by **National Express Eurolines** coach, **t** (0990) 143 219, in the UK, **t** (08) 36 69 52 52 in France; tickets are available from any National Express office. There are at least three journeys a week from London to Bordeaux and down the Landes to the Pays Basque and San Sebastian (26hrs) and to Toulouse (22hrs). The trip is long and slow but inexpensive, and has an open return. Going by coach also saves you the hassle of crossing Paris to change trains.

By Car

A car entering France must have its registration and insurance papers. If you're coming from the UK or Ireland, the dip of the headlights must be adjusted to the right. Carrying a warning triangle is mandatory, and it should be placed 50m behind the car if you have a breakdown. All cars in France are required to have rear seat belts and these must be worn by rear seat passengers. Drivers with a valid licence from an EU country, Canada, the USA or Australia don't need an international licence. If you plan to hire a car, look into air and holiday package deals to save money, or consider leasing a car if you mean to stay three weeks or more. Prices vary widely from firm to firm, and beware the small print about service charges and taxes.

If you're driving down from the UK you may face going through or around Paris on the abominable *périphérique*, a task best tackled on either side of rush hour. To avoid it, seasoned travellers favour the Portsmouth-

Car Hire Offices in France

Avis, **t** (01) 55 38 68 68
Budget, **t** (08) 00 10 00 00
Europcar, **t** (01) 30 43 82 82
Hertz, **t** (01) 39 38 38 38
Rent-a-Car, **t** (01) 45 22 28 28/08 36 69 46 95

Caen ferry, offering a direct and not too frenetic drive via Le Mans, Tours and Poitiers. Caen (360 miles to Périgueux) and Le Havre (390 miles to Périgueux) are the closest Channel ports to the southwest. From Caen or Le Havre take the N158/N138 to Le Mans and Tours, and continue on the N10 to Poitiers, from where you can branch off for either Bordeaux, via Angoulême.

Another Bordeaux alternative is the *autoroute* A10 from Tours. If you're visiting the west end of the region, you might also consider sailing to St-Malo and taking in Rennes, Nantes, La Rochelle and Saintes, and picking up the A10 there towards Bordeaux. Another option is taking the ferry from Plymouth to Bilbao, which will leave you only a three- to four-hour drive to Biarritz.

The **Channel tunnel** provides another option for drivers. Eurotunnel carries cars and their passengers from Folkestone to Calais on a simple drive-on-drive-off system (journey time 35mins). Payment is made at toll booths (which accept cash, cheques or credit cards). Prepaid tickets and booked spaces are available, but no booking is necessary as you can just turn up and take the next available service. Eurotunnel runs 24 hours a day, all year round, with a service at least once an hour through the night. For information and bookings, contact **Eurotunnel Customer Services Centre**, PO Box 300, Folkestone, Kent CT19 4QW, **t** (08705) 353 535, *www.eurotunnel.com*.

Entry Formalities

Passports and Visas

Holders of EU, US and Canadian passports do not need a visa to enter France for stays up to three months, but everyone else still does. Apply at your nearest French Consulate; the most convenient visa is the *visa de circulation*, allowing for multiple stays of three months over a three-year period. If you intend staying longer, the law says you need a *carte de séjour*, a requirement EU citizens can easily get around as passports are rarely stamped. On the other hand, non-EU citizens had best apply for an extended visa at home, a complicated procedure requiring proof of income, etc. You can't get a *carte de séjour* without this visa, a trial run for the *ennui* you'll undergo in applying for a *carte de séjour* at your local *mairie*.

Health and Travel Insurance

Citizens of the EU who bring along their E-111 forms are entitled to the same health services as French citizens. This means paying up front for medical care and prescriptions, of which costs 75–80 per cent are reimbursed later – a complex procedure for the non-French. As an alternative, consider a travel insurance policy, covering theft and losses and offering 100% medical refund; check to see if it covers extra expenses if you get bogged down in airport or train strikes. Beware that accidents resulting from sports are rarely covered by ordinary insurance. Canadians are usually covered in France by their provincial health coverage; Americans and others should check their individual policies.

Getting Around

By Train

SNCF general information: **t** 08 36 35 35 35, *www.sncf.fr*.

The southwest has a decent network of trains, although many of the smaller lines have only two or three connections a day, making it rather difficult to see much of the country by rail; in places SNCF buses have taken over former train routes.

Prices, if not a bargain, are still reasonable, and **discounts** are available especially if you travel off-peak in a *période bleue* with a return ticket and go at least 1,000km (25% discounts). Couples are eligible for a **Découverte à Deux** tariff, which gives a discount of 25% on all trains when travelling together in a blue period. Anyone over 60 can purchase a **Carte Sénior** valid for a year and giving 25–50% off individual journeys according to availability, and 25% off train journeys from France to 25 countries in Europe. There is also a **12–25 Carte** which offers 50% reductions in blue periods and a 25% reduction in white periods. Anyone can save money by buying a second-class ticket at least a week to a month in advance (**Découverte J8 or J30**), the only condition being that you must use it at the designated time on the designated train, with no chance for reimbursement if you miss it.

Tickets must be **stamped** in the little orange machines by the door to the tracks that say *Compostez votre billet* (this puts the date on the ticket, to keep you from using the same one over and over again). Any time you interrupt a journey until another day, you have to re-*compost* your ticket.

Long-distance *Trains Corails* can be utterly delightful when they aren't too crowded. They have snack trolleys and bar/cafeteria cars (the food isn't bad), and some offer play areas for small children.

Nearly every station has banks of mechanical **lockers** (*consignes automatiques*) that spit out a slip with the lock combination when you use them; they take about half an hour to puzzle out the first time you use them, so plan accordingly.

By Bus

Do not count on seeing any part of rural France by public transport. The bus network is barely adequate between major cities and towns (places often already well-served by rail) and rotten in rural areas, where the one bus a day fits the school schedule, leaving at the crack of dawn and returning in the afternoon; more remote villages are linked to civilization only once a week or not at all.

Buses are run either by the SNCF (replacing discontinued rail routes) or private firms. **Rail passes** are valid on SNCF lines and they generally coincide with trains. Private bus firms, especially when they have a monopoly, tend to be a bit more expensive than trains; some towns have a *gare routière* (coach station), usually near the train station, while in others the buses stop at bars or any other place that catches their fancy. Stops are hardly ever marked, while on the other hand in some areas there are conspicuous bus stops everywhere, where in fact no service exists. The posted schedules are not always to be trusted. The tourist office or shopkeepers near the bus stop may have a more accurate instinct for when a bus is likely to appear.

By Car

Unless you plan to stick to the major towns, cycle, or walk, a car is regrettably the only way to see the southwest. This too has its drawbacks: high rental car rates and Europe's priciest petrol, and an accident rate double that of the UK (and much higher than the USA). The vaunted French logic and clarity breaks down completely on the asphalt. Go slowly and be careful; never expect any French driver to be aware of the possibility of a collision.

Roads are generally excellently maintained, but anything of less status than a departmental route (D road) may be uncomfortably narrow. **Petrol stations** are rare in rural areas and closed on Sunday afternoons, so consider your fuel supply while planning any forays into the back country – especially if you're on unleaded. The scoundrels will expect a tip for oil, windscreen-cleaning or air. The price of petrol (*essence*) varies considerably, with motorways always more expensive.

France used to have a rule of giving priority to the right at every intersection. This has largely disappeared, although there may still be intersections, usually in towns, where it applies – these will be marked. Watch out for the *Cédez le passage* (Give way) signs and be careful. Generally, as you'd expect, give priority to the main road, and to the left on roundabouts. If you are new to France, think of every intersection as a new and perilous experience. Watch out for byzantine street parking rules (which would take pages to explain: do as the natives do, and be especially careful about village centres on market days).

Unless sweetened in an air or holiday package deal, **car hire** in France is an expensive proposition (€90–120 per day, without mileage, for the cheapest cars).

Speed limits are 130km/80mph on the *autoroutes* (toll motorways); 110km/69mph on dual carriageways (divided highways); 90km/55mph on other roads; 50km/30mph in an 'urbanized area': as soon as you pass a white sign with a town's name on it and until you pass another sign with town's name barred. Fines for speeding, payable on the spot, can be astronomical if you flunk the breathalyzer. The French have one admirably

Useful Websites
Route planner: *www.iti.fr*
Autoroute information: *www.autoroutes.fr*
Roads and traffic information: *www.equipment.gouv.fr*

civilized custom of the road; if oncoming drivers unaccountably flash their headlights at you, it means the *gendarmes* are about.

If you wind up in an **accident**, the procedure is to fill out and sign a *constat aimable*. If your French isn't sufficient to deal with this, hold off until you find someone to translate for you so you don't accidentally incriminate yourself.

If you have a **breakdown** and are a member of a motoring club affiliated to the Touring Club de France, ring the latter; if not, ring the police, **t** 17.

By Bicycle

Tour de France champions pump straight up the steepest Pyrenees, but if you're looking for something a bit less to a lot less challenging, you'll find it along the plethora of tiny rural roads in Gascony and foothills of the Pyrenees. French drivers, not always courteous to fellow motorists, usually give cyclists a wide berth.

Maps and info are available from the **Fédération Française de Cyclotourisme**, 8 Rue Jean-Marie Jégo, 75013 Paris, **t** 01 44 16 88 88; in Britain information on cycle-touring in France is available from the **Cyclists' Touring Club**, Cotterell House, 69 Meadrow, Godalming, Surrey GU7 3HS, **t** (01483) 417 217.

Getting your own bike to France is fairly easy: Air France and British Airways carry them free from Britain. From the USA or Australia most airlines will carry them as long as they're boxed and are including in your total baggage weight. In all cases, telephone ahead. Certain French trains (marked with a bicycle symbol in the timetable) carry bikes for free; otherwise you have to send it as registered luggage and pay a fee, with delivery guaranteed within five days.

Bike Hire

The French are keen cyclists, and if you haven't brought your own bike, the main towns and holiday centres always seem to have at least one shop that hires out **mountain bikes** (*VTT*) or **touring/racing bikes**; local tourist offices have lists. Be prepared to pay a fairly hefty deposit on a good bike (from 1,000F) and you may want to enquire about theft insurance.

You can also hire bikes of widely varying quality (most of them 10-speed) at most SNCF stations and in major towns. The advantage of hiring from a station means that you can drop it off at another, as long as you specify where when you hire it. Rates run at around 50F a day, with a deposit of 300–400F and credit card number.

On Foot

A network of long-distance paths, the *Grandes Randonnées*, or GRs for short (marked by distinctive red and white signs), take in some of the most beautiful scenery in Gascony and the Pyrenees, and the Pyrenees make up some of the most gorgeous walking territory in Europe. Each GR is described in a Topoguide, with maps and details about camping sites, *refuges*, *gîtes d'étape* and so on, available in area bookshops or from the **Centre d'Information Sentiers et Randonnée**, 64 Rue Gergovie, 75014 Paris, **t** 01 45 45 31 02. A good source in the UK is **Stanford's International Map Centre**, 12–14 Long Acre, Covent Garden, WC2E 9LP, **t** (020) 7730 1354.

The most popular trail is the **GR 10**, which goes straight across the Pyrenees, passing through many villages, and is accessible to any fit walker; also the more difficult **Haute Randonnée Pyrénéenne**, higher up and more or less following the French-Spanish frontier, and passing through fewer villages.

In the Pyrenees, the best maps and trail guides and much of the mountain accommodation is administered by the **Randonnées Pyrénéennes**, and there are a number of places that can give you all the details, among them the **Centre d'Information sur la Montagne et les Sentiers (CIMES)**, BP 24, 65420 Ibos, **t** 05 62 90 09 92, **f** 05 62 90 67 61. In the Ariège, pick up a free copy of the *Guide des Promenades et Randonnées en Ariège, Pyrénées*, from the **Comité Départemental Ariègeois de la Randonnée Pédestre**, BP 143, 09003 Foix Cedex, **t** 05 61 02 30 70.

Special Interest Holidays

There are a number of ways to combine a holiday with study or a special interest. For more information, contact the **Cultural Services of the French Consulate**, 23 Cromwell Rd, London SW7 2DQ, **t** (020) 7838 2055, or at 972 Fifth Avenue, New York, NY 10021, **t** (212) 439 1400.

Allez France, 27 West St, Storrington RH20 4DZ, **t** (01903) 748 100, organizes gastronomic holidays to *auberges* and châteaux-hotels in Aquitaine.

Alternative Travel Group, 69–71 Banbury Rd, Oxford OX2 6PE, **t** (01865) 315 678, *www.atg-oxford.co.uk*, arranges visits to top wine estates in Gascony.

Bike and Sun Tours, 42 Whitby Ave, Guisborough TS14 7AN, **t** (01287) 639 739, *www.bikeandsuntours.co.uk*, arranges two-week guided motorcycle tours in the Pyrenees.

Erna Low Consultants, 9 Reece Mews, London SW7 3HE, **t** (0207) 594 0290, *www.ernalow.co.uk*, provides spa holidays in Biarritz, Dax, Anglet and Hendaye.

Exodus Travel, 9 Weir Rd, London SW12 0LT, **t** (020) 8675 5550, *www.exodustravel.co.uk*, arranges easy to fairly strenuous trekking in the Pyrenees.

French Expressions, 13 McCrone Mews, Belsize Lane, London NW3 5BG, **t** (020) 7431 1312, plans tailor-made tours to Armagnac.

Gascony Secret, **t** (01284) 827 253, *www.gascony-secret.com*, will organize rentals and holidays based around walking or the Mariac jazz festival.

Headwater Holidays, 146 London Rd, Northwich CW9 5HH, **t** (01606) 813 333, provides unescorted or escorted walking holidays in the Pyrenees.

Inntravel, Hovingham, York YO6 4JZ, **t** (01653) 628 811, arranges fly-fishing, walking and horse-riding holidays in the Pyrenees.

La France des Villages, Model Farm, Rattlesden, Bury St Edmunds IP30 0SY, **t** (01449) 737 664, organizes residential courses at a health farm in the Pyrenees.

LSG Theme Holidays, 201 Main St, Thornton, Coalville LE6 1AH, **t** (01509) 231 713, is a French-operated company offering language courses, painting and drawing, nature and walking holidays in the Pyrenees, and spa holidays in Salies-de-Béarn.

St Peter's Pilgrims, 87A Rushey Green, London SE6 4AF, **t** (020) 8244 8844, organizes pilgrimages to Lourdes by air for three, four or seven nights.

Practical A–Z

05

Average Maximum Temperatures in °C /°F

	Jan	Feb	Mar	April	May	June
Dax	11/52	13/55	15/59	17/63	20/68	25/77
Bayonne	13/55	14/57	16/61	18/64	21/70	25/77
Tarbes	12/54	13/55	14/57	16/61	21/70	25/77
	July	**Aug**	**Sept**	**Oct**	**Nov**	**Dec**
Dax	27/81	26/79	24/75	20/68	15/59	10/50
Bayonne	28/82	27/81	26/79	24/75	19/66	13/55
Tarbes	29/84	28/82	27/81	24/75	18/64	14/57

Climate and When to Go

Gascony's climate is that of the Aquitaine Basin, shielded from intemperate continental influences by the Massif Central. It is a fairly balmy, humid climate, strongly influenced by the Atlantic, with long hot summers broken by moist winds off the ocean. Early spring and late autumn usually get the most rainfall – and it can rain for weeks or even months at a time. The lush green western Pyrenees get masses of precipitation, on average over 200 days a year all along the Spanish border, including some 50 or so days of snow. Winters along the Atlantic coast are fairly mild, with fewer than 40 days of frost a year, while the inland valleys and the great forest of the Landes are usually a few degrees warmer or colder; the pocket around the Basque coast and southern Côte d'Argent enjoys something of a micro-climate, with winters as warm as the Mediterranean coast, although a good deal wetter.

Unless you're coming to ski or learn about the intricacies of preparing foie gras, **winter** is the bleakest time to visit; accommodation, restaurants and sights simply close down, and the skies are often cloudy all day. Up in the Pyrenees, unless it's an exceptional year, the ski season doesn't really start until January or reach its full stride until February. No matter how lovely the weather is, nothing under the snow line really opens up until the first tourist rush of the year – Palm Sunday and Easter week. The weather from March into May is wonderfully inconsistent: it can be hot enough for a dip in the pool or so cold that you need a heavy coat, and can vary from week to week. May and June are often good months to come: usually summer has set well in, and it's hot enough for swims in the coastal lakes, the sights are open, hotel rates are still low. Hot July, August and early September are French school holidays, when everything is packed, prices are high, and the Pyrenees are apt to be pummelled by sudden and very violent thunderstorms. On the bright side, there are scores of village fêtes, fairs, festivals, concerts and races. The region often looks its best in October, when most of the tourists have gone (although late August–October are fine months for surfing); the mountain trails are empty, while down in Armagnac and the other wine regions everyone is concentrating on the *vendange*. November and December can be dismal, but wild mushrooms, game dishes and masses of holiday oysters and foie gras offer some consolation.

Crime and the Police

Southwest France isn't exactly a high crime area. Isolated holiday homes get burgled, as anywhere else; cars are occasionally broken into or stolen. Generally the police are more annoying than the crooks, especially the customs officers; these can turn up anywhere in the interior, and they have nothing better to do than arbitrarily stop cars from outside their department and give them the once-over. Report thefts to the nearest *gendarmerie*: not a pleasant task but the reward is the bit of paper you need for an insurance claim. If your passport is stolen, contact the police and your nearest consulate for emergency travel documents. By law, the police in France can stop anyone anywhere and demand ID; in practice, they tend only to do it to harass minorities, the homeless, and scruffy hippy types. If they really don't like the look of you they can salt you away for a long time without any reason.

The **drug** situation is the same in France as anywhere in the West: soft and hard drugs are widely available, and the police only make an issue of victimless crime when it suits them (your being a foreigner may just arouse them to action). Smuggling any amount of marijuana into the country can mean a prison term, and there's not much your consulate can or will do about it.

Disabled Travellers

When it comes to providing access for all, France is not exactly in the vanguard of nations; many Americans who come over are appalled. But things are beginning to change, especially in newer buildings.

Access and facilities in 90 towns in France are covered in *Touristes Quand Même! Promenades en France pour les Voyageurs Handicapés*, a booklet usually available in the tourist offices of large cities, or write ahead to the **Comité National Français de Liaison pour la Réadaptation des Handicapés** (CNRH), 236 bis Rue de Tolbiac, 13th, Paris, **t** (01) 53 80 66 63. The **Association des Paralysés de France**, 22 Rue du Père-Guérain, 13th, Paris, **t** (01) 44 16 83 83, publishes *Où Ferons-Nous Étape?* listing French hotels and motels accessible to those with limited mobility. Hotels with facilities for the handicapped are listed in Michelin's Red Guide to France.

The **Royal Association for Disability and Rehabilitation (RADAR)**, Unit 12, City Forum, 250 City Rd, London EC1V 8AF, **t** (020) 7250 3222, **f** (020) 7250 0212, can give specialist advice (*open Mon–Fri 10–4*) and sell *Getting There* (£5; send an SAE), a guide to facilities in airports. If you wish to visit Lourdes, **Tangney Tours**, 73 Crayford High St, Crayford DA1 4EJ, **t** (01732) 886 666, organize travel by ambulance carriages in special trains.

The Channel Tunnel is a good way to travel to France by car from the UK, since disabled passengers are allowed to stay in their vehicles. By train, Eurostar gives wheelchair passengers first-class travel for second-class fares. Most ferry companies will offer facilities if contacted beforehand. Vehicles fitted to accommodate disabled people pay reduced tolls on *autoroutes*. An *autoroute* guide for handicapped travellers (*Guides des Autoroutes à l'Usage des Personnes à Mobilité Réduite*) is available free from the Ministère des Transports, Direction des Routes, Service du Contrôle des Autoroutes, La Défense, 92055 Cedex, Paris, **t** (01) 40 81 21 22.

Other Useful Contacts

Access Ability, *www.access-ability.co.uk*. Information on travel agencies catering specifically for disabled people.

Alternative Leisure Co, 165 Middlesex Turnpike, Suite 206, Bedford, MA 01730, **t** (718) 275 0023, **f** 275 2305, *www.alctrips.com*. Organizes vacations abroad for disabled people.

Association des Paralysés de France is a national organization with an office in each *département*, with in-depth local information; headquarters are in Paris, **t** 01 40 78 69 00, **f** 01 45 89 40 57, *www.apf.ass.fr*.

Australian Council for Rehabilitation of the Disabled (ACRODS), PO Box 60, Curtin, ACT 2605, Australia, **t/TTY** (02) 6682 4333, *www.acrod.org.au*. Information and contact numbers for specialist travel agents.

Comité National Français de Liaison pour la Réadaptation des Handicapés, 236 bis Rue Tolbiac, 75013 Paris, **t** 01 53 80 66 66. Information on access and useful guides to various regions in France.

Disabled Persons Assembly, PO Box 27–254, Wellington 6035, New Zealand, **t** (6404) 801 9011, *www.dpa.org.nz*. All-round source for travel information.

Holiday Care Service, Imperial Building, Victoria Rd, Horley, Surrey, RH6 7PZ, **t** (01293) 774 535, **f** 784 647, Minicom **t** (01293) 776 943, *holiday.care@virgin.net*, *www.holidaycare.org.uk*. Publishes an information sheet on holidays in France (£2.50).

Mobility International USA, PO Box 10767, Eugene, OR 97440, USA, **t/TTY** (541) 343 1284, **f** 343 6812, *www.miusa.org*. Information on international educational exchange programmes and volunteer service overseas for the disabled.

RADAR (Royal Association for Disability and Rehabilitation), 12 City Forum, 250 City Road, London ECIV 8AF, **t** (020) 7250 3222, **f** 7250 0212, Minicom **t** (020) 7250 4119, *www.radar.org.uk*, *radar@radar.org.uk*. Information and books on travel.

Calendar of Events

Please note that dates can vary: contact the local tourist office to confirm. *Départements* are abbreviated as follows: 32 Gers, 40 Landes, 64 Basques, 64B Béarn, 65 Hautes-Pyrénées, 31 Haute Garonne, 09 Ariège.

January

Last Tues and Wed *Foire aux Pottoks*, Basque horse fair, Espelette 64

2nd half Festival of the Pyrénées, with theatre and music, Gavarnie 65

February

Sometimes Dogsled races and ice sculpture competitions, Arrens 65

March

Mid-month International organ competitions, Biarritz 64

April

Good Friday–Easter Sacred music festival, Lourdes 65

1st Sun after Easter *Coupes de Pâques*, auto races, Nogaro 32; Easter Fair, Tardets 64

8–10 Ham fair, Bayonne 64

Last Sun Flower market, Fourcès 32; Hesteyade, Occitan choir festival, at Ibos 65

May

1 Fête de Mer, Mimizan 40

2nd Sun Festival of Bandas y Penas, Condom 32

Sometime Onion festival, Trebons 65

Ascension Day Fête des Fleurs, Riscle 32

Pentecost Bullfights and festivities at Vic-Fézensac 32

June

1st Sun after Pentecost Battle of Saracens and Christians, Martres-Tolosane 31

2nd Sun after Pentecost *Processions de la Fête-Dieu*, Bidarray 64 and Iholdy 64

2–6 *Fêtes patronales*, Grenade-sur-l'Adour 40

1st week *Fête de Mer*, Capbreton 40; *Fêtes locales*, Boucau 64, Urcuit 64

2nd Sun Cherry festival, Itxassou 64

2nd week *Fêtes locales*, Arcangues 64

Throughout month Music Festival, Auch 32

Sometime World Cricket Trainers' Championship, Lavardens 32

20 Aire-sur-l'Adour fête, with *courses landaises* 40

21 Fire festival for St-Jean, at St-Lizier 09; summer equinox gatherings and fireworks, Montségur 09

24–27 St John's Day festival, Labastide d'Armagnac 40, St Jean-de-Luz 64

25 St-Sever 40, big fête with a *course landaise* 40

Last week *Fêtes locales*, St Pierre-d'Irube 64, Hasparren 64

Last Sun World Well-Water Drawers' Championship, Pavie 32

Last week/10 days in July *Festival de Pau* 64B with theatre, dance and music

July

Early July *Festival d'Art Flamenco*, Mont-de-Marsan 40; *fêtes locales* St-Pée-sur-Nivelle, St-Jean-Pied-de-Port and Lahonce 64; *fêtes patronales*, Eauze 32

July–Aug *Festival du Comminges*, concerts at St-Bertrand-de-Comminges 31; Sunday concerts, Abbaye de l'Escaladieu, Bonnemazon 65

Embassies and Consulates

The only consulate in the region is:

UK: 353 Bd de Président Wilson, Bordeaux, **t** 05 57 22 21 10.

Embassies and consulates in Paris include:

Australia: 4 Rue Jean-Rey, 15th, **t** 01 40 59 33 00, Ⓜ Bir-Hakeim. *Open Mon–Fri 9–6; visas Mon–Fri 9.15–12.15.*

Canada: 35 Av Montaigne, 8th, **t** 01 44 43 29 00, Ⓜ Franklin D. Roosevelt. *Open Mon–Fri 9–12 and 2–5.* Visas: 37 Av Montaigne, **t** 01 44 43 29 16. *Open Mon–Fri 8.30–11.*

Ireland: 12 Av Foch, 16th, **t** 01 44 17 67 00, Ⓜ Charles de Gaulle/Etoile. Consulate: 4 Rue Rude, 16th, as above. *Open for visits Mon–Fri 9.30–12; by phone Mon–Fri 9.30–1 and 2.30–5.30.*

New Zealand: 7 Rue Léonard de Vinci, 16th, **t** 01 45 00 24 11, Ⓜ Victor-Hugo. *Open for visa enquiries Mon–Fri 9–1.*

South Africa: 59 Quai d'Orsay, 7th, **t** 01 53 59 23 23, Ⓜ Invalides. *Open Mon–Fri by appointment 8.30–5.15; consulate open Mon–Fri 9–12.*

1st two weeks *Nuits Musicales en Armagnac* and International Folklore Festival of Gascony, Condom 32
2nd Sun Tuna Festival, St-Jean-de-Luz 64
Mid-month Jazz festival and medieval market, Bayonne 64; international piano recitals, St-Jean-de-Luz 64; sheep festival, Lannemezan 65; Jazz Altitude festival, Luz 65; Festival de Germ, Vallée du Louron 65
13 *Fête du Chipiron*, Hendaye 64
13–14 Big Bastille Day celebrations at Arcachon 40, Mimizan 40, Nogaro 32, Eugénie-les-Bains 40, Castets 40
15 Re-enactment of a Basque wedding, St-Etienne-de-Baïgorry 64
Mid-month Medieval Days in Foix 09 (music, medieval markets, jousts)
3rd week *Fête de la Madeleine*, Mont-de-Marsan 40; surfing championships and Basque folklore, Biarritz 64; Festival des Pyrénées, Gavarnie 65
3rd Sat and Sun Fair of Yesteryear, St-Béat 31
23 Tuna festival, Hossegor 40
25 *Fêtes locales*, Gotein-Libarrenx 64
End of month International festival of humorous drawing, Anglet 64; *Fête de la Madeleine*, with a competition of the unusual, St-Palais 64; *Fêtes locales*, Lasbastide-Clairence 64 and Arbonne 64; Lou Gran Marcat, an old-fashioned market, Rabastens-de-Bigorre 65; international theatre festival, Pamiers 09
Last week in July, festival of Salsa, Vic-Fézensac 32
29 July–3 Aug *Fêtes patronales*, Montfort-en-Chalosse and Peyrehorade 40
Last week July–1st week Aug Fantasia, classical music festival at St-Lizier 09

August

1 Sheepdog competitions, St-Jean-Pied-de-Port 64; Foire de Garris, cattle fair, St-Palais 64
Early Aug festival of wheat and good bread, Sarlabous 65; cheese fair, Loures-Barousse 65
3–8 *Fête*, with fireworks and *courses landaises*, Hagetmau 40
1st Wed Beginning of huge 5-day *Fêtes de Bayonne*, Bayonne 64
4–9 *Fêtes patronales*, Amou 40; Basque sport finals, Biarritz 64
1st weekend *Fêtes Basques*, Hendaye 64; crafts fair, Mauléon Soule 64
1st Sun Pastorale, shepherds' festival, Gotein Libarrenx 64
1st week in Aug *Festival de la Marionnette*, Mirepoix 09; folklore festival, Sentein 09
2nd week *Fêtes locales*, St-Etienne-de-Baïgorry 64, Cambo-les-Bains 64; humour festival, Lourdes 65; world pig-snorting championship, Trie-sur-Baïse 65
1st half Musical evenings, Cologne 32; in even-numbered years, *Festival des Pyrénées*, with dancers from around the world, Oloron 64B
Throughout month Le Houga 32 hosts three Gascon world championships: dove-cooing, *quilles à l'Escabeilhe* and eating *demoiselles* – fat-coated duck carcasses
Mon after 2nd Sun World Snail Speed Championship, Lagardère 32
12–17 *Fête patronale* at Dax, with *courses landaises* 40
Mid-month Big jazz festival at Marciac 32; World Championship of Melon Eaters, Lectoure 32
13 Basque shepherd hollering contest, Hasparren 64; sardine festival, Ustaritz 64

UK: 35 Rue du Faubourg St-Honoré, 8th, **t** 01 44 51 31 00, Ⓜ Concorde. *Open Mon–Fri 9.30–1 and 2.30–6.* Consulate: 16 Rue d'Anjou, 8th, **t** 01 44 51 33 01/01 44 51 33 03, Ⓜ Concorde. *Open Mon–Fri 2.30–5.30.*
USA: 2 Av Gabriel, 8th, **t** 01 43 12 22 22, Ⓜ Concorde. *Open Mon–Fri by appointment only 9–6.* Consulate/Visas: 2 Rue St-Florentin, 1st, **t** 01 43 12 22 22, Ⓜ Concorde. *Open Mon–Fri 8.45–11; provides a passport service and information on visas Mon–Fri 9–3.*

Festivals

Every single village or town in this book puts on a party at least once a year, usually in honour of its patron saint. The pronounced Spanish influence in Gascony and the Pyrenees, added to the inhabitants' natural panache, tends to make these fêtes among the liveliest in France. Many are accompanied by bullfights, either Spanish *corridas* or the bloodless *course landaise* (*see* p.23), while the Basques have a *pelote* match and perform astounding feats of strength running races

13–25 Assumption Day fête, Bayonne 64, Moliets 40, Ainhoa 64
14 Festival of Basque song, Garindein 64
15 Re-enactment of a Basque wedding, St-Etienne-de-Baïgorry 64; *Nuit Féerique* and fireworks, Biarritz 64; Espadrille festival, Mauléon Soule 64; crafts fair of the Val d'Aran, St-Béat 31; Madiran Wine Festival, 65; *Fête de Mer*, Arcachon 40
1st weekend after 15 Aug Big flower festival, Bagnères 65
18–23 *Fêtes patronales*, St-Julien-en-Born 40
19 Cheese fair, Tardets 64
19–21 Volkswagen Beetle rally, Soustons 40; gastronomic and crafts fair, St-Jean-Pied-de-Port 64
20 International Professional Cesta Punta finals, St-Jean-de-Luz 64
21 Mountain-climbing contests, Auzat-Vicdessos 09
3rd week Rip Curl Pro, World Surfing Championships at Hossegor/Seignosse 40
3rd Sun Smugglers' cross-country race, Sare 64; Force Basque festival, St-Palais 64
Last week *Fêtes locales*, Bassussarry 64

September
1st two weeks Local fête, Foix 09
1st half Quiksilver Surf master championships and *Musique en Côte Basque*, big name recitals, Biarritz 64; *corridas*, Bayonne 64; *Fêtes patronales*, Urrugne 64
3 World lark whistling contest and other events, Vieux-Boucau 40
1st Sat *Fêtes du ttoro*: best Basque fish soup competition, St-Jean-de-Luz 64
1st Sun Famous pilgrimage at Sarrance 64B; local fête, Le Mas-d'Azil 09
2nd Sun Fêtes de Sare, Sare 64; *foire aux côtelettes*, lamb chop fair, Arrens 65
16–17 Fiesta at Ordino, Andorra
19 *Fête des Corsaires*, St-Jean-de-Luz 64
3rd week Festival of stories and storytellers from around the world, Hasparren 64
End month International Festival of Latin American cinema and culture, Biarritz 64; world champion fishing from boats competition, Anglet 64; *foire aux côtelettes*, Luz-St-Saveur 65

October
1st Sun Formula III Grand Prix at Nogaro 32; also, every 3 years, the Championnat de France des Ecarteurs (*courses landaises*); Forum de la Marionette, Bagnères-de-Bigorre 65
2nd week Antiques fair, Mont-de-Marsan 40
Mid-month Important international theatre festival, Bayonne 64; *Haricot Tarbais festival*, bean fête, Tarbes 65
3rd weekend Wine harvest festival, Geaune 40
Last weekend Kite-flying contest, Hossegor 40; horse fair, Aspet 31
Last Sun *Fête du Piment*, Espelette 64

November
7–11 *Fêtes du St-Martin*, Biarritz 64
2nd weekend St-Martin's Fair, Aurignac 31
30 Ste-Catherine's Fair, Aspet 31

December
Throughout month *Marchés de gras* – foie gras, fattened ducks and geese markets – are held in most towns
4–5 *Fêtes patronales*, Guéthary 64

with 100lb weights in each hand, for instance; the local *bandas* (brass bands of 20 or 40 local musicians in dashing costumes) play Basque or Navarrais tunes all night long in the streets, and there are usually fireworks too. Larger villages will have a circus or a funfair. There is invariably plenty of what the French call *animation* (everything from a local merchant chattering away on a portable microphone to jumping motorcycles, or dogs pulling sleds on wheels) and plenty of dancing, from performances of the local folklore societies to *bal musette*, accordion tangos for the older generation and loud local rock bands for the young. Nearly all of the really goofy festivals listed above happen in the Gers.

Food and Drink

Intensely rural, sprinkled with small traditional family farms and overflowing with the good things of the earth, southwest France serves up a hearty cuisine of fresh ingredients, so delicious that eating and drinking are two of the most compelling reasons to visit. Each region in this book has its own specialities, but they overlap quite a bit. *See* pp.29–33 for information on the various regional cuisines.

Restaurant Basics

Restaurants generally serve between 12 and 2pm and in the evening from 7 to 9pm, with later summer hours. In the southwest people tend to arrive early, to have a better choice of dishes and to get a crack at the specials or ***plats du jour*** – turn up at 1 for lunch or 8 for dinner and your choice may be very limited. All restaurants post menus outside the door so you'll know what to expect; if prices aren't listed, you can bet it's not because they're a bargain. If you have the appetite to eat the biggest meal of the day at noon, you'll spend a lot less money. Almost all restaurants have a choice of **set-price menus**, usually featuring three to four courses, and often with a few choices among the starters, main courses and desserts. Many expensive places offer a cheaper lunch special – the best way to experience some of the finer gourmet temples. Eating *à la carte* will always be much more expensive, in many cases twice as much.

Menus sometimes include the house wine (*vin compris*); if you choose a better wine anywhere, expect a scandalous mark-up. Don't be dismayed, it's a long-established custom (as in many other lands); the French wouldn't dream of a meal without wine, and the arrangement is a simple device to make food prices seem lower. If service is included it will say *service compris* or s.c., if not *service non compris* or s.n.c. Some restaurants offer a set-price gourmet ***menu dégustation*** – a selection of chef's specialities, which can be a great treat. On the other end of the scale, in the bars and brasseries, is the no-choice *formule*, which is more often than not steak and *frites*.

A full French meal may begin with an apéritif served with little savoury snacks called *amuse-gueule*; hors d'œuvres, a starter or two (soup, asparagus, *charcuterie*, *pâté*, *crudités* and so on); followed by the main course (or two), cheese, dessert, coffee and chocolates, and perhaps a *digestif* to finish things off. If you order a salad it may come before or after, but never with, your main course. In everyday eating, most people condense this feast to a starter, main course, and cheese or dessert.

If you're a **vegetarian**, you may have a hard time in the restaurants of Gascony and the Pyrenees, especially if you don't eat eggs or fish. But most establishments will try to accommodate you somehow.

When looking for a restaurant, homing in on the one place crowded with locals is as sound a policy in France as anywhere. Don't overlook hotel restaurants, some of which are absolutely top notch. To avoid disappointment, call ahead in the morning to reserve a table, especially in the summer.

One thing you'll notice in the cities is a growing choice of ethnic restaurants, mostly North African (a popular favourite for their economical couscous, Asian (usually Vietnamese, sometimes Chinese, Cambodian or Thai), and Italian, the latter sometimes combined with a pizzeria (the pizza will be all right if there's a proper pizza oven).

Throughout this guide we rate restaurants as *expensive* (a full meal will cost more than 200F per person), *moderate* (a meal for one will cost between 100 and 200F) and *cheap* (you can eat for under 100F per person). Where a restaurant offers fixed-price menus, we state the prices of these in the text.

Markets, Picnic Food and Snacks

In most villages, market day is the event of the week, and rightfully so. Celebrated for their fresh farm produce, markets are fun to visit on their own, and become even more interesting if you're cooking for yourself or are just gathering the ingredients for a picnic. In the larger cities they take place every day, while smaller towns and villages have markets but one day a week, and double as social occasions for the locals. Most markets finish up around noon, when the lunch siren goes off at the *mairie* (an old custom, designed to reach farm workers out in the fields). Other good sources for picnic food are the *charcuteries* or *traiteurs*, both of which sell prepared dishes by weight in cartons or tubs. You can also find similar counters in the larger supermarkets. Cities are snack-food wonderlands, with outdoor counters selling pastries, *crêpes*, pizza slices, *frites*, *croque-monsieur* (toasted ham and cheese sandwiches) and a wide variety of sandwiches made from baguettes (long thin loaves of bread).

Drinking

That venerable French institution, the **café**, is not only a place to drink but for many people a home away from home, a place to read the papers, play cards, write letters, read a book, meet friends, and just unwind. Prices are listed on the *Tarif des Consommations*: note that they go up depending whether you're served at the bar (*comptoir*), at a table (*la salle*) or outside (*la terrasse*).

French **coffee** is strong and black, but lack-lustre next to the aromatic brews of Italy or Spain (you'll notice an improvement in the coffee near their respective frontiers). If you order *un café* you'll get a small black espresso; if you want milk, order *un crème*. If you want more than a few drops of caffeine, ask them to make it *grand*. For **decaffeinated**, the word is *déca*. The French only order *café au lait* (a small coffee topped off with lots of hot milk) when they stop in for breakfast. There are baskets of croissants and pastries, and some bars will make you a baguette with butter, jam or honey. If you want to go native, try the Frenchman's Breakfast of Champions: a *pastis* or two, and five non-filter Gauloises. *Chocolat chaud* (hot chocolate) is usually good; if you order *thé* (tea), you'll get an ordinary bag. An *infusion* is a herbal tea – *camomille, menthe* (mint), *tilleul* (lime or linden blossom), or *verveine* (verbena). These are kind to the all-precious *foie*, or liver, after you've over-indulged at the table.

Mineral water (*eau minérale*) can be addictive, and comes either sparkling (*gazeuse* or *pétillante*) or still (*non-gazeuse* or *plate*). If you feel run-down, Badoit has lots of peppy magnesium in it – it's the current trendy favourite. The usual international corporate soft drinks are available, and all kinds of bottled fruit juices (*jus de fruits*). Some bars also do fresh lemon and orange juices (*citron* or *orange pressé*). The French are also fond of fruit syrups – red grenadine and ghastly green *diabolo menthe*.

Beer (*bière*) in most bars and cafés is run-of-the-mill big brands from Alsace, Germany, and Belgium. Draft (*à la pression*) is cheaper than bottled beer. Nearly all resorts have bars or pubs offering wider selections of draughts, lagers and bottles; some even do cocktails. The strong spirit of the Midi comes in a liquid form called ***pastis***, first made popular in Marseilles as a plague remedy; its name comes from the Latin *passe-sitis*, or thirst quencher. A pale yellow 90° nectar flavoured with aniseed, vanilla and cinnamon, *pastis* is drunk as an apéritif before lunch and in rounds after work. The three major brands, Ricard, Pernod, and Pastis 51 all taste slightly different; most people drink their '*pastaga*' with lots of water and ice (*glaçons*), which helps make it taste more tolerable.

Wine

One of the pleasures of travelling in France is drinking great wines for a fraction of what you pay at home, and discovering new varieties that you've never seen in your local shop. Unless someone else is paying, smart restaurants are the last place to make your discoveries, with their prices marked up to triple or quadruple the retail. If you love wine but have to watch expenses (and who doesn't?), buy it direct from the producers, the *vignerons* or the *caves coopératives*. In the text we've included a few addresses for each wine to get you started. Tours of wineries or ***chais*** (a Gascon word meaning the building where the wine is stored in oak barrels before being bottled and laid in the *cave* or cellar) are often possible, except during the grape harvest when everyone is busy. If you're buying direct from the producer, you'll be offered glasses to taste, each wine older than the previous one, until you are feeling quite jolly and ready to buy the oldest (and most expensive) vintage. On the other hand, many small proprietors sell loose wine à la petrol pump, or *en vrac*; many *chais* even sell the little plastic barrels to put it in.

Don't neglect the wines with less exalted labels, especially those labelled VDQS (*vin de qualité supérieure*), such as Vin de Tursan or Côtes de St-Mont, or *vin de pays* – guaranteed to originate in a certain region – with *vin ordinaire* (or *vin de table*) at the bottom, which may not send you to seventh heaven but is usually drinkable and cheap. In a restaurant if you order a *rouge* or *blanc* or *rosé*, this is what you'll get, either by the glass (*un verre*), by the quarter-litre (*un pichet*) or bottle (*une bouteille*). *Brut* is very dry, *sec* dry, *demi-sec* and *moelleux* are sweetish, *doux* and *liqueroux* sweet, and *méthode champenoise* sparkling.

Health

Local hospitals are the place to go in an **emergency** (*urgence*). If you need an ambulance (SAMU) dial **t** 15; police and ambulance, **t** 17; fire, **t** 18. **Doctors** take turns going on duty at night and on holidays even in rural areas: pharmacies will know who to contact or else telephone the local **SOS Médecins** – if you don't have access to a phone book or Minitel, dial directory assistance **t** 12. To be on the safe side, always carry a phone card (*see* 'Post Offices and Telephones', p.52). If it's not an emergency, pharmacies have addresses of local doctors (including those who speak English), or outpatient clinics (*Centres Hospitaliers*). **Pharmacists** themselves are trained to administer first aid, and dispense free advice for minor problems. In cities pharmacies open at night on a rotating basis; addresses are posted in their windows or in the local newspaper. In most rural pharmacies you can ring the doorbell after hours and roust out the pharmacist on duty.

Money and Banks

1 Jan 1999 saw the start of the transition to the **Euro**. On that date it became the official currency in France (and ten other nations of the European Union) and the official exchange rate was set at 6.55957F. Straight away shops and businesses began indicating prices in both currencies and some people began opening Euro accounts even before the Franc was finally phased out. Euro coins and notes began to be circulated in 2002 and the Euro is now the only legal currency in France.

Travellers' cheques are now available in Euros and are the safest way of carrying money. Major international **credit cards** are widely used in France. Visa (in French, Carte Bleue) is the most readily accepted, although for the French Carte Bleue is a direct-debit bank card. American Express is often not accepted, however. French-issued credit cards have a special security microchip (*puce*) in each card. The card is slotted into a card reader, and the holder keys in a PIN to authorize the transaction. UK cards are different, because the information is held on a magnetic strip, and this sometimes causes problems because the French machines can't read them. Your card is valid, and the French Government Tourist Office suggests you use the following phrase to explain the problem: '*Les cartes internationales ne sont pas des cartes à puce, mais à bande magnétique. Ma carte est valable et je vous serais reconnaisant d'en demander la confirmation auprès de votre banque ou de votre centre de traitement.*'

In case of credit card loss or theft, call the 24-hour services, which have English-speaking staff: American Express **t** (01) 47 77 72 00, Diners Club **t** (01) 49 06 17 17, MasterCard **t** (01) 45 67 84 84, and Visa **t** (08) 36 69 08 80.

Under the Cirrus system, withdrawals in Euros can be made from bank and post office automatic cash machines (ATMs), using your UK PIN. The specific cards accepted are marked on each machine, and most give instructions in English. Credit card companies charge a fee for cash advances, but rates are often better than bank rates.

Banks are generally *open 8.30–12.30 and 1.30–4*; they close on Sunday, and most close either on Saturday or Monday as well. Exchange rates vary, and nearly all take a commission of varying proportions. Places that do nothing but exchange money (and hotels and train stations) usually have the worst rates or take out the heftiest commissions, so be careful. It's always a good bet to purchase some Euros before you go, especially if you are planning to arrive during the weekend or late at night.

National Holidays

On French national holidays, banks, shops, and businesses close; some museums do, but most restaurants stay open.

1 January
Easter Sunday
Easter Monday
1 May
8 May (Victory Day)
Ascension Day
Pentecost and the following Monday
14 July (Bastille Day)
15 August (Assumption)
1 November (All Saints')
11 November (First World War Armistice)
Christmas Day

Opening Hours, Museums and National Holidays

Most **shops** close down on Sunday afternoons and some Mondays, though some grocers and *supermarchés* open on Monday afternoons. In many towns Sunday morning is a big shopping period. **Markets** (daily in the cities, weekly in villages) are usually open mornings only, although clothes, flea and antique markets run into the afternoon.

Museums, with a few exceptions, close for lunch as well, and often on Mondays or Tuesdays, and sometimes for all of November or the entire winter. Hours change with the season: longer summer hours begin in May or June and last until September – usually. Some change their hours every month. We've done our best to include them in the text, but don't be surprised if they're not exactly right. Most close on national holidays and give discounts if you have a student ID card, or are an EU citizen under 18 or over 65 years old; most charge admission.

Churches are usually open all day, or closed all day and only open for Mass. Sometimes notes on the door direct you to the *mairie* or priest (*presbytère*) where you can pick up the key. If not, ask at the nearest house – they may well have it. There are often admission fees for cloisters, crypts and special chapels.

Post Offices and Telephones

Known as the PTT or Bureau de Poste and marked by a kind of blue bird on a yellow background, French **post offices** in the cities are *open Mon–Fri 8am–7pm, Sat 8am–12*. In villages offices may not open until 9am, close for lunch, and close at 4.30 or 5. You can receive mail *poste restante* at any of them; the postal codes in this book should help your mail get there in a timely fashion. To collect it, bring some ID. You can purchase stamps in tobacconists as well as post offices.

Post offices offer free use of a **Minitel** electronic directory; they've done away with printed directories, and using these slow, cumbersome and complicated technological marvels can be a major nuisance. Offices usually have at least one telephone booth with a meter – the easiest way to phone overseas. Almost all other public telephones have switched over from coins to *télécartes*, which you can purchase at newspaper kiosks, tobacconists and the post office.

The French telephone system was overhauled in 1996. Eight-digit numbers were extended to 10 digits and the following regional telephone numbers gained a prefix: Paris and the Ile de France region 01, northwest 02, northeast 03, southeast and Corsica 04, and southwest 05. When dialling from outside the country, omit the initial 0.

To make an **international call** from France, dial 00, then the country code, followed by the area code (omitting any initial 0) and the number. International dialling codes include: Australia 61, Canada 1, Southern Ireland 353, UK 44, and USA 1.

France's **international dialling code** is 33. For directory assistance, dial 12; international directory assistance is 003312 followed by the country code, but note that you'll have to wait around for them to ring you back with your requested number.

Sports and Activities

The great outdoors is one of the main reasons for visiting this corner of France, with its rare combination of ocean, lakes, rivers, and mountains. Below is a far from all-inclusive listing of possibilities.

Bicycling

For doing it yourself, *see* 'Getting Around', p.41. Any mountain resort of any size will rent out **VTT**, or mountain bikes. In the summer throngs come down to watch the Tour de France, which usually tackles at least the near-vertical Col de Peyresourde.

Fédération Française de Cyclotourisme, 8 Rue Jean-Marie-Jégo, 75013 Paris, **t** 01 44 16 88 88.

Bullfights

Aficionados call the *corrida* an art, not a sport, and it's big in Dax, Mont-de-Marsan, Bayonne, Estang, and Vic-Fézensac. Many people in the region prefer the bloodless *course landaise* (*see* p.23).

Bungee-jumping

According to the Académie Française, this is called *saut à l'élastique*. You can do it at Le Mas-d'Azil in the Ariège, **t** 05 61 74 64 00, or from the Pont Napoléon in Barège (Hautes-Pyrénées).

Canoeing and Kayaking

The **Fédération Française de Canoë-Kayak et des Sports Associés en Eau-Vive** is at 87 Quai de la Marne, 94340 Joinville-le-Pont, **t** 01 45 11 08 50, **f** 01 48 86 13 25.

In the Hautes-Pyrénées, **Le Relais d'Isaby**, Villelongue, **t** 05 62 92 20 77.

The Leyre, in the Parc Naturel des Landes de Gascogne, offers genteel five-day canoe trips (*see* pp.71 and 77).

Canyoning

Outings and all the necessary equipment are provided by **Loisirs Aventures** (*see* 'white-water rafting', below); **Adrénaline Passion**, **t** 05 62 98 73 25; and, for the Luz and the Gavarnie, with the **Bureau des Guides**, Luz-St-Saveur, **t** 05 62 92 87 28, in the Hautes-Pyrénées.

Car-racing

You can get a taste for it at Nogaro in the Gers, in a Renault Clio 16S Coupé or a Formule Renault.

Caves

Speleology, potholing, spelunking – whatever you want to call it, it's very popular. In Haute-Garonne, seek out the **Maison des Gouffres**, Herran-Labaderque, 31160 Aspet, **t** 05 61 97 53 30; and in the Pays Basque, **Tendance Sud Loisirs**, Oloron Ste-Marie, **t** 05 59 34 39 00. Alternatively, contact the **Fédération Française de Spéléologie**, 130 Rue St-Maur, 75011 Paris, **t** 01 43 57 56 54; or the **Comité de Spéléologie Régionale Midi-Pyrénées**, 7 Rue André-Citroën, 31130 Balma, **t** 05 61 11 71 60.

Deep-sea Diving

The Côte Basque has a number of schools and hires out equipment: try the **Union Sportive de Biarritz**, Allée des Passereaux, **t** 05 59 03 29 29. For further information, contact the **Fédération Française d'Etudes et des Sports Sous-Marins**, 24 Quai de Rive-Neuve, 13284 Marseille, **t** 04 91 33 99 31.

Fishing

You can fish in the sea without a permit as long as your catch is for local consumption. Freshwater fishing (extremely popular in this region of rivers and lakes) requires an easily obtained permit from a local club; tourist offices can tell you where to find them. Often the only outdoor vending machine in a town sells worms and other bait. Ocean-fishing excursions (for tuna and other denizens of the deep) are organized by the day and half-day, arranged in advance; contact local tourist offices for details.

Gambling

You'll find casinos with at least slot machines at the main coastal and mountain resorts or you can do as the locals do and play for a side of beef, a lamb or a VCR in a Loto, in a local café or municipal *salle de fêtes*. Loto is just like bingo, including the way some of the numbers have names: 11 is *las cambas de ma grand* (my grandmother's legs) and 75, the number of the *département* of Paris, is *los envaïssurs* (the invaders). Everybody bets on the horses at the local bar.

Golf

This is one of the prime golfing regions of France, with the oldest and most beautiful greens and fairways; the very first course in France is in Pau, and between Bordeaux and Biarritz you'll find 20 courses open to the public year-round; summer green fees for 18 holes are between €42–50. There are also courses in the mountains at Montrejeau and Luchon (Haute-Garonne), and La Bastide de Serou (Ariège), Laloubère, near Tarbes, and Lourdes (Hautes-Pyrénées), Auch, Eauze, L'Isle-Jourdain, Fleurance and Masseube. **Fédération Française de Golfe**, 69 Av Victor-Hugo, Paris, **t** 01 44 17 63 00, **f** 01 44 17 63 63.

Horse-riding

Each tourist office has a list of Centres Hippiques or Centres Equestres that hire out horses. Most offer group excursions, although if you prove yourself an experienced rider you can usually head off down the trails on your own. Contact the **Fédération des Randonneurs Equestres**, 16 Rue des Apennins, 75017 Paris, **t** 01 42 26 23 23.

Parachuting

Lessons for beginners (minimum age 15), jumps and gear are available from the **Centre Ecole de Parachutisme du Bassin d'Arcachon**, Aérodrome de Villemarie, La Teste 33260, **t** 05 56 54 73 11.

Paragliding, Hang-gliding and Microlites

Paragliding (*parapente*), a cross between parachuting and hang-gliding, has become quite popular in the Pyrenees year-round: the *parapente* itself weighs only 3 to 5kg and folds into a backpack; you ski or run down a slope until lifted off the ground, and with a good updraft sail several miles before gently descending. Because of the volatile winds near the coast, paragliding is restricted to the higher Pyrenees. Learn how to do it at **Les Aigles** at Montcalm, **t** 05 61 64 80 00; or **Odyssée**, in Moustajon, **t** 05 61 79 89 89. In the Hautes-Pyrénées, try **Air Aventures Pyrénées**, Barèges, **t** 05 62 92 91 60; **Centre Ecole Régionale des Pyrénées**, Aucun, **t** 05 62 97 43 00; or **Ecole Pyrénéenne de Vol Libre**, Génos, **t** 05 62 99 68 55.

For Microlite clubs (ULM in French), in the Pays Basque, try **Escary Espace Découvertes**, Aramits, **t** 05 59 34 11 34.

Pétanque

Like *pastis* and a twangy lilting accent, *pétanque* is one of the essential ingredients of the whole south of France, and even the smallest village has a rough, hard court under the plane trees for its practitioners – nearly all male, although women are welcome to join in. It's similar to *boules*: the object is to get your metal ball closest to the marker (*bouchon* or *cochonnet*). Tournaments are frequent and well attended.

Pelote and other Basque Sports

See pp.152–3.

Rock-climbing (*Escalade*)

The French love to dress up in bright colours and climb and dangle up vertical rock faces. If you want to join them, some places to try with rock faces of varying levels of difficulty are the **Base de Plein Air de Vacabrère** (*see* canoeing, above); the **Office de la Montagne**, 18 Allée d'Etigny, 31110 Luchon, **t** 05 61 79 21 21, and **Pyrénées Plaisirs**, Rue de la Grotte Huos, 31210 Montrejeau, **t** 05 61 95 68 01, all in the Haute-Garonne; also the **Maison de Montaigne** at Luz St Sauveur (Bureau des Guides, **t** 05 62 92 87 28) in the Hautes-Pyrénées.

Rugby

Since 1900 rugby, perfectly adapted to the Gascon temperament and broad-shouldered physique, has been the national sport of the southwest, the cradle of most of the players on the national team. There's a women's version without tackling called *barette*.

Sailing and Windsurfing

The *étangs*, or lakes, just along the inner edge of the sand dunes along the Côte d'Argent are ideal for easy sailing and windsurfing, or just learning how. The coast is framed on the north and south by ocean pleasure ports: Arcachon in the north and Guéthary, Hendaye and St-Jean-de-Luz in the south.

Skiing

The Pyrenees don't get as much of the white stuff as the Alps and the snow the mountains do get has been fiendishly unpredictable of late. The mountains in this book, the western and central Pyrenees, generally have the most snow. Besides skiing down pistes, the relative lack of avalanches and crevices make the Pyrenees perfect for off-piste, cross-country and mountaineering skiing. You may be best off just going down to the mountains and ringing around to see who has the best snow; besides February, the busiest month (when French schools take their two-week ski holidays), finding accommodation on the spot usually isn't a problem. Just don't expect much Alpine cuteness. Resorts in this book from east to west are:

Ariège: Ascou-Pailhères (1,500–2,000m), **t** 05 61 64 60 60; Ax-Bonascre (1,400–2,400m), **t** 05 61 64 20 64; Guzet (1,100–2,100m), **t** 05 61 96 00 11; Monts-d'Olmes (1,400–2,000m), **t** 05 61 01 14 14; Goulier-Neige (with a ski stadium, 1,500–2,000m), **t** 05 61 64 88 99; Mijanès-Donezan (downhill and cross-country, 1,530–2,000m), **t** 05 61 20 41 37; Chioula (cross-country only, 1,240–1,650m), t 05 61 64 60 60; Etang de Lers (cross-country and ice skating, 1,300–1,615m), t 05 61 04 91 13; Tour Lafont (cross-country, 1,250–1,500m), t 05 61 65 12 12. For general information, contact **Ariège Ski de Fond**, Hôtel du Départment, BP 143, 09004 Foix Cedex, t 05 61 02 09 70.

Haute-Garonne: Bourg d'Oueil (1,200–1,600m), t 05 61 79 34 07/05 61 79 21 21; Luchon-Superbagnères (1,800–2,260m), t 05 60 79 21 21/05 61 79 11 23.

Hautes-Pyrénées: La Mongie/Barèges, the biggest in the Pyrenees (1,750–2,245m), t 05 62 91 94 15; St-Lary-Soulan (1,900–2,400m), t 05 62 39 50 81; Gavarnie-Gèdre (one of the best for downhill and cross-country, bobsleighing and ice skating, 1,460–2,300m), t 05 62 92 49 10; Hautacam (1,500–1,810m), t 05 62 97 00 25; Cauterets (1,850–2,300m), t 05 62 92 50 27; Piau-Engaly (the most futuristic, 1,850–2,100m), t 05 62 39 61 69; Luz-Ardiden (with trails, 2,000–2,450m), t 05 62 92 81 60; Payolle/Campan (cross-country), t 05 62 91 70 36; Val d'Azun-Arrens Marsous (cross-country), t 05 62 97 49 49; Nistos Cap Nestes (cross-country), t 05 62 39 74 34; Peyragudes (1,600–2,400m), t 05 62 99 69 99; Val Louron (1,450–2,200m), t 05 62 98 64 12; Guzet-Niege (1,110–2,061m), t 05 61 96 00 01.

Pays Basque/Béarn: Iraty (cross-country, 1,200–1,500m), t 05 59 28 51 29; St-Jean-Pied-de-Port (cross-country and snow shoes, 1,000–1,450m), t 05 59 28 51 29.

For further information, contact the **Fédération Française de Ski**, 50 Av des Marquisats, 74000 Annecy, t 04 50 51 40 34, *www.ffs.fr*.

For skiing in Andorra, *see* p.332.

Skittles

In some places in the area, especially Armagnac and the Chalosse, 6- or 9-pin skittles, or *jeu de quilles*, the ancestor of bowling, is more popular than *pétanque*; tourist offices in the Gers and Landes have a complete calendar of tournaments.

Surfing

Surf bums from all across Europe flock in late summer to ride the big rollers that hit the Côte d'Argent from the Bay of Biscay. Hendaye, Anglet, Guéthary, Biarritz, Hossegor-Seignosse, Mimizan-Plage and Biscarrosse are the main centres, where there are schools to learn and world championships to watch, but you'll find plenty of small clubs in between that hire out both surfboards and body-boards.

Walking

See 'Getting Around', p.41. The **Fédération Française de Randonnée Pédestre** is at 14 Rue Riquet, 75009 Paris, t 01 44 89 93 90, f 01 40 35 85 48. One unusual mountain trek of three to seven days is run by **Gaves du Sud**, 64390 Laas, t 05 59 67 08 69, in the Pays Basque, with little Basque *pottok* horses carrying the luggage and/or children (from Easter to mid-Nov).

Water-skiing and Jet-ski

These are practised on the larger coastal *étangs* and at St-Jean-de-Luz and Ciboure.

White-water Rafting/Hydrospeed

From early April to the end of September, you can go white-water rafting down the rivers shooting out of the Pyrenees – the Gaves, the Noguera Pallareasa (the mightiest river in the Pyrenees, just over the border in Spain) and the Neste d'Aure; spring is the most thrilling time to go, while summer is recommended for beginners. Contact **Loisirs Aventures**, t 05 62 39 44 79, f 05 62 39 44 01, or write to **M. Christian Noly**, Cadeilhan-Trachée, 65170 Saint-Lary Soulan, or the Relais d'Isaby, both in the Hautes-Pyrénées. In Béarn, try **Rafting Eaux-Vives**, Place des Casernes, 64190 Navarrenx, t 05 59 66 04 05.

Tourist Information

Every city and town, and most villages, have a tourist information office, called either a *Syndicat d'Initiative* or an *Office du Tourisme*. In smaller villages this service is provided by the town hall (*mairie*). They distribute free maps and town plans, hotel, camping, and self-catering accommodation lists for their area, and can inform you about sporting events, leisure activities and wine estates open for visits and festivals. Addresses and telephones are listed in the text, and if you write to them, they'll post you their booklets to help you plan your holiday before you leave.

Where to Stay

Hotels

Like most countries in Europe, the tourist authorities grade hotels by their facilities (not by charm or location) with **stars** from four (or four with an L for luxury – a bit confusing, so in the text luxury places are given five stars) to one. There are even some cheap but adequate places undignified by any stars at all. Some places with good facilities have no stars at all, simply because the hotel owners have not applied to be graded.

Almost every establishment has a wide range of rooms and prices – a very useful and logical way of doing things, once you're used to it. In some hotels, every single room has its own personality and the difference in quality and price can be enormous; a large room with antique furniture, a television or a balcony over the sea and a complete bathroom can cost much more than a poky back room in the same hotel, with a window overlooking a car park, no antiques, and the WC down the hall. Some proprietors will drag out a sort of menu for you to choose what sort of price and facilities you would like. Most two-star hotel rooms have their own showers and WCs; most one-stars offer rooms with or without. The following guide will give you an idea of what prices to expect from the different star ratings. Throughout the guide, we state the price ranges of hotels according to the list below, and give the star rating as well.

Although it's impossible to be more precise, we can add a few more generalizations. **Single** rooms are relatively rare, and usually two-thirds the price of a double, and rarely will a hotelier give you a discount if only doubles are available (again, because each room has its own price); on the other hand, if there are three or four of you, triples or quads or adding extra beds to a double room is usually cheaper than staying in two rooms. **Prices** are posted at the reception desk and in the rooms to keep the management honest. Flowered wallpaper, usually beige, comes in all rooms at no extra charge – it's an essential part of the French experience. **Breakfast** (usually coffee, a croissant, bread and jam for €4–6) is nearly always optional: you'll do as well for less in a bar. As usual rates rise in the busy season (holidays and summer, and in the winter around ski resorts), when many hotels with restaurants will require that you take **half-board** (*demi-pension* – breakfast and a set lunch or dinner). Many hotel restaurants are superb and described in the text; non-guests are welcome. At worst the food will be boring, and it can be monotonous eating in the same place every night when there are so many tempting restaurants around. Don't be put off by obligatory dining. It's traditional; French hoteliers think of themselves as innkeepers, in the old-fashioned way. In the off-season board requirements vanish into thin air.

Your holiday will be much sweeter if you **book ahead**, especially from May to October. July and August are the only really impossible months; otherwise it usually isn't too difficult to find something. Phoning ahead a day or two is always a good policy, although beware that hotels will usually only confirm a room on receipt of a cheque covering the first night (not a credit card number). Tourist offices have complete lists of accommodation in their given areas or even *départements*, which come in handy during the peak season; many will even call around and book a room for you on the spot for free or a nominal fee.

Chain hotels (Climate, Formula One, etc.) are in most cities, but always dreary and geared to the business traveller more than the tourist, so you won't find them in this book. Don't confuse chains with the various umbrella organizations like Logis et Auberges de France, Relais de Silence, or the prestigious Relais et Châteaux, which promote and guarantee the quality of independently owned hotels and their restaurants. Many are recommended in the text. Larger tourist offices usually stock their booklets, or you can pick them up before you leave from the French National Tourist Office. If you plan to do a lot of driving, you

Hotel Price Ranges

Note: all prices listed here and elsewhere in this book are for a double room.

luxury €230 and over
very expensive €150–230
expensive €100–150
moderate €60–100
cheap under €60

may want to pick up the English translation of the French truckers' bible, *Les Routiers*, an annual guide with maps listing reasonably priced lodgings and food along the highways and byways of France (Routiers Limited, 25 Vanston Place, London SW6 1AZ).

Bed and breakfast: in rural areas, there are plenty of opportunities for a stay in a private home or farm. ***Chambres d'hôte***, in the tourist office brochures, are listed separately from hotels with the various *gîtes* (*see* below). Some are connected to *ferme-auberge* restaurants, others to wine estates or a château; prices tend to be moderate to inexpensive. Local tourist offices will usually provide you with a list if you ask them.

Youth Hostels, *Gîtes d'Etape*, and *Refuges*

Most cities have **youth hostels** (*Auberges de Jeunesse*) which offer simple dormitory accommodation and breakfast to people of any age for around €12 a night. Most offer kitchen facilities as well, or inexpensive meals. They are the best deal going for people travelling on their own; for people travelling together a one-star hotel can be just as cheap. You should also bear in mind that most are in the most ungodly locations – in the suburbs where the last bus goes by at 7pm, or miles from any transport at all in the country. In the summer the only way to be sure of a room is to arrive early in the day. To stay in most hostels you need to be a member of Hostelling International, which you join by becoming a member of your national YHA organization. Contact the following for more information:

Fédération Unie des Auberges de Jeunesse (FUAJ), 27 Rue Pajol, 75018 Paris, **t** (01) 44 89 87 27, **f** (01) 44 89 87 10.

Youth Hostels Association (YHA), Trevelyan House, 8 St Stephens Hill, St Albans, Herts AL1 2DY, **t** (01727) 855 215. To book youth hostels abroad, **t** (01629) 581 418, or **f** (01629) 581 062.

American Youth Hostelling International, PO Box 37613, Dept USA, Washington DC 20013/7613, **t** (0202) 783 6161.

Another option in cities are single sex dormitories for young workers, ***Foyers de Jeunes Travailleurs et de Jeunes Travailleuses***, which rent out individual rooms if available for slightly more than a youth hostel.

A ***gîte d'étape*** is a simple shelter with bunk beds (but no bedding) and a rudimentary self-catering kitchen set up by a village along GR walking paths or scenic bike routes. In the Pyrenees, the *gîtes d'étape* are administered by the Randonnées Pyrénéennes. Again, lists are available for each *département*; the detailed maps listed on p.41 mark them as well. In the mountains similar rough shelters along the GR paths are called ***refuges***; most of them are open in summer only. Both charge around 50F a night.

Camping

Camping is a very popular way to travel, especially among the French themselves, and there's at least one camp site in every town, often an inexpensive, no-frills site run by the town (Camping Municipal). Other camp sites are graded with stars like hotels from four to one: at the top of the line you can expect lots of trees and grass, hot showers, a pool or beach, sports facilities, and a grocer's, bar, and/or restaurant, and prices rather similar to one-star hotels (although these, of course, never have all the extras). Camping on a farm is especially big in the southwest, and is usually less expensive than organized sites. If you want to camp wild, it's imperative to ask permission from the landowner first, or you risk a furious farmer, his dog and perhaps even the police.

Tourist offices have complete lists of camp sites in their regions. If you plan to move around a lot, the *Guide Officiel Camping/Caravanning* is available in most French bookshops. A number of UK holiday firms book camping holidays and offer discounts on Channel ferries: **Canvas Holidays**, **t** (01383) 644 000; **Eurocamp Travel**, **t** (01565) 625 544; **Keycamp Holidays**, **t** (020) 8395 4000. The French National Tourist Office has complete lists. The Michelin Green Guide: *Camping/ Caravanning France* is very informative and also lists sites with facilities suitable for disabled visitors. In the UK, a couple of useful organizations are **Camping and Caravanning Club**, 11 Lower Grosvenor Place, London SW1; and **Caravan Club**, East Grinstead House, East Grinstead, Sussex RH19 1UA.

Self-catering Organizations

Companies are springing up offering information and on-line booking only. Try *www.francedirect.co.uk*, who have a large selection of cottages and villas.

In the UK

Allez France, 27–9 West St, Storrington, West Sussex RH20 4DZ, **t** 0800 731 2929, offers a wide variety of accommodation, from apartments to *gîtes*, villas and cottages.

Bowhill Holidays, Mayhill Farm, Mayhill Lane, Swanmore, Southampton SO32 2QW, **t** (01489) 877 627, arranges accommodation from simple two-bed cottages to 12-bed luxury.

Dominique's Villas, 13 Park House, 140 Battersea Park Rd, London SW11 4NB, **t** (020) 7738 8772, has several large châteaux around Auch.

La France des Villages, Model Farm, Rattlesden, Bury St Edmunds IP30 0SY, **t** (01449) 737 664, arranges stays in private châteaux and manors in Aquitaine and the Pyrenees.

French Life Holidays, 26 Church Rd, Hosforth, Leeds LS18 5LG, **t** (0113) 239 0077, offers good-quality self-catering accommodation throughout the region.

French Villas, 175 Selsdon Park Rd, Croydon CR2 8JJ, **t** (020) 8651 1231, deals with farmhouses and villas along the southwestern coast from Arcachon to St-Jean-de-Luz.

International Chapters, 47–51 St John's Wood High St, London NW8 7NJ, **t** (020) 7722 9560, *www.villa-rentals.com*. Farmhouses, châteaux and villas.

Unicorn Holidays, 2 Place Farm, Wheathampstead AL4 8SB, **t** (01582) 834 400. Châteaux-hotels in Biarritz and St-Gaudens.

Vacances en Campagne, Bignor, Pulborough, West Sussex RH20 1QD, **t** (01798) 869 433, provides farmhouses, villas and *gîtes* in Gascony and the Pyrenees.

VFB Holidays, Normandy House, High St, Cheltenham GL50 3FB, **t** (01242) 240339, arranges accommodation from rustic *gîtes* to luxurious farmhouses.

In the USA

Absolutely B&Bs, Box 703, South Miami, FL 33143, **t** 800 380 7420, **t** (305) 666 0710, **f** (305) 666 0173. B&Bs, from châteaux to carefully selected private homes.

France by Heart, PO Box 614, Mill Valle, CA 94942, **t** (415) 331 3075, **f** (415) 331 3076, *www.francebyheart.com*. Over 200 properties throughout the country.

Hideaways International, 767 Islington St, Portsmouth, NH 03802, **t** 800 843 4433, **t** (603) 430 4433, **f** (603) 430 4444, *www.hideaways.com*. Villas, farmhouses and châteaux throughout France.

Overseas Connection, Long Wharf Promenade, PO Box 2600, Sag Harbor, NY 11963, **t** (516) 725 9308/1805, **f** (516) 725 5825, *www.overseasvillas.com*.

Gîtes de France and Other Self-catering Accommodation

Southwest France offers a vast range of self-catering accommodation, from inexpensive farm cottages to history-laden châteaux and fancy villas, or even on board canal boats. The Fédération Nationale des Gîtes de France is a French government service offering inexpensive accommodation by the week in rural areas. Lists with photos for each *département* are available from the French National Tourist Office, from most local tourist offices, or in the UK from the official rep: **The Brittany Centre**, Wharf Rd, Portsmouth, PO2 8RU, **t** 08705 360 360. In France, contact the **Maison des Gîtes de France**, 59 Rue St-Lazare, 75009 Paris, **t** 01 49 70 75 85, **f** 01 42 81 28 53. Prices range from €300 to 400 a week, depending very much on the time of year as well as facilities; nearly always you'll be expected to begin your stay on a Saturday.

Many *départements* also have a second (and usually less expensive) listing of gîtes in a guide called *Clé-confort*.

The Sunday papers are full of options, or contact one of the firms listed on this page. The accommodation they offer will nearly always be more comfortable and costly than a gîte, but the discounts holiday firms offer on the ferries, plane tickets, or car rentals can make up for the price difference.

The Landes

06

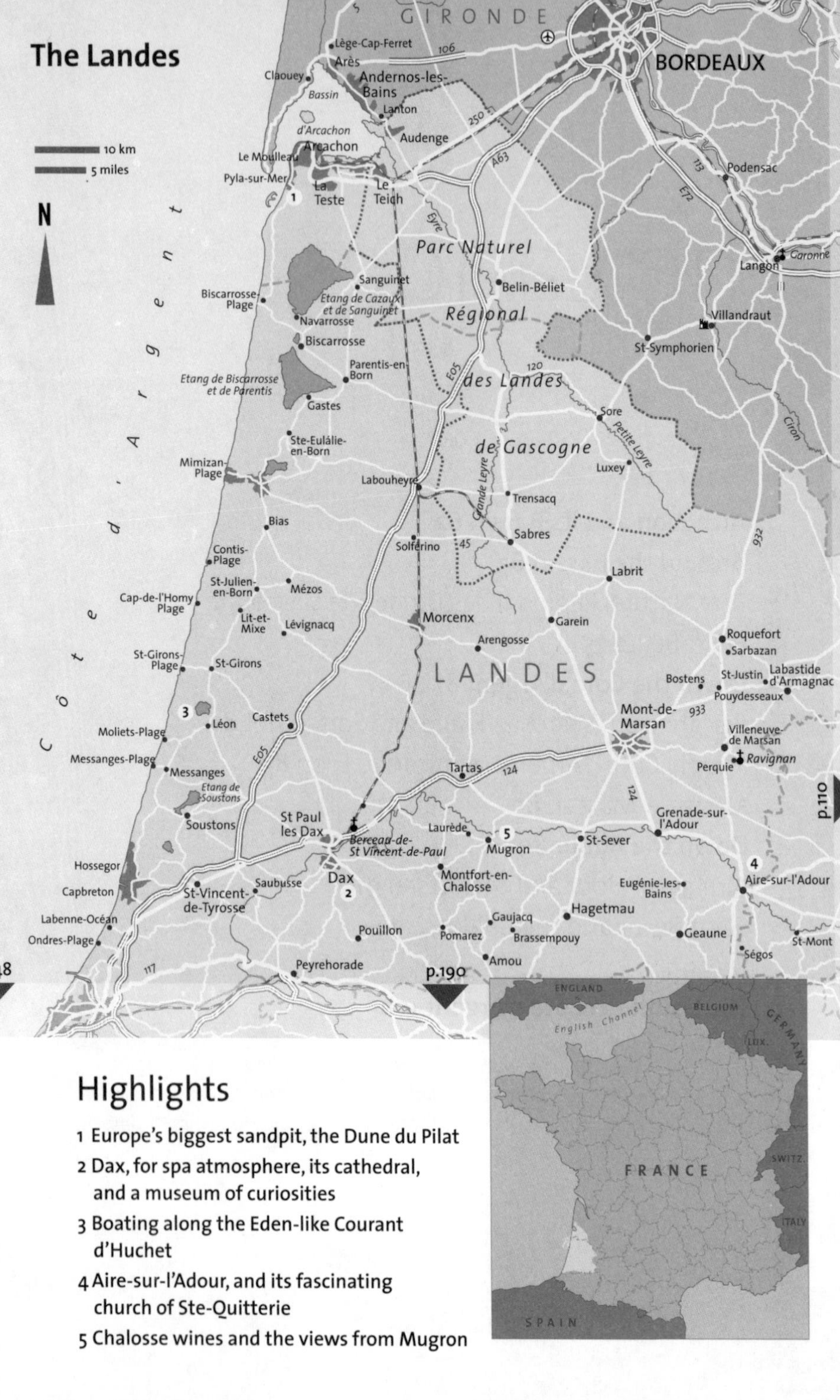

Highlights

1 Europe's biggest sandpit, the Dune du Pilat
2 Dax, for spa atmosphere, its cathedral, and a museum of curiosities
3 Boating along the Eden-like Courant d'Huchet
4 Aire-sur-l'Adour, and its fascinating church of Ste-Quitterie
5 Chalosse wines and the views from Mugron

These landes are sandy tracts covered with pine trees, cut regularly for resin. Historians report, that when the Moors were expelled from Spain, they applied to the court of France for leave to settle on and cultivate these landes; and that the court was much condemned for refusing them. It seems to have been taken for granted, that they could not be peopled with French; and therefore ought rather to be given to the Moors, rather than be left waste.

Arthur Young, *Travels in France*, 1790

...vastes perspectives, ouvertes à l'imprévu du songe.

Odilon Redon

In French 'Landes' means moors or heaths, but the moors that take up most of this, the second-largest *département* in France, have never had a Thomas Hardy to evoke their strangeness or grace them with romance or poetry; rather they have always been a territory outside the pale of civilization, the 'Desert of France', swept by legendary storms off the Bay of Biscay. In the old days, they say, you could hear the sea from 30 miles away, and the winds were powerful enough to lift hay wagons right off the ground. The storms sped dunes inland from the coast, burying villages in their wake and stopping up the rivers with sand, creating insalubrious marshlands. The only inhabitants were 'uncouth' Tartars, who lived a miserable life walking about on stilts, raising sheep for their manure, which was essential to grow their miserable crops of rye, as the land was too poor for wheat. Life was so hard that the Landais were 'condemned never to grow old'.

This all changed over 100 years ago, when France's desert was transformed into Europe's largest forest. It was Napoleon himself who first had the idea of doing something with the Landes: 'I will turn this country into a garden for my old guard,' he declared, although neither he nor most of his old guard survived to see any sign of a garden. Having heard the Landes region was a desert, he introduced dromedaries, which all perished from the excessive humidity in winter; he then brought in buffalo, which died from the excessive dryness in summer. In general discouragement, the Landes were relegated to the back burner until one summer day in 1856, when the little emperor's equally imperial nephew, Napoleon III, was changing trains at Labouheyre and was suddenly inspired to act on his uncle's idea (the fact that Napoleon III had acquired 7,400 hectares in the Landes naturally had nothing to do with it). He stoutly told everyone that he considered the Landes as a kind of local Algeria, his mission not to colonize but to promote business and capital first through drainage and irrigation schemes, followed by 'scientific exploitation' – not of timber, but of resin. On 19 July 1857, Napoleon III ordered the plantation of maritime pines across the Landes de Gascogne. At first the locals feared that the shade of the pines would make them ill, but it wasn't long before they found that the life of a lumberjack or resin-gatherer suited them just fine.

Although the invention of new solvents and foreign competition has cut into the Landes' resin revenues, the trees continue to thrive and supply a good portion of France's lumber, its paper and the 'pâte fluff' for its disposable nappies. Planted in a vast triangle between Bordeaux, Bayonne and Nérac, the forest covers 11,000 square

A note on the way this chapter is arranged

We begin with Arcachon and its Bassin in the southern Gironde, which marks both the northern limits of the Parc Naturel des Landes de Gascogne and the beginning of the Côte d'Argent. The Park follows, and then the northern Côte d'Argent; then it's down to the departmental capital of Mont-de-Marsan, the villages along the Adour and the pretty Chalosse region south of the river. Note that the part of Bas-Armagnac that is in the Landes is included with the rest of the Armagnac region in **The Gers**, *see* p.113.

kilometres, an area equal to two average French *départements* or a third of Belgium. The once plaguesome sand dunes of the coast have been converted into a holiday playground with big breakers, all polished and renamed the Côte d'Argent, the Silver Coast. The distinctive wide Landaise farmhouses or *bordas*, made of beams and white plaster, with a low sloping roof that often runs all the way to the ground on the west side (as protection from the mighty blasts from the Bay of Biscay), are being restored and converted into holiday *gîtes*. And the northern part of the Landes is now a Natural Park, determined to prove that the region is hardly dull, no matter what travellers down the straight, eternal A10 tunnel through the pines to Spain may say (in fact, the very first tourists to explore the area were English milords, who came down in the 1850s, a full half-century before any French tourists set foot in the Landes).

If nothing else, a look at the map may tempt you to explore. Although Gascon is the age-old language of the Landes, many place names have been traced back to the Celto-Iberians (mostly names endings in 'os'), the Romans (those ending in 'an' or 'acq') or Visigoths ('enx'). This helps in part to explain the piquant names of many Landais villages, which often look as if they came straight out of the Scrabble bag: Boos, Gaas, Buglose, Pissos, Stuc, Hinx, Arjuzanx, Bats, Uchacq, Yzosse, Goos, Le Barp, Le Bun and Gassies. Just try to pronounce them.

Arcachon and its Bassin

Gascony's inland sea and favourite playground, the 250-sq km Bassin d'Arcachon, not only sounds like something in your bathroom, but like a bathroom fixture the actual amount of water in it varies greatly, when the tide sweeps through twice a day – at low tide large sections turn into sandy mud pies.

Despite its location near Bordeaux, the Bassin managed to stay out of history most of the time; the Romans and Rabelais wrote admiringly of its oysters, and in the Middle Ages it belonged to the redoubtable Capitals de Buch, English allies in the Hundred Years' War. In the 18th century Louis XVI thought to make the Bassin into a military port and sent down an engineer of the Ponts et Chaussées, Brémontier, to fix the shifting sands. Brémontier built tall palisades 80 yards in from the high tide, halting the wind-borne sand to create barrier dunes between 30 and 40ft high, which he anchored with a long-rooted grass called *oyat*. To stop the dunes from wandering inland, he spread a mix of seeds of gorse, broom and maritime pines under a network of branches. The gorse sprouted up quickly, and helped hold down the soil as the slower pines established themselves.For all that, the Revolution intervened before the military port project ever got under way, leaving the Bassin to daydream to the ebbs and flows of its tides until the mid-19th century, when it discovered its double destiny as a massive nursery for oysters and a summer resort for the Bordelais; these days the gargantuan Dune du Pilat, just south of Arcachon, alone attracts a million visitors a year. Yet many corners have been left untouched by mass tourism: the little villages in the back Bassin could be part of a 17th-century Dutch landscape painting, with their ports sheltering the Bassin's small, shallow-keeled sailing boats called *pinasses* (or *pinassayres*, in Gascon), painted the colour of the owner's house, usually green, light pink or straw yellow.

Getting There and Around

There are **trains** nearly every hour from Bordeaux to Arcachon, and, in the summer, TGVs direct from Paris Montparnasse (Bd du Général-Leclerc, **t** 08 36 35 35 35).

Several CITRAM **buses** a day from Bordeaux (from 8 Rue Corneille, **t** 05 56 43 68 43, or from the station coinciding with the TGVs) serve Andernos, Arès, Cap Ferret, Pyla-sur-Mer and Pyla-Plage. **t** 05 57 72 45 00. Autobus d'Arcachon runs tourist trips of the area.

For a **taxi**, **t** 05 56 83 30 03.

The UBA, *Union des Bateliers Arcachonnais*, from the Thiers and d'Eyrac jetties (**t** 05 57 72 28 28) make frequent half-hour **ferry** crossings between Arcachon and Cap Ferret and Le Moulleau and Cap Ferret in the summer, and run a Bateau Bus in season between Arcachon's Port de Pêche, Petit Port, Jetée d'Eyrac, Jetée Thiers and Le Moulleau.

Bicycles are a convenient way to get around, and the Bassin has many cycle-tracks; you can hire bikes in all the villages, and in Arcachon at Locabeach, 326 Bd de la Plage, **t** 05 56 83 39 64; and Dingo Vélo, Rue Grenier, **t** 05 56 83 44 09.

Tourist Information

Arcachon: Esplanade Georges Pompidou, **t** 05 57 52 97 97, **f** 05 57 52 97 77, *www.bassin-arcachon.com. Open July–Aug daily 9am–7pm; Jan, Feb, Nov, Dec Mon–Sat 9am–6pm.* From Monday to Saturday in season they offer hour-long guided tours of the Ville d'Hiver.

Pyla-sur-Mer: Place du Figuier, **t** 05 56 54 02 22 *www.pyla-sur-mer.com. Open July–Aug daily 9am–1pm and 2–7pm; Sept–June Mon–Fri 9am–1pm and 2–7pm.*

Market Days

Arcachon: daily, in the covered market in Place de Gracia during the summer and Wed, Sat and Sun mornings in winter.

Where to Stay

Arcachon ✉ 33120

Hotels in fashionable Arcachon are in general more expensive than anywhere else in this book. Book months in advance for anything in July or August. All the places below have rooms in both price categories; rates rise considerably for a sea view.

****__Arc-Hôtel sur Mer__, 89 Bd de la Plage, **t** 05 56 83 06 85, **f** 05 56 83 53 72, *www.arc-hotel-sur-mer.com* (*expensive*). A stylish hotel where the rooms, all with balconies, overlook either water or garden; a sauna and a 'Californian' Jacuzzi are among the other amenities. *Open all year.*

***__Les Vagues__, 9 Bd de l'Océan, **t** 05 56 83 03 75, **f** 05 56 83 77 16, *www.hotel-les-vagues.com* (*expensive*). You can't stay much closer to the ocean. Decorated with a fresh, light touch. *Open all year.*

***__Grand Hôtel Richelieu__, 185 Bd de la Plage, **t** 05 56 83 16 50, **f** 05 56 83 47 78, *grand-hotel-richelieu@wanadoo.fr* (*expensive*). An old-fashioned hotel dead in the centre of town, right across from the beach. *Closed Nov–mid-Mar.*

Arcachon

Arcachon was a small fishing village until 1841, when its life was turned upside down by the building of a railway line from nearby La Teste de Buch to Bordeaux. This new link neatly coincided with the new fashion for sea-bathing launched by the Duchesse de Berry. Private villas went up here and there, but the resort really took off after 1852, when a pair of brothers, Emile and Isaac Pereire, took over the railway line and extended it to Arcachon. The Pereire brothers were descendants of Spanish Jews who found a safe haven in Bordeaux during the Inquisition; their grandfather, Jacob, was famous for inventing the first sign-language alphabet for deaf-mutes in the 1700s. The Pereire brothers proved just as inventive, but as property speculators, and laid out their new resort with cute winding lanes according to the Anglophile tastes of Napoleon III.

★★**Le Nautic**, 20 Bd de la Plage, **t** 05 56 83 01 48, **f** 05 56 83 04 67 (*inexpensive*). A hotel with a Spanish touch. *Open all year.*

★★**Les Mimosas**, 77 bis Av de la République, **t** 05 56 83 45 86, **f** 05 57 22 53 40, *www.bassin@arcachon.com* (*cheap*). Tidy if somewhat bland rooms not far from the sea in the Ville d'Eté. *Closed Jan and Feb.*

★**Saint-Christaud**, 8 Allée de la Chapelle, **t** 05 56 83 38 53 (*cheap*). If you book early you can get a room near the beach at this family-run, friendly place; half-board required in July and August. *Open all year except Christmas.*

Le Dauphin, 7 Av Ground, **t** 05 56 83 02 89, *hotel@dauphin-arcachon.com (moderate).* A typical 19th-century Arcachon villa, close to the beach. The bedrooms are small but comfortable. *Open all year.*

Le Provence, 106 Bd de la Plage, **t** 05 56 83 10 78 (*cheap*). Half a kilometre from the port, a simple, family-run inn, with a restaurant. *Closed Nov and Dec.*

Des Abatilles, **t** 05 56 83 24 15. The municipal campsite; nothing fancy, but clean and cheap. Camping club d'Arcachon. 1.8 km from beach and town. *Open all year.*

Pyla-sur-Mer ✉ 33115

★★★**Haitza**, Pl Louis-Gaume, **t** 05 57 52 79 27, **f** 05 56 22 10 23, *Haitza@wanadoo.fr* (*moderate*). Among the nicest here, set in the pine woods, a stone's throw from the beach. *Closed Oct–Mar.*

★★**La Corniche**, 46 Av Louis-Gaume, **t** 05 56 22 72 11, **f** 05 56 22 70 21, *www.corniche-pyla.com* (*moderate–cheap*). By the beach and at the foot of the mighty dune, a neo-Basque wood and brick hotel built in 1932, with spacious balconies and a stairway down to the beach. The restaurant is good too. *Menus from €13. Closed Nov–Mar.*

★★**Ttiki-Etchea**, 2 Pl Louis Gaume, **t** 05 56 22 71 15, **f** 05 56 22 15 99 (*moderate*). Basque-style, charming, set among the tall pines next to the sea. *Open May–Sept.*

★★**Côte Sud**, 4 Av de Figuier, **t** 05 56 83 25 00, **f** 05 56 22 70 21 *www.cote-du-sud.fr* (*expensive–moderate*). In a 1940s villa in the pines, a 5-minute walk from the beach; the restaurant offers a good value €20–27 menu, with plenty of seafood and game dishes in season. *Restaurant closed Dec and Jan.*

There are several excellent **camp sites** south of the dune although beware that they are often packed cheek by jowl in the summer: **Camping La Dune**, **t/f** 05 56 22 72 17; **Pyla Camping**, **t** 05 56 22 74 56, **f** 05 56 22 10 31, closer to the beach; and **Camping Panorama**, Rte de Biscarosse, **t** 05 62 22 10 44. Also try **Camping du Val de L'Eyre**, 8, Route de Minoy, 33770 Salles, **t** 05 56 88 47 03. Family camp site.

Eating Out

Seafood in all its forms is one of the reasons the French flock to Arcachon..

L'Ombrière, 79 Cours Héricart-de-Thury, **t** 05 56 83 42 52. Arcachon's classiest garden terrace serves delicious seafood platters as well as duck and veal dishes, and a good selection of wine (*menu €22*). *Open daily Apr–Oct; closed Sun and Mon in winter.*

They divided the residential sections into four subdivisions, each named after one of the four seasons. Although Spring and Autumn never really caught on, the **Ville d'Hiver**, the area best sheltered from the ocean winds and always 3°C/37°F warmer than the rest of Arcachon, attained full fashion status by the 1860s – Gounod, Debussy, Alexandre Dumas, Napoleon III, Marie Christine of Austria and her future husband Alfonso XII of Spain (who came incognito) were all habitués. For a centre-piece, the Ville d'Hiver has the **Parc Mauresque**, named after its fabulously outlandish pseudo-Moorish casino (1864), inspired by the Alhambra and the Great Mosque of Cordoba – but tragically destroyed by a fire in 1977. Inspired by its fantasy, the usually staid 19th-century Bordelais who built second homes in the Ville d'Hiver let their hair down, indulging in neo-Gothic, Tyrolean, Tudor, pseudo-medieval and other fond fancies; some 200 of these lacy gingerbread villas survive, many now owned by

Le Patio, 10 Bd de la Plage, **t** 05 56 83 02 72. Surrounds diners with vines, a waterfall and delicious aromas from specialities such as lobster salad and oysters in flaky pastry (*fixed menu €28.10*). *Closed Tues.*

Restaurant l'Avenue, 196 Bd de la Plage, **t** 05 56 83 43 98. Plain, simple good-value restaurant despite its prime location opposite the casino. Splendid seafood platters, rich *bouil-labaisse* and paella (*menus €15–29*). *Closed first two weeks in Dec.*

Diego Plage, Bd Veyrier Montayneres, Diego Plage, **t** 05 56 83 84 46. Enjoying a prime location overlooking the beach, with generous helpings of fresh fish and seafood platters (*menus €19–28*). *Open daily.*

Chez Yvette, 59 Bd Général Leclerc, **t** 05 56 83 05 11. More formal, with an enviable reputation for its superbly fresh seafood for the past 30 years, and a cellar of white Bordeaux wines to go with it. Expect to pay around €28 *à la carte*, or try the €14 *Escale Gourmande*, which begins with oysters. Set menu €16.50. A la Carte. €23–50. *Open all year.*

Chez Pierre, 1 Bd Veyrier-Montagnères, **t** 05 56 22 52 94. In the waterfront pedestrian zone, offering a well-prepared variety of seafood and luscious desserts in its cosy interior or out on the terrace, with fine views of the Bassin (*menus from €14*). *Open all year.*

La Plancha, just behind the market at 17 Rue Jéhenne, **t** 05 56 83 76 66, *www.la-plancha.com*. For under €14 you can fill up on *gambas à la plancha* and other Spanish-style seafood treats. Lunch menu from €6.40. Dinner €10.50. *Closed Sat and Sun lunch.*

Aux Mille Saveurs 25 Bd General Leclerc. (Opposite Arcachon Station). **t** 05 56 83 40 28. Lacks a view, but makes up for with its cuisine, notably the *jambonneau de canard* (stuffed duck thigh). Lovely desserts. Menus (lunch) €22–29. *Open daily July and Aug; closed Sun eve and all day Mon rest of the year. Closed November.*

Restaurant Le Chipiron, 69 Bd Chanzy, **t** 05 57 52 06 33. An authentic little Spanish bistro near to the marina, serving tapas, delicious baby squid and other offerings with a good value *set menu* at lunchtimes. Weekday menu €11, à la carte €30. *Closed Sun, Mon plus Tues eve (winter); closed Wed all year.*

Entertainment and Nightlife

After dark, much of Arcachon's life gravitates around the **Casino d'Arcachon**, 163 Bd de la Plage, **t** 05 56 83 41 44, where the roulette and blackjack tables open after 9pm; the complex includes bars, a restaurant, and a disco **Disco Le Scotch** **t** 05 56 83 41 43, open from midday.

The local **discos** put on a number of special nights in the summer: in Arcachon, try **Le Cotton Club**, 4 Bd Mestrézat, **t** 05 56 54 87 69; and **L'Escorida**, 177 Bd de la Plage, **t** 05 56 22 55 07.

If you've got any kids in tow, they might like an evening out watching and envying the daring cyclists run showily through their acrobatic stunts at **Dingovélos**, Rue Grenier, **t** 05 56 83 44 09, *www.dingovelos.com* (*open summer only, until midnight*).

wealthy retirees. Don't miss the fine overall view of the Bassin from the Parc Mauresque gardens, its **Passerelle Saint-Paul** (over adjacent Allée Pasteur), built by Eiffel in 1862, and the observatory, reached by a 19th-century lift.

The **Ville d'Eté**, facing the Bassin and cooler in the summer, has most of Arcachon's tourist facilities, seaside promenades, sheltered sandy beaches and the **Musée-Aquarium** (*Rue Professeur-Jolyet, **t** 05 56 83 33 32; open mid Feb–Nov 10–12 and 2–7; July and Aug 9.30–12.30 and 2–8*), with a pretty collection of tropical fish, tortoises, seashells, stuffed weasels and shark skeletons. The Ville d'Eté's most notorious resident was Toulouse-Lautrec, who had a house by the ocean and liked to swim in the nude, offending the sensibilities of his neighbours. To pacify them, he erected a fence between his house and the beach – then mischievously covered it with obscene drawings. The furious neighbours eventually bought the house and gleefully burned the fence. Their descendants have never really forgiven them. (They should consider the chagrin of the heirs of the young man in the Marquesas Islands, charged with tidying up Gauguin's hut after the painter's death. Finding it cluttered with sculptures and paintings, he loaded everything on to his boat and dumped the lot into the Pacific.)

Since 1950, a new crop of villas has gone up on the ocean front in **Parc Pereire**, overlooking Arcachon's best beach, Plage Pereire. As incredible as it seems, in 1922 someone had the chutzpah to drill for oil right in the middle of the park, but instead of black gold discovered, at 1,600ft down, a natural spring of mineral water, known as **Les Abatilles**, which is exploited and bottled in the spa (*on Bd de la Côte d'Argent, **t** 05 56 22 38 50, free tastes from the tap and guided tours every Wed in July and Aug at 10.30am*). Further south, along Boulevard de la Plage, a casino has been installed in the more Disneylandish than outlandish **Château Deganne**, with a congress centre, the Palatium, to keep it company.

The Dune du Pilat

As the afternoon draws to a close in Arcachon, the thing to do is drive or cycle 8km south, through the resorts of **Moulleau**, **Pyla-sur-Mer** and **Pyla-Plage**. In the pine trees, there's a pay car park where you can leave your vehicle, and, beyond that, the

Excursions

The UBA (*see* 'Getting Around') offer two hour-long excursions to the **Ile aux Oiseaux** at 3.30pm, all year long.

The Bassin's only island, the Ile aux Oiseaux is government-owned and given over to sea birds as well as oyster farms and sailing boats. In the old days, herdsmen in boats would have their horses swim over to the sweet islet pastures. The Ile aux Oiseaux's landmarks are its picturesque *cabanes tchanquées*, huts perched on stilts.

In July and August the UBA also offer day-trips to the shadeless, hot and sandy **Banc d'Arguin**, a wildfowl refuge at the entrance to the Bassin; in June sandwich terns by their thousands nest here (bring a picnic). Guided tours of the **oyster beds** are available, and four-hour trips up the cool, forested **river Leyre** (*see* below).

The Bataliers Arcachonais, departing from all Bassin jetties, also cross to **Cap Ferret**, and make summer excursions to the ocean, up the **Leyre river** *bayous* and to the **Banc d'Arguin**, as well as night trips in July and Aug.

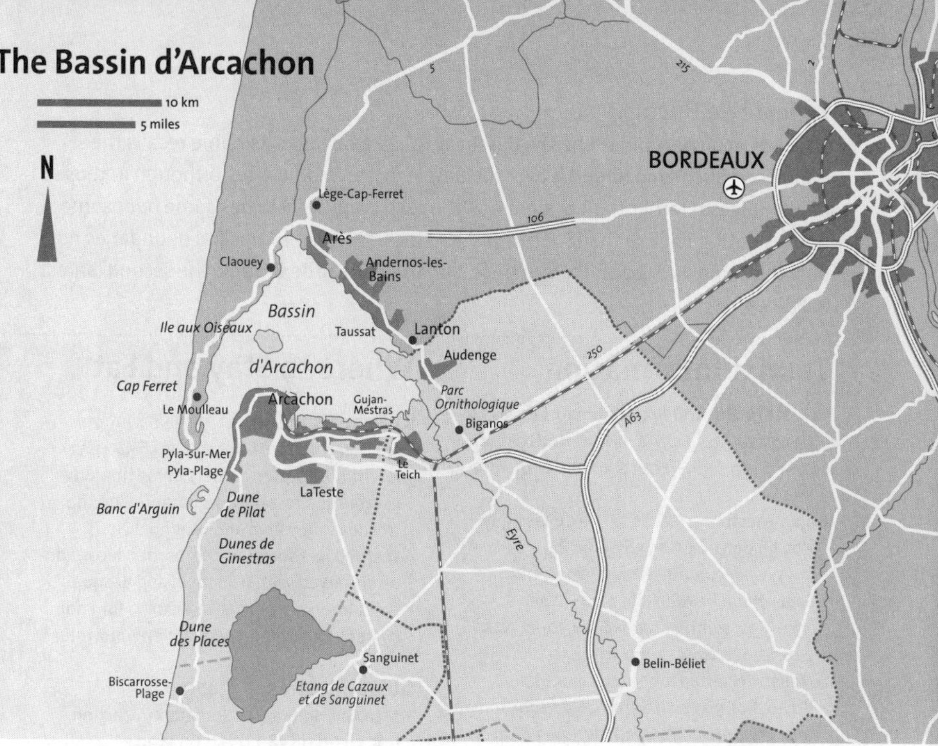

awesome, terrible, extraordinary sight of the Moby Dick of dunes, the **Dune du Pilat**, at 347ft the highest pile of sand in Europe, at 1.7 miles (2.7km) the longest, and at 550 yards the widest. Excavations in this little chunk of the Sahara have found that Pilat began to form 8,000 years ago, and more or less reached its present dimensions in the 17th century. Like all dunes, it's in a constant state of flux, and every year it inches about 15 yards, consuming the pines and forcing the camp sites and cafés at its rim (*see* 'Where to Stay, p.64) to move a bit further inland. A wooden stair with 190 steps helps you get to the top of the steep behemoth for an unforgettable view – especially at sunset. If you can't resist the urge to roll and slide and scamper down the ocean-side slope, be prepared to face the torturous return trip back up the slippery sands. Often included in the sundown view are schools of bottlenose dolphins and porpoises, who like to frolic just offshore.

South of the sand-monster there's **Le Petit Nice beach**, and beyond that a naturist beach, both with lifeguards and snack bars.

Around the Bassin

Ten *communes*, picturesque little ports with wooden oyster shacks, beaches, a river delta and a bird sanctuary, and a score of rather more commercial amusements wait to be savoured around the rim of the Bassin. Try at least once to cross the water the traditional way, in a *pinasse* – promenades are offered from the ports of Arcachon, Arès, Andernos and Lège-Cap-Ferret.

La Teste de Buch

East of Arcachon, pines line the Bassin at La Teste de Buch. Its name recalls the Captals de Buch who lorded it over the Bassin in the Middle Ages, although in those days pine resin rather than oysters was the cash crop. La Teste has some handsome houses dating back to the 18th century, and includes in its municipal boundaries not only the Dune du Pilat and a race track, but also the **Lac de Cazaux**, the second largest in France.

Tourist Information

La Teste de Buch: Pl Jean Hameau, **t** 05 56 54 63 14, **f** 05 56 54 45 94, *www.latestedebuch.com. Open Mon–Fri 9–12.30 and 2–6, Sat 9–12 and 2–5.*

Gujan-Mestras: 41 Av de Lattre de Tassigny, **t** 05 56 66 12 65, **f** 05 56 66 94 44, *www.ville-gujanmestras.fr. Open mid Sept–mid June Mon–Sat 8.30–12 and 1.30–5.30; summer Mon–Sat 8.30–12.30 and 2–6.30; Suns and hols 9.30–12.30.*

Le Teich: Pl Pierre-Dubernet, **t** 05 56 22 80 46, **f** 05 56 22 89 65, *office-de-tourisme-le-teich@wanadoo.fr. Open Mar–Aug Mon–Sat 10–1 and 2.30–6, Sun 10–1; winter Mon–Fri 10–12.30 and 2.30–5.*

Andernos-les-Bains: Esplanade du Broustic, **t** 05 56 82 02 95, **f** 05 56 82 14 29, *www.andernoslesbains.fr. Open all year Mon–Sat. 9.30–12.30 and 3–6; July and Aug Mon–Sat 9.30–1 and 2.30–7, Sun 10–1 and 3–7.*

Arès: Esplanade G. Dartiguelongue, **t** 05 56 60 18 07, **f** 05 56 60 39 41, *office–tourisme–ares@wanadoo.fr. Open July and Aug Mon–Sat 8.30–7 and 2–7; winter Mon–Sat 8.30– 12.15 and 4–7.*

Lège-Cap-Ferret: 1 Av Gén. de Gaulle, **t** 05 56 03 94 49, **f** 05 57 70 31 70, *www.lege-capferret.com. Open July and Aug 10–6.30, Sun 10–1 and 3–6.30; June and Sept Mon–Sat 10–1 and 3–6.*

Biganos t 05 57 70 67 56, *www.villedebiganos.fr. Open all year.*

Market Days

La Teste de Buch: Thursdays and Sundays, in the covered market. *Covered market daily in season. Open-air Tues, Sat and Sun in season.*

Where to Stay and Eat

La Teste ✉ 33260

Chez Diego, Centre Captal, **t** 05 56 54 44 32. A family of oyster farmers owns this long-established restaurant guaranteeing the freshest of oysters and other delicious seafood in a south-of-the-border décor, and often served with a Spanish and Basque twist (*menus from €13–25*).€10.50 for 1 doz oysters. *Closed Mon plus Sun eves in winter.*

Gujan-Mestras ✉ 33470

*****La Gueriniѐre**, Rte Bordeaux-Arcachon, **t** 05 56 66 08 78, **f** 05 56 66 13 39, *www.lagueriniere.com* (*expensive*). The most elegant place to stay here, with airy modern rooms set around a garden and pool. There's also an elegant restaurant. Exotic garden terrace. A la Carte €30–65. *Open all year.*

***Il Bacio**, 8 Av de L. de Tassigny, La Hume, **t** 05 56 66 12 12 (*cheap*). Set in a garden, this family-run hotel has 17 rooms overlooking the marina and beach, with a pretty, shady patio serving up a tasty paella and other succulent *fruits de mer* (*half-pension mandatory*). *Closed Oct.*

Les Viviers, Port de Larros, **t** 05 56 66 01 04 (*cheap*). The light-filled dining room and terrace restaurant offers a wide selection of shellfish and other denizens of the deep, as well as a tasty beef brochette with *cèpes*. Menu €19. *Open daily. Closed Nov–Feb.*

Le Teich ✉ 33470

The Maison de la Nature, **t** 05 56 22 80 93, doubles as a hostel, with 36 beds, communal kitchen and bikes and canoes to hire by groups.

Ker Helen, near the port on the D650, **t** 05 56 66 03 79, *www.kerhelen.com.* A good camp

La Hume

In the same area, La Hume has sprouted three other roadside attractions to keep mom and dad in the poorhouse: a 'zoo' of domestic animals, the **Parc Animalier La Coccinelle** (**t** *05 56 66 30 41; open June–mid Sept daily 10–7. Until 7.30 July and Aug*), where children can feed the baby lambs and goats; **Aqualand** (**t** *08 92 68 66 13; open June–mid-Sept daily 10–7; adm*), for a day splashing around in rivers, pools with waves, and every kind of waterslide imaginable.

site, with caravans or bungalows to hire. *Open Mar–Nov.*

Biganos ✉ 33380

★**Hôtel de France**, 99 Av de la Libération, **t** 05 56 82 61 08 (*cheap*). A good choice if you are on a tight budget. *Closed last week in Aug and 1st three weeks in Sept.*

Andernos-les-Bains ✉ 33510

L'Esquirrey, 9 Av Commandant-Allègre, **t** 05 56 82 22 15. A haven for oyster-lovers – the freshest of bivalves served in a real *cabanon* at friendly prices – along with the freshest, tastiest fish the Bassin has to offer. A la Carte only approx €30. *Closed mid Nov–mid Feb and Mon lunch in season.*

Lège-Cap-Ferret ✉ 33970

Cap Ferret is the trendiest spot on the Bassin these days, and there are plenty of bars, restaurants and camp sites, but only a handful of hotels; quite a few people sleep out under the stars. The lists below take the hamlets from north to south.

Chez Auguste, Le Petit Piquey, **t** 05 56 60 52 12. The local oyster bar to see and be seen in, with a terrace overlooking the sandy Dune du Pilat. *Closed Oct–Easter and Tues in season.*

Pat-à-Chou, Le Grand Piquey, **t** 05 56 60 51 38. The best home-made ice-cream on the whole Bassin. *Open 7–1 and 3.30–8; closed Mon.*

Chez Pierrette, 9 Impasse des Sternes, Piraillan, **t** 05 56 60 50 50. In a traditional Basque house, with a good reputation for unfussy dishes, based on the market and the day's catch, but there are meat specialities as well. Menu a la Carte in summer €25–30. Winter menu €25. *Closed Tues and Wed lunch in summer and all day Tues and Wed in winter.*

Hotel de la Plage 1, Rue des Marins–L'Herbe, **t** 05 56 60 50 15 (*expensive*). A delightful, simple 8-room wooden hotel by the beach, with a good restaurant, although the menu is rarely committed to paper. €37–40. *Closed Jan.*

Rond-Point, **t** 05 56 60 51 32, Port de l'Herbe. An equally simple décor but more pretensions in the kitchen, preparing abundant portions of seafood (monkfish sautéed in Vieux Médoc, for instance) as well as land food, served inside or out on the terrace Menu €25–30. *Open daily June–Sept; closed Tues and Wed Oct–May.*

★★**Des Dunes**, 119 Av de Bordeaux, Cap Ferret, **t** 05 56 60 61 81, **f** 05 56 03 61 66 (*expensive*). A little dune-side hotel. *Open April–Nov.*

★★**La Frégate**, 34 Av de l'Océan, Cap Ferret, **t** 05 56 60 41 62, *www.hotel-la-fregate.net* (*moderate–inexpensive*). Modern hotel complete with a pool. *Open April–Aug; closed Nov–Jan.*

★★**Hotel des Pins**, 23, Rue des Fauvettes, Cap Ferret, **t** 05 56 60 60 11 (*moderate*). A good small hotel with a decent restaurant, set in a 1920s house with garden. *Open April–11 Nov.*

Auberge de Jeunesse, 87 Av de Bordeaux, Cap Ferret, **t** 05 56 60 64 62. So many customers that many end up under tents.

Chez Hortense, Av du Sémaphore, Cap Ferret, **t** 05 56 60 62 56. The best restaurant in this corner, offering a wide variety of seafood, prepared in a wide variety of styles. Around €45 for a la Carte. *Open July–Aug and weekends from Easter to early Sept.*

L'Arrimeur, 58 Av de l'Ocean, Cap Ferret, **t** 05 56 60 60 60. A restaurant with a decided Basque influence (*Menus* €11–17). Also has 13 rooms (*moderate*). *Open daily in season; closed Sun eves Sept–May.*

The Oyster's their World

Oysters from the Bassin were popular among rich Romans of Burdigala, who would set up relays to have them brought to their tables in a few hours, where they would slurp them raw with garum, the prized and mysterious fish-gut sauce that culinary archaeologists guess was something similar to Vietnamese *nuoc nam*. By the Middle Ages, when the old Roman roads were full of mud and potholes, tastes turned to dried oysters put up in barrels, eaten in a sauce or fried. The Bassin's industry remained small and local, however, until 1850, when once again speedy transport, in the form of the railway, allowed the tasty bivalves to chug post-haste to Bordeaux, and then on to Paris in 1857 – at a time when restaurant diners thought nothing of beginning a meal with 10 or 15 dozen. Twice, however, Arcachon's bread-and-butter industry was devastated by oyster parasites; the first, in 1922, wiped out Arcachon's flat, native *gravettes*. These were replaced by *portugaises*, which in turn fell prey to a new parasite in 1970. Since 1972, the oysters farmed in the Bassin belong to two different species – a new *gravette*, a flat hybrid of Charente and Breton oysters, and a parasite-resistant, elongated Japanese oyster, the *huître creuse*, or *gigas*.

Today the Bassin d'Arcachon is the fourth-largest oyster producer in France, but the first in Europe to 'trap' microscopic oyster embryos and larvae swishing about the sea in search of a home – they simply can't resist stacks of Roman roof tiles, bleached in a mix of lime and sand. After eight months clinging to a tile, the baby oysters are moved into calm nurseries in flat cages; the next year, they are moved once more to oyster parks, in fresh plankton-rich waters, where the oyster farmers defend them the best they can against greedy starfish and crustaceans, who will nevertheless devour 15 to 20 per cent of the crop over the next three years. In the parks, the oysters are constantly turned, to encourage them to develop a nice shape and a hard shell. When at long last they're ready to go on the market, they are placed for up to four days in special pools that trick them into no longer trusting the tide, so that they remain sealed tight while they are shipped and sold by size, from 6 (the smallest) to 0 (the largest and best).

'Now if you're ready, Oysters dear/We can begin to feed,' as the Walrus said. To prepare the little rascals *à la mode d'Arcachon*: count on a dozen oysters per person (or more if you're really greedy), four (or more) *crépinettes* (small flat sausages cooked in white wine), plenty of thinly sliced rye bread and butter and glasses of dry white Graves, properly chilled at 6–8°C (44°F). Open the oysters and keep cool, fry or barbecue the sausages just before serving and eat – slurp down a cold oyster, take a bite of hot sausage with a bit of buttered bread and wash it down with a swallow of wine.

Gujan-Mestras

Next to La Hume, the Bassin's oyster capital, Gujan-Mestras, has seven little ports crowded with *oustaous* (oyster huts), which provide the perfect backdrop for ordering a plate of oysters *à déguster,* as the French say. The critter on Gujan's coat-of-arms, however, is the ladybird beetle, the *barbot* in Gascon, a name that goes back to the early days of the phylloxera epidemic, when the locals noticed that their infected vines invariably swarmed with ladybirds. They accused those helpful insects of spreading the plague, while in fact they were gobbling down the real culprits as fast as they could; the priest at Gujan even held *barbot* exorcisms in the vineyards. When the real, much tinier lice-like pests were discovered, the villagers of Gujan became the butt of jokes from their neighbours, who called them the *barbots*. By the 1920s, Gujan had learned to laugh at itself, and adopted the ladybird bug as its own, even naming its rugby team the Barbots.

Le Teich: the Delta of the Leyre

At Le Teich, the Leyre (or L'Eyre), one of the most important rivers of the Landes, drains into the Bassin d'Arcachon, forming the kind of marshy delta beloved of migratory waterfowl flying between Africa and Scandinavia. In 1972, Le Teich's rare environment of saltwater and fresh-water bayous was set aside as the **Parc Ornithologique** (*t 05 56 22 80 93, www.parc-ornithologique-du-teich.com; open daily 10–6, summer 10–8; adm; bring your binoculars, or rent them on the site*). The delta is the nesting ground for several species, especially grey herons, black cormorants, white storks, black and white oystercatchers, egrets, kingfishers, dabbling garganeys and spoon-billed shovelers. Altogether some 280 different species have been sighted. One of the big success stories has been the return of the mute swan, which vanished from France at the time of the Revolution. For general information, visit the park's **Maison de la Nature** (*t 05 56 22 80 93, f 05 56 22 69 43*).

The Parc Ornithologique is divided into four sections, and by taking the marked 3.5km (2-hour) path from the Maison de la Nature you can visit them all. The largest section, the vast **Parc de Causseyre**, has several hides and observation posts where you can watch a score of different year-round residents; the **Parc de la Moulette** is where the geese, swans and ducks are concentrated; the small **Parc des Artigues** has a collection of ducks from around the world, at liberty, and large aviaries; and the inaccessible **Parc Claude Quancard** is for wading birds (although there are two observation posts). There's a fine viewpoint over the entire delta from the **Observatoire du Delta de Leyre**.

The Back Bassin, Around to Cap Ferret

At **Biganos**, north of the Leyre delta, many of the old picturesque oystermen's *cabanons* have been converted into pretty holiday homes, while the poor old oystermen, one presumes, now work in the local paper mill. The next town, **Audenge**, is a sleepy fishing village where the day's catch is trapped in reservoirs left by the

Excursions

The Leyre delta is an especially fun part of Gascony to explore by canoe or kayak, especially if you are a keen birdwatcher, and there are several places to hire one by the day or half-day from June to September: the park's **Maison de la Nature** (*book in advance, t 05 56 22 80 93*); **Villetorte Loisirs**, 30 Rue du Pont Neuf, Le Teich, **t** 05 56 22 66 80; or **Club du Pont de Lamothe**, 1 Av de la Côte d'Argent, Gujan-Mestras, *t 05 56 22 67 57*.

retreating tide – a method of fishing that inspired someone to dig similar tide-fed reservoirs for humans; if the tide is out you can join the locals for a refreshing dip in the public seawater pools. Next to the north is **Lanton**, which has a long beach and a 12th-century church, the oldest to be found on the Bassin. **Andernos-les-Bains**, a lively summer resort with splendid views across the water, and **Arès** both have beaches safe for children.

The northwestern curve of the Bassin is sprinkled with little oyster-port resorts set between the calm waters and rough Atlantic. All belong to the *commune* of **Lège-Cap-Ferret**. The prettiest of these ports is **L'Herbe**, an intimate hamlet of wooden houses on tiny lanes founded in the 17th century. The *commune*'s 21 miles of ocean beaches culminate in the sandy tail of **Cap Ferret**, which has long been doing its damnedest to close off the mouth of the Bassin; long before anyone had even heard of global warming the sea was nibbling away at the land and in the past 200 years the cape has grown 2½miles and gobbled up several fashionable villas in its wake.

A path leads around to the tip of the cape, with splendid views of the Dune du Pilat, most breathlessly from the top of the 255 steps of the **lighthouse** (*Open all year. Contact tourist office for guided tours*). The cute little **Tramway du Cap-Ferret** links the end of the road to the ocean beaches, where surfers ride the big rollers expedited by the Bay of Biscay.

Tchanquayres: Why the Landais Wore Stilts

If maritime pines are synonymous with the Landes today, in the past the region's symbol was something straight out of Monty Python: shepherds on stilts, dressed in fleecy sheepskin coats and boots and black berets. Introduced only in the 16th century under somewhat mysterious circumstances, the traditional Landais stilts, or *tchanques*, are about a yard high and strapped three times around the calves; the foot rests on a shelf, the *paouse pé*, and the leg of the stilt, the *escasse* (hence the French word for stilt, *échasse*) ends in a point made of horn or hard wood. The stilts were handy for walking quickly through marshy land (wet on top, but with a solid sand base below), but woe to the *tchanquayres* who met a mole hill, far from the perches they had at home to hoist themselves up on to the stilts. Because of the flat terrain, the higher altitude provided by the *tchanques* was all a shepherd required to keep track of straying lambs. The last piece of essential gear for a shepherd was his little knitting bag, or *braguète*, which occupied many a weary hour high over the moors. Once they had mastered their stilts, the shepherds (and shepherdesses) took to dancing on them as well.

Although the stilts have become as obsolete as the sheep, some twenty societies in the Landes keep up the lofty tradition today, dancing high at local fêtes, or running races like drunken flamingos. Stilt-racing enjoyed something of a fad in the 1890s, and no one has yet topped the feat of Sylvain Dornon, the *échassier national* who, in what the French like to term their 'world-record-breaking spirit', climbed up to the second platform of the Eiffel Tower on stilts, and topped it off by running on his *tchanques* from Paris to Moscow and back again in 1891.

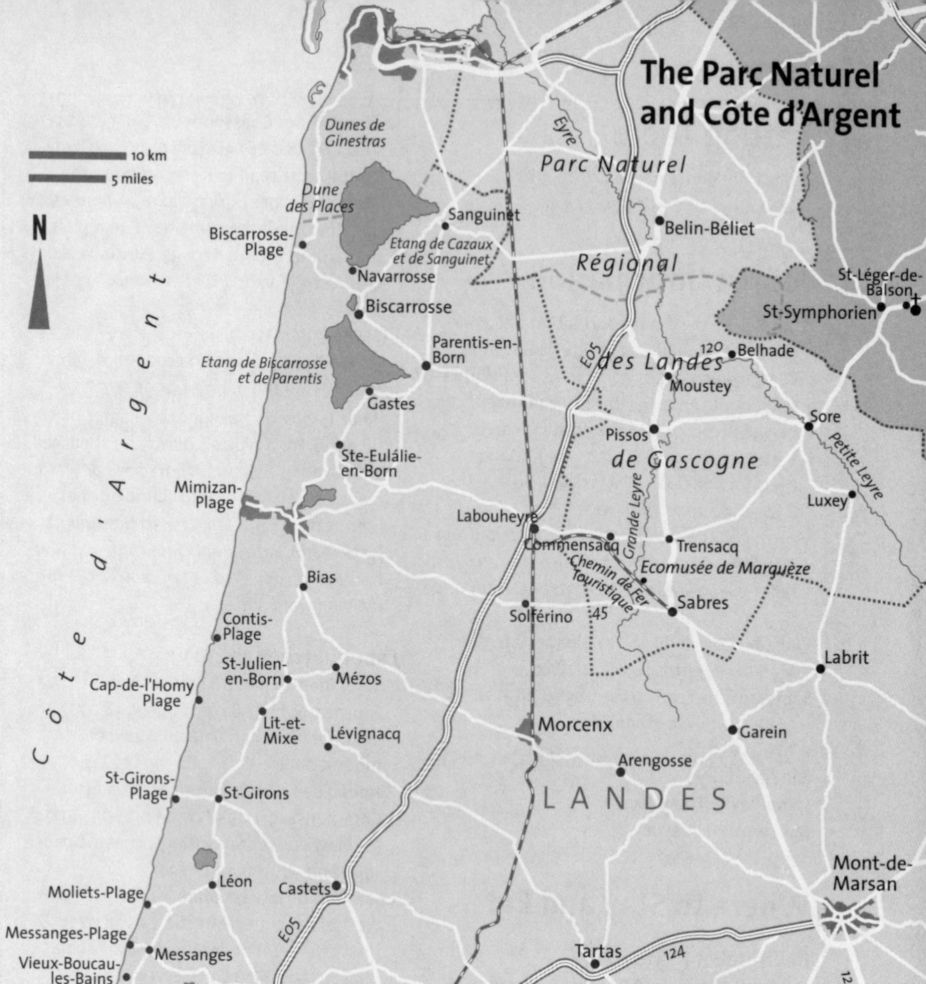

Parc Naturel Régional des Landes de Gascogne

The Parc Naturel des Landes de Gascogne (which includes the Parc Ornithologique of Le Teich, *see* above) was created in 1970, with the same goal as other natural parks in France, to both safeguard and promote an underpopulated region with a distinct environment and traditions. Managed by landowners, local business people and regional politicians, the park made one of its main goals to suck in excess visitors from the coasts and create jobs through tourism.

The park covers 290,000 hectares, including large swathes of two *départements*, the Gironde and the Landes, stretching from the Bassin d'Arcachon in the north and Brocas in the south. There's no finer place to take your first steps in the secret world of the Landes: the park encompasses the delta of the Leyre (also spelled l'Eyre: there are two intransigent orthographic camps) and the lovely rivers of the Grand and Petite Leyre, immersed in lush greenery and perfect for canoeing. A network of walking paths and little rural roads will get you into the pinewoods, passing by

Getting There

Trains from Bordeaux pass through Labouheyre, **t** 05 58 97 00 24.

Tourist Information

Belin-Béliet: the main information office for the Parc Régional is at 33, Rte de Bayonne, **t** 05 57 71 99 99, **f** 05 57 88 12 72. For information about the town the office number is **t** 05 56 88 00 06. Main website for area, *www.parc-landes-de-gascogne.fr* Market every Fri am. *Open all year Mon–Fri 8.30–12.30 and 1.30–5.30.*

Mousty: Mairie, **t** 05 58 07 71 26. *Open July and Aug Mon–Fri 9–12 and 2–5.30; rest of the year Mon–Wed 9–12 and 2.30–5.30 plus Thurs and Fri 9–12.*

Belhade: **t** 05 58 08 20 72 Belhade. *Open Mon–Fri 9–12.30; closed Tue, Wed 2–5.*

Sabres: at the Eco-musée, **t** 05 58 08 31 31. *Open Mon–Fri 9–12 and 2–6.*

Market Days

Labouheyre: Thursdays.

Morcenx: Wednesdays.

Where to Stay and Eat

Bélin-Beliet ✉ 33830

Madame Clements, 11 Rue du Stade, **t/f** 05 56 88 13 17 (*inexpensive*). A *chambre d'hôte* in the centre of the village, a 19th-century house surrounded by a garden with lovely views from the rooms. *Table d'hôte* available. *Open all year.*

Moustey ✉ 40410

La Haut Landaise, Pl des Platanes, **t** 05 58 07 77 85, a 17th-century *auberge* in the middle of Moustey. Some of the best cooking in the area. €15–36. *Closed Mon April–Sept. Closed school holidays in winter.*

Sore ✉ 40410

The *commune* operates nine woody cottages, or *gîtes forestiers*, and a camp site with a pool; to book, ring the *mairie*, **t** 05 58 07 60 06.

Restaurant des Chasseurs, Lot Barthe, 404330, Sore, **t** 05 58 07 62 36. For some excellent fills, take the road to Pissos as far as the *quartier* Barthes (around 4km), where you can dine under the plane trees on regional charcuterie. Menus €20–35. Lunch weekdays €11. *Closed Mon and Tues eve and all of Mar.*

Pissos ✉ 40410

To rent one of Pissos' 20 economical *gîtes forestiers*, ring the *mairie*, **t** 05 58 07 70 23.

Café de Pissos, on the edge of village, **t** 05 58 08 90 16. For a typical country feast packed with Landais delights, from *salmis de palombe* and foie gras to salmon dishes. Menus from €15. *Closed 15–30 Nov and 1st week in Jan. Restaurant closed Sun and Tues eves plus all day Wed out of season. Open daily July and Aug.*

Labouheyre ✉ 40210

***Hôtel Brémontier**, 110 Rue des Hauts-Fourneaux, **t** 05 58 07 01 13, **f** 05 58 07 13 40, *www.bremontier.fr* (*cheap*). *Menu €16.* (A modest choice. *Open all year. €23–28.*

Château de La Bouheyre, on the road to Commensacq, **t** 05 58 07 04 05, **f** 05 58 07 15 32 (*inexpensive*). Surprisingly cheap. *Open July–Sept, must book ahead.*

Chambres d'Hôte Loustau, set in a park 5km west of Labouheyre at Lüe, **t** 05 58 07 11 58 (*inexpensive*). A delightful, typical Landais *maison du maître*. *Open Easter–end Sept.*

L'Auberge Landaise, Lüe, **t** 05 58 07 06 13. A traditional half-timbered farmhouse with a terrace, serving up heaped portions of confits, roast pigeons, roast lamb, foie gras, game dishes, and other delights (*9 set menus from €10–30*). *Closed Sun eve, Mon, and the month of October.*

Sabres ✉ 40630

****Auberge des Pins**, Rt de la Piscine, **t** 05 58 08 30 00, **f** 05 58 07 56 74, *www.auberge-des-pins.com* (*moderate*). The complete Landais experience: renovated rooms in a typical country house, set in a pretty park, with an excellent restaurant; English spoken. *Menus €18–61. Closed Jan and Sun eve and Mon outside of season.*

villages and medieval churches from the days when most visitors in the Landes were pilgrims en route to Santiago de Compostela. Several museums, especially the excellent Ecomuseum at Marquèze, offer insights into life in this unique region.

Belin-Béliet

Located both on the Leyre and the N10 from Bordeaux to Biarritz, Belin-Béliet is a modest place, best known today as the seat of the Parc Naturel administration. Until the 11th century, however, Belin was the capital of old kings of Gascony and a fierce rival of Bordeaux; it was the birthplace of Eleanor of Aquitaine in 1122, and (some say) of her second and favourite son, Richard the Lion-Heart. The castle where the most fascinating woman of the Middle Ages first saw the light of day is now little more than a low mound, marked by a stele, located just west of the village centre.

The church of **St-Pierre-de-Mons** on the outskirts of Belin was built during Eleanor's reign, although its bell tower was only fortified a century later, during the Hundred Years' War – that time bomb left behind by her French and English marriages. Inside are four archaic capitals, carved with scenes of mysterious import; pilgrims to Compostela would stop to pray by the scented sepulchre of Charlemagne's paladins, whose bodies were miraculously brought here after Roncevalles (*see* pp.182–3; Saint-

The Queen from Belin

Eleanor's father was the powerful Count of Aquitaine, her mother an heiress from the House of Toulouse; her grandfather, Count Guillhaume IX of Aquitaine, was the very first troubadour of them all and a rascally adventurer. As the sole heiress to Aquitaine and Poitou, she was the marriage prize of the century; after wedding the cold, pious Louis VII in 1137, accompanying him on a crusade to the Holy Land and bearing him two daughters, she had had enough by 1152 and insisted on dissolving the marriage. Even more galling to Louis was her re-marriage, only two months later, to his arch rival Henry Plantagenet, heir not only to the throne of England but of the counties of Anjou and Brittany. One of his first acts, and one that did much to make the English popular from the start, was to grant the common people of Aquitaine the right to hunt – 600 years before the rest of feudal France won the same right in the Revolution.

Like her son Richard, whom she made her heir as Count of Aquitaine, Eleanor spent as little time as possible in England, preferring to rule over her court of love at Poitiers, where her eldest daughter, Marie of Champagne, helped to write much of the code of courtly love. Yet her later years were bitter. Henry imprisoned her in England for her political intrigues, invariably in favour of her beloved Aquitaine, and as she lived to the then incredibly ripe old age of 82 she saw much of her hard work and travels come to nought as three of her four sons by Henry predeceased her, leaving only John Lackland, the one she loved least and the baddie in the Robin Hood legends, to try to fit into the shoes of his extraordinary parents.

Seurin in Bordeaux and the Alyschamps in Arles had similar tombs, but perhaps there were enough bodies to go around). The local **Musée d'Histoire** (*Open 1 June–Sept 30; July and Aug 10–12 and 2–7; June and Sept 2–6*) has a number of curiosities, including two megaliths, ancient sarcophagi, Iron Age vases, local costumes, items related to traditional Landais industries, and *grimoires* – old books of magic.

From Belin-Beliet, take the D110 west and turn right just before the A63 for the abandoned village of **Vieux Lugos**. In 1869 it moved to higher, healthier ground further west, leaving behind the fortified Romanesque church of Saint-Michel, now isolated in a clearing, of interest for its frescoes dated *c.* 1500 of the Seven Deadly Sins being led off to Hell on the right wall, and Works of Mercy on the left.

Up the Petite Leyre

Moustey stands at the confluence of the Grande Leyre and the Petite Leyre. Unusually, its central square has not one but two churches side by side, both from the end of the 1200s: one, Saint-Martin, was built as the village parish church; the other, Notre-Dame, with a handsome bell tower rising directly from the façade (a typical feature of southwestern Romanesque churches), was the chapel of a pilgrims' hostel-hospital, demolished in 1870. Notre Dame now houses the Parc Naturel's **Musée de Patrimoine Religieux et des Croyances Populaires** (*open daily*, Call Mairie ***t*** *05 57 71 99 99; open Tues and Thurs 3–7, July and Aug only. All other times, call ahead to arrange a visit*), with two changing exhibits on popular beliefs and superstitions.

From Moustey the D120 follows the valley of the Petite Leyre. Unlike the Grande Leyre, the Petite is not kept clear of dead trees and vegetation, but its waters, rich in eels and pike, are specially reserved for fishermen – and otters, if you're lucky enough to see one. The first village up the Petite Leyre is **Belhade** (Gascon for 'beautiful fairy'),

Liquid Diamonds

When American imports were cut off during the Civil War (1861–5), the price of resin, 40 francs a barrel back in the 1850s when Napoleon III first planted the pine forests, soared to 245F. This began a golden era in the Landes; at the beginning of the 20th century, when the stuff was in great demand for making turpentine and rosin, there were 30,000 *gemmeurs*, or resin-tappers, employed in the giant forest; today there are a mere 50. It's hard, seasonal labour; the average *gemmeur* works between 12 and 15 hours a day between April and October (the heat makes the pines 'bleed' more easily), collecting the resin from 1,000 to 1,500 trees. Since 1960, new techniques using sulphuric acid have doubled the yield; now, instead of 1,000, the *gemmeur* only has to visit 500 trees in five days to fill a 200-litre barrel. Pines are first tapped when they're between 17 and 20 years old. Some specimens have been tapped for 200 years; others, destined for the chop, are bled dry. In the old days the *gemmeurs* used stilts to tap high up the trunk, using a little reversible container called a *pot Hugues*; now even these have been replaced by plastic sacks.

Excursions

Few rivers in France are as ideal for rowing gently downstream as the Grande Leyre and the Leyre, whether you want to spend a day's outing or a week going the whole distance from Mexico (no kidding) on the Grande Leyre to Le Teich. Lined with white sandy cliffs, little beaches and lush foliage (willows, ferns, alders), the water is perfectly clear, albeit with a slight orange tint from iron oxide in its sandy bed. And life can seem to be but a dream: no motor boats intrude, and glimpses of civilization are limited to the rare village or small nautical bases where you can spend the night camping out or in a *gîte*.

The season runs from May to September. In July and August be prepared to share the river; with Arcachon nearby it's no secret. The slow, tranquil waters of the Leyre/Eyre make it the perfect place for beginner canoeists and children. The only qualification is knowing how to swim. The bases along the river hire canoes at around €21 a day for two people and tents, and can arrange to pick you up downstream (you pay by the kilometre). This list starts with the furthest upstream and gives distances and times from the previous base.

Base de Mexico, on the D626, 3.5km from Commensacq, **t** 05 58 07 05 15, has a *gîte* and camp site. *Open all year.*

Halte Nautique, at Trensacq, 5km/2hrs downstream, **t** 05 58 07 04 41, with a *gîte* and a *gîte d'étape*. *Open July and August only.*

Base de Testarouman, Pissos, 21km/7hrs downstream, **t** 05 58 08 91 58, with camping and a group *gîte*. *Open all year.*

Base de Saugnac, Saugnacq-et-Muret, 15km/5hrs downstream, **t** 05 58 07 73 01, the main centre on the river, with *gîtes* and camping. *Open all year.*

Centre de Graoux, Belin-Béliet, 15km/5hrs downstream, **t** 05 57 71 99 29, *gîtes*. *Open all year.*

Salles, 10km/3hrs downstream, **t** 05 56 88 20 53. Canoes and kayaks for hire. *Open May–Sept.*

Mios, 9km/3hrs downstream, **t** 05 56 26 69 82, with a camp site. *Open mid-June–mid-Sept.*

Maison de la Nature du Bassin d'Arcachon, Le Teich, 10km/3hrs from Mios, **t** 05 56 22 80 93, with *gîtes collectives* for groups of 15 or more; booking essential. *Open all year.*

set in an old oak forest and the seat of the oldest barony of the Landes. The château with its moat and three towers is on the edge of town, built over a prehistoric camp, while in the centre of the village is a little 11th-century Romanesque church with a *clocher-mur* and a portal adorned with very curious sculpted capitals on its columns: a mermaid pulls a boat with two sailors, a serpent eats a man, birds ride animals.

The Petite Leyre has a **Sore** on one of its elbows – a village founded in the Middle Ages. Of the Albrets castle that once stood here, only the moat and a gate survived the Wars of Religion; there's a 12th-century fortified mill and a church from the same period, with an unusual arcaded bell tower. **Luxey** is a sweet little village and site of the **Atelier de Produits Résineaux**, in an old resin distillery behind the church (***t** 05 58 08 31 31; open April–May 2–6; June–mid Sept 10–12 and 2–7; Sept–Nov 2–6; guided tours at 10 and 11 in the morning, and at 3, 4, 5 and 6 in the afternoon; adm*), where you can learn all about the sticky liquid diamonds that were the forest's first cash crop.

Up the Grande Leyre to Sabres

South of Moustey, **Pissos** provides a popular base with its 20 *gîtes forestiers* and Maison des Artisans, with a display of crafts from the area. Its church, Saint-Jean-de-Richet, has a Romanesque apse, decorated with pretty modillons, and inside,

14th-century frescoes rediscovered in 1969. To the south, at Trensacq, turn west 6km on the D45 for **Commensacq** and its 11th-century church of Saint-Martin. The vaults are decorated with 15th-century paintings of Adam and Eve, and there's a pretty baldachin and altar that somehow survived the usual depredations of French churches. Best of all, the central pillar has a carved frieze of musicians, including a pig playing the bagpipes, a rabbit playing the violin and a wonderfully sensual mermaid. Mermaids, or sirens, turn up with some frequency on Romanesque churches, often spreading their tails to display the entrance into the womb. It is a symbol steeped in medieval mysticism, perhaps not entirely inaccessible to the modern imagination. Some scholars believe the sirens represent desire and act as intermediaries by which nature's energy and inspiration are conducted into the conscious world. Others claim that they betray the existence of an ecstatic cult, based on music and dance and descended from ancient Dionysian rituals.

Further west on the D45 is **Labouheyre**, an important market and *gîte* centre that first grew up along a Roman road, then along the pilgrimage road, and then along the N10; the old town gate and the church of Saint-Jacques, with a 15th-century portal, are its chief monuments. A narrow road south of Labouheyre leads to **Solférino**, founded as a model village around a model estate by Emperor Napoleon III in 1863, just as his great forestation project was proving a success. It was to be something of a social laboratory as well; remembering his vaguely progressive politics from his exile in London, the emperor constructed cottages for his 'colonists' which they could eventually own with two hectares of land by working for free for 75 days a year for 10 years. In 1905, Empress Eugénie sold Solférino to another family, the Schneiders.

Sabres to the east attracts plenty of tourists on their way to the Eco-musée, but don't neglect a glance at its 11th-century church, with a towering triangular *clocher-mur* and richly carved portal, decorated with saints and imaginary flowers and beasts. Even in this century Sabres was so cut off from the rest of the world that when the first German soldiers in their long black coats marched through the village in 1940, some old women were heard to cry in terror that the Huguenots were back in town. Six km southwest of Sabres on the D77 you can visit one of the best dolmens in the Landes, the **Pierre de Grimann**.

Marquèze and the Eco-Musée de la Grande Lande

Open April, May and Nov Mon–Sat, 5 trips from 2–6.40; Sun and hols, 9 trips 10.10–4.40; adm.

The only access to Marquèze, the pride of the Parc Naturel, is by a delightful old steam train that chugs 5km from Sabres in 10 minutes. 1 June–30 Sept, nine departures daily, 10.10–5.20. Last return from Marquèze 7pm. On Suns and holidays, all nine trains run. Admission; discount combination tickets available for Marquèze, Luxey and Moustey. There's a snack bar and mediocre restaurant on the site, or you can bring a picnic lunch. Optional guided tours (in French) last an hour and a half; a brochure is available in English so you can wander about on your own. Reservations and information, **t** *05 58 08 31 31.*

Until about 50 years ago, the Landes were divided into agricultural *quartiers*. Each *commune* had between six and twelve *quartiers*; the most important was the site of the church and cemetery and, over the years, of the school, *mairie* and shops. The other *quartiers* were all more or less alike, little islands of civilization in the desert of the Landes: in the centre would be the *maison du maître*, or landowner's house, along with the servants' house, the shepherds' houses, the miller's house, and the *maisons des métayers*, or farm labourers' houses (although '*métayer*' means sharecropping in French, in the Landes the word refers to any kind of farming). Other houses belonged to the *brassiers*, who lived only from the strength of their *bras*, or arms. Around the houses were buildings that look remarkably like smaller versions of the houses: barns, sheds, pigsties, mill, ovens, sheepfolds, hives and chicken coops (on stilts, to protect them from the foxes), located on a lawn known as the *airial*, planted with oaks and chestnuts.

Marquèze was an abandoned *quartier* of Sabres, rescued in 1978 by the board of the Parc Naturel to become the first *eco-musée* in France. Most of the buildings to be seen on the site date from the end of the 19th century; a few come from other *quartiers* and have been reconstructed on the *airial*. Marquèze's surroundings have been meticulously maintained as well, including the orchard and stream, the fields and forests and Landais sheep chomping in the meadow; one goal of all *eco-musées* is to conserve old varieties of seeds, trees and domestic animals in danger of being lost forever.

South of Sabres

There are only a few points of interest between the Parc Naturel and Mont-de-Marsan. Southeast on the N134 from Sabres, in **Garein**, the 11th-century church has frescoes of the coronation of the Virgin, rediscovered in 1900 when parts of the plaster crumbled off.

Labrit, east of Sabres, was the humble cradle of, and gave its name to, the d'Albrets, the most influential and powerful of all Gascon families, who out of this little Landais nowhere blazed like a comet across the history of 15th- and 16th-century France. Their rise to riches, fame and royal favour was no accident: they were faithful agents of the French Crown, at a time when Gascony/Aquitaine had few natural ties to France, but was a patchwork of regions accustomed to a fair amount of independence under English sovereignty and the feudal anarchy that preceded it. In return, the kings of France showered every sort of prize on the d'Albrets, not the least of which were advantageous marriages. With their help Henri d'Albrets became king of Navarre and husband of François I's sister, the talented Marguerite d'Angoulême; their hellcat daughter, Jeanne, grew up to be one of the most fanatical leaders of the Protestant camp in the Wars of Religion. Jeanne's Protestant son in turn became King of France as Henri IV, who converted to Catholicism ('Paris is worth a Mass') and put a truce to religious bigotry in his Edict of Nantes. But what remains of the d'Albrets in Labrit? Not a trace.

Southwest of Sabres, in **Arengosse**, the feudal motte of Bezaudun marks the home of the ancient kings of Gascony, though it was occupied until the 1840s by the Cagots (*see* **Culture** pp.24–6). **Morcenx** grew up around the railroad and owes its big spot on the map to the fact that it's the only town for miles around and a lunch stop en route to Dax.

Getting Around

You need a car to get around, as public transport is pretty thin on the ground. Buses link Arcachon to Biscarrosse in the summer; contact Autobus d'Arcachon, 47 Bd Général Leclerc, for information, **t** 05 56 83 07 60. Others go down to Mimizan, ring **t** 05 58 09 10 89 for schedules.

Tourist Information

Biscarrosse-Plage: 55 Pl G. Dufan. **t** 05 58 78 20 96, **f** 05 58 78 23 65, *www.biscarrrosse.com. Open Jan–Mar Mon–Fri 9–6, Sat 10–12; April, May, June and Sept Mon–Fri 9–6, Sat and Sun 10–12 and 2–5; July and Aug open daily 9am–8pm; Oct and Dec Mon–Fri 9–1 and 2–9.*

Sanguinet: Mairie, **t** 05 58 78 67 72, *www.sanguinet.com. Open July and Aug Mon–Sat 9.30–12 and 2–7 plus Sun am; rest of the year 9.30–12 and 2–5.30.*

Parentis: Pl du Général-de-Gaulle, **t/f** 05 58 78 43 60, *www.parentis.com. Open July and Aug Mon–Sat 10–1 and 3–7, Thur 9–1 and 3–7, Sun 9–1; the rest of the year Mon–Sat 9–12.15 and 1.45–5.30.*

Market Days

Biscarrosse: Fridays.
Parentis: Thursdays.

Where to Stay and Eat

Biscarrosse ✉ 40600

★★★**La Forestière**, Av du Pyla, Bicarrosse-Plage, **t** 05 58 78 24 14, **f** 05 58 78 26 40, *www.hotellaforestiere.com* (*expensive–inexpensive*). The nicest place on the sea, and also has a pool. *Open from April until mid Oct.*

★★**Atlantide**, in Pl Marsan, **t** 05 58 78 08 86, **f** 05 58 78 75 98, *www.hotelatlantide.com* (*inexpensive*). 33 pleasant, modern rooms. *Open all year.*

★★**La Caravelle**, at Ispe (5314 Rte des Lacs), **t** 05 58 09 82 67, **f** 05 58 09 82 18, *www.lacaravelle.fr* (*inexpensive*). Near the golf course, a lovely, quiet place, right on the Etang de Cazaux et de Sanguinet; but the food is so good that many non-guests drop in for a meal (*menus around €13*). *Closed Nov–mid Feb.*

★★**La Transaquitaine**, 15 Rue des Parterres. Navarrosse, **t** 05 58 09 83 13, **f** 05 58 09 84 37 (*inexpensive*). Also overlooks the lake and has a swimming pool besides. *Open April–mid Sept.*

Auberge Regina, 34 Av de la Libération 40600, Biscarosse Plage, **t** 05 58 78 23 34, *www.auberge-regina.com* (*moderate*). A couple of minutes walk from the beach, this pretty auberge run by a gay couple is the trendiest place to stay in Biscarosse Plage. Bedrooms are chalet-like with a distinct Mediterranean feel. All bedrooms have internet access – cyber-café meets beach house. Regional menu €15–16. *Open daily all year.*

Chez Camette, 532 Av Latécoère, **t** 05 58 78 12 78. For a good, honest meal. Lunch menu €10. Menus €15–22. *Open daily July and Aug. The rest of the year closed Fri eve and all Sat.*

Parentis-en-Born ✉ 40160

Cousseau, 11 Rue St-Bartélémy, **t** 05 58 78 42 46. Long the place to dine in Parentis, with a typical French provincial atmosphere but serving up tasty sea and land food, sometimes deliciously combined as sole prepared with *girolle* mushrooms; also *foie gras* prepared in a variety of ways and a wide choice of wine. (*Daily changing menu starts at €10; gourmet menus begin at twice that.*) *Closed Fri and Sun eve, and two weeks Oct. Open daily in July and Aug.*

Omelette aux Cèpes

This favourite way of cooking *cèpes* in the Landes is very easy to prepare and is absolutely delicious. In a frying pan, brown a handful of sliced fresh *cèpes* in a little oil; add salt and pepper. Drain off the oil and set the mushrooms aside; return the frying pan to the heat and stir up a spoonful of freshly chopped parsley with a bit of garlic (what the French call a *persillade*), and set it aside as well. Then heat up the oil from the mushrooms in a large frying pan. Whip seven or eight eggs with a little salt, pepper, a spoon of oil and one spoonful of *crème fraîche*. Pour the egg mixture into the very hot oil, add the mushrooms and parsley and cook at as high a temperature as you dare. *Serves four*.

Down the Côte d'Argent

Nearly dead straight and practically endless, the 'Silver Coast' as it was dubbed by a Bordeaux newspaperman in 1905, is the biggest beach in Europe, some 140 miles of pale sand between the deep green forest and the bracing blue Atlantic. It stretches from Médoc's Pointe de Grave at the mouth of the Garonne and, after a momentary interruption at the mouth of the Bassin d'Arcachon, continues all the way down to Bayonne, offering broad vistas of empty space rare in Europe. Backing the beach is a long chain of carefully tended, artificial dunes (which you should only cross at the specially arranged points); the first task when sowing the pine forest was to follow Brémontier (*see* p.62) in planting tufty *oyat* grass to anchor the moving sands into dunes, breaking the winds and sheltering the first pine saplings.

The Golfe de Gascogne, or Bay of Biscay, sends so many big rollers special delivery to the coast that the Côte d'Argent is up in the same league as California, Australia, Hawaii and Tahiti for surfing; the sport was introduced to France in 1955 when a Californian student visiting the area was impressed enough to have his board shipped over. If that's not enough, just on the other side of the dunes are a score of freshwater lakes and ponds formed by the numerous streams that crisscross the Landes' forests. Lined with sandy beaches, not only are they ideal for calmer swimming and sports like windsurfing and sailing, but they also happen to lie on one of the continent's major flyways for migratory birds. The whole is one of France's largest outdoor playgrounds: the pleasures of surfing, *char à voile* (land yachting), windsurfing, sailing, fishing, bird-watching, hang-gliding, golfing, cycling, or just building sand castles on the beach see nearly 3 million summer visitors and 600 tonnes of sunscreen lotion every year.

Biscarrosse, Biscarrosse-Plage and Sanguinet

Biscarrosse is a big town but a fairly dull one, and owes much of what panache it has to its land-of-lakes setting. Just north is the vast Etang de Cazaux et de Sanguinet, while the town itself is set between the Petit Etang de Biscarrosse and the vast Etang de Biscarrosse et de Parentis. And when the lakes seem too tranquil, the thumping waves of the Atlantic are only 10km away.

For years Biscarrosse was an important seaplane port, a past remembered at the **Musée Historique de l'Hydraviation** (*332 Av Louis Bréguet, **t** 05 58 78 00 65; open July and Aug daily 10–7; rest of year 2–6; closed Tues and holidays in winter; adm*), stocked with models, mementos of great aviators, and photos; a video fills in the rest. Although it's been a while since a seaplane landed here, rockets occasionally blast off from the Centre d'Essai des Landes, which keep a large slab of the Côte d'Argent – between Biscarrosse-Plage and Mimizan-Plage – strictly off limits.

Biscarrosse's other claim to fame revolves around its centuries-old elm in the main square. The story goes that the unfaithful wives of Biscarrosse would be brought here under its shade, so that their guilt would be publicly exposed. One day, however, one of the women was innocent, a fact the elm recognized by forming a white crown of leaves over her head. The elm has re-created the curious white crown every year since. Antoine de Saint-Exupéry, who besides writing *Le Petit Prince* was one of France's star pilots in the early days of airmail, loved to sit in its shade when he was in Biscarrosse on a mission. Nearby, the town church hides a fine 14th- to 15th-century Gothic interior.

The prettiest part of Biscarrosse is up around the three tiny pleasure ports on the clear waters of the **Etang de Cazaux et de Sanguinet**, just north of Biscarrosse town: Ipses, Navarosse, and Port-Maguide, the latter with a pretty beach and windsurfing.

Sports are what bring most summer visitors to Biscarrosse and its seaside annexe, **Biscarrosse-Plage**, a rather characterless, purpose-built resort that sprouted up in the 1970s by the beach; one of the best things to do is take the coastal road north towards Arcachon for the magnificent views of coast and dunes. In August and September, white sea daffodils (*Pancratium maritimum*) scent the dunes so sweetly that many people unfortunately cannot resist picking them, although they play a vital role in anchoring the dunes. Little by-roads, some drivable, lead down to the beach, where no one cares if you've brought your bathing costume or not.

If the Atlantic is too rough for a satisfying swim, the lakes around Biscarrosse, especially the Etangs de Cazaux et de Sanguinet, have sandy beaches as well. Before the dunes blocked off its mouth, this lake was one of the Landes' many rivers, or *courants* as they're called. In 1977, archaeologist-divers found signs of ancient settlements 22ft under the lake, dating from the Bronze Age to the Gallo-Roman period, when the Roman Via Antonina passed here. Canoes, ceramics, coins, jewellery and other artefacts are now displayed in the **Musée des Traditions** (*216 Rue Louis Bregnet, **t** 05 58 78 77 37; open June–Sept daily 10–12 and 3–7; Oct–May Tues–Sat 10–12 and 3–7, Sun 3–7, closed Mon; adm*), in the Place de la Mairie in **Sanguinet**, 13km up the lake shore. Sanguinet itself stands over the Gallo-Roman village of Losa, located along the Roman road from Bordeaux. Its submerged stone temple can be seen some 12ft under the surface of the lake.

In between Biscarrosse and Sanguinet is an old **forest** of pines and oaks growing atop ancient dunes; ferns and heather cover the lower regions, a prime area for finding wild mushrooms in the autumn, especially *cèpes*, *chanterelles*, and the orangish-yellow *bidaou*, or *tricholome équestre*.

Parentis-en-Born

'Here is a village where life flows like honey,' wrote Saint-Exupéry when he saw it, but if Biscarrosse has had something of its tourist potential compromised by the adjacent rocket-testing area, Parentis-en-Born and its lake have been more dismally undermined, since 1955, by the presence of petroleum derricks – the first lake platforms in Europe, busily sucking up the contents of France's biggest oil field and sending them down the pipeline to refineries on the Gironde. If you want to learn more, there's a little **petroleum museum** on the Route des Lacs (*t 05 58 78 43 60; currently closed for renovations, due to re-open summer 2004*), or you can take an hour-long boat ride out among the derricks for a really good time (*open June–Sept daily 11–7*). Parentis is also proud of its turn-of-the-century arena and its recently restored 15th-century church; during the restoration, some medieval muskets were found from the days when the church was fortified.

The 'Born' in Parentis refers to the surrounding region, for a long time beyond the *bornes* or boundaries, a kind of end of the world. Besides the lakes, there isn't a whole lot to see in the Born. Along the D652 towards Mimizan, **Gastes** makes a nice stop for a lake swim; Sainte-Eulalie-en-Born, with its statue of Saint Eutrope by a fountain that once enjoyed a certain renown for healing lame children, lies on the river or *courant* of the same name, linking the Etang de Parentis with that of Aureilhan, one of the prettiest of all Landes lakes.

Middle Côte d'Argent: Mimizan to Léon

Mimizan and Mimizan-Plage

May God keep us from the song of the Siren, the tail of the whale,
and the bell tower of Mimizan.

An old Gascon sea-dog saying

With all these pine trees, there has to be a paper mill somewhere, and Mimizan, at the mouth of the *courant* that flows through Sanguinet, Parentis and Aureilhan lakes, won the prize; its Papeteries de Gascogne claims to be the largest producer of brown paper in the world. But don't let the threat of a change in wind and the occasional gust of stink put you off: unlike Biscarrosse, which is similarly endowed with the combined pleasures of ocean and lake, Mimizan, the 'Pearl of the Côte d'Argent' has some history and character. Once the Roman port of *Segosa*, it had an important **Benedictine abbey**, built in the 12th century, of which only the brick *clocher-mur* and beautifully carved Gothic portal have survived the usual vicissitudes, not the least of which was being half buried in sand, along with the rest of the town, in 1342. In the old days, the abbey and town were granted the right of asylum, or *sauveté* (the four stone pillars marking the boundaries still stand). Not only could any fugitive from justice find safe refuge within the magic square, but the inhabitants of Mimizan enjoyed salvage rights that made them the dread of sailors; whenever a ship was seen to be floundering, the abbey bell would toll and the village would pounce on the

Tourist Information

Mimizan: 38 Av Maurice-Martin, Mimizan-Plage, **t** 05 58 09 11 20, **f** 05 58 09 40 31, *www.mimizan-tourisme.com. Open Oct–April Mon–Sat 9–12 and 3–6 plus Sat am; May, June and Sept Mon–Fri 9–12 and 3–6 plus Sat 10–12 and 3–5; July and Aug Mon–Sat 9–7, Sun 10–12.30 and 3–7.*

Mézos: Av du Born. **t** 05 58 42 64 37, **f** 05 58 42 64 89, *www.ot-mezos.fr. Open July and Aug Mon–Sat 10–12 and 3–7; June and Sept Mon–Sat 10–12 and 5–7.*

Vielle-Saint-Girons: Rte de Linxe, **t** 05 58 47 94 94, **f** 05 58 42 90 00, *www.tourisme-vielle-st-girons.com.*

Where to Stay and Eat

Mimizan ✉ 40200

★★★**Au Bon Coin du Lac,** right on the lake at 34 Av du Lac, **t** 05 58 09 01 55, **f** 05 58 09 40 84, *www.jp-caule.com* (*expensive–moderate*). If your pockets are deep enough or you want to splash out, this peaceful and stylish place is hands-down the most delightful place to sleep and eat in Mimizan. There are only 4 luminous, elegant rooms and 4 apartments; tables from the equally attractive restaurant spill out along the lakeside terrace, where you won't go wrong trying one of the house specialities. The desserts, prepared by a special pastry chef, are out of this world, and the cellar offers a magnificent array of wines. *Menus €28–56. Open mid May–end Sep; closed Sun eve.*

★★★**Côte d'Argent**, 6 Av M-Martin, **t** 05 58 09 15 22, **f** 05 58 09 06 92, *www.hotelcotedargent.com* (*inexpensive*). Best by the beach, and only 5mins from the sea; the restaurant enjoys a huge view of the coast. Restaurant is now closed but the hotel has an arrangement with a neighbouring restaurant for visitors who want half board.

★★**L'Emeraude des Bois**, 68 Av du Courant, **t** 05 58 09 05 28, *emeraudedesbois@wanadoo.fr* (*inexpensive*). Set among lofty old trees a few minutes from the centre of Mimizan, an attractive old house, with a range of rooms in a range of prices; the restaurant is excellent and serves many old French favourites. *Menus €16–26. Restaurant open eves only.*

★★**Hôtel de France**, 18 Av de la Côte d'Argent, Mimizan-Plage, **t** 05 58 09 09 01, **f** 05 58 09 37 67 (*inexpensive*). Bright, welcoming rooms with bathrooms, some overlooking a courtyard. *Closed Oct–April.*

Camping Municipal de Mimizan-Plage, **t** 05 58 09 00 32. There are plenty of camp sites around Mimizan: one of the nicest is this one, nearest the sea. *Open May–Oct.*

Hotel de la Foret, 39 Avenue Maurice Martin, Mimizan Plage, **t** 05 58 09 09 06, *(moderate)*. Pleasant Logis de France opposite tourist office. Pretty terrace and garden. *Menus €15–23. Open all year.*

★**Hôtel du Centre**, 2 Rue de l'Abbaye in Mimizan-Bourg, **t** 05 58 09 37 70, **f** 05 58 09 46 33. Similar fare is served at similar prices in this hotel's pretty dining room; also has rooms (*cheap*). *Menus €9–11. Open all year.*

cargo, free to drink as much of the alcohol they could hold and cut off bolts of cloth to make clothes.

Across from the remains of the abbey is the modest little **Musée d'Histoire de Mimizan** (***t*** *05 58 09 00 61. Open 15 June–15 Sept Mon–Fri 10.30–7. Guided tours 11am, 3, and 7pm. You must phone ahead.*), with a few bits on local geography, and ancient and medieval history.

North of Mimizan, the sweet verdant banks of the **Etang d'Aureilhan** have been planted with exotic trees, flowers and shrubs, making for a lovely lakeside promenade. This lake enchanted the Duke of Westminster, who in 1910 built himself a Tudor-style manor called Wolsack. King Gustav II of Sweden, Coco Chanel and Winston Churchill were frequent guests between the wars; today only the façade and two wings are intact, along the D87. The big wide beach, **Mimizan-Plage**, is divided by the *courant* running into the ocean, and has four areas with lifeguards, both to the north and south of the bridge.

South of Mimizan

This is the least populated stretch of France's Atlantic coast. There are a number of small villages with road access to the beaches: **Bias** is one and **St-Julien-en-Born** is another, located near the *courant* leading down to **Contis-Plage**; you can get there by road or by taking a boat from the Pont Rose. Contis-Plage has a couple of hotels and a **lighthouse** with 192 steps you can climb for the view (*ring ahead*, **t** *05 58 42 80 08*). Just inland from Saint-Julien, **Mézos** is a pretty village with a good 14th-century church, built by the Knights of Malta in the local stone, called *garluche*. Further south, there is access from Lit-et-Mixte, with its old wooden bullring, to **Cap-de-l'Homy Plage** ('Man's Head Beach') with a summer lifeguard. The coastal route, the D652, continues south from Lit-et-Mixte to **St-Girons**, with a road to the beach of the same name.

Inland, **Uza** overlooks a pretty little man-made lake, dammed back in the 18th century to supply water power for the local iron forges. The owners of the forge built themselves a little Italianesque loggia to live in as well as the village church, which contains three painted wooden Renaissance-era statues. Further inland through the forest, **Lévignacq** is just as picturesque, an old village with an old *lavoir*, a watermill and a remarkable church. Built and fortified in the 1200s, the church tower is topped by a pointed roof and a curving steeple; inside the wooden ceiling is covered with paintings from 1715, and frescoes from the 15th century were found in the choir during the recent restoration. For Léon and the southern Côte d'Argent, *see* p.104.

Mont-de-Marsan

Birthplace of French prime minister Alain Juppé and the biggest town in the Landes with all of 32,000 souls, Mont-de-Marsan isn't exactly cosmopolitan and urbane – except for six days during the last two weeks of July when it explodes in honour of the Magdalene, with *corridas*, *courses landaises* and a megaton of fireworks. Located where the rivers Douze and Midou meet to form the Midouze, an important tributary of the Adour, the site was inhabited in prehistoric times, although the traces of these first settlers were bulldozed in 1980. One apocryphal text claims the medieval town was founded by Charlemagne, but the real founders were the abbots of Saint-Sever, who built a priory dedicated to the Magdalene here, and a certain Pierre de Lobaner, the lord of Marsan, who founded a *castelnau*, or new town, nearby in 1140. The town prospered by transporting the wines and wheat of Armagnac down the Midouze to the Adour and the sea. Made departmental capital in the Revolution, it owes much of what character it has to the neoclassical administrative buildings erected under Napoleon. During the Second World War, the Germans enlarged the airport, making it one of the most important in France in terms of size; it is now used as a testing ground for the newest Mirages and other military aircraft.

Getting There and Around

Although Mont-de-Marsan owed its importance in the last century to rail, few trains on the Bordeaux–Tarbes line pass through its little station at the south end of town. For information on the *département's* bus network and schedules, you can contact RDTL, 99 Rue Pierre Benoit, **t** 05 58 05 66 00, **f** 05 58 75 34 00.

Tourist Information

6 Pl du Général-Leclerc, **t** 05 58 05 87 37, *open Mon–Sat 9–12.30 and 1.30–6, summer 9–6*. For general information on the sights and what is going on in the whole *département*, contact the Comité Départemental, 22 Rue Victor Hugo, **t** 05 58 06 89 89, *www.mont-de-marsan.org. Open July and Aug Mon–Sat 9–6.30; rest of the year Mon–Sat 9–12.30 and 1.30–6.*

Market Days

Food market: Tuesdays and Saturdays.

Flea market: the first Wednesday of each month, all day in Place Saint-Roch – a bustling local market with plenty of colour and not a few bargains.

Where to Stay and Eat

Mont-de-Marsan ✉ 40000

Book early for the Feria de Ste Madeleine.

★★**Richelieu**, Rue Wlérick, **t** 05 58 06 10 20, **f** 05 58 06 00 68 (*inexpensive*). The Richelieu has recently been refurbished in a retro Art Deco style, but still has the air of the old classic. Very comfortable. Restaurant is lacking in ambiance but makes up in cuisine; the chef has come from the same family for three generations. Try the brochettes de langoustine on a bed of risotto. *Menus €16–30. Open all year. Restaurant closed Sat.*

★★**Sablar**, Place Jean-Jaurés, **t** 05 58 75 21 11, **f** 05 58 75 67 31, *www.hotelsablar.fr* (*inexpensive*). Usually has a simple room not occupied by a travelling salesman. *Open all year.*

Le Midou, Pl Porte Campet, **t** 05 58 75 24 26. Fine, and smack in the centre of town, this restaurant has a good menu, specializing in regional dishes. Menus €11–28. *Closed Sat lunch and Sun.*

Around Mont-de-Marsan ✉ 40000

For more luxurious lodgings, look on the periphery.

★★★**Abor**, on the Grenade Road, **t** 05 58 51 58 00, **f** 05 58 75 78 78, *www.aborhotel.com* (*moderate–inexpensive*). Clean and modern. Set in the forest, air-conditioned, with a pool and a good restaurant, L'Airial, with a garden terrace and generous regional cuisine (*menus €11–24*). *Open all year.*

★★★**Le Renaissance**, Rte de Villeneuve, **t** 05 58 51 51 51, **f** 05 58 75 29 07, *www.lerenaissance.com*. Neoclassical in spite of its name, a handsome manor house set amid verdant lawns, with a pool. The rooms are large and comfortable and the bathrooms totally luxurious. The restaurant draws in hungry clients from all over the area with delicately prepared dishes based on regional products; try the *magret de canard* with peas. *Menus €22–68. Nov–May the restaurant is closed weekends. Summer closed Sat lunch plus Sun eves. Closed the last week in July.*

Hotel-Restaurant Zanchettin, 1565 Av de Villeneuve, **t** 05 58 75 19 52 (*cheap*). Just outside Mont-de-Marsan en route to Villeneuve, a small family hotel-cum-bar and tabac, which has cheap rooms and menus in its tiny terrace and restaurant. *Menus €11–25. Open all year; closed Sun eve and Mon.*

Didier Garbage, due west of Mont-de-Marsan on the RN 134 in Uchacq-de-Parentis, **t** 05 58 75 33 66, may have a name that sounds rather unappetizing in English, but the food here is just the opposite; try the *flambéed* pigeon. *Menus €12–15; closed Sun eve and all Mon.*

Auberge de Lapouillique, Mazerolles 40090, **t** 05 58 75 22 97, 4km east of Mont-de-Marsan (signs will guide you; book in advance). A big old inn under the oaks, serving Landais specialities. *Menus €16–28. Closed all day Sun, Mon and Tues eves.*

Around Town

In the narrow confines between the Douze and Midou, the fortified *ville médiévale* is the most interesting part of Mont-de-Marsan. The walls were built in the 14th century by Gaston Fébus. There are a pair of 13th-century houses along Rue Maubec, and in the centre, along Rue Victor Hugo and its extension, Rue Dulamon, a cluster of First Empire public buildings and mansions. To create a harmonious ensemble, the creators of the new departmental capital demolished the Gothic church of the Magdalene and replaced it with the nondescript current neoclassical model; its marble high altar is by the Mazetti brothers from Avignon, who travelled across the Landes in the 18th century and left works in a number of churches. Every now and then they were even inspired.

But the main attraction is the **Musée Despiau-Wlérick**, (*6 Pl Marguerite-de-Navarre (just south of Rue Victor Hugo),* ***t*** *05 58 75 00 45; free on Mondays*) installed in 1968 in the 14th-century Lacataye donjon (*open daily exc Tues and holidays, 10–12 and 2–6; adm*). It is dedicated to two sculptors born in Mont-de-Marsan. The more important, Charles Despiau (1874–1946), was the son of a local plasterer who became Rodin's assistant from 1907. In 1914, Despiau reacted against Rodin's romanticism and left his workshop to develop his own, far more classical style; he is best known for his sensitive, psychologically penetrating female portrait busts. The second, Robert Wlérick (1882–1944), had a Belgian father and belonged, like Despiau, to the group of Independent Sculptors, but concentrated more on genre works until he got the commission to sculpt half of all the Monuments aux Morts in the Landes (or so it seems); his greatest claim to fame is having carved large parts of the equestrian statue of Maréchal Foch on the Trocadéro Esplanade in Paris. The museum prides itself on being the only one in France solely devoted to modern figurative sculpture. The ground floor is devoted to works by Despiau, the first floor to sculptures by Wlérick, while the second and third floors have works by their contemporaries; along the stair are pretty 18th-century ceramic works from Samadet. Don't miss the view over the town from the donjon's terrace. In 1988 Mont-de-Marsan decided it was time to give some of the museum's bronze and marble inhabitants a breath of fresh air and in May you can see them standing around the town's streets, waiting for something to happen.

North of the Douze and the *ville médiévale* is a pleasant garden, the **Parc Jean Rameau**, decorated with sculptures by Despiau; nearby Place Francis Planté is named after another son of Mont-de-Marsan, one of the great virtuoso pianists of the 19th century. During the Feria de Ste Madeleine, the action takes place down by the train station at the venerable **Arènes du Plumaçon**, built in 1889.

The east end of Mont-de-Marsan, the **Quartier Saint-Médard**, is named after the church of Saint-Médard, first built in the Middle Ages, although its chief glories are from the 17th and 18th centuries, especially its carved wooden door and retable. Nearby, the **Parc de Nahuques** (*open Mon–Fri 9–12 and 3–7; Sat, Sun and holidays 3–7; 2–6 in the winter; adm*) is Mont-de-Marsan's biggest recreation area; part of it is home to swans, donkeys, Tibetan goats and other small animals, who live at liberty. West of town, **St-Pierre-du-Mont** has been absorbed by the capital, and is the site of

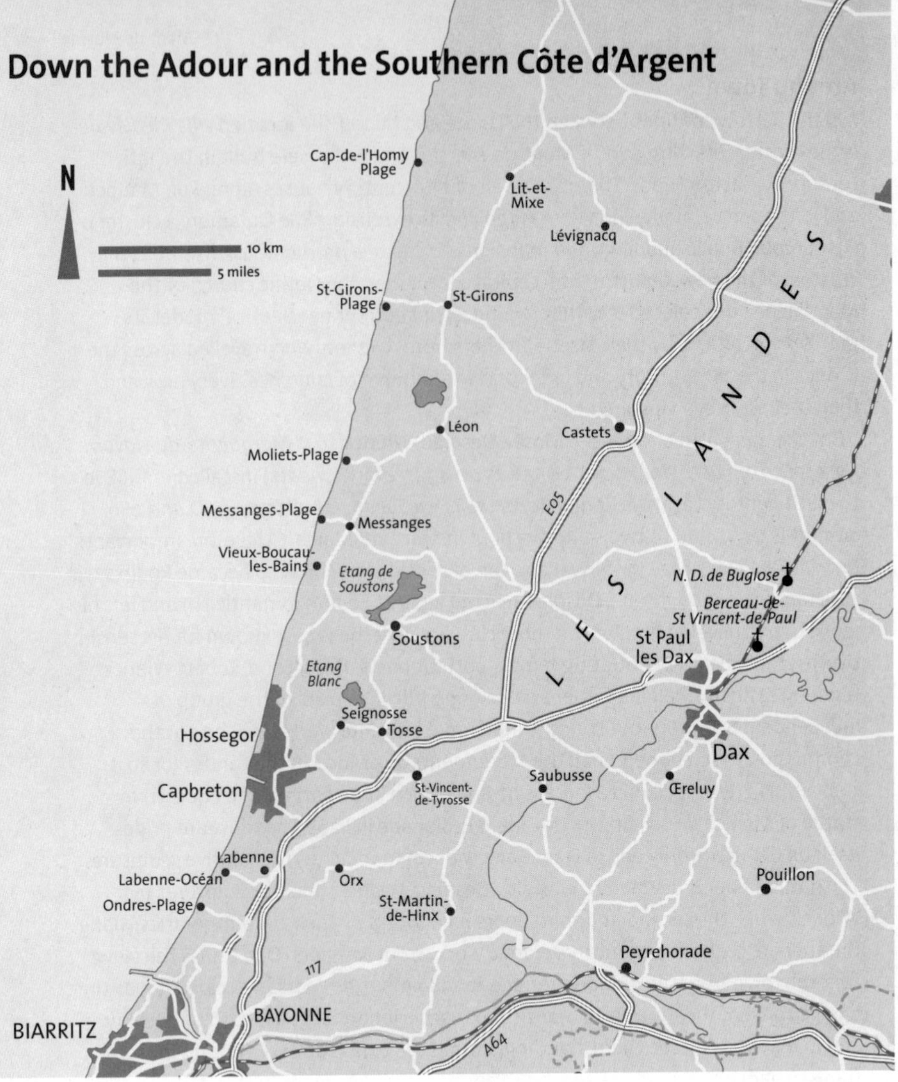

the Romanesque church of St-Pierre, part of the priory founded by the abbots of Saint-Sever in the 10th century. It has a fine wooden door similar to Saint-Médard, and a marble altar and stucco decorations by the Mazetti brothers.

Northeast of Mont-de-Marsan, Towards Roquefort

In its heyday in the 11th and 12th centuries, the abbey of Saint-Sever founded a string of churches and priories this way, along a branch of the **Compostela pilgrimage route** that descended from Langon through Mont-de-Marsan, now followed by the D932. The first church, **Ste-Marie**, is in Bostens, and has an interesting bell tower decorated with carvings as well as sculpted modillons. The second is in **Sarbazan**, defended by a massive tower and containing a few carved capitals inside. A **Gallo-Roman villa** with

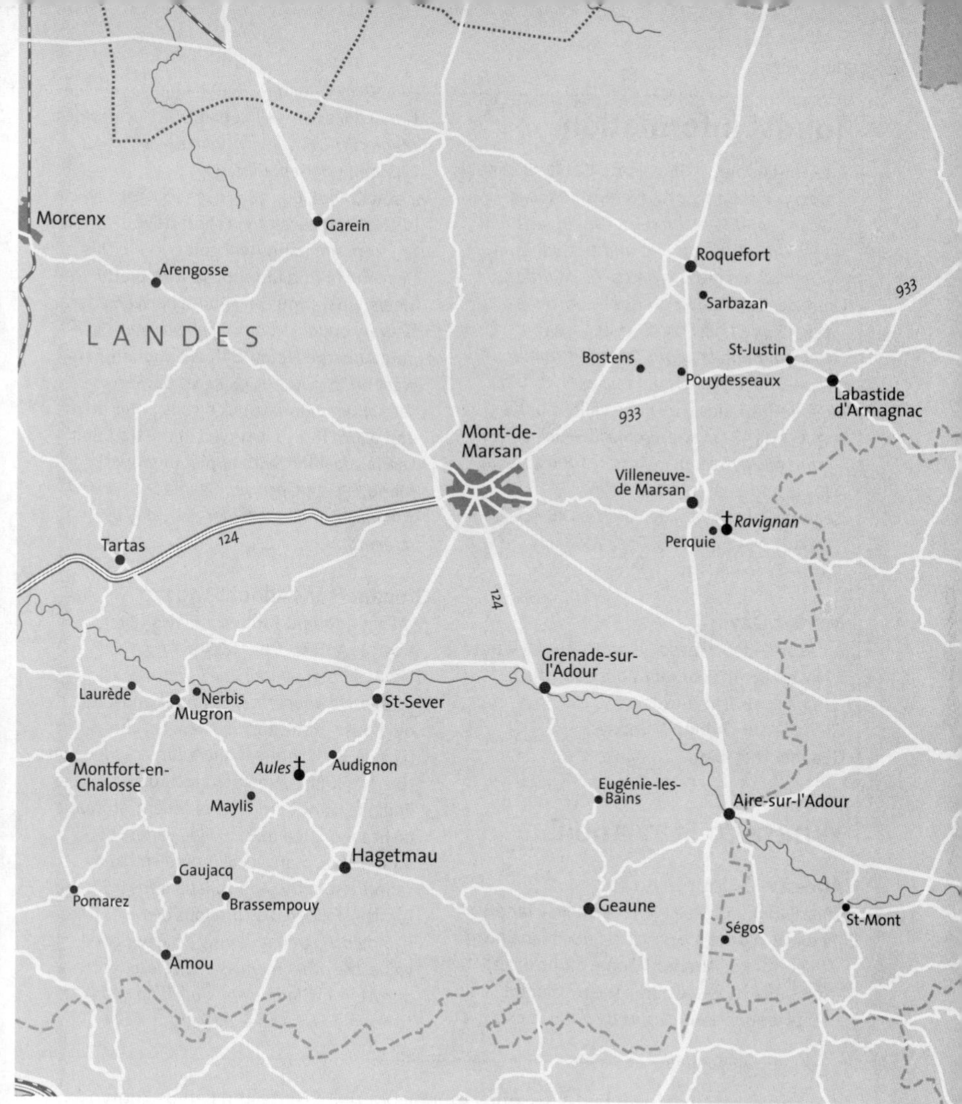

mosaics was excavated nearby. The third is up in **Roquefort**, where the fortified church of Notre-Dame dates from a 12th-century priory; much of it was rebuilt in the Gothic period.

East of here the pretty region of Armagnac touches the Landes: *see* p.113.

Down the Adour

South of Mont-de-Marsan the very first toes of the foothills of the Pyrenees embrace the Adour, one of the most important rivers in southwest France, its green-blue waters rich in salmon, shad, pike, eels and other tasty fish. The Adour is so prone to flooding in the winter and early spring that once it reaches the Landes it forms for

Tourist Information

Aire-sur-l'Adour: Pl Charles-de-Gaulle, B.P. 155, **t/f** 05 58 71 64 70, *otsi.aire@wanadoo.fr. Open Sept–May Mon 9–12, Tue–Fri 9–12 and 2–5; June Mon–Sat 9–12 and 2–5; July and Aug Mon–Fri 9–12.30 and 2–6, Sat until 5.*

Grenade-sur-l'Adour: 1 Pl des Déportés, **t** 05 58 45 45 98, **f** 05 58 43 45 55, *www.tourismgrenadois.com. Open in summer Mon–Thurs 8.30–12 and 1–5.30, Fri 8.30–12.*

Eugénie-les-Bains: Rue René Vielle, **t** 05 58 51 13 16, **f** 05 58 51 12 02, *www.ville-eugenie-les-bains.fr. Open Mon–Fri 9.30–12 and 2–6, Sat 10–12 and 2.30–4.*

Geaune: Pl de l'Hôtel de Ville, **t** 05 58 44 50 01, **f** 05 58 44 53 10. *Open Mon–Fri 8.30–12.30 and 1.30–5.30.*

Market Days

Aire-sur-l'Adour: Tuesdays and Saturdays; from November to February, goose and duck market, also on Tuesdays.

Grenade-sur-l'Adour: Mondays.

Geaune: Thursdays.

Where to Stay and Eat

Aire-sur-l'Adour ✉ 40800

Chez l'Ahumat, 2 Rue Pierre-Mendes-France, **t** 05 58 71 82 61 (*cheap*). On a quiet lane near the centre of Aire, with some of the nicest low-price rooms around. The restaurant features delicious *cuisine landaise* at exceptional prices as well, served with local wines. *Menus €11–26. Open all year except 15–30 Mar and 1–15 Sept.Closed Wed.*

Maison Crabot, **t** 05 58 71 91 73 (*cheap*). Some of the best places are a short drive away. Five km from Aire, signs will guide you to this peaceful hilltop farmhouse with pretty views, where you can choose between the flowery or dolls' room. *Open all year.*

Ferme Auberge Fléton, Bahus-Soubiran, 6km west on the D2, **t** 05 58 44 40 64. Serves satisfying regional duck dishes, *poule au pot* and warm foie gras served in the traditional Landais fashion, with apples or grapes; Menu €13–23. *Open year-round Sat eve and Sun lunch, and in summer every day by reservation.*

Grenade-sur-l'Adour ✉ 40270

★★★**Pain Adour et Fantaisie**, Pl des Tilleuls, **t** 05 58 45 18 80, **f** 05 58 45 16 57, *www.chateauxhotels.com/fantaise* (*expensive–moderate*). Set in a handsome old house in the arcaded heart of the *bastide*, with comfortable rooms overlooking the river and a celebrated restaurant, where Philippe Garret prepares excellent, aromatic dishes prepared from a wide variety of ingredients, many local (home-smoked salmon from the Adour, asparagus from the Landes), followed by luscious desserts (*the €30 menu is tremendously delicious good value; the other menu is €82*). *Closed Sun eve and Mon, exc in July and Aug; it's a good idea to reserve. Hotel open all year.*

itself an extra-wide river bed, a swampy muddy prairie of islets and canals known as the *barthes*. The *barthes* are one of the secret ingredients that make the spa of Dax so popular; they are also a special environment, host to some 130 species of bird, a little 8-inch terrapin the French call the *cistude d'Europe*, and 50 or so little *poneys barthais* (or *landais*), the last members of a native species living in semi-liberty along the Adour. It's not only their survival that is in doubt, but that of the *barthes* themselves, threatened especially west of Dax, where the demands of civilization are drying the *barthes* for suburban plots, industrial areas or farmland.

The fertile hills south of the Adour are divided into three small regions, the Tursan, Chalosse, and Pays d'Orthe. All three offer a striking contrast to the dreamlike infinity of flat pine forests to the north. Here the main tree is oak, standing in groves amid rolling fields of grain and vineyards, pastures and spring vegetables. Everything is more self-contained, plumper, richer, glossier, more solid (especially the houses,

Hôtel de France, 3 Pl des Tilleuls, **t** 05 58 45 19 02 (*cheap*). Restaurant only. No Hotel. *Menus €16–32. Restaurant closed Sun and Thurs eve plus all day Mon.*

Eugénie-les-Bains ✉ 40320

Eugénie-les-Bains is the fief, or rather little paradise, created by Christine and Michel Guérard. Set in a beautiful 30-acre wooded park full of rare trees and flower gardens, *****Les Prés d'Eugenie**, **t** 05 58 05 06 07, **f** 05 58 51 10 10, *www.michelguerard.com* (*luxury*) is one of the dreamiest small hotels in all France; romantic rooms with wrought-iron balconies occupy the main neoclassical wing, while others, exquisitely furnished with antiques, are in a 19th-century convent near the herb garden. A gymnasium, billiards hall, sauna, beauty centre, tennis courts, heated pool and thermal slimming centre are on the grounds, and guests can join in courses on nouvelle cuisine. *Closed Dec–28 Mar. Menus €120–165, restaurant closed Mon eve exc July and Aug plus Jan–Mar.* Christine Guérard has also refurbished and redecorated ****La Maison Rose** (same phone), a charming country inn in the estate grounds (*expensive–moderate*), where most rooms come with kitchenettes. The restaurant, the one which attracts visitors from around the world to this remote corner of the Landes, is best known by the name of the legendary sorcerer of saucepans, Michel Guérard. After installing himself in Eugénie-les-Bains in the early 1970s, Guérard hit the world of *haute cuisine* like a comet, earning a constellation of stars and toques from the guides. He has remained firmly at the summit ever since that time, continuously improving and adding new imaginative dishes to his repertoire, which is based using only the finest natural ingredients and especially products from the Landes – many of them, like the herbs, are picked fresh the same day. The wonderful Baroque dining room provides an exquisite stage setting for each exquisite dish, which is every bit as beautiful to look upon as it is to taste, with Guérard's flawless combination of flavours and textures. The wine list covers most of the great vineyards of the southwest, and includes the excellent white Baron de Bachen vin de Tursan that Guérard produces in his own vineyard; (for a table, book as far in advance as possible, **t** 05 58 05 06 07, **f** 05 58 51 13 59. *Closed Thurs lunch and Wed, except in high season; also closed Dec–mid Feb.*

Another recent Guérard acquisition, **La Ferme aux Grives**, at Les Charmilles, is an old Landais farm and specializes in the kind of delicious food that the original owners may well have dined on themselves. Among the delicious items on the menu are some wonderful country hams, melt-in-your-mouth roast suckling pig, and magnificent desserts that will send you waddling over to make an urgent appointment at the slimming centre . Menus €40–60. *Closed Wed in low season and Jan–mid Feb.*

which are made out of stone). The one out of every five Landais who is a farmer lives south of the Adour, and like their brethren in Armagnac they prefer to play 6- or 9-pin *quilles*, or skittles, rather than the more traditional *pétanque*. And there are other surprises, too.

Aire-sur-l'Adour and the Tursan

Aire-sur-l'Adour, 'Capital of Foie Gras'

Aire is a hoary old town, founded by the Tarusates, a Celtic tribe. Crassus conquered it for Rome in 50 BC and it went on to become the occasional capital of the Visigothic kings of Aquitaine in the 5th century. The Visigoths were Arians – heretics according to the Church – and they weren't above tormenting the Catholics in their realm. Their most memorable deed during their stay in Aire involved a young Catholic princess named Quitterie. Quitterie had refused to marry a local Visigoth lord and took refuge in Aire, where she performed a number of miracles. Eventually the rejected suitor found her, and when Quitterie still refused him he cut off her head. In the age-old tradition of decapitated saints, her trunk picked up her head and walked up the hill, choosing the site of her tomb; a miraculous fountain at once gushed forth. In the obscure associative logic of religion, Quitterie and her fountain were soon performing miraculous cures of headaches and mental illness. She is the patron saint of Gascony, and her cult is widespread on both sides of the Pyrenees.

The church of **Ste-Quitterie**, a not unpleasant mix of Romanesque, Gothic and 18th-century, presides over the upper level of Aire, known as the Quartier du Mas. In the old days, a constant stream of pilgrims and the faithful (it served as a cathedral from the 12th to the 18th centuries) assured that it was always open; nowadays you have to check the notice board to arrange for a tour with the church's guides (*to visit the church call* **t** *(06) 77 02 43 44 or* **t** *05 58 71 47 00*). The main western façade dates from the 14th century and presents a rather sad, forgotten face to the world, with much of its original decoration chewed away by Huguenots, Revolutionaries and the weather. However, the portal, tucked under the the square brick bell-tower porch, is still mostly intact and decorated with an impressive Gothic tympanum showing scenes from the Last Judgement. The righteous are given robes to wear by an angel, the damned are led off in a chaingang into the maw of hell in the form of a monster, while those doomed to purgatory are stewed in a big pot. The whole is set in luxuriant floral motifs, with the ranks of angels, apostles and prophets in attendance.

The interior was reworked in reheated Baroque by the Mazetti brothers; their choir in coloured marbles remains intact, while the Romanesque capitals that were long masked have been uncovered, some carved with biblical scenes, others with plants, animals or monsters. The crypt was originally part of a Roman temple to Mars; it had a miraculous spring where the baptistry is now. In the old days there were cells nearby, where the mentally ill were locked up in hope of a cure. The magnificent 3rd- or 4th-century white marble sarcophagus of Ste-Quitterie is carved with scenes from the Old and New Testaments: God, dressed in a Roman toga, is seen creating man, the 'Synagogue' is symbolized by a veiled Roman woman, Daniel is in the Lions' Den, Lazarus comes back to life. On the sides Jonah is sleeping under a tree, thrown into the sea and vomited forth by the whale, and Tobias battles the fish. A sacrificial altar, probably from the Roman temple, is in the little chapel opposite; test the chapel's bizarre acoustics by speaking towards the altar.

The palace of Alaric II, the king of the Visigoths, occupied the same spot as the nearby **Château du Mas** (*not open*). In the lower town there are a few buildings of note: the 17th-century **Hôtel de Ville**, originally the Bishops' Palace, with a fine stone stair and, tucked below it, a few mosaics and other minor archaeological finds. The adjacent cathedral, rebuilt and reworked from the 12th to the 19th centuries, lost its title to Dax in 1933. In the Place du Commerce is a handsome **covered market** built in 1860, converted into a theatre and abandoned: nowadays Aire's lively fruit and

Vin de Tursan and Coteaux de Chalosse

The Tursan and Chalosse had their golden age in the 17th and 18th centuries, when they imported wine down the Adour to Bayonne, and from there to England and Holland, at a time when Bordeaux controlled all the production up its own river, the Garonne, and did everything it could to stifle competition. Neighbouring on the prestigious Madiran growing region, the hills around Geaune have grown vin de Tursan since the 12th century on. The reds made of tannat, cabernet and égiodola, have a pleasant supple quality, a wine for bons vivants that goes well with the regional duck and goose cuisine, while the whites, made from an unusual medieval variety called baroque, as well as chasan and aribola, are fruitier and excellent with asparagus dishes.

Vin de Tursan was granted the *appellation* VDQS in 1958, and most of it is produced through Geaune's co-operative, the **Caves des Vignerons du Tursan** (*open for tours and tastings, Mon–Fri 8–12 and 2–5; but ring ahead* on **t** 05 58 44 51 25, *to let them know you're coming*).

To the west, the Vin de Pays Coteaux de Chalosse is made from similar varieties, but suffered a dire setback in the 1860s when the vines were ruined by oïdium. Replanted this century and commonly regarded as a 'petit vin', the vintners have been striving to improve the quality and structure in their wines. You can see, or rather taste, how they're doing in Mugron, down the Adour from Saint-Sever, at the **Caves des Vignerons des Coteaux de Chalosse** (Av Réné-Bats, *open for visits Mon–Sat 8.30–12 and 2–6,* **t** *05 58 97 70 75*).

vegetable market and winter Marché de Gras, 'Fat Market', spilling over with geese and ducks (alive or dead, whole or in pieces), takes place under a roof along Rue Henri-Labeyrie. The 15th-century **Maison de l'Officialité**, at 6 bis, was originally the seat of the local court.

Grenade-sur-l'Adour and Our Lady of Rugby

The first town of importance down river, Grenade-sur-l'Adour is a pretty *bastide* town founded in 1322; its *cornières* are still intact, and the church conserves a pretty flamboyant Gothic retable. Grenade is better known, however, for its unusual chapel just across the river at La Rivière, **Notre-Dame-du-Rugby** (turn left up the narrow road). Dedicated to the 'Virgin supporter of teams from the Landes', it is hung with the jerseys of players who came to leave their prayers inscribed in the 'golden book'. The stained glass and other art is what stays with you, however, especially the statue made by an old rugby captain of a young Jesus handing off the ball to his Mother.

To the north of Grenade on the D406, in **Bascons**, the Virgin supports another local craze in the chapel of **Notre-Dame-de-la-Course-Landaise**, set in the midst of corn fields, but don't come looking for statues of Jesus or the Apostles dodging bulls. There's a small **museum** dedicated to the sport (**t** *05 58 52 91 76; open Wed, Thurs and Fri 2–7*).

The Tursan

An agricultural region of uneven, broken valleys south of Aire and Grenade, the Tursan is the source of most of the geese and ducks in the Fat Market, as well as the corn that feeds them, dairy cattle and wine. It also has a spa, **Eugénie-les-Bains**, named after its godmother, the Empress Eugénie, wife of Napoleon III, although by rights it should be renamed Michel-Guérard-les-Bains after the famous chef who put it on the map when he transformed the dowdy baths into a health-orientated *nouvelle cuisine* pleasure dome (*see* p.91). Eugénie's waters are used for treating obesity and digestive troubles – hence the *Premier Village Minceur de France*, 'France's Top Slimming Village'.

To the south, **Geaune**, the capital of the Tursan, was founded as a *bastide* in 1318 by a *sénéchal* from Genoa, who named it after his home town (*Gênes* in French). It has a 15th-century southern Gothic church with an enormous bell tower and porch, and is the centre of local wine production.

Samadet

West of Geaune, Samadet is a pleasant hilltop village synonymous with the lovely dinnerware made by the **Manufacture Royale de Fayance de Samadet**, in business for just over a century (1732–1840). Founded when the Marquis and Abbé of Rochépine, Charles Maurice de Bouzet, obtained the necessary royal work permit, the industry is remembered in the **Musée de la Faïencerie**, near the church (***t*** *05 58 79 13 00; open Jan–Mar 2–6; April–Oct 10–12.30 and 2–6.30; the rest of the year 2–6; closed Mon and hols; adm*).

After Louis XIV bought his first faïence (after having had to melt down all his gold and silver plates to pay for his endless wars), it became fashionable on the tables of French aristocrats, and various factories were set up to meet the new demand. Made from the excellent local clay, sand and marl, Samadet table services are characterized by their delicate, highly stylized animal and floral *motives* or hunting scenes, painted in rich pure colours. Often imitated, Samadet has rarely been equalled, and pieces sell for small fortunes today. Besides a display of 250 plates and bowls, a workshop has been recreated in the museum to show how it was done; other artefacts evoke traditional rural life in the Tursan. Near the museum, a new atelier has been set up to recreate Samadet pieces – at almost affordable prices.

St-Sever and the Chalosse

St-Sever, site of the Landes' most important abbey in the Middle Ages, enjoys a superb setting, high on a balcony between the gently rolling hills of the Chalosse and the endless sea of pine forests to the north. The Chalosse, a region even lusher than the Tursan, is known as the 'Secret Garden of the Landes'. Good food is a near-Pantagruelian obsession in its little hilltop villages; the excellent quality of the corn grown here gives the foie gras from the Chalosse its national prize-winning finesse and fattens a unique race of beef cattle.

Tourist Information

St-Sever: Pl du Tour-du-Sol, **t** 05 58 76 34 64, **f** 05 58 76 43 55, *www.saint-sever.fr. Open Mon–Fri 9.30–12 and 1.30–5.30, Sat 9.30–12 and 1.30–4.30.*

Hagetmau: 56 Pl de la République, **t** 05 58 79 38 26, **f** 05 58 79 47 27, *www.tourismehagetmau.com. Open Mon–Sat 9–12.30 and 2.30–6.30.*

Market Days

St-Sever: Saturdays.
Hagetmau: Wednesdays.**Amou:** Mondays.
Pomarez: Mondays.
Mugron: Thursdays.
Montfort-en-Chalosse: Wednesdays.

Where to Stay and Eat

St-Sever ✉ 40500

★★Le Relais du Pavillon, Quartier Péré (at the crossroads of the D924 and D933), **t** 05 58 76 20 22, **f** 05 58 76 25 81, *www.hotellandes.com. Route de Grenade. Menus €14–45.* (*inexpensive*). A peaceful modern haven in a garden with pool, where the chef prepares a tasty *pot-au-feu de canard* and other tasty delights from the regional repertoire (*menus €20–40 with lots of* foie gras). *Closed Sun eve and Mon; closed 1st two weeks in Jan.*

Camping des Rives de l'Adour, **t** 05 58 76 04 60. A pleasant site on the river, near the canoe and kayak base. *Open July and Aug.*

Hagetmau ✉ 40700

★Le Jambon, 27 Rue Carnot, **t** 05 58 79 32 02, **f** 05 58 79 34 78 (*inexpensive*). You can check in here at the 'Ham', a good standard provincial hotel, and feast by the fireplace on Chalosse beef steaks, fresh salmon with crayfish and other delights. *Menus €23–30. Closed Oct.*

Mugron ✉ 40250

Ferme-Auberge Marquine, t 05 58 97 74 23. Good fills, with a meaty menu – country ham, *rillettes de canard*, foie gras, a choice of duck *magrets* or *confits*, with a traditional *tourtière* to finish off. *Menus €13–31. Open daily all year, but ring ahead.*

Maylis ✉ 40250

Ferme-Auberge Caboué, t 05 58 97 91 74. Colette Laborde's restaurant has both set menus *Menus €15–29.* and an *à la carte* menu featuring foie gras, quails stuffed with foie gras and capon *confits*, as well as the more common duck *magrets* and *confits*. *Open Sat and Sun year round, and other days by reservation only.*

Montfort-en-Chalosse ✉ 40380

★★Aux Tauzins, on the D2 towards Hagetmau, **t** 05 58 98 60 22, **f** 05 58 98 45 79 (*inexpensive*). This cosy old family-run country inn has been open for decades, with comfortable rooms, set in a garden with a pool. The restaurant makes excellent use of the good things from the Chalosse, as in *foie frais aux raisins* or *tournedos landais. Menus €18–35; A la Carte about €40. Closed Sun eve and Mon out of season, Jan, and first 2 weeks Oct. Also closed 1–15 Feb.*

Domaine Testilin, Baights, **t** 05 58 98 61 21, *www.domaine-de-testilin.fr* (*inexpensive*). Twelve lovely rooms in a magnificent, warm friendly *maison de maître*, set in a park; the food is equally lovely, featuring succulent *magrets* and other regional specialities, washed down with vin du Tursan. *Menus €22–31. Open all year except for the 1st two weeks in Oct; closed Sun and Tues eves plus all day Mon.*

St-Sever, the 'Cap de Gascogne'

Naturally defensible, St-Sever has been inhabited since the dawn of time; since the Middle Ages it has been divided into two districts. One, the lofty plateau of Morlanne, was the site of the Roman *castrum*, where the Pope's emissary St Severus converted the 5th-century Roman governor Hadrian (before the Vandals lopped off his head). Not a stone remains of this, but you can drive up to the Belvedere for the view, shared by a statue of General Lamarque, a patriotic stalwart of the Revolution born in St-Sever in 1770, whose funeral in Paris in 1828 ignited a bloody riot (see Victor Hugo's account in *Les Misérables*). Below stretches the formerly walled Cité of St-Sever – the centre of the modern town – that grew up around the Benedictine abbey, an important pilgrimage stop on the Limousine branch of the Compostela road. Although for centuries the French believed the Landais were really Tartars, St-Sever hosted the only authenticated Tartars to cross through the area: the emissaries of the Khan Argoun, who stayed in St-Sever in 1287 on their way to the court of the Black Prince in Bordeaux. Since the mid-19th century, St-Sever has been the goose-feather capital of the Landes, stuffing the downy by-product of the regional foie gras industry into duvets, sleeping bags and jackets.

Although a handful of 18th-century *hôtels particuliers* survive in the centre of St-Sever (among them, the building housing the tourist office), the star attraction is the **Benedictine abbey**, founded in 988 by the count of Gascony, Guillaume Sanche. It reached its golden age under the reign of Abbot Grégoire de Montaner of Cluny (1028–72) who rebuilt the abbey on a grand scale, with seven staggered apses, here and there reusing Gallo-Roman marble columns. Work proceeded throughout the 12th century: the church floor was covered with a splendid mosaic (of which some fragments remain behind the choir), and several different workshops of sculptors carved the capitals. Heavily damaged in the Hundred Years' War, the nave was rebuilt with Gothic arches in the 14th century; the cloister and monastery buildings date from this period.

Worse was yet to come: the Protestants in 1570, statue-guillotining Revolutionaries, and, to top it off, 19th-century restorers from the *Monuments Historiques* whose leaden neo-Romanesque touch destroyed much of the abbey's charm. Fortunately, the restorers left the capitals alone. Those from the 11th century have simple, decorative floral designs. Sculptors from the early 13th century added (in the south apses) figures amid the leaves and stems: birds, grinning lions, and Daniel in the Lions' den (definitely the favourite subject of 12th-century sculptors in the Midi – but no one really knows why). The finest capitals of all, in the north tribune (at the end of the transept), are believed to have been carved by the vigorous School of Toulouse, with the Feast of Herod and Beheading of St John the Baptist. Also note the sculpted wooden case of the organ (1711).

In 1280 Eleanor of Castile, wife of Edward I of England, founded another monastery in St-Sever, the Dominican **Couvent des Jacobins** (*To visit call* **t** *05 58 76 34 64. Phone ahead for guided tours.*) Restored after the Wars of Religion, it did duty as a school and agricultural college after the Revolution until 1970; since then the town has been slowly restoring it bit by bit as a cultural centre. The church, its plan strict and plain compared to the elaborate apses of the Benedictines, has a Gothic portal and rose window; the chapterhouse, entered through the right, has retained some of its murals from the 14th and 15th centuries; the adjacent refectory has a painting of a monk kneeling before St Dominic and a cardinal. The cloister was completely rebuilt in the 17th century and now houses the little **Musée des Jacobins**, with Gallo-Roman and medieval artefacts, items relating to the pilgrimage route, old postcards and a display devoted to the celebrated illuminated 11th-century *Apocalypse of Saint-Sever* (now in the Bibliothèque National in Paris), a creation of the wonderfully inventive school of painting founded by Grégoire de Montaner.

South of St-Sever

After St-Sever, pilgrims en route to Compostela passed through **Audignon**, 5km southwest, where there was a hospital and a gem of a Romanesque church to receive them, with a beautiful apse decorated with carved modillons and capitals. The bell tower doubled as a donjon, and the doorway, decorated with masks, dates from the 14th century. Inside, there's a superb 15th-century stone retable with frescoes from 1550, and stone blocks cut with distinctive masons' marks. Two kilometres to the south of Audignon on the D21, **Aulès** has another good Romanesque church with carved capitals on its exterior.

Further south, **Hagetmau** means 'bad beech tree' in Gascon (there must be a story there somewhere, but we don't know it) and takes no little pride in being 'The Chair Capital of Europe', producing everything from the straw-seat country farm chair to Louis XV armchairs – but don't expect any factory outlets. Instead, Hagetmau offers more Romanesque art in its atmospheric **Crypte de Saint-Girons**. This is all that remains of a Benedictine abbey, built over the 4th-century tomb of St Girons, evangelist of the Chalosse. Although the vaults of the crypt are more recent, the 14 elaborately sculpted capitals are fascinating: there's a *tête à tête* between a man and a dragon, the story of Lazarus, and the Deliverance of St Peter from prison.

On the Hagetmau–Mugron road (the D18) you can visit a modern pilgrimage site: **Maylis**, the 'Mother of Lilys', where the Olivetan **Abbaye Notre-Dame de Maylis** (***t*** *05 58 97 72 81*). has Romanesque and Gothic elements in its old church and a 12th-century statue of the Virgin. The monks cultivate a special plant used in treating liver and kidney ailments, run a shop and sing Gregorian chant Masses every day at 11.45, and Sunday at 6.30pm.

Brassempouy, southwest of Hagetmau, is famous as the source of the unique Venus of Brassempouy, or the *Dame à la Capuche*, 'the hooded lady'. Carved in mammoth

Salade Landaise

You'll see this *salade composée* listed as a starter on many menus throughout southwest France, and it's easy to prepare, especially if you're self-catering: the average supermarket carries all the ingredients. The following serves six people. First, mix a dressing using a tablespoon of hazelnut oil and two tablespoons of sunflower oil, a tablespoon of wine vinegar, pepper and a bit of salt. Wash and drain whatever lettuce is in season. In a frying pan, heat up 6 sliced *gésiers confits* (gizzards preserved in fat), 12 thin slices of dried duck breast (they come ready in packages from the *charcuterie* counter, labelled *aiguillettes de magret séché*), and 12 thin slices of fresh *magret de canard*; put them on paper towels to soak off any excess fat, and let them cool. Meanwhile place the lettuce around six plates, embellish with the meat slices, dress the salad and place a medallion of *foie gras de canard* in the centre of each plate; serve preferably with a dry Jurançon.

Capcazal

Capcazal, 'first house', is the local word for a place occupied and cultivated since the beginning of time, or almost. Owners of such houses, who occupied a midway point between the nobility and the commoners, enjoyed a variety of privileges, such as the right to own a dovecote and complete freedom from the feudal system.

ivory and measuring 3.5cm – about an inch – this is the oldest known human portrait, going back 23,000 years. It was discovered in 1894 in the Grotte du Pape just outside the village, where excavations continue apace in the summer, when you are allowed to visit. Current finds are in a small **Musée de la Préhistoire** (***t*** *05 58 89 21 73; open daily exc Mon, Oct–May 2–6; summer daily 10–1 and 2–7*). Although the original was whisked off to Paris' Museum of St-Germain-en-Laye, the museum has a copy of the Dame à la Capuche; note that her so-called 'hood' could just as easily be an elaborate corn-row hair style. Also worth a look is Brassempouy's fortified 12th-century church of **Saint-Saturnin**; you can climb the slightly dangerous stairs to the top of the bell tower for an excellent view.

West of Brassempouy, the 17th-century **Château de Gaujacq** (or de Sourdis), standing on the ruins of a Roman *castrum* just outside the village of the same name, is open for guided tours (***t*** *05 58 89 01 01; open all year; winter Mon, Tues, Thurs–Sun 3–5*). The de Sourdis family were so fond of the Carthusians that they built their home in the form of a Charterhouse, complete with an interior cloister; here the Marquis de Montespan came to retire and die after his wife became the mistress of Louis XIV. The rooms are noted for their lovely panelling and furnishings from the 17th to 19th centuries. The colourful botanical garden is used to propagate endangered species.

Another road from Brassempouy, the D21, leads southwest to the happy little town of **Amou**, a town originally called Amor by the Romans, hence the town's motto '*Amor que so*', or 'I am Love'. Set on the banks of the Luy de Béarn and surrounded by orchards, its Romanesque church boasts a colourful rococo altar, and its 17th-century château, built to the designs of Mansart, offers a rare look at French Classicism in this neck of the woods. West of Amou, **Pomarez** is the 'Mecca of Bullfighting' (in this case, the *course landaise*), which it loves so well that it built the first covered arena in France, with seats for 3,000 – more than the village itself can begin to fill. The great local rendezvous of aficionados is the **Café Laborde**, whose owner has a huge collection of posters, videos and other memorabilia upstairs in a small museum.

Back Along the Adour

The Adour is most scenic between St-Sever and Mugron, where the *villages perchés* sit on natural terraces over the water. Here **Montaut** has been a stronghold since the Middle Ages, and as such was destroyed by the Huguenots in 1569. The village **cultural centre** (***t*** *05 58 76 05 13; open mid June–mid Sept daily 3.30–6.30*) displays tools and explanations from the nearby Solutrean-era *gisement d'Arcet*, where flint tools were manufactured between 20 and 15,000 BC. **Brocas**, 5km south of Montaut, has a fine 12th-century church, Saint-Pierre, all that remains of an abbey. **Mugron**, the 'Belvedere of the Chalosse', enjoys a superb view (especially from its church) of the great forest to the north. The centre of the Chalosse wine production (*see* p.93), Mugron's old *chais* can still be seen along the river, where the wine was stored before shipment to Bayonne. Just north, the pretty 11th-century church at **Nerbis** was another foundation of Saint-Sever.

An interesting museum can be found in the 13th-century *bastide* of **Montfort-en-Chalosse**, which was founded by the king of England and remains one of the prettiest villages in the Chalosse. The **Musée de la Chalosse** (***t*** *05 58 98 69 27; open April–Oct Tues–Fri 10–12 and 2–6.30; weekends and hols 2–6.30; winter Tues–Fri 2–6; closed mid Dec–mid Jan*) is contained in the Domaine de Carcher, a master's house preserved and furnished as it was at the end of the 19th century, complete with barns and outbuildings and an exhibit on wine. The church of Montfort is equally worth a look, a charming combination of Romanesque and Gothic, heavily fortified in the 15th century; but as with many villages in the Chalosse, many people come to Montfort just to eat.

Dax

With five deep wells bored into the left bank of the Adour pouring out over 7 million litres of hot water steeped in sodium chloride, calcium and magnesium sulphates every day, Dax easily makes its living as France's top thermal spa. It's a busy, pleasant

Dax Facts

Back in the 19th century, a visiting doctor caused a stir when he accused Dax of lax hygiene for mixing something that looked like cow dung into the Fontaine Chaude. An inquiry revealed that the stuff was really algae, and although you won't see it floating around the Fontaine Chaude any more (thanks to a cement bottom added in 1961), it is one of the keys to Dax's fame as '*La Première Station de Pélothérapie*', which translates something like 'First in Hot Mud Pie Cures'. The earliest thermal mud installations were pits dug along the banks of the river; whenever the Adour overflowed, the mud from the *barthes* oozed into the pits where everyone could wallow to their heart's content. These days, the mud is scientifically gathered, filtered and mixed with hot water from the fountain, and spread out to ripen for four to six months in large solar basins – artificial *barthes*. Here greenish algae and bacteria incubate in the mud mix (it looks like the picture of proto-evolutionary primordial soup in your biology schoolbook) which contribute in some mysterious way to the anti-inflammatory, soothing effect when the sticky, plasticky grey mud, now called *peloïde de Dax*, is heated and applied to aching joints and bad backs. The spas apply 1,000 cubic metres of the stuff every year, by prescription only; if you'd like to try a bath, however, the Thermes Borda, 30 Rue des Lazaristes, t 05 58 74 86 13, is open every afternoon except Sunday from *3–8; closed Jan–Feb*.

Getting There and Around

A special **bus** service links Dax to Biarritz and Bordeaux airports; to reserve a place, ring the Dax tourist office with the time of your arrival. The more people in your party, the cheaper it is per head.

The **train** station (on the TGV Atlantique route from Paris) is on the north bank of the Adour, half a kilometre north of the centre. (The Bordeaux–Dax track is almost dead straight after Arcachon and there are never any cows on it: the French make use of it whenever they're trying to break speed records with a new TGV engine.)

For regional **bus information** (RDTL), call **t** 05 58 56 80 80. For a taxi, call **t** 05 58 74 71 53 or 05 58 57 15 11 or 05 58 91 25 25.

Tourist Information

By the river in Pl Thiers, **t** 05 58 56 86 86, **f** 05 58 56 86 80, *www.dax.fr. Open 9.30–12.30 and 2–6, non-stop in the summer; closed Sun, July and Aug 9.30–7.*

Market Days

The big Saturday market by the cathedral, established in 1356 by order of the Black Prince, is especially colourful and packed with geese and ducks.

Flea market: first and third Thursday of each month, Pl Camille-Bouvet.

Saint-Paul-lès-Dax: Thursdays.

Where to Stay

Dax ✉ 40100

An unusual feature of Dax is that 16 of the town's 58 hotels are directly connected to thermal establishments. High season is September and October, when it can be hard to find a place that will take you in for just one or two nights. Note that at least *half-pension* is obligatory in nearly every hotel.

★★★**Hôtel Splendid**, 2 Cours Verdun, **t** 05 58 56 70 70, **f** 05 58 74 76 33 (*expensive*). If you can afford the experience, check into this recently renovated hotel, built in 1928, with its enormous lobby, Art Deco furnishings and grand old bathrooms intact; along with a spa cure there's a health centre on the premises, and lounging about in white bathrobes is *de rigueur. Menus €23–32. Closed Jan and Feb.*

★★★**Grand Hôtel**, Rue Source, **t** 05 58 90 53 00, **f** 05 58 74 88 31, *www.thermes-dax.com* (*expensive*). Large, well-lit rooms, each individually furnished, and its own baths, the Thermes-Adour. *Menus €14–22. Closed for Christmas.*

★★**Miradour**, Av Eugène Millès-Lacroix, **t** 05 58 56 77 77 (*moderate; full pension only*). Overlooking the river, modern and very pleasant, with direct access to its own bath. *Menus €11–17. Open all year.*

★★**Auberge des Pins**, 86 Av Francis-Planté, **t** 05 57 74 22 46, **f** 05 58 56 05 62 (*inexpensive*). A charming little inn with a large garden just outside the centre; country family-style meals (but they will adapt to any diet), with free minibus service to the baths. *Menus €10–20. Closed mid Dec–mid Jan.*

★★**Beausoleil**, near the centre at 38 Rue du Tuc-d'Eauze, **t** 05 58 74 18 32, **f** 05 58 56 03 81, *www.hotel-beausoleil-dax.fr* (*inexpensive*). This white, old-fashioned hotel oozes charm and comfort, peace and quiet and offers lots of personal attention. *Menus €11–32. Closed Mon eve plus Christmas–mid Feb.*

★★**Le Richelieu**, 13 Av Victor-Hugo, **t** 05 58 90 49 49, **f** 05 58 90 80 86, *www.le-richelieu.fr* (*inexpensive*). Centrally located and recently renovated, with a pleasant patio for sunny

town of 20,000 – a metropolis by Landais standards – full of flowers, mimosa and minivans transferring patients to and fro between the hotels and the baths. If you're aching, scores of doctors are on hand to prescribe a cure; if you're French, it's a bargain – a fat section of the prospectus the tourist office sends out is devoted to analyzing all possible Social Security reimbursements for soaking in the water or getting plastered in mud. And all cures seem to last three weeks.

days and a restaurant that tries harder than most; the owners have recently opened a 'Club Rétro' on Rue St Eutrope where for a €5 cover charge you can dance and sing to French golden oldies. *Menus €19–34.*

****Hôtel de la Paix**, Rue des Pénitents, **t** 05 58 90 16 46/**t** 05 58 90 00 16 (*inexpensive–cheap*). Near the pedestrian-only centre, and linked by a lift to the Thermes Romains. Special rates for 3-week stays and big discounts to a second person. *Closed Dec–Feb.*

***Au Fin Gourmet**, 3 Rue des Pénitents, **t** 05 58 74 04 26 (*moderate–inexpensive*). Right in the centre of town by the Fontaine Chaude, this elegant hotel has rooms ranging from the very basic to others with private bathrooms and TVs as well as studios. Half- or full-pension is mandatory, but the food is very good with many Landais recipes on the menu (try the delicate *cèpe* omelette) served in a choice of pretty little rooms *Menus €12–26. Closed Dec and Jan.*

***Hôtel de la Nehe**, Rue de Fontaine Chaude, **t** 05 58 90 16 46 (*inexpensive–cheap*). Like the Paix, linked by a lift to the Thermes Romains, and offering special rates for 3-week stays and big discounts to a second person. *Closed Dec–Feb.*

Hôtel Loustalot, 60 Pl Joffre, **t** 05 58 74 04 13 (*cheap*). Just over the bridge from the centre of Dax on the right bank of the Adour; the décor inside is more modern than the exterior might suggest, and there is a good chance of finding a room with a bathroom for only one or two nights. *Open all year.*

Les Chênes, just west of Dax in the Bois de Boulogne, **t** 05 58 90 05 53, **f** 05 58 56 18 77, *www.camping-les-chenes.fr*. An excellent camp site with clean showers, good facilities and very reasonable rates. *Open mid May–mid Sept.*

Eating Out

L'Amphitryon, 38 Cours Gallieni, **t** 05 58 74 58 05. As most guests dine in their hotels, Dax has relatively few restaurants. Besides the Au Fin Gourmet mentioned above, try this friendly place for constantly changing menus that feature plenty of delights from Amphitryon's watery realm. *Menus €20–37. Closed Sun eve plus Mon and Sat lunch. Closed Jan and end Aug–5 Sept.*

Restaurant du Bois de Boulogne, Allée du Bois-de-Boulogne, **t** 05 58 74 23 32. With a shady summer terrace, overlooking the Adour, this is another good bet for seafood-lovers, but the chef also does good regional meat dishes . *Menus €10–27. Closed Sun eve.*

Le Moulin de Poustagnacq, Saint-Paul-lès-Dax, **t** 05 58 91 31 03, **f** 05 58 91 37 97. When the Dacquois do dine out, they usually get in their cars and head out of the centre. This popular place overlooks a forest and pond; the kitchen uses local ingredients to create imaginative dishes such as crayfish tempura seldom seen in the Landes, served with a wide choice of wines. *Menus €21–54. Closed Sun eve plus Mon and Tues lunch.*

Ferme Auberge de Thoumio (6km south) 40180 Saint Pandelon, **t** 05 58 98 73 41, offers Landaise specialities using their own farm produce; plenty of foie gras and duck. *Menus €12–26. Open 1 Mar–15 June and 16 Sep–20 Dec on reservation only. Mid June–mid Sept open daily exc Sun eve and Wed.*

Auberge La Chaumière. Rte de Bayonne, Quartier Hardy, St–Paul–les–Dax (3km west of Dax). This place has been in business since 1868, and offers a Basque–Landaise gastronomic journey with a full use of regional and seasonal produce. Try the *gratin de tourteau* or the lamb with sweet peppers and *cèpes*. *Menus €16–31. Closed Mon eve and Tues.*

The first known Dacquois were the Tarbelli, a tribe of Gauls defeated by Caesar's lieutenant Crassus in 56 BC. A Roman garrison town, *Aqua Tarbellica*, was set up next to the Gaulish village. It owed its first fame to a shaggy dog legend: one of the centurions stationed in the garrison had an old dog that was stiff with rheumatism, so he left it behind when he was sent over the Pyrenees to crush a Spanish revolt. When he returned, he was amazed to see old, infirm Fido frisking about like a pup. No one could explain the change, but the centurion was curious enough to follow the dog one day on his rounds. To his surprise, the dog went mucking through the shallow *barthes* along the Adour and jumped into a pool of hot mud. The centurion, who had a few aches and pains himself from a winter spent in the Pyrenees, joined his dog in the mud, enjoyed the experience and quickly spread word of a miraculous cure.

The good news or mud's theraputic qualities reached all the way to Rome, where Julia, the man-eating daughter of Augustus, was also afflicted with rheumatism. Not wanting to miss out, she became the first celebrity to take the muds and in gratitude renamed the garrison *Aqua Augustus* after her dad. By the 2nd century AD, the garrison had grown into a proper town with at least one temple; in the 4th century it was walled in as its name gradually contracted on Gascon tongues to Dax. In the 12th century Richard the Lion-Heart gave it a castle, but it was razed to the ground in 1891. Its current career as a full-time spa took off after the construction of the railway from Bordeaux in 1854.

A Walk Through Old Dax

From the 4th century to the mid-1800s, Dax was corseted in its town walls on the left bank of the Adour; only a part of these and eight of the original 49 towers have survived near the river. It has the perfect centrepiece for a spa town, the neoclassical arcaded **Fontaine Chaude**, built in 1818 around the steaming source. Known by the Tarbelli Gauls and the Romans as the fountain of the naiads, or La Néhe, this is the most generous of the 50 hot springs in France, pumping out 2,400 cubic metres of water a day at 64°C (147°F); in Gascon it's called *Lou Bagn Bourren*, the Boiling Bath, and was an old favourite of housewives for cooking hard-boiled eggs, dipping chickens for easy plucking and washing the sheets.

From the Fontaine Chaude, Rue Cazade leads to the **Musée de Borda** (***t** 05 58 74 12 91; open 2–6 daily; closed Sun–Mon and hols*), housed in the 16th-century Hôtel de Saint-Martin-d'Agès, where Mazarin lived while arranging the marriage of Louis XIV (*see* p.172). The collection was founded as a cabinet of curiosities by Dax's most famous son, Jean-Charles de Borda (1733–99), a member of the Académie de Sciences who did much to improve the technology of the French fleet and invent new navigational instruments at the time of the American War of Independence. The museum houses an important collection of engraved ivories from the Upper Palaeolithic era and another cast of the famous *Dame à la Capuche*, from Brassempouy (*see* above). There's a large collection of Roman votives from Dax and Aire, some impressive bronzes found under Dax's *halles* in 1982 (note especially the Mercury, with a little goat, and the cockerel that became the symbol of Gaul) as well as Gallo-Roman mosaics and a statue of *Sleeping Eros* discovered embedded in the town walls when they were levelled in 1850.

In the medieval section are a pair of Merovingian sarcophagi from St-Vincent de Xaintes, the first church in the Landes, founded in the 4th century, and a stone where debtors who couldn't pay up were made to sit in Rue du Mirailh; every time someone passed by they had to receive three smacks on the behind. The coin collection ranges from the ancient Greek to the curious ceramic pennies minted by the Weimar

Republic in the 1920s, and a display tells the history of the *course landaise*. Opposite the museum, you can see the foundations of a Roman temple and house, the **Crypte Gallo-Romaine** (*same hours as the museum*), discovered in 1979.

Rue Cazade continues south to Rue Saint-Pierre, site of the new Hôtel de Ville and the 4th-century city gate; beyond the gate is another section of walls, repaired in the 19th century by the Monuments Historiques. West of the Hôtel de Ville towers the ponderous bulk of the **Cathédrale Notre-Dame** (***t** 05 58 74 27 66*) completed in 1894, the third church built on the site. The original Romanesque cathedral was bombed to bits by the English in 1295; its splendid Gothic replacement collapsed in 1645. St Vincent de Paul convinced Anne of Austria, Louis XIV's mother, to raise a special tax for its rebuilding, but it still took 275 years to complete. The resulting mongrel Baroque-classical interior is morose and frumpy, but there's an impressive organ case from the 17th century, said to be carved from the chestnut trees that were once used by Dax's hangman.

From the Gothic cathedral were salvaged 80 choir stalls from the mid-16th century, lovingly carved with a Renaissance lunatic asylum of bizarre figures twisting about the seats like circus contortionists. Best of all is the 12th- or early 13th-century **Portal of the Apostles** installed inside the left transept in 1890 to protect it from the elements. One of the few southern Gothic portals to escape the Revolution, the 19th-century wrecking ball and the grasp of American museum collectors (only because it was forgotten, wedged into a wall between 1642 and 1890), its tympanum depicts a favourite medieval subject, the Weighing of Souls. Over the centre pillar Christ holds the book of the Seven Seals, while around him stand expressive life-size statues of the twelve Apostles with their various emblems. Along the lintel, the dead rise from their graves, the blessed from smart tombs on the right, while on the left the reprobates are pursued and chewed by devils, monsters and Deadly Sins.

Behind the cathedral, pedestrian-only Rue Neuve has some of Dax's finest buildings from the 17th century; at the top of the street, turn left in Cours de Verdun to see the handsome **Atrium Casino**, built in 1929 and scarcely touched since. Up the Adour, in the riverside Parc Théodore Denis, the rather elegant white **Arènes** with its domed towers is the busiest arena in the Landes, with both *courses landaises* and Spanish *corridas* from June to October.

On the west side of Dax, the former village of **Saint-Vincent-de-Xaintes** was annexed to Dax in 1950. A church from the 1890s stands on the site of the 4th-century church of St-Vincent (although it conserves a Gallo-Roman mosaic in the choir), while the old oak forest belonging to the parish is now the attractive public park of the **Bois de Boulogne**, a great place for a picnic, pony rides, fishing in the pond or whacking a golf ball on the driving-range. Other attractions in Dax include **Le Pavillon du Foie Gras** (***t** 05 58 56 73 21; open May–Oct Mon-Fri 10–12 and 3–6pm*), where you can tour the factory, see how it's made and buy direct; and the **Musée de l'Aviation Légère**, (*58 Av de l'Aérodrome, **t** 05 58 74 66 19; open daily 2–6; closed Sun and hols*) with a collection of old fighter planes, 'Bananes' helicopters and their prototypes.

Around Dax

Just over the Adour from Dax, **St-Paul-lès-Dax** is worth a visit for its 12th-century church, in particular for the eleven sculpted capitals and niches around the exterior of its apse, beautifully carved in white and coloured marble with floral designs, monkeys, musicians and fantastic animals. The white marble niches show a curious mix of biblical scenes – Samson and the Lion, St Veronica wiping Christ's face with a handkerchief, the Last Supper, the Crucifixion, two Angels at the Tomb, the Resurrected Christ, and flame-spitting monsters.

Six km northeast of Dax, the village of Ranquine was renamed **St-Vincent-de-Paul** after the saint born here in 1581. In a small complex known as **Le Berceau de St-Vincent-de-Paul**, run by the Sisters of Charity, his half-timbered house has been restored with original furnishings; a neo-Byzantine chapel of dubious taste was plumped next door, and in the grange you can watch a video on the life of the saint, who as a young shepherd kept the family flock in the shade of the huge oak tree nearby. His family, noting his piety, sent him off to study with the Franciscans in Toulouse, and he was ordained at the age of 20. In 1605 he was captured by Barbary pirates and enslaved, an experience that gave him a deep empathy with the world's outcasts. When he managed to escape to Paris, he devoted his life to charity, during a time when it was common for poor parents to drop unwanted babies off at hospitals, which commonly sold them for a few pennies to beggars who would break their limbs to incite the pity of passers-by. Vincent de Paul formed an institute known as the Priests of the Mission, or Lazarists, in 1625, and in 1633 founded the Sisters of Charity to help him in his work. His reputation was so great that Louis XIII summoned him to his deathbed to perform the last rites; one of his last tasks was chaplain to galley slaves. He died in 1660 and was canonized in 1737, declared the patron saint of all charitable societies.

Nevertheless, the chief pilgrimage destination in the Landes is the ornate 19th-century **Notre-Dame de Buglose** just north, where the towers have a 66-bell carillon and a 900lb painted stone Virgin holds pride of place. Note, from a less ambitious era, the 17th-century reliefs showing the Sisters of Charity in the chapel of St-Vincent-de-Paul, just left of the choir.

The Southern Côte d'Argent

The playground continues; one thing not to miss is the descent down the Huchet, where Landais gondoliers will punt you through semi-tropical lushness worthy of the sets in *The African Queen*. *See* map pp.88–9.

Léon, its Lake and the Courant d'Huchet

Traditional houses give the old village of Léon its tone, while the most lush and beautiful river in all the Landes, the **Courant d'Huchet**, brings it visitors from far and wide. The Huchet flows 12km down to the sea, passing under a canopy of alders, pines, and willows hung with garlands of ivy and creeper, through giant tamarisks, majestic ferns called *osmondes royales*, wild hibiscus and waterlilies. Apparently it was something of a secret until 1911, when Gabriele d'Annunzio among others discovered it while hurtling through the Landes on a cross-country car race. Throughout April to the end of October, the flat-bottomed boats of **Les Bateliers du Courant d'Huchet** make the trip, lasting up to four hours (*2hr trips daily at 8am, €9; 3–4hr trips daily at 2.30pm, €11; book ahead – up to two weeks ahead in August – on* **t** *05 58 48 75 39; children 10 and under half-price*).

The region south and west of the Etang de Léon has been set aside as a nature reserve, a good place to observe the local water-loving birds. The nearest beach is **Moliets-Plage**, the seaside extension of **Moliets-et-Maa**, best known for its golf course. Just down the coast, **Messanges** was long famous for its *vin des sables*, where vineyards planted in the hollows of the dunes yield a now-rare red wine with the perfume of violets.

The next town south has a double-double-barrelled name, **Vieux-Boucau-Port-d'Albret**. Just Port d'Albret back in the Middle Ages, it marked the spot of the sometime mouth of the mighty Adour; so great was the force of the river's waters that the sandy soil of the Landes could not begin to contain it in a proper bed, and when huge Atlantic storms battered the coast and stuffed its mouth with sand, the Adour would change direction. For a long time its mouth was at Capbreton; it moved to Port d'Albret in 907; in 1164 it went south to Bayonne, and then to Capbreton; in the 14th century it went back to Port d'Albret, which prospered – until 1578 when the Adour once again curled to the south. But this time, Bayonne, distressed at seeing its own port silt up with sand, asked King Charles IX for help, and he sent down an engineer who dug a canal for it to ease into. And there it has stayed – thanks to constant dredging. These days Port-d'Albret, spread around the banks of a salt-water lake, is the name of a purpose-built holiday resort annexe of the pleasant old village of Vieux-Boucau ('Old Mouth').

Inland, **Soustons** manufactures corks for Bordeaux wines and is the most important market town for the region. It has its own lake, the Etang de Soustons, while to the south lie two more small lakes, now part of a nature reserve: the Etang Noir (named after its black mud) and the Etang Blanc (named after its fine sandy bottom). Near them, **Tosse** has an 11th-century church with an apse decorated with exterior carvings. **Seignosse** is an old village just south of the Etang Noir, while all the beach action as usual happens a few kilometres away in **Seignosse-le-Penon**, which grew up in the 1960s as one of the surfing capitals of the coast. If the waves are too much, there are two vast sea-water pools on the beach.

Capbreton-Hossegor

Two separate *communes*, divided by the Bourret Canal, are responsible for this booming resort's name, and a unique setting with the Pyrenees hovering on the horizon has made it the biggest holiday centre between Arcachon and Biarritz: besides the usual ocean beach, it has a warm, sandy tidal lake (another former mouth of the Adour), two rivers and a canal. The older town, Capbreton, was an important whaling and fishing port before the 14th century, when the Adour graced it with its

Getting There and Around

No trains pass through here; the nearest stations are in Dax and Bayonne, and from there **buses** travel to the main points on the coast.

Tourist Information

Léon: Pl Jean-Baptiste Courtiau, **t** 05 58 48 76 03, **f** 05 58 48 76 03, *www.ot-leon.fr. Open July and Aug Mon–Sat 9–1 and 3–7, Sun 10–1; the rest of the year Tues–Sat 9–12 and 2–7.*

Moliets-et-Maa: Rue du Général Caunègre, **t** 05 58 48 56 58, **f** 05 58 48 52 93, *www.moliets.com. Open Oct–April Mon–Fri 9–12.30 and 2.30–6; July and Aug Mon–Sat 9–1 and 2–7 plus Sun 10–1 and 3–6; the rest of the year Mon–Sat 9–12.30 and 2.30–6.*

Vieux-Boucau-Port-d'Albret: Le Mail 11, **t** 05 58 48 13 47, **f** 05 58 48 15 37, *www.ot-vieux-bocau.fr. Open July and Aug Mon–Sat 9–12 and 2–6.*

Soustons-Port d'Albret: Grange de Labouyrie, **t** 05 58 41 52 62, **f** 05 58 41 30 63, *www.mairie-soustons.fr. Open July and Aug Mon–Sat 9.30–1 and 2.30–7, plus Sun am; the rest of the year Mon–Fri 9.30–12.30 and 2–6; June and Sept Sat am.*

Seignosse: Av des Lacs, **t** 05 58 43 32 15, **f** 05 58 43 32 66, *www.seignosse.com. Open all year. Mon–Sat 9–12 and 2–6;July and Aug Sundays 10–1.*

Hossegor: Pl des Halles, **t** 05 58 41 79 00, **f** 05 58 41 79 09, *www.hossegor.fr, www.ville-soorts-hossegor.fr. Open July and Aug Mon–Sat 9–12 and 2–6, Sun 10–1 and 3–7; the rest of the year Mon–Sat 9–12 and 2–6.*

Capbreton: Av Georges Pompidou, **t** 05 58 72 12 11, **f** 05 58 41 00 29, *www.landes-cote-sud.com. Open July and Aug 9–7 plus Sun 10.30–12.30 and 4–7; the rest of the year Mon–Sat 9–12 and 2–6.*

Market Days

Soustons: Mondays.

Capbreton: Saturdays, but daily in the summer, flea market second Sunday in June.

Hossegor: Monday, Wednesday, Friday and Sunday mornings.

Labenne: Wednesdays.

Where to Stay and Eat

Léon ✉ 40550

★**Hôtel du Lac**, **t** 05 58 48 73 11, *www.hoteldulac-leon.com.* (*moderate*). The only hotel here, but it's simple and nice enough. *Closed Oct–Mar.*

Moliets ✉ 40660

Hotels here are built around the golf course.

★★★**Green Parc Océan**, Rue des Croquillots, **t** 05 58 48 57 57, **f** 05 58 48 57 58, *www.maeva.com. Maeva-Green Parc* (*inexpensive*). Large, attractive and well-run – as well as rooms you can rent a modern cottage in the trees by the night or week; there are pools and tennis courts, and a disco; *half-pension* mandatory. *Closed Oct–Mar.*

★★**Hotel de l'Océan**, Av de l'Océan, **t** 05 58 48 51 19, **f** 05 58 48 51 19 (*cheap*). For something cheaper in Moliets, this place fits the bill; most rooms have sea views. *Open all year.*

Soustons ✉ 40140

Saint Christophe, 15 Pl Sterling, **t** 05 58 41 15 16 (*inexpensive*). *Open all year.*

★★★**Relais de la Poste**, **t** 05 58 47 70 25, **f** 05 58 47 76 17, *www.relaischateaux.fr/poste* (*expensive*). The very best place to eat and stay, 10km east of Soustons, at Magescq, with comfortable rooms set in a park with huge pines, a heated pool and tennis court. But it's the exquisite Landais cuisine, prepared by Bernard and Jean Coussau, that has made it renowned: the pigeon with *girolle* mushrooms, the foie gras, duck fillets, and potatoes sautéed in goose fat that melt in your mouth, accompanied by warm, crisp bread made in the Relais' special oven, a superb list of wines from Bordeaux and Burgundy as well as the finest armagnacs, not to mention perfect desserts as full of rich flavours as all the other courses. *Menus €50–75. Closed Mon and Tues from Oct–May. Open daily in season; closed 11 Nov–20 Dec.*

Seignosse ✉ 40510

★★★**Golf Hôtel de Seignosse**, Av du Belvédère, **t** 05 58 41 68 40, **f** 05 58 41 68 31, *www.golfseignosse.com* (*expensive–moderate*). Built in the style of a Louisiana plantation house, in the heart of the golf course, with a pool and pretty terrace and *restaurant gastronomique*; rooms are well equipped with satellite TV, minibars, etc. *Menus €26–35. Closed Jan and Feb.*

★★**Hotel du Golf**, 2 Av de la Brasérade, **t** 05 58 41 68 40, **f** 05 58 41 68 41 (*expensive–moderate*). On the edge of the golf course towards the ocean; pleasant quiet rooms, a pool, terrace and private parking. Good restaurant. *Open all year.*

Du Lac Blanc: 'Chez Tonton', **t** 05 58 72 80 15, *www.cheztonton.com* (*inexpensive*). A quiet little inn by the the Etang Blanc with regional cuisine. Restaurant. *Closed Oct–Easter.*

Campeiole Les Oyats, Rte des Casernes, **t** 05 58 43 37 94, *www.campeole.fr.* A camp site near the sea with lots of shade and a pool for the small fry. *Open 10 May–14 Sept.*

Hossegor ✉ 40150

Of the two linked towns, Hossegor has the nicer places to stay, many set back in the trees.

★★★**Le Mercedes,** Av du Tour du Lac. **t** 05 58 41 98 00, *www.hotelmercedes.com.* A lovely white and blue Art Deco exterior, sparkling on the edge of the lake, and the best place to stay in town. The rooms are spacious and decorated in cool pastels. *Open Easter–mid Nov.*

Restaurant le Cottage, 1 Av Jean Moulin, 40510 Seignosse (Fond du lac d'Hossegor), **t** 05 58 43 31 39. A pretty restaurant with a lovely terrace set in its own woods back from the road. The chef spent time in Provence where he discovered an ancient Provençal cookbook, and many of his wonderful recipes have been adapted from this: the aubergine terrine with a sweet pepper sorbet, a preferred dish of the 'Papes des Vignes', the wine lords of Provence, followed by the chef's fish stew (recommended) or char-grilled sea bream. The use of fresh herbs is ambitious and refreshing. Or you could clear your pleasantly bombarded taste buds with a dish of three sorbets: rosemary, thyme and lavender. Menus (€18 for lunch only) €30 plus à la carte. Charming and efficient service. *Closed Mon and Tues plus 6 Jan–12 Feb.*

★★**Les Hortensias du Lac**, Av du Touring Club, **t** 05 58 43 99 00, **f** 05 58 43 42 81, *www.hortensais-du-lac.com.* Av Du tour du lac (*expensive–moderate*). Between ocean and lake, built in the local style, and friendly and comfortable, too. No restaurant.

★★**Les Huîtrières du Lac**, 1187 Av du Touring Club, **t** 05 58 43 51 48, **f** 05 58 41 73 11 (*inexpensive*). Owned by a family of oystermen, on the main lake road. Rooms are pleasant and immaculate; be sure to reserve one with a view. The restaurant naturally features oysters and other seafood, is also good. *Menus €19–33. Open all year.*

Dégustation du Lac, 1830 Av du Touring Club, **t** 05 58 43 54 95. Besides the hotel restaurants, Marianne Lamoliate's restaurant is worth trying for its exquisite seafood platters and fish soup at very reasonable prices. *Menus start at €16. Closed Tues exc July and Aug. Open April–Sept.*

Le Pizzaïol, Av du Touring Club, **t** 05 58 43 57 04. The décor with all the Chianti bottles may be a bit corny, but it has the best pizza in town. *Open till 1 am in July and Aug.*

Amigo, Pl des Landais, **t** 05 58 43 54 38. For *gambas*, sardines or tapas. *Open daily from April until the end of Oct.*

Capbreton ✉ 40130

★★★**L'Océan**, a big white hotel near the port at 85 Av G-Pompidou, **t** 05 58 72 10 22, **f** 05 58 72 08 43, *www.hotel-capbreton.com* (*moderate*). The nicest here, with large, comfortable soundproofed rooms. *Closed mid Nov–mid Dec and some of Jan.*

★★**Bellevue**, Av G-Pompidou, **t** 05 58 72 10 30, **f** 05 58 72 11 12 (*inexpensive*). Twelve recently refurbished rooms and a delightful restaurant. *Menus €15–26. Closed Nov–Jan.*

Regalty, Port de Plaisance, **t** 05 58 72 22 80. In the fishermen's quarter, head for where the nautical style is a backdrop to excellent fish dishes. *Menu €28. Closed Sun eve and all Mon.*

Pêcheries Ducamp, 4 Rue du Port d'Albret, **t** 05 58 72 11 33. Pescophobes should stay away from this fishmonger's converted into a restaurant, where waitresses in plastic boots and aprons serve nothing but the freshest of fish and shellfish. *Menu €21–44. Closed Tues and Fri lunch out of season.*

presence. When the Adour moved and the port silted up, Capbreton rapidly declined; the few people who stayed around grew table grapes. It began to perk up again in the 18th century, when Napoleon III built a long jetty and it began to farm oysters. In the early 1900s, artists and writers from Biarritz set up a colony around the Lac d'Hossegor, with the idea of living fraternally together in an ideal, highly charged cultural milieu. It did produce one painter of interest, Roger Sourgen (1883–1979), son of a Landais customs officer, who learned enough of his father's trade to become a successful smuggler as well as a naïf artist, painting the lakes and pines around Hossegor. In the 1930s the property developers followed (see the luxurious villas around the golf course) and ever since the resort has grown, sacrificing any charm the centre of Hossegor once had. Besides all the usual beach things, climb up the high dune known as **Super-Hossegor** for the view.

Capbreton has been filled to the hilt with new building, preserving only a few old houses in the very centre that somehow escaped the voracious cement-mixer. One feature of Capbreton that may never be exploited is its unique underwater canyon, or the **Fosse de Capbreton**, 2km offshore, an abyss plunging 100m down, ten times deeper than anywhere nearby. Louis XIV's great engineer Vauban back in the 17th century was the first to propose it as a deep-water port. It's still an idea that crops up every now and then; for the time being the resort contents itself with a marina – the only one between Arcachon and Bayonne – named *Mille Sabords* (translated as 'Blistering Barnacles!' whenever Capt. Haddock says it in *Tintin*), and the **Ecomusée de la Pêche et de la Mer**, in the municipal casino (***t** 05 58 72 40 50; open daily July and Aug 9.30–12 and 2–6.30; April–May, June and Sept daily 2–6; Oct–Mar, Sun and hols only 2–6*) with an aquarium, ships' models, fossils, shells, and a film. Along the ocean beach, you should only swim in the designated areas, protected by lifeguards; the big rollers that bring champion surfers to Capbreton hit the coast just to the north, towards Seignosse.

South of Capbreton-Hossegor

There are two more small resorts along the coast before Bayonne: **Labenne-Océan** and **Ondres-Plage**. Labenne is just west of the Marais d'Orx, a favourite nesting marsh of migratory birds, especially ducks and geese, which was recently purchased by the WWF and the Conservatoire du Littoral. It was drained by Napoleon III and given as a present to his cousin, Count Walewsky, the natural son of Napoleon I. Over the years it filled up with water again, much to the delight of the 150 species that stop here throughout the year.

Between here and the Adour to the east, the villages have interesting churches (especially **St-Martin-de-Hinx** and **Biarrotte**) and the occasional château.

The Gers
The Heart of Gascony

07

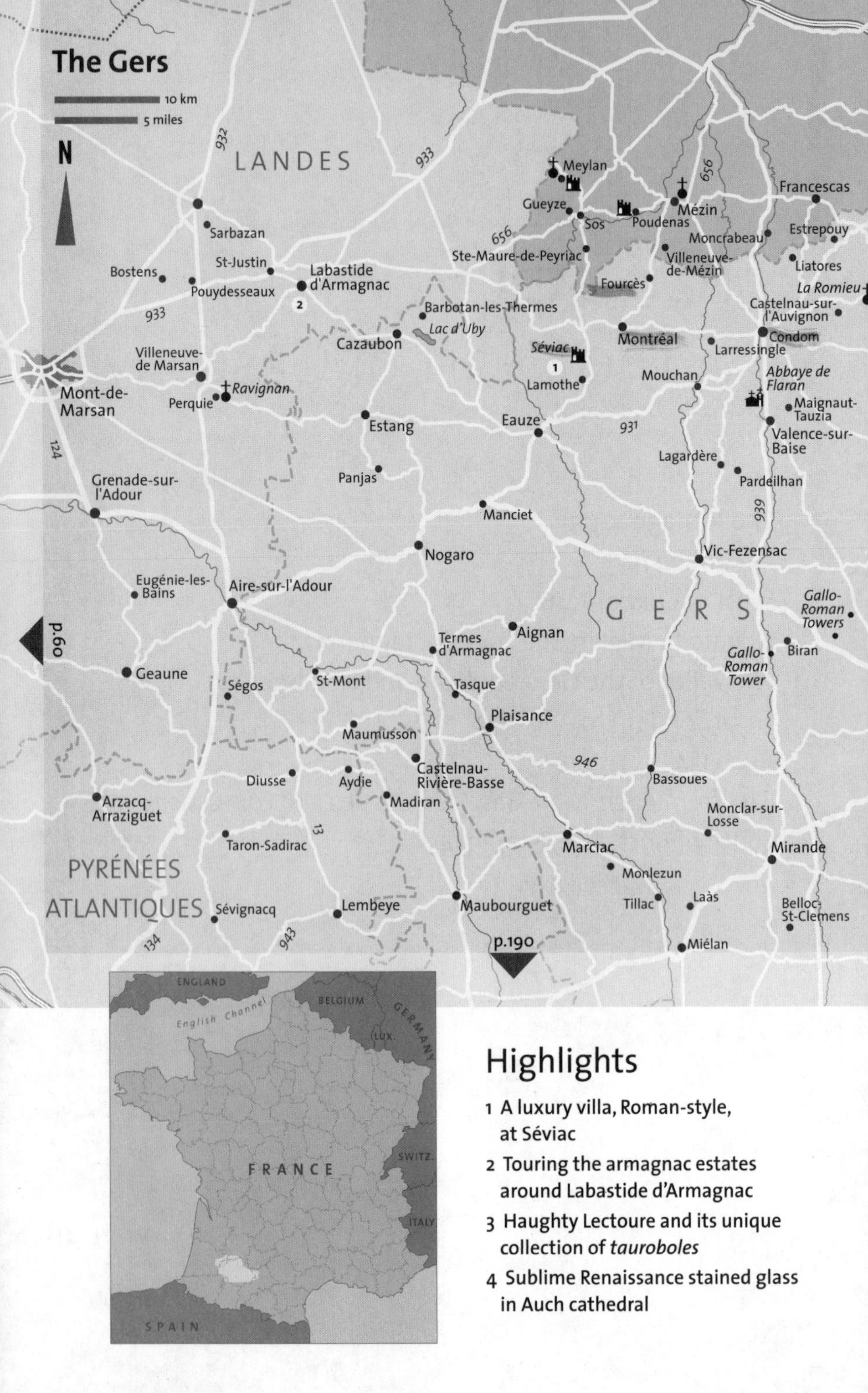

Highlights

1. A luxury villa, Roman-style, at Séviac
2. Touring the armagnac estates around Labastide d'Armagnac
3. Haughty Lectoure and its unique collection of *tauroboles*
4. Sublime Renaissance stained glass in Auch cathedral

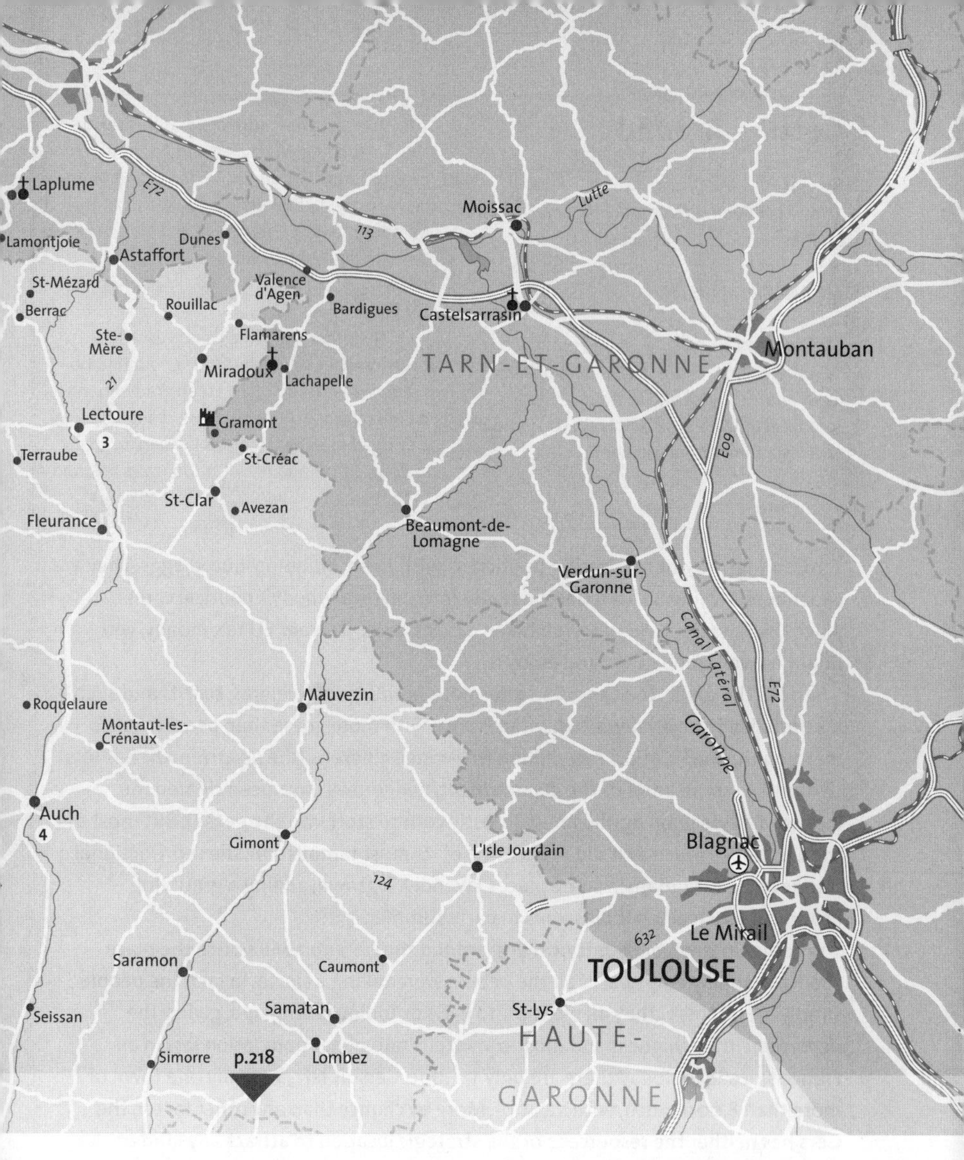

You've seen the Eiffel Tower and Mont Blanc, but have you been to the *département* that produces more garlic than any in France? No doubt everyone knows the Gers as home of the World Championship Snail Races (in Lagardère) and the World Championship Melon Eating Contest (in Lectoure), but beyond these, *département* number 32 may seem a bit obscure. Its own tourist literature proudly claims it as the 'most discreet province of France'; the Gersois are probably aware that jokes are made at their expense in sophisticated, up-to-date metropolises like Pau and Agen.

Most of the Gers is serious farmland and, not surprisingly, the *département* is one of the stoutest strongholds of *Coordination Rurale*, the militant group that is always in the news dumping tons of manure on a local *préfecture* or truckloads of potatoes

Getting Around

By Car

You aren't going to get very far here without a car. Even more than the rest of the southwest, public transportation in the Gers is rudimentary at best.

By Rail and Bus

From Auch, there are rail connections to Agen (via Fleurance and Lectoure), and to Toulouse; the *Ville Rose* is only 1½ to 2½ hours away (via Gimont and l'Isle-Jourdain).

Auch is also the centre of what bus service there is (ring **t** 05 62 05 76 37 in Auch): daily runs to Tarbes, Bordeaux, Toulouse and Mont-de-Marsan; slightly more frequently to Mirande, Condom, Vic-Fézensac, Fleurance, Lectoure and nearby villages.

By Bicycle

On the other hand, the Gers is excellent country for bicycling: just hilly enough to be scenic without too many steep gradients, and plenty of shade along the back roads. If you're driving, remember that this is a very sparsely settled region, and petrol stations are few and far between.

across a highway, or splattering politicians with fresh, home-produced eggs. They are capable of sticking a sharp Gascon rapier into nearly anybody's political career, so places like the Gers are very well taken care of. Since it's your EU tax money, you might as well come down and enjoy it.

Besides the garlic, the Gers is an enormous producer of foie gras, *confits* and such – it's probably the only *département* in France with more geese than people, not to mention the ducks, and a few million free-range chickens (the *département* has lots of room). In some parts of the *département*, hedgerows have been cleared for industrial-style grain agribusiness (mostly corn to stuff into the geese). But most of the Gers looks much as it did in the time of its most famous son, the semi-fictional musketeer d'Artagnan; in some places lavender is grown, adding a gratifying Provençal touch when it blossoms in early summer.

Whether in town or country, driving around the Gers you will notice the place seems strangely empty, as if all the people were taking a siesta. In fact, the people simply aren't there; they all went off to Paris or Toulouse long ago, giving the *département* the highest and most consistent rate of net population *loss* in all France since 1850. Today there are only 174,000 Gersois left, and only one town of more than 8,000 (Auch, with 22,000). More by chance than any other factor, the Gers has neither the resources nor the strategic location to attract any kind of industry whatsoever. But what's bad news for the *syndicats d'initiative* may be good in the long run for the Gers, and for now, at least, it makes the heart of Gascony the perfect place for anyone who wants a dip into *la France profonde* at its unspoiled best.

Besides that, the Gers has some genuine attractions: the great art of Auch cathedral, unmatched in the southwest, a number of medieval abbeys, such as La Romieu and Flaran, and a surprisingly large number of gracious châteaux, most of which can be visited. Above all the Gers is a land of bastides – over a hundred of them, ranging from charming Mirande, which has almost grown into a town, to little arcaded squares lost in the woods that never got more than half built in the Middle Ages and have been declining genteelly ever since.

The Armagnac

This is more of a fond old expression than a term with any precise geographical meaning. 'Armagnac' can mean the old territories of the counts of Armagnac, the big bosses in the heart of Gascony before the French rubbed them out and gobbled up their lands in 1473. But to people today it is more likely to mean the area where little-a armagnac is produced, the finest of French brandies (cognac? they've never heard of it). This area, roughly, includes everything west and north of Auch, and armagnac is still its name and its fame. Touring it can seem truly civilized; where else in the world can you stop in at a château for a shot of eau-de-vie every five minutes?

Condom

With such a name, what's a town to do? The natural instinct of the Gascon, of course, would be to flaunt it, as with the fellow on France's national rugby side who called himself 'Condom' after his home town, and proudly carried the name into international combat until his retirement a few years back, no matter what the nasty Britons were mumbling in the scrum. Lately, the whole town has decided that they might as well make the best of it and recently opened the **Musée des Préservatifs**

Tourist Information

Condom: Pl Bossuet, **t** 05 62 28 00 80, **f** 05 62 28 45 46, *www.gers-gascogne.com. Open July–mid Sept Mon–Sat 9–7, Sun 10.30–12.30; the rest of the year Mon–Sat. 9–12 and 2–7.*

Market Days

Condom: Wednesdays.

Where to Stay and Eat

Condom ✉ 32100

★★★**Hôtel des Trois Lys**, right in the centre on Rue Gambetta, **t** 05 62 28 33 33, *www.les-trois-lys.com* (*moderate*). Occupying an 18th-century mansion, this hotel has a warm, welcoming atmosphere and is well kept. It has just enough room at the back for a small swimming pool. *Menus €18–30. Restaurant closed all Sun and Mon lunch plus Feb.*

★★**Logis des Cordeliers**, Rue de la Paix, **t** 05 62 28 03 68, **f** 05 62 68 29 03, *www. logisdes cordeliers.com* (*inexpensive*). Pool but no restaurant. *Closed Jan.*

Camping Municipal, across from the centre, on the river on Av des Mousquetaires, **t** 05 62 28 17 32. An inexpensive site. *Open April–Sept.*

Hôtel le Continental. 20 Av Maréchal Foch, 32100 Condom, **t** 05 62 68 37 00, *www. lecontinental.net*. Pleasant enough if nondescript hotel next to the bridge overlooking the Baïse. The modern restaurant is brightly decorated with local artists' work. The menu is regional – plenty of beans and duck. *Menus €21–30. Lunch €13. Closed Christmas and 5–12 Jan.*

Moulin du Petit Gascon, out on the D931 towards Eauze, **t** 05 62 28 28 42. Foie gras and duck of course, but you might wish to hold out for the *filet aux morilles* when there are morels to be had. Very good desserts. *Menus €12–32. Closed in Nov. Closed in winter, Sun eve and all Mon.*

La Romieu ✉ 32480

Camp de Florence, just outside the village, **t** 05 62 28 15 58 (*cheap*). Pool, tennis, a few rooms, and a restaurant. Snack bar and pizzas too. *Menus €15–29. Restaurant closed Wed and Nov–Mar.*

Ferme de Gratazous, Blaziert, **t** 05 62 28 44 54 (*inexpensive*). This farm offers *gîtes*.

(**t** *05 62 68 25 69; open daily June–Sept 9–12 and 3–7; adm*). If you're hoping for some grisly examples of our rubber friends down through the ages, no such luck – the museum places its emphasis firmly on the modern context. They have the first machine ever to produce them en masse, and three rooms extolling the virtues of condoms against AIDS.

Nobody knows where the name came from. The best guesses imagine some Roman place name, such as *Condatum* or *Condominium*. As a town, though, Condom did not appear until the Middle Ages, when it grew up around a Benedictine monastery, now long disappeared. Ask any of the farm boys, slouching in the bars on a Saturday evening, and they may well tell you that the name is entirely deserved; one senses they feel the bright lights of Auch or Agen calling them away.

Condom's one sight is its **Cathédrale de Saint-Pierre**, begun in 1507 (the same year that the archbishops of Auch began the ambitious decorative programme in their cathedral; the armagnac business must have been thriving). This is a magnificent building, though it has taken its bumps over the centuries, from Montgomery's Protestants in the Wars of Religion, to the mobs of the Revolution and the 19th-century restorers. The most decorated portal, on the southern door, was finished in 1531, and Montgomery's men smashed it up only 38 years later. An excellent example of the southern approach to the flamboyant Gothic of the era, the church's interior features complex vaulting and big gallery windows. A few of the stained-glass windows are original, though most were installed in the 19th century, done in the style of Arnaut de Moles's windows at Auch. About the same time, the stone enclosure was added around the choir. Outside there is a simple 16th-century **cloister**, now used as offices by the *mairie*.

Nearby on Place Lannelongue, the bishops' stables have been converted into the **Musée de l'Armagnac** (**t** *05 62 28 47 17; open April–Oct 10–12 and 3–6; winter 2–5; closed Mon, Tues and hols*), with a collection of farm bric-a-brac and exhibits on making armagnac the old-fashioned way. If you miss this one, don't worry – the *département* has many more like it.

Another summer activity for tourists is an excursion boat up the Baïse, on which you will end up at another armagnac *chai* and a glassblower's workshop; ask at the tourist office for details.

La Romieu

The nearby abbey of Flaran (*see* p.132) gets most of the tour buses, but **La Romieu**, east of Condom on the D41, would be a much more rewarding place to visit if you only have time for one.

On the way, you can take a short detour to **Castelnau-sur-l'Auvignon**, for a look at the simple Templar commandery there. The Templars, along with the other orders of crusading knights, had buildings like this throughout Europe, local headquarters from which to oversee the vast lands they owned. The building isn't anything special, but it is one of the few such buildings to survive intact.

La Romieu itself, with its towers dominating a wide panorama of farmland, makes a memorable sight, one that has changed little over the centuries. The name means 'pilgrim', one who has been to Rome; a pilgrim named Albert founded a monastery here in 1082, acting on behalf of the powerful Abbey of St Victor in Marseilles, the force behind scores of new foundations in the Midi.

It was not until the 14th century, though, that La Romieu grew into the lavish complex we see today. From the village that grew up around the abbey came a young nobleman named **Arnaud d'Aux**, whose luck it was to see his friend and cousin become pope – Clement V, the Gascon elected with the connivance of the king of France, who moved the papacy to Avignon and began the 'Babylonian Captivity' (as the Italians call it).

Thanks to his family connections, Arnaud was named a cardinal, serving as the papal chamberlain, and occasionally as ambassador to Edward II, King of England and Duke of Aquitaine, while piling up plenty of absentee bishoprics, and plenty of revenues from them. Interestingly, he also presided over the trial of the Templars in 1307, and must have picked up lots of confiscated loot from them too (perhaps the lands around Castelnau). In 1312, he began spending much of the booty on the enlargement of the abbey in his home town, along with a palace for himself and his family.

The palace is mostly gone, leaving only the **Tour de Cardinal** (***t** 05 62 28 86 33; open May–Sept 10–7; the rest of the year 10–12 and 2–6*). Together with the two larger towers of the adjacent **Collegiate church**, it dominates La Romieu's impressive little skyline. All three towers are very good examples of the showy, sophisticated architecture that was spreading at the time from the papal court at Avignon. The church's bright and airy interior, full of flowers, is a delight, but the real treasure here is the adjacent building called the **sacristy**, on the ground floor of the larger of the towers.

Most likely, this octagonal hall was originally intended as a tomb for Arnaud d'Aux and his family. The entire interior is painted with well-preserved frescoes: beautiful angel musicians on the vaulted ceiling, and portraits of family members and biblical personalities on the walls. Along with these is a real puzzle, a set of peculiar, carefully painted designs. They might be simply abstract decoration, or perhaps some sort of symbol of esoteric significance (there are a few hints of such intent in the architecture of the church). If they do have some kind of religious significance, no one so far has even managed a good guess at what they might represent; nothing like them appears anywhere else.

If you can find someone around who has the keys, ask to see the unusual double-spiral staircase, an architectural trick with separate flights for ascending and descending wound together. Outside, there is a fine Gothic **cloister**, which was heavily damaged in the Wars of Religion.

The picturesque village that grew up around the abbey was a *sauveté*, a place under the protection of the Church and off limits to all armies and fighting. Parts of its fortifications survive, as a reminder that the arrangement didn't always work out well in practice. The village was built around an arcaded square; like the bastides, many of these *sauvetés* were planned foundations.

Around La Romieu

North of La Romieu, delightful back roads like the D41/D266 and its continuations will take you through an odd little *pays* called the **Fimarcon**, after the medieval lords who owned most of it. Caught in one of the worst places to be during the Hundred Years' War, these barons and their people made almost every one of their villages into little fortresses. Fragmentary remains of their work – castles and blockhouses, fortified churches, defensive trenches and such – are everywhere, especially around the villages of **Berrac**, **St-Mézard**, and **Estrépouy**. **Liatores**, west on the D267, has a fine country Romanesque church.

West of Condom

The countryside is green and delicious, though you might find it somewhat disfigured by the signs for the armagnac estates that pop up at every crossroads. The main route west, the D15, passes **Larressingle**, the 'Carcassonne of the Gers' – a wonderful specimen of rustic Gersois hyperbole, but just the same this medieval fortified village (the smallest one in France) makes a striking sight. Its walls, built in the 13th century,

Tourist Information

Montréal: Pl de la Mairie, **t** 05 62 29 42 85. *Open July and Aug daily 9–12 and 2–6; rest of the year Mon–Fri 9–12 and 2–6; closed Jan.*

Eauze: Rue Félix Soulès, next to the church, **t** 05 62 09 85 62, **f** 05 62 08 11 22, *www.eauze.net. Open 25 June–2 Sept Mon–Sat 9–12 and 1.30–7.30, Sun 10–2; rest of the year Mon–Sat 9–12 and 2–6.*

Barbotan-les-Thermes: Av des Thermes, **t** 05 62 69 52 13, **f** 05 62 69 57 71. *Open 9–12 and 2–6, also Sun summer only 10–12 and 3–6.*

Labastide d'Armagnac: **t** 05 58 44 67 56, *Open Mon–Sat 9.30–12.30 and 2–6.30 plus Sun in summer 10–12 and 3–6.*

Market Days

Montréal: Fridays.
Barbotan: Wednesdays.
Cazaubon (near Barbotan): Fridays.
Eauze: Thursdays.

Where to Stay and Eat

Montréal ✉ 32250

Chez Simone (opposite the church), **t** 05 62 29 44 40. This fine old building decorated with frescoes shelters a superb restaurant. It is well known in the area for its duck and foie gras though the truffle omelettes and old armagnacs are pretty good too. The lunch menu is a bargain, otherwise *menus range from €13 to €25. Closed Sun eve and all Mon and Tues.*

Fourcès ✉ 32250

Château de Forcès, **t** 05 62 29 49 53, **f** 05 62 29 50 59, *www.chateau-fources.com* (*expensive–moderate*). A superbly restored château on the edge of this bastide village, with some fine spacious rooms, a ravishing garden and a swimming pool. The food here is also a treat, professional and inventive, and service is friendly. *Menus €18–45. Open April–Oct.*

L'Auberge, **t** 05 62 29 40 10. This restaurant on Fourcès' circular square offers simple, good-value warming local food such as cassoulet and duck breasts. There's a terrace in summer and roaring fire in winter. *Menus €15–22. Closed Wed in winter.*

Sos ✉ 47170

★Le Postillon, Pl Delbosquet, **t** 05 53 65 60 27 (*inexpensive*). This hotel-restaurant is in a restored smithy, with a few cosy rooms are almost entirely intact, and the tiny village tucked inside seems to have changed little since then; the unusual church is partly Romanesque, with some carved capitals. South of Larressingle, there is another good medieval church at **Mouchan**, built as a stop for pilgrims along the route to Compostela; it has some of the earliest Gothic vaulting in the south. The **Château du Busca Maniban**, 5km from Cassaigne on the D229 at Mansencome (***t*** *05 62 28 40 38; open April–1 Nov daily except Sun 2–6; winter open by appointment only; adm*) is a beautiful 17th-century castle boasting the oldest distillery still in use, dating back to 1693. The guided tour includes a free tasting of some very fine Armagnac. The **Château de Cassaigne** (***t*** *05 62 28 04 02, www.chateaudecassaigne.com. Closed Mondays mid Sept–mid June*), just up the D208, was the residence of the bishops of Condom. The 16th-century building is open for visits, offering a look at its old-fashioned kitchens and armagnac cellars.

East from Larressingle on the D15, the next village is **Montréal**, a sleepy balcony of a town that seems almost forgotten on its hilltop. Montréal is an English bastide, founded in 1289, though the site was occupied even in Celtic times. The village's immediate ancestor, however, lies down on the plain at **Séviac**, one of the most important Roman-era finds in southwest France.

and nice fat *magrets* and *confits* with *cèpes* out on the terrace. *Menus €15–20. Closed Feb.*

Barbotan-les-Thermes and Cazaubon ✉ 32150

★★★**Bastide Gascogne**, Barbotan, **t** 05 62 08 31 00, **f** 05 62 08 31 49 (*expensive–moderate*). A gracious, restored 18th-century *chartreuse* (a Carthusian monastery – and 18th-century Carthusians were known for a certain *joie de vivre*; all over southern Europe they left monasteries like this one that look more like palaces). It's a Relais et Châteaux establishment, with a pool and garden, and a lovely terrace for dining. The restaurant is one of the best in the area, its *cuisine soignée* is a real bargain. *Closed for renovations. No date given for completion.*

★★★**Château Bellevue**, Rue Joseph-Cappin, Cazaubon, **t** 05 62 09 51 95, **f** 05 62 09 54 57, *www.chateaubellvue.org*. Here there are 25 rooms in an old mansion set in a garden, with a pool and an excellent restaurant. *Menus €18–40. Closed Sun eve and Monday all day. Closed Jan and 1st week in Feb.*

Eauze ✉ 32800

Municipal Campground, just outside town at Moulin de Pouy, **t** 05 62 09 86 00. This camp site has a pool.

Café Commercial, under the arcades across from the church, **t** 05 62 09 82 12. A popular bar and lunch spot serving tasty sandwiches and cool drinks plus the opportunity to take a breather and watch the world go by. *Open daily.*

Auberge du Moulin de Pouy, Moulin de Pouy, **t** 05 62 09 82 58. A pretty terrace and home cooking on menu makes this a good choice. *Menus €15–39. Closed 1st two weeks of Sept plus Sun eve and all Mon.*

Manciet ✉ 32370

★★**La Bonne Auberge**, Pl du Pesquerot, **t** 05 62 08 50 04, **f** 05 62 08 58 84 (*inexpensive*). This hotel, right in the centre of the town, has as its major advantage a restaurant that people come all the way from Auch and even Bordeaux to visit. Among the attractions are the many game dishes, including a wonderful roast pigeon with apples. *Menus €23–43. Closed Sun eve and all Mon. Closed 1st week in Jan.*

★★**Le Moulin du Comte**, out in the hamlet of Bourrouillan, just to the north, **t** 05 62 09 06 72 (*inexpensive*). This hotel-restaurant occupies a restored old mill in a nice setting by the river, with spacious and comfortable rooms and a big pool. *Menus €16–38. Open daily all year.*

A Little Place in the Country

The way we learned it in school, the Roman age was a wonderfully civilized time when everyone wore togas and recited Latin verse in the Forum – until those malodorous barbarians barged in to spoil the party. But for a moment, try and imagine a place like the Gers in the 4th century AD, as it really was. Grass is growing in the streets of *Augusta Auscorum* (Auch) and the other towns. Trade is rotten, the currency's worthless, and crushing imperial taxes are forcing what's left of commerce into extinction; legions of bureaucrats wait to squeeze out every last *denarius*, while telling you what you can and can't do, according to the emperor's restrictive and increasingly bizarre edicts on economic planning. Everything belongs to a small handful of colossally wealthy families: all the land, all the money, and even most of the people. There have always been armies of slaves on the big estates, but beyond these, the majority of free citizens have already become serfs, giving up their lands and selling themselves into bondage with the big landowners, just to get off the tax rolls and avoid prison and torture when they couldn't pay. Anyone with any nerve, an increasingly scarce commodity in the Roman twilight, has gone off to the woods to join the *bagaudae*, the guerrilla bands that haunted Gaul and Spain in the last two centuries of Roman rule.

Despite the advantages that accrued to them under the imperial system, landowners had by this time completely abandoned the decomposing state, avoiding all taxes and contributing no time or talent to saving the Empire or trying to reform it. They had also abandoned the cities, preferring to spend their time at their country villas far from crime, decay, and the other troubles of the day. With their owners' monopoly of wealth, these villas often grew into full-sized towns in themselves – private towns replacing public ones, devoted to the pleasure and wellbeing of a single family, and staffed by hundreds or even thousands of slaves, as well as private armies, when necessary to keep the *bagaudae* at bay. The complexes were built around one or a number of courtyards, and included elaborate baths and temples.

The landowning families were never too seriously inconvenienced by the barbarian invasions; for a while, after the Empire collapsed, they formed a committee at Arles and ran southern Gaul for themselves. After that, they easily reached an accord with the new Gothic and Frankish overlords. The old and new groups gradually intermarried, and over the generations metamorphosed into something new – the feudal aristocracy of medieval Europe. But history has had its way with these villas, as with all vanities. While their owners were turning into feudal barons, their homes made a parallel transition into feudal castles. Especially after the invasions of the Vikings and Arabs, defence was all-important, and hilltop sites came into favour. The villas, often built in lovely natural settings near water, were abandoned (such as Montmaurin, east of Lannemezan), or, more often, turned into simple villages, housing the descendants of Roman slaves and serfs. The villagers recycled the stone for their own houses, and the foundations and the mosaics simply disappeared, under the dirt floors of the peasants the villa's builders had oppressed for so long. Undoubtedly, there are still some that have not yet been discovered.

The Roman Villa of Séviac

The first to call attention to this site was a local boy named Lannelongue, who went up to Paris and became an Academician, and personal physician to Sarah Bernhardt. No one bothered to start digging, however, until 1961. The site, as with so many of the mega-villas of Roman Gaul, was hidden well enough. Now it has been completely excavated, and the foundations exposed under plastic-roofed pavilions. Like most Roman villas, this one was built on a peristyle plan, meaning that it has a central rectangular courtyard around which the rooms were arranged. The most impressive of the ruins are the **baths** and **pool**, the former with vestiges of proper Roman hypocaust central heating – a space under the floor propped on columns, where heat from a fire in another room could circulate. There are also some well-preserved **mosaics** with floral and geometric motifs, and an especially good one with a goldfinch among vines. The excavators found two skeletons from the 6th or 7th century, and they have named them 'Les Amants' and put them under glass for your inspection. More finds from Séviac can be seen in the small **museum** on the site (***t*** *05 62 29 48 57, www.seviac-villa.fr.st. Open daily July and Aug 10–7; March, June, Sept, Nov daily 10–12 and 2–6; adm*).

North of Séviac

North of Montréal on the D29, **Fourcès** is worth a detour if you have the time. It was one of the few medieval bastides laid out in the form of a circle, with a castle at the centre that was a frequent bone of contention in the Hundred Years' War. The castle was demolished long ago, leaving a pretty circular square shaded with plane trees. The people of Fourcès today haven't been shy about taking advantage of it; they've tarted it up as cute as can be – it could be a village in a model train layout. Parts of the wall remain, along with the 15th-century Tour de l'Horloge, overlooking the little river Auzoue.

Beyond Fourcès, the D29 will take you to a little corner of the Bas-Armagnac district currently in the *département* of Lot-et-Garonne. **Mézin**, the biggest village, was the home of Armand Fallières, president of France from 1906 to 1913. Fallières' presidency caused no embarrassment to Mézin, and the villagers have named their main square after him. There is a small **museum** (***t*** *05 53 65 68 16; open Tues–Fri 2–6.30*), with exhibits on Fallières' life and on corks – cork oaks being one of the area's traditional crops – and also a Roman statue of Jupiter. Mézin grew up around an important Cluniac abbey, and it retains the **abbey church of St-Jean** – Romanesque in the apse while the rest is graceful Gothic (though the builders may have botched it; currently there are cracks in the vault, and iron girders holding up a tilted column). On the vault over the altar, note the whimsical carving of a grimacing giant and a pot of flowers. The tympanum on the north door must have been destroyed in the Revolution; replacing it you can still make out part of some painted revolutionary slogan about the 'Supreme Being'. These are common enough in French village churches; the radicals in Paris were telling the peasants it was still all right to believe in God, though not necessarily the God of the Christian church.

All For One and One For The Road: Armagnac and Floc

The vines in the Gers date back at least 1,000, if not 2,000 years, but until the Middle Ages the 10° white wine they produced had the reputation of barely being able to travel across the table, let alone to other parts of France. The main variety of grape, *folle blanche*, was nicknamed *picquepoul*, 'tingle-lips', for the extremely dry, acidic sensation it gave the unwary.

Turning tingle-lips into a fine amber brandy was an idea introduced in 1285 by Arnaud de Villeneuve, a medical student at the University of Salerno, who joined the University of Montpellier and went on to become the personal doctor of the first Avignon pope, Clement V of Bordeaux (whom he inadvertently killed by prescribing a plate of ground emeralds for a stomach upset). In 12th-century Salerno, the Arab-Italian faculty had perfected the ancient Egyptian art of distilling the essences from plants and fruits, and the first record of the Gascons applying this fine art to grapes dates from 1411 (upstart cognac, armagnac's arch rival, dates only from the early 17th century). As far as anyone knows, armagnac is the oldest eau-de-vie distilled from grapes in the world, and to give you some idea how closely the brandy is intertwined with the Gascon mystique, one of the larger producers stores his in three great barrels known as Athos, Porthos and Aramis.

Although Gascony's first guild of *vinaigriers-distillateurs* dates from as far back as 1515, it wasn't until the 17th and 18th centuries that armagnac was produced on a wide scale. The first market was Dutch; before setting out on a long voyage, Dutch ships were fitted out with a large barrel of '*vin brûlé*' or brandy, and as most ships made a final call at Bordeaux or Bayonne before crossing the Atlantic, Dutch shipowners encouraged the production of armagnac.

By the late 19th century, armagnac was so successful that 100,000 hectares of vines were planted – just in time for the disastrous phylloxera epidemic, which devastated nearly the entire lot. The vines were replanted with resistant varieties (ten different kinds of white grapes are allowed, the main ones being bacco 22 A, a hybrid of picquepoul and noah, saint-émilion and colombard) although they were hardly replanted on the same scale: today less than 20,000 hectares are under production, in an area strictly limited in 1909 by Armand Fallières, the Gascon vintner from Mézin who also happened to be president of France.

You could get lost for a long time in the lush countryside around Mézin and never mind it. On the stretch of the D656 that follows the valley of the Gélise, you'll pass things like a pretty country chapel and a traditional *pigeonnier* on stilts, and plenty of farmers hang out signs to sell you asparagus and *cèpes*, foie gras and *floc*. At **Poudenas** there is a fine Italianate château to visit; built largely in the 17th and 18th centuries, it has some period furniture and paintings (*advisable to telephone in advance,* **t** *05 53 65 78 86 or 05 53 65 70 53; open 14 July–31 Aug, Tues–Sun 3–6; adm*). There are Romanesque churches at **Sos** and **Gueyze**, and a fortified church from the 13th century at **Villeneuve-de-Mézin**, south of Mézin. **Meylan**, just inside the pine forest of Les Landes, is a tiny village that seems to consist of a swing set, a *mairie* in a shed, a picnic table and a war memorial, yet it contains so many curiosities that the

The production of armagnac isn't exactly coterminous with the boundaries of the Gers. AOC armagnac can be made as far north as Agen, as far west as Mont-de-Marsan and in the south almost to the Pyrenees; it hardly ever crosses the Adour. There are three sub-regions: limestone Haute-Armagnac or 'Armagnac Blanc' which includes almost everything east of the river Baïse, with Auch as its centre, although only 500 hectares are under vines; Ténarèze, in the middle, a mix of limestone and sandy soils stretching south from Condom (8000 hectares); and Bas-Armagnac or 'Armagnac Noir' (10,000 hectares) on fawn-coloured sand amid deep oak forests around Eauze, Nogaro and Aire-sur-l'Adour. Some experts consider armagnac from Ténarèze to be the finest, especially a well-aged Ténarèze with its strong perfume of violets, while the majority stand behind Bas-Armagnac, plummier in the nose and quicker to mature, though any controversy of this sort is liable to lead to fisticuffs, if not swordplay.

What all armagnac has in common, however, is the use of acidic, low-alcohol white wine (the humid Atlantic air currents are mostly responsible for this), which makes it perfect for distillation. The essential technique for making armagnac hasn't changed since 1818, when the Marquis de Bonas patented an armagnac still that permitted a single-pass distillation process as opposed to the two-step process formerly used (the two-step process is still used to make cognac).

Some time between December and April, when the wine has finished fermenting, it is distilled. This is a delicate process and two specialists known as *brûleurs* are called in to watch carefully over the still day and night to maintain a constant temperature. If the temperature becomes too hot then the brandy will taste harsh. If the temperature is too low then the brandy will be uneven (these days, however, gas burners have been installed to replace the wood fires, making the *brûleurs'* job much easier).

It is during distillation that the distinctive armagnac aromas are formed in their most embryonic forms, depending on the quality of the soil, wine, and distillation. Fresh from the still, the armagnac is a rough brandy with an alcohol content ranging from 58 to 63°. To soften it up, it is put in a 400-litre cask made from the dried heart of black oak from the forests around Monlezun and shut away in a darkened storeroom at a constant temperature. In the first ten years of ageing some 6 per cent of the brandy is lost every year through evaporation ('the angels' share') and is carefully

Meylanais have drawn out a little itinerary of them, posted in front of the *mairie*. The circuit includes the château and unusual Romanesque church of **St-Pau**, a small cromlech hidden in the pine woods, called Las Naous Peyros, and **Lac Sans-fond**. As the name implies, no one has yet found the bottom of this mysterious little lake. There are a number of legends: about the phantom that haunts it, and about the church that once stood on its bank; the lake swallowed it up one Sunday morning, parishioners and all.

Eauze and the Bas-Armagnac

South of Montréal, on the way to Eauze, on the D29, you'll pass **Lamothe** and its landmark, a three-storey medieval defence tower called the Tour de Lamothe.

replenished by distilled water; it's also at this time that the brandy receives its distinctive burnished golden hues, by dissolving the tannins of the wood. The tannins make the brandy bitter, although after three to ten years the bitterness gives way to the natural armagnac fragrance. After ten years it is transferred into old casks that no longer have any tannin. As no additives of any kind are permitted at any stage from grape to bottle, armagnac is advertised as the 'most natural brandy in France'.

To be sold as genuine 'armagnac' the brandy has to spend at least two years ageing in the oak cask; anything less is sold as an *eau-de-vie de vin du pays gascon* which is often ideal for the many recipes that call for dishes flambéed in armagnac, or served well-iced with smoked fish instead of vodka or schnapps, or drunk between courses of a meal as a *trou gascon*. The finest brandies are aged in oak barrels for up to 40 years, demanding continual attention and checking. When the head magician or *maître de chai* decides that the armagnac has at last reached its quintessential apogee of taste and finesse, further evolution is stopped by transferring it to glass vats or bottles.

Everywhere that armagnac is produced, you'll also find *floc de Gascogne*, the 'Flower of Gascony', an aperitif that has been made here since the 1500s and has recently started to become popular once more.

Essentially, *floc* is grape juice mixed with armagnac, but don't sniff – it has been strictly AOC since 1989, divided into the same three regions as armagnac. It follows similarly strict rules: after the addition of armagnac (which prevents the fresh juice from fermenting, setting the alcoholic content at 16 to 18°, the *floc* is aged for a year in oak casks. Fresh and fruity, it goes down quite well properly chilled in the hot months; *floc rosé*, made from merlot, cabernet sauvignon and cabernet franc grapes, is an especially good accompaniment to melons from Lectoure and sheep cheeses from the Pyrenees, while *floc blanc*, made from colombard, ugni blanc (saint-émilion) and gros manseng, is a favourite aperitif or dessert wine, especially good with a *tourtière* or slice of Roquefort cheese. Uniquely in France, *floc* owes its revival and success almost exclusively to women, who in 1980 formed the only French female wine confraternity (perhaps consorority is the proper word), the Dames du Floc de Gascogne. Their symbol is a bouquet of violets, roses and plum flowers – the traditional perfumes of armagnac.

Everyone in the Bas-Armagnac comes to the Thursday morning market at **Eauze**. A true *gros bourg*, as the French like to say, Eauze is the centre of the armagnac trade and the biggest agricultural market of the eastern Gers. Originally the capital of a Celtic tribe called the *Elusatii*, it was an important town in Roman and Merovingian times, with its own bishops. The Vikings trashed it thoroughly in one of their bold inland raids in the 840s, and nothing but *eau-de-vie* has come out of it since. The market takes place on the edge of the old town, in a delightful open place where the branches of the plane trees have been tied together to make a roof. A few blocks away in Place d'Armagnac, the tall brick church of **St-Luperc** dominates the centre, a rugged work of the 15th century. Facing it, a 15th-century half-timbered building bears a plaque marking it as the **Maison de Jeanne d'Albret**. Half the towns in Gascony have a house where Jeanne once slept, though it's a wonder they care to remember the nasty old bag; if she hadn't been Henri IV's mother they probably would have knocked the place down long ago. Today it houses the convivial Café Commercial, centre of all Eauze's comings and goings, with a rugby mural on the wall. The only other noteworthy thing about Eauze is its *war memorial*, which won fourth prize in a contest in the 1920s, back when every town and village in France was erecting one.

The big news these days is the **Eauze Treasure**, housed in a new museum of its own on Place de la République (***t** 05 62 09 71 38; open June–Sept 10–12.30 and 2–6; Feb–May and Oct–Dec 2–5; closed Jan, Tues and hols plus 1st weekend in July*). Discovered in 1985, this is the only ancient treasure in France saved in its entirety. Excavated from a prosperous Roman colony dating from the 1st to 4th centuries, the treasure consists of 28,003 coins and about 50 precious objects, including jewellery and statues.

Head east from Eauze and you will be entering one of the real empty quarters of the southwest. The scenery is pleasant enough, a typical Gersois landscape of oak forests and rolling hills, but there is nothing to detain you long in any of the area's scores of humble villages, or in its humble spa town, **Barbotan-les-Thermes**, where there is plenty of mineral-rich mud to help you with your rheumatism, varicose veins and gout; of course the Romans sojourned here too, though remains are few. Just outside the village, the **Lac d'Uby** is a small man-made lake with a sandy beach built in, along with water sports facilities. Barbotan has a simple Romanesque church, St-Pierre, and there are others to be seen in the neighbourhood, at **Panjas**, **Saint-Cane** and **Estang**.

A Dip into Les Landes: Labastide d'Armagnac

One little piece of the Bas-Armagnac has been left out in the cold, in the *département* of Les Landes; even so, the armagnac brandy produced around here is rated among the very best. At its centre, **Labastide d'Armagnac** is a bastide of considerable charm, one that has changed little since the Count of Armagnac, Bernard VI, and his liege lord, Edward I of England, got it started in 1291. There's little more to it than the central Place Royale, with its typical arcaded buildings, and a small grid of streets with many half-timbered houses; Henri IV spent some time here before he became king, and the locals claim their square provided the inspiration for the famous Place des Vosges Henri built in Paris. Labastide became a Protestant stronghold in the Wars of Religion, and where the D626 passes through the village stands the **Temple** (all Protestant meeting houses were called temples). This one, built in the 1600s before Louis XIV revoked the Edict of Nantes and put an end to religious tolerance, looks more like a barn. Today it houses a small **museum** (***t** 05 58 44 80 06. Call Mairie to visit; adm*) dedicated to bastides, the 'new towns' of the Middle Ages, and their role in building the southwest. Labastide also has the **Eco-musée de l'Armagnac** (***t** 05 58 44 81 08; open Mon–Fri 9–12 and 2–6, April–Oct also weekends 3–6; adm free*), dedicated to vines and spirits, naturally, but they also arrange nature trips around the surrounding countryside.

Just east of the village on the D626, bicycle fans will want to make their pilgrimage to **Notre-Dame-des-Cyclistes**, a small country chapel (*open daily 10–12 and 2–6*) that is the official sanctuary for France's bicycle racers.

Some of the other attractions in this region include **Saint-Justin**, a bastide only a decade older than Labastide, and **Villeneuve-de-Marsan**, the biggest village in the region, known for its fois gras markets in winter and for its restaurants. Anyone who ever gets just a little nostalgic for the *ancien régime* will enjoy a trip to the **Château de Ravignan**, near Perquie (***t** 05 58 45 28 39; summer visits Mon–Fri 4 and 5pm; winter Sat and Sun 3 and 5pm*). Begun in the time of Louis XIII, the château includes a collection of court costumes from the 18th century, period furniture and paintings. It's still in the family, but they'll take you around for tours of the house, formal gardens and *chais*.

Not to be outdone by the cyclists, the serene toreros of the Landes have created a chapel and museum dedicated to their art at Bascons, just southeast of Mont-de-Marsan, the **Musée et Chapelle de la Course Landaise** (***t** 05 58 52 91 76; open 15 May–15 Oct, Wed, Thurs and Fri 2–6*), with exhibits on the history of the sport and costumes.

Nogaro to Miélan: the Pays d'Artagnan

The biggest village in the eastern end of the Armagnac, **Nogaro** has plenty of brandy and foie gras, but likes better to dress up in racing colours and expound on the joys of speed – heady stuff, for a place where every day seems like Sunday and dogs are wont to sleep in the middle of the street. Nogaro started out as the Roman *Nogarolium*, but its current pride is its race track, the **Circuit Paul Armagnac**, which hosts a full schedule of events in summer. There's a school of race driving attached, with courses for beginners, and also a small airport where you can learn to pilot gliders and sailplanes. If that isn't why you came to the Gers, visit the town's entirely sedentary **church**, originally part of the monastery around which Nogaro grew up. Begun in the 11th century, it has some lively capitals (*Daniel in the lion's den, David playing a rebec*), delicately carved arcades in the courtyard, and a colourful window of the *Coronation of the Virgin*, claimed to be a work of Arnaut de Moles.

Espagnet and **Toujouse**, west of Nogaro, also have Romanesque churches; the people of the latter village have assembled a collection of old farm gear, furniture and such, called the **Musée du Paysan Gascon** (***t** 05 62 09 67 33; open June–Oct Daily 2–6*). South of Nogaro, you're heading towards the green **valley of the Arros**. The landscapes are a little wilder and emptier here, the villages fewer and smaller. From any height, you'll be able to see the taller peaks of the Pyrenees to the south; the further you go, the grander the panoramas. Most of this area produces armagnac, but it is also part of the Madiran AOC wine region (*see* p.209) – some vintners make both.

Termes-d'Armagnac takes its name from the Latin *terminus*; this village was the boundary between those Kilkenny cats, the Dukes of Armagnac and Viscounts of Béarn. Termes sits under a commanding height with a tremendous view, and naturally it had a strong castle, partly built by Thibaut de Termes, who fought alongside

Tourist Information

Nogaro: 81 Rue Nationale, **t** 05 62 09 13 30, **f** 05 62 69 06 79, *www.nogaro.fr. Open July and Aug Mon–Sat 9.30–12.30 and 2–6.30; the rest of the year Mon–Sat 10–12 and 2–6.*

Aignan: **t** 05 62 09 22 57. *Open July and Aug Mon–Fri 10–12 and 2–6; the rest of the year Mon–Fri 10–12 and 2–6.*

Termes-d'Armagnac: **t** 05 62 69 25 12, *www.tourdetermes.com. Open summer 10–7.30;winter Mon–Fri 2–6.*

Plaisance-du-Gers: 4 Rue Ste-Quitterie, **t/f** 05 62 69 44 69. *Open Tues–Sat 9.30–12.30 and 2–6.*

Marciac: Place du Chevalier, **t** 05 62 08 26 60. *April–Sept daily 9.30–12 and 2.30–8; the rest of the year closed Mon morning and Sat.*

Market days

Nogaro: Wednesdays and Saturdays.
Riscle (near Termes): Fridays.
Plaisance: Thursdays.
Miélan: Thursdays.

Where to Stay and Eat

Nogaro ✉ 32110

★★**Hôtel du Commerce**, in the village centre, **t** 05 62 09 00 95 (*inexpensive*). Basic but reasonably priced accommodation. *Closed Fri eve and Sat lunch.*

Auberge du Bergerayre, 10km south of Nogaro on the D25, in St-Martin-d'Armagnac, **t** 05 62 09 08 72, **f** 05 62 09 09 74 (*inexpensive*). A much nicer alternative, with a pool and also a small lake nearby. The restaurant offers a choice of menus and the *magret* with *cèpes* and foie gras is a treat. *Menus €19–34. Closed Tues and Wed plus Jan and Feb.*

Plaisance-du-Gers ✉ 32160

★★**Ripa-Alta**, Pl de l'Eglise, **t** 05 62 69 30 43, **f** 05 62 69 36 99 (*inexpensive*). In this small hotel in the village centre there's also a restaurant that's been a favourite in the area for decades, with complex cuisine. *Menus €14–34. Closed Jan. Closed Sun eve and Mon lunch from Oct–June.*

Ségos ✉ 32400

★★★★**Domaine de Bassibé**, **t** 05 62 09 46 71, **f** 05 62 08 40 15, *www.bassibe.fr* (*expensive*). If you really want to get away, you couldn't get farther than this hamlet in the western corner of the Gers, and the nine lovely rooms set in the various buildings of a former estate, all restored with taste and style. It's a bit expensive, but they have a regular clientele that doesn't seem to mind. The restaurant, set in what was once the estate's *chais*, serves up a very sophisticated cuisine with imaginative foie gras starters; good wines from nearby Madiran and Bordeaux. *Menu a la carte €43. Except for July and Aug restaurant closed Tues and Wed.*

Marciac ✉ 32230

La Petite Auberge, on the arcaded square, **t** 05 62 09 31 33. This is a popular spot for lunch, with a simple and filling four-course meal at a reasonable price. Go for the pricier menus if you want the duck. *Menus €10–30. Closed Wed eve and Thurs exc for July and Sept.*

Joan of Arc. Only one tower remains of it now, a striking landmark outside the village, and they have kitted it out as the **Musée du Panache Gascon**, with dioramas of historical scenes (*open June–Sept daily 10–7.30; closed Tues mornings; the rest of the year open 2–6*).

Just down the D3, **Tasque** had an important Benedictine monastery, until Montgomery's Protestant raiders torched it on Christmas Eve, 1570. The church remains, with a Romanesque portal portraying Christ in a mandorla. Inside is a weird, Celtic-looking cross, probably from as far back as Charlemagne's time. Note the old mechanical clock with its heavy weights. Though no longer working, it's one of the last survivors of its kind.

West of Termes on the river Adour, **Saint-Mont** has another old church worth a look, with some early, strangely carved capitals and scanty fragments of medieval painting. **Aignan**, set in the middle of some delicious countryside east of Termes, must be one of the most attractive villages in the Gers, and a major producer of armagnac, with plenty of old-fashioned cellars to visit in the hinterlands. The original seat of the counts of Armagnac, Aignan was wrecked by the Black Prince in 1355, but it retains its arcaded square and a good 12th-century church. Charles de Batz, the legendary D'Artagnan, was born at the **Château de Castelmaure** (privately owned) north of nearby Lupiac.

Plaisance and Bassoues

South and east of Termes, the countryside gradually rumples into the contorted topography of the Vic-Bilh (*see* p.208). **Plaisance-du-Gers**, little capital of the 'Pays d'Artagnan', hasn't done much for itself since the Black Prince burned it down on his 1355 tour. It's nice enough, but besides a few old half-timbered houses Plaisance's only monument is a ghastly Victorian Gothic church by one of the architects of Lourdes.

Just south of Plaisance, the D946 branches eastwards for Auch. It's a beautiful drive, a natural balcony with views of the Pyrenees in many places. At the end of the best part of the drive stands **Bassoues**, one of the most interesting of the Gers's many bastides. Bassoues was a strategic possession of the archbishops of Auch, who laid it out in the 1280s to accompany their strong **castle**, much of which remains today, including a stout 140ft **donjon** (***t*** *05 62 70 97 34; open July and Aug daily 10–7; April, May, June, Sept and Oct 10–12 and 2–6; closed Tues all of Jan; open the rest of the year weekends and Weds 10–12 and 2–5*).

Bassoues also has a 15th-century church, the old archbishop's palace, a wooden *halle*, and, out by its cemetery, the **Basilique Saint-Fris**. The crypt contains the relics of this obscure saint, really a warrior cousin of Charles Martel, who defeated the Arabs in a battle near Bassoues in 732, when the invaders were in retreat after the great battle of Poitiers.

Marciac, Monlezun, Tillac and Miélan

Continuing south from Plaisance, the D3, main drag of this corner of the *départe-ment*, takes you to the busy village of **Marciac**, a late 13th-century bastide that now stands the Gers on its ear each August with one of France's biggest jazz festivals, **Les Territoires du Jazz** on Place du Chevalier (*ring the tourist office for details*). Marciac is also known for furniture-making, and for the tallest **tower** in the Gers, the 293ft steeple of its church, a glorious 14th-century building with some good sculptural work inside.

The imposing landmark that is clearly visible from the D3 at **Monlezun** is that village's ruined **castle**, yet another casualty of the Hundred Years' War. It belonged to a certain Count Géraud of Pardiac, who was the brother of the powerful Count Bernard IV of Armagnac who after 1407 was the leader of the 'Armagnac' faction, siding with the king against the English. Suspecting Géraud of intrigues against him, he attacked the castle by surprise one night, capturing the unfortunate Géraud and his family.

Bernard then razed the place and starved all the Pardiacs to death. The locals like to joke that the surviving tall tower, sticking up like a finger, is Géraud's last, eternal gesture of defiance.

Next along the route comes **Tillac**, a little medieval jewel consisting of a pretty single arcaded street of half-timbered buildings and a 15th-century church, unfortunately partially destroyed by fire. Tillac grew up around a castle, of which only two defence towers remain. Just up the D16, **Laas** is nothing but a few houses on the site of a long-demolished château. The house was abandoned because it was haunted, but the ghosts stayed – and they've been puttering around at night for the last 300 years or so.

Miélan is another typical bastide founded by the Sénéchal de Beaumarchais, who planted scores of them around the southwest for the king of France, and who liked to name them after famous places. Just as Fleurance is named after Florence, Miélan was after Milan (the Sénéchal also founded Cologne and a Pavie – Pavia – near Auch). West of here on the N21 there is a famous viewpoint where you can enjoy a tremendous panorama over the Pyrenees, the **Puntous de Laguian**.

The Valley of the Gers: Lectoure and Fleurance

The eastern end of the Gers is a *pays* called the **Lomagne** that extends eastwards into the *département* of Tarn-et-Garonne. It is a country of knobby hills where both the roads and the little rivers such as the Arrats and the Auroue meander around, not in much of a hurry to get anywhere. The Lomagne is known for wheat and garlic (a third of all the garlic in France!) and not much else, but it does the best with what it has.

Lectoure

The French were often unkind to Lectoure. First they burned it down, and then they took away its ancient distinction as a capital by creating the *département* of the Gers and moving the seat of authority to Auch. Today the town (a population of 4,000 is enough to qualify as a town around here) has an aristocratic and somewhat forlorn air about it, sitting up on its lofty cliff with its monuments and its memories.

History

Lectoure occupies a strategic spot; an easily defensible site overlooking the Gers, it has always been the military key to Gascony. A Celtic tribe called *Lactoratii*, the first recorded residents, were famous for being one of the very few Celtic tribes to sit out the Gallic Wars, even going so far as to sign a treaty with the Romans. Collaboration paid off; the *Lactoratii* were the only Gauls to retain control over their affairs, forming a little republic under Roman protection with the blessing of Julius Caesar. Roman *Lactora* was one of the important cities of the southwest in Roman times, spreading down on to the plain from its original site; the old Celtic *oppidum* served as a kind of acropolis, with temples to Jupiter and Cybele.

Tourist Information

Lectoure: *mairie*, Pl de la Cathédrale, **t** 05 62 68 76 98, **f** 05 62 68 79 30. *Open April, June and Sept Mon–Sat 9–12 and 2–6, Sun 2.30–5.30; July and Aug Mon–Sat 9–12.30 and 2–7, Sun 9.30–12.30 and 3–7; the rest of the year Mon–Sat 9–12 and 2–5.*

Miradoux: **t** 05 62 28 63 08. *Open Tues–Fri 9–12 and 3–6.*

Saint-Clar: Pl de la Mairie, **t/f** 05 62 66 34 45. *Open Mon–Fri 10–12 and 2–6.*

Fleurance: 112 bis Rue de la République, **t** 05 62 64 00 00, **f** 05 62 06 27 80, *www.gascogne.com/fleurance. Open July and Aug Mon–Sat 9–6.30 also Sun 9.30–12.30; the rest of the year Mon–Fri 10–12 and 2–6.*

Market Days

Lectoure: Fridays.

Saint-Clar: Thursdays.

Fleurance: Tuesdays.

Where to Stay and Eat

Lectoure ✉ 32700

****Hôtel de Bastard**, Rue Lagrange in the centre, **t** 05 62 68 82 44, **f** 05 62 68 76 81, *www.hotel-de-bastard.com* (*inexpensive*). The best thing about staying in this hotel is of course sending a card home from it. The nobleman who built this stately town mansion in the 1700s may well have been a real bastard, but the current owners are actually quite amiable. The atmosphere is conservative French provincial and the rooms airy and tasteful. There is also a fine terrace with a pool looking out over the rooftops of Lectoure and even room for a small garden. In the restaurant, along with traditional Gascon fare on offer, the cooking takes some welcome detours, usually in the direction of Italy, with dishes such as *carpaccio* and lasagne with lobster. *Menus €14–54. Closed Sun eve and Mon Oct–Mar and also at Christmas.*

Bellevue, 55 Rue Nationale, **t** 05 62 68 80 06 (*inexpensive*). This place does indeed offer a *belle vue* from some of its rooms. The restaurant has a good menu with the accent on honest regional cooking. *Menus €11–18. Closed Mon in winter and Jan.*

Auberge des Bouviers, Rue Montebello, **t** 05 62 68 95 13. This is a happy place where the windows are full of flowers and the cooking is first class. *Menus €13–23. Closed Sun and Mon.*

Le Gascogne, 121 Rue Alsace Lorraine, **t** 05 62 68 77 57. This is a classic French establishment, with a pretty terrace, specializing in fish and wood-fire *grillades. Menus from €11. Closed Wed.*

Lectoure retreated back to the hilltop during the invasions that followed, but still suffered some rough handling from both the Visigoths and the Normans. During the Middle Ages, it became the capital of the counts of Armagnac, and remained so until 1473. At that time, France was beginning to recover from the Hundred Years' War, and King Louis XI took the opportunity to assert greater control over the south. His army attacked Lectoure, defended by Count Jean V in person. After a long siege, the two sides agreed on a peace by which the Armagnacs would recognize the authority of the king, and in turn the rights of both the Armagnacs and the town would be confirmed.

The French, unfortunately, were not being entirely truthful, and when Jean V opened the gates they immediately poured in, then sacked and burned the town. Their soldiers treacherously murdered the gullible count, and most of the population along with him. That put an end to the Armagnacs once and for all, and, as a result, to the independence of Gascony.

Louis XI rebuilt the city, and in the Wars of Religion Lectoure had the good sense to side with Henri of Navarre – the future Henri IV. As king, Henri and his son Louis XIII favoured Lectoure, but with the Revolution, and the dividing of France into *départements*, Lectoure lost out to Auch, and has dwindled in importance ever since.

The Musée Lapidaire

Lectoure's *mairie* occupies the old episcopal palace; underneath, in the bishops' cellars, the town has an excellent, recently redesigned **museum** (***t** 05 62 68 70 22; open Mar–Sept 10–12 and 2–6; the rest of the year the same hours but closed Tues and hols.*). The collection was begun a century ago, when workmen excavating underneath the cathedral discovered a score of Gallo-Roman *tauroboles* – funeral monuments in the form of altars, decorated with bulls' heads. These are remarkable, in that they are dedicated not to the usual gods of the classical world, or even those of the Celts, but to Cybele, the Great Goddess of Asia Minor whose cult became widespread in Gaul and the rest of the western Empire in the first three centuries AD. Translations of the inscriptions on the monuments have been posted (into French), giving a fascinating insight into life in ancient *Lectora*.

Along with them is an early Christian marble sarcophagus carved with vine leaves, typical of the fine work that was still being turned out in Aquitaine throughout the twilight of the Roman Empire. The museum also has on display an interesting collection of jewellery from Roman and Merovingian times, as well as bits of mosaics found around the town, including one labelled *Ocianus* – a very strange face, full of foreboding.

Upstairs in the *mairie*, you can ask to see the two rooms of memorabilia of Lectoure's two famous sons: Maréchal Lannes, who fought in the Napoleonic Wars, and Admiral Boué-de-Lapeyrère, navy minister during the First World War (he tried, unsuccessfully, to talk Winston Churchill out of the Gallipoli landings).

Another room houses a restored pharmacy and laboratory of the 18th century. Nearby on Rue Ste-Claire is a new **Centre de Photographie** (***t** 05 62 68 83 72; open daily July and Aug 2–7; winter 2–6; closed Mon)* with a wide variety of summer exhibitions.

Lectoure's **cathedral** is dedicated to Saint Gervais and Saint Protais, a very obscure pair of 4th-century martyrs in Milan; this suggests this church was around at a very early date, though most of its present incarnation was begun in 1488, as part of Louis XI's rebuilding programme. There is little of note inside the cathedral, only a small collection of religious paraphernalia – but if the sacristan is around, ask if you can go up the bell tower, for a view that takes in half the Gers and, on a clear day, the Pyrenees.

Failing that, the view from the **Bastion** on the eastern edge of the town is almost as good. Lectoure's old neighbourhoods, trailing on the slopes of the hill, are peaceful and lovely for walking, especially around **Rue de la Barbacane**. This quarter will show you a number of old convents, half-timbered houses and the 13th-century **Tour d'Albinhac**, part of a fortified town residence, of the sort that was more common in Italian cities at that time.

Into the Lomagne: Villages and Châteaux

Northeast of Lectoure, the D23/D953 is a pretty road for an aimless ramble; it passes through **Miradoux**, the first bastide founded in the Gers (1252), and **Flamarens**, a very picturesque village that has been saved from decrepitude by a number of private restoration projects in recent years. A perfect example of this is Flamarens magnificent château (*open July and Aug 10–12 and 3–7; closed Tues)* that was destroyed by a fire and has just completed a long programme of restoration. Some other villages of note in the vicinity are **Sainte-Mère**, west of Miradoux, with a well-preserved medieval castle, and, just to the north at **Rouillac**, a château built by another of the relatives of Pope Clement V (*see* La Romieu); and another bastide, **Dunes**, with a richly decorated 15th-century church. At **Plieux** the château has been superbly restored by the celebrated local writer Renaud Camus and it is now open as a **contemporary-art museum** (***t*** *05 62 28 60 86; open July and Aug Mon and Wed–Sun 3–7; rest of the year Sat and Sun 3–7*).

There are quite a few interesting châteaux that can be visited in this out-of-the-way region: the **Château de Lacassagne**, just outside Lectoure on the N21, was built by a grand prior of the Knights of Malta; the place is still in the family, and they occasionally open it up (*ask at the Lectoure tourist office*). Some of the rooms are reconstructions of halls at the Knights' headquarters in Valletta, Malta, decorated with a series of big paintings of famous episodes in the Order's history.

At **Gramont**, where the D25 crosses the river Arrats, the lovingly restored château (***t*** *05 63 94 00 08; open May–Sept daily 10–12 and 2–6; winter 2–6; closed Mon; adm*) is a fine example of a Gascon nobleman's house of the 17th century, complete with period furniture and tapestries.

And at **Terraube**, west of Lectoure on the D42, there is a mostly 16th- to 18th-century château (*closed Sat and Mon 10–12 and 3–7 in summer only*) that once belonged to a renowned warrior of the Hundred Years' War, Hector de Galard. This fine fellow lives on as the Jack of Diamonds in the French pack of cards (in France, all the face cards are representations of historical personages). Terraube also has a famous (or infamous) well – it was into this that Blaise de Montluc's merry men stuffed all the local Protestants, in one of the opening atrocities of the Wars of Religion.

For another Lomagne excursion, take the little unnumbered road south from Lectoure that follows the valley of the Gers. The road is marked for the Lac des Trois Vallées, a popular recreation area. Eventually it turns into the D45 and takes you to **Saint-Clar**, the garlic capital of the area. This singular village is actually made up of two separate bastides, each with its own arcaded square (one was laid out in the 14th century, but nobody could be bothered to build on any of the lots until five centuries later), as well as an original *castelnau*, which has a 13th-century church and a crumbling feudal castle as well as a later *faubourg*. To the north, the little church in **Saint-Créac** preserves some very early, Byzantine-style medieval frescoes. Just south of Saint-Clar, **Avezan** has a striking castle, which is currently under restoration, overlooking the Arrats.

Fleurance

Yet another bastide, one of the earlier ones (1272), Fleurance was also one of the few to grow into a real town. From the time of its prosperity, in the 18th century, there is an elegant ensemble of buildings around the central **Place de la Halle**, including the mairie, market-building, and a fountain with bronze allegories of the Four Seasons. The real reason for stopping, though, is three more stained-glass windows of Arnaut de Moles, as good as the ones in Auch cathedral and perhaps even more colourful. They are found in the **Eglise de Notre-Dame**, a Gothic church of brick and stone built mostly in the 14th-century – how they got it up in the middle of the Hundred Years' War is something of a mystery. The windows, in the apse, catch the eye as soon as you enter the church: on the left, St Lawrence, Mary Magdalene and St Augustine; in the centre, the Virgin with the Trinity; and on the right a wonderful 'Tree of Jesse' (a common subject in medieval glass, a genealogical tree showing the descent from Jesse of Mary and Jesus).

South of Fleurance, the N21 follows the river Gers closely on the way to Auch, the only distractions along the way being another restored 17th-century château, the **Château de Rieutort** near Roquelaure, and **Montaut-les-Crénaux**. This fortified village has only fragments of its walls and castle, but its 12th-century church of St-Michel survives intact, one of those rare Romanesque jewels you can find in out-of-the-way French villages. Not much has been changed in 800 years; the church still has its original stone altar, along with some fragments of Roman mosaics that were found in the vicinity and set up for safekeeping here.

Tourist Information

Valence: t 05 62 28 59 19. *Open Mon–Fri 9–12 and 2–6.*

Vic-Fézensac: t 05 62 06 34 90. *Open daily 10–12 and 2–7; closed Sun Sept–June.*

Lavardens: t 05 62 58 10 61.

Market Days

Vic-Fézensac: Fridays.

Where to Stay and Eat

Valence ✉ 32310

★★**Ferme de Flaran**, t 05 62 28 58 22, f 05 62 28 56 89, *www.gascogne.fr/hotels/ferme-flaran* (*inexpensive*). This restored farmhouse stands just off the D930 south of Condom, within easy walking distance of the abbey. There is a pool, and friendly management who are very dedicated to Gascony and its traditions, going out of their way to help visitors discover the region. This dedication also extends to the restaurant, where all the southwestern favourites you would expect turn up. *Menus €17–29. Closed Sun eves and Mon exc for July and Aug.*

Castéra-Verduzan ✉ 23410

Hôtel Ténarèze, t 05 62 68 10 22, f 05 62 68 14 69 (*inexpensive*). Halfway between Condom and Auch, this village offers an inviting stop for lunch or dinner. It's an old, family-run place, with a dozen pleasant rooms, and the family happens to have a very good cook. At its restaurant (confusingly under a different name, the Auberge Le Florida), t 05 62 68 13 22, both the lunch and dinner menus have a good range of seafood choices, some game (when in season) and of course the duck and foie gras. There is a good selection of local wines on the menu, too. *Menus €12–38. Restaurant closed Sun eve and Mon, exc July and Aug plus 1 week Feb/Mar. Hotel closed Nov–Mar.*

From Condom to Auch

The Abbaye de Flaran

t 05 62 28 50 19; open July–Aug daily 9.30–7; Feb–June and Sept–first week in Jan daily 10–12.30 and 2–6; closed last 3 weeks in Jan and hols; guided tours; adm.

Just south of Condom on the outskirts of the village of Valence, the Abbaye de Flaran was founded by the Cistercians in 1151. The great leader of this order, St Bernard of Clairvaux, never tired of preaching how beauty in architecture or decoration was nothing but worldly vanity, and this substantial complex is less remarkable for these than for the fact that nearly all of the monastic buildings have survived intact. The *département* has recently done a thorough restoration, and operates the complex as a cultural centre.

Though Cistercians did not care to dress up their buildings, they were hardly a lot of otherworldly mystics. Following the lead of St Bernard, one of the most mean-spirited ayatollahs in history, they did have two little weaknesses: money and power. In the order's golden age, the 12th century, they acquired vast lands across Europe, and used the most up-to-date agricultural methods to exploit them, while their leaders meddled in political and moral affairs everywhere. Bernard was the great enemy of Abelard and the universities, and Cistercians dedicated themselves especially to stamping out free-thinking wherever they could find it.

As such, they weren't warmly welcomed in the south, and, though Cistercians founded hundreds of monasteries across Europe, this is one of their few colonies in

Tourist Information

1 Rue Dessoles, **t** 05 62 05 22 89, **f** 05 62 05 92 04, *ot.auch@wanadoo.fr. Open Mon–Sat 9–12 and 2–6, Mon open at 10 plus Sun 10.15–12.15;July and Aug daily 10–12 and 3–6.*

Market Days

Saturday is the big market, but also Thursdays.

Where to Stay

Auch ✉ 32000

★★★★**Hôtel de France**, Pl de la Libération, **t** 05 62 61 71 71 (*expensive–inexpensive*). Few hotels in all of France have as many stories to tell. As the Armes de France it was a noted establishment 200 years ago. The Auscitains claim that no less a personage than the son of Louis XVI, the poor Dauphin Louis, was smuggled out of Paris during the terror and ended up here, working as a stable boy (until recently, his descendants still lived in the area, though no one took their claim to the throne very seriously outside the Gers). For all that, it is a thoroughly modern hotel, with luxurious rooms and amenities including a sauna. No pool, but they will arrange sports such as riding and golf out in the nearby countryside. *Open all year.*

★★★**Le Robinson**, just south of Auch, **t** 05 62 05 02 83, **f** 05 62 05 94 54, *www.hotelrobinson.net* (*inexpensive*). In a beautiful forest setting, this hotel has clean and stylish modern rooms with balconies and television.

★**Hôtel de Paris**, Av de la Marne near the train station, **t** 05 62 63 26 22, **f** 05 62 60 04 27 (*inexpensive*). This is a family-run, well-cared-for hotel. *Closed Nov.*

Camping Ile St-Martin, on the N 21 towards Tarbes, **t** 05 62 05 00 22. This site is well equipped and municipally run. *Open mid April–mid Oct.*

what was then Aquitaine. The **church**, begun in 1180, shows the restrained elegance common in the best Cistercian buildings, with simple arcading, and just a touch of stonecarving around the cornices and windows for decoration. It is always interesting to see how the medieval master masons responded to the Cistercian beliefs – a 'less is more' approach to architecture that many minds of that fertile age must have found wholesome and satisfying. Among the other buildings are an equally austere cloister, the main halls, a lovely **chapter house** built with some reused Roman columns, the refectory (dining hall) and library.

Around the Abbey

The Cistercians usually chose their sites well. The little river Baïse is navigable along most of its length, and this was an important trade route in medieval times. As another testimony to this, the area is littered with **castles**, usually in varying stages of ruination. Some of the better ones are at **Tauzia**, only a few kilometres from Flaran, across the D930, and further south at **Pardeilhan** and **Lagardère**. One of the largest can be seen at **Herrebouc**, overlooking the Baïse.

If you're passing by Tauzia you might also wish to stop in at the **Château-Monluc** at St-Puy, which is some 8km further east. This was the home of Blaise de Monluc, Maréchal de France under Henri II and less a fierce Catholic bigot than a simple soldier following orders. His spree in the 1550s, massacring Protestants wherever he could find them, contributed as much as anything to setting the tone for the Wars of Religion. Today the château is better known for the liqueur it produces: *Pousse-Rapier*, based on armagnac with an orange flavour; the vaulted *chais* from the 1500s are worth a visit.

Eating Out

Jardin des Saveurs, in the Hotel de France (*see* opposite), **t** 06 62 61 71 71. This famous hotel also claims the highest-rated restaurant of the *département*, with new chef Roland Garreau as accomplished as his legendary predecessor, André Daguin. The lunch menu goes for €25 with wine; otherwise you'll find *menus for* €11–14 in the brasserie, and €22–78 in the restaurant. And for that, they lay it on thick: the very best foie gras, perhaps with a hint of truffles, along with all the other natural delights of the southwest. Some of the dishes on offer are traditional favourites (it's a surprise to find *cassoulet* on the menu in such a place), others inspired flights of fancy. For accompaniment, they have probably the best cellar in the southwest. *Menus €22–78; try 4 different flavours of foie gras. Closed Sun eve.*

Claude Lafitte, Rue Desoules, **t** 05 62 05 04 18. Here is a champion of regional cooking and fresh local ingredients. You will get *charcuterie* and a Gascon favourite such as Henri IV's *poule au pot*; there are also formidable menus which are not to be entered into lightly. Menus €12–61. *Closed Sun and Tues eve plus all Mon.*

Hôtel de Paris, Av de la Marne, **t** 05 62 63 26 22. This hotel (*see* above) has an acceptable if unexciting restaurant. *Menus €10–18. Closed Sun eve and Nov.*

★★**Relais de Gascogne**, 5 Av de la Marne, **t** 05 62 05 26 81. This hotel-restaurant delivers good local cuisine such as *daube à l'armagnac*, *cassoulet*, duck and fish. *Menus €15–26. Closed end Dec–mid Jan.*

Le Chouan, Rue Mazagran, **t** 05 62 05 08 47. This choice offers a *plat du jour* and menus which often include seafood. *Menus €7–10. Closed Sun.*

Café Gascon, Rue Lamartine, **t** 05 62 61 88 05. After visiting the cathedral nearby, a good light lunch can be had here. *It closes Wed and Sun out of season.*

Vic-Fézensac isn't exactly on the way to Auch. It isn't really on the way to anywhere, and seems to know it. The biggest village and market of the area, it comes alive twice each year and only twice: for its bullfights, which take place around Pentecost, and for its popular Sulsa festival (*last weekend in July, call* **t** *05 62 06 56 66 for info*).

A Roman Mystery: the *Tourasses*

Rather than detour to Vic-Fézensac, you might wish to take a ramble through the countryside between **Biran** and **Saint-Lary**, to seek out the *tourasses*. These unusual towers, built of neat masonry and usually about 30ft tall, are a speciality of the Gers; the *département* has over a dozen of them, and the greatest concentration is here, on or around the Roman road that once ran up the valley of the Baïse. Nobody knows exactly what purpose the *tourasses* (as the locals call them) originally served. They may have been trophies, erected to commemorate some military feats, like the famous trophy of Augustus at La Turbie in Provence, or more likely they served some religious purpose. Nearly all of them have a niche for a statue, but since all the statues are missing we'll never know; Christians turned them all into shrines long ago. There is one on the opposite side of the D930 from Saint-Lary, off on a side road, and two others further west on the road to the hamlet of Lat Roque. Perhaps the best-preserved and easiest to find is just south of **Biran**, on the road to Le Mas on the eastern bank of the Baïse. Biran, built around its ruined castle, is an attractive village; its church has an enormous marble altarpiece, in the cold style of the age of Louis XIV.

If you're out looking for towers, though, you might bypass a genuine attraction on the other side of the D930. **Lavardens** looks to have been a serious and busy place long ago, a densely built fortified village on a lofty site. The castle attatched to it was a stronghold of the counts of Armagnac. Henri of Navarre captured it from the Catholics and destroyed it, but a century later a local nobleman rebuilt it as residential château. For a while this château belonged to the Marquis of Mirabeau, father of the famous Revolutionary orator; after falling into decay it has been completely restored (by a private society of '*amis du château*', like Flamarens and so many others in France) and is open for visits (**t** *05 62 58 10 61; open daily in July and Aug 10–7; April, May, June, Sept and Oct 10.30–12.30 and 2–6; the rest of the year 10.30–12.30 and 2–5; closed mid Jan–mid Feb; adm*). The best feature is the intricate pavements, done in patterns of different kinds of stone. Lavardens will do its best to entertain you; in summer the village hosts a competition for trainers of crickets, and another for the prettiest scarecrow.

Auch

Auch could be a lovely little town, if it wanted to. The metropolis of the *département*, with its 23,000 people, has all the ingredients: a pretty setting overlooking the river Gers, and a rather elegant core of monuments and squares inherited from the days when the town was run by its archbishops. Unfortunately, Auch seems to have no ambitions to be anything more than an overgrown farmers' market. The

Auch Cathedral

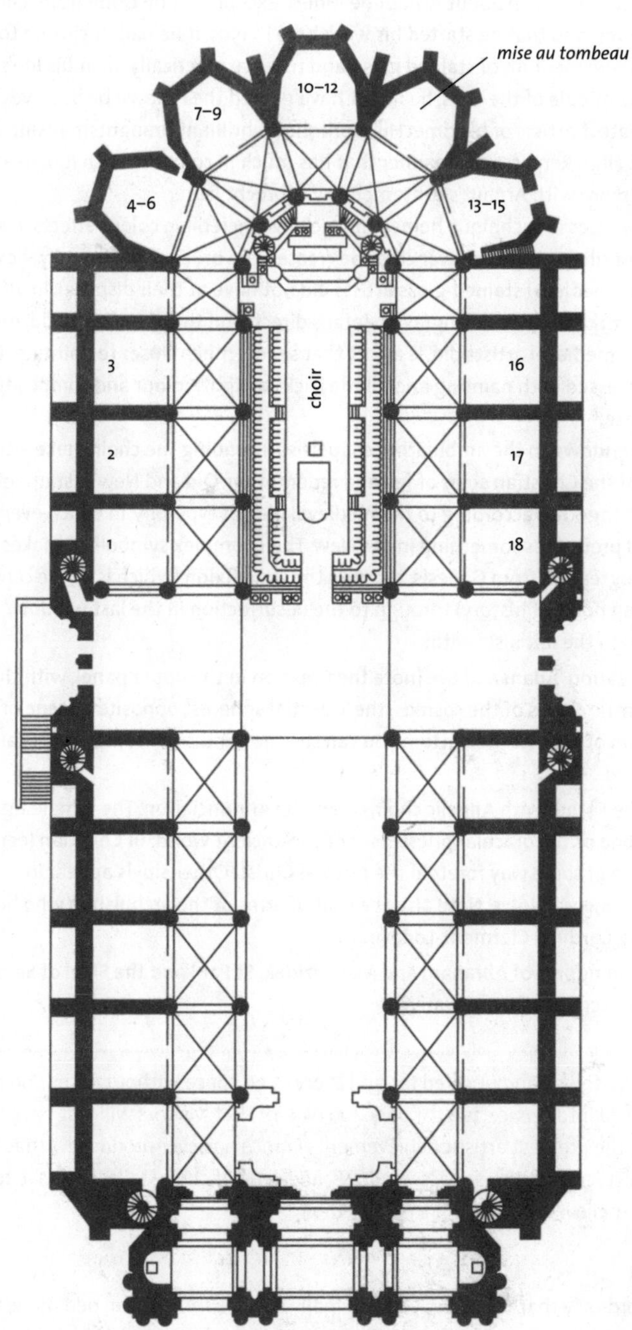

The Stained Glass (*see plan, previous page*)

Nobody knows much about Arnaut de Moles, except that he came from Saint-Sever in the Landes, and that he started his work here in 1507. If he hadn't chosen to work in the obscure medium of stained glass, and to leave practically all of his life's work here in the middle of the Gers, he might have gained the renown he deserves as one of the greatest artists of his time. His work shows brilliant draughtsmanship, in an Olympian High Renaissance manner that has much in common with Italian artists, and even more with Arnaut's contemporary, Albrecht Dürer.

New advances in technique helped him achieve incredible colour effects. A stain made from silver nitrite or silver chloride created the brilliant golds and yellows, something medieval stained-glass artists did not have at their disposal. In all, Arnaut's work, in which he engraved details directly on the glass with acid, much more than medieval artists did, is an art that seems much closer to painting, born of an age obsessed with painting and all the tricks of light, colour and composition it could create.

The 18 windows, in the ambulatory chapels surrounding the choir, make a complete account of the Christian story of fall and redemption. Old and New Testament figures are mixed together according to the medieval idea of typology, in which everything in the Old prefigures something in the New. Their complex symbolism makes a fascinating progression from Genesis, through the Crucifixion (which is at the centre as the turning point of history) through to the Resurrection in the last window.

It begins in the left aisle with:

1 The Creation, Adam and Eve (note the Creation in the upper panel, with the concentric circles of the cosmos, the 'celestial spheres', opposite a scene of the creation of Eve). At the bottom you can see the expulsion from paradise and Cain and Abel.
2 God the Father with Angelic choir, Noah, the Annunciation. The female figure is a sibyl, one of the oracular priestesses of the ancient world; in Christian legend each of these in some way foretold the birth of Christ. Other sibyls appear in succeeding windows. Note also the coat of arms of the archbishop who hired Arnaut, Cardinal Clermont-Lodève.
3 Graceful figures of Abraham and Melchizidek, St Paul and the Sibyl of Samos; below, sacrifice of Isaac, Nativity.

centre looks dowdy and uncared for, and every open space without exception has been pressed into service as a car park. Too bad for that: visitors will just have to settle for two of the greatest artistic achievements France has ever produced: Arnaut de Moles' spectacular stained-glass windows, and a set of choir stalls that have to be seen to be believed. Both are in the cathedral.

History

The records say that this town was originally called *Elimberris*, an odd name that suggests a Basque origin. When it first appears in history, though, it was inhabited by

4 The Virgin Mary with Old Testament prophets; in a medallion, portraits of the cathedral architect, Pierre de Beaujeu, and his wife.

5 Jacob, Jonah, St Mark; below, Jonah and the whale; a medallion portrait of Jean V, the last count of Armagnac.

6 Moses, a sibyl, Enoch; below, the burning bush, the sibyl of the Capitoline Hill with Emperor Augustus.

7 Joseph, St Andrew, Joel; below, Joseph sold by his brother.

8 Some charming angel musicians; above, Joshua, a sibyl, Amos; below, the flight into Egypt.

9 Caleb, Bartholomew, Abdias; above, the 'Holy Women' including Mary Magdalene.

10 Isaiah, St Philip, Micah.

11 The central window: Crucifixion, with St John and Mary Magdalene. This window, like the two flanking it, displays big *fleurs-de-lys* in honour of the King of France.

12 David, St James the Greater, in the costume of a pilgrim to Compostela, Azarias. The next chapel was originally the entrance to the sacristy, and hence has no window. It does, however hold a remarkable work of Renaissance sculpture, a *mise au tombeau* (entombment of Christ, a common subject in the 15th century); Joseph of Arimathea and Nicodemus hold the body, while St John, the three Marys and Mary Magdalene look on. Note the figures of the soldiers on the side, dressed in typical military costume of the 1500s. This work too is traditionally attributed to Arnaut de Moles, who was also a sculptor; no one knows for sure.

13 Jeremiah, a sibyl, Nahum; below, the flagellation of Christ.

14 Daniel, a sibyl, St Matthew; below, Daniel in the lions' den.

15 Sophonias, Elias, Uriah.

16 Esdras, Habbakuk, and an exceptionally lovely Tiburtine Sibyl. Here too are portraits of King Louis XII and former archbishops including Jean de Lescun.

17 More portraits, including the king's son, the future François I; Elisha, Judas and a sibyl; below, the crown of thorns.

18 Christ, flanked by a doubtful-looking Thomas and a believing Magdalene; below, the Last Supper. At the end, the artist signs off: 'On the 25 June 1513 these present works were completed for the honour of God and Our Lady. *Noli me tangere*. Arnaut de Moles.'

a Celtic tribe called the *Auscii*, and consequently it became known in Roman times as *Augusta Auscorum* (the *Augusta*, as in so many towns across the Empire, denotes a special sign of favour from Augustus or one of the later emperors; there would have been a ceremonial 'refounding' and renaming, perhaps accompanied by a new temple or amphitheatre or some such work, which would have been financed from Rome). Auch survived the Dark Ages by retreating up to the high ground around the cathedral and building a set of walls. After the Vikings had their way with Eauze in the 870s, the archbishops moved from there to Auch, and the town began to grow again. Though nominally under the suzerainty of the counts of Armagnac, it was the archbishops, and the town's elected consuls, who made most of the decisions during the Middle Ages. In fact the situation was far more complicated than that; in typically intricate and balanced medieval fashion, Auch was a schizophrenic three cities in one. The archbishops looked after the centre, around the cathedral; the counts and their vassals, for their part, took care of the settlement that grew up around their castle of Fézensac, now demolished; while a third nucleus appeared to the north, which was owned by the Priory of Saint-Orens – all three contained in an area of less than a square mile.

After the French crushed the Armagnacs and put an end to their dynasty in 1473, they wasted little time in occupying Auch. For the next three centuries it was ruled by *intendants* appointed by the king, and these added some gracious embellishments, including the Allées d'Etigny, a grand promenade of plane trees off central Place de la Libération. Since then Auch's destiny has mirrored that of the Gers as a whole: no economic activity to speak of besides farming and government, and probably about the same population as it had in the 14th century.

Cathédrale de Sainte-Marie

t 05 62 05 72 71; open April–Sept. 8.30–12 and 2–6. July and Aug open all day until 8.30. Oct and Mar. 9.30–12 and 2–5.

'A cathedral like this should be put in a museum!', Emperor Napoleon III is recorded as saying after a visit to Auch; we can only suppose that one of history's happiest philistines was intending a compliment. At first sight, though, this wonderful building is a bit disconcerting, with its strange façade looming over central Place de la République. This is one of the last cathedrals in France to be completed – not surprisingly, for such an ambitious work in such a small town – and the west front was not added until the 17th century.

The French would call the façade's style *classique*, which means lots of bits and pieces from Italian Renaissance style books pasted together every which way. The bits go together harmoniously enough; there isn't another façade quite like this one anywhere in the south of France. The façade has been recently cleaned, which has brightened up Auch substantially. Walking around the sides, you can see the flamboyant Gothic intent of the original architects, with impressive ranks of buttresses and arches, and an elegant apse.

Auch began its cathedral in the 14th century, but the work didn't really get rolling until 1463, under an archbishop named Jean de Lescun. Thus, despite its Gothic form, built on a plan inspired by the great cathedrals of the Ile-de-France, this cathedral is essentially a child of the Renaissance. When Renaissance ideas and styles really took root in France, in the early 1500s, Auch was fortunate to have another forceful archbishop, one who had travelled in Italy – and one who had access to some serious money; Cardinal Clément-Lodève was the brother of Georges d'Amboise, who at different times filled the offices of chief minister to King Louis XII, and papal legate to France. Under him, the most important features of the interior were begun, the choir and the stained glass.

The Choir Stalls

The choir is an unusual feature, completely enclosed as in a Spanish cathedral. It is usually locked, but someone is sure to be around with the key. Though worth seeing, the stalls are badly lit and you might find it handy to bring a torch. The entire space is filled with a set of 113 choir stalls, in which the monks of the cathedral chapter would celebrate the Mass. Made of heart of oak, soaked in water for fifty years to harden it and permit carving of the tiniest of details, this ensemble is one of the masterpieces of Renaissance woodcarving. It is also one of its most ambitious projects; two centuries ago, a monk of Auch tried to count all the figures on the stalls, and came up with over 1,500.

Elaborate sets of choir stalls such as this one were common enough in Europe in the 15th to the 18th centuries, but this one would be hard to beat. At first glance, expending so much time and talent on a locked-up place for monks to plant their behinds might seem a mad obsession, somewhat like making a model battleship out of toothpicks. But take this rather as an eccentric but glorious example of that Renaissance innovation: art for art's sake. These choir stalls took over fifty years to make, and many hands assisted in the work.

One theory has it that this was a special project of the *compagnie des sculpteurs* (like the masons, every other art and craft in medieval times was organized into a self-governing brotherhood); journeyman woodcarvers would make a trip as a kind of artistic pilgrimage, a *devoir de liberté*, and contribute some work to the whole. This would explain the wide range of styles in the work, and also the great freedom of subject matter. Unlike Arnaut's windows, and entirely contrary to the encyclopaedic, carefully thought-out decorative plans in earlier cathedrals, there is no grand scheme here, reflecting the truth of scripture and the organization of the cosmos. Rather, within limits each artist seems to have done as he pleased. Some of the works mirror the figures in the stained glass, which was under way at the same time; others represent other biblical personages or vignettes. Mythology is represented – even Hercules makes an appearance, slaying the giant Antaeus – and others are pure flights of fancy.

Unfortunately, none of the artists added much to their works that would clear up exactly who all these figures really are. Perhaps this was by design; certainly, this is one of the first – if not the first – great works executed for the Church in France where religious symbolism takes a back seat to pure artistic expression. The same monk who tried to count all the figures also attempted to identify them all. Though he did his best, the result is probably extremely unreliable. You can get a brochure with his guesses from the caretaker. At any rate, the main panels, above the seats, echo a motif of the windows, with pairs of male and female figures, beginning with Adam and Eve and continuing through sibyls, saints and and Old Testament figures.

The vast majority of the figures, however, are concealed among the magnificent carved Gothic traceries, on the arms or under the seats; you'll find something beautiful in every corner, or at least something that will surprise you or make you laugh. It will take two hours or so to look the thing over carefully. This is a wonderful place to bring children, and even for adults the endless details of the stalls make one of the best treasure hunts imaginable. See if you can find the *camel*, the *winged bulldog*, the *skeleton*, the *baby snake*, the *saw*, the *two-headed monk*, the *unicorn*...

The man with the keys will also let you down to see the **crypt**, where there is a 7th-century sarcophagus and a number of other relics from local saints, as well as the cathedral treasure, with plenty of old church bric-a-brac and busts of Henri IV and Marguerite of Valois. A different generation of woodcarvers, Parisians this time, contributed the cabinet for the great **organ**, a work of architecture in itself (1694).

The Monumental Stair

Auch turns its back towards the river Gers, as you will see if you come from Mirande or Comminges; just the same, this is its best face, with a quiet river-front boulevard (Avenue Sadi Carnot) and the **monumental stair**, built in the 1860s, leading down from the apse of the cathedral. There are 370 steps if you're going that way, and landings with a **statue of d'Artagnan** (Charles de Batz never would have dreamed...) and a bizarre modern work that consists of the story of Noah, in Latin, engraved in the pavement.

Also behind the cathedral you can see the striking 14th-century tower called the **Tour d'Armagnac**, one of the landmarks of the city and a proud monument for all Gascons. Unfortunately, the tower and the building to which it is attached, the Palais de l'Officialité, never belonged to the Armagnacs or had any connection with them whatsoever. Rather, they served as the offices of the archbishops of Auch, and their prisons.

South of the stair and the cathedral is one of the oldest neighbourhoods of Auch, the **Quartier du Caillou**, a forbidding tangle of narrow hillside street alleys that often turn into stairways. The locals call these old streets the '*pousteries*', a fittingly strange setting for a place that briefly was the home of Nostradamus. The wizard spent some time in Auch in the 1540s, and taught at the old Jesuit College on Rue de la Convention.

There's more life on the streets north of the cathedral. In Rue Dessoles, just off Place de la République, stands the lovely half-timbered **Maison Fedel** from the 15th century, which now houses the tourist office; one of the oldest houses in Auch, it leans in so many directions at once that it seems to be made of pastry. Rue Dessoles is the main street of the old town; at its opposite end are some walls and a tower, relics of the **Priory of St-Orens**, once one of the most powerful monasteries in Gascony.

Musée des Jacobins

*Place Louis-Blanc, **t** 05 62 05 74 79; open Tues–Sun 10–12 and 2–6 (closed Mon and hols exc July and Aug); adm.*

From here, heading down towards the river, find your way to Rue Daumesnil and the **Musée des Jacobins**, housed in a monastery that dates mostly from the 17th century. Founded in the middle of the French Revolution, in 1793, this is one of the best-run little provincial museums in France, even if the collections are a bit like grandma's attic; everything is atractively presented and good fun. The small archaeological rooms display some 1st-century frescoes from a Roman villa near Auch (in the 'late Pompeiian style', meaning still good, though the inspiration is wearing a bit thin), and a scant few relics from *Augusta Auscorum*, including a big statue of Emperor Trajan with a big Roman nose (any archaeological museum worth its salt has one of these: it's paradoxical, though, that one of the greatest and most intelligent of emperors should have been the most enamoured of financing statues of himself everywhere, all bigger than life). The epochs that follow offer a grab-bag of items: a number of medieval tombs and tombstones, including a fine Renaissance *gisant* of Cardinal Jean d'Armagnac, and some beautifully made musical instruments, such as a harpsichord from the time of Louis XV.

Holding pride of place among the museum's paintings are the works of a local boy named Jean-Marie Roumeguère, who seems to have specialized in sunrises, sunsets, and burning houses. The upstairs holds a large collection devoted to traditional Gascon crafts, with furniture, costumes, lace and samplers, an exhibit on the life of d'Artagnan, and a room with some lovely 18th-century faïence – Auch and Samadet (*see* p.94) in the Landes were ceramic centres at the time.

The museum is laid out to save the best and most surprising for last: a collection of pre-Colombian and colonial **Latin-American Art**, gathered by an Auscitain named Pujols who travelled over the continent for most of his life and then came home to run this museum. He brought back pottery, figures and fabrics from Teotihuacan and the other Mexican cultures, from Peru (including a statue of Manco-Capac, founder of the Inca dynasty) and from the Caribbean Indians. Some of the best of these works are 19th-century fakes, of which every collector must have picked up a few; here they have been proudly given a display case of their own. From after the Spanish conquest there is mostly naive religious art and folk crafts, such as some wonderful carved stirrups and a bolo from Argentina.

East from Auch: More Bastides, Castles and Foie Gras

Mauvezin, on the D928, grew into a town in the 13th century and has been dwindling ever since. A stronghold of Protestantism in the Wars of Religion, the town was known as 'Little Geneva' but still somehow managed to survive. Mauvezin's landmark is its **halles**, a stone and timber construction that has lasted since the 14th century. The town is Saint-Clar's redoubtable rival in garlic, and tries to keep its name in the headlines with the annual Garlic Festival, and the beauty pageant to select the Garlic Queen. **Cologne**, 10km to the east, doesn't have such an impressive market, but the centre of this bastide of the 1280s is one of the prettiest sights in the Gers: a typical square, surrounded by an ensemble of comfortable-looking old houses of brick and half-timber. The *halles* here may be smaller, but it is another fine example of traditional carpentry, built also in the 14th century; note the old standard measures, carved into the stone pillars that support it.

Tourist Information

Mauvezin: t 05 62 06 79 47. *Open July and Aug Mon–Sat 9–12 and 2–6 plus Sun 9–12; closed Wed; the same for the rest of the year but closed at 5.30.*

Cologne: t 05 62 06 99 30, f 05 62 06 77 30. *Open Tues–Fri 9–12 and 2–5 plus Sat and Sun am in July and Aug.*

Gimont: 83 Rue Nationale, t 05 62 67 77 87, f 05 62 67 93 61, *www.ot-gimont.com. Open Tues–Sat 9.30–12.30 and 2–6.*

L'Isle-Jourdain: t 05 62 07 25 57, f 05 62 07 24 81. *Open Mon–Sat 9.30–12.30 and 1.30–5.30; July and Aug 6.30.*

Samatan: t 05 62 62 55 40, f 05 62 62 50 26. *Open July and Aug daily 10–12 and 3–6; the rest of year 9–12 and 3–5; closed Sun and Tues.*

Market Days

Both Samatan and Gimont are famous for their *marchés au gras*, which are held from April to October, every Monday morning in Samatan and Sunday morning in Gimont. Samatan's may well be the biggest foie gras market to be found anywhere in the world, and it can be particularly frantic, especially in December. Half the foie gras in France disappears in the week between Christmas and New Year's Day; Paris alone gobbles up a staggering 2,000 tons of the stuff during the festive period.

Though great fun to watch, these markets are mostly intended for the pros – including some of the great chefs of the southwest, who send somebody to get the best right at the source – but if you happen to be around, you can pick one up too.

As for the regular weekly markets:

Mauvezin: Mondays.
Cologne: Thursdays.
Gimont: Wednesdays and Sundays.
L'Isle-Jourdain: Saturdays.
Samatan: Mondays.
Saramon (west of Samatan): Tuesdays.

Where to Stay and Eat

Mauvezin ✉ 32120

Auberge Cheval Noir, t 05 62 06 83 94. Typical country inn serving regional cuisine with a little twist. *Cassoulet de Cabecou* (goat cheese). *Menus €13–26. Closed Sun eve.*

Gimont ✉ 32200

★★★**Château de Larroque**, just east of the village on the N 124, t 05 62 67 77 44, f 05 62 67 68 90, *www.chateau-larroque.com* (*expensive–moderate*). The château is a stately country house of a century ago, set in an enormous park. A Relais et Chateaux member, it offers plenty of peace and quiet, a pool and tennis, and an excellent restaurant (but it's one of the most expensive places in the Gers). The kitchen is fittingly distinguished. In the capital of foie gras, you can be sure of getting the best, and the restaurant here does quite a lot of it, in salads, or in unusual combinations with *cèpes* or even oysters. There's also a memorable *daube* with scallops and crayfish. The cellars are more than well stocked. *Menus €22–49. Oct–May closed Mon and Tues eve plus Nov.*

L'Isle-Jourdain ✉ 32600

Hostellerie du Lac, near to the lake, t 05 62 07 03 91 (*inexpensive*). Pretty bedrooms, a swimming pool, and a restaurant with a huge shady terrace. *Menus €11–35. Closed Sun eve Sept–June.*

★**Hôtel du Centre**, t 05 62 07 00 23 (*cheap*). A venerable choice. *Closed Oct.*

Puits Saint-Jacques, Pujaudran, 7km along the N 124, t 05 62 07 41 11. Set in a restored medieval stable with a pleasant terrace, this restaurant is very good for seafood. It is well known for the *écrevisses*, or river crayfish, that are one of the favourite dishes in the Gers. *Menus €20–76. Closed Sun eve and Mon, except hols, 22 Feb–10 Mar and 28 Aug–10 Sept.*

Just 5km east of Cologne, just over the border in the Haute Garonne, you can visit the grand Renaissance **Château de Laréole** (*t 05 61 06 33 58; open 10–6 Wed, Sat, Sun in May and June; daily July and Aug; Sat and Sun only in Sept, free*), recently restored and opened to the public. Begun in 1579 by Pierre de Cheverry, son of a great Toulouse pastel merchant who went on to fame and fortune as the treasurer of France, it was finished in only three years thanks to the tremendous sums at his disposal. The Wars of Religion were raging, so defence was an important consideration – hence the four towers and moat – yet style wasn't overlooked, either, most strikingly in the stone and brick stripes that decorate both the exterior and central courtyard. Unfortunately the original furnishings are long gone, but there's an exhibition on the history of the château and its owners over the centuries. You can also visit the surrounding park, laid out in the 18th century according to the geometric theories and perspectives of Le Nôtre; although neglected in the last century, it too is being restored to its original form.

The N124 stretches from Auch into the furthest eastern reaches of the Gers, passing through **Gimont**, another distinctive bastide and one of the centres of the foie gras trade. The village's church of Notre-Dame possesses a Renaissance triptych of the crucifixion. East of here, both the countryside and the villages begin to change. We're entering the valley of the river Save, whose waters flow almost to Toulouse before they find their way into the Garonne. Toulouse isn't far away, and the *Ville Rose* shows its influence in the predominantly brick churches and buildings of villages like **L'Isle-Jourdain**, the biggest centre of the region. L'Isle's history is wrapped up with the ancient family of the same name, who took on the 'Jourdain' because one of their members was baptized in the Jordan, while his parents were off in the First Crusade. Cardinal Richelieu, who made the guidebook writer's job considerably easier by knocking down hundreds of castles around France (to decrease the chances of rebellion among their noble owners), got rid of L'Isle's, but one of its towers suvives as the bell tower of the brick church of **Saint-Martin**. The *halles* is brick too, and now houses the **Musée Campanaire** (*t 05 62 07 30 01; open mid June–mid Sept 10–12 and 2.30–6.30; winter closed at 5.30; closed Tues*), devoted to bell-ringing. There is a handsome bridge over the Save, built just outside town in the 12th century.

Twelve km southwest on the D39, the **Château de Caumont** (*t 05 62 07 94 20; open May, June, Sept and Oct weekends and hols 3–6; July and Aug daily 3–6*) was built in the late 16th century by a favourite of King Henri III. Outside, the château looks all business – the memory of the Wars of Religion was still warm when it went up – but inside you'll find one of the most luxurious mansions in the southwest, complete with some wonderful rooms redone in the mock-medieval style of the Victorian era (*open July–Aug daily 3–6; otherwise call* **t** *05 62 07 95 87*).

At Caumont, you are already halfway to the next village, **Samatan**, the real foie gras capital of the Gers. Nothing much here is very old, partly because the Black Prince smashed up the place in 1355, and partly because Samatan is really only the successor to a truly old and somewhat peculiar place, **Lombez**, just 2km down the D632. Lombez was an important settlement for a very long time. Remains from the Celts and even earlier have been found here, and the town enjoyed prosperity as the Roman *Lumbarium*. From the Middle Ages until 1789 it was the seat of a bishopric; Petrarch stopped in to visit a cleric friend of his in the 1330s. From then, it has all been downhill. Lombez today is left with some 1,200 people, and the brick **Cathédrale Sainte-Marie** (*for info call Lombez tourist office* **t** *05 62 62 37 58*) topped by an attrac-

It Looks Potentially Wonderful, But What Does One Do With It?

Such is the common reaction of the uninitiated to a foie gras in its natural splendour. So we'll tell you. Wherever you get a chance to purchase a fresh foie gras (goose or duck), at a market or even better, from a farmer, look for one that is firm, and light in colour with a touch of pink to it – not yellowish. Don't worry about the size. Once you've got it home, carefully cut out all the blood vessels and bile ducts as well as you can, along with any greenish bits. Then soak it overnight in water with a bit of vinegar (1/4 cup).

The next day, dry it well, and sprinkle it all over with salt and pepper (and maybe a little armagnac). If you want it *au naturel*, now wrap the foie up tightly in a thin cloth, cover with foil and put it in the refrigerator (very cold, but not freezing) for 3–5 days. Some people like it just like this, sliced into very thin medallions and served well chilled. Others cook it in a sealed jar immersed in boiling water; one hour per kilo, or proportionately less according to weight. *Mi-cuit* ('half-cooked') seems to be the favourite way throughout the southwest. This can mean roasting it in a medium oven in a sealed container with a half-inch of water in it, for a half-hour or maybe more (don't overcook it; as soon as the inside is good and hot it's done). Or else, get yourself a mess of goose fat (*graisse d'oie*, which the same farmer can probably supply), melt it down and cook the foie gently in it for about ten minutes. This way, you can store the cooked foie in a canning jar, covered with the fat used in cooking. It keeps for a long time in the refrigerator, and you can use the fat to make a *tourin* or fry potatoes.

The great chefs of the southwest worry themselves endlessly, thinking up clever new recipes for foie gras. But hardly anyone else here does; they're perfectly happy to eat it on toast, or to put it in a proper *salade composée* with thin slices of *magret* (or *magret séché*) or *gesiers* (gizzards), or maybe all three, along with lettuce, oil and vinegar – and, most importantly, a sprinkling of hazelnut oil. Everybody has their own variation and their own name for this kind of salad; throw in what you like. Another simple and traditional way of doing foie gras is to slice it (before cooking) into thin escalopes, dust with flour and fry gently in oil. Then put aside and use the same pan to fry some sliced potatoes. If the grease from the foie gras isn't enough to do this, add some *graisse d'oie*. (Face it; if you mean to get serious about southwestern cooking, you're going to be keeping a jar of goose fat in the back of the refrigerator. The family will eventually get used to it.) Serve the potatoes with the *escalopes de foie gras* arranged on top. Or instead of potatoes, after the *escalopes* are cooked add some white grapes to the pan (with a little armagnac), and cook for about 5 minutes, and then serve with the foie – this is a favourite in the Landes.

tive bell tower in the style of Toulouse's St-Sernin. Inside, copying Auch's cathedral, there is a fine set of stained-glass windows, said to have been done by followers of Arnaut de Moles, and a set of carved wooden choir stalls to match. The church *trésor* has some items that go back to the 13th century.

South of Auch: the Astarac

In this gritty, homespun *pays*, the landscapes are a continuation of the jumbly Pyrenean valleys just to the south. A row of no fewer than eight rivers, each about 5km from the next where they enter the *département*, flow in from the mountains, spreading out like a fan across the Astarac; the roads from east to west go up and down like rollercoasters.

Mirande, the little capital of the Astarac, is a rarity in the Gers: a bright little metropolis of 4,000 souls with an evident civic pride – a place that, though not in any hurry, seems to be going somewhere. In 1994 the women's basketball team were French champions. The town is now becoming famous for its country music festival. Yet another typical bastide, with its straight streets and arcaded square (graced with a Victorian bandstand), Mirande is a lovely place to stroll around. The main street is closed to traffic; here you will see the town's most notable embellishment, the spire of the Eglise Sainte-Marie, supported by a flying buttress and arch that crosses over the street. Inside, there are some good stained-glass windows from the early 16th century. Just around the corner, Mirande has proudly opened a tiny **Musée des Beaux-Arts**, on 13 Rue de l'Eveche (***t** 05 62 66 68 10; open Mon–Sat 10–12 and 2–6; closed Sun and hols; adm*), with a collection of paintings and ceramics.

Tourist Information

Mirande: 13 Rue de l'Evêché, **t** 05 62 66 68 10, **f** 05 62 66 78 89/87 09. *Open all year Mon–Fri 9–12 and 2–6, Sat 10–12 and 3–6 plus Sun in July and Aug 10–12.*

Simorre: Rue de la Mairie, **t** 05 62 65 36 34.

Market Days

Mirande: Mondays.

Seissan: Fridays (also a big *marché au gras* from October to April).

Where to Stay and Eat

Mirande ✉ 32300

★★Hôtel des Pyrénées, Av d'Etigny, **t** 05 62 66 51 16, **f** 05 62 66 79 96 (*moderate–inexpensive*). A very gracious establishment but a good bargain, with a pool included, and for dinner you won't do better anywhere else south of Auch: a wide choice of menus from *€14 (lunch) to €35*. It's perhaps worth paying a little more for dishes like the *tournedos de canard* or *bœuf en croûte*. There's also a good choice of Madiran and local wines.

Europ-hôtel Maupas, at the northern edge of town, **t** 05 62 66 51 42 (*inexpensive*). There are nice rooms and a more than ample *€12 menu*, which may include duck or possibly grilled salmon. *Open daily all year.*

Camping de l'Isle du Pont, just outside town on the N21, **t** 05 62 66 64 11, **f** 05 62 66 09 86, *www.camping-l'Isleduport.com*. Gîtes and chalets plus a number of activities. Canoes, pool, tennis and kids' club. Tent and caravan park. *Open April–Sept, chalets and park open all year.*

Grand Café, on the main street. This old-fashioned place packs them in for its *€9 plat du jour*.

Pizzeria Lo Squadro, on the main street. Decent and cheap pizza and pasta dishes.

Masseube ✉ 32140

Hôtel du Parc, **t** 05 62 66 00 32 (*cheap*). Set in this cheerful bastide, just south of Seissan, this is a good example of what you will find in the hardly touristed wilds of the Astarac: cheap rooms, people glad to see a genuine novelty like you, and a *€10 menu* you'll find nothing to complain about. *Menus €10–22. Closed Mon and Jan.*

If you like Mirande you may be inspired to press further into this region of narrow, exasperating roads, minuscule villages and plenty of forests; there are some modest but beautiful surprises, such as **Montclar-sur-Losse**, on the D159 just west of Mirande, nothing more than a château and a church lost in the trees, but a corner of France that sticks in the memory. Everything further west is described above (*see* pp.124–7); if you're going east, get out the magnifying glass and look on the map for **Belloc Saint-Clamens**, where there is a rare early Romanesque church, substantially unchanged in 900 years. **Seissan**, another foie gras village, is south of Auch along the river Gers; the windows in the old church (there are two) are attributed by the locals to Arnaut de Moles, but we have our doubts. There are better ones from the same period at **Simorre**, where the very interesting church of the early 1300s was once part of a Benedictine abbey. Viollet-le-Duc, the famous restorer of Paris's Notre-Dame and Carcassonne, fixed up Simorre too, and it is to him we owe the leering gargoyles and much of the other sculptural detail.

The Pays Basque

08

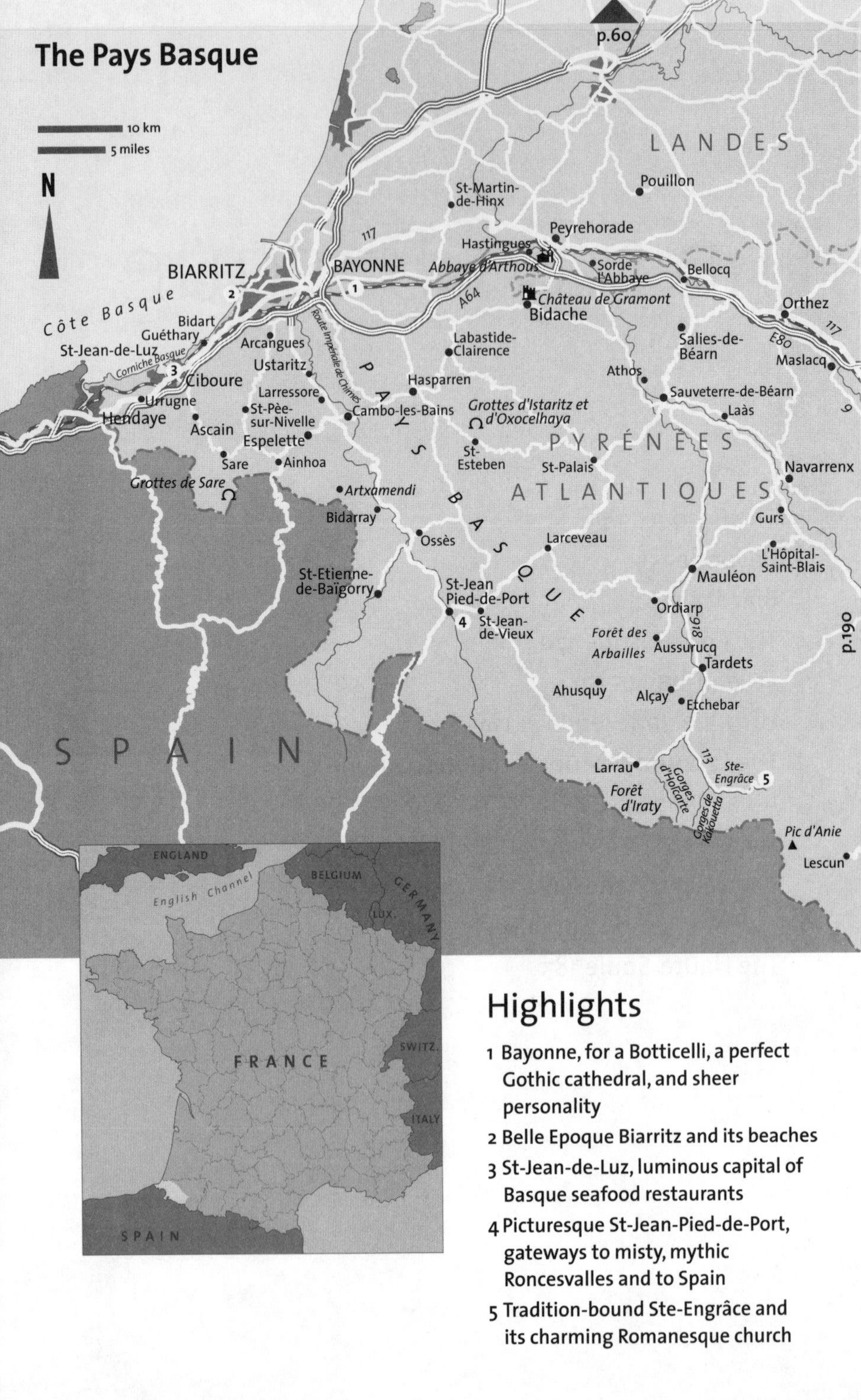

Highlights

1 Bayonne, for a Botticelli, a perfect Gothic cathedral, and sheer personality
2 Belle Epoque Biarritz and its beaches
3 St-Jean-de-Luz, luminous capital of Basque seafood restaurants
4 Picturesque St-Jean-Pied-de-Port, gateways to misty, mythic Roncesvalles and to Spain
5 Tradition-bound Ste-Engrâce and its charming Romanesque church

Of all the *départements* of France, number 64 is the one with the most remarkable split personality. Béarn, occupying the eastern half of the *département*, is a resolutely Gascon province redolent of garlic and castles and good Jurançon wine; it has personality enough of its own, discussed on pp.189–218. But cross the Gave d'Oloron, a national boundary that does not appear on any map, and you're entering an entirely different world: specifically, the land of the Basques, Euzkadi, the oldest nation of Europe. You'll know you're there when you find a village with a *fronton* (*pelote* court) in the middle, one where the shop signs are packed full of 'z's and 'x's, and where everything except the dogs and cats is painted red, white and green. Those are the eternal colours of the Basque flag, which waves proudly over the autonomous Basque provinces across the border in Spain, but is discouraged by the authorities over here. Three of the seven traditional provinces of Euzkadi are in France, laid out in vertical stripes across the western half of the Pyrénées-Atlantiques *département*: first, the coastal Labourd (from *Lapurdum*, the Roman name of Bayonne), a delightful land full of beautiful villages, which also includes Bayonne and Biarritz where Basques have long been a minority; next, inland, the Basse-Navarre, with Pyrenean valleys in the south and hardworking farmers in the humble lowlands; and finally the even humbler Soule, around Mauléon.

One doesn't visit the Basque country to see the sights, which are few and far between. The real attraction is the Basques themselves, a taciturn though likable lot, and their distinctive culture and way of life. The setting also helps to make the trip worthwhile, emerald landscapes that have been well tended by the same people for millennia (and well they should be emerald; the Basque country gets as much rain as the west of Ireland). The Basques' tremendously long but thoroughly uneventful history is covered in **History**, pp.5–16, but to really appreciate this world-in-itself, here is a brief primer in things dear to Basque hearts, from *ttoro* to tombstones.

The Basques

Language

Want to impress your hosts with a few words of Basque? Go ahead and try it! The Basques point out with great pride that their language is not only Europe's oldest, but by far the most difficult. There are four distinct dialects, and in each the grammar is Kafkaesque, to put it mildly. Verbs, for example, can vary according to the gender of the person you are addressing. The vast number of grammatical tenses includes not only a subjunctive, but two different potentials, an eventual, and a hypothetical. But grammatical complexity permits beauty and economy; you can express anything in Basque in far fewer words than in most other languages.

Basque is maddeningly, spectacularly indirect. For example, to say 'I am spinning', comes out *Iruten ari nuzu*, or literally, 'In the act of spinning doing you have me!' Or try out this proverb: *Izan gabe eman dezakegun gauza bakarra da zoriona*. 'Having without, give (*Izan gabe eman*), we can (*dezakegun*), one thing only is (*gauza bakarra da*), happiness (*zoriona*)' – 'happiness is the only thing we can give without having'.

Pronunciation, thank God, is not such a problem; it's phonetic, and there are only a few letters you need to know: **e**, as long 'a'; **u**, as 'oo'; **j**, as 'ee'; **s**, as something halfway between 's' and 'sh'; **tz** or **z**, as 's'; and **x**, as 'sh'. Pronounce all the vowels, and don't make any soft consonant sounds; practise on the village of Azcoitia (ahsko-IT-ee-ah). One of the peculiarities of the language is its habit of doubling words for effect, unknown to any European tongue but common among the Polynesians. In Basque, something very hot is *bero-bero*; a glutton makes *mauka-mauka*, and when a Basque walks on all fours this is called *hitipiti-hatapata*. Like eskimos, who know no generic word for 'ice', the Basques have no word for 'tree' or 'animal'. And being the democratic folk they are, there is no word for 'king' either – they had to borrow one from the French and Spanish potentates to whom they were forced to pay taxes.

In all the Basque lands, on average only a third of the inhabitants still speak their language. Owing to the severe cultural oppression in Spain under Franco, the percentages are much higher on the French side: 72 per cent in Basse-Navarre and 60 per cent in the Soule. But following the example of the Catalans in Spain, Basques on both sides of the border are actively promoting their own language in the schools, with some success. It's important to remember that Basque is a living literary language, the centrepiece of a living culture. The plays known as *pastorales*, possibly descended from medieval mystery plays, are still written and produced at festival times, and Basques pay great reverence to the *bertsulari*, poets who have memorized a vast repertoire of traditional pieces and who are also skilled at improvisation.

The Basque Cuisine

Basques know how to eat. Go into a village restaurant at nine in the morning on a market day, and watch the boys tuck into their three-course breakfasts – soup, tons of meat, fish and potatoes, with a gallon or so of wine for each. Fortunately for them, the Basques also know how to cook. Their distinctive cuisine will be one of the delights of your visit to the Basque country, and your one chance for something piquant in France, a nation pathologically disdainful of anything too spicy. Like the Greeks, the well-travelled Basques took their culinary skill with them everywhere. Basque restaurants turn up in unlikely places all over France, and it isn't unusual to drive through a dusty, one-horse town out in the American west where the only restaurant serves up good Basque home cooking.

Not surprisingly, Basque cooks exert most of their talents on seafood. Marseille has its *bouillabaisse*, among a score of other exotic and treasured fish stews of southern Europe, but the Basques stoutly maintain that their version, called *ttoro* (pronounced tioro), is the king of them all; naturally there is a solemn *confrérie* of the finest *ttoro* chefs. A proper one requires a pound of mussels and a mess of crayfish and congers, as well as the head of a codfish and three different kinds of other fish. They say the cooks of St-Jean-de-Luz and Hendaye make the best ones; St-Jean holds an annual *ttoro* festival with a competition and *dégustation* in early September. Currently, a very popular dish is *piquillos aux morue*: skinned red peppers stuffed with a purée of cod, potatoes, butter, parsley and a little garlic. Other seafood delights include *thon basquaise*, fresh tuna cooked with tomatoes, garlic, aubergine and spices.

Another icon of the kitchen is the red pepper, the *piment d'Espelette*; Basque housewives still hang strings of them on the walls of their houses for drying (and for decoration). Some of these go into *piperade*, the relish of pepper, tomato, egg, ham and garlic that can accompany almost any Basque dish. Milder peppers turn up everywhere: in omelettes, or in the common stewed chicken, *poulet basquaise*. Other treats, made the old-fashioned way, include the *pur brebis* sheep cheese from the Pyrenees, the best in France, and the famous Bayonne ham, which is hung for over a year; it has a strict set of rules and an *appellation contrôlée* status like fine wines.

As for drinks, there is AOC Irouléguy wine from the Pyrenean foothills, and plenty of special herb liqueurs, from home-made specialities you'll find in restaurants to Bayonne's famous green Izarra. The Basques are also fond of good hard cider. They claim to have taught the more famous cider-makers of Normandy and Asturias their secrets long ago, and back in the 1500s Basque fishermen used to trade the stuff to the American Indians for furs.

Folklore

The Basques are not alone. In fact, their long intimacy with their land has forced them to share it with an unreasonably large number of gods, demons, spirits and fairies, creatures of one of the richest mythologies of Europe. Many tales are connected to the dolmens and other Neolithic monuments that grow so thickly on the mountains here; often their names connect them to Mari, the ancient Basque great goddess. The dolmens were built by the *jentillak*, the race of giants that once lived side by side with the Basques. The *jentillak*, often a great help to their neighbours, invented metallurgy and the saw, and introduced the growing of wheat. One day a strange storm cloud appeared from the east, and the wisest of the *jentillak* recognized it as an omen and interpreted it as the end of their age. The giants marched off into the earth, under a dolmen (still visible in the Arratzaran valley in Spanish Navarre). One was left behind, named Olentzero, and he explained to the Basques: 'Kixmi [Jesus] is born and this means the end of our race.' Olentzero lives on today, as the jolly fat doll or straw figure prominent in the Basques' celebrations of Christmas and New Year's Day.

Other familiar creatures include the *laminak*, originally small female fairies with a capacity to help or harm, now a sort of leprechaun that gets blamed for everything that goes wrong. And where mythology fades off into nursery-lore we have the 'man with the sack' who comes to carry off naughty children, and a large bestiary with jokes like the elusive *dahu*, a kind of lizard with legs shorter on one side – the better to walk the Pyrenean slopes. Along with the myths goes a remarkable body of pre-Christian religious survivals, including rituals that lasted well into the 20th century; many old Basques in isolated villages can remember festivals with Midsummer bonfires in their childhood. If you'd like to learn more about this bottomless subject, an excellent introduction is the *Petit Dictionnaire de Mythologies Basque et Pyrénéenne* by Olivier de Marliave (Editions Entente).

Basques are passionately fond of music, whether it's choral music at Mass (which they do extremely well), Basque rock (rare, perhaps fortunately), or traditional tunes played on the *dultzaina*, a primitive bagpipe, and a flute called the *txistu*. Dozens of traditional dances are still current, and small groups in many villages keep them up; you'll have a chance to see them at any village fête.

Basque Accessories

No old Basque gentleman would be complete without a beret (most of which are made in Béarn), and a walking stick, or *makila*. These are taken very seriously. Made out of seasoned and dried medlar wood, they are exquisitely carved and decorated with silver trim. By tradition, there is always a coin built into the *makila*, and each one will usually carry an inscribed motto, such as *hitza hitz* – 'one's word is one's word'. If you want one to take home, the best place is the 200-year-old family firm of **Ainciart-Bergara**, in the village of Larressore, or else the **Fabrique de Makilas** on Rue de la Vieille Boucherie in old Bayonne – but they don't come cheap. With a striking, healthy inclination for combining beauty and utility, Basque artisans excel at the simple things of everyday life: furniture and woodcarving, and especially embroidered linens. *Linge basque*, whether factory-made or woven on an old wooden loom, may be your best bet for a beautiful and practical souvenir.

Basques have their own distinctive style of 'discoidal' or round-headed tombstone. Archaeologists have dug up some models 4,500 years old, and they've been using them ever since. The earliest ones often had human figures, sun symbols or other symbols carved on them; since the coming of Christianity the stones usually show crosses. You will see them in any churchyard, usually turned south so that the sun shines on the carved face all day.

One thing the Basques are very good at is houses. There's nothing in the southwest as pretty, simple and functional as a traditional Basque *etche*, or cottage, with its distinctive long, low gable along the façade, and half-timbering and shutters – inevitably painted deep red or green, of course (really more maroon than red, a colour called 'bull's blood'). Originally this was a simple farmhouse, where the lower storey was a wine cellar or given to other farm business; examples of these, some 300 or 400 years old, can still be seen in many villages. One particularity of the older houses, here and in neighbouring Béarn, is the carved lintels over the main door, with the year and name of the builder, accompanied by odd symbols or a sententious inscription. In the last century these houses evolved into the modern Basque villa. The style became extremely popular throughout France in the 1920s and '30s, and you'll see versions of it with a bit of Art Deco trim in suburbs everywhere.

Sporting Life

The real national sport, of course, is smuggling. But the Basques love to play, and over the millennia they have evolved a number of outlandish games that are unique in the world. Many of these are based on pure brute strength, the celebrated *force basque* that provides a major element of the national mystique. One can imagine them, back in the mists of time, impressing each other by carrying around boulders – because that's what they do today, in a number of events generally called the *harri altxatzea*, literally stone-lifting. In one, contestants see how many times they can lift a

500lb stone in five minutes; in others, they roll round boulders around their shoulders. Related to this is the *untziketariak*, in which we see how fast a Basque can run with 100lb weights in each hand. They're fond of the tug-of-war too; they probably invented it. Besides these you will see them at village festivals pulling loaded wagons, racing with 200lb sacks on their shoulders, or chopping huge tree trunks against the clock. Don't fool with these people.

The miracle is that at the same time they could develop a sport like *pelote*, the fastest ball game in the world. Few sports in the world can offer an image as beautiful and memorable as the *pelotari* in his traditional loose, pure white costume, chasing down the ball with a long, curving *chistera*. *Pelote* takes a wide variety of forms, but the basic element is always the ball: a hard core, wrapped tightly with string and covered with hide – like a baseball, only smaller and with much more bounce; in a serious match this ball can reach speeds of 150 mph. The oldest form of the game is *rebot*, played without a wall. This is done bare-handed; other versions, played in an outdoor *fronton* (court), may be bare-handed, with a leather glove (*pasaka* or *joko garbi*), or with the *chistera*, made of leather and osier, which enables a player to scoop up the ball and fling it back in the same motion. Whatever the game, it usually requires teams of two players each. The ground in front of the wall is marked off in *cuadros* every 4m from it; to be in, a ball bounced off the wall must usually hit between the 4th and 7th *cuadros*, if it is not returned on the fly. Games are usually to 35 points.

Every Basque village has a *fronton* as its principal monument, usually right in the centre. On some village churches from as far back as the 1600s you can see how the architects left one smooth blank wall to accommodate the game. Besides the *fronton*, the game may be played in a covered court (*trinquet*), or one with another wall on the left side, a *jaï-alaï*, in which case the game is called *cesta punta*, the fastest and most furious form of *pelote* (thanks to Basque emigrants this has become a popular sport around the Caribbean).

If you want to get in a little action yourself, you might try to talk your way into it at any village *fronton* when they're practising (they'd be charmed), or else contact the Fédération de Pelote Basque at the Trinquet Moderne in Bayonne, *60 Av Dubrocq*, ***t** 05 59 59 22 34*; they set up training courses in summer for beginners. As for getting in on the gambling aspect of *pelote* – go ahead and throw your money away if you want to. A list follows of towns where you're likely to see a match in summer; matches take place at least once a week, but times and days change, so ring the local tourist office to ask for the most up-to-date schedule. Towns include: Anglet, Ascain, Biarritz, Bidart, Cambo-les-Bains, Guéthary, Hasparren, Mauléon, St-Etienne-de-Baïgorry, St-Jean-de-Luz, St-Jean-Pied-de-Port, St-Palais, St-Pée-sur-Nivelle and Sare.

In addition, there are games indoors year-round in the *trinquets*: at Bayonne, in the Trinquet St-André; at St-Jean-Pied-de-Port, in the Trinquet Garat; and usually something at the weekends in St-Jean-de-Luz.

Most of the big championships are held in July and August, often in Biarritz or St-Jean-de-Luz. *Force basque* competitions are usually held in July and August; many villages put something on for Basque Sports Week, the second week in August; the big festivals are at St-Palais (late August) and St-Etienne-de-Baïgorry (mid-July and early August). Bayonne has a bullfight season in August and September.

Nationalism

Basque nationalism is hardly a recent phenomenon. In its modern version, it started in the 18th century, with a community of liberal bourgeois in Bilbao and the other outward-looking port cities of Basque Spain; these supported Enlightenment thinkers such as Manuel de Larramendi, who developed a concept of Basque nationhood based on language and tradition. Throughout the 19th century, nationalist thought and the development of Basque culture proceeded apace in Spain, while at least on the political side it ran into a stone wall in the much more repressive climate of France. French Euzkadi thus became a sideshow to main events, while in Spain, the PNV, the first Basque nationalist party, controlled a majority of the region's parliamentary seats from 1917 on. Franco's rule was a catastrophe for the Basques: over 100,000 prisoners and 200,000 exiles after the Civil War, including the entire intelligentsia and political leadership. Resistance groups did not start forming until 1952. ETA (Euzkadi ta Askatasuna, or Basque Homeland and Liberty) was founded in 1959. Its bombing campaign near the end of Franco's reign was singularly effective – notably when they blew the car carrying Franco's successor, Carrero Blanco, over the roof of a Madrid church. In the new Spain the Basques got all they wanted: full autonomy and the right to their language and culture; this left ETA out in the cold as a band of die-hards demanding total independence. That did not keep them from continuing their terror tactics up until the present day, with help and safe havens among the Basques over the border in France.

A few years ago, when the French government started cracking down on ETA operatives and sympathizers, the organization responded by bombing Renault dealerships around Spain. They've stopped that, which suggests somewhere a deal has been cut. France may be a democratic country, but in affairs like this we know as little of what goes on as we do about political factions in China. ETA does seem to be on its last legs – widespread disgust among Spanish Basques at terrorist tactics have made them pariahs in many circles, and the organization was conspicuously silent in Spain's magic year of 1992.

Though most French Basques decided long ago that being French wasn't so bad after all, there are in fact plenty of nationalists; hang around for a while and you'll meet them. The police watch over them and manipulate them silently and skilfully. This is something at which the French have had centuries of practice – all over the Midi, as well as in Brittany, Corsica and the colonies – and they're extremely good at it, probably the best in the world. Basque nationalism within France, such as it is, is also not an issue that the media are often permitted to emphasize. We met one nationalist supporter, a young mechanic on his way to a ping-pong tournament. With an earnest look in his eyes, he told us: 'They'll never let the Basque lands unite, because together we would be stronger than either France or Spain.' A marvellous people, bless them.

Bayonne

Arthur Young, the famous English traveller of the 1780s, called it the prettiest town he'd seen in France. Young had a good eye; even today, Bayonne is as attractive and lively an urban setting as you'll find in the southwest. Despite a remarkable history, a majestic cathedral and a delicious medieval centre full of brightly painted old half-timber buildings, Bayonne doesn't attract much attention these days, lost as it is in the sprawling conurbation that includes Biarritz, the ports and industry of Boucau and the bedroom community of Anglet. Nevertheless, if you enjoy good cities or if you need a break from the beaches, spend a day in Bayonne.

History

Bayonne began in the 3rd century AD as a Roman *castrum* called *Lapurdum*, home to the cohort that guarded *Novempopulania*. Nothing, however, is heard from it until the booming 12th century, when it adopted its present name and grew into an important port town. From the beginning, Bayonne was not Basque but in fact a predominantly Gascon town; the two peoples have been getting on well enough ever since. From 1151 until 1452, the English ruled Bayonne. As in Bordeaux, it was an arrangement enjoyable to both sides; Bayonne gave the Plantagenets a strong base at the southern end of their continental empire, and the town enjoyed considerable privileges and freedom, not to mention a busy trade with Britain. At the same time, the intrepid Basques began sailing around the Atlantic in (as any reader of *Moby Dick* knows) the world's first whale fishery. They taught whaling to the Dutch, who taught the English, who taught the Massachusettsans.

All that ended when King Charles VII marched in at the end of the Hundred Years' War. Not long after, an even bigger disaster hit – the River Adour suddenly picked itself up and moved to a new bed, leaving the port high and dry. But Bayonne, close to the border with Spain, was important to the French; in 1578 they sent down engineers to dig a canal and redirect the Adour, and the port was back in business. A century later, Louis XIV dispatched his famous military engineer, Vauban, to make Bayonne an impregnable stronghold; the sprawling, state-of-the-art fortifications he designed, along with the Citadelle, are a striking feature of the cityscape even today.

Bayonne's military vocation flourished in the 18th century. An armaments industry grew up and gave the world the word 'bayonet', while Basque and Gascon corsairs, with letters of marque from the king, sallied out to snatch what they could from the Spanish, the English and North Africans. Besides weapons, the city's other passion was sweets. Jewish refugees from Spain introduced chocolate to Bayonne in the 1600s, and Louis XIV and his courtiers spread it across France when the king passed through on his way to marry the Spanish infanta in 1659. Bayonne's *chocolatiers* gradually built up a reputation as the best in France – there are still quite a few in the old town who keep up the tradition. Two of the best are Daranatz and Cazeneuve, both located under the arcades of the Hôtel de Ville. (Back in the 17th century, incidentally, chocolate was thought of only as a drink, and a century later a Basque pirate captain

named Sopite thoughtfully provided something to sprinkle on top – bringing the first cinnamon to France from Sumatra in a daring trip ordered by royal command in the middle of a war; his ship, *La Basquaise*, met five English vessels on the way home and beat them all.)

Bayonne lost its status as a free port, and most of its trade, with the Revolution, and there were more troubles to come. Vauban's walls proved their worth in the

Napoleonic Wars. Coming up from Spain, Wellington's army twice besieged the city, in 1813 and 1814; they took it on the second try, by stringing a bridge of ships across the Adour and dragging artillery across it to bombard the city from both sides. Recovery came only with the arrival of the railway from Paris in 1854. Industrialization proceeded apace after that, and now Bayonne's little jewel of a historic centre is wrapped in the 'BAB' (Bayonne, Anglet, Biarritz), a metropolitan area of over 100,000 people, counting Biarritz and smaller towns.

Grand Bayonne and the Cathedral

Bayonne's main street is a river, the little Nive, and it is one of the most delightful centerpieces a city could ask for, lined on both sides with busy quays and old tall houses with trim painted in bright colours (mostly red and green, but no prizes for guessing that). The Nive also marks the division between the two old quarters of the walled town, Grand Bayonne and Petit Bayonne. The former is the business end, jammed with animated, pedestrian-only shopping streets.

Cathédrale Ste-Marie

t 05 59 59 17 82; open Mon–Sat 10–11.45 & 3–5.45, Sun and hols 3.30–5.45. No visits during services.

One of these, narrow Rue Argenterie, will take you from the quays to Bayonne's landmark and symbol, the **Cathédrale Ste-Marie**. It is also a symbol of the coming of French control – one of the few examples of the northerners' Gothic style in the southwest, and certainly one of the best. Begun in the 12th century, most of the work was done in the 13th. Some was still going on in the 1500s, when the south tower went up, and the arms of the King of France were added to the sculptural decoration of the portal in honour of Bayonne's new rulers. Throughout, the building was largely financed by Bayonne's whalers. The bishops exacted a tenth of the profits from them, also claiming 'by divine right' the most prized parts of each whale for themselves – the tongue and the fat; nobody really knows what they did with them. Despite all the city's loot from cetaceans, piracy and chocolates, however, the cathedral still wasn't finished until the 1800s, when followers of Viollet-le-Duc oversaw a thorough restoration and added the matching north tower.

So far from the Ile-de-France, and so long in building, it isn't surprising that there are no unusual stylistic departures here. What is surprising is how well it all fits together. Best of all, it still enjoys the sort of setting a Gothic cathedral should have – among narrow streets and tightly packed tall buildings, where its presence and verticality can make exactly the impression its designers intended.

Individual details worth calling attention to are few; this cathedral was thoroughly trashed in the Revolution. Inside, there's no need for detail; the rise of the slender pilasters that carry the rib-vaulted nave permit a lofty interior that no church in the southwest save the Jacobins in Toulouse can match. There is some good Renaissance stained glass in the nave windows, heavily restored a century ago. Note the scene of Adam and Eve, where the serpent (with a female head) wears the bonnet of a medieval doctor of philosophy – just to show what a subtle argument she was

Getting Around

Bayonne is a stop along the main **rail** line from Paris through Bordeaux and down to the Spanish border. There are plenty of trains along this run; most of them also stop at Biarritz. There will be a few TGVs each day; and these also stop in Biarritz (contact SNCF information in Bayonne **t** 05 59 55 20 45, Biarritz **t** 05 59 50 83 07). Other lines from Bayonne go up the Gaves to Orthez and Pau in Béarn, and down the valley of the Nive to St-Jean-Pied-de-Port.

There is a parallel and equally convenient **bus** service down the coast run by the ATCRB line, **t** 05 59 26 06 99 – about a dozen a day from Bayonne and Biarritz to St-Jean de Luz and Hendaye, and buses for San Sebastian, Spain, on Tues, Thurs and Sat.

Public transportation in the Bayonne-Biarritz area is run by an aggressive-sounding line called STAB (info and tickets: Bayonne, Pl du Géneral de Gaulle, **t** 05 59 59 04 61; Biarritz, Av J Petit, **t** 05 59 24 26 53; Infobus provides information on all local services, **t** 05 59 52 59 52). Regular city buses connect the two cities, from the Hôtel de Ville in Bayonne to the Hôtel de Ville in Biarritz – line 1 or 2, or faster, the Express BAB. Biarritz's SNCF **station** is far from the city centre; the no.2 bus terminates here.

The no.6 bus from Biarritz goes to the city **airport**, the Aérogare de Parme, **t** 05 59 43 83 83, with four or five flights a day from Paris Orly with Air France, **t** (08) 20 82 08 20, and three a day from Charles de Gaulle. Ryanair, **t** 05 59 43 83 93, flies daily from London Stansted.

Tourist Information

Pl des Basques, **t** 05 59 46 01 46, **f** 05 59 59 37 55, *www.bayonne-tourisme.com*. Culture website *www.ville-bayonne.fr*. Ask them about their guided historical tours of the city. *Open July and Aug Mon–Sat 9–7, Sun 10–1; the rest of the year Mon–Fri 9–6.30, Sat 10–6.*

Market Days

Markets are held on Monday to Saturday mornings in Les Halles and all day on Friday. Place des Gascons holds a market on Wednesday and Saturday mornings; Quais de la Nive has one on Tuesday, Thursday and Saturday mornings; Rue St-Catherine has one on Friday and Sunday mornings; and Polo Beyris holds one on Friday morning.

Where to Stay

Bayonne ✉ 64100

If you're not too concerned about proximity to a beach, the animated streets of Bayonne might make a nice, cheaper, alternative to staying in Biarritz.

capable of. In the left aisle, the **Chapel of St Jerome** has one of the best windows (1531), a scene of the Canaanite woman (from Matthew, 15:22) crowned by a salamander, the symbol of King François I. The **sacristy** shelters the only original 13th-century sculptures that survived the Revolution: one tympanum of the Last Judgement, with the Devil boiling a king and a bishop in his cauldron, and another of the Virgin Mary, surrounded by angel musicians. This leads to a lovely **cloister**, also much damaged in the Revolution.

Château-Vieux

Just behind the cathedral, on Rue des Gouverneurs, the **Château-Vieux** was the city's stronghold and the seat of its governors: first the English (parts of what you see are from the 12th century; one of the governors was the Black Prince), and then the French (the outworks were added in the time of Louis XIV to guard against revolts by the Bayonnais).

★★★**Best Western Grand Hôtel**, 21 Rue Thiers, **t** 05 59 59 62 00, **f** 05 59 59 62 01 (*expensive–moderate*) All the city can offer in terms of luxury; it is bland but stately.

★★**Hotel Ibis**, 44–50 Bd Alsace-Lorraine, Quartier St-Esprit, **t** 05 59 50 38 38 (*inexpensive*). A functional chain hotel with a small garden and a restaurant. *Open all year.*

★**Des Arceaux**, 26 Rue du Port-Neuf, **t** 05 59 59 15 53 (*inexpensive–cheap*). One of the best options, near the cathedral. *Open all year.*

★**Monbar**, 24 Rue Pannecau, **t** 05 59 59 26 80 (*inexpensive*). Well kept little hotel on a lively street in Petit Bayonne, across the Nive. *Open all year.*

Eating Out

Like other cities of the coast, Bayonne does much better with restaurants than with hotels. Many of the best inexpensive places can be found in Petit Bayonne, either on the quays along the Nive or in the back streets behind them.

Le Cheval Blanc, Rue Bourg Neuf, just round the corner from the Musée Bonnat, **t** 05 59 59 01 33, **f** 05 59 59 52 26. At the top of the heap, by popular acclaim. Even though the Tellechea family has been running this place for a long time, they never get tired of finding innovative twists to traditional Basque cooking: stuffed squid or *poulet basquaise* with *cèpes*. *Menus €23–60. Closed Sun eves and Mon except in Aug. Closed 1st week in July and 4–18 Feb.*

Francois Miura, 24 Rue Marengo **t** 05 59 59 49 89. A stylish small restaurant with modern furniture and contemporary paintings, specializing in fish dishes. *Menus €19–30. Closed Sun eves and Wed.*

The Bayonnais, 38 Quai des Corsaires, **t** 05 59 25 61 19, **f** 05 59 59 01 33. Traditional Basque restaurant in the old town, with décor dedicated to local sporting heroes. *Closed Sun in winter. Closed Mon in July and Aug.*

Le Petit Chalut, **t** 05 59 25 54 60. A hole-in-the-wall on Quai Galuperie. It offers fresh seafood on a set *menu*: grilled fish or *thon à la basque*. *Menus €17–22. Open daily all year.*

Hotel Loustau, 1 Pl de la République, **t** 05 59 55 08 08, *www.hotel-loustau.com*. Comfortable, well run hotel, overlooking the Pont St Esprit and the Ardour. *Menus €17–25. Restaurant closed Sun eves in winter.*

Hotel Paris-Madrid, Pl de la Gare 64100 Bayonne, **t** 05 59 55 13 98. A little bit different: a family run hotel with most rooms looking over a quiet courtyard, creating a little peace in the middle of Bayonne. Decorated throughout with paintings and murals contributed by all members of the family. A bit worn but colourful, clean and reasonably comfortable for the price. *€28. Closed for Xmas and weekends in winter unless you phone ahead.* The owners speak English.

Though usually closed to visitors, the tours organized by the Syndicat d'Initiative will take you through here, and also through the amazing expanses of underground chambers that underlie much of the city, some of them as properly vaulted as the cathedral's aisles. In medieval times they were used for storing wine.

Petit Bayonne

The smaller but livelier side of Bayonne, this is a *rive gauche* on the right bank of the Nive. The narrow back streets of Petit Bayonne are crowded with popular neighbourhood bars and restaurants – you won't see the likes of an old, unspoiled city neighbourhood like this in many places in southwest France. Right in the middle, on the Quai des Corsaires, is the **Musée Basque** (***t*** *05 59 46 61 90; www.musee-basque.com; Open May–Oct 10–6.30; Nov–April 10–12.30 & 2–6; open Tues–Sun all year; Closed bank hols*). This 16th-century building facing the Nive started out as a convent, and later did long service as a customs house. In 1922 the city of Bayonne took it over as a museum that gradually turned into the largest collection of objects on Basque culture and folk life anywhere. Recently modernized and reopened after a long absence, the collection includes over 100,000 items covering every aspect of Basque life with interactive displays, from agriculture to seafaring, with special sections on the old Basque talent for wood and stone carving, religious and folklore traditions, and modern Basque art. The Museum's special exhibitions are held in the Château Neuf (*see* p.161).

The Musée Bonnat

5 Rue Jacques Laffitte, **t** *05 59 59 08 52, www.musee–bonnat.com, open Wed–Mon 10–12 and 2.30–6.30pm, Fri until 8.30, closed Mon and hols; adm.*

Bayonne's own Léon Bonnat was one of the best-known salon painters of late 19th-century France, the sort of happy Philistine who got rich painting celebrity portraits, collected prizes and medals, and sneered at the Impressionists when he served as a judge in the Salon competitions. When he died, in 1922, Bonnat left his own considerable collection of art to Bayonne, and it has become the nucleus of one of the finest museums in the southwest.

Some of Bonnat's work takes pride of place in the museum's main hall: portraits of shiny bankers and blooming society ladies in corsets – another world. There's a portrait of Puvis de Chavannes, by Bonnat, and one of Bonnat himself – done by Degas, of all people. If you want to do the museum chronologically, however, start upstairs, with the late medieval and early Renaissance works the French, ignorantly and infuriatingly, still call 'primitives'. Besides works of *quattrocento* masters Domenico Veneziano and Maso di Banco, there are some obscure delights: a Christ and Virgin of the Toulouse school, better than most of their work you'll see in any churches, and a number of Catalan-Aragonese paintings from the same age, with the Catalan love of extreme stylization and rich gold backgrounds. As always with this art, the works range from the really excellent, such as the *Saint Martin* of the unknown 'master of the Musée Bonnat', to some that are almost *naïf* – a bit of precocious Diego Rivera with halos and gold leaf.

There is a fine *Madonna* by Botticelli, from the late period when the artist renounced his magical mythological works and lapsed into extreme piety. It didn't always work; this one, despite the Christian trappings, is still plainly Botticelli's *Venus*. From the late Renaissance and Baroque there are some good Flemish tapestries, two El Greco portraits, and an entire room devoted to Rubens.

Almost all the great schools of 17th- and 18th-century painting are represented here. Standouts include a Murillo, *Daniel in the Lions' Den*; a bit of chilly militarism from the time of the Thirty Years' War in Jan Bronkhorst's portrait of *General Octavio Piccolomini*, and an equally disturbing, untitled painting by Ribera of a distraught girl combing her hair. This work, in its weird intensity, seems to prefigure Goya, and there are some Goyas here in the museum to compare it to, including a fascinating self-portrait.

There's no telling whose face is going to turn up on the walls of this museum. Among the English paintings you will see Lawrence's portraits of the composer Karl Maria von Weber and Johann Heinrich Füssli – better known as Henry Fuseli, crazy painter and friend of William Blake. Ingres, one of the spiritual fathers of salon painting, was understandably a favourite of Bonnat's; among ten of his works here is an unspeakable portrait of the unspeakable last Bourbon, King Charles X.

An important part of Bonnat's collection was the 36 works by his friend Antoine Barye, the most popular sculptor of his day. Nearby, not always open, is the *cabinet des dessins*, a collection of almost 2,000 drawings and prints from the Renaissance up to the 20th century. Down in the basement is the museum's archaeological collection. Many of these works were Bonnat's: Greek pots and Roman glass, votive reliefs, and lovely statuettes of various goddesses that caught the painter's fancy.

Château-Neuf

***t** 05 59 59 08 98; open June–Sept 10–6.30; winter 10–12.30 and 2–6; closed Mon exc July and Aug.*

On the eastern edge of the walls, the Château-Neuf looms over the town, a stronghold begun in 1460 by the French to consolidate their control over the city. Some rooms are devoted to temporary exhibitions from the Museé Basque. The adjacent parts of Vauban's walls, however, were tidied up by the city and opened to the public a decade ago. On these **Remparts de Mousserolles** you can see what was going through Vauban's mind, and what war was like in the late 17th and 18th centuries. To defend a city properly, it was usually necessary to destroy at least half of it for the fortifications. Baroque fortifications are notable for the space they take up: one or two rings of low-slung, zig-zagging ramparts, with a complex of earthen salients and trenches beyond them, all designed to counter artillery rather than repulse a direct attack, which with the improved firearms of the age would have been suicidal.

Today the Mousserolles ramparts are an attractive city park, with a lagoon and open-air theatre.

Quartier St-Esprit

The third district of Bayonne, cowering under Vauban's haughty Citadelle and half-demolished 150 years ago for the rail station, is the Quartier St-Esprit, reached by the long bridge across the Adour. At the end of the bridge, the **St-Esprit** church was a gift of Louis XI, that most excellent monarch who wore old clothes and kept a troupe of dancing pigs to entertain him when he was blue. This 15th-century Gothic building retains from its original decoration an unusual wood sculptural group of the *Flight into Egypt* in the left aisle.

On the other side of the Citadelle, the working end of Bayonne, an impressive stretch of docks and factories, follows the wide Adour down to the sea. At the northern edge of town, off Avenue Louis de Foix, is the **English cemetery** from Wellington's campaigns; Queen Victoria and other members of the royal family always came to visit when they were in Biarritz.

Biarritz

For their 1959 season, the designers at Cadillac came up with something special: a sleek and shiny convertible, nearly 25ft long, with the highest tailfins in automotive history (22 inches). They called it the *Biarritz*, a tribute to the Basque village that was chosen by fortune, for a few decades at the end of the 19th century, to become the most glittering resort in Europe. Nowadays, there's still enough Ritz in Biarritz to support six luxury hotels (among 65 more modest establishments). But, freed from the burden of being the cynosure of fashion, the resort has become a pleasantly laid-back place, where anyone, wealthy or not, can have an unpretentious good time.

Come in the off season, and you'll notice the otherwise inconspicuous major phenomenon of Biarritz today – it's becoming the retirement capital of France, a Gallic Bournemouth or Florida. Already 34 per cent of the population are retirees, and the number goes up each year. Another statistic: 45 per cent of all the housing is holiday homes; you'll certainly notice that after September, when Biarritz declines into an overgrown village. Then everybody knows everyone else; they shake hands and exchange pleasantries on street corners, or lounge in the bar talking about how nice and quiet it is.

History Under the Palms

Local historians claim that both Biarritz and its landmark, the Atalaya, are names bestowed by the ancient Phoenicians, who may well have used the port as a stage on their trade routes to Britain. Biarritz is said to mean something like 'safe harbour', and

Getting Around

Javalquinto, t 05 59 22 37 10, *www.biarritz.fr. Open July and Aug daily 8–8; the rest of the year 9–6 plus Sun 10–5.*

Tourist Information

Square d'Ixelles (next to the town hall), **t** 05 59 22 37 00, **f** 05 59 44 14 19, *www.tourisme.fr/biarritz.*

Sports and Activities

Golf thrives in Biarritz. There are 10 courses around the town and several more in St-Jean-de-Luz, ranging from lush, professional-length links with an ocean view to dinky three-par places to practise your iron shots. At least one important tournament is held in Biarritz each season. Serious courses include the Golf de Chiberta in Anglet, Bd des Plages; Golf d'Arcangues in Arcangues, south of Biarritz; Golf de Chantaco, Rte d'Ascain, St-Jean-de-Luz; and Golf de la Nivelle, Pl Sharp, Ciboure. For more information contact the **Association Golf Côte Basque–Sud Landes** on **t** 05 58 48 54 65.

If you should feel a sudden desire to take up **surfing**, there are five schools in Biarritz and Anglet, and plenty of places to rent equipment. Some useful contacts are **Biarritz Surf Training**, 4 Impasse Hélène Boucher, **t** 05 59 23 15 31/**t** 05 59 43 74 25, *www.surftraining.com* and Ecole de Surf Moraiz, 4 Pl Bellevue, **t** 05 59 24 22 09/**t** 05 59 22 16 28.

You may not have heard of **thalassotherapy t** 05 59 41 30 01, *www.thalassa.com* – the use of sea water for aiding stress, fitness or recovery from diseases – but in France it is big news; Biarritz has two of the most up-to-date establishments, the **Institut Thalassa**, 11 Rue Louison Bobet, and **Les Thermes Marine**, 80 Rue de Madrid, **t** 05 59 23 01 22.

For other watersports, you might do better in some of the smaller resorts down the coast. St-Jean-de-Luz has plenty of places that offer deep-sea fishing excursions or rent sailing boats, including the **Ecole Nationale de Voile, at Socoa, t** 05 59 47 06 32, which also offers courses in windsurfing and such. Or else, you can fritter away your money on the *tiercé*, *quarté* and *quinté* at the Hippodrome de la Cité des Fleurs on Av du Lac Marion, still one of France's premier racing venues.

Where to Stay

Biarritz ✉ 64200

Don't let Biarritz's past fool you into thinking there's no place for the likes of you and me here. In fact the vast majority of people who come these days are looking for a bargain, and they have little trouble finding it, although Biarritz is somewhat lacking at the lower end of the scale – if you arrive without a reservation in July or August you might get pushed up into the higher brackets. The tourist office on Place d'Ixelles can help you find a room.

Luxury

******Hôtel du Palais**, 1 Av de l'Impératrice, **t** 05 59 41 64 00, **f** 05 59 41 67 99, *www.hotel-du-palais.com.* Probably the most prestigious address on France's west coast. Built in Biarritz's glory days on the site of Napoleon and Eugénie's villa, this compound on the beach has a circuit of old wrought-iron fences to separate you from the rest of the world. For a while in the 1950s, the Palais was closed, but the city got it fixed up and reopened, under a determined mayor who had campaigned under the simple slogan: 'No Palace, No Millionaires'. Some of the rooms are palatial, many with period furnishings. *Menus €50–80. Closed lunch July and Aug; closed Feb.*

Atalaya a kind of tower (like the *talayots* of Minorca, an important landmark visible to the early, coast-hugging sailors.

Before the 1860s, Biarritz was never more than a simple fishing village. But in the Middle Ages, even more than Bayonne it was the heart of the Basque whaling fleet. *Cachalots* and other species of whales were once common in the Bay of Biscay. A

★★★★**Miramar**, 13 Rue LouisonBobet, **t** 05 59 41 30 00, **f** 05 59 24 77 20, *www.thalassa.com.* The younger contender for the luxury prize. Modern and up-to-date, this hotel may not have the panache of the Palais, but compensates with very high standards in every respect: one of Biarritz's best restaurants, a pool, sauna, and even its own thalassotherapy centre. *Menus €50. Open all year.*

Expensive

★★★**Plaza**, Av Edward VII, **t** 05 59 24 74 00, **f** 05 59 22 22 01. Built in 1928, with a touch of restrained Art Deco elegance. It has retained much of its original decoration, with a quiet sense of decorum to match. *Open all year.*

Moderate

★★★**Maison Garnier**, 29 Rue Gambetta, **t** 05 59 01 60 70, **f** 05 59 01 60 80, *www.hotel-biarritz.com* is currently fashionable, set in a 19th-century Basque house. There are seven exquisitely restored rooms, all with antique furniture.

★★★**Louisiane**, Rue Guy Petit, **t** 05 59 22 20 20, **f** 05 59 24 95 77, *www.louisiane-biarritz.com.* Worth a try despite its unprepossessing modern exterior. This is a conveniently located, well-managed chain hotel with its own swimming pool, a boon for those who want to swim rather than surf.

★★★**Château de Clair de Lun**e, 48 Av Alan Seeger, **t** 05 59 41 53 20, **f** 05 59 41 53 29, *www.chateauduclairdelune.com.* An alternative far from the centre. It's in a Belle Epoque villa in a delicious park, with tranquillity assured, and lovely rooms, though it's a bit expensive.

Inexpensive

★★**Hostellerie Victoria**, 11 Av Reine Victoria, **t** 05 59 24 08 21, is in a delightful villa from the old days, close to Grande Plage. *Closed mid Oct–1 April.*

★★**Hôtel du Rocher** de la Vierge, 13 Rue du Port-Vieux, **t** 05 59 24 11 74. At the centre of the action in the old town. *Open all year.*

★★**Palacito Hotel**, 1 Rue Gambetta, **t** 05 59 24 04 89, **f** 05 59 24 33 43, *www.palacito.com.* A traditional small hotel right in the middle of town.

★**Palym**, 7 Rue du Port-Vieux, **t** 05 59 24 16 56, **f** 05 59 24 96 12. A family-run, old-style place popular with surfers.

Camping

While every other town on the coast has a huge choice of places, Biarritz doesn't. You'll do better looking in nearby Bidart, which has 12 of them.

Biarritz Camping, 28 Rue Harcet, **t** 05 59 23 00 12. *Closed Oct–10 May.*

Eating Out

Expensive

La Rotonde, Hôtel du Palais, **t** 05 59 41 64 00, may be the southwest's ultimate trip in luxurious dining: a magnificent domed room with its original decoration, and views over the beach and sea. There is a formidable wine list. *Menus €50–80. Closed for lunch July and Aug exc Sun; closed Feb.*

Le Relais, Miramar Hotel, **t** 05 59 41 30 00. Without the posh ambience of the former, but you can eat as well for a bit less. Seafood is the main attraction, cooked with a delightful lightness and savour: a *fricassée* of sole and *langoustines*, or lobster ravioli with *cèpes*. *Menus €50.*

Les Jardins de l'Océan, Hôtel Régina et Golf, 52 Av de l'Impératrice, **t** 05 59 41 33 00. Good for a slightly more modest seafood extravaganza. Prices are reasonable but you may be tempted to splurge for the *grand plateau de fruits de mer*, including lobster. *Menu €34 plus à la carte. Closed 5–20 Jan.*

permanent watch was kept on the Atalaya, and whenever one was sighted, the entire village would row out and try to nab it; the Biarrots were probably the inventors of the harpoon, and a harpooner once figured on the village's coat of arms. When the whales caught on and started avoiding the area, the Biarrots and the other Basque whalers bravely sailed out into the open sea after them.

Café de Paris, 5 Pl Bellevue, **t** 05 59 22 19 53. Stylish brasserie and restaurant specializing in southwestern cuisine, with excellent crab and lobster. *Menus €43–73. Closed for lunch exc Sun; closed Tues.*

Campagne et Gourmandise, 52 Av Alan Seeger, **t** 05 59 41 10 11. In a Basque farmhouse in the grounds of the Château de Claire de Lune (see 'Where to Stay', above). You can dine on a terrace with splendid panoramic views of the Pyrenees. Typical dishes include *fricassée de champignons en cappuccino d'herbes, queue de bœuf à la tranche de foie gras*, and pigeon tart. *Menu €35. Closed Sun eve exc July and Aug. Closed Mon lunch and Wed all year.*

Moderate

Chez Albert, Port des Pêcheurs, **t** 05 59 24 43 84. This may at first glance look like a typical tourist restaurant, but it's popular year round with visitors and Biarrots alike for quality seafood at reasonable prices. Squid in its own ink is a speciality. *Menu €29. Closed Wed exc July and Aug plus 1–15 Dec and 6–10 Feb.*

Goulue, 3 Rue E. Ardouin, **t** 05 59 24 90 90. A Belle Epoque-style restaurant with attentive service of classic local dishes; try a plateful of baby squid or monkfish cooked with bacon. *Menus from €24. Closed all Mon and Tues lunch.*

Le Clos Basque, 12 Rue Louis Barthou, **t** 05 59 24 24 96. An authentic little bistro with stone walls and Spanish tiles inside, and a charming terrace outside. Local specialities such as squid with peppers are served. *Menu €23. Closed Sun eve exc July and Aug and Mon all year.*

Café de la Grand Plage, 1 Av Edouard VII, **t** 05 59 22 77 88. 1930s-style brasserie-café, facing the ocean and overlooking the Grand Plage. Part of the casino, it has a wide range of drinks and light meals. *Open daily all year.*

Le Surfing, 9 Bd Prince de Galles, **t** 05 59 24 78 72. Overlooks the Plage des Basques and is the place for fashionable surfers to peel off their wetsuits and enjoy a décor of surfboards and Hawaiian shirts. It specializes in fish but serves lots of good salads too. *Menu €24. Closed Mon and Tues eves and Wed exc school hols.*

Blue Cargo, Villa Itsasoan, Av Ibarritz, **t** 05 59 23 54 87. In a villa perched right on the beach of Ibarritz, on the outskirts of Biarritz. It's perfect for sunset-over-the-sea drinks or simple seafood meals.

Bistrot des Halles, Rue du Centre, **t** 05 59 24 21 22. Usually crowded for both lunch and dinner. As in any French town, you won't go wrong looking around the market, and you won't do better than the daily special (usually a grilled fish or steak). *Menu €16. Closed Sun exc for school hols plus 15–31 Oct.*

Cheap

The Players, Esplanade du Casino de Biarritz, **t** 05 59 24 19 60. Can't be beaten for good cheap seafood and vast pizzas. It's right next to the Grand Plage, with views out to sea. *A la carte €7–15. Closed Nov and 1st week Dec.*

Bar Jean, 5 Rue des Halles, **t** 05 59 24 80 38. A Biarritz classic; the place to go for superb fresh tapas, oysters and a good choice of wines in a traditional Spanish tiled *bodega. Closed Tues and Wed from Oct–Apr plus Jan and Feb.*

El Callejon, 5 Rue Monhaut, **t** 05 59 24 99 15. A good tapas bar. *Open eves only exc Sun.*

Pâtisserie Miremont, Pl Clemenceau. Port des Pêcheurs is the site of several good tapas places. This is the place to go while you're waiting for dinner: today, as in the Belle Epoque, an essential part of the Biarritz experience is to drop in at four in the afternoon for a coffee and a little pastry that's much too pretty to eat. The pâtisserie retains its original décor, with rooms overlooking the sea.

There doesn't seem to be any conclusive evidence for it, but the Basques will tell you they discovered Newfoundland in the 14th century, and probably other parts of the Americas as well (Columbus did after all take a Basque along to be his navigator). By 1800, Basque whalers couldn't keep up with the British and Americans, but Biarritz was beginning to make part of its living from a new and unprecedented phenomenon, the desire of northerners to come and spend a holiday beside the sea.

Eugenia Maria de Montijo de Guzmán, to whom Biarritz owes its present status, came from a minor Spanish noble family a bit down on its luck. But even as a young girl, fortune-telling gypsies and nuns forecast a brilliant future for her; 'an eagle will carry you to the heavens and then drop you,' one of them supposedly said. Eugenia also had a scheming, social-climbing mother, who got her daughter as far as the court of the new Emperor Napoleon III in Paris in 1852. This striking 26-year-old blonde was more than capable of doing the rest of the job herself. A brilliant horsewoman who liked to smoke a cigar now and then, she made quite an impression. But there was a cold, unapproachable side to her too, and she used it to win the Emperor's heart by being the only girl in Paris the old rogue couldn't have. It is claimed he found his way into her bedroom one night; meeting a chilly reception, he asked the way to her heart. 'Through the church,' she replied.

As Empress Eugénie, she helped inaugurate the cult of fashion in Paris, making the fortune of Worth, first of the celebrity couturiers. With a political outlook somewhat to the right of Attila the Hun, and a near-total control over Napoleon, she was able to exert a tremendous influence over the policies of the government, presiding gloriously over the orgy of greed, corruption, décolletage and waltzes that was the Second Empire. It took a woman historian, Edith Saunders, to notice this strangely significant bit of the world's secret history. In her lovely book, *A Distant Summer*, she wrote:

> *...Eugénie had risen like a brilliant star, to create not only new fashions but a new taste in beauty, a new type of woman. The old type, which had lingered on in England and was represented in the pages of Dickens, belonged to Europe's Romantic period and was open-mouthed, angelic and mawkish. The new type, with its prediliction for blonde hair and its hard expression, is still with us. The Empress set the modern standard of highly polished perfection which is maintained today by Hollywood film stars and mechanically transmitted to entranced millions who follow in the measure allotted by their circumstance. To look like a film star is the dream of the present day woman of the industrial age; in 1855 everyone dreamed of looking like Eugénie.*

As a girl, Eugénie and her mother had often vacationed at the just 'discovered' village of Biarritz. As Empress, she dragged Napoleon back down with her and established the summer court on the beach. Having invented the new woman, Eugénie now made some great contributions to the modern concept of the seaside resort. The imperial couple didn't stay in a hotel; Eugénie had a palace – the Villa Eugénie – built on the most prominent spot along the beach in 1854. Everybody who was anybody in Paris soon followed, along with grand dukes, petit dukes, every sort of count and baron, and plenty of factory owners with marriageable daughters. The royal families of Spain and Belgium came; the English were already here, laying out golf courses, while Count von Bismarck canoodled with the wife of the Russian ambassador.

The Fall of France in 1870 put an end to the Second Empire, and to Eugénie's fairy-tale. In 1881, the government of the Third Republic demolished the Villa Eugénie after a fire, and divided the estate into building lots. But you can't keep a good princess down; Eugénie lived a romantic if somewhat melancholy life in exile, an object of fascination wherever she travelled. She died in Madrid in 1920, at the age of 94.

Even without her, Biarritz carried on. More Russian princes and even Queen Victoria came to visit (in 1889); the Prince of Wales left so much money in the casino that they named two different streets after him. The Belle Epoque brought a tidal wave of building: grand hotels, the casino, a salt-water spa and acres of wealthy villas in every imaginable style. It wasn't a wild scene like the Côte d'Azur in the 1920s. The swells followed a respectable and rather bland daily schedule, starting with a morning promenade past the shop windows on Rue Mazagran at 10, followed by an hour on the beach, dressing for lunch at 11.30, and so on. The First World War started Biarritz's fall from fashion; in the '20s everybody started shifting to Nice and Cannes where life promised a bit more excitement.

Biarritz has begun to shake off its dusty image with dramatic refurbishment of its hotels and fine buildings, in architectural styles ranging from Belle Epoque to Art Deco and Art Nouveau. These include the splendid Municipal Casino, which dominates the Grand Plage, with its restored casinos, entertainment centres and an old-style grand café overlooking the beach.

Despite its hordes of retirees, Biarritz is hardly behind the times. France Telecom has made it the experimental city for the communications of the future, wiring up the town with a single fibre optic cable to provide cable TV, telephone, '*visiophone*', '*télétel*', 'interactive communications' and God knows what else. And plenty of young people still come in the summer for one unexpected reason – surfing. Stuck in its odd angle of coastline, Biarritz provides what many claim are the only perfect waves on the Atlantic; French hot-doggers and surf bunnies have made it the modest Malibu Beach of Europe. And lots of good Frenchmen who have never heard of surfing, and who would never dream of sitting on a beach, know Biarritz for its crack rugby squad – the great Serge Blanco played here until his retirement in 1992 (now the local hero runs a thalassotherapy centre down in Hendaye).

The Atalaya

Here, on the tip of old Biarritz's little peninsula, is the height where in the old days the watch would send up smoke signals when whales were sighted. To the right, the Port des Pêcheurs now holds only pleasure craft. To the left is the old fishing port, long ago unusable and filled up with the beach of Port-Vieux, and also the best place in Biarritz for a stroll, the **Rocher de la Vierge**. Napoleon III and Eugénie are responsible for this system of causeways and tunnels, connecting a number of crags and tiny islands into a memorable walk just above the pounding surf; the biggest rock carries a marble statue of the Virgin Mary.

Up on top of the Atalaya, the **Musée de la Mer**, (*t* *05 59 22 75 40 or 05 59 22 33 34, www.museedelamer.com; open daily July and Aug 9.30–midnight, Easter, June and Sept 9.30–7; rest of year 9.30–12.30 and 2–6; closed Mon Nov–Mar exc school hols plus last 2 weeks Jan; adm; the seals are fed at 10.30 and 5*), in a clean Art Deco building, contains an imaginatively decorated old aquarium for a look at what's down below the surface of the Bay of Biscay, along with exhibits on the natural history of the sea, whales and whaling, navigation, etc.

Descending eastwards from the Atalaya, the Bd Maréchal Leclerc takes you to the church of Ste-Eugénie, another modest contribution of the Empress's; the big organ inside won a prize at the 1900 Paris World's Fair. It faces one of the centres of resort life in the old days, the beautifully restored Casino Bellevue, now converted to residences and exhibition and conference rooms. Not far away, by the city marketplace on Rue Broquelis, is the **Musée de Vieux Biarritz** (*t* *05 59 24 86 28; open 10–12 and 2.30–6; closed Sun and Mon; adm*) set in a former Anglican church, this is a small exhibition of photos and mementos of the good old days. There is also an interesting museum of oriental art, **Asiatica**, 1 Rue Guy Petit (*t* *05 59 22 78 78, www.museeasiatica.com; open Mon–Fri 10.30–7, Sat and Sun 2–8*), with a collection which includes jades, bronzes and porcelain from China, Nepal and India, and many Tibetan *thangkas* (paintings on silk).

Beaches and Villas

Below this, the shore straightens out into the long, luscious expanse of the Grande Plage, which before Eugénie was called (for reasons not entirely clear) the Plage des Fous, dominated by the magnificently restored casino. Farther up the beach, behind the wrought-iron fences, is Biarritz's stately landmark, the sumptuous Hôtel du Palais. This is the spot where Eugénie built her palace, destroyed by fire in 1881. The present hotel, begun in 1905, is the successor to an even grander one that also burned down. Across the street, the Russian aristocrats built their onion-domed church of St-Alexandre-Nevsky (1908).

Avenue Edward VII, which becomes Avenue de l'Impératrice further on, was the status address of Belle Epoque Biarritz, lined with ornate hotels and residences now largely converted to other uses. In the shady streets behind them, all originally part of the imperial estate, scores of wealthy villas still survive, in a crazy quilt of styles ranging from Art Nouveau to neo-Moorish to Anglo-Norman. Some of the best can be seen on and around Avenue Reine Victoria. Also in this area, you can have a look at what passed for piety in the Second Empire – another creation of Napoleon and Eugénie, the 1864 **Chapelle Impériale**, on Avenue Reine Victoria at Rue Pellot. Unfortunately the lavish neo-Byzantine interior is currently closed for renovation. Due to reopen early in 2004, though no details at the time of writing.

At the end of Plage Miramar stands the landmark on this stretch of the coast, the 143ft **Phare St-Martin** (*t* *05 59 22 37 10; open July and Aug 10–12 and 3–7; closed Mon; open weekends and hols from mid April 3–7*), a rare example of an old-fashioned lighthouse: built in 1834, and little changed since. It has only 249 steps to climb.

As for beaches, there is a wide choice of places to plant your towel, and you should be able to find a spot that's not too crowded even in the height of summer. From south to north: at Biarritz' southern limits is the broad expanse of the Plage de la Milady, Plage Marbella and the Côte des Basques, a favourite of the surfing set. Under the old town is the tiny but pleasant Plage du Port Vieux. The Grande Plage and Plage Miramar, the centre of the action, are lovely if often cramped, but further out, stretching miles along the northern coast in the suburb of Anglet, there are plenty more. When the beach traffic's too terrific in summer take the special Navette des Plages bus from Place Clemenceau or Avenue de l'Impératrice (*summer only, otherwise the infrequent no.4 line*) to the above-mentioned beaches, or go north and take your pick among the Plage de la Chambre d'Amour, the Plage des Corsaires, de la Madrague, de l'Océan, des Dunes, and Plage des Cavaliers. The first one takes its name from a number of caves, now mostly submerged, that served as lovers' trysts long ago. Plenty of different stories have grown up around the place – about pairs of lovers who took refuge here and were tragically drowned with the tide – but the notorious French witch-hunter de Lancre, who wrote a report on witchcraft in the Labourd in 1609, said that this was known locally to be none other than the birthplace of Venus, where the goddess rose up from the foam of the sea.

For a break from the city, in 10 minutes you can drive from the beach to **Arcangues**, a lovely village on a height south of Biarritz. In the centre, a fine 16th-century church shares space with the *fronton* and a bust of Arcangues' son Luis Mariano, celebrated singing star of some really excruciating French film musicals of the 1940s and '50s.

Tourist Information

Guéthary: Rue du Comte Swiecinsky, **t** 05 59 26 56 60, **f** 05 59 54 92 67, *www.guethary-france.com. Open summer Mon–Fri 9–7 plus Sun 10–12.30; winter Mon–Fri 9–12 & 2–5.30 plus Sat 9–12.30.*

Where to Stay and Eat

Bidart ✉ 64210

Elissaldia Hotel, Pl de la Mairie, **t** 05 59 54 90 03 (*inexpensive*). A cheap, authentic place to stay within a *pelote* ball's throw of the church and *fronton* court. It's a snip with sea views thrown in. There's also a bar and restaurant. *Open daily all year.*

Table des Frères Ibarboure, Rte Ahetze, **t** 05 59 54 81 64, *www.freresibarboure.com* (*expensive*). One of the region's most celebrated restaurants. It's a family establishment, but the cuisine is predictably perfect and abstrusely *soignée*, from the *encornets farcis* (stuffed squid) and oysters with caviar to the rich and extravagant desserts. *Menus €32–77. Closed Sun eves plus Mon lunch in July. Also closed mid Nov–mid Dec and three weeks in Jan.*

Guéthary ✉ 64210

★★★Hotel Villa Catarie, Av du Géneral de Gaulle 64210 Guéthary. (Opposite the Mairie and *fronton*), **t** 05 59 47 59 00, *www.villa-catarie.com*. This old Basque villa has been beautifully restored. Comfort, romance and luxury classically done. A bit pricey but a lovely place to stay and feel pampered.

Restaurant Madrid, right in the village centre on Pl Toulet, **t** 05 59 26 52 12, is cheery and homey and serves mostly seafood. *Menus €18. Closed last two weeks in Nov plus Jan and Feb.*

Kandela, **t** 05 59 47 77 57, also in the centre, is a tiny restaurant with a terrace specializing in grills, fish and seafood, with a good local wine list. *Menus €17–23. Closed Sun eve and Mon exc July and Aug.*

The Côte Basque

If Biarritz is too big and cosmopolitan, there's St-Jean-de-Luz down the coast, and if St-Jean is still too frenetic, you've got two very amiable choices in between, Bidart and Guéthary. Both are perfect Basque villages, with church, *mairie* and *fronton* right in the middle, and both have good beaches. If they do get a bit crowded at the height of summer, it's much too early to call them spoiled yet. Leaving Biarritz on the coastal N10, **Bidart** comes first, with a grand view across the coast from the pilgrimage chapel of Ste-Madeleine. Bidart's parish church, in the centre, has some painted altar-pieces and a quite unusual Slavic baptismal font – a gift of Queen Natalie of Serbia, who spent a lot of time here before the First World War, in a palace called the Pavillon Royal above the beach. Sleepy **Guéthary** has been a resort as long as Biarritz, though

Tourist Information

Place Maréchal Foch, **t** 05 59 26 03 16, **f** 05 59 26 21 47, *www.saint-jean-de-luz.com; open Mon–Sat 9–12 & 2.30–6.30; July and Aug 9–7.30, Sun and hols 10–1.*

Market Days

St-Jean-de-Luz: Markets are held on Tuesdays and Fridays, and also Saturdays in summer. There are also markets all year round in Les Halles from Monday to Saturday, and on Sunday as well from July to mid-September.

Ciboure: Sundays.

Where to Stay

St-Jean-de-Luz ✉ 64500

If St-Jean has one drawback, it's finding a reasonably priced place to stay – rates here are even higher than in Biarritz. The top spots here are not by the beach.

★★★★**Chantaco**, Route d'Ascain, **t** 05 59 26 14 76, **f** 05 59 26 35 97, *www.hotel-chantaco.com* (*luxury–expensive*). The emphasis is on golf, with the area's most famous course next door. The hotel, in a 1930s-style Andalucían villa, with a patio covered in vines, is set in a lovely park, and offers tennis courts and a pool in addition to golf. Here you'll find deluxe rooms and service, with prices to match. No restaurant. *Closed Nov–April.*

Hôtel les Almadies, 58 Rue Gambetta, **t** 05 59 85 34 48, *www.hotel-les-almadies.com*. A lovely hotel in the heart of town in the main pedestrian zone. Seven good-sized bedrooms with balconies and new bath-rooms. The hotel has been renovated and now has a clean, crisp and modern design. Very light and airy. The owners are friendly and helpful.

★★★★**Parc Victoria**, 5 Rue Cèpe, **t** 05 59 26 78 78, **f** 05 59 26 78 08, *www.parcvictoria.com* (*expensive*). A gracious mansion on the outskirts of town. It's a beautifully deco-rated, intimate place (only eight rooms and four suites). It has its own park with a pool. *Closed Nov–April. Restaurant closed Tues in winter.*

★★★**Hôtel de la Plage**, 33 Rue Garat, **t** 05 59 51 03 44, **f** 05 59 51 03 48, *www.hoteldelaplage.com* (*moderate*). As its name suggests this hotel is right on the beach. Recently refurbished it has just earned its third star. Spacious, bright modern bedrooms. The owner's brother has a restaurant next door. (*see* below). A comfortable hotel. *Closed 11 Nov–25 Dec plus 5 Jan–5 Feb.*

★★**Ohartzia**, Rue Garat, **t** 05 59 26 00 06, **f** 05 59 26 74 75, *www.hotel-ohartzia.com* (*moderate*). Very pretty, family-run hotel, situated in the middle of St-Jean, with a lovely terrace and garden on the first floor. Neat as a pin. *Closed Dec–Jan.*

★★★**De la Poste**, 83 Rue Gambetta, **t** 05 59 26 04 53, **f** 05 59 26 42 14, *www.grandhoteldelaposte.com* (*inexpensive*). Right in the centre (with the added bonus of its very own snooker table). *Open all year.*

Bakea, 9 Place Camille Julian, across the harbour in Ciboure, **t** 05 59 47 34 40, *www.hotel-bakea.fr.st* (*inexpensive*). Twelve rooms. *Closed Dec–Jan.*

it never made it big. It has a pretty, Basque-style *mairie*, which must get a window broken every now and then from the *fronton* right in front of it, along with a tiny port and a beach.

St-Jean-de-Luz

For those who do not naturally gravitate towards the sun and fun of the beach, a seaside resort needs a certain special, intangible quality. Like the theatre, a good resort must be able to make one suspend one's disbelief. In all of southern France, there are very few places that can do this: one is Collioure on the Mediterranean, another St-Jean-de-Luz. The name is perfect. Light and colour can be extraordinary

Restaurant le Brouillarta, menus €11–25. Lunch weekdays only €12. A busy brasserie next door to the Hôtel de la Plage. Decorated with bright Basque paintings, it is a popular lunch spot. *Open daily in July and Aug. The rest of the year, closed Sun eve and Mon plus Dec and Jan.*

Eating Out

St-Jean-de-Luz ✉ 64500

Everyone knows St-Jean as the capital of Basque cuisine in France, and there is a marvellous collection of restaurants around the centre. Competition keeps the quality high.Rue de la République, just off main Rue Gambetta near the port, must be counted among the sights of the Basque coast no one should miss. It's almost entirely lined with seafood restaurants, each one with its beautifully arranged table of *fruits de mer* out front.

Auberge Kaiku, 17 Rue de la République, **t** 05 59 26 13 20. The oldest house in St-Jean (1540) rolls out one of the most sumptuous tables (*expensive*); but you can negotiate your way to a fine marine repast between. Menu €34 plus à la carte. Service can be slow when busy. *Closed Tues and Wed all year plus Mon–Fri lunch in July and Aug.*

Bakea, 9 Place Camille Julian, across the harbour in Ciboure, **t** 05 59 47 34 40, has outside tables right on the port (*moderate*). It is a local favourite for *ttoro* and grills This is also a charming hotel. *www.hotel-bakea.fr.st. Menus €16–30.*

Le Portua. 18 Rue de la République. **t** 05 59 51 01 12. Oysters, salmon for starters, a satisfying *ttoro* and grills. *Menu €23. Open daily all year.*

Restaurant Chez Maya, 2 Rue St. Jacques, St-Jean, **t** 05 59 26 80 76. This place is very popular with the locals and tourists alike for its simple and authentic Basque cuisine. Good value. *Menus €19–26. Closed Thurs lunch and Wed plus 20 Dec–20 Jan.*

Pasaka, 11 Rue de la République, **t** 05 59 26 05 17. A cosy interior and two terraces, where you can feast on local grilled sardines, or *ttoro*, a satisfying Basque fish soup with potatoes and saffron. *Menus €17–23. Closed Mon and Tues plus last week in Dec and all Jan.*

Chez Pantxua, Port de Soccoa, **t** 05 59 47 13 73. A long-established local favourite decorated with Basque paintings, serving *fruits de mer* and fish according to the catch of the day. A la carte only, around €36 including wine. *Closed Mon and Tues out of season, plus 15 Nov–1 Feb.*

Le Patio, Rue de l'Abbé-Onaïndia, **t** 05 59 26 99 11, is a place with a Spanish accent that serves up a very gratifying *parillada* (seafood mixed grill) with just about everything you can imagine, including lobster.

Vieille Auberge, 22 Rue Tourasse, **t** 05 59 26 19 61. For a filling Basque meal in the company of Luziens that usually include grilled fish and sometimes paella.

Le Peita, Rue Tourasse, **t** 05 59 26 86 66. All the Basque seafood favourites; full meals *à la carte* average around €23. Lunch menu €12. *Closed Tues all year, plus Wed in winter and 1–15 Dec, 1–15 Feb and 2 weeks in June.*

St-Jean – Petit Paris

It was a party to remember, and without its tourists St-Jean would be left only with the memory of that one glorious month when it seemed the centre of the world. In 1659, Spain and France signed the Treaty of the Pyrenees, putting an end to a century and a half of almost continuous hostility. To ice the deal, a marriage was arranged between Louis XIV and the Spanish infanta, Maria Teresa. Preparations went on for a year, and this obscure whaling and fishing port, roughly halfway between Paris and Madrid, was chosen as the venue. In May 1660, *everybody* came to St-Jean, including nearly the entire French court. 'Monsieur' (Louis's neurotic uncle) and Cardinal Mazarin were there; the 'Grande Mademoiselle' (Louis's flamboyant cousin) and her lover floated down, and all the dandies and popinjays of Versailles followed in their wake. Louis himself arrived last, in a gilded carriage. One observer, Madame de Motteville, marvelled at how everyone was covered in lace and feathers and tassels. So were the horses. It reminded her of King Cyrus and ancient Persia.

Years before, a gypsy fortune-teller had predicted that peace between France and Spain would finally come 'with a whale'. And on the day that Maria Teresa and the Spaniards arrived in St-Jean, a great whale was sighted just off the harbour. The courtiers rushed to the shore to watch the town's seamen give chase. Young Louis, however, took the opportunity to barge in on his future bride in her chambers; he surprised her *en déshabillé* and they had an intimate lunch together. For the wedding, there were Basque dancers, mock naval battles offshore, a bullfight and a grand ball in the main square, now Place Louis XIV, illuminated with thousands of candles and torches. Louis and his bride lived happily ever after (though the France Louis ruled suffered greatly); when the queen died, Louis remarked that her death was 'the only chagrin she ever caused me'. The peace with Spain has lasted up to the present, save for the unfortunate interlude of Napoleon. As for the whale, they caught it, and the bishop of Bayonne, who performed the wedding ceremony, took the tongue and fat of it back to Bayonne with him.

here, illuminating an immaculately white Basque town and the acres of glistening rose-silver seafood its restaurants roll out on tables to lure in customers. Even in the Basque lands, St-Jean's cooks are renowned for their skill and imagination. The beaches are fine, and, best of all, this is not the sort of town to have entirely succumbed to the tourist tide; the fishermen on the quay still strut around as if they own the place. What more could you ask?

Unfortunately, the name really has nothing to do with light (*luz* in Spanish). Gradgrind etymologists have traced it back to a Celtic or Latin word *louth* or *lutum*, meaning mud, the same as Paris's original name, *Lutetia* – Mudville. St-Jean, or rather *Donihane Lohitzun*, as the Basques know it, grew up in a swampy nowhere that coincidentally happened to have a good harbour. It began to thrive as a fishing port when the river Adour started silting up the harbour of Bayonne in the Middle Ages. The Luziens shared fully in the French Basques' whaling and buccaneering adventures up until the Revolution. It's tuna and sardines they're after now, and tourists.

The Port

A casual visitor could walk around St-Jean all day and never notice it had a beach, but it's a good one, long and deep, tucked away on the northern side of town; the beach is protected by a jetty, and very safe for swimming. At its centre is the lavish **casino**, built in 1924.

St-Jean naturally turns its face to the port, lined with blue, red and green fishing boats, and a broad quay where the fishermen spread their nets; St-Jean is home to the biggest tuna fleet in France. There will be boats offering excursions around the area, or to the Spanish coast. Some, like the *Marie Rose*, also offer deep-sea-fishing trips. Behind the port is the town hall and the adjacent **Maison de Louis XIV** (*Place Louis XIV, **t/f** 05 59 26 01 56; open daily June–30 Sept 10.30–12 and 2.30–5.30 (6.30 July and Aug); adm*), where the Roi Soleil stayed for his wedding. A typical Basque town-house, built in 1643, it is occasionally open for tours. The nearby **Pavillon de l'Infante** (*Pavillon visits mid-June–mid-Oct 11–12.30 and 2.30–6.30; closed all Sun and Mon am*) has been turned into a wax museum of characters from Louis' time, a branch of the **Musée Grévin** (*7 Rue Mazarin, **t** 05 59 51 24 88, open daily April–Oct 10–12 and 2–6; July and Aug till 6.30; for the rest of the year open afternoons during school hols).*

From the port, the main stem, pedestrian Rue Gambetta, takes you to **St-Jean Baptiste**, largest and greatest of all the Basque churches to be found in France, where Louis XIV and Maria Teresa were married. The church is a lesson in Basque subtlety, plain and bright outside, and plain and bright within; any Baptist or Methodist would feel at home here. The aesthetic is in the detail, especially the wonderful wooden ceiling formed like the hull of a ship, and the three levels of wooden galleries around both sides of the nave, carved with all the art and sincerity the local artisans could manage.

The church was begun in the 1300s, but such wooden galleries do not last forever, no matter how well made; this latest version, probably much like those that preceded it, was completed in the 1860s. Another feature, also typical of Basque churches such as this, is the ornate gilded altarpiece, dripping with Baroque detail. The main door of the church was sealed up after Louis and Maria Teresa passed through it on their wedding day.

Ciboure

Right across the port from St-Jean, over a little bridge, this is the less-touristy, working member of these twin towns. Ciboure is the home of the composer Maurice Ravel, who was born at No.12 Quai Ravel, and who once started a concerto based on Basque themes and rhythms (called *Zaspiak Bat*), but never finished it.

The town has a mirror-image of St-Jean's picturesque port, though this side is mostly used by pleasure boats. Behind the port, there are pretty streets of old Basque houses such as **Rue de la Fontaine**, and the simple St-Vincent, a 16th-century fortified church with an octagonal tower. On the northern end of town, facing the coast, is the quarter of **Socoa** with its **castle**, begun by Henri IV which today houses a surfing and windsurfing school.

Urrugne and Hendaye

To get to Hendaye, you have a choice of either the coastal road, the scenic Carniche Basque (the D912), or else the more inland N10 or the motorway; these two pass through **Urrugne**, where the church of **St-Vincent** has a Renaissance portal with some excellent reliefs, which were damaged somewhat by English artillery in 1814. Note the famous, if somewhat gloomy, inscription on the tower's sundial: *vulnerant omnes, ultima necat*, referring to the hours – 'each one wounds, the last one kills'. Inside, there is more good sculptural work, notably on the bishop's chair, supported by a figure the locals call 'Samson'; they say if you pull his nose you will grow strong, and you can bet all the aspiring Basque barrel-lifters and wagon-pullers stop in to visit. The **Château d'Uturbie** (*t 05 59 54 31 15, www.chateauduturbie.fr; open daily 2–6 from mid-Mar–31 Oct; adm*), was the home of the medieval viscounts of the Labourdan. The castle in its present incarnation dates from the 1340s, though each century up until the Revolution added its bits and pieces; Wellington made it his headquarters briefly in 1814. The interior has some impressive 17th- to 18th-century furnishings, and a fine set of Flemish tapestries.

From the village, a winding road leads up to the pilgrimage chapel of **Notre-Dame-de-Socorri**, with views over the mountains; it's a lovely spot for a picnic (though it may be disconcerting to know that nearly all the souls sleeping in the chapel's oak-shaded cemetery were victims of cholera epidemics).

Tourist Information

Hendaye: 12 Rue des Aubépines, **t** 05 59 20 00 34, **f** 05 59 20 79 17, *www.hendaye.com; open July and Aug Mon–Sat 9–7.30 plus Sun 10–1; rest of the year Mon–Fri 9–12.30 and 2–6 plus Sat 9–12.30.*

Market Days

Hendaye: Wednesdays and Saturdays.

Where to Stay and Eat

Urrugne ✉ 64122

Chez Maïté, Place de la Mairie, **t** 05 59 54 30 27. Handy if you're stopping for lunch after a visit to the Parc Floral Florenia gardens. Try seafood, *poulet basquaise* and a choice of very special homemade desserts. There are cheap set menus, but it's worth paying a little more for the specialities *à la carte*. Menus €26 and *à la carte* for about €39. *Closed Tues eve and Wed plus Mon in summer and Sun eve in winter; closed Jan.*

Hendaye ✉ 64700

Rather less attractive than Biarritz or St-Jean, Hendaye is correspondingly less posh.

*****Hôtel Serge Blanco**, Bd Mer, **t** 05 59 51 35 35, **f** 05 59 51 36 00, *www.thalassoblanco.com* (*expensive*). Named after the famous Basque rugby star who is the proprietor and whose empire features a thalassotherapy centre and restaurant on the beach. *Closed Christmas.*

****Lafon**, 99 Bd de la Mier, **t** 05 59 20 04 67, **f** 05 59 48 06 85, is a hotel (*inexpensive*) that serves menus at €17–23. *Open Easter–31 Oct.*

****Santiago**, 29 Rue Santiago, **t** 05 59 20 00 94, **f** 05 59 20 83 26, *www.hotelsantiago.net* (*cheap*). One of the least expensive hotels. *Open Mar–Oct.*

Fuenterrabia (Spain)

Parador El Emperador, Plaza Armas del Castillo, Fuenterrabia, Spain, **t** 64 21 40. An option over the border. This *parador* is lovely, though expensive, and in a 16th-century castle, the Palacio de Carlos Quinto.

Just outside Urrugne, anyone who likes gardens won't want to miss the 30,000 trees and million flowers of **Parc Floral Florenia** (***t** 05 59 48 02 51, www.florenia.com; open mid-Mar–mid-July 10–7, summer daily 10–9, mid-Aug–mid-Sept 10–7; Oct–Nov 2–6. Closed Mon except July and Aug; adm*). It will seem hard to believe, but Florenia opened only in 1993. An official of the Pyrénées-Atlantiques council named François Girard was on a mission to Canada. Visiting a famous park in Vancouver, the Butchert Gardens, he was inspired to create something like it back home. With determination and persistence, Girard got everyone else in the area involved with the project, lined up 20 million francs in financing, and made his dream come true in only three years. The park covers 45 acres, and, young as the plantings are, it's already quite impressive.

A booming resort and the border crossing-point into Spain, **Hendaye** is divided into two distinct units, the old town and **Hendaye-Plage** on the coast. Hendaye's border location on the River Bidassoa puts it in the news every century or so. There is a small, uninhabited island in the Bidassoa called the **Ile des Faisans** (also known as Ile de la Conférence) that belongs to neither country; a traditional meeting place for kings and ministers since the 1400s, it is still under an unusual joint administration – the Spanish watch over it from February to July, the French the rest of the year. Here in 1526, King François I was returned after a year of imprisonment, when he was captured in battle at Pavia, Italy, by the Spanish King and Holy Roman Emperor Charles V. In 1659, the Treaty of the Pyrenees was signed here, and the following year representatives of both sides came back to plan the marriage of Louis XIV and Maria Teresa. A special pavilion was erected for the occasion and decorated by Velazquez – who caught a bad cold doing the job that eventually killed him. In October 1940, Hendaye's train station was the scene of the famous meeting between Hitler and Franco. Hitler had come down in his private rail car to bluster the Caudillo into joining the war; later he said he would rather have his teeth pulled out than talk to such a stubborn character again.

The **beach** is long and broad, though as a resort Hendaye can't match the charm of the other towns along the Côte Basque. The old town offers nothing particularly special to draw you out of your way, and the beach area is a bland place lined with old villas, gradually being replaced by concrete hotels, the preserve of family vacations. Occasionally, tours are offered at the **Château Antoine d'Abbadie** (***t** 05 59 20 04 51; open Feb–May and Oct–Dec Mon–Fri 10–12 & 2–5; June–Sept Mon–Fri 10–6, Sat 10–1 and 2–6, Sun 2–6; adm*), an eccentric Disneyland-Gothic castle set on a hill at the southern end of the beach. It was built by Viollet-le-Duc for an Irish-born traveller son of a Basque family named Antoine d'Abbadie who spent a lot of time in Ethiopia; there's a large collection of mementoes from that country, an observatory, and **Le Domaine** (***t** 05 59 20 37 20*), an exotic 110-acre park. The villa is covered with inscriptions in Amharic and Gaelic.

Looking over into Spain, you can practise rolling your Spanish 'r's on the town of Fuenterrabia. Spain announces itself even before you get there, with the striking Baroque bell tower of Fuenterrabia's church, visible from Hendaye's beach. It's a beautiful village, full of flowers and brightly painted houses, and if you want to press on further the big resort of **San Sebastián**, the Spanish Biarritz, is just down the coast.

The Labourd Interior: Around La Rhune

The name of La Rhune, westernmost monument of the Pyrenean chain, comes from the Basque *larrun*, or pastureland. It's full of cows and sheep all right, just as it has been for the last few millennia. The tracks around its slopes have been one of the main Basque smugglers' routes for centuries. A Basque tale has it that La Rhune was once covered in gold. Some evil men came to take it away; they cut down the trees and burnt them to get at it, but the gold all melted and flowed away. The mountain's summit also had a reputation as an *akelarre*, a ritual ground for witches and sorcerers; up until the 18th century the mayors of the villages around it always paid a monk to live on top as a hermit for a term of four years, to keep the witches away and to pray for good winds.

Ascain and Sare

Coming in from Hendaye or St-Jean, the first of the villages below La Rhune is **Ascain**, with its landmark three-arched medieval bridge over the Nivelle, and a 16th-century church on its lovely square. From here a hiking trail leads up to the 892m/2925ft summit of La Rhune, or else you can take the D4 up to the Col de St-Ignace, where there is another trail and also an old, open tramway to the top, the **Petit Train de la Rhune** (*__t__ 08 92 39 14 25, www.rhune.com; open mid-March–mid-Nov daily every half-hour from 9am, and 8.30am in summer, plus night runs in July and Aug*).

In Neolithic times, La Rhune was a holy mountain, as evidenced by the wealth of monuments around its slopes. The rites of the ancient Basque religion were usually celebrated on mountain tops, hence their reputation in Christian times as haunts of sorcerers. You'll need a *série bleue* map and a day's hiking (at least) to find the monuments; there are eight small stone circles around a place called the **Crête de Gorostiarria**, and several dolmens and circular tumuli on the northern and western slopes. On the slopes of La Rhune towards Sare, the easiest to find are the four dolmens at a farm called **Xominen**, just off the Col de St-Ignace; further away at the **Aniotzbehere** farm are two more. The northern side of the **Pic d'Ibanteli** has four of them.

Just beyond the pass lies **Sare**, one of the true capitals of the Basque soul. For its isolation and its traditionally independent ways, people jokingly call it the 'Republic of Sare'. Since the 1400s, the republic was one of the main centres for what the Basques call *gabazkolana*, or 'night work' – smuggling. Folks on both sides of the border never really saw the logic of paying duties on moving their flocks around to French and Spanish foreigners. Smuggling sheep and cows gradually led to other things too. The French authorities usually treated all this with commendable humanity. The story is still told of a zealous customs man, just arrived from Alsace in the 1920s, who shot a local man in the leg while he was taking some cows over the slopes of La Rhune. His superiors went to the mayor of Sare and to the man's family to explain the situation and express their regrets, and then sent their officer over to

Tourist Information

Ascain: *mairie*, **t** 05 59 54 00 84, out of season **t** 05 59 54 68 34. *Open winter Mon–Fri 9–12.15 & 2–5.15; July and Aug Mon–Fri 9.30–12.30 and 2.30–7 plus Sat 9.30–12.30 and 2.30–7, plus Sun 10.30–1.*

Sare: *mairie*, **t** 05 59 54 20 14, **f** 05 59 54 29 15, *www.sare.fr. Open Jan–Mar & Oct–Dec Mon–Fri 1.30–5.30; July and Aug Mon–Fri 9.30–12.30 & 3–6.30, rest of the year 9.30–12.30 & 2–6.*

St-Pée-sur-Nivelle: Place de la Poste, **t** 05 59 54 11 69, **f** 05 59 54 17 81. *Summer open Mon–Sat 9–12.30 & 2–7; winter Mon–Fri 9–12 & 2–6.*

Where to Stay and Eat

Prices for both rooms and meals in the Labourd will be a relief after the coast. And you'll never be disappointed with the quality of either – in fact the modest joys of an old Basque country inn may be one of the major reasons for coming here.

Ascain ✉ 64310

★★**Du Pont**, Route de St-Jean-de-Luz, **t** 05 59 54 00 40 (*inexpensive*). Rooms overlooking the Nivelle and its bridge and a delightful restaurant with a garden terrace: *feuilleté de langoustines* and other delicate dishes. *Menus €14–22. Open daily 1 Mar–31 Oct.*

★**Achafla Baïta**, Route d'Olhette, **t** 05 59 54 00 30 (*cheap*). Out in the peaceful countryside. There is also a good restaurant with lots of fish in a variety of sauces, from *cèpes* to *beurre blanc*. *Menus €19–32. Closed Mon and Tues eves in winter plus Nov.*

Sare ✉ 64310

In the Labourd, hotels tend to be sweet and simple, with immaculate rooms in white traditional buildings with red shutters and oak beams. Sare provides a bewildering choice of these, all wonderfully inviting.

★★★**Arraya**, Place du Village, **t** 05 59 54 20 46, **f** 05 59 54 27 04, *www.arraya.com* (*moderate*). Quite expensive for the area, but with a memorable restaurant. Menus are reasonable; might want to surrender a little more for specialities such as the *mesclange*, veal stuffed with foie gras, artichoke and *morels*. *Menus €21–31. Closed Nov–March*

Pikasseria, just outside Sare at Lehembiscay, **t** 05 59 54 21 51, **f** 05 59 54 27 40 (*inexpensive*), also has a good restaurant. *Restaurant closed Sun eves and Mon lunch except July and Aug.*

★**Col de St-Ignace** (*inexpensive*), at the pass on the D4 near the Rhune cable car, **t** 05 59 54 20 11, has a simple restaurant. *Menus €25–28. Open 1 April–11 Nov.*

Les Trois Fontaines, Col de St-Ignace, **t** 05 59 54 20 80 (*moderate–cheap*). A country *auberge* near the cable car. There's a charming terrace and garden, serving Basque specialities. *Menus €15–25. Closed 20 Dec–15 Mar.*

Ainhoa ✉ 64250

Itthurria, Place du Fronton, **t** 05 59 29 92 11, **f** 05 59 29 81 28, *www.itthurria.com* (*moderate*). A large Basque house with a celebrated restaurant, featuring dishes such as pigeon with garlic, and local foie gras. *Menus €28–43. Restaurant closed Wed plus Thurs lunch except July and Aug. Closed Nov–mid-Apr.*

★★**Oppoca**, Place du Fronton, **t** 05 59 29 90 72, **f** 05 59 29 81 03 (*inexpensive*). On the main street of this pretty village, in a restored 17th-century post house. Lovely rooms, some furnished with antiques. There is also a fine restaurant with a terrace, serving seafood and *confits*. *Menus €16–36. Closed mid-Nov–20 Dec*

Espelette ✉ 64250

★★ **Euzkadi**, Rue Principle, **t** 05 59 93 91 88, **f** 05 59 93 90 19, *www.hotel-retaurant-euzkadi.com*. Worth travelling out of your way for, even in an area rich in good restaurants. There are nice rooms with a small pool and tennis, and a remarkable restaurant where the chef is passionate about traditional Basque recipes and traditions. Some of the house specialities are things you won't see elsewhere, such as *axoa*, a stew of veal and peppers, and *tripoxa*, a black pudding in a pepper and tomato sauce. *Menus €16–27. Closed Nov and Dec, also closed Mon and Tue except July and Aug.*

The *Pottok*

It has a face that would make you suspect there was a camel somewhere in the family tree – but a sweet face just the same, with big soft eyes and a wild shaggy mane. It is quite shy, hiding out on the remotest slopes of the western Pyrenees, but it's not afraid of you; come too close and you'll get a bite to remember. The *pottok* is the wild native pony of the Basque country. They've been around for a while; drawings of *pottoks* have been found in the prehistoric caves up in the Dordogne.

Though they're hard to catch, people have been molesting the poor *pottoks* for centuries. A century ago, they were shipping them to Italy to make salami, or to Britain to pull mine cars, a dismal task for which their strength and small size made them perfectly adapted. Annual horse fairs took place in the villages of Espelette and Hélette. Business was so good that the unfortunate *pottoks* were on the road to extinction only a few decades ago. Then, a famous mayor of Sare, the late Paul Dutournier, stepped in, and got the government to set up a reserve for them on the slopes of La Rhune.

the hospital to make his apologles. In 1938 and '39, Sare's night workers found a more rewarding if less lucrative business – helping their countrymen from the Spanish side escape Franco's troops; a few years later, they were doing great work smuggling Allied pilots and spies back the other way.

Sare's **church** is a wonderful example of the traditional Basque style, with its three levels of wooden balconies; memorials inside include the tombs of one of the early figures of Basque literature, the 17th-century Pierre Axular. More than most villages, Sare has retained a number of fine **town houses** with carved lintels, both in the village and in the *quartier* of Lehenbizkai to the south – in the Basque country, outlying hamlets are considered as 'quarters', or neighbourhoods of the main village.

South of town, a side road off the D306 takes you to the **Grottes de Sare** (*t 05 59 54 21 88; open Easter hols 2–5; Easter until the end of June 10–6; July and Aug 10–7;Sept 10–6; Oct 10–5; Nov and Dec 2–5; closed Christmas day and Jan; adm; guided tours and sound and light show*), with Palaeolithic drawings largely destroyed by vandals in 1918; it's said that you can go in here and find your way out at the Cuevas de Bruja, across the border in Spain, but no one has tried it lately. The D306 continues on to the Col de Lizarrieta and the Spanish border on its way to Pamplona.

Saint-Pée-Sur-Nivelle and Ainhoa

In the late 1500s many gypsies and converted Muslims fleeing from Spanish persecution took refuge in the Labourd. In that most credulous of ages, all manner of stories about sorcerers and heathen rituals started circulating. The trouble began in 1609, started not by the Church's Inquisition, but by the Parlement de Bordeaux. A lawyer named de Lancre was sent, and like most professional witch-hunters this one revealed himself as a murderous psychotic. De Lancre installed himself in **Saint-Pée**'s château, and soon accused the baroness herself of forcing him to participate in a black Mass, where the Devil himself was present. With authority from the king, de

Lancre started a reign of terror that lasted three years. Relying largely on the testimony of children and tortured women, he had several hundred people condemned to the stake over the next three years. When he started barbecuing parish priests too, the Bishop of Bayonne finally put an end to it.

Ainhoa, one of the southernmost of all bastides, was founded in the days when the English were fighting with the Navarrese for control of this disputed region. A 13th-century Navarrese baron started it, not only to keep the English out, but with the intention of charging tolls and otherwise making money off pilgrims to Compostela. Despite the straight streets, Ainhoa is another lovely *Labourd* village with many old houses – note the lintel over the door of the **Maison Gorritia** on the main street, telling how a mother built it in 1662 with money sent home by her son in the West Indies. For a pleasant if steep walk, take the path up to the pilgrimage chapel of **Notre-Dame-de-Aranzazu**, with panoramic views over the valley.

From either St-Pée or Ainhoa, the next step is **Espelette**, the village famous for red peppers; in the late summer you'll see them hanging everywhere. Here too are many attractive old houses, a church with a Baroque altarpiece, and an interesting cemetery full of discoidal stones; you might note an odd modernistic one, marking the tomb of a local girl who became the first Miss World.

The Valley of the Nive

The little river that comes to such a handsome end among the quays and half-timbered houses of Bayonne has a long way to go before it reaches that city. Starting in the Spanish Pyrenees, it opens out into a narrow valley that cuts a diagonal swath across the Basque country. The D932/D918 that follows it is the high street of the Labourd and Basse-Navarre.

Hasparren to St-Etienne

From Bayonne, an alternative route to the D932 into the heart of the Basque country is the D22, the **Route Impériale des Cimes**, a beautiful road over the hilltops that was built in the time of Napoleon. It will take you to Hasparren, a grey, hard-working town where there is an unusual Roman altar behind the church. Nearby La Bastide-Clairence was founded by the king of Navarre in 1314; settled by Gascons, it long remained an ethnic enclave among the Basques. Just outside the village is a Jewish cemetery, from the community of Spanish refugees that formed here in the 1600s.

Southeast of Hasparren, near the village of St-Esteben, the **Grottes d'Istaritz et d'Oxocelhaya** (***t*** *05 59 29 64 72, www.grottes-d'istaritz.com; open daily Mar–May plus Oct and Nov 2–5; June–Sept 11–12 and 2–5; July and Aug 10–12 and 1–6; guided tours*) are one of the most important prehistoric sights of this region; tools, paintings and other relics, including a musical instrument, have been found here going back some 40,000 years. Most of these have been spirited off to museums though, and visitors will have to content themselves with a look at the underground stretch of the river

Irouléguy

From the sunny Palaeozoic Basque highlands come the red, rosé and white wines of Irouléguy, the wine that 'makes girls laugh'. Tucked in sheltered pockets in the mountains, and trained on vertical espaliers to protect the vines from frost, the once vast number of grape varieties has been limited since 1952, when Irouléguy was given its AOC status: cabernet (or acheria, 'fox' in Basque) and tannat for reds, and courbu and menseng for whites. Try the generous, sombre red Domaine de Mignaberry, the leading label produced by the co-operative Maîtres Vignerons du Pays Basque in St-Etienne-de-Baïgorry (*t 05 59 37 41 33, open Mon–Fri 9–12 and 2–6*) or the co-operative's fine fresh rosé, Les Terrasses de L'Arradoy. Of the independent growers, Domaine Brana, 3 bis Av du Jaï Alaï, St-Jean-Pied-de-Port (*t 05 59 37 00 44, open July–15 Sept daily 10–12 and 2.30–6.30*), has bottled some excellent, peppery reds (especially '91); Domaine Ilarria, in Irouléguy (*t 05 59 37 23 38, call ahead to visit*) produces a lovely rosy rosé.

Arbéroue, and some exceptional cave formations – delicate stalactites that have grown down to the floor to become columns.

On the main road, the D932 up the Nivelle valley, the first big village is **Ustaritz**, once the meeting place of the Biltzar. Next comes **Larressore**, known for the manufacture of *makilas*, and then the biggest village of the interior, **Cambo-les-Bains**. The name of this placid and genteel spa seems to come from a Roman army camp; locals called the site 'Caesar's camp' long ago. The spa grew up in the 16th century, and became briefly fashionable when Napoleon III and Eugénie visited from Biarritz. The Prince of Wales (Edward VII) also liked to drop in during his Biarritz holidays to see a legendary pelote star named Chiquito de Cambo play. Cambo's attraction is the **Villa Arnaga** (*t 05 59 29 70 57; open daily in April–Sept 10–7; closed Oct–Mar*), the home of dramatist Edmund Rostand, who came here in the 1900s to treat his pleurisy at the baths . The house contains mementos from his life and the Paris of the turn of the 20th century; the real attraction however is the splendid 18th-century-style French garden.

After Cambo, the foothills begin rising steadily. Nearby off the D918 is the sweet tiny village of **Itxassou**, famous for cherries. From here, through the hamlet of Laxia, a steep and difficult road can take you to the summit of 918m/3,010ft **Artxamendi** on the Spanish border, another ancient holy place. Besides a number of natural wonders, including waterfalls, small herds of *pottok* and rock needles, this 'mountain of the bear' has human remains ranging from long-abandoned iron mines and shepherds' huts to Neolithic dolmens and cromlechs.

From here, you cross the ancient boundary from the Labourd into Basse-Navarre. The next villages down the valley are **Bidarray** and **Ossès**, centres of a rich rolling country known for its *pur brebis*. Their prosperity 300 years ago has given both a number of fine houses, many with 17th-century inscriptions. Bidarray has a graceful medieval bridge, the Pont d'Enfer, and a rare 12th-century church, once the chapel of a hospice for Compostela pilgrims. If medieval churches are rare in these parts, it is only because of Basque tidiness; just as families rebuild their houses every few centuries on the same site, so they cannot stand to see an old church or any other building looking frowzy. Ossès's church, St-Julien, was entirely rebuilt by the villagers in the 1500s, with a built-in *fronton*, a later Baroque façade and a rich interior decoration similar to the churches of Spanish Navarre. The hills around the nearby modern village of **St-Martin-d'Arossa** offer three examples of another peculiarity of the Basque

Tourist Information

Ustaritz: Centre Lapurdi, **t** 05 59 93 20 81, **f** 05 59 70 32 80; *open all year Mon 2–6 Tues–Fri 9–12 and 2–6 plus Sat 9–12.*

Hasparren: 2 Place St Jean, **t** 05 59 29 62 02, **f** 05 59 29 62 02.

Cambo-les-Bains: Av de la Mairie, **t** 05 59 29 70 25, **f** 05 59 29 90 77; *open winter Mon–Fri 8.30–12.30 & 2–6 plus Sat 8.30–12 & 2–5.30; July and Aug 8.30–6.30 plus Sat 8.30–12.30 & 2–5.*

Market Days

Hasparren: every other Tuesday, and Saturday for farm produce.

Espelette: Wednesday mornings, and Saturday in July and August.

Ossès: Saturday mornings (summer only).

Where to Stay and Eat

Cambo-les-Bains ✉ 64250

★★**Bellevue**, Rue des Terrasses, **t** 05 59 93 75 75, **f** 05 59 93 75 85 (*inexpensive*). An old, pleasant establishment with a view, near the top of town. The restaurant serves menus costing €15–28. *Lunch €10. Closed Mon and Sun eve plus Nov–Mar.*

★★★**Hostellerie du Parc**, Place de la Mairie, **t** 05 59 93 54 54, *www.hotels-basque.com* (*inexpensive*), in the lower part of town, offers 10 pretty rooms, a little garden, and a reasonable restaurant. There is outside dining in summer. *Menus €16 plus* à la carte. *Closed Tues.*

★★**Chez Tante Ursule**, Bas Cambo, **t** 05 59 29 78 23, **f** 05 59 29 28 57 (*inexpensive*). Small rustic hotel with a modern annexe. There is also an excellent restaurant. Try the pimentoes stuffed with *morue* or salads with foie gras or *boudin noir*. *Menus €15–34. Closed Tues all year; closed mid Feb–mid Mar.*

Domaine de Xixtaberri, Quartier Hegala, **t** 05 59 29 22 24 34, *www.xixtaberri.com* (*moderate*). Bright colourful rooms. A *ferme-auberge* up in the hills that is simpler but equally special. The restaurant menu is full of duck and foie gras. The hotel opens year-round, but the restaurant opens Oct–May only for the winter season. *Menu €25.*

Itxassou ✉ 64250

Itxassou Hotel, Ixistulari direction St-Jean-Pied-de-Port, **t** 05 59 29 75 09. Traditional Basque villa that has been modernized. Well run and neat as a pin. Nice terrace plus pool with lovely views. Regional cuisine, popular with the locals. *Menus €15 plus à la carte; lunch weekdays €12. Restaurant closed Sun eves plus 3 weeks in Dec and 1 week Jan.*

★★**Fronton**, Place du Fronton, **t** 05 59 29 75 10, **f** 05 59 29 23 50, *www.hotelrestaurantfronton.com* (*moderate–inexpensive*). The hotel of choice in the village. The restaurant has a room with a view, and the artichoke hearts with foie gras followed by a fillet of sole St-Jacques or a *confit* make a satisfying dinner. *Menus €16–29. Closed Wed in Jan and Feb plus 1 week in Dec.*

★★**Etchepare Sallaberia**, Place de la Mairie, **t** 05 59 29 75 14. *Menus €13–23. Closed mid-Nov–Mar.*

Bidarray ✉ 64780

Hôtel Barberaenea, Place de L'Eglise 64780 Bidarray, **t** 05 59 37 74 86, *www.hotel-barberaenea.fr.* The Bidarray offers a perfect setting, nestled in rolling hills with mountain views, nothing but the odd bleat or sheep's bell to break the quiet. The hotel is at the top of the village in the square opposite the 12th-century church. There are three leafy terraces and the interior is a step back in time; flagstone floors, rustic beams and antique Basque furniture. The same family has run an inn here since 1875. Bedroom are a good size, comfortable and immaculate. The restaurant serves traditional fare. *Menus €16–22. Restaurant closed Tues–Wed and Thurs Jan–April. Closed 15 Nov–15 Dec.*

Roland the Rotter

All over the south of France, the very mountains and rocks carry the memory of Roland – the Brèche de Roland in the High Pyrenees, hewn with a mighty stroke of the hero's sword Durandal, or a cleft in a great boulder where touched the hoof of his horse. From France, his fame spread across Europe, remembered in everything from Ariosto's Renaissance epic *Orlando Furioso* to the ancient, mysterious statue of 'Roland the Giant' that stands in front of the city hall in Bremen. But who is this Roland really?

Outside the *Chanson de Roland* and the other versions of the legend, information is scarce. The chronicler Eginhardt, writing *c.* 830, mentions a certain Roland, Duke of the Marches of Brittany, who perished in the famous ambush in the Pyrenees in the year 778, without according him any particular importance. Two hundred years later, this obscure incident had blossomed into one of the great epics of medieval Europe. Here is the mighty hero, with his wise friend and companion in arms Oliver. He is the most *puissant* knight in the army of his uncle Charlemagne, come down from the north to crusade against the heathen Muslims of Spain. Charlemagne swept all before him, occupying many lands south of the Pyrenees and burning Pamplona to the ground before coming to grief at an unsuccessful siege of Zaragoza. On their return, Roland and Oliver, with the rearguard, are trapped at the pass of Roncevaux, the 'Gate of Spain', thanks to a tip from Roland's jealous stepfather Ganelon. Numberless hordes of *paynims* overwhelm the French; though outnumbered, they cut down Saracens by the thousand, like General Custer or John Wayne against the

country, the *gaztelu*. This is an earth- and rock-built hilltop fortress dating from the Iron Age; no one knows if the native populations or invading Celts built them.

St-Etienne-de-Baïgorry, the principal centre for the production of Irouléguy wine, is really a collection of villages around the Nive and its branch, the Nive des Aldudes. St-Etienne, the centre, has another lovely humpbacked medieval bridge, and the château of the feudal *seigneurs*, the Etxauz.

St-Jean-Pied-de-Port

This town's real name, in Basque, is *Donihane Garazi*, and they have spelled it out in flowers at the entrance to remind us. The French name is even more curious, but *port* is an old mountain word for a pass, and St-Jean, or Donihane, stands at the foot of the pass of Roncevaux, the 'Gate of Spain' of medieval French legend and poetry. The location has made it a busy place. From the 8th century, Arab armies must have passed this way many times on their way to raid France; Charlemagne and Roland came back the other way to raid Spain, and pass into legend along the way. Pilgrims from all over Europe came through on their way to Compostela, and another famous visitor, Richard the Lion-Heart, put the original town – now nearby St-Jean-le-Vieux – to siege in 1177. When he took it, that most pitiless and destructive of warriors razed it to the ground; the kings of Navarre refounded St-Jean on its present site soon after.

savage Injuns. Finally Roland, cut with a hundred wounds, sounds his horn Oliphant to warn Charlemagne and the main army, alas too far away to rescue them. In vain the dying Roland smites his sword against the rock to break it, meaning to keep it from the hands of the infidels. As he dies, the angels Michael and Gabriel appear to carry his soul to heaven (and as for his sword, though it isn't mentioned in the *Chanson de Roland*, he throws Durandal into the air and it lands in the rock of Rocamadour, an important pilgrimage site in the Lot).

History says it wasn't a Muslim horde at all, but rather the Basques who did Roland in. And why shouldn't they get their revenge on these uncouth Franks who were invading and devastating their lands, trying to force this democratic nation to kneel before some crowned foreign thug who called himself their king? We might excuse a people who did not even have a word in their language for 'king', if they were not much impressed either with Charlemagne or his duke. The exact process by which this affair metamorphosed into an epic will never be known, but tales and songs in the oral tradition must have spread and refined themselves constantly over those two centuries, until the caterpillar Roland of history re-emerged into the written word as the mythological butterfly of the *Chanson*. As in many epics from Virgil to *El Cid*, a modicum of political propaganda is involved. For the French, up in Paris, glorification of Carolingian imperialism provided poetic justification for the expansionist dreams of the medieval Capetian kings. And replacing the embattled Basque farmers with bejewelled infidel knights for an enemy makes perfect sense: the time of the *Chanson* also witnessed the beginning of the Crusades.

Though it still holds four big fairs each year, just as in medieval times, St-Jean today makes more of its living from visitors; it's the main centre for mountain tourism in the Basque lands, and in summer it can be quite a crowded place. Bars, restaurants and souvenir shops pack the centre, along the D933 and the picturesque streets around the **Vieux Pont** over the Nive. Old houses with wooden balconies hang over the little river, and facing the bridge stands the church of **Notre-Dame**, originally built by Sancho the Strong of navarre in commemoration of the battle of Navas de Tolosa (1212), where the Christian Spaniards finally put an end to Muslim dominance of the peninsula. The current building is Gothic, rare in these parts, though it has been much reworked since. The old streets climb up from here to the house which the St-Jeanais have called the **Prison des Evêques** (*41 Rue de la Citadelle,* ***t*** *05 59 37 00 92; open Easter–early Nov daily 11–12.30 and 2.30–6.30; July and Aug 10–7*), and turned into a tourist attraction. The house in fact seems to have belonged to a merchant, and the unusual vaulted underground chamber may have been for storing his wares, like the similar cellars in Bayonne. The bishops who lived in the mansion above it *c.* 1400 weren't exactly kosher – supporters of the Antipope at Avignon during the great Schism – and the chains and shackles in the cellar wall were probably used by local authorities in the 18th century to lock up poor peasants who didn't pay their salt tax. If you climb to the top of the town for the view, you'll find the **citadel**, a castle last remodelled in the 17th century by Vauban.

Just east on the D933 stands St-Jean's original, **St-Jean-le-Vieux**. The town destroyed by the Lion-Heart has only the Romanesque tympanum of its church to remind it of its former importance. There are also scanty remains of a large Roman camp, including baths. North of St-Jean-le-Vieux, on a height above the D933, a venerable stone pillar with a cross on top is locally known as the **Croix de Ganelon**, supposedly the spot where Roland's treacherous stepfather was pulled apart by wild horses on Charlemagne's command.

South of St-Jean, the D933 leads down to the Spanish border and 16km beyond that, the cold, misty pass of Roncevaux itself. For an alternative, if you want to get really lost, take the D301 from St-Jean down to the pretty village of **Estérençuby**, hub of a wild maze of steep narrow roads and hiking trails around the border. With a good

Tourist Information

Place Charles-de-Gaulle, t 05 59 37 03 57, **f** 05 59 37 34 91, *www.terre-basque.com.* They offer free guided tours of the town on Mon and Fri mornings in summer. *Open July and Aug Mon–Sat 9–7; the rest of the year Mon–Sat 9–12 & 2–6.*

Market Days

Mondays.

Where to Stay and Eat

St-Jean-Pied-de-Port ✉ 64220

Being a popular tourist base, St-Jean's hotel prices are substantially higher than the other villages in the area.

Les Pyrénées, Place Général de Gaulle, **t** 05 59 73 01 01, **f** 05 59 37 18 97 (*expensive*) has a restaurant that is one of the most esteemed culinary temples in all the Basque country. Hotel is a member of Relais & Châteaux and has a pool and Jacuzzi. People come from miles around for cooking that, while not notably innovative, brings the typical Basque-Gascon repertoire of duck, foie gras and game dishes to perfection; they're especially noted for their desserts. A gratifying *menu* (*exc Sun*) puts Les Pyrénées within the reach of most. *Menus €40–86. Closed Mon eve from Nov–Mar and Tues exc July–Sept. Closed 20 Nov–20 Dec.*

Hôtel Central, Place Charles de Gaulle, **t** 05 59 37 00 22, **f** 05 59 37 27 79 (*moderate*). Old family hotel and restaurant with views over the River Nive, which according to the fishing season yields such delights as salmon and eels for the table. *Menus €19–42. Closed Tues in winter and Dec–Mar.*

★★**Ramuntcho**, 1 Rue France, **t** 05 59 37 03 91, **f** 05 59 37 35 17 (*inexpensive*). One of the nicest places to stay in the old town, just inside the Porte de France. Rooms have balconies and a view. The restaurant serves good simple dishes. *Menus €14–26. June and Sept closed Wed, Oct–May closed Tues and Wed plus mid-Nov–26 Dec.*

★★**Hôtel des Remparts**, Place Floquet, **t** 05 59 37 13 79, **f** 05 59 37 33 44, *www.touradour.com/hotel-remparts.htm* (*inexpensive*). The cheapest accommodation option. *Menus €11–19. Closed weekends Oct–April plus Nov and Dec.*

Pecoïtz, t 05 59 37 11 88, in Aincille, just south of St-Jean-le-Vieux on the D118 (*cheap*). Rooms cheaper than anything in the town, a quiet and lovely setting, and a very good restaurant that does game dishes in season, trout and *confits*. *Menus €14–23. Closed Thurs eve and Fri out of season and 1 Jan–15 Mar.*

Esterençuby

★★**Sources de la Nive, t** 05 59 37 10 57 (*inexpensive*), is in Esterençuby, 11km south of town. Set among the mountain forests, next to the river, it offers all the calm you can stand, as well as a restaurant that serves *salmis de palombe* (don't ask where the dove came from), and other rural treats. There is a swimming pool. *Menus €12–27. Closed Tues in winter and Jan.*

map, you can find your way to the abandoned **Château Pignon**, a battered old castle last rebuilt by Ferdinand of Aragon that saw trouble in every conflict up to the Napoleonic wars. Even better, take the D428 up to the **Col d'Arnostéguy**, passing the primeval beeches of the **Forêt d'Orion** in one of the remotest parts of the region; exactly on the border stands the mysterious **Tour d'Urkulu**, a circular platform of huge, well-cut stone blocks some 65ft in diameter. Some historians, for lack of a better explanation, suppose it to be the remains of a Roman victory monument, like the ones set up on the Mediterranean at La Turbie and Perthuis. It is just as likely, though, that it is far older; the surrounding slopes are littered with dolmens, cromlechs and other Neolithic remains, and arrowheads dated from the Bronze Age have been found on the site. Some have speculated that the name Urkulu, which has no meaning in Basque, might have something to do with Hercules.

The Haute-Soule

By now, the mountains are getting taller and so are the roofs: steep slate ones become more common than the Roman tiles of the coast. From St-Jean-le-Vieux, the D18 will take you deeper into the remotest corner of the French Basque country, the beautiful, seldom-visited Haute-Soule, a 50km stretch of Pyrenees with scarcely more than 1,000 inhabitants. From the village of Mendive, an alternative route is the D117, narrow but marvellously scenic, passing near several peaks of over 910m/3,000ft. The only settlement it passes is **Ahusquy**, a former spa; from here trails lead into one of the largest of Pyrenean forests, the **Forêt des Arbailles**.

The D18/D19 is just as good, though more difficult, crossing three mountain passes before it arrives at **Larrau**, the closest thing to a village the Haute-Soule can offer. The GR 10, the hiking trail that runs the length of the Pyrenees, passes nearby, among many other trails, and if you have some time to spare there are a number of attractions: west of Larrau is a small ski station called **Les Chalets d'Iraty**, set amidst another lovely beech forest, the **Forêt d'Iraty**. This area is a major transit point for many kinds of migrating birds; serious birdwatchers come from all over to see them in autumn. Hunters come too, and some of them still follow the practice of trapping doves by the thousands in great nets – remarkably this is still legal in France. Netting birds is turning into a hot issue, and considerable hostility surfaces each year between hunters, birders, environmentalists and the local authorities.

East of Larrau, the GR 10 leads you to the wild and spectacular **Gorges d'Holcarte**, a series of canyons explored for the first time only in 1908; now a trail runs along the top, with a cable footbridge across the gorge. Further east the GR 10 meets another, similar sight, the **Gorges de Kakouetta**, also accessible by car on the D113 (***t*** *05 59 28 60 83; tours from mid-March–mid-Nov daily 8am until dark*). Here too a trail has been laid out; there's a lovely waterfall at the end. The D113 continues to a dead end in the mountains, passing tiny **Ste-Engrâce**. This is one of the most isolated and tradition-bound of all Basque villages; the twisting road up to it was only built a decade ago. It is also the unlikely setting for one of the most fascinating medieval churches in the

Pyrenees. Built in the 12th century, this cockeyed church sits on a slope, tilted and asymmetric; pilasters added a century ago keep it from sliding away. The Romanesque tympanum shows the chrism, the monogram of Christ, in a circle supported by two flying angels – a remarkable example of the persistence of symbolism. Replace the chrism with a laurel crown and you have the emblem of the Roman Imperium from the time of Augustus. The carved capitals inside are painted in detail, as Romanesque sculpture was meant to be. One shows a pair of lovers; for lack of a better explanation they are said to represent Solomon and Sheba, accompanied by a medieval European's idea of what an elephant might look like; others seem to show Salome's dance and the three Magi. Behind the church is an old cemetery with some strange discoidal tombstones.

Heading north from the Haute-Soule, the D26/D918 follows the valley of the Saison (or Gave de Mauléon, depending to whom you're talking), a stream popular with canoeists. The valley is a rich land, thick with tiny villages of which the largest is **Tardets**. **Ordiarp** has an interesting Romanesque church and cemetery in a pretty setting. There are caves with prehistoric paintings around Ossas and Camou, but they are currently closed to the public. The peculiarity of this area is its large number of *gaztelu*; good examples can be found near the villages of Aussurucq, Ideaux-Mendy, Etchebar (an especially impressive one with three circuits of fortifications), Alçay, and Ordiarp; this must have been as hot a border region in the Bronze Age as it was in the time of Louis XIII.

East of Tardets, the D918 takes you to the villages of **Aramits** and **Arette**. The former is the home of Dumas's musketeer Aramis; there have always been some people here who won't admit he's a fictional character. The latter is largely new, rebuilt after a surprise earthquake in 1967.

The Inner Reaches of the Soule: Mauléon

At first glance, the temptation to leave this grey industrial town immediately might be irresistible. But hang around a while; Mauléon, the town of the evil lion (*mauvais lion*), has character. They make furniture, sheep cheese and fabrics here too, but everyone knows Mauléon as the world capital of the espadrille. And even though most of these classic French summer sandals may be produced in Asia these days (what isn't?), Mauléon's little factories still do their best to keep competitive. The capital of the Soule is a proper Basque village with its working clothes on, that's all.

To prove its Basqueness, there is the busy and famous *fronton* right in the centre, on the park called Les Allées. Mauléon's château faces it, the **Château d'Andurain du Maytie** (*1 Rue Jeu de Paume, **t** 05 59 28 04 18; open 1 July–20 Sept, visits at 11am and 3–6, last visit at 5.30; closed Sun am and Thurs; adm*), also known as the Hôtel du Maytie. This stern yet graceful building was erected in the early 1600s by a local boy who became bishop of Oloron-Ste-Marie in nearby Béarn. It is still in the original family; highlights are the Renaissance fireplaces and the grand oaken carpentry that holds up the steep roof, designed by a shipwright. Old Mauléon climbs precipitously up to the town's other castle, the **Château Fort** (*For information, call tourist office; **t** 05 59 28 02 37; open daily 15 June–15 Sept; adm*). There has probably been a castle on this site

Tourist Information

Mauléon: 10 Rue J. B. Heugos, **t** 05 59 28 02 37, **f** 05 59 28 02 21, *www.valleedesoule.com. Open all year Mon–Fri 9–12.30 and 2–6; July and Aug 9–1 and 2–7.*

St-Palais: Place Charles de Gaulle, **t** 05 59 65 71 78, **f** 05 59 65 69 15.

Market days

Tardets: every other Monday, and every Monday in July and August.

Mauléon: Tuesday and Saturday mornings.

St-Palais: Fridays.

Where to Stay and Eat

Mauléon ✉ 64130

★★**Bidegain**, Rue de la Navarre, **t** 05 59 28 16 05, **f** 05 59 19 10 26 (*inexpensive*). This friendly, immaculate hotel across from the château is highly praised in a guidebook from the 1920s that we chanced upon at an old book sale. The praise is still deserved, and what's more the place doesn't seem to have changed all that much in 80 years. The restaurant is a real winner, with tables set in a sweet covered terrace looking out on to the delightful gardens. *Menus €26 plus à la carte. Closed Sun eve and Mon in winter plus 2 weeks in Mar.*

Barcus ✉ 64130

★★**Chilo**, **t** 05 59 28 90 79, **f** 05 59 28 93 10 (*moderate*). Way out in the middle of nowhere, some 15km east of Mauléon, and it's worth the detour. Some rooms are fancy and furnished with antiques. This hotel has been in the same family for generations. There is also a pool. There's a fine restaurant, with a garden terrace, which is especially good for fish, along with starters like a salmon terrine and a wide range of tempting desserts. *Menus €15–60. Closed Sun eve plus Mon and Tues lunch in winter and Jan.*

St-Palais ✉ 64120

Hôtel de Trinquet, **t** 05 59 65 73 13, **f** 05 59 65 83 84 (*inexpensive*). Traditional hotel in the central square of this market town, with a classic wood-beamed restaurant. *Menus €16–26.*

for at least 3,000 years; this latest version dates from the 1300s, rebuilt after Richard the Lion-Heart chased out the French viscount and wrecked the place in 1261. Mauléon and the castle remained English until 1449, when the viscount of Béarn seized it. In 1642 Richelieu ordered it destroyed, but before the work was done he changed his mind and ordered it rebuilt, and sent a bill for 130,000 livres to the Mauléonais, causing a fierce but short-lived fracas called the Revolt of Matalas. A tour of the castle may be wonderfully evocative, but watch your step – parts of it could collapse at any minute.

St-Palais

The northeastern corner of the Basque lands is a humble country, where you'll see plenty of livestock and farming paraphernalia and little else. Its only centre is an equally humble though quite pleasant village with a memorable Friday morning market, St-Palais (*San Pelayo* in Basque). Once St-Palais had a viscount and a mint, and the village disputed with St-Jean-Pied-de-Port the honour of capital of Basse-Navarre; today it's best known as host to the annual *Festival de Force Basque* each August (and a lot of the farmers you'll see walking around on market day look as if they could be competitors).

From the old days all that survives is the mansion called the **Maison des Têtes** across from the chapel of St-Paul on Rue du Palais-de-Justice. A 17th-century house of a noble family, its façade is decorated with odd 'heads' including those of Henri IV and Jeanne d'Albret. Nearby, in the courtyard of the *mairie*, you can mull over St-Palais' history in the small **Musée de Basse Navarre** *(Place Charles de Gaulle,* ***t*** *05 59 65 71 78; open all year Mon–Sat 9.30–12.30 and 2–6.30).*

Béarn

09

Béarn

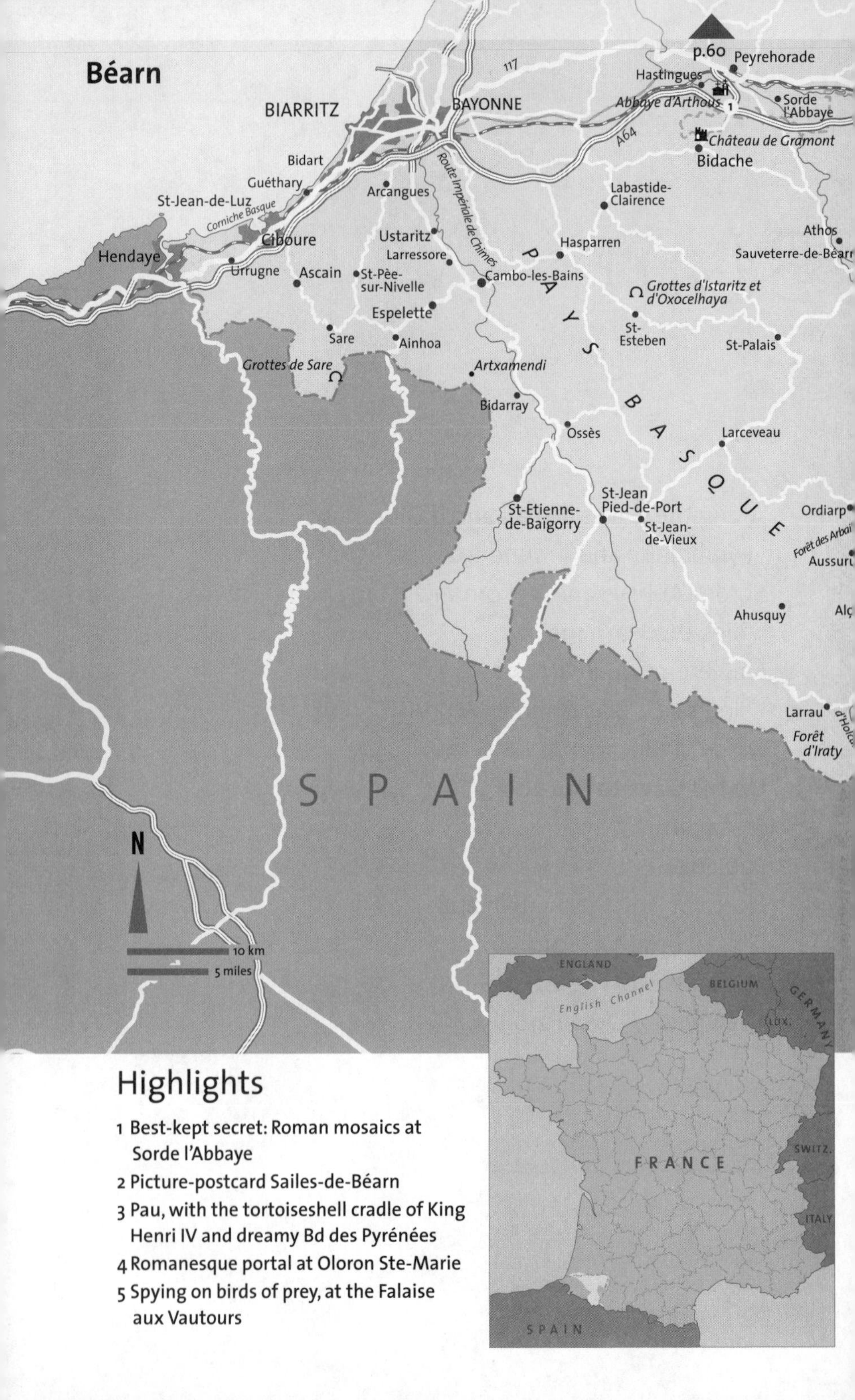

Highlights

1 Best-kept secret: Roman mosaics at Sorde l'Abbaye
2 Picture-postcard Sailes-de-Béarn
3 Pau, with the tortoiseshell cradle of King Henri IV and dreamy Bd des Pyrénées
4 Romanesque portal at Oloron Ste-Marie
5 Spying on birds of prey, at the Falaise aux Vautours

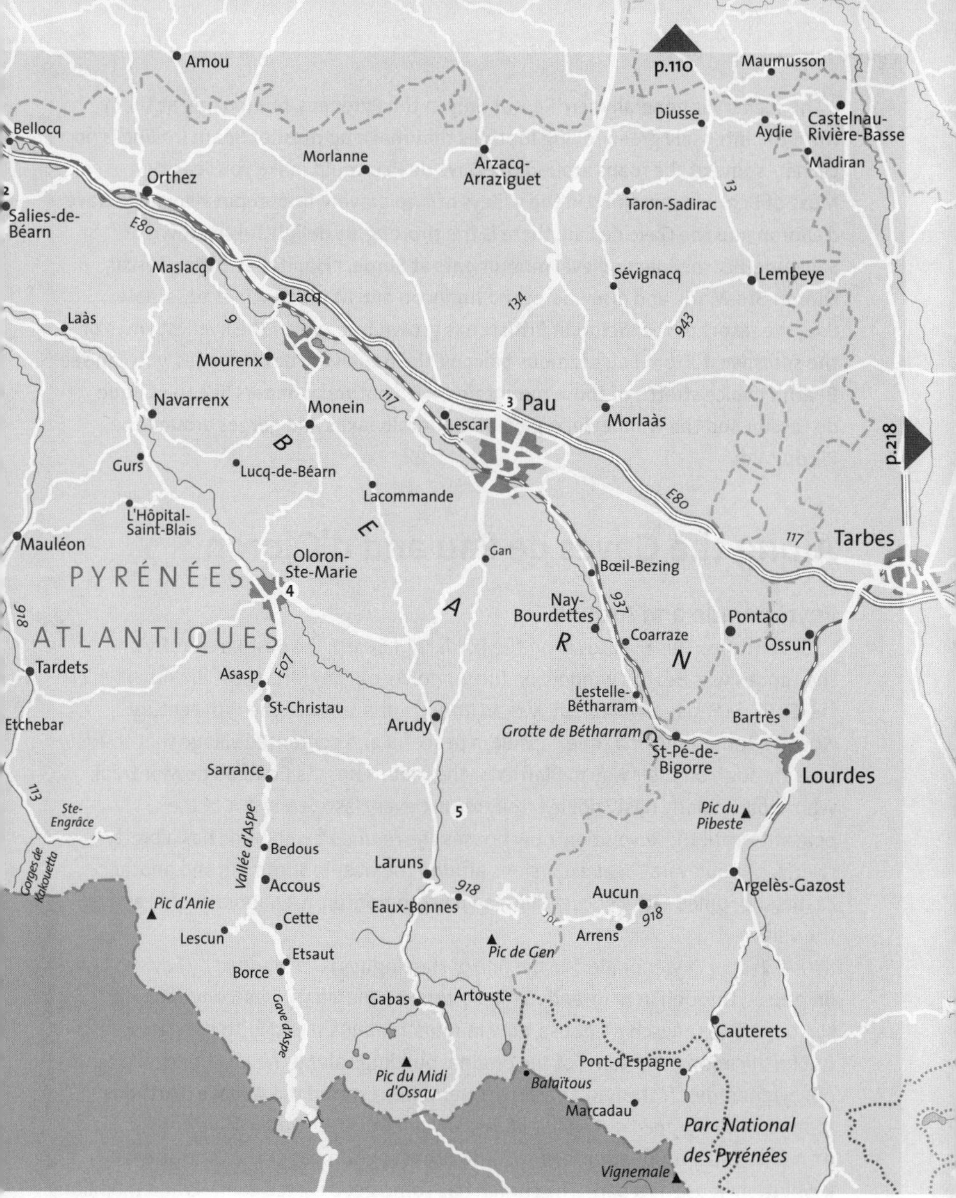

Anno 1609. Vive la Vache. That is the inscription we saw on a typical carved lintel over the door of a village house. The 'cow' is the proud device on Béarn's coat of arms, the symbol of this stalwart Pyrenean Ruritania. There are two cows really, sporting their cowbells, but sheep would have done just as well. From the earliest times, this isolated region of mountains and foothills has been above all a grazing land, its calendar punctuated by the annual descent and return of the shepherds and cowherds from the Pyrenean Vallée d'Aspe and Vallée d'Ossau. There isn't much else that is really distinctive about Béarn – what gives the region its identity is its long history as an independent state.

The scenery is generally terrific, not only in the Pyrenees, but looking at them from the intensely green rolling foothills that make up most of Béarn (*rolling* is no cliché – some of the roads around the Gave de Pau could make you seasick). Most of Béarn is contained in the valleys of two gravely, impetuous rivers, the Gave d'Oloron and the Gave de Pau; there is the thoroughly delightful spa town of Salies-de-Béarn; fine medieval monuments at Sorde, l'Hôpital-St-Blaise, Lescar, Oloron-Ste-Marie and elsewhere; and Jurançon and Madiran wines to sample. Pau, the resort of the Victorian British, has grown into one of the liveliest cities of the southwest. From Pau's famous balcony, the Boulevard des Pyrénées, you can see Béarn's choice stretch of those mountains, with natural wonders like the Cirque de Lescun and the wonderful region of mountain lakes and gorges around the Pic du Midi.

Along the Gaves de Pau and d'Oloron

Peyrehorade and Around

For centuries, this river town on the borders of Béarn, the Basque country and the Landes was Béarn's window on the world. As the point furthest inland at which the Gave de Pau is navigable, it was an important port until the 19th century. Now it's something of a time capsule, a peaceful and contented village that tourists pass through on their way to Biarritz or the mountains. Its **Château de Montréal**, whose particularly nasty noble family wrung every last penny out of the peasants until the Revolution, now houses the *mairie*. Peyrehorade has a pretty riverfront boulevard (boat excursions around the river in summer), and another castle, the ruined 13th-century **Château d'Aspromonte**, on a panoramic hill above the village.

Just west of Peyrehorade, the bastide of **Hastingues** was founded by Edward I when he passed through in 1289, and named after his seneschal of Gascony, John de Hastings. The seneschal's house, now in ruins, remains, along with the gates, parts of the fortifications, and some of the original buildings along the Rue Principale. South of Peyrehorade, off the D19, the department has restored the **Abbaye d'Arthous** (***t** 05 58 73 03 89; open 9–12 and 2–6pm, till 5pm Nov–Feb; closed Mon; adm*), a once-wealthy foundation, begun in 1167, that spent most of the time after the Revolution in use as a barn. The church has some good carved capitals and modillons, along with tympanum, recently discovered in pieces and restored; it shows an unusual subject, the *Adoration of the Magi*. Inside the cloister, a small museum of archaeological finds has been assembled.

Further south, on the borders of the Basque lands, is **Bidache**. By some quirk of history this village's lord owed no feudal allegiance to the viscount, the king of France, or anyone else, and Bidache remained practically independent up to the Revolution. Today, it offers the visitor the romantic ruined **Château de Gramont** along with the **Cité des Aigles** (*open June–Sept daily 2.30–6.30, closed Mon in Sept; the birds fly at 3.30 and 5pm; adm*), with trained eagles, vultures, falcons and kites.

Corisande

Diane d'Andouins, Comtesse de Guiche, was the daughter of the royal seneschal of Béarn. As a girl, she loved nothing more than reading the chivalric romances popular in the 16th century, the sort of books parodied by *Don Quixote*. So much was she taken with these fond medieval fantasies that she began calling herself 'Corisande', after the heroine of one of the most famous romances, *Amadis de Gaule*.

As this Corisande grew up to become one of the celebrated beauties of the age, she never lost her sense of chivalric virtue. Up at court in Paris, she was pressed into service by Catherine de' Medici for her famous *bataillon volant* of charmers, girls sent to seduce the notables of France and influence them to support the queen's endless political intrigues. It didn't work out; the accounts suggest Corisande wasn't up to the ultimate sacrifice the job occasionally required.

When her husband, Philibert de Gramont, was killed in the Wars of Religion, Corisande retired to his castle at Bidache. Already celebrated for her virtue in Catherine's court, as well as for her considerable intelligence and grace, she now became something of a legend, sitting up in her castle like the Lady of Shalott. It proved irresistibly attractive to young Henri of Navarre, the young firebrand who had already put in a night's wenching in every town between Flanders and the Pyrenees. Henri polished up his manners and came to Bidache to court Corisande. Although perhaps never consummated, it was a relationship that changed history. French historians credit Corisande with civilizing the Gascon warrior, with giving him some belated lessons in tenderness and courtesy. The two became friends for life, and Corisande contributed sympathy, good advice – and a good deal of cash – all through the campaigns that brought Henri IV to the throne of France.

Corisande's hour at the Château de Gramont was a brief moment of refinement in what was on the whole a pretty sordid story. The Gramonts began their career as the archetypal robber barons, the sort that medieval guidebooks warned pilgrims about. One of the main roads to Compostela passed near Bidache, and the Gramonts lived off what they could take, while cleverly playing the French, English, Spaniards and Navarrese against each other to maintain their independence. Corisande's own son, when he became lord of the manor, had his wife put to death for adultery. During the Revolution, the château was pressed into service as a military hospital. Its director had been embezzling funds and selling off medicines for profit. When he was found out in 1795, he torched the château and drowned himself in the River Bidouze.

Sorde-l'Abbaye and its Roman Villa

t *05 58 73 09 62; open Apr–mid-Nov Tues–Sun 10.30–12 and 2.30–6.30; rest of the year Mon–Fri 9–12 and 1.30–5.*

For one of the surprise attractions of this region, take the D29 east from Peyrehorade to Sorde, a tiny village on the Gave d'Oloron. The place has always been inhabited; prehistoric traces have been discovered in nearby caves, and Neolithic peoples added some curious earthworks outside the village at La Redoute. A wealthy

Tourist Information

Peyrehorade: *Mairie*, 147 Quai du Sablot, **t** 05 58 73 00 52, **f** 05 58 73 16 53; *open Sept–June Tues–Sat 9.30–12.30 and 2–5.30; July and Aug until 6.*

Salies-de-Béarn: Rue des Bains, **t** 05 59 38 00 33, **f** 05 59 38 02 95, *www.bearn-gaves.com. Open winter Mon–Fri 9.30–12 and 2–6; summer Mon–Sat same hours until 6 plus Sun am.*

Sauveterre-de-Béarn: Place Royale, **t** 05 59 38 58 65. *Winter open Tues–Sat 9–12 and 2–6; July and Aug same hours plus Mon am.*

Navarrenx: Pl des Casernes, **t** 05 59 66 14 93. *Open July and Aug daily 10–12.30 and 2–7; June and Sept Mon–Sat until 6; rest of the year Tues–Sat until 5.*

Market Days

Peyrehorade: Wednesdays.

Navarrenx: Wednesdays.

Where to Stay and Eat

Peyrehorade ✉ 40300

***Central**, Place Aristide Briande, **t** 05 58 73 01 44 (*inexpensive*). Opposite the village church; well-kept and correct; the hotel also has a restaurant – a simple, unpretentious room with nothing to offer but exceptional cooking, with treats like *pot-au-feu* with foie gras. *Menus €16–40. Open daily July–Sept. Other times closed Fri and Sun eves and Mon lunch plus Xmas and 3 weeks in Mar.*

Restaurant des Pêcheurs, on the road to Bidache, **t** 05 58 73 02 40. A basic pizzeria. *Closed Tues eve and Wed.*

Salies ✉ 64270

Salies is definitely the place to stay in this area, and there are plenty of choices.

Hôtel du Golf, **t** 05 59 65 02 10, **f** 05 59 38 16 41 (*inexpensive*). A posh-looking place with reasonable rates, a golf course and a good restaurant. *Menus €15–23. Restaurant closed Fri; hotel closed 3 weeks in Jan.*

***Hélios**, Domaine d'Hélios, **t** 05 59 38 37 59, **f** 05 59 38 16 41 (*inexpensive–cheap*). In the same complex as the Hôtel du Golf, but less expensive, with a garden setting and use of the golf course. *Open all year.*

Municipal camp site, Camping du Gave. Mosqueiros, **t** 05 59 38 53 30. Set in a lovely park with all the amenities. *Open Apr–mid-Oct.*

La Terrasse, Rue Saley, across from the church on Rue l'Oumé, **t** 05 59 38 09 83. For *confits* and suchlike, on a pleasant terrace overlooking the Saleys. *Menus €15–22. Closed Tues eve and Feb.*

Sauveterre-de-Béarn ✉ 64390

Hotel Reine Sancie, Rue du Pont, **t** 05 59 38 95 11, *www.lareinesancie.com*. A beautiful old house at the base of the village with a lovely terrace overlooking the river. Simple and classic décor and a good restaurant. *Usual menus €11–16. Open all year.*

Municipal camp site, **t** 05 59 38 53 30. Pleasantly situated under the trees by the river.

L'Hôpital-St-Blaise

***Auberge de Lausset**, opposite the church, **t** 05 59 66 53 03, **f** 05 59 66 21 78 (*inexpensive*). For a rural retreat amidst some delightful countryside, stop at this little-visited hamlet. Or at least stop for lunch at this modest family-run inn; it offers real country cooking where trout and other local favourites hold a prominent place on the menu. *Menus €12 (weekday lunch), €15–29. Closed Mon and 3 weeks Oct plus 2 weeks Jan.*

*****Hôtel du Commerce**, Place des Casernes 64190. Navarrenx, **t** 05 59 66 50 16, *www.hotel-commerce.fr*. This traditional Béarnaise house stands in the heart of the town. The interior is modern and comfortable whilst keeping its rustic charm. *Menus €16– 26. Closed 24 Dec–1 Feb.*

La Belle Auberge, 64270 Castagnéd (7km from Salies on D27), **t** 05 59 38 15 28. This simple looking auberge has the best reputation in the area. There is a very pleasant annexe with bedrooms, a large pool and garden but the real reason people travel for miles to the middle of nowhere is to enjoy the wonderful food. Excellent value. *Closed Sun and Mon eves plus 20 Dec–31 Jan and 1–15 June.*

Roman villa here metamorphosed into a Benedictine abbey during the Dark Ages. By the 12th century it was a major power in the area, owning vast lands, mills, forts and villages all around the Pays d'Orthe and beyond. The huge **church**, begun in the late 13th century, is as rough and crumbly as an oyster shell outside. Inside, there is no pearl, but a strange confusion of styles. While building was under way, in about 1290, this part of Aquitaine came under the control of the French king – meeting the threat of the English and their new settlement at Hastingues. The style of the church also changed, from southern Romanesque (as in the chapel to the right of the altar) to northern Gothic (chapel left of the altar).

In the jumble of half-ruined buildings behind the church, there are two things to see, but you'll have to dig up separate elderly caretakers for each. First, the half-ruined **abbey buildings**, in a picturesque state of medieval dilapidation; and secondly, the separate **abbot's residence**. The first clues to what's hidden inside are in the old abbot's gardens – walls and pavements carefully excavated by the archaeologist, along with fragments of mosaic. The abbot's residence, in fact, occupies the central part of the ancient Roman villa. Such historical continuity is not unusual; through the end of the Empire and the onset of the Dark Ages, the Roman élite gradually and gladly put much of its wealth and property in the hands of the Church, a Church that was after all their creation, and in which the élite's younger sons held all the positions of power. Some of Sorde's abbots may well have been lineal descendants of the Roman family that built the villa. The lady who looks after the place is a delight; rather formidably knowledgeable about the Romans and their works, she will give you a thorough tour of the **baths** that have been excavated underneath, along with the villa's residential quarters. Some of these contain mosaics with geometric and floral motifs, some with hunting scenes. Excellently preserved, with fresh colours and original designs, they are some of the best **Roman mosaics** discovered in southern France – and hardly anyone outside Sorde has ever seen them.

Salies-de-Béarn

'Salt City', they call it, and ever since Roman times an endless supply of the ever-popular NaCl has made this town's fortune. Salies may be the loveliest town in Béarn, a picture-postcard vision of steep-gabled houses overlooking the River Saleys. A mighty underground source, seven times saltier than the sea, once poured out enough water to make the whole area a saline swamp. Unsung engineers of the Bronze Age drained it for farmland, but it was probably the Romans who first found a way to put the waters to good use. Back at that remote date, life in Salies was probably much the same as documented in the 1500s: then nearly everyone lived from salt, collecting the water in great kettles, boiling it down, and carting the precious mineral off to the warehouse for their pay. Undercut by competition from Languedoc sea-salt in the 19th century, Salies found new life from the spring by becoming a spa. From the 1850s until the Second World War, Salies was in fashion with the Parisians; grand hotels, a Moorish-style bathhouse and even a casino were built.

Today the spa still does good business. And the Salies' tourist office still extols the virtues of its waters, with their 'excitative, but non-aggressive' properties, especially good for arthritis, gynaecological matters and underdeveloped children. Besides the sodium and chlorine they contain more magnesium than any other known spring in the world, a heavy load of sulphur, potassium and calcium, as well as bits of nickel, strontium, carbon, rubidium, boron, bromium, gallium and nearly everything else on the Periodic Table. There are veterinarians who will arrange a thermal cure to get your dog back into shape, or help its recuperation after surgery. The boosters have come up with a slogan for Salies tourism that might have been penned by Gertrude Stein: 'It's here; it's there ... it isn't anywhere else!'

From the Boar to the Baths

A walk through the old town, bordering the D933 that runs through Salies, is a delight. Start at the central Place du Bayaa, with the bronze boar's head of the salty **Fontaine du Sanglier**. An old legend of the founding of Salies had hunters on the track of this boar, who led them to the yet-undiscovered spring, where he was cornered and killed. The boar's motto is inscribed around Salies' coat of arms: *Si you nou y eri mourt arrès nou y bibéré* (had I not died here none of you would live).

Near the fountain are two small museums: a folkloric **Musée des Arts et Traditions Locales** (***t*** *05 59 38 00 33; open mid-May–mid-Oct Tues–Sat 3–6*) on Place du Bayaa, and on Rue des Puits-Salants, a 17th-century house that has been restored as the **Musée du Sel**, *(same number and hours as above)* where you can learn everything you wanted to know about salt-making in the old days. Many of the old half-timber houses on the surrounding streets still have the outdoor basins called *coulédés*, where they kept their salt.

The spa area is set in a park on the northern edge of town. Besides the *parfait*-striped Moorish bathhouse, there is the old casino, now a library, a Victorian bandstand, and the **Hôtel du Parc**, worth a look inside for its spectacular lobby, a tall skylighted court surrounded by mahogany-panelled galleries. Salies likes to keep its visitors busy: there are 'gondola' trips around the river in summer, a miniature golf course in the park, a salt-water swimming pool at the bathhouse, and opportunities for riding, tennis and most other sports; some of the streams in this area are extremely good for trout and salmon fishing; the tourist office has all the details. There is also a 12-hole golf course, at the Hôtel Hélios.

Around Salies

Bellocq, north of Salies, is the oldest bastide in Béarn; its rugged castle, under restoration, was built in the 1200s and hardly changed after that. South of Salies, **L'Hôpital d'Orion** was a commandery of the Knights of St John (the Knights Hospitallers) and a stop along the pilgrims' route to Compostela. From this survives an unusual 13th-century church. Gaston Fébus stopped at an inn here in 1391, after hunting the woods around Sauveterre. While cleaning up for dinner, a servant poured cold water over his hands. The count turned white and fell into his chair; he died half an hour later, probably from a cerebral haemorrhage.

Sauveterre-de-Béarn

A *sauveterre*, in the Middle Ages, was supposed to be a place of peace, exempt from all the terrors of feudal warfare; all the local barons, counts and dukes would promise faithfully to leave it alone. To show just how successfully this worked in practice, here is Sauveterre-de-Béarn, with the most imposing fortifications of any town in the region.

Viscount Centulle IV gave this sauveterre its charter in 1080, and for the next two centuries it prospered greatly, as evidenced by the ambitious Romanesque church of **St-André**, with its huge central tower and apse. There is some good sculpture here: a portal with Christ and the symbols of the Evangelists, and a few carved capitals.

Much of the walls survives, along with the gates and the huge bastion called the **Tour de Montréal**. The real attraction of Sauveterre, however, is its lovely setting on the wooded banks of the Gave d'Oloron, where you can see the town's landmark, a fortified, half-demolished medieval bridge called the **Pont de la Légende**. In 1170, the wife of Viscount Gaston V of Béarn, a Navarrese princess named Sancie, was charged with aborting her child. A trial by ordeal was decided, and Sancie was thrown from this bridge, tied hand and foot. She popped up like a cork and washed up on the bank 'three arrow shots downstream', as the chroniclers put it, and the judges were satisfied.

Around Sauveterre-de-Béarn

Laàs, 9 kilometres up the Gave from Sauveterre on the D27, has an 18th-century castle set in a gorgeous park; it was meticulously restored by a gentleman named Serbat, who was president of the French antique dealers association. Part of it is now open as a museum (***t** 05 59 38 91 53; open daily July and Aug 10–7; May, June, Sept and Oct 10–12 and 2–7; closed Tues and April 2–7; adm*) containing a rich collection of tapestries and furnishings from the 16th–18th centuries. There is also a good number of historical curiosities: a beautiful 14th-century book of hours that belonged to the Dukes of Burgundy, Mary Queen of Scots' sewing scissors, and the bed Napoleon slept in the night after Waterloo. Laàs will also seek to regale you with its Museum of Corn.

Athos, just northeast of Sauveterre along the Gave, is – could you doubt it? – the home of the first of the Three Musketeers; the village also has a pretty Gothic church.

Another village on the Gave d'Oloron, **Navarrenx**, has fortifications as good as Sauveterre's. These, however, aren't medieval, but the first modern anti-artillery walls in France. An Italian engineer named Fabrizio Siciliano designed them in 1521; the last word in military architecture for their day, a century and a half later not even the great Vauban, Louis XIV's chief fortress-builder, could find anything to improve here. The walls were only tested once, when Protestant refugees gathered here and held off a Catholic army for two months in 1569.

L'Hôpital-St-Blaise and its Moorish Church

Continuing down the Gave d'Oloron, you'll pass **Gurs**. This honest village has no touristic pretensions whatsoever; the big sign it has erected along the D936 spells out facts and figures – 'so that we remember'. In 1939, 30,000 Spaniards fleeing Franco's final victory were interned at a camp here; among them were many members of the International Brigade. A few years later, under the occupation, the camp held 30,000 Jews, most of them refugees from Germany. Most were shipped eastwards in 1944; those that died here are buried, along with many Spaniards, in the cemetery on the southern edge of town. It may be a discordant note in this serene countryside, but it is a memorable place to visit.

L'Hôpital-St-Blaise may be little more than a few houses in a forest clearing south of Gurs, but it is well worth a detour for one of the most unusual and beautiful churches in the southwest. Built in the 12th century, **Saint-Blaise** was attached to a hospice for pilgrims going to Compostela. At first sight, the Greek plan with its central dome is enough of a surprise, but then you notice the delicate stone latticework that fills some of the windows, an art that was popular in Islamic Spain and North Africa. Inside, the Muslim influence is striking. Doubtless the architects came from Spain, working in the Mudejar style common there throughout the Middle Ages. They skilfully wove Andalucian elements into the Byzantine plan: lobed arches in the apse, and a wonderful dome made of four pairs of round arches, interlaced to form an eight-pointed star; this was probably inspired by the one in the mihrab of the Great Mosque of Córdoba. Among the few carved decorations, note one very un-Christian symbol, the Pythagorean pentagram on the left transept; the church seems to be designed according to the proportions of this figure. The people of the village have cobbled together an endearingly screwy home-made *son et lumière* to entertain you; just drop a coin in the box by the door.

From Saint-Blaise, you can follow the D25 across the Gave d'Oloron to the attractive village of **Lucq-de-Béarn**, which takes its name from a holy grove (*lucus*) of ancient times. Another 12th-century church here, St-Vincent, has some carved capitals bizarre even by Romanesque standards. The altar is a 4th-century sarcophagus, with reliefs of Adam and Eve, Daniel in the lions' den, the sacrifice of Abraham and the raising of Lazarus.

Orthez

After seeing half a medieval bridge in Sauveterre, you might like to have a look at a whole specimen. Orthez, capital of Béarn when Pau was still a mere village, is the place to go. Orthez owed its medieval prominence to Viscount Gaston VII (1229–90), who made it his capital. Gaston Fébus, who built up Pau, nevertheless spent much of his time here; Froissart, the chronicler of the Hundred Years' War, came for a visit and wrote a glowing account of Fébus's wealthy and sophisticated court, with 'knights and squires coming and going, talking of arms and love', and where all the news from Scotland to Spain passed over the dinner table. Orthez was wakened from its medieval dream with a start in 1569, when Jeanne d'Albret's Protestant soldiers under Montgomery burned the place to the ground. Nothing has come along to disturb its peace since, and Orthez today with its 12,000 souls is as cheerful and contented a town as you'll find anywhere.

Tourist Information

Maison Jeanne d'Albret, Rue du Bourg Vieux, t 05 59 69 02 75/ t 05 59 69 37 50, f 05 59 69 12 60, *www.marie-orthez.fr. Open Mon–Sat 9–12 and 2–6; July and Aug open until 7 plus Sun am.*

Where to Stay and Eat

Orthez ✉ 64300

★★**La Reine Jeanne**, behind the tourist office on Rue du Bourg-Vieux, t 05 59 67 00 76, f 05 59 69 09 73, *www.reine-jeanne.fr* (*inexpensive*). Pleasant, simple rooms; the same can be said of the restaurant.Hotel has recently been refurbished with another 10 air–conditioned bedrooms. *Menus €15–34. Closed 2 weeks Feb–Mar.*

★★**Terminus**, 14 Rue St-Gilles, t 05 59 69 02 07 (*cheap*). The least expensive sleep in town. *Closed weekends exc July and Aug plus 20 Dec–8 Jan.*

★★**Auberge du Relais**, just west of Orthez, on the D933 at Berenxin, t 05 59 65 30 56, f 05 59 65 36 39, *www.auberge-du-relais.com* (*inexpensive*). In a rustic setting with a park and swimming pool; the restaurant has an outdoor terrace. *Menus €11–25. Closed Sat exc July and Aug plus Xmas and 3 weeks in Feb.*

Auberge St-Loup, 20 Rue du Pont Vieux, t 05 59 69 15 40. Orthez's long-time favourite restaurant has had its cuisine revitalized by a new young chef. Duck is the star of the menu – as *confits*, *aiguillettes*, in pies and everything else you could do to a quacker; also some interesting seafood dishes. Summer dining is in a pretty garden courtyard; it's just across the river near the medieval bridge. *Menus €21–38. Closed Sun eve and Mon plus Nov.*

The Pont Vieux

Orthez's centre having moved away from the riverfront over the centuries, this beautiful fortified bridge is now hard to find – go to the end of Rue du Bourg-Vieux from the tourist office, and take a right into Rue des Aiguilletiers. Gaston Fébus built it, *c.* 1370, though what you see now was heavily restored a century ago; the bridge had been seriously damaged by Wellington's army in 1814. In medieval times, criminals were often tossed off this bridge. Note also the little window in the side of the central tower; this was medieval Orthez's garbage disposal system – everything was simply tossed out into the Gave de Pau. The Protestants of 1569 expanded on the concept, using the window to dispose of all the town's priests and nuns.

In the centre of Orthez, a passageway off Rue du Bourg-Vieux leads to the tourist office, in the **Maison de Jeanne d'Albret**, a restored 15th- to 18th-century mansion built around a typical Béarnais pigeonnier and courtyard. Whether or not the countess actually did stay here is open to debate. Beyond this, Rue du Bourg-Vieux changes its name to Rue Moncade, with some of Orthez's oldest buildings, including the charming **Hôtel de la Lune**. A block away on Place St-Pierre, the town's main church, **St-Pierre**, barely survived the depredations of the Protestants. Most of what you see, including the bell tower, is 19th-century restoration, though some good original Gothic carvings remain on the capitals and portal.

The Tour Moncade

Further out, on the eastern edge of Orthez, Rue Moncade becomes the spine of another medieval bourg, one that grew up around the castle of the Béarn viscounts. All that's left of it, besides some bits of the outer wall, is the tall, five-sided keep, the

Feasts and Terrors of Gaston Fébus

The viscount cuts a dashing figure in French history; perhaps his greatest virtue was to embody better than anyone else the strong and hearty medieval spirit that has nourished so many legends. A great and flawed character, born to fight and hunt and lord it over meaty banquets in the hall with troubadours and dogs lurking around the tables, Gaston Fébus was made for Hollywood. His honorific, from Phoebus Apollo, was conferred early on for his long blond hair, which flowed in battle or the chase like the rays of the sun. His Pyrenean domains of Foix and Béarn felt his strong hand for 48 years (1343–91), and even though Fébus abrogated the charter, the *For de Morlaas*, not even the commoners grumbled too much; the viscount quite capably maintained the peace and liberties of his lands in a bad time, playing off the French, the English and his treacherous brother-in-law on the throne of Navarre, and keeping the troubles of the Hundred Years' War at bay.

Froissart, in Orthez, had a hard time finding out what had happened to the younger Gaston, the viscount's son. An 'old and distinguished squire' finally told him the story, how the viscount's wife had become estranged from him in a quarrel over money, and how she had gone to live with her brother, King Charles the Bad of Navarre. Young Gaston went to visit his mother, and when he was ready to return the king gave him 'a very fine little purse filled with a certain powder', explaining that it was a love potion – just sprinkle a little on the count's food, and he will have one desire only: to have his wife – your mother – back with him again. The youth believed everything, but back in Orthez his half-brother, the bastard Yvain, became curious about the purse and informed the viscount. Froissart recounts the scene in the great hall.

Tour Moncade, along with the adjacent residence of the counts, including the *tinel* or great hall of Gaston Fébus.

The Tour Moncade is haunted, though not by Gaston or any of his family. The ghost is the Princess Blanche of Navarre; caught up in a dynastic struggle in the 1450s, she was imprisoned here until her death – some say she was poisoned.

Up the Gave to Pau

If you follow the river, along the N117 or the A64 motorway, you'll run smack into an unexpected smear of industry around **Lacq**. The discovery of natural gas deposits here in 1951 sparked a little industrial boom that continues today. The earth might consider swallowing up nearby **Mourenx**, an industrial town laid out in 1957 and a good example of French planning at its most gruesome. A much prettier road, though slower, is the D9 through Maslacq, Mourenx and **Monein**, a village that still glories in the compliment of Henri IV, who called it the 'Paris of Béarn'. It isn't easy to see why, though you might stop for a look at its Renaissance church. If anyone's around, they'll take you up the steps to see the rather incredible forest of oak beams that supports its high-pitched roof, a virtuoso piece of carpentry whose 15th-century builder seems, from his master's mark, to have been a Scandinavian shipwright.

'Gaston, come nearer. I have something to say in your ear.' The young man came up to the table. The count gripped him by the chest and undid his tunic, then took a knife and cut the strings of the purse and held it in his hand.

Fébus sprinkled the powder on some bread and gave it to one of his greyhounds, which immediately rolled over and died. The viscount was barely prevented from slaying his son; instead he locked him up in the dungeon of the Tour Moncade.

Young Gaston was the viscount's only heir, and the barons of Béarn begged him to be merciful; even the pope at Avignon sent a cardinal to plead Gaston's case. Gaston, for his part, depressed and confused, said nothing, and refused to take anything of the meals that were brought him. One night the angry Fébus went down to the dungeon and touched the point of his dagger to his son's throat, saying 'Ha, traitor, why don't you eat?' He left the cell, not knowing that he had accidentally pierced a vein.

Gaston Fébus was never the same man after that; his last task on earth was to write a grim book of penitence and prayers called the *Livre des Oraisons*. When he died at l'Hôpital d'Orion, 11 years later in 1391, the first thought of every man present was for the continuity of the state – and for the vast treasure that was kept in the Tour Moncade. It was the loyal Yvain who took the initiative, seizing the viscount's ring and riding back to Orthez to take control of the fortress and the treasure. Yvain, who could not inherit either, ended up in Paris. Not long afterwards, dressed as a chained savage at a masque, his costume caught fire and he died a flaming torch before the eyes of the king and the court of France.

From Monein, another lovely country road, the D34, leads up into the valley of the river Bayse. **Lacommande** was another foundation of the medieval knightly orders, like l'Hôpital d'Orion, a hospice for Compostela-bound pilgrims. The hospice and commandery survive here, along with their **church of St-Blaise**, an exceptional Romanesque building with rich carvings and a Moorish-vaulted chapel in the transept.

Lescar

Any time someone digs a hole in Lescar, something Roman turns up; the most important city of the region in Roman times, *Civitas Beneharnum* was razed to the ground by Norman raiders in the 800s, and only reappeared under its modern name two centuries later when a monastery was founded on the site. Today, strikingly sited on a height over the valley of the Gave de Pau, Lescar is almost a suburb of Pau, though nevertheless an island of grace and tranquillity in this built-up part of the valley.

Lescar's monument is its **cathedral**, begun as the abbey church in 1141. Much of the bulding has suffered changes, but the apse, set in a cemetery that contains a good number of Basque discoidal stones, contains as complete a gallery of stone curiosities

Tourist Information

Place Royale, **t** 05 59 81 15 98, **f** 05 59 81 12 54, *www.marie-lescar.fr. Open all year Mon–Sat 10–12 and 1–6 (5 on Sat).*

Market Days

Tuesday mornings.

Where to Stay and Eat

Lescar ✉ 64230

Lescar, only 8km from the centre of Pau, makes a quiet alternative to staying in the city.

****La Terrasse**, 11 Rue Maubec, **t** 05 59 81 02 34, **f** 05 59 81 08 77 (*inexpensive*). Pleasant rooms and a reasonable restaurant with a menu beginning at €23. *Closed 1st 3 weeks of Aug and 2 weeks Dec–Jan.*

as any: lions and pussycats, a mermaid, monsters, serpents and plenty of characters that will never be identified. Before 1569, this was the Westminster Abbey of Béarn, and notables of the Foix-Béarn house buried here include Henri II d'Albret and Marguerite d'Angoulême. In that year, Montgomery's Protestants made a shambles of the place, wrecking the tombs and stealing anything of value inside. For 40 years after, this was a Protestant temple; fortunately, the real treasure was sleeping under plaster, not to be discovered until 1837: unique **mosaics**, odd hunting scenes featuring boars, fanciful lions, and a man with a wooden leg. These were part of the church's original decoration, and show a strong desire to recapture the forms of classical art. Some of the capitals are Corinthian, recycled from Roman buildings.

Across from the church is a small **museum of local archaeology**.

Pau

Perhaps your great-grandparents vacationed here, back in the 19th century when the Pyrenean air made Pau a popular resort. But resorts go in and out of fashion with the times, and few outside Gascony have heard of Pau now. It comes as a surprise to find such a big, up-to-date city so close to some of the choicest, most unspoiled parts of the mountains. Pau still has something of the air of a Ruritanian capital – it was one, until 1620, when the French took over Béarn.

History

The modern bridge just to the east of Pau's castle marks the site of a far earlier one, a wooden bridge that existed even in the Dark Ages along Gascony's high road – the route shepherds took to move their flocks from the Pyrenees to winter pasture in the Landes. The high cliffs over the Gave de Pau also made it the logical spot to control the river.

Though a castle and a small village stood on the site throughout the Middle Ages, it was Gaston Fébus in the 1370s who first realized the potential of the site; he expanded the castle and built a wall, intending to make Pau the capital of his domains. It was a popular residence with most of the later rulers of Béarn, including Henri d'Albret and Marguerite d'Angoulême, who brought down the latest Renaissance tastes from Paris and made the castle a showplace. Their grandson,

Jurançon and Béarn

Jurançon, Henri IV's favourite wine, is like Henri himself one of the most distinct products of Gascony. Grown on the hillside lining the south bank of the Gave de Pau, these white wines made from petit manseng, gros manseng and courbu grapes owe their striking individuality to a combination of factors: a gentle moist climate, buckets of sunshine, and dry, warm autumn winds that allow for a late harvest in November – essential for the overripened sweet vintage. The earth itself is sweet and clayey, laced with iron with an underpinning of siliceous or limestone rock. The vineyards themselves are rarely visible; most are tiny and tucked away on family farms, behind the trees and shrubs that help anchor down the slippery clay.

There are two AOC Jurançons. Golden sweet Jurançon offers a rarefied balance of the sumptuous, rich qualities of the finest *vin moelleux* with a fresh, tangy acidity. It never tastes heavy, nor can many wines match its astonishing fragrance, reminiscent of the exotic fruits that Carmen Miranda loved to stick on her head – guava, pineapples, lychees, passion fruit, or mangoes – each estate has its own individual taste; all are delicious with desserts or foie gras prepared with wild mushrooms. Their longevity is legendary; buy a few bottles now to serve at your grandchildren's baptisms, especially the superlative 1988s and '89s.

Straw-coloured Jurançon Sec, with a similar exotic bouquet and aftertaste, is one of France's great white *vins de garde*. In the past few years, three growers in the village of Monein have consistently produced wines that are a class apart: **Clos Uroulat** at Quartier Trouilh (***t** 05 59 21 46 19; phone ahead to visit*), the highest property in the *appellation*; **Domaine Cauhapé** (***t** 05 59 21 33 02; open Mon–Fri 8–6, Sat 10–6, closed Sun and hols*), whose vintner, Henri Ramonteu is a student of Bordeaux's star œnologue, Dubourdieu; and the traditional **Domaine Bru-Baché** (***t** 05 59 21 36 34*).

Part of the growing area for white, red and rosé AOC, Béarn touches the north-western edge of Jurançon, although the larger portion stretches west of Orthez. Beárn is an ancient vintage that was once part of the Bayonne wine trade, especially after the 17th century, when nostalgic Protestant émigrés created a demand abroad for the wines of the Pyrenees. The whites make use of the same grape varieties as Jurançon, with the addition of lauzet, camarelet, rafflat de mocade and sauvignon; reds and rosés can be no more than 60 per cent tannat, with cabernet franc, cabernet sauvignon, fer, black manseng and black courbu. Bellocq is the main centre, where you can visit the cooperative **Les Vignerons de Bellocq** on the outskirts of town (***t** 05 59 65 10 71*).

Henri IV, was born there, giving Pau its enduring claim to fame. While young Henri was off travelling and campaigning, his dour mother Jeanne d'Albret spent much of her time here, putting an end to the brilliant court life of the old days and turning most of the Palois into good Calvinists.

After Louis XIII and his army seized Béarn, Pau dwindled in size and importance, a medieval relic that would not reawaken until the 1840s.

In Pau's hotels and shops, you'll occasionally see old Victorian hunting and racing prints, the last reminder of the city's days as the Gascon outpost of the British Empire. The trend started with some of Wellington's veterans, who liked the country and came back in their retirement. The real impetus, however, came with a Scottish doctor named Taylor, who in 1869 wrote a book called *The Climate of Pau*, extolling the benefits of this part of the Pyrenean foothills for just about any affliction. After this, Pau rapidly became one of the star resorts of Europe. With few sights to see and little to do besides drink in the mountain air, the British (and a good number of Americans) had to bring their amusements with them. They built the first golf course on the continent, along with a racetrack and a casino; they established cricket and hunt clubs. The centre of the town filled up with fancy milliners' shops, travel agents and even tearooms, while wealthy foreigners lined the outskirts with luxurious villas. Fashion moved on to Biarritz after 1890, following the example set by Queen Victoria – by that time the seaside, not the mountains, was the place to see and be seen in. For a while, Pau struggled on as a resort, as Parisians and other northern Frenchmen replaced the Anglo-Saxons; they kept the clubs going, and a select few even learned to play cricket and drink tea.

On 3 February 1909 Wilbur Wright put on a demonstration of his latest aircraft in Pau for an audience that included the kings of Great Britain and Spain. Soon after that, France's first school of aviation was started here. Not much else happened until the 1950s, when the discovery of gas deposits at nearby Lacq fuelled a modest boom that continues today. Though aeronautics has moved on to Toulouse, the training school is still here, specializing in parachuting – boys in green dropping out of the sky are a common sight in the surrounding farmlands. Pau has a new university, a busy, rebuilt centre, a convention hall, an inexplicably large number of lingerie shops, a few nightclubs, and (following the Victorian tradition) an English bookstore (Scribes, on Rue Gassion) and a tandoori restaurant.

King Henri's Castle

***t** 05 59 82 38 19; www.musee-château-pau.fr. Open Nov–Mar daily; 9.30–11.45 and 2–4.15; April–mid-June and mid-Sept–Oct same hours until 5; mid-June–mid-Sept 9.30–12.15 and 1.30–5.45.*

Pau's restored old centre, the quarter called the Hédas, is a delightful place that any other French city might envy. Only a few medieval half-timber buildings survive in out-of-the-way places, but the streets around Nouste Henric's castle have become a pedestrian zone full of restaurants and cafés, the liveliest place in town. The castle itself, rising behind its moat, is a stunning vision of Renaissance turrets and gables, like a château on the Loire. Not all of them are original, though – the pretty **tower** on the end of the right wing, facing you, was done in the time of Louis Philippe, when restorations were begun after long centuries of neglect. The grim brick **donjon** on the left dates from the time of Gaston Fébus. Between these, the castle is entered through a beautifully carved marble **triple arch**, part of the 19th-century restorations but good enough to fool you into thinking it a Renaissance work. Beyond this is the elegant courtyard, the heart of the residential palace of the 1500s.

Getting Around

Pau is the centre for all transportation in this stretch of the Pyrenees.

The **rail** station, with connections to Bordeaux, Tarbes and Lourdes, is down by the river, underneath the Boulevard des Pyrénées on Av Jean Biray.

For the coast and the mountain villages, there are plenty of **buses**, most leaving from central Place Clemenceau. The TPR line (**t** 05 59 82 95 85) has frequent services (four or five a day) to Salies-de-Béarn, Bayonne, Biarritz, Nay-Lourdes, Mauléon, Monein, Mourenx and Orthez (via Lescar).

There are also services to Tarbes, Mont-de-Marsan, Oloron and up the Gave d'Ossau to Laruns and Gourette.

Tourist Information

Place Royale, **t** 05 59 27 27 08, **f** 05 59 27 03 21, *www.pau.fr. Open all year, Mon–Sat 9–6 plus Sun 9–1.*

Where to Stay

Pau ✉ 64000

While none of the '*grands hôtels*' of Pau's glory days survives, there are over 40 hotels around the city in all price ranges to ensure you have a pleasant stay. None, however, has anything special that would merit a splurge.

******Bristol***, 3 Rue Gambetta, **t** 05 59 27 72 98, **f** 05 59 27 87 80 (*inexpensive*). At the posher end of the scale, the Bristol is as old-fashioned as its name, but comfortable, quiet and reasonably priced, with good courteous service. *Open all year.*

*****Roncevaux**, 25 Rue Louis-Barthou, just off Place Royale, **t** 05 59 27 08 44, **f** 05 59 27 08 01, *www.hotel-roncevaux.com* (*inexpensive*). Similar to the Bristol (above).

****Grand Hôtel du Commerce**, 9 Rue Maréchal Joffre, **t** 05 59 27 24 40, **f** 05 59 83 81 74 (*inexpensive*). A traditional hotel close to the castle, with a decent restaurant. A good choice for sightseeing. *Menus €15–26. Open daily all year.*

*****Hotel Montpensier**, 36 Rue Monpensier, **t** 05 59 27 42 72, *www.hotel-montpensier.fr* (*inexpensive*). A charming, old-fashioned place; although there is no restaurant meals are available to order.

*****Regina**, 18 Rue Gassion, near the castle, **t** 05 57 27 29 19, **f** 05 59 27 04 62 (*inexpensive*). One of the nicest budget choices in the area, though it's on a busy street and some rooms can be noisy. *Open all year.*

***Hôtel Matisse**, 17 Rue Mathieu-Lalanne, near the Musée des Beaux-Arts, **t** 05 59 27 73 80 (*cheap*). A simple place, but a good choice in this price range. *Open all year.*

Logis des Jeunes, Base de Plein Air, Jelos, **t** 05 59 11 05 05. Youth hostel. *Open all year.*

Eating Out

There are several restaurants in the lively streets around the castle, many with outside tables.

Restaurant La Brochetterie, 16 Rue Henri-IV, **t** 05 59 27 40 33. Very popular for its grilled duck and spit-roasted pig and lamb . *Menus €11–20. Closed Sat lunch and Mon.*

Le Viking, 33 Bd Tourasse, **t** 05 59 84 02 91. Rustic and intimate, treating local produce with flair and not a little style; try their stuffed courgette flowers with *cèpes* or *poires williams* with Jurançon wine for dessert. *Menus €20–38. Closed Sat and Sun lunch plus all Mon.*

Chez Pierre, 16 Rue Louis-Barthou, **t** 05 59 27 76 86. A firm favourite, considered '*très* British' with its golf clubs over the bar, but serving firmly southwest French cuisine, notably foie gras and *béarnais cassoulet*. *Menus €31. Closed Mon and Sat lunch and all Mon.*

Au Fin Gourmet, 24 Av Gaston-Lacoste, down below the Boulevard des Pyrénées, **t** 05 59 27 47 71. Try here for a rather more ambitious dining experience. The fried crayfish tails with orange come specially recommended, as do the other fish dishes. *Menus €16 (lunch only), €34 and €55. Closed Sun eve, Wed lunch and Mon. Plus 2 weeks July–Aug and 2 weeks in Feb.*

Before 1620, this must have been one of the most lavishly decorated palaces in the south. Louis XIII, who had come down personally to oversee the conquest of Béarn, carried most of the furnishings back to Paris with him. For the next two centuries, the castle saw duty as a royal prison. In 1791, the revolutionaries in Paris declared it the 'property of the nation' but refrained from selling it off out of respect to the memory of Good King Henri. Nevertheless, it remained a prison until Louis Phillippe ordered restorations in the 1830s (the last and most famous of the prisoners was Abd el-Kader, the Algerian emir who led the resistance against the French occupation until his capture in 1848). The works continued through the reign of Napoleon III, who took a personal interest in the place and often came for visits in Pau's heyday as a resort. They were overseen by Viollet-le-Duc, famous restorer of Paris's Notre-Dame and so many other important buildings in France. It is to his workshop that we owe most of the fine sculpted detail around the courtyard. Since that time, enough of the original furnishings have been reassembled to make the excruciatingly detailed guided tour worth the trouble.

In the castle's other rooms, you will see a fine collection of **Gobelin and Flemish tapestries**, as well as a notable 16th-century series on the story of Cupid and Psyche, in the Salle Marquet de Vasselot, and another, the oldest in the castle, with scenes of the months and seasons.

Just east of the castle on Place des Etats stands a plain building dear to the hearts of Gascon patriots, the old **Parlement de Navarre**. Before the French kings installed their Parlement in 1620, this served as home of the Sovereign Council, Béarn's last independent government (parlements, in old France, were not legislative bodies, but judicial councils, packed with royal appointees). Another two streets east, stately **Place Royale** was laid out in the 18th century, a classically simple bit of town design from the Age of Enlightenment. Once lined with '*grands hôtels*' and cafés, it was the centre of the town's life, and the site of the evening promenade, in the days when the

King Henri's Cradle

As every Gascon schoolboy knows, this is the star attraction. In 1553, the pregnant Jeanne d'Albret was up in the north, keeping her husband Antoine de Bourbon company while he warred with Emperor Charles V. Both parents thought that the heir to Gascony should have his birthplace there, and Jeanne had to rush back home. Henri was born ten days after her arrival in Pau, and the affair was so hurried that no one could find a proper cradle for the baby – so instead Jeanne used a big tortoise's shell, which little Henri found quite cosy. This odd relic was preserved ever after – a loyal Gascon officer saved it from the revolutionaries by hiding it and putting another tortoise shell in its place. Now it is displayed here in a charming sort of shrine, along with Henri's helmet, an arch-Renaissance tapestry of the *Apotheosis of Henri IV*, and banners with the royal arms of France and Navarre. The guides are certain to mention how Henri's grandfather, Henri d'Albret, rubbed the newborn's lips with a little garlic and some Jurançon wine, just to make sure he started out in life as a proper Gascon.

English came to Pau. The swells of the Belle Epoque still went to church on Sunday, and for a suitably fashionable venue they built the impressive neo-Gothic **St-Martin**, nearby on Rue Henri IV.

The Boulevard des Pyrénées

Pau is an Occitan word for rampart or palisade, and the cliffs above the Gave de Pau that once made it an excellent place for a fortress now give the city its most memorable embellishment, the Boulevard des Pyrénées. Running from Henri's castle to the Parc Beaumont, it skirts the city centre, providing a dreamy panorama over a 50-mile stretch of mountains and the wooded foothills in front. The Palois never get tired of it. They come to mull over the view in the morning, they walk their dogs there in the afternoon, and they come back in the evening for the sunsets. The odd conical mountain rising just a bit higher than the rest is the Pic du Midi.

The Boulevard's charms can be dangerous. Charles Maurras, the writer and politician, had a kind of mystic experience here in the 1880s, when he first realized what he later called 'the natural necessity of submission for the order and beauty of the world'. Maurras went on to found the fascist Action Française, and he ended his life in prison as a Vichy collaborator.

At the eastern end of the Boulevard, **Parc Beaumont** was laid out as an English garden a century ago. At its centre, the old **casino**, long closed, is currently being restored as a convention-recreation centre.

Musée des Beaux Arts

10 Rue Mathieu Lalanne, ***t*** *05 59 27 33 02; open 10–12 and 2–6, closed Tues; adm.*

This surprisingly good collection is kept just north of the park on Rue Lalanne. The majority of the paintings are 18th- and 19th-century French, with Pyrenean landscapes naturally well represented, but there are also some choice works of the Italians, Flemish and Spaniards: an odd night scene by Luca Giordano, better known for painting Baroque ballroom ceilings, an equally unexpected *Last Judgement* from Rubens, even an El Greco, the *Ecstasy of St Francis*. Perhaps the best-known work is a classic of Degas, the *Cotton Brokers' Office in New Orleans*. The artist painted it on an American visit with his businessman father. Meant as a reference to Rembrandt's *Masters of the Cloth Hall* and other works of that Dutch genre, it was put on display at the Second Impressionist Exhibition in 1876. There is also a collection of modern art, and a section with medieval and ancient coins.

There isn't much else in Pau. Most of the city's churches were wrecked or turned into Protestant temples by Jeanne d'Albret, but there is another museum, a little house on Rue Bernadotte dedicated to the remarkable career of Pau's other favourite son, Jean-Baptiste Bernadotte. A soldier who worked himself up through the ranks to become a marshal and confidant of Napoleon, Bernadotte fell out with the emperor over his constant warmongering and was forced into retirement. The heirless king of Sweden made him an adopted son, and Bernadotte wound up leading troops against Napoleon in the Russian campaign. In 1826 he assumed the Swedish throne, and ruled for 26 years as Charles XIV, ancestor of the line of kings that continues today. The **Musée Bernadotte** (*Rue Tran*, **t** *05 59 27 48 42; open 10–12 and 2–6 pm, closed Mon; adm*) contains personal relics, paintings and period furniture. In the same neighbourhood, some of the villas of the English survive on the side streets off Rue Montpensier – notably Rue Planté and Rue Quin, where the visitors built an Anglican church.

North of Pau: the Vic-Bilh

Looking at a relief map, you'll see how the tremendous run-off from the well-watered Pyrenees creates wild landscapes of narrow, closely packed parallel valleys, each with its rushing stream or rocky *gave*. Nowhere is this more pronounced than in the area between Pau and Aire-sur-l'Adour, the tract of deepest Gascony people call the Vic-Bilh, the 'old country'. If you're really sincere about getting away from it all, France can offer few better opportunities. There are no trains, few buses, and no main routes through it. Trying to get across its tangle of winding back roads, especially from east to west, is utterly exasperating – so very few ever try.

Not that they're missing much. The landscapes, though clean and pretty, are generally unexceptional (though you'll usually get a view of the Pyrenees while crossing the crest of the roller coaster from one valley into another). The villages often have piquant names like Boueilh-Boueilho-Lasque, Coslédaa-Lube-Boast and Maspie-Lalonquère-Juillacq that are longer than their main street. They get such names from being consolidated – a typical result of rural depopulation over the last century.

There are a few medieval churches, as at **Taron-Sadirac** and **Diusse**, but the only one worth a detour is the late 11th-century church in the pleasant village of **Sévignac**. The local baron, the story goes, built it in expiation for a couple of murders. To remind himself and others just how easy it is to go astray, he had the artists embellish the portal with a full array of personified vices: a glutton patting his belly, another one vomiting, a merchant with a money-box, a pair of fellows arguing, and a man and a woman displaying parts of their anatomies not often seen on church portals.

At the western edge of the Vic-Bilh, in a little pays called the Saubestre (from the Latin sylvestrensia for its extensive forests) stands the village of **Morlanne**. The castle here, like Pau's and most of the others in this *département*, is the work of Sicard de Lordat, Gaston Fébus's personal architect. Half ruined by our century, it was purchased by a historian named Raymond Ritter (he wrote, among other things, a biography of Corisande), who spent the last decades of his life restoring it. He bequeathed it to the departmental government, which keeps it up as a museum (*not currently open; call the mairie at* **t** *05 59 80 61 23*). The restoration work was thorough and sensitively done, though don't expect furnishings to match; the collection of paintings, tapestries and furniture inside dates mostly from the 18th century.

Morlaas, on the borders of the Vic-Bilh just northeast of Pau, was the capital of Béarn for two centuries starting from the 10th century. Not much is left to testify to the town's medieval prominence, only the church of Sainte-Foi, built by the viscount

Madiran, Pacherenc du Vic-Bilh and Côtes-de-Saint-Mont

Madiran and Pacherenc du Vic-Bilh are two AOC wine areas that share the same frontiers in the hilly Vic-Bilh with the villages of Madiran and Maumusson in the centre. Here the climate is drier than anywhere elsewhere in Beárn and the hard clay soil isn't good for growing anything else. Two 11th-century abbeys, Madiran and Sainte-Foy, each developed their own wine-making traditions – the former made a deep, dark, full-bodied red wine from tannat and cabernet, while the monks of Sainte-Foy created a white wine from ruffiac grapes known as Pacherenc. Originally Pacherenc was dry, with a refreshing coarseness, although in recent years a sweet variety in the Jurançon mould has been developed as well.

Madiran is a class apart. The most tannic wine in France, powerful enough to drink with jugged game, strong mountain cheeses and *entrecôte béarnaise*, it is also one of the great success stories of recent years. For years, Madiran suffered a dark age so dark that the few wine drinkers who even knew its name shuddered to recall that astringent red toothpaint. Enter, in the 1970s, a new breed of wine-growers led by Alain Brumont, who by dint of hard work, inspiration and a dollop of public relations transformed the old wine into a drink so elegant, robust, and full of flamboyant Gascon character that Brumont was showered with awards as the vigneron of the 1980s. Headquartered in Maumusson, Brumont bottles his inky nectar under three different labels: at the top of the line, made from 100 per cent tannat are **Château Bouscassé Vieilles Vignes**, and the even more expensive **Château Montus Prestige** – the '88 and '91 are rated as simply phenomenal. The Montus Pacherenc Sec and Moelleux are equally superb (***t** 05 62 69 74 67*). To mention just a few of the many other excellent estates in the district: **Château d'Aydie**, a handsome, jagged-towered Béarnais manor in Aydie (***t** 05 59 04 08 00*) run by the Laplace family, who also played a major role in the rebirth of Madiran (also try their Pacherenc Moelleux, especially the 2001 and 2002); **Château Lafitte-Teston** in Maumusson,(***t** 05 62 69 74 58*), which produces another pure tannat Madiran; and the **Cooperative de Plaimont**, at Plaimont in St-Mont (*open July and August 9–7, Sept–June 8.30–12 and 2–6.30, closed Sun*), one of the largest in France, which produces consistently fine Madirans under its Collection label, but also Pacherenc du Vic-Bilh Moelleux under the Saint Albert label. It is also the most important bottler of Côtes-de-Saint-Mont, the adjacent appellation squeezed between Madiran and Bas-Armagnac. Red Côtes-de-Saint-Mont are similar to Madirans in their high tannic quality; Plaimont's very best wear the label of the 17th-century Château-de-Sabazan.

of Béarn, Centulle IV. The exterior has suffered considerably from fires and renovations over the centuries, though a wonderful portal survives: a tympanum of Christ and the Four Evangelists, surrounded by scenes of the Massacre of the Innocents and the Flight into Egypt, and a border of the 24 Apocalyptic Elders, a giveaway that the sculptors of the Toulouse-Moissac school were around.

On the northern edge of the Vic-Bilh, just over the border in the department of Hautes-Pyrénées, **Madiran** gives its name to the region's singular AOC wine district.

The centre of the wine trade in the area, Madiran has plenty of opportunities for cave visits, but little to see except for the remains of the village's Benedictine abbey (the monks here introduced vine growing to the area in the Middle Ages). There is a big, barn-like abbey church, with an unusual crypt, made for the veneration of holy relics and carved with some unusual, primitive capitals.

Oloron-Ste-Marie

Oloron, the gateway to the Béarnais Pyrenees, began as the Celtiberian *Illuro*, 'city of the waters'. Burnt by the Normans at about the same time as Lescar, it gradually reappeared as twin towns, Oloron on its high hill and Ste-Marie, a new medieval *bourg* across the river; they only merged in 1858. Since the Pyrenees' first hydroelectric plant was built here in the 1870s, Oloron has been a centre of manufacturing. Today, sprawling over hills and valleys, it looks uncannily like a Pennsylvania mill town – though the only real industries in Oloron make berets and chocolates.

Ste-Marie Cathedral

This is a typically bastard French church: Romanesque in front, Gothic behind and a little of everything else mixed in. Located in the bourg, near the river, it was begun in

Tourist Information

Allées du Comte de Treville. **t** 05 59 39 98 00, **f** 05 59 39 43 97, *www.ot-oloron-ste-marie.fr. Open summer Mon–Sat 9–7 plus Sun 10–1; winter Mon–Sat 9–12.30 and 2–6.30.*

Market Day

Friday.

Where to Stay

Oloron-Ste-Marie ✉ 64400

Rancèsamy, Quartier Rey 64290 Lasseube. About 2km out of Lasseube, which is 11km from Oloron on the D24 towards Pau, **t** 05 59 04 26 37, *www.missbrowne.com*. Isabelle and Simon Browne welcome you to their little oasis of tranquillity in a beautiful setting, with views of the verdant Vallée d'Ossau with mountains in the distance. It's an old stone house, lovingly restored and decorated throughout with objets d'art and furniture collected from all over the world. Bedrooms are spacious and comfortable and most have a view over the Mediterranean style courtyard. There's a lovely garden and pool. Two evenings a week, Mrs. Browne gets creative in the kitchen, using local and home-grown produce, she offers regional and international cuisine (€25). There is also a lounge and kitchen for communal use. *Open all year, on reservation.*

Château de Boués, just outside town on the D919, **t** 05 59 39 95 49 (*inexpensive*). A lovely château with a few guest rooms. *Open May–end Sept.*

★★**Bristol**, 9 Rue Carrerot, **t** 05 59 39 43 78, **f** 05 59 39 08 19 (*inexpensive*). Even cheaper than the above. *Menus €12–22. Closed Sun.*

★★**De La Paix**, Avenue Sadi Carnot, by the SNCF station, **t** 05 59 39 02 63, **f** 05 59 39 98 20, *www.hotel-oloron.com* (*inexpensive*). The least expensive, with a garden. No restaurant.

La Promenade. 64290 Lasseube, **t** 05 59 04 26 24. Locally popular, family-run *auberge* where the Brownes may send you when not serving dinner. No frills, regional fare. *Menus €15–29. Closed Mon, exc July and Aug, 2 weeks in Jan plus 2 weeks in Oct–Nov.*

the 12th century and largely completed by 1500. The **portal** is one of the finest in the southwest, a flight of medieval fantasy in the style of Moissac that includes two remarkable *voussures* around the tympanum, one carved with the 24 Elders of the Apocalypse playing their rebecs and viols; the other recalling the parable from Matthew:22 about the preparations for a wedding feast. The joys awaiting us in heaven are described in terms any true Gascon would appreciate: they're hunting the boar, fishing for salmon, bringing in the wine and cheeses, killing the fowls. At the top of the arch, a hellish demon serves to underline the parable's point that 'many are called but few are chosen'.

On the tympanum, by a different artist, is the *Descent from the Cross* with the Virgin, John the Evangelist and Joseph of Arimathea in attendance. On the right, the statue on horseback is Constantine, representing the true faith (some say he's really Gaston IV of Béarn); the poor wretch being devoured by a lion on the left reminds us of the passage through death to a new life. The *trumeau* (column between the doors) shows two Saracen captives carved in Pyrenean marble; they may be an allusion to Gaston IV's successes in the Crusades.

Inside, the choir and apses are quite impressive flamboyant Gothic work, rare in these parts. Gothic sculptors of the 1300s also added some fine capitals and an unusual baptismal font. There is a *trésor* containing some Italian Renaissance items. If it's near Christmas, you can see the cathedral's elaborate crêche, carved in about 1700. Surprisingly the Pyreneans always neglected this widespread folk art, and this is one of the few examples; some of the figures wear berets.

Quartier Ste-Croix

Modern Oloron spreads along three valleys, where the Gave d'Aspe and Gave d'Ossau come together to make the Gave d'Oloron. The Gave d'Ossau bridge is a 13th-century original, while the Pont de Ste-Claire over the Gave d'Aspe was an early iron work of engineer Gustave Eiffel; this leads to a delightful **Jardin Public** with a Victorian bandstand and statuary.

Between the two bridges, you can take the formidably steep Rue Dalmais up to the Quartier Ste-Croix, the acropolis of ancient Illuro and medieval Oloron. At the top, the square around **Ste-Croix** was the site of the important annual fair that made Oloron's prosperity in the Middle Ages; parts of the covered market hall that once surrounded the building can still be seen. Various restorations disfigured much of the church's exterior, though there is some good Romanesque carving on the apses. The interior rises to a splendid Moorish dome in the form of an eight-pointed star, like the one in l'Hôpital-St-Blaise. Carvings on the capitals include a full picture-book of biblical scenes, including some not often seen: Cain and Abel and Salome's Dance.

Rue Dalmais was the main street of the medieval town; along it you'll see the old town hall, the 15th-century **Maison du Sénéchal** and a 13th-century tower called the **Tour de Grède**, with an adjoining mansion of the 1700s. This houses the **Maison du Patrimoine** (***t*** *05 59 36 12 05, open daily; open Tues–Sun 10–12.30 and 3–7 July–Oct; adm*), a museum with archaeological finds, paintings, and an exhibit on the concentration camp at nearby Gurs (*see* p.198).

The Vallée d'Aspe

The N134 follows the Gave d'Aspe up towards the Spanish border. Footsore Roman legionaries once trod this path and the Romans gave the border pass, the Col du Somport, its name: *Summus Portus*, the highest gate.

South of Oloron, the first place of interest is off on a side road, the D918 from Asasp. The source at **St-Christau** has been known since ancient times, its waters a sure cure for skin diseases. One of the first spas of France, it was also one of the first to be forgotten. What's left of it stands in a quiet forest clearing: a park, two mouldering hotels of the 19th century, and a stately building called the **Rotonde** built over the source in the 1630s. A large number of Celtiberian relics, jewellery and figurines were found around the fountain, along with a grim mustachioed bust of a Celtic god, which is still on display in the Rotonde.

From here the serious mountains begin; your last chance to leave the valley is the D294, following a beautiful but lonely route through forests and up to the 1,026m/3,364ft Marie-Blanque pass, before finishing in the Vallée d'Ossau. The N134, meanwhile, continues south through a dramatic gorge, the **Défilé d'Escot**, and then skirts the charming village of **Sarrance**.

The chapel here was built to house an image of the Virgin that was found at a fountain by a shepherd; Sarrance has been a place of pilgrimage since the 1400s. The chapel has naïve painted reliefs telling the legend of the icon's discovery; nearby, there are similar items from around the Pyrenees that have been assembled in a **Musée d'Arts Religieux** (*t 05 59 34 55 51; open weekends and school hols 2–6*).

Tourist Information

Accous: Moulin Bladé, N134, **t** 05 59 34 71 48. *Open Mon–Fri 9–12.30 and 2–5.30.*

Market Days

Bedous: Thursdays.

Where to Stay and Eat

St-Christau ✉ 64660

★★★**Au Bon Coin**, on the D918 (Route des Thermes), **t** 05 59 34 40 12, **f** 05 59 34 46 40 (*inexpensive*). A modern hotel in a lovely forest setting. In this perfect isolation, there are pretty rooms at reasonable rates, a pool, gardens and an excellent restaurant serving both simple Béarnais favourites and some surprising seafood dishes – from peppers stuffed with crabmeat to lobster lasagne. *Menus €15–51. Closed Sun eve and Mon in winter.*

The Upper Aspe Valley

There are more interesting places to spend a night in these mountains than just a plain old hotel, including the mountain refuges at L'Abérouat and Arlet, both of which provide an opportunity to savour the mountain scenery.

Camping des 4 Saisons. Asasp, near St-Christau, **t** 05 59 34 43 10 (*cheap*). *Open June–Sept.*

Maison de l'Ours, Etsaut, **t** 05 59 34 86 38 (*cheap*). Rooms and meals, along with nature walks and activities. *Open all year.*

Réfuge des Ecuyers Montagnards, on the trails above Accous (✉ 64490), **t** 05 59 34 72 30, **f** 05 59 34 51 97, *www.auberge-cavaliere.com* (*cheap*). Accommodation and meals for hikers and riders.

Le Châlet Restaurant, **t** 05 59 36 00 60. No accommodation. *Open daily. Closed May.*

Youth Hostels

Lourdios, ✉ 64570, **t** 05 59 34 46 39. *Open all year.*

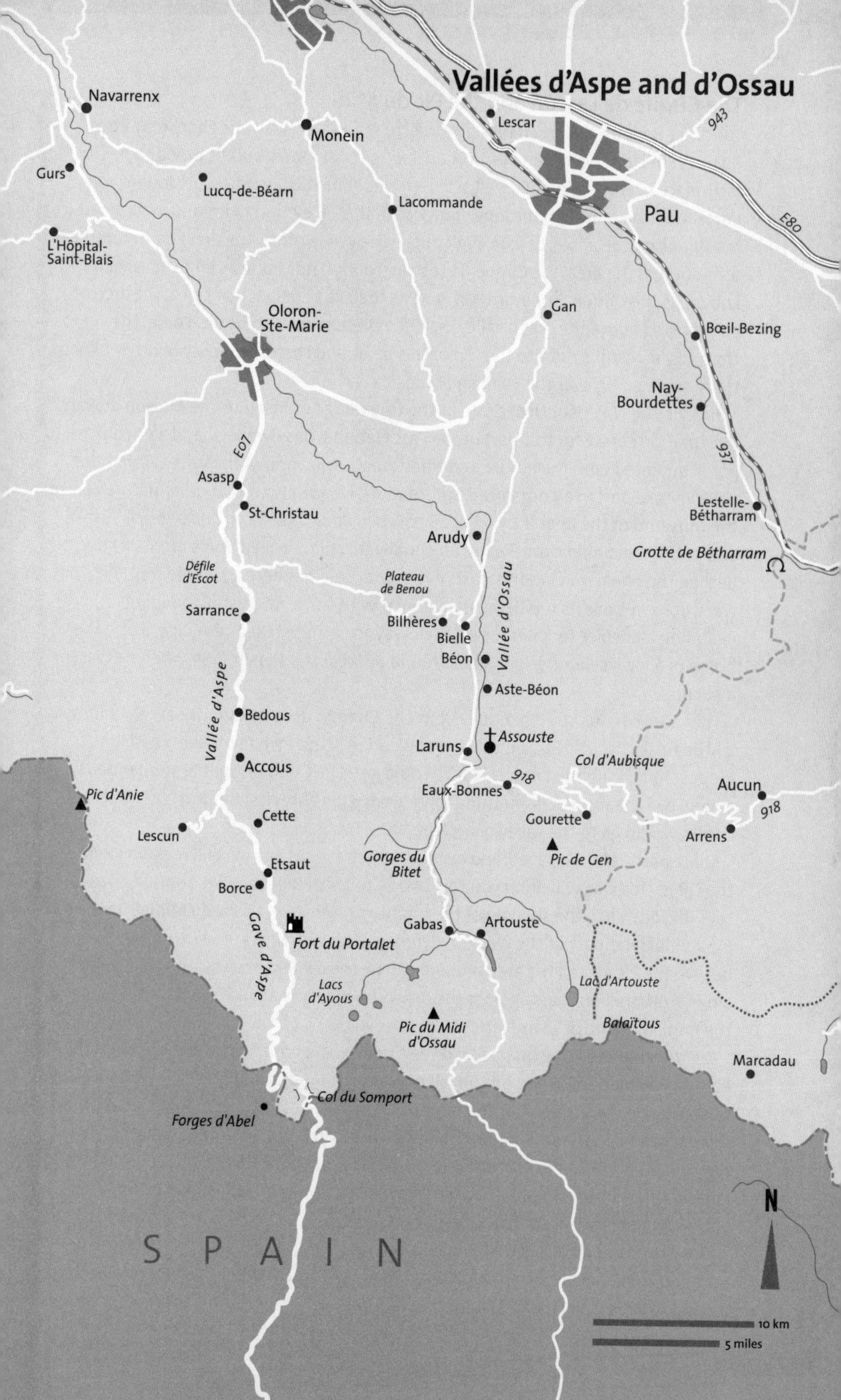

Vallées d'Aspe and d'Ossau
Navarrenx
Monein
Lescar
943
Gurs
Lucq-de-Béarn
Lacommande
Pau
E80
L'Hôpital-Saint-Blais
Gan
Oloron-Ste-Marie
Bœil-Bezing
Nay-Bourdettes
E07
937
Asasp
St-Christau
Lestelle-Bétharram
Arudy
Grotte de Bétharram
Défile d'Escot
Plateau de Benou
Vallée d'Ossau
Sarrance
Bilhères
Bielle
Béon
Aste-Béon
Vallée d'Aspe
Bedous
Laruns
Assouste
Accous
Col d'Aubisque
918
Eaux-Bonnes
Aucun
Pic d'Anie
918
Cette
Gourette
Arrens
Lescun
Pic de Gen
Gorges du Bitet
Etsaut
Borce
Gave d'Aspe
Gabas
Artouste
Fort du Portalet
Lacs d'Ayous
Lac d'Artouste
Pic du Midi d'Ossau
Balaïtous
Marcadau
Col du Somport
Forges d'Abel
SPAIN
N
10 km
5 miles

The Cirque de Lescun and the Pic du Midi

Around **Bedous**, the green hills give way to stark grey cliffs, and there may be a distinct chill in the air even in summer; Bedous isn't much, but it's proud to be the birthplace of the explorer Pierre Laclede, founder of St Louis, Missouri. **Jouers** and **Cette** have the only Romanesque churches in the valley, both with unusual carved modillons on the apses. **Lescun**, high above the valley, offers the greatest natural attraction of the area, the **Cirque de Lescun**. Though not quite as large or as well known as the Cirque de Gavarnie, it is nevertheless a spectacular sight. The arch of peaks rising above the green valley includes the 2,482m/8,138ft **Pic d'Anie**. The GR 10 from Lescun climbs right to the top of this peak, and there are plenty of other hiking trails, some going over the Spanish border.

Back on the N 134, south of Cette at the tiny village of **Etsaut** is the **Maison du Parc**, information centre for this part of the Parc National des Pyrénées, and a good place to get acquainted with the nature and traditional civilization of the valley. From here you can take part in an organized nature tours. Etsaut also has another nature centre, the **Museum of the Bear** (***t*** *05 59 34 88 30; open daily 9.30–12.30 and 2–6.30*). Just across the main road from Etsaut, an equally tiny place called **Borce** merits a short detour. The one hamlet in this part of the Pyrenees that never suffered from fires or wars, Borce retains its medieval appearance, with some interesting buildings including a hospice for pilgrims on their way to Compostela. The village is also the home of a local celebrity: Jojo, a bear found by local children in 1985, when he was a lost cub.

The most curious stretch of the GR 10, the **Chemin de la Mâture**, meets the highway a little further south. Back in the age of wooden ships, Pyrenean pines made the longest and straightest masts France could get. The Chemin, built at tremendous expense in the 1860s, was nothing more than a long steep slide, down which the trunks would go to the valley on rollers.

Some parts of it are paved, and over a kilometre is cut out of solid rock. Following the GR 10 this way will bring you to a barren but striking area of mountain lakes, the **Lacs d'Ayous**, all in the shadow of the mighty 2,920m/9,573ft **Pic du Midi d'Ossau**, the pyramidal landmark of the western Pyrenees. The geologists aren't sure, but they believe the Pic and all the area around it to be the caldera of a volcano that collapsed a mere 240 million years ago. For the Béarnais, the Pic is an old friend; people call it by the familiar name of 'Jean-Pierre'.

Overlooking the N134, just beyond the Chemin, the grim fortress on the hill is the **Fort du Portalet**. Following on the fall of France in 1940, Marshal Pétain sent a number of political leaders here after the famous show trial at Riom, including former prime ministers Paul Reynaud, Edouard Daladier and Léon Blum. After the Liberation, the new government found it a fitting lock-up for Pétain himself; the old scoundrel couldn't stand the cold, and they transferred him to a more agreeable prison after a year (Portalet is now private property; no visits).

Close to the new tunnel that will take the highway (*see* above) under the Col du Somport into Spain is an old ironworks called **Les Forges d'Abel**. The property used to belong to a local boy named Pierre Loustaunou, born in 1754. You'll hear lots of stories about him in the villages of the Aspe. As a young shepherd, he was taking somebody else's flock down to summer pasture when he had the inspiration to sell them; the money financed a huge personal adventure, culminating in a career as general to an Indian maharajah. Pierre eventually returned with a bag full of rubies, and bought the forge and many other things; ruined in the troubles of the French Revolution, he was last seen as a mendicant dervish preaching somewhere in the Levant.

The Vallée d'Ossau

Closer to the heart of the Pyrenees, this valley is a little wilder than the Aspe, with peaks crowding in against the road. The people who live here, a self-governing community of shepherds, in the old days always thought of themselves as set apart from the rest of the Béarnais; indeed they claimed not to be Gascon at all, and some have speculated that they are direct descendants of the Celtiberians, maybe with a little Moorish blood mixed in. Some smaller villages, like Assouste, still manage their affairs by the ancient *jurat*, a council of the heads of families.

Coming from Oloron or Pau, the entrance to the valley is the village of **Arudy**, centre of the Pyrenean marble trade. Here the **Maison d'Ossau** (***t** 05 59 05 61 71; open daily July and Aug 10–12 and 3–6, Jan–June and Sept Tues–Fri 2–5 plus Sun 3–6, Oct–Nov Sun 3–6; adm*), in a restored 17th-century house, provides a good introduction to the valley, including exhibits on nature, history and traditions of the area. From Arudy, the D934 leads into the valley, passing under the ruined medieval castle at **Castet**, and the beautiful white twin villages of **Bielle** and **Bilhères**. Bielle's name betrays its ancient origins – from a Roman villa the village gradually replaced. From its greatest period of prosperity in the 16th century, it has an attractive late Gothic church, St-Vivien, and an ensemble of houses to match, many with Béarnais carved lintels, the only decoration the austere Béarnais ever allow their homes. Above Bilhères, on the **Plateau de Benou**, a hiking path will take you near three small **Neolithic cromlechs** (stone circles). There are many natural springs on the plateau, and this must have been an important religious site.

Further south, around Béon and Aste, you can see the steep winding roads that lead up to the marble quarries; here you can also visit **La Falaise aux Vautours** (***t** 05 59 82 65 49, www.falaise-aux-vautours.com. Open daily June–Aug 10.30–12.30 and 2–6.30; May and Sept 2.30–6.30 plus school hols 2.40–5.30*), an educational and observation centre (with cameras hidden on the cliffs and interactive computers) for the many species of birds of prey that live around the mountain-tops: kites and eagles, and especially various species of buzzard – quite absurd creatures, some of them; if you're lucky in these parts, you may get to see the biggest of all in Europe, the rare and fearsome lammergeyer. Since 1998, Egyptian vultures have been nesting here, and a camera is installed in the nest. **Laruns**, the little capital of the Ossau, won't detain you long, unless you come on 15 August when everyone's out in traditional costume for the valley's big festival. **Assouste**, above Laruns, has a good Romanesque church.

Tourist Information

Arudy: *mairie*, **t** 05 59 05 77 11, **f** 05 59 05 80 31, *www.ot-arudy.fr. Open daily June–Sept 10–12 and 2–6; winter Tues 10–12 and 2–4 plus Sat 10–12.*

Laruns: Maison de la Vallée d'Ossau, **t** 05 59 05 31 41, **f** 05 59 05 35 49. *Open all year Mon–Sat, 9–12 and 2–6 plus Sun 9–12; July and Aug until 6.30 plus Sun pm.*

Artouste: Village de Fabrèges, **t** 05 59 05 34 00, *www.station-artouste.com.*

Market Days

Arudy: Tuesdays and Fridays.

Laruns: Saturdays.

Eaux-Bonnes: Wednesdays (summer only)

Where to Stay

Laruns and Environs ✉ 64440

Laruns is not a resort town, and there are only simple places to stay.

★★Le Lorry, Route des Cols, **t** 05 59 05 31 22 (*inexpensive*). The restaurant has *menus from €12. Closed Sun eve and Mon plus mid Nov–mid Dec.*

★★Hôtel de France, 1 Place de l'hôtel de Ville, **t** 05 59 05 60 16, *www.logis-de-france.fr* (*inexpensive*). *Closed Sat in winter plus May.*

★★Hôtel de la Poste, Eaux-Bonnes, **t** 05 59 05 33 06, **f** 05 59 05 43 03, *www.hotel-dela-poste.com* (*inexpensive*). Ten nice rooms and a restaurant (*see* below). *Open May–mid-Oct.*

★Le Glacier, **t** 05 59 05 10 18, **f** 05 59 05 15 14, *www.leglacier.fr.st* (*inexpensive*). The ski station at Gourette, high up at the Col d'Aubisque, can be a pain to reach but it promises some memorable scenery. Le Glacier is the least expensive. *Open mid May–30 Sept.*

Barthèque camp site, Laruns, **t** 05 59 05 38 88. Well equipped and with a swimming pool. *Open all year.*

Refuge d'Embaradere, Laruns, **t** 05 59 05 41 88. Cheap dormitory accommodation with meals for €11–16. *Closed Mon and Tues out of school hols.*

Village Résidentiel du Lac de Fabrèges, on the shore of the lake (write to Artouste Accueil, Maison de Fabrèges, ✉ 64440 Artouste), **t** 05 59 05 39 22. Studios to let for 4–6 people on the lake. *Open June–Sept and Dec–Apr.*

Eating Out

Auberge Bellevue, Rue de Bourguet, Laruns, **t** 05 59 05 31 58. One of the best places in the mountains, where you can have a fine Béarnais *garbure* or a *confit* at very reasonable prices. *Menus €14–28. Closed Tues eve and Wed, exc July and Aug, plus Jan and June.*

Hôtel de la Poste (*see* above). They put on a delicious €13 menu at this hotel: soup, salmon terrine and grilled lamb *persillade*; there are also *menus* €15–23.

Pic du Midi, Gabas. Hearty *garbure* and *confits*. *Menus €11–22.*

The Col d'Aubisque

From Laruns, you can detour eastwards on the marvellous, tortuous D918 (*completely open only from June to November*), a road that will make any car miserable – not to mention the bicyclists of the Tour de France, on those occasions when the sadists who run it steer the race this way. Still, it's 36km of Pyrenean scenery at its best, passing the little spa of **Eaux-Bonnes** and the modern ski resort at **Gourette**. Empress Eugénie, wife of Napoleon III, visited occasionally at Eaux-Bonnes; it was she who ordered this improbable road to be made. Eaux-Bonnes, like its matching book-end spa Eaux-Chaudes, back on the D934, still has a Second Empire look about it from the days when the Empress made it briefly fashionable. After Gourette, the D918 passes through the weird landscapes of the **Crêtes Blanches** before reaching the 1,694m/5,554ft Col, with spectacular views just under the summit of the peak called **Soum de Grum**. Carry on further and you'll be in the Vallée d'Arrens (*see* p.235).

The High Pyrenees

10

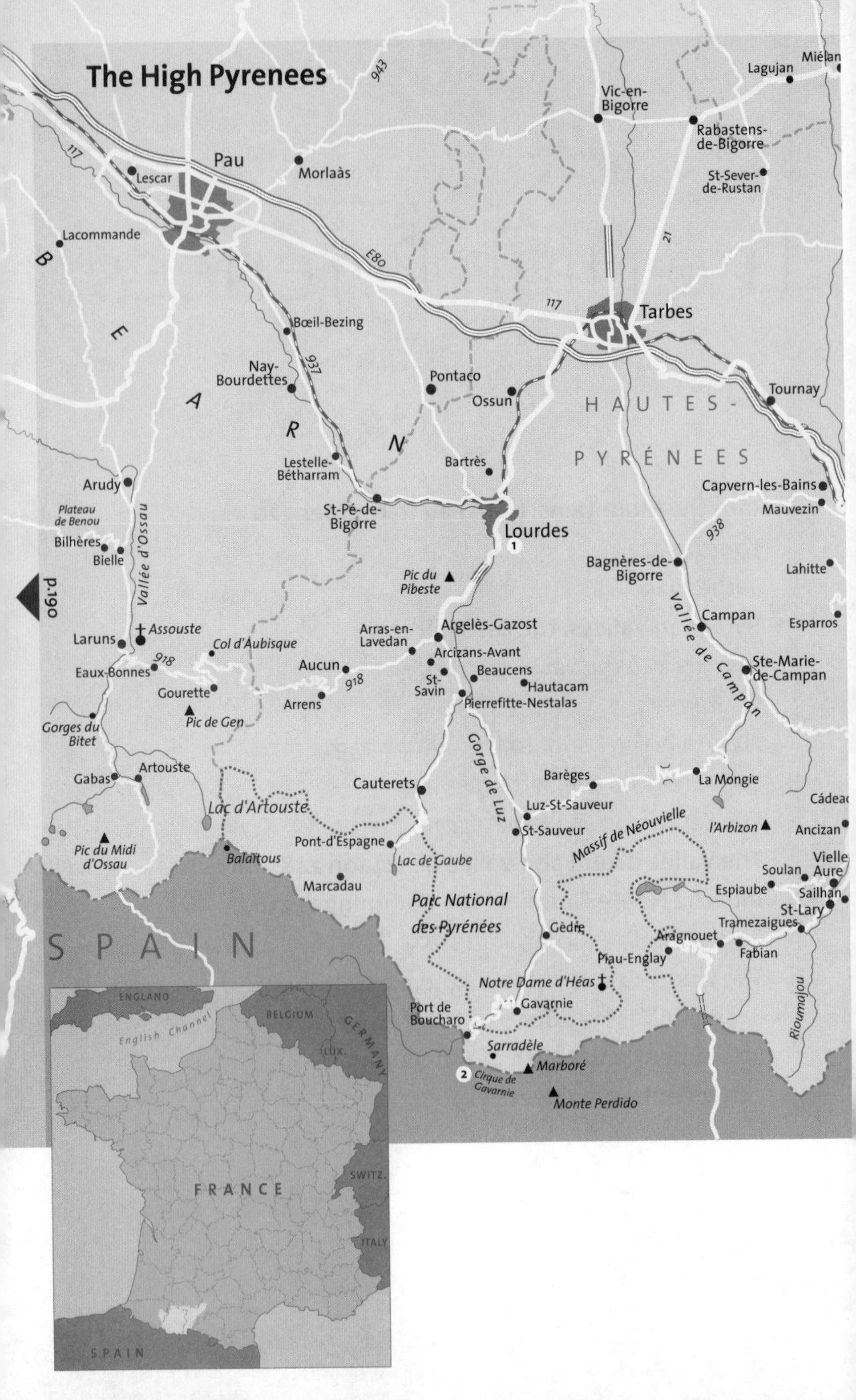
The High Pyrenees
Pau
Lescar
Morlaàs
Lacommande
Vic-en-Bigorre
Rabastens-de-Bigorre
Lagujan
St-Sever-de-Rustan
B E A R N
Tarbes
Bœil-Bezing
Nay-Bourdettes
Pontaco
Ossun
Tournay
HAUTES-PYRÉNEES
Lestelle-Bétharram
Bartrès
Arudy
Plateau de Benou
St-Pé-de-Bigorre
Capvern-les-Bains
Mauvezin
Lourdes
Bilhères
Bielle
Bagnères-de-Bigorre
Lahitte
Pic du Pibeste
p.190
Vallée d'Ossau
Laruns
Assouste
Col d'Aubisque
Arras-en-Lavedan
Argelès-Gazost
Campan
Esparros
Vallée de Campan
Eaux-Bonnes
Aucun
Arcizans-Avant
St-Savin
Beaucens
Hautacam
Ste-Marie-de-Campan
Gourette
Arrens
Pierrefitte-Nestalas
Pic de Gen
Gorges du Bitet
Gorge de Luz
Gabas
Artouste
Cauterets
Barèges
La Mongie
Lac d'Artouste
Luz-St-Sauveur
St-Sauveur
Massif de Néouvielle
l'Arbizon
Ancizan
Pic du Midi d'Ossau
Balaïtous
Pont-d'Espagne
Lac de Gaube
Soulan
Vielle Aure
Marcadau
Espiaube
Sailhan
Parc National des Pyrénées
St-Lary
Tramezaigues
Gèdre
Aragnouet
Fabian
SPAIN
Piau-Englay
Notre Dame d'Héas
Port de Boucharo
Gavarnie
Rioumajou
Sarradèle
Marboré
Cirque de Gavarnie
Monte Perdido
ENGLAND
English Channel
BELGIUM
GERMANY
LUX.
FRANCE
SWITZ.
ITALY
SPAIN

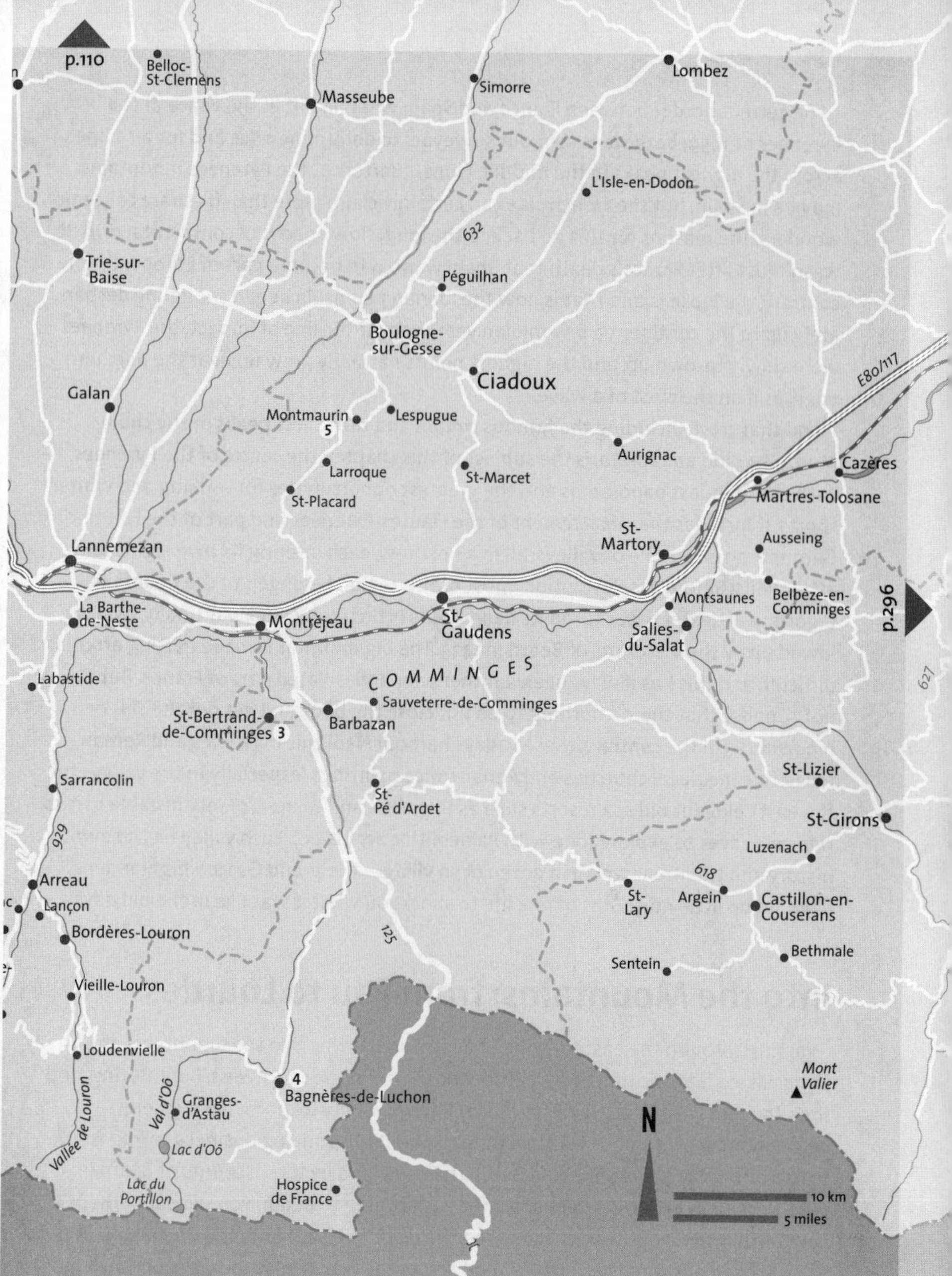

Highlights

1 Lourdes, to see what the all the fuss is about
2 The vertiginous, unforgettable Cirque de Gavarnie
3 Gothic beauty and Roman Lugdunum Convenarum, at St-Bertrand-de-Comminges
4 Luchon, immersed in fabled mountain scenery
5 The biggest Gallo-Roman villa ever discovered in France, at Montmaurin

The current border between France and Spain was laid out in the Peace of the Pyrenees of 1659; both sides sent out surveyors to determine once and for all a line across the highest peaks in the middle. Three-quarters of the Pyrenees mountains may be in Spain, but the French side can certainly claim more than its share of scenic wonders. The reasons for this go back to the long, slow epochs of continental drift. It wasn't just after Franco's death that Spain wanted to become part of Europe. On the contrary, the loose island that is now the Iberian peninsula began snuggling desperately up to the continent a few million years ago. At the line of impact, the Pyrenees were slowly thrown up, and the highest points naturally grew up near the northern edge, as if on the crest of a wave.

And that crest, including the famous *cirques* and the tallest peaks of the chain, Monte Perdido and Aneto, is the subject of this chapter: the centre of the Pyrenees, with the grandest panoramas and the greatest opportunities for walking and winter sports. It includes the *département* of the Hautes-Pyrénées and part of the Haute-Garonne, an ensemble of valleys, all in a neat row, each offering its own sights and attractions. Before the Revolution, most of this region belonged to the Counts of Bigorre, a little fief that caused its neighbours little trouble and was finally swallowed up by the Viscounts of Béarn in 1425. The big mountains made getting around difficult, and this has always been a rather poor and isolated part of France. But do not suppose that there's nothing to do but close the book and get out the skis or binoculars. On the contrary, these valleys harbour Neolithic mysteries and Roman relics, fine medieval churches and Renaissance paintings (especially in the valleys to the east), elegant old spa resorts such as Bagnères and Luchon, plenty of cable cars to ride, and caves to explore (one with Palaeolithic art inside). Each valley has its own history and traditions, and in a dozen or so villages the proud Gascon highlanders have set up little museums of folk life to show you what it was like in the old days.

Into the Mountains: from Pau to Lourdes

Passing through the eastern edge of Béarn, on the way into the mountains, the D937 passes first the most onomatopoetic village in the southwest, **Bœil-Bezing**, and then the most negative, **Nay**. This busy village lives mostly from making berets – before Atatürk's infamous Hat Law of 1925, Nay had a thriving business selling fezes to the Turks. Nay is a *bastide*, laid out in the usual grid by the viscounts of Béarn in 1302; despite a certain discreet charm, it has nothing to detain you, except perhaps a wonderfully ferocious war memorial on the *place*, with a First World War *poilou* about to hurl a grenade into the knitting shop across the way. Across the Gave de Pau from Nay, **Coarraze** will show you its castle, begun in the Middle Ages and converted into a proper château in the 18th century.

Next, as a prelude to Lourdes, there's **Lestelle-Bétharram**, one of the most peculiar holy sites anywhere. A chapel stood on the site from the earliest times, but not until the early 1600s, after Montgomery's Protestants sacked it in the Wars of Religion, was it promoted into a major pilgrimage site. Legends and miracles were concocted, and

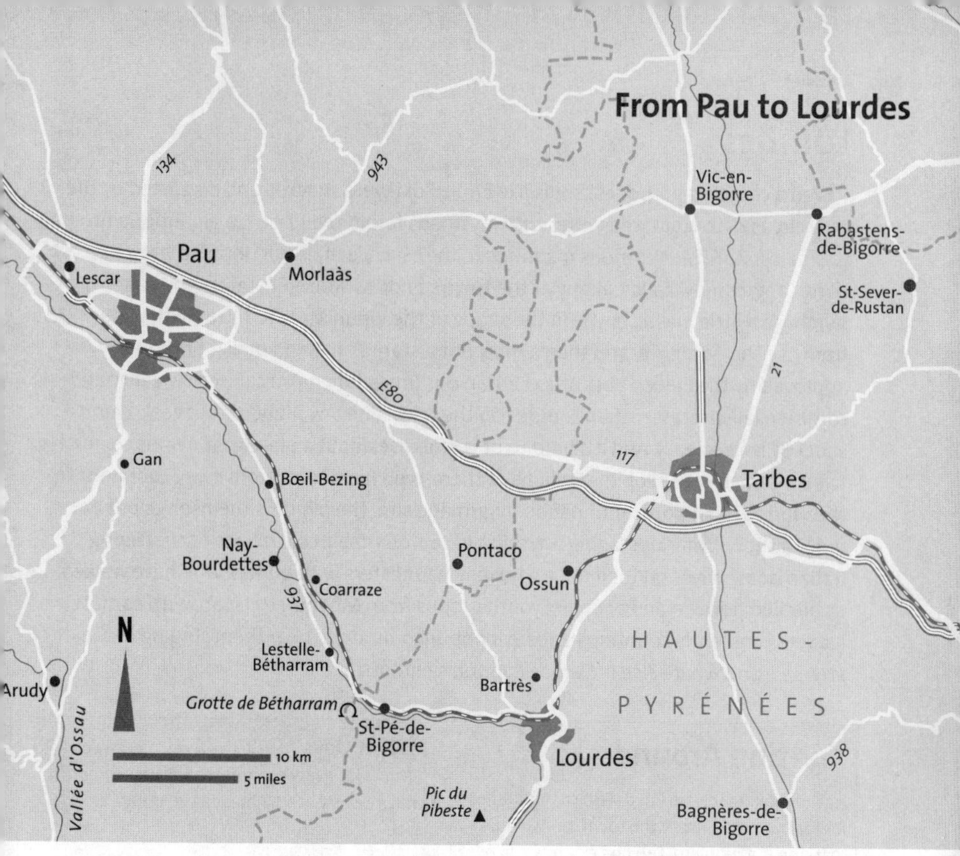

even the name of the place was changed, from Gatarram to Bétharram, supposed to mean 'the House of the Most High' in Hebrew. Soon pilgrims were pouring in by the thousands, and a major building programme was begun. The result, crowded on a hillside just south of the village, is an epitome of the religious architecture and religious sensibility of 17th-century France – weird, and a little sinister. The long, gloomy buildings lining the Gave de Pau belong to a religious college; behind them stands the chapel, jam-packed with paintings and dripping with gilt woodwork. Oddest of all is the **Calvary**, trailing up the hillside, a series of small stone chapels built in the 1800s that look like the mausolea in Victorian cemeteries.

Just south of the village off the D937 is a series of caves, the **Grottes de Bétharram** (***t*** *05 62 41 80 04, www.grottes-de-betherram.com; open 25 Mar–25 Oct, daily 9–12 and 1.30–5.30, 1 Feb–25 Mar Mon–Fri visits at 2.30 and 4*). So close to Lourdes, it isn't surprising they are so well laid out for tourists. Everyone rides a little train past the colourful stalactites; there's a boat ride across the underground lake, and commentary in nine languages.

Getting ever closer to Lourdes, the village of **St-Pé** had one of the biggest abbey churches of the southwest before Montgomery and the Protestants wrecked it in 1569. Over the next two centuries it was almost completely dismantled, though some good carved capitals survive in what's left. St-Pé (Peter) must really have stopped here – they've got his key in the village's parish church.

Lourdes

Even a century ago, honest souls like Emile Zola were shocked and disgusted by the holy circus of Lourdes; the writer J. K. Huysmans found the place '...a gigantic Saint-Louis Hospital' (Paris' famous madhouse), 'the essence of horror dripping from a barrel of gross joy'. Today, at any of the town's endless souvenir stands, you can purchase a little plastic bottle in the shape of the Virgin Mary to fill up with water from the sacred *source,* and then simply put a stamp on it and mail it home – they're approved by the French post office. But in our times, when you can see vulgarity and commercialism crasser than Lourdes on the television any night of the week, being shocked isn't so easy. And it's hard to be dismissive about a place that means so much to so many sincere people – millions of them, who have come from every continent to the world's most popular Christian pilgrimage site. The pilgrims themselves put on quite a show, by far upstaging anything in Lourdes itself: coachloads of chattering Italian housewives on their dream holiday, youngsters with guitars who have walked or hitched from Ireland or Spain; youth groups from Missouri or Japan, with earnest leaders constantly counting heads. It's not uncommon to hear them singing in the streets – and where else in Europe can you see that?

Getting Around

The main roads are lined with cars for miles before you even reach the town limits and parking is a problem. The no.1 city **bus** will be useful to all footsore pilgrims, shuttling between the rail station and the Grotte.

Lourdes has plenty of **travel firms** that organize day trips or half-day trips out to the mountains and even to the Basque country. Most of these go for about €20. (full day); for details, see the two Gares Routières d'Excursions on Bd du Lapacca and Av du Paradis.

Lourdes also has good **bus** connections to the Pyrenean valleys: there are at least eight buses a day up the valley to Argelès and Cauterets.

Tourist Information

St-Pé-de-Bigorre: Place des Arcades, **t** 05 62 41 88 10, **f** 05 62 41 87 70. *Open Mon–Fri 8–12 and 2–6; July and Aug daily 9–12.30 and 2–6.30.*

Lourdes: Place Peyramale, by the market, **t** 05 62 42 77 40, **f** 05 62 94 60 95, *www.lourdes-france.com. Open 10 Nov–2 Feb Mon–Sat 9–12 and 2–5.30; 3 Feb–6 April and 13 Oct–9 Nov 9–12 and 2–6; summer 9–6.30; July and Aug 9–7 plus Sun until 6.*

Market Days

Mon–Sat every morning in summer; *grand marché* every other Thursday year round.

Where to Stay

Lourdes ✉ 65100

In all France, only Paris has more hotel rooms. Nearly all of them close in winter. English, Spanish and German are spoken and most hotels accept pets and require half-board. In short, it's a factory; visitors aren't very demanding and nothing really stands out. Mid-range hotels crowd the Boulevard de la Grotte, just above or behind the souvenir shops. Away from the inferno, though, some quiet addresses may be found.

******Grand Hôtel de la Grotte**, 66 Rue de la Grotte, **t** 05 62 94 58 87, **f** 05 62 94 20 50, *www.hotel-grotte.com* (*moderate*). A traditional grand hotel just below the château, with ringside rooms overlooking the basilica. *Open mid April–end Oct.*

*****Moderne**, Av Bernadette Soubirous, **t** 05 62 94 12 32, **f** 05 62 42 10 07, *www.hotelmodernelourdes.com* (*moderate*).

History

Long before Bernadette, Lourdes was an important town. With a strategic location at the edge of the mountains, the site was occupied all through prehistoric times. The ancient Pyrenean Basques were here, and also the Celts, though the Romans were probably the first to fortify the heights overlooking the Gave. In the 8th century, Lourdes was briefly a stronghold of the Moors, invading from Spain, and after that it served for centuries as the chief bastion of the vassals Charlemagne appointed to keep the Moors out, the counts of Bigorre. Just the same, no one would ever have heard of the place were it not for a 14-year-old girl named Bernadette Soubirous (St Bernadette, since 1933), who saw the Virgin Mary and discovered the miraculous spring in 1858.

Apparitions of the Virgin are as common as sightings of izards in the Pyrenees, and it isn't likely that Bernadette's would have made much of a stir but for two factors. First, the spring early on developed a reputation for curing hopeless cases. Far more important, though, was active and heavy promotion by the Church, which historically has been inclined to look at apparitions and miracles with a sceptical eye. For Rome, Bernadette's visions couldn't have come at a better time. Only a decade earlier, the pope had briefly been toppled from his throne in the revolution of 1848.

Another real palace of the *belle époque*. *Open April–Nov.*

★★★**Hotel Beauséjour**, 16 Avenue de la Gare, **t** 05 62 94 38 18, *www.hotel-beausejour.com*. This fine old hotel opposite the station has recently been refurbished with a modern, glitzy interior; well-equipped, comfortable rooms. Although spacious, the rooms at the front can be noisy due to the large volumes of traffic. There is a *brasserie* with terrace and garden. *Menus €14–23. Open all year.*

St-Savin, Rue des Pyrénées, **t** 05 62 94 06 07, **f** 05 62 94 75 51 (*inexpensive*). Neat rooms on a street where you might even find a parking place, a consideration in Lourdes. *Open all year.*

★★**Hotel Majestic**, 9 Chaussée Maransin, **t** 05 62 94 27 23, **f** 05 62 94 64 91 (*inexpensive*). A good option not far from the shrines, with good comfortable rooms, a terrace and simple restaurant. *Open mid April–end Oct.*

There are plenty of places on the periphery of town and in neighbouring villages, where life can be more peaceful.

★★**Hotel Le Virginia**, Adé, 5km north of Lourdes on the N21, **t** 05 62 94 66 18, **f** 05 62 94 61 32, *www.hotelvirginia-lourdes.com* (*inexpensive*). A motel with separate cottages and a restaurant. Chalets €57. *Menus €15–26. Open all year.*

Eating Out

Lourdes' pilgrims do not much concern themselves with cuisine either.

Le Magret, 10 Rue des 4 Frères-Soulas, **t** 05 62 94 20 55. Worth a visit for good unpretentious local cuisine and southwest wines. *Menus €14–38. Closed Mon and Jan.*

Pizzeria da Marco, Rue de la Grotte. **t** 05 62 94 03 59. An inexpensive oasis for Italian pilgrims, with a menu, Italian pasta and wines. *Menus from €11. Closed Sat lunch and Mon.*

La Bodega, Rue Basse. A popular and chaotic self-service with a Spanish touch, offering paellas and *zarzuela*, but also *confits*; average dishes about €11.

A La Petite Bergère, Bartrès, **t** 05 62 94 04 28. It's worth travelling out to Bartrès for the food here. On the garden terrace, you can try lamb and chicken dishes, shad and salmon, prepared in often surprising ways. *Menus €11–30. Open all year (closed Wed).*

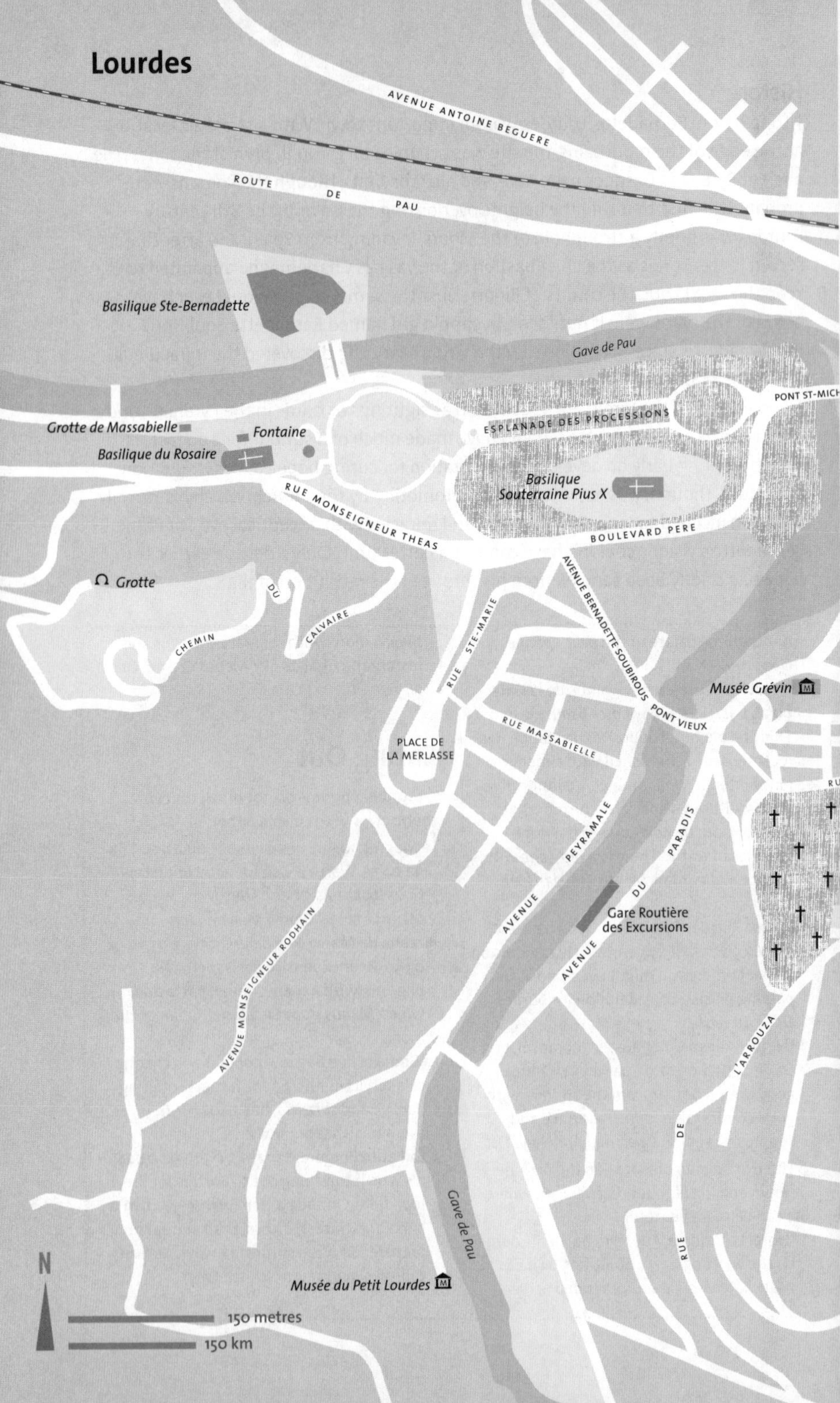
Lourdes
AVENUE ANTOINE BEGUERE
ROUTE DE PAU
Basilique Ste-Bernadette
Gave de Pau
PONT ST-MICH
ESPLANADE DES PROCESSIONS
Grotte de Massabielle
Fontaine
Basilique du Rosaire
Basilique Souterraine Pius X
RUE MONSEIGNEUR THEAS
BOULEVARD PERE
Grotte
CHEMIN DU CALVAIRE
RUE STE-MARIE
AVENUE BERNADETTE SOUBIROUS
PONT VIEUX
Musée Grévin
RUE MASSABIELLE
PLACE DE LA MERLASSE
AVENUE PEYRAMALE
AVENUE DU PARADIS
Gare Routière des Excursions
AVENUE MONSEIGNEUR RODHAIN
RUE DE L'ARROUZA
Gave de Pau
Musée du Petit Lourdes
N
150 metres
150 km

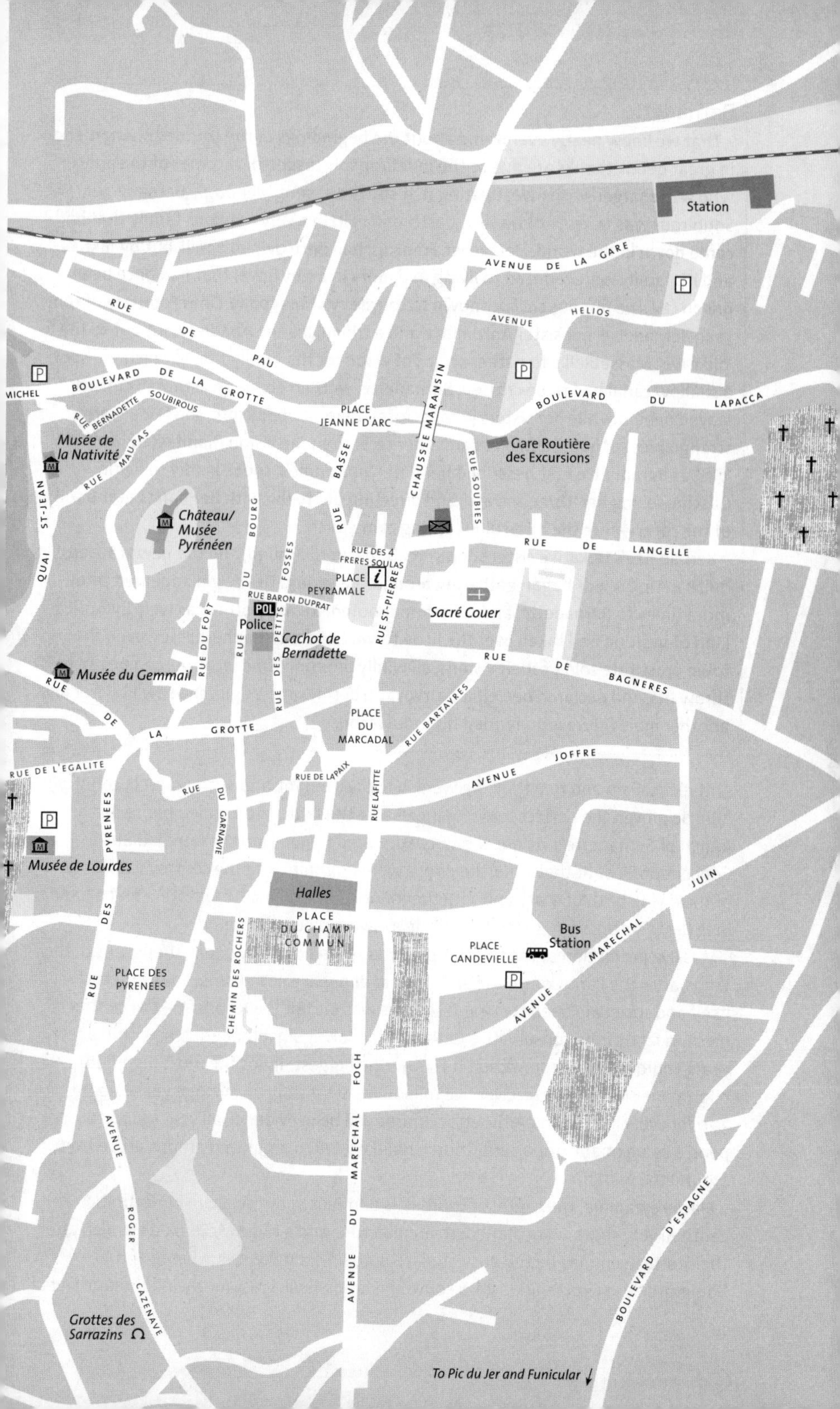

Station
Avenue de la Gare
Avenue Helios
Rue de Pau
Michel
Boulevard de la Grotte
Rue Bernadette Soubirous
Rue Maupas
Musée de la Nativité
Quai St-Jean
Château/ Musée Pyrénéen
Place Jeanne d'Arc
Chaussee Maransin
Rue Basse
Boulevard du Lapacca
Gare Routière des Excursions
Rue Soubies
Rue de Langelle
Rue des 4 Freres Soulas
Place Peyramale
Sacré Couer
Rue Baron Duprat
POL
Police
Cachot de Bernadette
Rue du Bourg
Rue des Petits Fosses
Rue du Fort
Rue St-Pierre
Musée du Gemmail
Rue de la Grotte
Rue de Bagneres
Place du Marcadal
Rue Bartayres
Avenue Joffre
Rue de l'Egalite
Rue de la Paix
Rue Lafitte
Rue du Garnavie
Musée de Lourdes
Rue des Pyrenees
Halles
Place du Champ Commun
Bus Station
Place Candevielle
Avenue Marechal Juin
Place des Pyrenees
Chemin des Rochers
Avenue du Marechal Foch
Avenue Roger Cazenave
Boulevard d'Espagne
Grottes des Sarrazins
To Pic du Jer and Funicular

Bernadette

That we know nearly everything about the beginnings of the Lourdes phenomenon in great detail, thanks are due to the indefatigable Inspector Jacomet of the police, who was charged with investigating it. It starts out simply enough. Bernadette Soubirous was 14 years old, a sickly, asthmatic girl in a very religious family that had come down in the world. Her father, François, had once owned a mill, but by 1858 he and his family were reduced to living in penury in a tiny hovel that had once been a prison cell, the famous *cachot* shown to Lourdes visitors today. On 11 February of that year, Bernadette, her sister Antoinette and a friend, Jeanne Abadie, went out to the 'old cave', Massabielle, to gather scraps of wood for the family fire. To reach the spot, a shallow canal had to be crossed. Bernadette, worried about an asthmatic attack, stayed behind while her sisters went across. There, at about 1pm, she felt a warm, strange breeze that seemed to caress her face. Then the vision manifested itself. A 'girl', as Bernadette first described her (later '*une dame*'), spoke kindly to her in Gascon, telling her 'three secrets', and directing her to dig with her hands in the soil of the cave, where the miraculous spring came forth.

Bernadette's talkative sister soon spread the word around, and the news caused quite a stir. Crowds began gathering around the spring. The Virgin appeared three more times to Bernadette, and, as Jacomet noted, to many others as well. By April a kind of hysteria had taken over the little town. Children, shepherdesses, even the town prostitute told of their visions, all wildly differing. One local woman began to throw fits, and declared herself a clairvoyant; besides the Virgin, she saw St Peter and another male figure who twirled his moustache.

Anti-clericalism and free thinking were in the ascendant, and such a simple country miracle proved the perfect tonic for increasing the faith. As an added bonus, in the fourth of Bernadette's visions the Virgin declared to her, 'I am the Immaculate Conception.' Just at that time, the popes were promulgating the controversial dogma of the divine birth of Mary, and, whether or not a little clerical prompting had a hand in it, Bernadette's word helped greatly in swaying pious opinion.

Massive promotion of the Lourdes pilgrimage did not really begin, though, until the 1870s, after the Paris Commune and the end of papal rule in Rome. The Church saw itself and society in deep crisis, and Lourdes was part of the response – the centre-piece, in fact, of the conservative Catholic reaction against modernism. Within a few years, Lourdes had become what it is now: the biggest (if not the most dignified) pilgrimage site anywhere. Over five million people visit in an average year – about 300 for every inhabitant. Although pilgrims will be in evidence all year round, most people come on the important Church holidays, when organized groups arrive from around the world.

Place Peyramale, the centre of Lourdes, is dominated by the tourist information centre, a very sharp work of modern architecture, and a huge McDonald's, which after the Grotte itself may be the busiest place in town. From here, Rue Basse and Boulevard de la Grotte, lined with souvenir stands, head west for the pilgrimage sites,

Miracles could not be far behind. The first was bestowed on Louis Bouriette, a man who worked with Bernadette's father in a stable. Blind in one eye, he procured some mud from around the spring and made a compress of it, and regained his sight. Newspapers began to pick up on the story, and both the bishop of Tarbes and the authorities came to investigate. As soon as word got around, Lourdes became a very busy place.

Throughout the holy carnival that followed, Bernadette seemed to be the only one to keep her head. Always the very picture of sincerity and simplicity, she never encouraged any sensationalism or commercialization. She continued to have her visions, and described them politely to anyone who troubled to ask; that was all. Bernadette was a girl of few words. A famous sculptor came down to try and reproduce the Virgin as Bernadette saw her, and spent days talking with the girl, making sure he had the description down perfectly. When it was finished, he asked her if it was a good resemblance. 'Not at all,' was the reply.

Bernadette entered a convent up north in Nevers in 1866. By some accounts, she was forced into it – Lourdes had become big business, and there was always the chance she might say something the Church would find inconvenient. In Nevers she led a quiet, secluded life. Always subject to bouts of ill health, she died there in 1879, at the age of only 35. A movement for canonization sprang up almost immediately, though with the Church's accustomed deliberation it took 54 years to finally make Bernadette a saint.

As for her role in history and religion, her own wishes sum it up best: 'The less people say about me,' she once said, 'the better.'

while Rue St-Pierre bears south, towards the workaday Lourdes of the Lourdais, with its lively market – two worlds, giving the impression that they like to keep a certain distance from each other.

Above it all, on the hill overlooking the town, is the **château**. The site has been occupied at least since Roman times. Legend states that the castle was occupied by Moors from Spain, who seized it on their retreat home after the Battle of Poitiers. Later, under a chief named Mirat, the Muslims were besieged by Charlemagne. During the fighting, a salmon fell miraculously from the sky at Mirat's feet; he sent it as a present to the Frankish king, saying that he had no worry about holding out indefinitely, since heaven itself was providing provisions for him. The siege dragged on, and only ended when the bishop of Puy-en-Velay, who was with Charlemagne, suggested a compromise – the Muslims all converted to Christianity, swore fealty to Charlemagne and the bishop, and got to keep the castle (unfortunately, like so many other similar legends, it seems this one was invented in the later Middle Ages to support the Church's claim to part of the castle's rents).

Throughout medieval times, the castle was a stronghold of the counts of Bigorre; most of what you see today, though, dates from the 1590s, after a rebuilding ordered by Henri IV. Today it houses the **Musée Pyrénéen** (***t** 05 62 42 37 37; open daily all year Oct–Mar 9–12 and 2–6 (5 on Fri); summer 9–12 and 1.30–6.30*), with farm paraphernalia and objects of everyday life from the time of Bernadette Soubirous, along with a stuffed bear and exhibits on the Pyrenees and mountain-climbing.

The *Cité Religieuse*

When the pilgrims are in town, the **Boulevard de la Grotte** is the closest thing the Pyrenees can offer to a North African souk – jam-packed with people babbling in every imaginable tongue, and vast heaps of glittering merchandise spilling out into the street from every shopfront. Every bit of that merchandise, though, is a holy souvenir: sea-shell shrines, medallions, patches, Virgin Mary toaster-covers, gargantuan rhinestone rosaries, and gilt plastic-framed magic pictures that show Bernadette in the grotto when you look one way, and a smirking pope when you look the other. Though quality has been dropping off in recent years, for connoisseurs of kitsch this is still the next best thing to paradise.

After running the gauntlet, you'll cross the little bridge over the Gave de Pau and enter the '**Domaine de la Grotte**' – no shorts or beach clothes, no dogs, no smoking. Everything is impeccably organized, as it has to be, and there are guides, maps and signposts everywhere, along with visitors' centres that speak every language known to Catholicism. The Domaine begins with the pretty **Esplanade des Processions**, with room for 40,000 people – and it's often full in the evening when groups from all over the world parade up and down with their home-town banners. At the end of this stands the **Basilique du Rosaire**, built in 1883. Unlike the souvenirs, this bit of kitsch fails to amuse. The 'Romanesque-Byzantine' style, invented in 19th-century France, undoubtedly marks the low point of Christian sacred architecture, a degenerate parody of the medieval Age of Faith; Emile Zola found it 'ugly enough to make one cry'. The frescoes and mosaics within match the architecture perfectly, and may even surpass it.

Even when it was new the Basilica often proved too small to accommodate the crowds, but not until the '50s was a larger facility built. The chilly **Underground Basilica Pius X**, to the left of the Esplanade, seats 20,000. Walk around the back of the Basilique du Rosaire to see where it all started, the little **Grotte de Massabielle**, and the adjoining spring, where the water that doesn't get packed into little bottles is channelled into pools to bathe the sick. Up above on the hillside, pilgrims trek a **Calvaire** made of giant bronze statues.

Roadside Attractions and More Mysteries

Beyond the *cité religieuse* Lourdes has a formidable array of holy sites and dubious 'museums' to entertains its pilgrims. Among many others, there's the **Musée de Lourdes**, at the car park l'Egalité (***t*** *05 62 94 28 00; open April–Oct daily 9–11.45 and 1.30–6.45, to 6.15pm the rest of the year; adm*), with dioramas of little Bernadette's vision and village life in the 1850s. Of course there's also a branch of the **Musée Grévin** (*87 Rue de la Grotte,* ***t*** *05 62 94 33 74; open April–Oct daily 9–11.30 and 1.30–6.30, also July and Aug evenings 8.30–10pm; adm*), with more of the same, along with Jesus and 12 pasty-faced Apostles reproducing Leonardo's *Last Supper*. And if you can stand any more, there's the **Musée de la Nativité** (*21 Quai St-Jean, **t** 05 62 94 71 00; open Easter–Nov daily 9–12 and 1.30–7 plus evenings in July and Aug 8.30–10; adm*), and the **Musée du Petit Lourdes** (*67 Av Peyramale, **t** 05 62 94 24 36; open April–Oct daily 9am–7pm, closed for lunch April–June and mid Sep–Oct; adm*), with the village of Bernadette's time in miniature and some toy trains. On Rue des Petits-Fosses, a building that was once a prison and later the home of Bernadette's family can be visited: **Le Cachot**, 'the cell' (***t** 05 62 94 51 30; open daily in summer 9–12 and 2–7, Oct–April daily 3–5*).

Visitors also like to take trips up the mountains that fringe the town; you can ride to the top of the 3,081ft Pic du Jer on a **funicular railway**; there is a grand view, and **caves** to explore near the summit (***t** 05 62 94 00 41, www.picdujer.info; open May–Aug daily 9.30–12 (last descent at 11.50) and 1.30–6.30, April and Oct 1.30–6.30. Closed Nov–Easter; adm includes fare and cave visit*). More caves await atop the slightly shorter Le Béout, which also has a cable railway to the top.

If you want to see some stalactites without the trouble of going up into the mountains, there is the **Grottes du Loup**, near the Basilica on Chemin des Bottes (***t** 05 62 94 20 91; open daily Easter–Oct, 9–7*).

Just west of town, off the D937, the **Lac de Lourdes** is one of the largest natural lakes of the Pyrenees, today a favourite picnic ground. Until recent times, however, its overgrown banks were a sinister, cursed place, seldom visited. Legends said that the lake could swallow up swimmers or boatmen and hold their souls for eternity. According to another story, there once was a city here, that sank under the waters as punishment for its sins; fishermen claimed they could sometimes hear its church bell ringing under the surface. Now, you can rent a canoe and listen for yourself.

Bordering the lake to the north is a long stretch of empty countryside around the village of Bartrès. This area, as far north as Pontacq and Ossun, was a major **necropolis** and perhaps a religious site in Neolithic times. Dozens of tumuli and standing stones can still be seen, a small fraction of the original total; farmers were still ploughing them under a decade ago. Survivors include some of the largest mounds in the south of France – one over 170ft in diameter. Others have stone corridors inside with branching funeral chambers. In this lonely, haunted landscape, a little girl named Bernadette Soubirous used to spend long days alone, watching the sheep. Maybe it had an effect on her. Bernadette's family lived for a time in **Bartrès**, where both the family's house and the sheep barn have been converted into shrines.

Tarbes

Almost half the 220,000 people of the Hautes-Pyrénées live in or around this grey, unfathomable toadstool of a departmental capital. There's precious little to see or do here; upon careful consideration, you might be inclined to agree that among all the cities of southern France, Tarbes is the one most sadly wanting in personality and character (Salon-de-Provence comes in a close second). It has long been a military town (like Salon), and do not doubt there is a connection.

History

According to legend, Tarbes was founded by an Ethiopian queen named Tarbis. Having been defeated in battle by the Pharaoh's army – commanded by none other than Moses – she offered Moses her hand and half her kingdom. When he refused, the queen was so distracted that she went off to the south of France with her sister Lorda (who founded Lourdes). More likely, the city started out as a trading post for Aquitaine merchants on the Adour, *c.* 300 BC. It grew into a Roman town, and after being destroyed by the Normans in the 9th century reappeared under the leadership of its bishops. Being sited on a plain made defence difficult, and medieval Tarbes grew up in the odd form of six walled, self-contained *bourgs* strung in a row (nothing of

Getting There and Around

Tarbes-Ossun-Lourdes **airport**, halfway between the Hautes-Pyrénées' two cities, has a daily flight from Paris on Air France. For information in Tarbes, ring **t** 05 62 32 92 22.

Another easy way to get into the region is the **TGV** from Paris to Tarbes; there are usually four a day, as well as night trains and motorail.

Tarbes is the hub for **bus** connections. Most buses start from Place du Forail near the market (but ring F.A.L.T. on **t** 05 62 34 76 69 for complete information). There are at least a dozen runs a day to Lourdes, and many continue on from there to Argelès, Arrens and Pierrefitte.

Tourist Information

Tarbes: 3 Cours Gambetta, **t** 05 62 51 30 31, **f** 05 62 44 17 63, *www.tarbes.com. Open all year Mon–Sat 9–12.30 and 2–7.*

Vic-en-Bigorre: 2 Rue Jacques Fourcade, **t** 05 62 96 80 38. *Open all year Tues–Fri 8–12.30 and 2–5.30 plus Sat 9–12.*

Market Days

Tarbes: Thursdays.

Vic-en-Bigorre: Saturdays.

Where to Stay and Eat

Tarbes ✉ 65000

As at Lourdes, you'll do better just outside town. Tarbes has plenty of accommodation for visiting salesmen; it's never crowded and rooms are generally much cheaper.

***__Henri IV__, 7 Av Bertrand Barère, between the rail station and Place de Verdun, **t** 05 62 34 01 68, **f** 05 62 93 71 32 (*moderate–inexpensive*). A good bargain, with helpful staff and very comfortable rooms. *Open all year.*

__Hôtel de l'Avenue__, Av Bertrand Barère, **t/f 05 62 93 06 36 (*cheap*). Basic, with the cheapest rooms in town. *Open all year.*

***__Hôtel l'Aragon__, Juillan, on the D921 towards Lourdes, **t** 05 62 32 07 07, **f** 05 62 32 92 50, *www.hotel-aragon.com* (*inexpensive*). A modern but gracious establishment set in spacious gardens. Even if you don't stay you should try to drop in for dinner. The restaurant, **t** 05 62 32 07 07, is run by the Cazaux brothers (one cooks, one looks after the wine). It's quite popular, with a reputation for the best food around; ring ahead for their famous salads with quail or foie gras. *Menus €30–52. Closed Xmas, 9–25 Feb and 4–20 Aug.*

L'Isard, Av Maréchal-Joffre, near the rail station, **t** 05 62 93 06 60. Usually crowded at lunch time, with filling menus *€13–31. Closed Sun eve.*

L'Ambroisie, 48 Rue Abbé, **t** 05 62 93 09 34. A popular local restaurant in an old presbytery, with a terrace and garden. Tuna steak and beef roasted with Madiran wine are especially recommended. *Menus €28–50. Closed Sun and Mon.*

L'Asia, 77 Av Régiment-du-Bigorre, **t** 05 62 93 03 43. As its name implies, this offers tasty specialities from China, Japan and elsewhere, including a Vietnamese fondue, plenty of seafood and dramatically flambéed fruits for dessert. *Menus €16–28. Closed for lunch exc Sun plus Sept.*

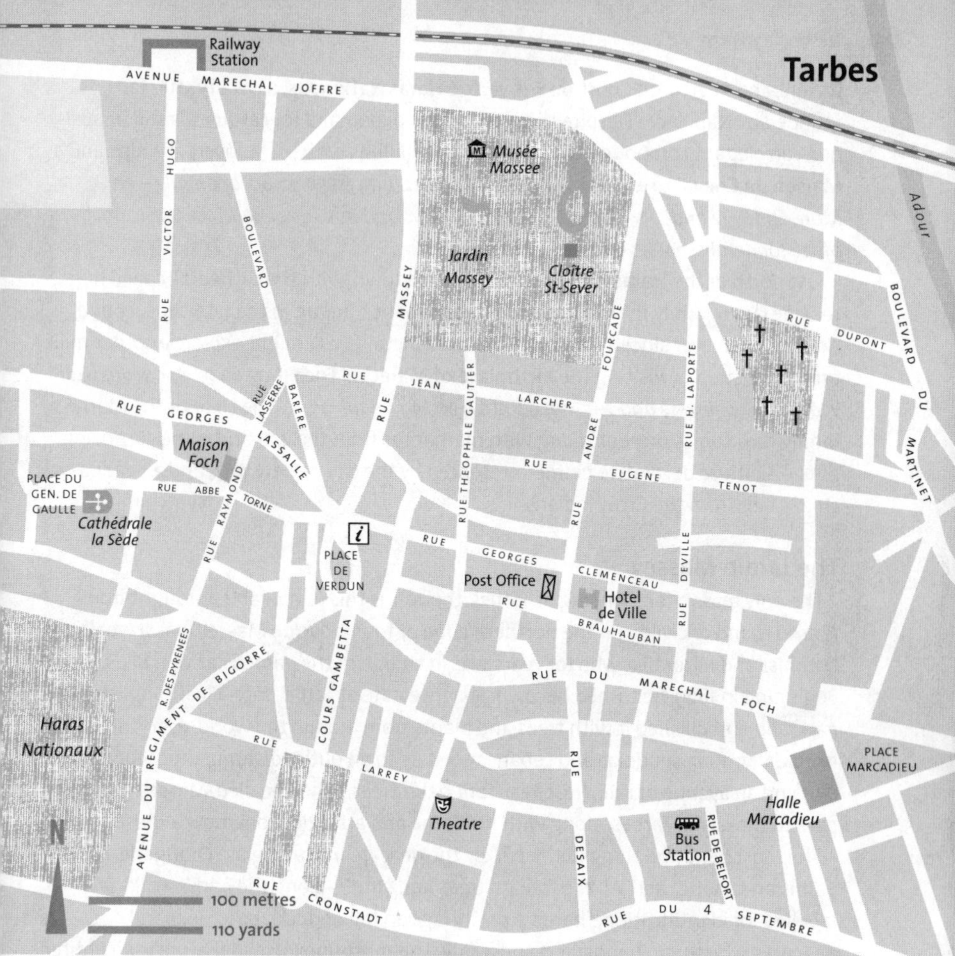

these survives today). The counts of the Bigorre fixed their residence here, and Tarbes acquired its status as capital of the region. Slow but steady industrialization after the railroad arrived in 1859 made Tarbes what it is today. Among other things, Tarbes makes aeroplane parts, and the local resistance won the Croix de Guerre for effectively sabotaging the plant in 1944.

For all its industry, and the fact that it is the administrative capital of the Hautes-Pyrénées, Tarbes is still really just a big market town, and its liveliest corner is still the Place Marcadieu, where the enormous Thursday farmers' market spreads out around the big metal *halles*, built in 1880. The *place* got its centrepiece about the same time: the Fontaine Duvignau. Four local sculptors combined to make this fountain, a complex allegory representing the four valleys that stretch up to the mountains from around Tarbes, dripping with cute allegorical maidens as well as bears, izards and other Pyrenean wildlife.

Besides the market, Tarbes is also an army town. There are large and stately barracks, belonging to a division of *hussards parachutistes* on the Allées Général

Leclerc, and nearby, on Cours de Reffye, the **Haras Nationaux**, a cavalry stud farm founded by Napoleon. Despite the current lack of demand for cavalry, it's still in business, an elegant compound of Empire-style buildings with some lovely gardens and a **Maison du Cheval** to explain what it's all about (***t** 05 62 56 30 80; open July–Feb Mon–Fri 10–12 and 2–5; also open some Sundays and public holidays, ask the tourist office for details; horses out to stud Feb–July*).

Just north of the Haras is the heart of the old town, with the **cathedral**, called here La Sède, an ungainly thing full of Baroque fripperies, begun in the 12th century and tinkered with ever since. Nearby, on Rue de la Victoire, you might explore another military connection by visiting the **birthplace of Maréchal Foch** (***t** 05 62 93 19 02; open all year Thurs–Sat 9–12 and 2–5, open until 6.30 May–Sept; adm*). The Hero of the Marne's family furniture is present, along with mementos from the war and some surprising gifts – a bizarre decorative helmet presented by the city of New York, and a beaded chief's belt from the Crow Indians .

The Jardin Massey

The only reason for stopping at Tarbes, though, is this remarkable, wrought-iron-fenced island of civility on the northern edge of town. Placide Massey was a wealthy botanist and naturalist who for years was in charge of the gardens at Versailles. Beginning in 1829, he turned his own 35-acre estate at Tarbes into a lush, English-style park, and embellished it with trees and plants from around the world: everything from Californian sequoias and Lebanese cedars to an outlandish, gigantic Siberian elm and an avenue of rare, frost-resistant palm trees. When he died, Massey left the park to the city of Tarbes, along with his home and art collections, now a museum.

The most beautiful thing in the park is the delicate iron and glass **Orangerie**, full of palms and exotic cacti. All the foreign trees and shrubs along the park's walks are labelled for identification; there's a pretty lagoon full of ducks, baby deer and peacocks, a Victorian bandstand and a café. The most unexpected feature is an entire medieval **cloister**, reassembled here from St-Sever-de-Rustan. The 14th-century carving is first-rate, on some of the strangest capitals ever: besides more conventional scenes you'll notice birds pulling a woman's toes, swans killing a bear, boiling martyrs, and a fellow chasing a lady with a long knife. The peculiar building with the neo-Moorish tower near the Orangerie, once Placide Massey's home, now houses the **Musée Massey** (***t** 05 62 36 31 49; at time of writing the museum is undergoing major restoration and is only open for the first week in the month until Autumn 2004, Sun–Fri 10–12 and 2–5*). The star of its small archaeological collection is a bronze mask of about the 3rd century BC, a curly-haired figure supposed to represent the Pyrenean god Ergé; dozens of votive altars to this divinity have been found in the High Pyrenees, possibly an equivalent of Ares or Mars. There's also a picture gallery, with a view of Tarbes under snow by Utrillo, a work attributed to the Mannerist Pontormo, and some ripe Dutch works of the 1600s. Most of the space, however, is taken up with the Musée Internationale des Hussards (*closed for renovation at the time of writing*). Tarbes' hussars may jump out of aeroplanes now, but this museum will remind you that the idea of 'hussars' as a flashy élite cavalry goes back to Hungary in the 15th century. Other countries, including France, developed corps of their own; with their élite training and fancy uniforms hussars were singularly effective in terrorizing natives in the colonies and rebellious workers at home. Most of the museum consists of paintings and empty uniforms on horseback and it's all very colourful. There is also a **Musée de la Déportation et de la Résistance** (*63 Rue Georges Lassalle,* **t** *05 62 51 11 60; the museum is currently short-staffed, call ahead to visit*).

Around Tarbes

The northernmost part of the Hautes-Pyrénées, very much a continuation of Béarn's Vic-Bilh, is a jumbled-up land of parallel river valleys only a few miles apart, full of innumerable tiny villages. If anything, the area is famous for beans, the *haricots tarbais* without which no *cassoulet* would be right. **Vic-en-Bigorre**, the only large village, could be Tarbes in a nutshell, built around its old market *halles* and 15th-century church. **Rabastens-de-Bigorre**, a 14th-century *bastide*, claims to be the national centre for milk-fed veal, most of which gets sent to Italy to make *scallopine* and *osso buco*. East on the D6, you can see what's left of the abbey at **St-Sever-de-Rustan**: the 12th-century abbey church, remodelled in the Renaissance, and the Pavilion des Hôtes from the 1700s. Apparently the mayor of St-Sever sold the cloister to Placide Massey to make a quick buck in 1890, and you'll have to go to Tarbes' Jardin Massey to see it.

Pyrenean Valleys: the Lavedan

This is the highest of the High Pyrenees, and the most famed for its scenic wonders. A trio of the chain's giants, Balaïtous, Vignemale and Monte Perdido, look down on a host of smaller fry – mere 7,500-footers – as well as the most astounding sight the mountains have to offer, the great natural wall of the Cirque de Gavarnie. The mountain views are never short of spectacular, a paradise for skiers and hikers, though beyond sports and activities there isn't a lot to do. The difficult terrain has always kept the Lavedan out of the mainstream of culture and history. Today, the valleys that run down from the heights get more than their share of tourists year-round. Cauterets and Gavarnie, in fact, were the first fashionable resorts in the Pyrenees, back in the early 19th century when mountain-touring first became popular.

Tourism remains the sum total of the Lavedan economy, though this was not always the case. Busy and heavily populated by a Gaulish tribe called the *Levitani* in ancient times, when mountain pasture-land was a greater asset than it is now, the Lavedan lived as a world in itself, where Romans and Franks were but distant nuisances who would come sniffing around for tax money. Charlemagne created a viscount of the Lavedan to do the job better, and his successors ruled the valleys as their private preserve up to the Revolution. All the while, people made a comfortable though never luxurious living from their cows and sheep, guiding them up to the heights in summer and back down again when the leaves started to turn. Because the Lavedan valleys provided a way into the mountains but not through them, the region has always been more isolated than the valleys to the west; proper roads were not built until the 18th century. You won't get trapped at a dead end at the Spanish border, however. A good number of rivers flow down from the highest peaks of the Pyrenees to form the Adour and the Gave de Pau, and there will be several chances to branch off along the way and follow them.

Tourist Information

Argelès-Gazost: Grande Terrace, **t** 05 62 97 00 25, **f** 05 62 97 50 60, *www.argeles-gazost.com. Open Mon–Sat 9–12.30 and 2–7 plus Sun 9–12 in peak season.*

Pierrefitte-Nestalas: Av Jean-Moulin, **t/f** 05 62 92 71 31, *www.pierrefitte-nestalas.net. Open Mon–Sat 10–12 and 2.30–6.30.*

Market Days

Argelès-Gazost: Tuesdays and Saturdays.

Pierrefitte-Nestalas: Saturdays.

Where to Stay and Eat

Argelès-Gazost ✉ 65400

★★Bon Repos, Av des Stades, **t** 05 62 97 01 49, **f** 05 62 97 03 97, *www.bonrepos.com* (*inexpensive*). Sometimes we take France for granted, but it's gratifying to think that nearly always, when you find a hotel with a name like this, the establishment is likely to provide just that. There are 18 rooms, a pool, a welcoming family and very reasonable rates. *Closed mid Oct–Easter.*

★★Beau Site, **t** 05 62 97 08 63, **f** 05 62 97 06 01, *www.hotel-beausite-argeles.com* (*inexpensive*). Typical old French inn, full of big flowery wallpaper and old furniture. A bit shabby but comfortable none the less. *Menu €16. Closed 5 Nov–15 Dec.*

★Victoria, on the N21, **t** 05 62 97 08 34 (*inexpensive–cheap*). The cheapest option to be found in town and quite acceptable if a bit scruffy. *Open all year.*

Estaing ✉ 65400

★Hôtel du Lac d'Estaing, **t/f** 05 62 97 06 25 (*inexpensive–cheap*). Out by itself in the mountains, on the road to the lake, the hotel offers generous helpings of peace and quiet, nice rooms, and a restaurant worth the detour. There's a lunch menu, but it's worth going for the spectacular local *charcuterie*, river fish, and main courses such as the delicious stuffed *roulade d'agneau*. *Menus (lunch €14 up to €39). Open daily May–mid Oct.*

St-Savin ✉ 65400

★★Le Viscos, **t** 05 62 97 02 28, **f** 05 62 97 04 95, *www.hotel-leviscos.com* (*inexpensive*). On the edge of the village, with beautiful views over this exceptional corner of the valley, this hotel has functional rooms, but a restaurant you are bound to remember. M. Saint-Martin presents innovative dishes that are never over the top; everything seems just right, as in the *lotte* (monkfish) in a casserole with ham. Also wonderful are simple desserts such as tarts made with wild strawberries. *Menus €15–49. Restaurant closed Sun eve and Mon exc July and Aug; closed Jan.*

★★Panoramic, a block from the church, **t** 05 62 97 08 22 (*inexpensive–cheap*). The hotel alternative is this venerable village inn with mountain views. *Open Easter–end Sept.*

Arcizans-Avant ✉ 65400

★★Le Cabaliros, **t** 05 62 97 04 31, **f** 05 62 97 91 48, *www.auberge-cabaliros.com* (*inexpensive*). You might not think of basing yourself in this out-of-the-way hamlet, but Arcizans has one sweet little hotel, offering 8 nice rooms with a view, and dinner on the terrace. *Menus €16–40. Open 4 Feb–4 Nov.*

Château du Prince Noir, Arcizans–Avant, **t** 05 62 97 02 79, *www.prince.noir.free.fr.* For a big gulp of history and amazing views at nearly 2,000 ft up this is the place to stay. The oldest part of this historic building dates back to before the prince's time, to 1120 (*see* p.263.) The ruin was bought and totally renovated by André Doyen in 1972. It now has 3 guest-rooms and although they don't appear to have been decorated since he moved in, they're spacious and full of character. *Open June–Oct, and on reservation for the rest of the year. Closed Dec.*

Argelès and the Val d'Azun

Heading south from Lourdes on the N21, the big mountain on your right is the **Pic du Pibeste**, a fine area for hiking, its slopes crisscrossed with trails. Herds of mouflons, deer, eagles and vultures are commonly sighted here. The next town is **Argelès-Gazost**, one of the main centres of mountain tourism. Argelès has a split personality: an attractive and well-kept medieval centre of stone houses and narrow alleys, and below that a spacious spa resort laid out in the 1890s.

The Val d'Azun

From Argelès, there is a choice of roads: either straight down the D921 into the heart of the mountains, or a detour west on the D918 into the Val d'Azun. It's a lovely detour, passing through unspoiled medieval villages like **Arras**, with ruins of a castle and a Romanesque church that has a low Gothic *porte des Cagots*. From Arras, you can really get away from it all by detouring even further down the D103 (or the main Pyrenean hiking route, the GR 10, which parallels it) up the **Vallée d'Estaing**, an isolated region in the shadow of 8,853ft Moun Né; the road ends at a pretty mountain lake, the Lac d'Estaing.

The D918 continues west to **Aucun**, with another Romanesque church; this one conserves truly unusual holy water stoups and baptismal fonts from its original equipment, covered with naïve carvings. Aucun also has a small folk museum, the **Musée du Lavedan** (***t*** *05 62 97 12 03; open daily during school holidays, 9–12 and 3–6; adm; phone ahead and book for the rest of the year*).

Further west, there are more churches worth a look at **Arrens**: the 12th-century St-Pierre, with a stoup 'of the Cagots', and, just south of the village, **Notre-Dame-de-Pouey-Lahün**, called the 'Golden Chapel' because of its extravagant gilded wood-carved decoration inside; this chapel is a pilgrimage site much like Lourdes, commemorating an appearance of the Virgin to a shepherd long ago. From here the D105 will take you up to the slopes of **Balaïtous** on the Spanish border, a sparse region of mountain lakes created by dams; the big glacier that covers Balaïtous' northern face is the dominant sight. Go any further on the twisting, gear-grinding but exceptionally scenic road west from Arrens and you'll be approaching the Col d'Aubisque, gateway to the Vallée d'Ossau in Béarn (*see* p.218).

St-Savin and the Gave de Pau

South of Argelès, the D921 passes through one of the most densely inhabited valleys of the Pyrenees, dotted with minuscule villages on both sides of the Gave de Pau. On the left bank of the Gave, beautifully sited on a shelf above the valley with a wonderful view, **St-Savin** goes back quite a way for a tiny village. Founded on the site of a Roman villa, it was sacked by the Arabs and Normans, and then rebuilt under Charlemagne. Later it became a *sauveté*, and the home of a Benedictine abbey favoured by the counts of Bigorre.

From this busy history only the **church** of St-Savin remains, but it is one of the medieval treasure houses of the western Pyrenees. The austere exterior is punctu-

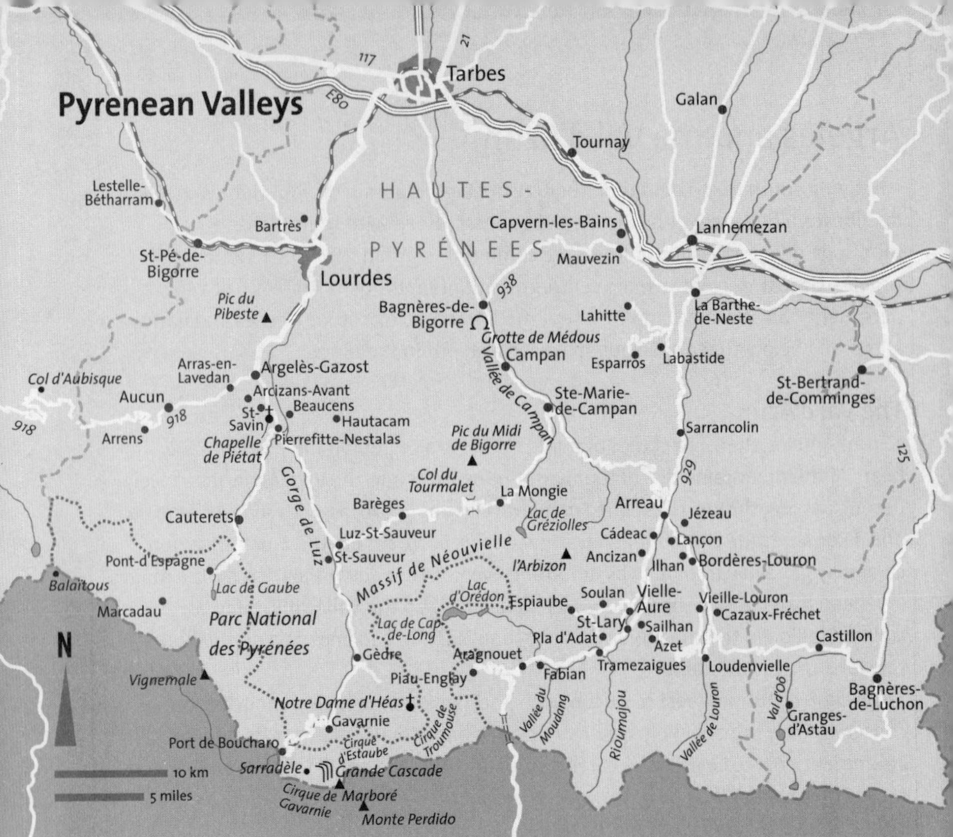

ated by 12 buttresses (to represent the Twelve Apostles, as the novices were no doubt told when they entered the abbey). Savin was a 6th-century hermit – or 8th-century, according to some; there's nothing definite known about him, though in the apse a painter of the 15th-century did his best to portray Savin in fresco. Some odd Renaissance paintings can be seen around the altar: mythological figures, allegories of the liberal arts, a sun and moon and orrery. The abbot who commissioned them in 1546, an interesting character named François de Foix-Candale, was a translator of the mystic books of Hermes Trismegistus, and also one of the first recorded mountain-climbers; he made it up the Pic du Midi in the same year. Among the paintings are three carved grimacing faces, the '*barabouts*' – comically representing the three men it took to work the organ. Note the painted wooden *Crucifixion* from the same period; like many others of this popular Spanish genre, Christ seen from one side seems to be dead, while alive from the opposite angle. Note also the *bénitier des Cagots*, the holy water stoup reserved for the Cagots, carved with a rabbit's foot. Adjacent to the church, the chapter hall of the abbey also survives. The church treasure, housed here, contains some unique baubles, including a Renaissance gold box holding the relics of St-Savin and two medieval statues of the Virgin Mary.

The beautifully forested slopes around St-Savin and on the opposite side of the Gave make one of the most delightful corners of this valley. Below the village, the chapel of **Notre-Dame-de-Piétat** stands on a height in a setting worthy of a jigsaw puzzle picture. From St-Savin, you can detour up the pretty D13 to **Arcizans-Avant**, with its 'Castle of the Black Prince' (that's the traditional name, though most of it dates from much later than Edward's day). It has been thoroughly restored and is now a chambre d'hôtes (*see* p.234). Continuing this route, you'll cross over back towards the Vallée d'Estaing (*see* above).

Down in the valley beneath St-Savin, stop for a minute as you pass through **Adast** to see the singular Romanesque portal on its church: a woman with a dragon, along with dancing figures. On the opposite side of the Gave de Pau, no fewer than 12 small villages occupy a strip of fertile mountain slope 8km long; in the Middle Ages, when the Pyrenees became densely populated, no bit of space went to waste. **Beaucens** was the old headquarters of the viscounts of Lavedan, and they left a well-preserved medieval **castle** to explore, now housing the Donjon des Aigles (***t*** *05 62 97 19 59, www.donjondesaigles.fr; open spring school holidays to end Sept daily 10–12 and 2.30–6.30; flights 3 and 5, July and Aug 3, 4.30 and 6; adm*), a zoo for birds of prey like the one in Bidache, in Béarn, with eagles, kites, vultures, owls and such; in season they let them fly about. Just to the south is the ski resort of Hautacam. At **Pierrefitte-Nestalas**, a sizable village, the unlikely attraction is the **Aquarium Tropical du Haut Lavedan** (***t*** *05 62 92 79 56; open daily 9.30–12 and 2–6; closed Mon am exc July and Aug; adm*), with coral and exotic specimens from the South Seas.

From Pierrefitte, you have the choice of heading right, towards Cauterets, or left, towards Luz-St-Sauveur and the Pays Toy.

Cauterets

The only real town close to the mountains owes its founding to the presence of mineral waters. This seems to be one spring the Romans missed, but one of the earliest documents concerning the Lavedan, from *c.* 950, records Count Raymond of Bigorre handing the property over to the abbot of St-Savin, in return for the monks building and running baths. Lacking anything better, people used the waters to treat many more ailments than we do now. Gaston Fébus, one of the first celebrity visitors, came here to try and cure his growing deafness. In the 18th century, Cauterets became fashionable among French aristocrats, and with the rediscovery of the beauties of nature in the Romantic era, people began to pour in from all over Europe, including Napoleon's brother, the 'King of Holland', with his Queen Hortense (the Bonapartes liked to keep everything in the family: Hortense was none other than Josephine de Beauharnais' sister, and the mother of Napoleon III, whose solicitous attitude towards these valleys may well have been the result of his having been conceived in a Gavarnie hotel). Cauterets remained fashionable for another century, drawing crowned heads and several presidents of France to take the waters.

Though most of the bath establishments have closed, Cauterets is still a major tourist centre, albeit one comfortably down at heel and in need of a lick of paint. The narrow valley and the steep mountain walls on both sides make it seem a bit claustrophobic at times, but Cauterets is still the essential base for seeing this corner of

Tourist Information

Place du Maréchal Foch, **t** 05 62 92 50 50, *www.cauterets.com. Open Mon–Sat 9–12.30 and 1.30–7.*

Market Days

Thursdays, June–Sept.

Where to Stay and Eat

Cauterets ✉ 65110

***Hotel Club Aladin, **t** 05 62 92 60 00, **f** 05 62 92 63 30, *www.hotel-balneo-aladin.com* (*expensive*). Such luxury as Cauterets can provide is limited to this modern hotel, with a pool, in-room TVs and gym. *Closed Oct–Dec plus 1st week in June.*

Hôtel Edelweiss, 7 Bd. Latapie Flurin, **t 05 62 92 52 75 or 06 81 61 08 26, *www.edelweiss-hotel.fr*. Pleasant, family-run hotel in the centre of town. Light, airy bedrooms and a very reasonable restaurant; good value all round. *Menus from €15. Open mid Dec–end of Sept.*

Lion d'Or, Rue Richelieu, **t/f** 05 62 92 52 87, *www.hotel-lion-dor.net* (*inexpensive*). This simple place, also a survivor from a bygone age, is on a thoroughly grim, narrow street that provides an interesting contrast to the Pyrenean glory to be found all around. *The restaurant open to residents only menus €17–23. April–Sept restaurant open daily for lunch and dinner, the rest of the year evenings only.*

Hôtel César, 3 Rue César, **t** 05 62 92 52 57, *www.cesarhotel.com* (*inexpensive*). This hotel is conveniently situated for the *thermes* and ski lift alike, with a good traditional restaurant. *Menus €19–29. Closed Wed in winter plus May and first 3 weeks Oct.*

the Pyrenees. It has also become a ski resort, with a *téléférique*, one of the longest in the Pyrenees, leading up to the slopes on the **Cirque du Lys**, tucked under 2,698m/8,853ft **Moun Né.** A chairlift from here goes 7,000ft up the slopes of Moun Né's slightly shorter sidekick, the **Soum de Grum** (not to be confused with the mountain of the same name further west). The *téléferique* runs in summer too (*19 June–19 Sept 8.45–5.45*), an easy way to enjoy the views.

In the old days, your introduction to Cauterets would have been the **railway station**, an 1890s wooden confection now used as a coach station. The other remarkable feature of the town is the **Gave de Cauterets** and its rapids, flowing right through the centre with houses closely built up along both sides. Most of the old bath establishments have been closed, and you can see some once-glorious pavilions in the centre that have been converted into a cinema and shops. One of the old hotels, the Résidence d'Angleterre, has been turned into the **Musée 1900** (*t 05 62 92 02 02; open daily for summer and winter hols 10–12 and 3–6.30; closed Sun and mid Nov–mid Dec*) with displays of 18th- and 19th-century costumes. The turn-of-the-last-century grand hotels are in much better shape, along with the recently restored casino, on Boulevard Latapie-Flandrin.

If you're headed further into the mountains, an indispensable stop is the **Maison du Parc** on Place de la Gare. Run by the Parc National management, this includes a small museum, exhibits on Pyrenean wildlife, and occasional films (*t 05 62 92 52 56; open daily June–Sept 9.30–12 and 3–6.30; rest of the year closed Wed, Thurs am and Sun pm*).

For children and bee lovers, the **Pavilion des Abeilles** offers a big glass beehive and guided tour through the world of bee-keeping (*Av du Mamelon Vert; t 05 62 92 50 66; open daily July and Aug 10.30–12.30 and 2.30–7; rest of the year closed Sun–Tues*).

Still, the best thing to do here is to get up into the mountains. The road south of Cauterets will take you a difficult 8km further, as far as the locality called **Pont d'Espagne**. For hikers, the GR 10 follows the road on the opposite side of the Gave; from Pont d'Espagne it branches off into two paths: one for the **Vallée du Marcadau**, a lovely area forested with pines, and the other up to the Lac de Gaube and then to the *refuges* for people scaling **Vignemale**. For determined hikers only, it continues from there around the northeastern face of the mountain, practically under an enormous glacier, and then descends into the Vallée d'Ossoue. To have a look at Vignemale the easy way, there is a **chair lift** from Pont d'Espagne up to the Lac de Gaube (*runs continuously every day June–10 Oct and Dec–April for skiers; adm*).

Gavarnie: the Route to the *Cirques*

The other road from Pierrefitte-Nestalas, the D921, will probably be a little busier. This is the road that leads up to the *cirques*, the most obviously spectacular and most-visited sites the Pyrenees have to offer. A *cirque* is a freak of erosion on a grand scale. The centre of the Pyrenees may be good hard granite, pushed up from below when the mountains were formed, but there are layers of mostly limestone to either side. In places like Gavarnie, these strata were pushed up almost vertically to form the highest peaks of the chain. In geological periods when the climate here was much warmer than today, rainfall on the northern face started to erode the soft limestone into something like its present form, and in the Ice Ages glaciers finished the job, leaving landforms that seem to have been gouged out by an ice-cream scoop, one several miles wide.

First, though, the road passes through the long Gorge de Luz, and arrives at **Luz**, the biggest village in the valley. This is a medieval-looking place of not much interest, except for its 14th-century church, **St-André**. Though often called the 'Templar church' by locals, it was really largely built by their Crusading rivals, the Knights Hospitallers (Knights of Malta); perhaps they picked up an earlier church on the site with the rest of the booty they acquired after the suppression of the Templars in 1307. Though a stout, fortified church, it has a touch of striking grace on its porch: a carved tympanum of Christ and the four Evangelists. Inside, some frescoes remain, as well as a church treasury that holds some fine works of medieval sculpture. Across the Gave de Gavarnie from Luz stands another spa: **St-Sauveur**, the younger half of the consolidated village of Luz-St-Sauveur. Here you can find sulphurous waters to fix up your aching bones, and an impressive arched bridge embellished with imperial eagles, the gift of satisfied spa customer Napoleon III.

Continuing south toward the *cirques*, the D921 traverses more gorges, and then passes the Pyrenees' biggest hydroelectric plant, at Pragnères. From any high ground at **Gèdre**, the next village, you may catch a first glimpse of the Cirque de Gavarnie, along with the famous notch in the wall, the Brèche de Roland, over 10km away. Two roads go south from Gèdre, and both of them lead to *cirques* – there are three of them in a row, an almost continuous, thrice-indented wall almost 18km in length. The right turn is only a steep and very difficult track up to the Cirque de Tramouse, and if you have a car you'll be going the other way, to Gavarnie, the highest village in the Pyrenees and the traditional base for seeing the area.

Cirque de Gavarnie

There are two ways to see the Cirque de Gavarnie: either walking (about 4hrs) or on the back of a donkey. (The families with the donkeys have been serving as guides for generations. Usually they only take you one way; if you want them to wait for the trip

Tourist Information

Luz-St-Sauveur: **t** 05 62 92 81 60/**t** 05 62 92 30 30, **f** 05 62 92 87 19, *www.luz.org. Open summer Mon–Sat 9–7.30, plus Sun.9–12.30 and 4.30–7.30; rest of the year closed 12–2 and Sun.*

Gavarnie: Route Nationale, **t** 05 62 92 49 10, **f** 05 62 92 41 00, *www.gavarnie.com. Open daily all year 9–12 and 2–6, plus July and Aug 9–7.*

Barèges: **t** 05 62 92 16 00, **f** 05 62 92 69 13. *Open all year Mon–Sat 9–12 and 2–6.30, plus Sun in July and Aug 10–12 and 4–6.*

Market Days

Cauterets: Thursdays, from June through to Sept.

Luz-St-Sauveur: Mondays.

Arrens-Marsous: Sundays, in July and Aug.

Sports and Activities

As far as activities go, as you would imagine in this busy area nearly everything is on offer, and all well-organized: nature walks, courses in rock-climbing and ornithology, children's activities, photo safaris, mountain lake fishing, telemark and cross-country skiing, paragliding, canoes and kayaks and so on.

All the local tourist information offices are well-informed, and worth writing to in advance if you have a special field of interest; Luz and Argelès (*see* p.261) are particularly good.

Maisons du Parc

Besides the tourist offices, you can find out everything about the natural wonders of the area, plus information on hiking, sports, flora and fauna, at the Maisons du Parc, run by the administration of the Parc National des Pyrénées. They also have regular schedules of films, exhibits and activities.

Cauterets: **t** 05 62 92 52 56.

Luz: **t** 05 62 92 38 38.

Gavarnie: **t** 05 62 92 49 10, **t** 05 62 92 42 48.

Where to Stay and Eat

Luz-St-Sauveur ✉ 65120

*****Le Montaigu**, on the D172 to Vizos, **t** 05 62 92 81 71, **f** 05 62 92 94 11, *www.hotelmontaigu.com* (*moderate–inexpensive*). This is a modern building in a traditional style. Rooms are spacious and comfortable, some with balconies, all with a great view. A pleasant hotel in a beautiful setting. *Menus €20. Restaurant open eve only. Closed Oct and Nov.*

Les Cimes, in the centre of Luz, **t** 05 62 92 82 03, *www.cimes.fr.st* (*cheap*). A good choice.

Hôtel–Restaurant Panoramic, 30 Av Impératrice Eugénie, Quartier Thermal, 65120 Luz, **t** 05 62 92 80 14, *www.hotel-panoramic-luz.com.* A fine old family hotel that must have been quite grand in its day; though a bit faded now, the bedrooms are modern, clean and functional. The restaurant offers honest, regional cooking at €13. Excellent value with a pretty summer terrace overlooking the town. *Closed Oct, Nov and April.*

Gèdre ✉ 65120

****Brêche de Roland,** **t** 05 62 92 48 54, **f** 05 62 92 46 05, *www.gavarnie.com/hotel-la-breche* (*inexpensive*). One of the famous old hotels of the Pyrenees, this is an old mansion, all mountain austerity outside but retaining many of its original furnishings and walnut back, make arrangements in advance.) On the way, you will pass the Jardin Botanique, part of the Parc National, with hundreds of Pyrenean species in a rugged setting.

One of the oddities of seeing the *cirque* is reflecting that at the top of the wall lies Spain; the border follows the crests of all three of the *cirques*. The panorama takes in a view of almost 4km: 2,300m/7,547ft Pic des Tantes on the right, then fragments of the tremendous glacier that once covered all of Gavarnie. Near the centre, at an altitude of 2,781m/9,123ft, is the huge gash in the wall, the **Brèche de Roland**. In local legend, the hero smote at the mountain with his sword Durendal in futile rage when he was

panelling within. A sauna and a lift have recently been added. There is a garden and a restaurant with outdoor terrace, and the management helps arrange winter sports and helicopter rides. *Menus €16–35. Closed Oct–Dec. Open in winter for school hols only.*

****Hôtel des Pyrénées, t** 05 62 92 48 51 (*inexpensive*). Another lovely old establishment, in the centre of town. No restaurant. *Closed mid Nov–mid Dec.*

Gavarnie ✉ 65120

If you're spending the day here and decide to stay the night, book early, every room is taken by hikers or skiers by about 5pm. Parking in a private hotel you will also avoid the exorbitant €4 (for 5 minutes or 5 hours) that is mandatory for public parking.

*****Hôtel-Club Vignemale, t** 05 62 92 40 00, *www.hotel-vignemale.com* (*expensive*). This hotel has little to justify its rates, but its restaurant is the best in the valley: mountain trout and *écrevisses*, and good desserts on a pretty outdoor terrace. Restaurant is open for group bookings only. *Open mid May–mid Oct.*

****Le Marboré, t** 05 62 92 40 40, **f** 05 62 92 40 30, *www.lemarbore.com* (*inexpensive*). Set in a distinctive 19th-century building, with a sauna and gym. Like many French hotels recently, this lovely old building has been totally modernised inside. Still, it's clean and comfortable and at a good price. *Menus €20. Closed mid Nov–mid Dec.*

Refuge des Espuguettes, on the trail from Gavarnie to the Cirque d'Estaubé, **t** 05 62 92 40 63 (*cheap*). For hikers, this is the best base for a thorough exploration of the *cirques*. Be sure to book ahead, especially for July and August.

Barèges ✉ 65120

Hôtel Compostelle, t 05 62 92 49 43, *www.compostellehotel.com*. Very simple, more like a posh refuge. *Open 26 Dec–30 Sep.*

****Hôtel de l'Europe, t** 05 62 92 68 04, **f** 05 62 92 65 29 (*inexpensive*). The games room is the highlight of this modern, functional and somewhat faceless hotel. *Menus €13–22. Closed Oct–1 May.*

Auberge du Lienz, just east, near the cable car up the Pic de l'Ayre, **t** 05 62 92 67 17. In an idyllic mountain setting, this lovely auberge has been a haven for hikers and skiers since 1905. Louisette is passionate about maintaining mountain traditions, and adamant, (almost religious) about using only locally farmed produce. The only access in winter is by ski, and after being totally cut off for weeks once, she now bakes her own bread daily and smokes her own trout. *Menus from €23 but it's worth going for the à la Carte at around €40.*

La Ribère, on the road to Luz, **t** 05 62 92 69 01. This is a good site on the edge of town. *Closed mid Oct–mid Dec.*

*****La Grange,** aux Marmottes et Les Campanules Viscos 65120. On D149 off the D921, **t** 05 62 92 91 13, *www.lagrange auxmarmottes.com*. Ancient stone and slate buildings joined together on different levels make up the two hotels oozing rustic charm. The restaurant is a member of Les Tables Gourmand. *Menus €20–39. Closed mid Nov–mid Dec.*

Hôtel Central, 11 Rue Raymond, Barèges, **t** 05 62 92 68 05, *www.fhr.fr/hotelcentral65*. High ski season €51. As name implies, in the middle of town. A well-run modest hotel with a garden. *Menus €13–22. Closed mid Oct–30 Nov.*

surrounded by the Saracens (never mind that the ambush happened at Roncesvalles, far to the west; relics of Roland, his horse's footprints and so on, turn up all over Europe). One of the most spectacular sights (if you can get close enough to it), the **Grande Cascade** is the highest waterfall in Europe; the water drains out of semi-frozen marshes, high above on the Spanish side. On the eastern edge loom two formidable mountains: **Marboré** (which means 'marble' in Gascon) and behind it, visible from some angles, the second-tallest peak of the entire chain, 3,323m/10,904ft **Monte Perdido**, entirely on the Spanish side of the border.

It's hard to believe, looking up at it, but you can actually walk to the top of the *cirque*, or at least near it, in the summer months. A trail leads up to the Sarradets *refuge*, and reaches the crest from there, though you'll have to cross some difficult patches of glacier to make it all the way. For one additional attraction, if you get to the top you can have a look inside some of the biggest and highest-altitude **ice caves** in the world, first explored by Norbert Casteret in the 1920s. All are on the slopes of Marboré and Monte Perdido, and unless you are an experienced spelunker it isn't wise to go too far into any of them – there are some surprise drops of hundreds of feet.

For another view of the *cirque*, there is a steep road (the D923) from Gavarnie village up to **Port de Boucharo** on the border, where it peters out into a hiking trail; this is the only reliable path into Spain in a stretch of some 40km, and a long-favoured route of smugglers and bandits. Along the way, you can get out and climb without too much difficulty up to the top of Pic des Tantes, for a grandstand seat that takes in the entire area.

The Cirque de Troumouse and Cirque d'Estaubé

Anywhere else, this would be a three-star attraction, but next to the more awesome Gavarnie the Cirque de Troumouse gets stuck with the role of little sister. Just as broad as Gavarnie, it is much lower, with neither a waterfall nor a *brèche* – but it may afford you a bit more peace and quiet in summer, when all the trails around Gavarnie are packed. To get there, take the D922 from Gèdre up the Gave de Héas. This passes a dammed lake, the **Lac des Gloriettes**, and the **chapel of Notre-Dame de Héas**, commemorating yet another apparition of the Virgin, back in 1349. The last part of the route is a toll road, but it leads up to a 1,981m/6,500ft peak for a grand view of the *cirque*.

Even less visited is the *cirque* in the middle, the Cirque d'Estaubé, smallest of the three. A hiking trail from the Lac des Gloriettes is the only way in.

Barèges and the Col de Tourmalet

On the way back, instead of returning to Lourdes, you can take a convenient short-cut into the next valley, the **Vallée d'Aure**, by means of the D918 from Luz (or by the ubiquitous GR 10). This is big-time skiing country, beginning with **Barèges**, an old thermal resort (the highest one in France) that has successfully made the transition to concentrating on winter sports. Barèges and **La Mongie**, just down the road, have between them the biggest ski area and greatest number of pistes in the Pyrenees. Besides skiing, the thing to do here is to take the funicular railway up the Pic d'Ayre; a path from the end of the line will have you at the summit in 1½ hours. This whole area is an *Aire Pastoral*, which means you quite often have to stop for the herds of sheep, cattle or horses that roam free. This just adds to the beauty of this breath-taking mountain pass, and makes the first glimpse of La Mongie and its concrete tower blocks quite jarring.

Further along the D918, the views take in a chain of big peaks to the north, culminating in the 2,838m/9,312ft **Pic du Midi de Bigorre**, and to the south, the **Massif de Néouvielle**, a huge region of lakes that is easily accessible only from the south (*see* p.254). Halfway to the Vallée d'Aure the road crosses over the Col de Tourmalet, where the waters of the Gave de Pau and those of the Adour divide. On the way you can see the **Jardin Botanique de Tourmalet** (*t 05 62 92 18 06; open mid-May–mid-Sept daily 10–6; adm*), a two-hectare garden which presents wild flowers of the Pyrenees in appropriate settings, from rocks to forest. Nearly every year, the Tour de France bicycle race is routed over this pass, providing the ultimate test of stamina for the riders (and filling all the hotels and blocking up the roads for everyone else, for a few days in mid-July). Along the route you'll notice the competitors' names, painted on the roads in huge letters, along with contributions from local graffiti artists and ETA supporters.

At the top of the Pic du Midi is a magnificent **observatory**, built by the University of Toulouse in 1881, which has one of the biggest telescopes in Europe. It has recently been opened to the public as a **Musée des Etoiles** (*t 05 62 56 71 11, www.picdumidi.com.fr; open June–Sept 9.30–4.30; closed Nov*) with splendid viewing platforms and observatories, terraces with spectacular views of the Pyrenees, and a restaurant. Access is by *téléférique* from La Mongie. Further east, another cable car leads up to the EDF dam and its lake, the Lac de Greziolles; beyond the hairpin bend there's a favourite postcard subject, a waterfall called the **Cascade de Garet**.

Bagnères and the Baronnies

Bagnères-de-Bigorre

Bagnères-de-Bigorre is a wonderful town for eating ice cream and turning your brain off. Sitting in the cafés, under the plane trees of the Coustous, the world seems far away. This is what Bagnères is for, and the city on the Adour has had centuries of practice as a resort to perfect its charm. The Romans, who liked nothing better than taking the waters, built the town of *Vicus Aquensis* ('Waterville'), and it has known the favours of rulers since, from Alaric the Goth to Napoleon III and Eugénie. Bagnères is also the only town in the Pyrenees to have a subatomic particle named for it (the hyperon, after the Boulevard de l'Yperon by the casino; the scientists of the Observatoire du Pic du Midi, who do a lot of work on cosmic rays, have their main laboratories here).

The old town extends westwards from a pretty square, the Allées des Coustous, on the site of part of the old town walls. In one corner, the church of **St-Vincent** has a good Renaissance portal. Other monuments can be found on the narrow streets that begin on the opposite side of the square: yet another Maison de Jeanne d'Albret, on

Tourist Information

Bagnères: 3 Allées Tournefort, **t** 05 62 95 50 71, **f** 05 62 95 33 13, *www.bagneres debigorre.com. Open all year Mon–Sat 9–12 and 2–6.*

Tournay: **t** 05 62 35 79 67.

Capvern-les-Bains: Place de Thermes, **t** 05 62 39 00 46, **f** 05 62 39 08 14, *www.capvern-tourisme.com. Open Nov–Mar Mon–Fri 9–12 and 2–6; April–Oct Mon–Sat 9–12.30 and 3–6.30.*

Sarlabous: Maison des Baronnies, **t/f** 05 62 39 05 14. *Open daily 15 June–15 Sept 9–12 and 2–7. Other times phone only.*

Market Days

Bagnères: Saturdays.

Capvern-les-Bains: Tuesdays April–Oct.

Where to Stay and Eat

Bagnerès ✉ 65200

More than just a stopover, this town can be a good place to relax for a few days.

****Le Trianon**, Place des Thermes, **t** 05 62 95 09 34, **f** 05 62 91 12 33, *www.perso.wanadoo.fr/hoteltrianon* (*inexpensive*). Not quite up to the standard of its namesake palace at Versailles, but you won't find a more gracious hotel round here: set in a shady park near the baths. *Open May– Oct.*

****Hôtel Les Vignaux**, **t** 05 62 95 03 41, **f** 05 62 95 42 24 (*cheap*). This budget option is a good choice. *Closed Dec–mid Jan.*

Le Bigourdin, Rue Victor Hugo, **t** 05 62 95 20 20. This is a good stop for lunch in the centre, offering traditional treats, and also pizza. *Closed Sun eve and Mon.*

Capvern-les-Bains ✉ 65130

There are plenty of choices in town, which is good to know as you aren't going to find anything in any of the Baronnies villages. Capvern being one of the more humble spa resorts, accommodation here tends to be modern and functional.

****Lemoine**, **t** 05 62 39 02 18, **f** 05 62 39 04 20 (*inexpensive–cheap*). This is well-priced and pleasant enough for an overnight stay. *Closed Nov–April.*

Rue Daléas (rheumatic Jeanne was a frequent visitor), and around the corner the Gothic **Tour des Jacobins**, from a monastery now largely demolished.

The spa zone begins at the opposite side of the old town, at **Place des Thermes**, with the imposing neoclassical Etablissement Thermal, built in 1823, and the casino from the 1890s, now a cinema. Next door, the **Musée Salies** (*t 05 62 91 07 26; open July–Aug daily 3–7, Sept–Nov and May–June Tues–Sun 3–6; adm*) has a small collection of art from the Renaissance to modern times, including a work of the Dadaist Francis Picabia and drawings by Honoré Daumier.

Bagnères has another museum, devoted to farm life and crafts of the central Pyrenees, the **Musée du Vieux Moulin** (***t*** *05 62 91 07 33; from Oct– April call ahead, otherwise open all year Tues–Fri 10–12 and 2–6; adm*).

Into the Baronnies

A beautiful country, and sometimes a sad country, the Baronnies is a *pays* in the foothills east of Bagnères: no great elevations, but plenty of cliffs and valleys, and tortuous narrow roads connecting a score of villages, most of which are nothing more than a handful of old stone houses. Many of these are either empty or restored holiday homes, for few places in all the depopulated rural areas of the Midi have lost so many people in the last century.

The Baronnies takes its name from the four little lords who divided the area amongst themselves. Tradition has it that they would meet once a year, at a spot in the Forêt des Baronnies where each of their domains met (south of Arrodets), and have a drink, each with one foot on his own land and one on his neighbour's. Its inhabitants always held themselves a bit apart from the other *pays* around them. In fact they were different – research on their blood types has established that the people of the Baronnies are of Basque origin, a pocket of the Basques who once inhabited all the Pyrenees; here, they managed to hold out in this backwater and resist assimilation much longer than the others. They scraped by on their sheep and cows for millennia, building distinctive houses out of the local limestone with heavy *lauze* roofs. But their land is too poor and too hilly for modern farming, and, lacking thermal waters or any other tourist attractions, the *pays* has watched its people simply drain away.

From Bagnères, the main road across the Baronnies is the D938, a green and lovely drive that follows the river Luz. It crosses the river at the **Abbey of Escaladieu** (***t** 05 62 39 16 97; open May–Sept daily 10–1 and 2–7; Oct–April 10–12 and 2–5, closed Tues*) the first Cistercian foundations in the Midi (and the mother house of Flaran, in the Gers). The church, built with the usual Cistercian austerity, nevertheless has a wonderful pavement of stones of different colours, arranged in geometric patterns. The chapter house also survives, along with some of the other buildings; restoration work is under way, and the organization that is overseeing it uses the abbey for Sunday concerts and exhibitions. Just a few kilometres up the road stands **Mauvezin**, worth a stop for its **castle**, built in the 12th–14th centuries. Over the gate an odd inscription can be read: JAY BELLE DAME, 'I have a beautiful lady'. Southern scholars like to argue about it, and some claim it was put there by one of the castle's lords, none other than Gaston Fébus of Béarn. Whether true or not, the castle is currently occupied by the Escole Gaston Fébus, a literary society dedicated to keeping alive the Gascon language and culture. They maintain a large Gascon library here, and hold meetings and poetic competitions in the manner of the Félibres of Provence. The castle keep has a view over most of the Baronnies, and down in the court you can inspect some modern reconstructions of catapults and other medieval engines of war.

Capvern-les-Bains, in the hills above Mauvezin, is a thermal spa with little of the glamour of Bagnères, though it too has been around since Roman times. **The Musée Christhi /Musée de la Calligraphie** (*166, rue de Thermes; open daily 20 April–20 Oct 10–6, rest of the year 3–6*), offers an exhibition on the history and mechanics of handwriting, with many examples and some old instruments.

North of the D938, where the Tarbes–Toulouse motorway breaks the stillness of the Baronnies, **Tournay** is a *bastide* founded in 1307 and the largest village in the *pays*.

Another very scenic road traverses the southern end of the Baronnies, the D84/D26, which also begins in Bagnères. The D84 passes over the **Col des Palomières**, with a lovely view, before entering the nest of tiny villages that make up the heart of the region. **Esparros**, a representative hamlet with only about 200 people, a quarter of what it had a century ago, is a place that won't go down without a fight. The village has become famous, with annual appearances on the French television news for its *foire aux célibataires*, where the Baronnies' bachelors put themselves on display to try and attract some womenfolk, all for the worthy cause of repopulating the region. The lord of Esparros, one of the four old barons of the Baronnies, laid out **Labastide** with the same thing in mind, back in the 1300s. It never was much of a success, and Labastide is even smaller than Esparros. Near the village is a cave with colour paintings from the Palaeolithic era, discovered by Norbert Castaret, the Gouffre D'Esparros (***t*** *05 62 39 11 80; www.gouffre-esparros.com; open all year for hols and weekends 10–12 and 1.30–6; daily June–Sept; visit lasts for about 50 mins. Advisable to call ahead; adm*). Discovered only in 1938, the caves were not opened to the public until 2000; you'll see immense carpets of what looks like delicate coral, and huge caves draped with stalactites in a vast array of colours.

For anyone interested in prehistory, **Lahitte** will prove the main attraction of the Baronnies. Near the village is a major Neolithic site, with nearly fifty burial tumuli, all in a neat row, along with menhirs (*hitte* is a Gascon word for menhir); nothing like it exists anywhere in the Midi.

South of Bagnères: the Vallée de Campan

Following the river Adour southwards, the D935 offers glimpses of the Pic du Midi de Bigorre and another giant that has strayed from the centre of the range, 9,285ft **L'Arbizon**, just behind it. Just south of Bagnères, signs point the way to the **Grotte de Médous** (***t*** *05 62 91 78 46, www.grottes-medous.com; open April–June and Sept–mid-Oct daily 8.30–11.30 and 2–5.30, July–Aug daily 9–12 and 2–6, mid-Oct–March for groups by appointment only; note that only 12 people are allowed in at a time; adm*). Discovered only in 1948, it offers some magnificent sights, including a grotto of colourful formations called the 'Hall of Orchids' and a branch of the Adour that flows underground; they'll take you down it in a boat.

Campan, one of the prettier villages in this part of the mountains, is built around its wooden *halles* and a 16th-century fountain; many of the houses have half-timbering and corbelled second floors.

If you pass through this pretty village during the summer, at first glance you might think it's a very busy place – full of industrious little people up ladders cleaning windows, fixing cars, getting married or just hanging around chewing the fat. On closer inspection of course, you'll realize that they're all rag dolls, about 4ft high, stuffed with hay and fully dressed in various costumes. The custom of the mounaques comes from the old days, when folks in Campan did not take kindly to one of their girls marrying an outsider, especially if she was the heiress to a house or farm. When that happened, the young people of the village would demand a 'tribute' from the prospective bridegroom– enough money to throw a fête for the village. If he didn't come through, they would appear every night outside the girl's house with cowbells around their necks for mocking serenades. And on the wedding day, they would make sure that the procession had to pass under a pair of satirical effigies of the wedding couple– the origin of the mounaques. Nowadays, no such reason is needed; the locals just like the look of them decorating the village.

At Ste-Marie-de-Campan, the road meets the D918 from the Col de Tourmalet (*see* above); the only other alternative is to continue on eastwards, with another beautiful but taxing drive over the **Col d'Aspin**, and so into the valley of the Aure (*see* below).

The Lannemezan Plateau

Set on a high, flat, semi-arid plateau of reddish-brown rock and gravel dumped by a glacier in the Quaternary age, *Lannemezan* means the '*Lande du Milieu*' or 'Middle Moor'. Windswept or fog-bound much of the winter, covered with broom, heather and ferns, the Middle Moor has never been good for much, except perhaps for escaping the heat that can poach the surrounding valleys in the summer. It has long been a place to hurry through rather than stay in; the Neolithic salt road passed across it, as did age-old transhumance trails from the mountains and the Roman road from Dax to St-Bertrand-de-Comminges. In the Middle Ages it was widely believed that witches gathered on the forlorn corners of the plateau for their Sabbaths, presided over by the devil himself in the form of a he-goat (*bouc* – hence Lannemezan's older name, the *lande de bouc*. Packs of wolves and large bands of bandits and ruffians terrorized the population. Once oak trees dotted the plateau, and accounts say they were never, never without a body or two hanging in the wind, under the plateau's famous *ciel d'airain*, sky of bronze.

Tourist Information

Lannemezan: 73 Rue Jean Jaques Rousseau, **t** 05 62 98 08 31, **f** 05 62 40 21 50, *www.lannemezan.fr. Open Mon–Fri 9–12.30 and 2–5.30 plus Sat 9–12.30.*

Castelnau-Magnoac: Maison du Magnoac, Ariès-Espenan, **t** 05 62 39 86 61. *Open July and Aug Mon–Sat 9–12 and 2–6; rest of year closes at 5 and Sat pm.*

Market Days

Lannemezan: Wednesdays.
Trie-sur-Baïse: Tuesdays.
Castlenau-Magnoac: Saturdays.

Where to Stay and Eat

Lannemezan ✉ 65300

***De La Gare**, Av de la Gare, **t** 05 62 98 00 10 (*inexpensive–cheap*). This place is okay for a night, and open all year.

***Le Madrigal**, 45 Rue du 8 Mai 1945, **t** 05 62 98 02 13 (*cheap*). This is also an unremarkable choice. There is also a restaurant. *Menus €12–16. Closed Fri and Sun eves.*

Castelnau-Magnoac ✉ 65230

Moulin d'Ariès, 2km from Castelnau at Aries-Espenan, **t** 05 62 39 81 85, *www.poterie.fr.* (*inexpensive*). Five handsomely furnished *chambres d'hôte* have been installed in a lovingly renovated mill, with a garden and tennis court. *Evening meals only €18. Closed Jan–mid May.*

Le Petit Château, 65130 Laborde. On D26 coming from Esparros. **t** 05 62 40 90 16, *www.petitchateau.com.* July and Aug weekly bookings only; €1,350 for 2 adults and 2 children, this includes half board, wine and juice. Sept–June rms €55. This beautiful white house set in its own park is a welcome contrast to the usual grey stone and slate of the Baronnies. The owners are very keen for all guests to have a wonderful, fun-packed holiday. Children are obligatory in July and Aug, but they'll take them off your hands for 25 hours a week and entertain them with various themes; in the evening they'll set up a native American camp, a circus or Pyrenean folk dancing whilst the parents enjoy a candle-lit supper. There is also a full itinerary for the adults; aesthetic not athletic, we are assured.

Hôtel–Restaurant du Mont d'Aure, 65250 Lortet, **t** 05 62 39 02 43, *www.baronnies.com.* Pleasant auberge on the river. The décor is a bit arty and a little scruffy, the bedrooms simple yet comfortable. The restaurant offers generous portions of regional cuisine, nicely presented. *Menu €16. Closed Tues in summer and Wed Sept–June, plus Jan and one week at end of August.*

For the last hundred years, the plateau has been tamed to provide a livelihood from the rearing and marketing of piglets and lambs. If snubbed by Mother Nature, the otherwise empty wastelands around Lannemezan are ideal for setting up hydro-electric plants, chemical and fertilizer plants.

Founded as a *bastide* in 1270 to defend the surrounding area from bandits, **Lannemezan** is now the market town of the eastern Hautes-Pyrénées: come if you can on a Wednesday, when the main square is packed with shoppers twanging away in Gascon, while in the nearby Halle du Nébouzan, broad-shouldered farmers mutter in their berets around the biggest sheep market in the Pyrenees. And once you've seen that, and the excellent **retable** (1703) in the choir of its church, you've seen the sights of Lannemezan. However, in the grounds of the electrochemical plant along the D939 to La-Barthe-de-Neste, you can see the large if low Neolithic **tumulus of Pierrehitte** crowned by an oak tree. The mound marks the old crossroads of the salt road and the ancient route to Spain through the Vallée d'Aure, a road known as the Ténarèze, and was originally crowned by a large stone that stood equidistant from the sources of the rivers Save, Gers and Baïse.

Heading north across the plateau of Lannemezan towards Armagnac on the D939, you can look in at the *bastide* of **Galan** (1318), which has kept much of the medieval character that Lannemezan has lost, with its half-timbered houses and fortified Gothic church. Further north, fortified **Trie-sur-Baïse** (founded in 1323), 'France's biggest piglet market', is similar, preserving its precise grid plan and arcaded central market square. Unusually, Trie built its largest church smack in the middle of the market square; this dates from the 15th century and has a Gothic portal.

East of Trie, on the river Gers, **Castelnau-Magnoac** was once the capital of its own little region, the Magnoac; it now boasts of rivalling Trie in piglet sales. It has a handsome collegiate church from the 15th century, but most of the piety in the Magnoac is concentrated to the south, where in 1520 the Virgin Mary appeared to a shepherdess and requested that a church be built on the site. And so it was, called the **Chapelle de Notre-Dame Garaison**. It drew its fair share of pilgrims in its day, and has pretty if very provincial 16th- and 17th-century frescoes on the miracles of Our Lady of September.

The Vallée d'Aure and Vallée de Louron

The sunny mountains and valleys south of Lannemezan are sometimes called 'the Pyrenees of the Nestes of the Garonne' – not that the mighty river Garonne hatches out of bird's nests, but from *nestes*, the Gascon word for river. Since the invasion of the Visigoths and Moors, the westernmost valleys and *nestes* (the Aure, Barousse, Basse-Neste and Magnoac valleys) have been known as the **Pays des Quatre Vallées**, a province jointly administered by Bigorre, Comminges and Aragon. Throughout the Middle Ages, the various lords of the Quatre Vallées adroitly maintained their independent political arrangements and pacts, and the region prospered perhaps more than most Pyrenean valleys, especially after 1492, when Spain's demand for wool for the uniforms of its troops in the Americas brought a small economic boom to the

Pyrenees. All the private dealing, however, gradually ended between 1473 and 1715, when through marriages and treaties the four valleys were gobbled up by the French Crown. This had a dark side: France's wars with Spain cut off the valleys' natural political and economic outlets. The Industrial Revolution and the First World War only aggravated the decline, as people headed north in search of easier jobs and better pay. During the Spanish Civil War, the population picked up a bit, most dramatically in June 1938 when the Republic's 43rd Brigade, trapped at Bielsa, was pushed over the border into the Vallée d'Aure, with hundreds of civilian refugees. During the Second World War, the traffic went the other way, as local shepherds, woodcutters and others helped Jews, German dissidents and escapees from French political prisons to flee over the mountains; in the Aure Valley alone, an estimated 1,500 of the 2,000 who made the attempt survived to make it to Spain.

The Vallée d'Aure: Sarrancolin to St-Lary

Moulded by ancient glaciers into a giant fishhook around the formidable peaks of the Massif de Néouvielle, the Vallée d'Aure not only receives more sunshine than most French valleys, but is blessed by a warm Spanish wind, known locally as the *et bentthat*, which sweeps the surrounding peaks clear of clouds and mists. Perhaps because of its sunny disposition, the Vallée d'Aure was one of the first valleys, back in the 1950s, to reverse its decline by attracting tourists and skiers. Another feather in its cap is the recent opening of the Aragnouet–Bielsa tunnel, confirming the Aure's age-old links with Spain that began with the 'royal way' or Ténarèze (a peculiar Gascon word, apparently derived from the Latin words *in itinere* or itinerary), used at least from Neolithic times to link the valleys of the Garonne and hence the Atlantic with those of the Ebro and the Mediterranean.

Sarrancolin

From La Barthe-de-Neste (just south of Lannemezan and the A64) the D929 follows the route of the Ténarèze through rather dismal scenery to Sarrancolin. The Romans loved it for its red marble with grey veins, and in more recent years the quarries have been reopened to decorate Versailles and build the famous grand stair of the Paris Opéra. The medieval town was once heavily fortified, although today only a tower gate remains, the **Porte Sainte-Quitterie**, carved with the arms of France. The lanes here, especially the picturesque Rue Noire, are lined with 15th- and 16th-century houses (note the dates on the marble lintels). The pride of Sarrancolin is the handsome church and bell tower of **St-Ebons**, begun in the 12th century in the form of a Greek cross. Inside, the relics of St Ebons (or Ebontius, *d.* 1104), the first bishop of Roda de Isabena in Aragon after its reconquest from the Moors, are preserved in a magnificent 13th-century gold and copper enamel casket made in Limoges, decorated with medallions showing scenes from the New Testament and the figures of Christ, the Apostles, St Louis and St Ebons. Carefully preserved through centuries of troubles, the casket was stolen in 1911, and, to the dismay of Sarrancolin, given up for lost – until

Getting Around

All **trains** between Pau, Tarbes and Toulouse stop at Lannemezan, and from there **buses** continue south 3 or 4 times a day to Sarrancolin, Arreau and St-Lary. Once a day there's a direct connection between Tarbes and St-Lary.

For information, call **t** 05 62 98 00 49.

Tourist Information

Sarrancolin: Rue de l'Hôtel de Ville, **t** 05 62 98 79 88. Information point open during school hols,.

Arreau, for the Aure and Louron valleys: Place du Monument, **t** 05 62 98 63 15, **f** 05 62 40 12 32, *www.vallee-aure.com. Open summer Mon–Sat 9–12.30 and 1.30–7 plus Sun 9–12; winter hols Mon–Sat 9–12 and 2–6; the rest of the winter Mon–Fri 9–12 and 2–6.*

St-Lary: Rue Principale, **t** 05 62 39 50 81, **f** 05 62 39 50 06, *www.saintlary.com. Open daily for all school hols. The rest of the year Mon–Sat 9–12 and 2–7.*

Piau-Engaly: Maison du Tourisme, **t** 05 62 39 61 69, **f** 05 62 39 61 19. *Open July–Aug Mon–Fri 9–12 and 2–7; peak winter 9–7; the rest of the year 9–12 and 1–7.*

Bordères-Louron: Maison du Tourism, **t** 05 62 99 92 00, **f** 05 62 99 92 09, *www.lelouron.com. Open all year. Mon–Sat 9–12.30 and 2–6 plus Sun mornings July and Aug.*

Market Days

La Barthe-de-Neste: Sunday *marché au gras*, May–Oct and Christmas.

Sarrancolin: Tuesdays and Saturdays.

Arreau: Thursdays.

St-Lary: Saturdays.

Where to Stay and Eat

Sarrancolin ✉ 65410

Marie Menvielle's Chambres d'Hôte, Quartier Porailhet, **t** 05 62 98 77 60 (*inexpensive*). Bed and breakfast place in a woodland setting. *Open all year.*

Jeanne Puchol's Chambres d'Hôte, Route du Tous, **t** 05 62 98 78 18 (*cheap*). Here there are three rooms in a typical Pyrenean house in the trees. *Open all year on reservation only.*

Arreau ✉ 65240

****Hôtel d'Angleterre**, on the edge of town, **t** 05 62 98 63 30, **f** 05 62 98 69 66, *www.angleterre-hotel.com* (*moderate–inexpensive*) A big comfortable country inn, with a garden terrace to sit out on; the owners arrange rafting or hang-gliding excursions. Half board obligatory mid July–mid Sept. Heated pool. The restaurant serves good hearty food – *garbure*, *confits* and regional dishes – perfect for high-altitude appetites. No restaurant in winter. *Closed 1 Oct–26 Dec. Open June–Sept also weekends and holidays in winter.*

Hôtel de France, t 05 62 98 61 12. On the main street, a traditional family hotel with a pleasant garden terrace. *Menus €12–20. Closed mid Oct–mid Dec and April–May. Restaurant closed Tues eves and all day Wed.*

****Hostellerie du Val d'Aure**, just south of Arreau in Cadéac, **t** 05 62 98 60 63, **f** 05 62 98 68 99, *www.hotel-valdaure.com* (*inexpensive*). Lovely family-run hotel set in some pretty woods with a pool. *Menu lunch €23. Closed Tues and Thurs lunch. Closed April–15 May and 27 Sept–26 Dec. May–Sept restaurant open to all. In winter, residents only.*

one dry year, when the waters in the Neste d'Aure were exceptionally low and it was spotted in the middle of the river where the thief had dropped it. Also of interest are the 17th-century paintings on wood by the entrance and the carved choir stalls, where the usual funny faces seem to groan and grimace under the weight of the churchmen who once sat there.

Next to St-Ebons are the scant remains of a Benedictine **priory**, founded in 1032 by the abbot of Simorre in the Gers. Four centuries later it was used as the residence of the lovely but singularly unhappy Isabelle, made the 'Dame des Quatre Vallées' by Jean V, Count of Armagnac, her brother and husband. The story goes that Jean V had

St-Lary-Soulan ✉ 65170

In the town that helped inaugurate package ski holidays in the Pyrenees, there are no bargains. The restaurants in St-Lary, such as they are, are notoriously mediocre.

****Hôtel de la Neste**, **t** 05 62 39 42 79, **f** 05 62 39 58 77, *www.hotel-delaneste.com* (*moderate–inexpensive*). By the river, the hotel enjoys a grand view of the mountains; all rooms have bath, TV and mini-bar. A little over a kilometre from the village centre. Do not be put off by the ugly modern exterior. Clean, comfortable well-run hotel with a pool. The restaurant serves meals. The restaurant offers simple regional fare. *Menus €20. Closed Nov.*

*****La Pergola,** 25 Rue Vincent MIR 65170 Saint-Lary, **t** 05 62 39 40 46, *www.hotellapergola.fr.* This hotel is set in a lovely park with peak views. Bedrooms are comfortable and have balconies or terraces facing the mountains. Some bathrooms have massage showers. There are two restaurants: one has traditional rustic décor and offers good regional fare, the other, L'Enclos des Saveurs (open in winter only), offers a gastronomic tour of nouvelle cuisine. *Menus €21–60. €8 for an excellent buffet breakfast.*

La Grange, Quartier d Autan St-Lary (on D118 on the outskirts, coming from Arreau), **t** 05 62 40 07 14. The young chef is obviously trying to get St-Lary on the gastronomic map with a very ambitious menu. Try the *millefeuille de crab aux tomates*, or the Gascon *jambon de cochon noir*, or the *escalope de foie frais* with caramelized peaches. The décor is cosy and rustic and there is a pretty summer terrace. *Menus €24–38. Closed Tues eve and Wed plus mid Nov–mid Dec and 15 April–7 May.*

****La Terrasse Fleurie**, 21 Rue Principale, **t** 05 62 40 76 00, **f** 05 62 39 50 10, *www.la-terrasse-fleurie.com* (*inexpensive*). In the town centre, a nice comfortable hotel with wooden balconies.

***Pons 'Le Dahu'**, Rue de Couderes, **t** 05 62 39 43 66, **f** 05 62 40 00 86, *www.hotelpons.com* (*inexpensive*). An inexpensive and sunny choice. *Open all year.*

La Détente, Route de Cap-de-Long, **t** 05 62 39 53 09 (*inexpensive*). This is the place for longer stays, with studio apartments with kitchenettes, sleeping 2 to 4, and a play area for the children. *Open all year.*

Marius Verdier, Azet, **t** 05 62 39 43 97 (*cheap*). Six tranquil rooms at a very good price. Restaurant is open to non-residents by reservation. *Open June–Sept.*

Chez Lulu, in Sailhan, **t** 05 62 39 40 89. Here you can dine pleasantly on the summer terrace. There are Gascon favourites on the menus. *Menus €14–21. Closed Mon plus May, Nov and Dec.*

Vallée de Louron ✉ 65590

Le Relais d'Avajan, Avajan, **t** 05 62 99 67 08 (*moderate*). A handful of reasonably priced rooms and a stout menu. *Menu €12. Open all year exc Wed in winter.*

Auberge des Isclots, overlooking the Lac de Loudenvielle at Aranvielle, **t** 05 62 99 66 21 (*inexpensive–cheap*). Utterly pleasant, with doubles, or cheaper *gîte d'étape* rooms in a dormitory. *Menus €14–20. Open all year.*

Accueil sans Frontière Pyrénées, Germ, **t** 05 62 99 65 27, **f** 05 62 99 63 22 (*cheap*). A popular complex of well-furnished *gîtes* and hostel accommodation, with a camp site, good food, swimming pool and loads of information and equipment for summer and winter sports in the area.

been separated from his sister until she turned 18, and when he saw her he fell passionately in love with her. So potent was this affection that he even found a bishop to try to justify their incestuous love to the pope, using the gods of Olympus as a precedent for their unnatural union. Isabelle bore him three children before he was assassinated (*see* p.128), then spent the rest of her life secluded at Castelnau-Magnoac, dying of a disease given to her by her brother. Her subjects in the Quatre Vallées apparently felt sorry for their lady, and never caused her any more trouble than she already had, but when she died they were quick to offer their allegiance to Louis XI rather than face one of her heirs.

Lastly, if you're in Sarrancolin and it's time for a picnic and just a view of the surroundings, take the steep *route forestier*, which winds 8km to the east up to the panoramic **Col d'Estivère** (1,217m/3,993ft).

Arreau

The main valley road continues 7km south to Arreau, the pretty, slate-roofed capital of the Quatre Vallées, located at the meeting of the Aure and Louron rivers and various roads, including the route up to the Col d'Aspin (*see* p.246). Like the Aure itself, Arreau's name comes from the Celtic Arebaci, the original inhabitants of Pamplona, whom Pompey defeated and relocated here when re-founding the town in his own name. Now a popular base for walks, rafting, hang-gliding and skiing (at **Val-Louron**, 1,450–2,150m/4,757–7,054ft), Arreau used to attract merchants and wheeler-dealers from all across the Pyrenees, who met in the centre of the village under the 17th-century *halles*. Just opposite, the most beautiful house in the village, the 16th-century **Maison des Lys**, is named after the fleurs-de-lys carved in the timber – a testimonial to local enthusiasm for distant French rule after the too-close-for-comfort Armagnacs. At the top of the Grand Rue, the parish church of **Notre-Dame** is worth a look for its elegant and colourful retable from the 18th century and the arm reliquary of St Exuperius. Exuperius (born in Arreau, died 411) was one of the first bishops of Toulouse, and a good friend and benefactor of St Jerome. He was famous for his generosity, sending food to the poor as far away as Palestine and Egypt. The diminutive **Château des Nestes** contains the tourist office and an intriguing Musée des Cagots *(Museum is open the same times as the tourist office)*. Over the river, below the Château de Ségur (where there's convenient parking), stands the 16th-century **Chapelle St-Exupère**, with an octagonal bell tower and a Romanesque portal with carved capitals. By the entrance, an old *coffre* was set up for offerings, in the style of St Exuperius himself; if the chapel's open, note the fine 16th-century wrought-iron screen.

Around Arreau

The best church around, however, is 3km east of Arreau at **Jézeau**, beautifully set on the mountain flank over the medieval hamlet. Ask at the *mairie* (*call ahead, mornings only*) for the key before setting out because the interior is what you've come to see: when it was remodelled and enlarged in the 16th century, the church was given a magnificent brightly painted Renaissance retable, several polychrome statues and, on the wooden ceiling, vigorous, imaginative paintings by an unknown hand, including a remarkable *Last Judgement* that has inspired Jézeau's enthusiasts to call it 'The Sistine Chapel of the Pyrenees'.

Continuing up the Neste d'Aure from Arreau, **Cadéac-les-Bains** is a spa down on its luck since the Second Empire, with the 19th-century fountains and the donjon of a 13th-century castle built by Sancho of Aragon as its landmark. Next is **Ancizan**, an important textile centre in the 16th century, when many of the houses were built and the villagers plumped for the fine *mise au tombeau* in the parish church. You can discover what life was like around here not even a hundred years ago at the **Musée de**

la Vallée d'Aure (*Route de St-Lary,* **t** *05 62 39 97 75; open school hols daily 10–12 and 2–7; rest of the year open same hours until 6, closed Mon, Tues and Thurs*).

For a mighty dose of scenery, turn up the D113 for the **Hourquette d'Ancizan** (1,538m/5,975ft), passing by way of **l'An Mil**, a fortified 11th-century village with heather-thatched roofs – constructed a few years back as a film set. Beyond Hourquette, the D113 continues to Payolle, where you can circle back to the Vallé d'Aure by way of the dramatic Col d'Aspin.

A by-road to Compostela passed through the Vallée d'Aure, but few traces remain of the pilgrims' passing; one is the **Chapelle d'Argos**, south of Guchen, all that survives of a hospital set up by the Knights Hospitallers. The next village south, **Vielle-Aure**, has a sweet little Romanesque church, with 15th-century frescoes inside and a gilded Renaissance retable, and many houses from the 16th to 18th centuries in the centre (and plenty of condominiums and pseudo-Pyrenean bungalows from the 20th century on the outskirts, part of the sprawl from St-Lary).

Even better are the murals in the church of **Notre-Dame-de Bourisp**, just to the east over the Neste d'Aure (*open periodically in the summer, and every Sunday for Mass at 10am*). In 1542, two painters named Jean Berneil and Jean Boé embellished the interior with scenes from the *Life of Christ* and *SS. Stephen and Sebastian*, but when it came to painting the *Seven Deadly Sins* Berneil and Boé showed their misogynist colours – all the sins are represented by fashionably dressed women, riding beasts symbolic of their various vices (Pride on her lion, Avarice on what looks like a wolf). All are escorted by the most kindly, solicitous demons imaginable; each has three faces, butterfly wings, and stands lightly on the beast's hindquarters like a circus performer.

St-Lary

St-Lary claims (as do several other towns) to be nothing less than the biggest winter/summer sports resort in the Pyrenees. It certainly had a head start. Back in the 1950s, when all the workers who built the dams and hydroelectric plants in the valley had finished their tasks and gone home, St-Lary was left so empty and disconsolate that its bigwigs decided immediate action was called for. By 1957 the town had built its first aerial **cableway**, at the time the largest in the world, to the ski slopes of Pla d'Adet (these days it looks quite puny); most recently (1988) it built a deluxe modern **spa** at Soulan, to treat rheumatism and nose-ear-throat troubles in the hopes of attracting tourists in the dead periods of May, October and November.

Another recent project has been the restoration of the old core of St-Lary, including the 16th-century Maison Fornier in Place de la Mairie, now home to the **Musée du Parc National** (**t** *05 62 39 40 91; open mid-Dec–end Oct Mon–Fri 9–12 and 2–6.30 plus Sat and Sun in July and Aug*), with audio-visual information on the fauna of the Pyrenees. But it's the great outdoors that brings most people to St-Lary – in the winter, ice-skating and skiing on the 33 pistes at Pla d'Adet, where you can ride all the way up to the **Soum de Matte** (2,477m/8,174ft) for the eagle-eye views; in the summer, paragliding, riding, rock climbing, canyoning and walking take over. The popular three-day trek known as the Tour de la Vallée d'Aure begins at **Vielle-Aure**, as does the D123 up to the old village of **Soulan** (annexed by St-Lary) and **Espiaube**, where in the winter the *téléférique* lifts punters up to the stupendous **Col de Portet** (2,215m/ 7,309ft).

Around St-Lary

Nearby **Ens** is a typical mountain village, with a Romanesque church in a superb setting. The unpaved but driveable D225 from Sailhan rises up to the remote old village of **Azet** with more grand views, then crosses the mountains for the Vallée de Louron to the east.

Continuing up the valley from St-Lary, the small village, sheer rock and ruined 11th-century castle of **Tramezaïgues** (from the Latin *inter ambas aquas*, 'between two waters' – the Neste d'Aure and the Torrent de Rioumajou) stand like an exclamation mark at the beginning of the deep green, arcadian 12km-long **Vallée du Rioumajou**. The driveable track that cuts up the middle is the heir of the Ténarèze; you can drive or walk this ancient route as far as the Hospice de Rioumajou (1,560m/5,118ft), and join the High Pyrenees trail (HPH) or continue south of the border from **Port d'Urdisseto** (2,403m/7,884ft). Daniel Defoe came this way in 1689, during one of the worst winters in history, and was lucky to come out uneaten by the ravenous wolves; he fictionalized the experience in a chapter of *Robinson Crusoe*. The next little valley, the **Vallée du Moudang**, was a favourite smugglers' route; a bad road braves it part of the way, from where it's an easy walk to a curious village of barns, the **Granges de Moudang**, where shepherds lodged in the summer.

The D929 continues to Fabian, the crossroads for the Routes des Lacs and the Réserve Naturelle de Néouvielle (*see* below), and then to Le Plan d'Aragnouet. Here a very photogenic Templars' chapel has a charming if unusual *clocher-mur* with windows at the top, although all attempts to find any esoteric meaning in it have fallen flat. At Le Plan a road branches off for **Piau-Engaly**, the highest and snowiest ski resort in the Pyrenees (1,400–2,500m/4,590–8,200ft), and certainly the most futuristic, with 35 pistes, 21 lifts, and illuminated night skiing to prolong the thrills. There are a number of trails passing near the station, including a link up to the National Park and Gavarnie. The D929 continues to the **Tunnel de Bielsa** to Spain and the dry, wild mountains of Upper Aragon (*tunnel open April–Sept 24hrs; Oct–April closes Sat–Thurs 11pm, Fri midnight*).

The Réserve Naturelle de Néouvielle: the Route des Lacs

In 1935, the great south-facing granite *massif* of Néouvielle became the first nature reserve in France; the French call it the Parc National *bis*. It's an especially good place for bird-watching, with golden eagles soaring high overhead. The reserve also has the highest growth of pines in Europe (the *massif* is wooded up to 2,400m/7,920ft), thanks to a sunny micro-climate that supports another 1,250 known species of plants, not a few of which are in and around its score of lovely lakes. Early July, when the rhododendrons burst into bloom, is the perfect time for a visit. Thank the French power monopoly, EDF, for the narrow road up from Fabian, which for a few months in the summer allows you (and half the population of St-Lary in August) to motor as far as the Lac d'Orédon and Lac de Cap-de-Long, both within easy striking distance of other lakes. There are several *refuges* (at Barstan and Orédon) and a wide range of easy to difficult and dangerous paths; an easy, classic circuit on the GR 10 and GR 10c includes most of the lakes and an overnight stay at Barstan; the main GR 10 continues west to Barèges (*see* p.242).

The Vallée de Louron

Arreau (*see* p.276) stands at the foot of the 25km-long Vallée de Louron, green and tranquil compared to its neighbours, the Vallée d'Aure to the west and the Vallée de Luchon to the east. It has a pair of ski resorts, at **Val-Louron** (2,260m/7,415ft) and **Peyresourde** (2,241m/7,352ft), and is increasingly a popular base for hang-gliding and paragliding daredevils; the 'altiport' at Peyragudes is unique in the Pyrenees. Water sports are another focus on the new large man-made **Lac de Loudenvielle**, a mirror under a 12th-century castle.

The Valley of Romanesque Churches

By the 16th century, the wool and cloth business in the Vallée de Louron was good enough for the inhabitants of its villages to pool their money to hire painters to decorate their churches. Unfortunately they are often locked; the afternoon tours offered on Thursdays by the Maison du Tourism at Bordères is the easiest way to get into them (***t** 05 62 99 92 00; ring ahead*). Heading up the valley, **Lançon** (take the D219 from Arreau) has a Romanesque church, not with murals but an unusual bell tower topped with a pepperpot roof; **Ilhan** just south has fine views of the valley. South of Bordères-Louron, **Vielle-Louron**'s church has both walls and ceilings covered with 16th-century paintings. From **Génos** you can take the road past the Val-Louron ski resort over the mountains to the Col de Peyrefitte (1,578m/5,177ft) for the majestic views, then descend down the unpaved road to St-Lary.

Loudenvielle, south of its large man-made lake, and the power station at **Tramezaïgues** 8km further south, are the bases for walks in the upper Vallée de Louron. Other good Romanesque churches are just to the east: one at **Cazaux-Fréchet** and another at **Armenteule**, isolated and decorated with a curious carved frieze. **Mont** has the finest frescoes in the whole valley, painted in 1573 by one Melchior Rodiguis of St-Bertrand-de-Comminges, who decorated both the interior and exterior and the cemetery chapel with charming provincial Renaissance paintings on the *Lives of the Virgin, John the Baptist and Christ*. Lastly, tucked off the main route, is a clean and pleasant little hamlet lost in nature called **Germ** (yes, really), named after a saint so obscure that he never made it out of the valley. Beyond the turn-off for Germ, the main D618 continues up to the **Col de Peyresourde**, with beautiful views back to the Vallée de Louron. If you don't want to backtrack, it continues down to Bagnères-de-Luchon (*see* p.292).

Into the Haute Garonne: The Comminges

East of the Vallée de Louron extends the southernmost bit of the *département* of the Haute-Garonne, lodged in between the Hautes-Pyrénées and the Ariège like an insistent jigsaw puzzle piece. Before the bureaucrats of the Revolution changed all the political contours, this bit of the puzzle was the county and bishopric of the Comminges, one of the most venerable provinces of Gascony.

Located exactly midway between the Atlantic and Mediterranean, the Comminges encompasses the upper valley of one of France's four great rivers, the Garonne, and has been inhabited, literally, since the cows (and bison and woolly mammoths) came home in the last Ice Age; one of the villages gave its name to the misty Aurignacian era. The Iberians, Celts and especially the Romans, beginning with Pompey, recognized its strategic and commercial importance as a natural crossroads. Although few places in the Pyrenees have as many proud relics of the prehistoric, Roman and medieval past, tourism is a fairly recent phenomenon in the region, with the exception of the grand old spa of Bagnères-de-Luchon.

South of the Garonne: Montréjeau to St-Béat

Approaching the Comminges from the west on the N117, the first town is Montréjeau. From there we move south into the spiritual heart of the Comminges, at St-Bertrand, then continue into the Pyrenees; if you're going north from Montréjeau into the 'Petites Pyrénées', *see* p.296.

Montréjeau

At the confluence of the Neste and Garonne, Montréjeau stands on a natural terrace, where it was founded as a *bastide* in 1272, called Mont-Royal before Gascon tongues tried to fit around it. It has lovely views over to the Pyrenees from its two main squares, central arcaded **Place Valentin Abeille** and **Place Verdun**, with the market and public garden; on Bd de Lassus, skirting the edge of the plateau, an orientation table has been set up. Montréjeau's **church**, first built in the 12th century, has a handsome octagonal bell tower, typical of the hinterland of Toulouse. The **Château de Valmirande** (*route de Tarbes*, **t** *05 61 95 78 31; guided tour daily at 3, July–mid-Aug. Call ahead to book at other times; adm*) is a fairytale castle designed by Louis Garros in the late 19th century, a folly of different façades with a Gothic chapel, all set in a park and formal gardens.

The Grotte de Gargas

***t** 05 62 39 72 39; open daily July and Aug 10–11.45 and 2–6.15; April–June and Sept 10.15–11.15 and 2.15–5.15; Jan–Mar and Oct–Dec 10.30–11.15 and 2.30–4.*

There's always an ineffable quality to prehistoric caves, perhaps because the thoughts and dreams of our remote ancestors can never be recaptured; no amount of study nor comparative science can really fathom the Palaeolithic mind or the

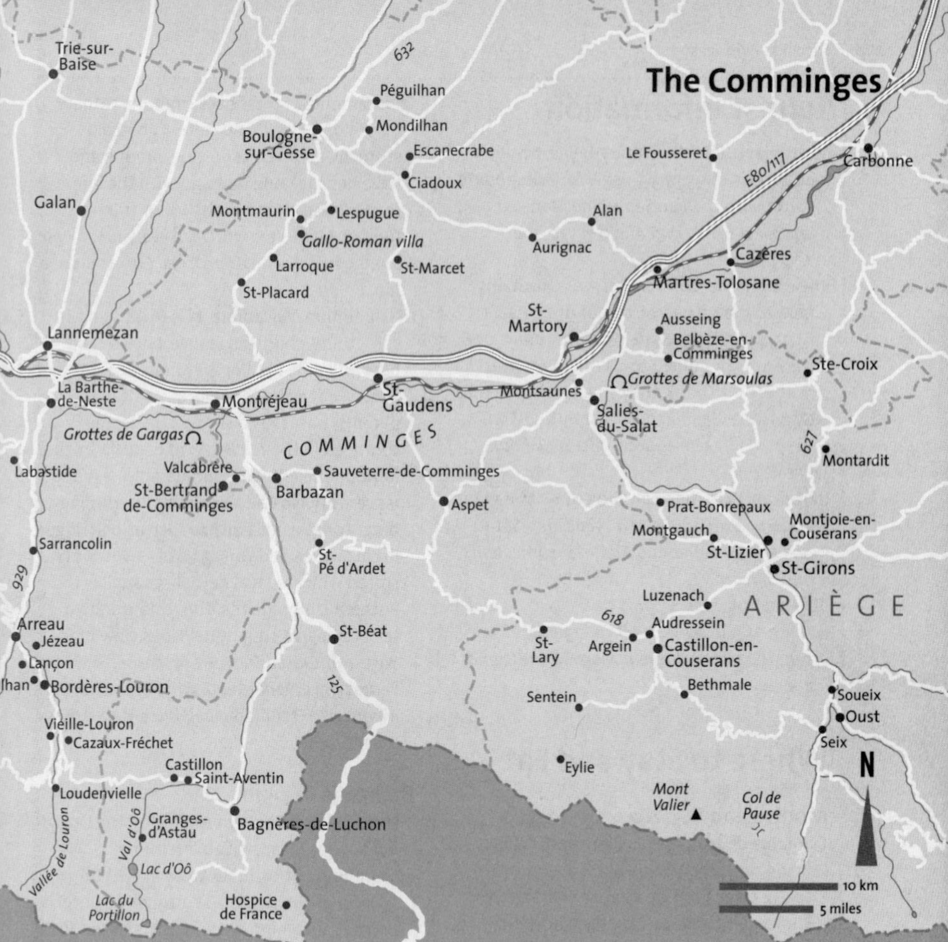

meaning behind the often stunning, often inscrutable works left behind by humanity's first artists.

The Grotte de Gargas, south of Montréjeau on the D26, is even more uncanny and troubling than most. Gargas is one of the oldest-known decorated caves in France, dating from the Aurignacian era, the period of the first figurative art (*c.* 33,000 BC), and its oldest paintings and engravings of bison, horses, mammoths, bulls, deer and goats (and, unusually, two birds) are still rather awkward and archaic, compared to the more graceful and lively works of the Magdalenian era (*c.* 12,000 BC) made famous at Lascaux; a few examples here testify to millennia of use following the last Ice Age.

But what sets Gargas apart are its bizarre, **mutilated hands** – 231 pictures in different sizes and different colours (red ochre or black magnesium oxide), made by blowing paint through a tube around a hand. Nearly all are somehow deformed or missing parts of or whole fingers. Evidence of fingerprints in the clay seem to show that both living hands and amputated hands were used for models, and guesses are that they were damaged either through frostbite, disease, accidents or ritual

Tourist Information

Montréjeau: Place Valentin Abeille, **t** 05 61 95 80 22, **f** 05 61 95 37 39, *www.tourisme-haute-garonne.com. Open Sept–June Mon–Sat 9–12 and 2.30–6, July and Aug 9–12.30 and 2.30–6.30 plus Sun 10–1.*

St-Bertrand-de-Comminges: 'Les Olivetains', next to the cathedral, **t** 05 61 95 44 44, **f** 05 61 95 44 95, *open Easter–October daily 10–6*; they run 3hr guided tours of the town and, as there's no bank, they change money, too. *Open June–Sept daily 10–6, July and Aug 10–7; winter Mon–Sat 10–5; closed in Jan. Phone only.*

Barbazan: Parc Thermale, **t** 05 61 88 35 64, **f** 05 61 94 96 64. *Open all year Tues–Sat 10–12 and 2–6, July and Aug Mon–Sat same hours plus Sun am.*

St-Béat: **t** 05 61 79 45 98, **f** 05 61 79 57 07. *Open July and Aug Mon–Sat 8.30–7.30 plus Sun 9–7; the rest of the year Mon–Fri 10–12 and 2–6.*

Where to Stay and Eat

Montréjeau ✉ 31210

Domaine de Jean-Pierre, 8km west in Pinas (✉ 65330), **t/f** 05 62 98 15 08 (*inexpensive*). If you're after something with character, this choice has three very pretty rooms in a typical country house immersed in creeper, set in a large park. *Open all year, book ahead in winter.*

St-Bertrand-de-Comminges ✉ 31510

★★**L'Oppidum**, up in the medieval town, **t** 05 61 88 33 50, **f** 05 61 95 94 04 (*inexpensive*). This pretty place has 15 comfortable rooms, some sleeping as many as six. The restaurant serves local specialities: stuffed trout, veal dishes and a delicious mousse with caramel and walnuts. *Menus €14–35. Closed mid-Nov–mid-Dec. Closed Sun eves and all Mon except July and Aug.*

★**Hôtel du Comminges**, facing the cathedral, **t** 05 61 88 31 43, **f** 05 61 94 98 22. An old ivy-covered building that was once a private house, this option has nicely furnished large rooms, and an interior garden to sit in as well as the terrace in front. *Closed Nov–Mar.*

Chez Simone, a street back from the cathedral, **t** 05 61 94 91 05. If you crave a good old stuffed Gascon chicken, ring Simone and have her cook one up to go with the home-made desserts and pretty views from the terrace. *Menus €13–16. Open every lunch and dinner for July and Aug; closed Christmas and Jan.*

Le Lugdunum, Valcabrère, **t** 05 61 94 52 05. For something unique in France, book a table here and dine like Pompey himself. Here chef Renzo Pedrazzini (born locally of Italian parents) bases his dishes on the recipes compiled in the *Ten Books of Cooking* by the famous ancient gastronome Apicius in the 1st century. No Caesar salads or humming-birds' tongues, but dishes such as partridge in cold sauce and young boar, served with spiced wines; a local herbalist supplies the authentic ingredients. The restaurant terrace has an equally delicious view of St-Bertrand. *Closed Tues out of season.* Mr Pedrazzini is very friendly and enthusiastic. *Menus €30–50. Closed in winter Mon–Thurs except for school hols.*

Barbazan ✉ 31510

★★★**Hostellerie des Sept Molles**, on the D9 just east of Barbazan, in Sauveterre-de-Comminges, **t** 05 61 88 30 87, **f** 05 61 88 36 42 (*expensive–moderate*). The all-white hotel is perched on a high hill and offers luminous rooms, spread out in several buildings, with a heated pool, tennis, and bubbling stream in the grounds. The restaurant has a lovely terrace for summer dining, or a roaring fire in the winter, and specializes in baby lamb with *mounjetado*, the local version of *cassoulet. Restaurant closed mid-Feb–mid-Mar.*

Châteaux et Hôtels de France, *www.hotel7molles.com. Restaurant open daily May–Sept. Closed Tues–Wed and Thurs lunch Oct–April. Closed all Tues, Wed, Thurs and Fri lunch. Menus €30–47.*

★★★**L'Aristou**, on the road to Sauveterre, **t** 05 61 88 30 67, **f** 05 61 95 55 66 (*inexpensive*). Small and cosy, in a 19th-century house. *Closed Christmas–Jan.* There's also a good restaurant. *Menus €18–35. Closed mid Dec–Feb. Restaurant closed Sun and Mon Sept–April.*

mutilation. The painted outlines of hands are found everywhere in Upper Palaeolithic art, almost as if they were signatures, but rarely are any mutilated and nowhere else do they appear in such quantity. The only other cave where similar mutilated hands have been found is in the Grotte de Tibiran, the nearest cave to Gargas (*not open to visitors*).

Curiously enough, Gargas has long had a rather nefarious reputation. Its name is derived from the giant Gargas who lived there, the precursor of Rabelais' giant Gargantua. In the 18th century, the national newsapaper, the *Mercure de France*, claimed it was the abode of a cannibal named Blaise Ferrage, who ate a few dozen shepherds and local women and couldn't be caught because he also ate a certain magic plant called *herba Heraclea* that gave him jaws of iron. In the 19th century, tourists en route to Luchon would stop at Gargas for a *frisson* and were shown a bunch of bears' bones by the guides, who claimed they were the remains of Blaise's unnatural dinners. All along, no one 'saw' Gargas' prehistoric art: no one even imagined anything of the sort existed until the early 1900s.

As for Blaise the anthropophage, he was apparently based on a ruffian named Chaillet, who was condemned to death in 1782 in Toulouse for his crimes, although chewing up the local citizenry wasn't one of them.

St-Bertrand-de-Comminges

Until the Virgin Mary appeared at Lourdes, the religious centre of the central Pyrenees was St-Bertrand-de-Comminges. Magnificently placed on an isolated promontory where the river Garonne curls about a fertile plain, the massive Gothic church of **Ste-Marie** makes for an unforgettable sight, a kind of inland Mont-St-Michel, as the French like to say, with its nearly windowless walls, tower and buttresses rising up like an ocean liner, dwarfing the village below. The important remains of St-Bertrand's Roman predecessor and a fine Romanesque church nearby are added attractions, along with a unique restaurant that specializes in ancient Roman cuisine.

The Citadel of the Rising Sun

St-Bertrand was settled by Iberians from around the river Ebro, who built the first *oppidum* on the naturally fortified site of the cathedral. Their Celtic cousins, the Volcae Tectosages (the founders of Toulouse), gave it its name, *Lugdunum*, which can be literally translated as the 'Citadel of the Rising Sun'. A temple to Lug, the Celtic sun god, stood in the centre of the *oppidum*, and there may have been a market nearby – Iberian coins have been found in excavations under the square in front of the cathedral. By 76 BC, when Pompey was campaigning in Spain, the Iberians had been chased to the south and the region was largely empty except for various guerrilla tribes holding out against the joys of Roman rule. They were collectively known as the *convenii*, the 'robbers of souls', and they were determined and tough enough to make even a great general like Pompey think twice before taking to the hills to exterminate them. Rather, he decided to win them over by kindness; he declared them to be Roman colonists and granted them the fertile region around *Lugdunum*, henceforth *Lugdunum Convenarum*.

The ferocious *Convenii* turned out to be excellent citizens. Set at the crossing of two major Roman roads, *Lugdunum Convenarum* grew by leaps and bounds: by the time of Augustus the town covered much of the plain, and the temple, the baths and forum were built. The great 1st-century-AD Jewish historian Josephus wrote that *Lugdunum* received the Tetrarch Herod and his family in 39 AD, when Caligula exiled them from Palestine (perhaps to keep company with Mary Magdelene and the other Marys, Martha, Veronica and Zaccheus and other New Testament characters who supposedly ended up in France). Local legend has it that one winter Herod's famously wicked stepdaughter Salome fell into a lake and drowned, so that only her head stuck out of the ice, as if on a great white platter – just as she had demanded John the Baptist's head in exchange for her dance. A square tower, known as Herod's tomb for as long as anyone can remember, stands by the Garonne on a rock known as the **Mail de Martrouilh**.

The first Christian basilica was built in the lower town shortly after the Comminges was annexed by the Visigoths of Toulouse in 410. But by then *Lugdunum Convenarum* was in decline; final disaster arrived in the form of Gondowald, the bastard son of Clotaire II, king of the Franks. Gondowald had been raised by Narses, the eunuch governor-general of Italy in the name of Byzantium. Always keen to undermine the pretensions of the pope in Rome, who was increasingly infringing on the rightful domain of the emperor of Constantinople, Narses sent his ward Gondowald to take power in Gaul. Waiting for a local uprising of the Gascons and an army from Spain, Gondowald holed up in the fortress of *Lugdunum* (585), but in the meantime the new king of the Franks, Childebert, allied with the king of the Burgundians, led a forced march on *Lugdunum*, hurled Gondowald over a precipice, and proceeded to vent their feelings about Byzantium on the town and its citizens in a murderous, fiery rampage. For centuries the once-rich town of *Lugdunum Convenarum* became a stone quarry for southwest France, while its statues fed the local limekilns.

The town next appears in the 11th century, in the biography of Bertrand de l'Isle-Jourdain, a cousin of the extraordinary count of Toulouse, Raymond IV, who fought with El Cid in Spain and led the First Crusade. Bertrand shared much of Raymond's energy and zeal; when appointed bishop of Comminges he rebuilt both the church and the town and presided there for 50 years, performing enough miracles to be canonized by popular demand in 1175. In the late 13th century, another Bertrand, Bertrand de Got of Bordeaux, was named bishop and replaced his predecessor's Romanesque church with the grand Gothic edifice that stands today. When Bertrand de Got was elected Pope Clement V, he remembered his old see and confirmed the canonization of the first Bertrand in 1309, putting his bull of approval on the pilgrimage to his tomb and personally visiting to render homage before the saint's relics. Decline began with the Wars of Religion and quickened with the Revolution, when the episcopate was suppressed; today fewer than 300 people call St-Bertrand home.

The Ste-Marie Cathedral

t 05 61 89 04 91; open daily except Sun; Feb–April 10–12 and 2–6, May–Sept 9–7; Oct 10–12 and 2–6, Nov–Jan 10–1 and 2–5.

When Bertrand de Got rebuilt St Bertrand's cathedral, he left the 100ft bell tower-cum-donjon and the rather severe façade intact; if you look carefully, you can see that a number of stones used in the construction were first cut as pagan tombstones. At the top of the well-worn marble steps, the richly decorated portal also dates from the 12th century, its tympanum carved with the Three Magi (and the future St Bertrand) paying their respects to the Virgin, seated on a throne holding a crowned Jesus the size of an 8-year-old child, an image known in the Pyrenees as 'the Seat of Wisdom'. Imaginary animals look down from the capitals, while on the left side of the door demons daintily drop sinners into the maw of hell. As you enter, don't miss the embalmed crocodile, hanging on the right over the parish altar; no one knows who left it here, but guesses tend towards a passing Crusader. Note, too, the fine altar front, made of Cordoba leather. On the left, columns support one of the most lavish **Renaissance organs** in France, known as 'the Third Wonder of Gascony', built in the 16th century and decorated with finely carved wooden panels representing the labours of Hercules. Although its 3,000 pipes were purloined in the Revolution, the organ was restored in the 1970s and still works a treat, as you can hear every Sunday at 10.30am.

The nave is closed off from the choir by an opulently carved Renaissance rood screen, but to continue any further down the nave you have to buy a ticket (*tours are optional, but you have to at least tag along with one to get into the treasury*). The delightful 12th- to 13th-century **cloister**, just to the right of the ticket desk, is another legacy of St Bertrand d'Isle-Jourdain; squeezed onto the edge of the promontory, it's small and irregularly shaped, and has an open gallery with a charming view over the wooded hillside. The west gallery is the oldest; among the carved capitals are fighting cockerels and Adam and Eve, while in the centre you'll find one of the cathedral's prizes, the **Pillar of the Evangelists**, carved with four column-like figures, the whole topped with a capital showing the Labours of the Months and signs of the Zodiac, although they're not easy to make out. Tombs, inscriptions and coats of arms line the walls, including one in the east gallery belonging to Canon Vital d'Ardengost, who died in 1334 and was given a pungent epitaph: *Hic jacet in tumba rosa mundi, non rosa munda, no redolet, set olet quod redolere solet*. (Here in the tomb lies a rose of the world, but no longer a rose intact. She no longer perfumes, but smells of what she should smell.)

The superb **choir stalls** were carved between 1523 and 1551 on the order of Jean de Mauléon, 52nd bishop of the Comminges. He hired a workshop of sculptors from Toulouse influenced by the Italian Renaissance. Inspired perhaps by the great choir stalls then under way at Auch, they expressed a large part of their humanistic view of the universe on the 66 stalls: wicked sins and somberly elegant religious and secular scenes intermingle with an imaginary bestiary. One of the most prominent stalls has an abbot caning a bare-bottomed monk. Along the top of the choir are the twelve Sibyls, prophets, Christian virtues, and knights (among them Roland and Oliver), and over the rood screen an intricate Tree of Jesse. Here and there you can make out Bishop Jean de Mauléon's motto, *Omnis amor tecum*,'All my love is for you', addressed to his beloved cathedral. Behind the high altar, a small chapel holds the tomb of St Bertrand, decorated with folksy 15th-century paintings from his life. The last scene shows Pope Clement V venerating the saint's relics; because of his importance, the painters made him as big as the Jolly Green Giant.

Upstairs, still off the right side of the nave, is the sacristy with the cathedral **treasury**. The two exquisite medieval copes are believed to have belonged to Clement V, who also donated what was long the cathedral's most precious valuable, the *alicorne*, a horn from a *narwhal* that was long believed to come from a unicorn. Any water that passed through the *alicorne* was considered a sure-fire antidote for any poisoned food eaten by man or beast. Medieval popes put a lot of faith in such talismans, and as Clement lay dying in Avignon from a stomach ache he must have wished he had kept his unicorn horn. Centuries later, Catherine de' Medici, a deep believer in every kind of juju and hocus-pocus on the market, coveted St-Bertrand's *alicorne* and did all she could to get her son Charles IX to add it to the royal treasury, without success. In 1594 a band of Huguenots under Corbeyran d'Aure stole it along with much of the cathedral treasure, but even Corbeyran feared the vengeance of St Bertrand, and he returned the alicorne in exchange for a complete amnesty for his theft. And it's in the treasury to this day.

In the easternmost chapel are three surviving 15th-century stained-glass windows, while around the choir on the left side of the nave, the Gothic **Chapelle Notre-Dame** contains the finely sculpted **tomb of Hugues de Châtillon**, the bishop who designed the chapel in the 14th century. The bishop's alabaster effigy sits atop a black marble slab, itself finely carved with some 70 figures in a funerary procession.

Around the Town

There are a number of fine old buildings here and there around the upper town, still enclosed behind its three gates (you'll drive through one as you leave the village car park; if you're in a van or a Cadillac, don't even try to squeeze through it, but reverse out of the entrance). One of the prettiest buildings of all, the 15th-century **Maison Bridault**, now houses the local post office.

Lugdunum Convenarum

To visit the excavations of Roman *Lugdunum Convenarum*, first check the opening hours with the tourist office, and then follow the road for Valcabrère. Since 1913, large sections – although hardly all – of the Roman town have been revealed amid more recent buildings. In the centre of *Lugdunum* (opposite the school building), the **Forum temple** with its impressive podium was built *c.* 15 AD and is believed to have been dedicated to the cult of Rome and the Emperor. As evidence of *Lugdunum*'s prosperity, originally a lavish covered portico, 24ft wide, enclosed the temple's *temenos* or sacred area. A courtyard separated the temple from the baths, or **Thermes du Forum**, built about the same period; you can make out the hot and cold rooms (*caldaria* and *frigi-*

Ste-Marie Cathedral

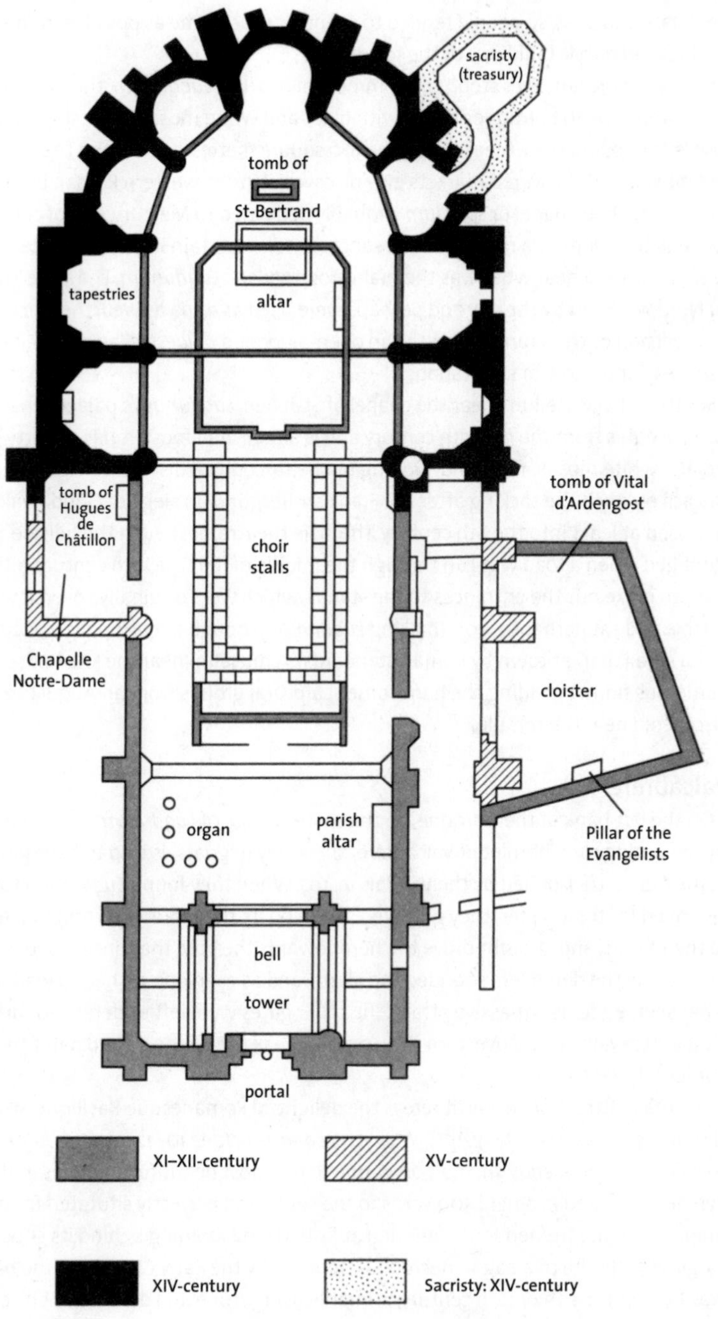

daria) and much of the plumbing. Bathing in Roman times was hardly the quick private affair it is today, but a long-drawn-out afternoon social ritual, a place to meet friends and talk business and politics. Most private houses or apartments at the time were dark and poky, so people tended to spend as much time as possible in the airy, marble-clad public buildings of the forum.

Across the present D26 stood the commercial heart of *Lugdunum*, the **market**, or *macellum*, with 26 boutiques paved with black and white mosaics – a 1st-century AD covered shopping mall. Measuring over 500 square metres, it is among the largest and most opulent covered markets ever discovered in the western Roman Empire. It had an attached chapel or *sacellum*, probably dedicated to Mercury, god of commerce. Towards the car park, a raised circular sanctuary of uncertain import has recently been unearthed near what was the main crossroads of *Lugdunum*. The large **Thermes du Nord** were run by the city and perhaps were used as a spa as well; they included an early version of the sauna, as well as an open-air pool, a *palaestra* (an open-air exercise area), and a row of small shops.

South of the Macellum, near the chapel of St-Julien, *Lugdunum*'s palaeochristian **Basilica** dates from the mid-5th century and is larger than most; it has a pretty green red and white mosaic floor, and, judging by the sarcophagi discovered here, the basilica escaped the sacking after the Frankish-Burgundian siege of Gondowald and was used at least into the 8th century. The little **theatre**, nestled in the hillside, was damaged when a road was run through the middle of it in the 18th century, although you can make out the entrances to the stands, which were originally covered with marble and sat perhaps 2,000 (making *Lugdunum*, though a metropolis in Gaul, still just a small market town by Roman standards). A **museum** near the site houses the numerous finds, including the handsome sculptural groups from an Augustan trophy discovered near the temple.

Valcabrère

On the left bank of the Garonne, on the eastern edge of *Lugdunum Convenarum*, the charming rural hamlet of Valcabrère, 'the valley of goats', is said to have got its name from a trick pulled by the Vandals in 407. When they found *Lugdunum* too well defended for their tastes, they gathered all the goats they could find and tied torches to their horns, and at night drove the herd towards the gate that once stood in Valcabrère. The defenders sounded the alarm, and as everyone rushed to ward off what seemed to be a massive attack, the other gates were left undefended for the Vandals to waltz in and overturn the wagons, break the windows and paint their names all over the walls.

The main attraction in Valcabrère is the delightful Romanesque **Basilique St-Just** (***t*** *05 61 95 49 06; open daily April–May 10–12 and 2–6, June 10–12 and 2–7, July and Aug 9–7; Oct–Mar weekends and hols only*), one of the most beautiful churches in the Pyrenees, isolated in a field 500 yards to the south and perfectly situtated for photographs with the tremendous cathedral at St-Bertrand looming behind its shoulder. Originally the site of a pagan necropolis, adapted by the early Christians, the basilica was built in the 11th or 12th century, primarily using stone and decorative bits cannibalized from *Lugdunum*; its importance yet relative isolation have led some scholars to guess that St-Just stands on the site of the first cathedral of *Lugdunum*, before St Bertrand arrived and built his new church on the other hill.

The square apse, with radiating polygonal chapels, is a lovely and unique essay in medieval geometry, as well as a veritable collage of Gallo-Roman bits; note the theatre mask embedded in the wall, and a relief of a supper party. The portal was inspired by the Roman models so near at hand, crowned with a tympanum showing Christ in majesty and the four Evangelists, while on the sides are marble column statues believed to represent SS. Just and Pastor, brothers martyred in Spain under Diocletian, as well as St Stephen. The fourth, a woman holding a cross, is believed to be St Helen; the capitals over their heads show various forms of martyrdom with vigour and relish. The interior, beautiful in its simplicity, has fine acoustics (classical music concerts take place here in the summer Festival de Comminges); note the re-use of antique columns and Roman and Merovingian capitals. A parchment discovered in the masonry of the high altar dates its consecration to October 1200. The sarcophagus behind it, sheltered under a Gothic ciborium, perhaps originally held the relics of St Just. Near the main entrance note the 4th-century Christian tombstone of a certain Valera Severa and two holy water stoups made from Roman columns.

South of St-Bertrand: Along the Garonne

The glacial valley of the 'laughing' Garonne offers a few tempting stops along the way to the mighty mountains of the Haute-Garonne. **Barbazan**, just across the river from Valcabrère, is an old spa trying to get back into the business; its water is rich in magnesium and calcium, and reputed for its digestive qualities. The Thermes building has recently been restored; see, too, the Baroque church with a gilded interior. In nearby **Sauveterre-de-Comminges**, you can visit and take home a souvenir puppet from L'Atelier des Marionnettes (*ring ahead*, **t** *05 61 88 36 04*).

More typically Pyrenean, perhaps, is the 11th-century church at **St-Pé-d'Ardet**, 15km south on the D33, decorated with excellent wall paintings by a 15th-century itinerant artist (if it's not open, the neighbour has the key). The altars to the right of the high altar were originally part of a Gallo-Roman temple. The road continues to the small lake of **Géry**, formed when the giant Gargas (*see* p.282) was walking through the valley and answered a gigantic call of nature.

St-Béat

Further south, squeezed in between the Cap det Mount and the Cap d'Ayre mountains, St-Béat has long been known as the 'Key to France'; any army from Spain marching down the narrow defile of the Garonne from the Val d'Aran would have to beat its way past St-Béat and its citadel, so naturally well defended that it could be held with only a handful of men. Another nickname, although this one doesn't always look so good on the tourist brochure, is 'the shadiest town in the Pyrenees'. It was the home of the ancient *Garunni*, the tribe who gave their name to the River Garonne; in 75 BC Pompey founded a fort here, which he called *Passus Lupi* (Wolf Step). While in the area, he might have noticed that the two mountains that enclose St-Béat were made of white marble. One massive vertical excavation in the flank of Cap det Mount is said to have been carried off to Rome to become Trajan's column; an altar discovered nearby, guarded by two ancient marble quarrymen, was dedicated to the gods of the wood and mountain for allowing them to extract such a sizable chunk without accident. Some of the mountain now decorates the garden of Versailles, but these days St-Béat can't keep up with the even whiter marble of Carrara. The tourist office can help if you want to visit the Roman quarries.

Not surprisingly, much of St-Béat is built of marble, including the donjon (now the town clocktower), all that remains of its once nearly impregnable 11th-century castle, and the Romanesque **church**, from the same century. It has a portal with a sculpted tympanum and carved capitals, while inside is a small museum with some fine Renaissance statues and the relics of St Privat. Nearby, note the houses overhanging the Garonne. Elsewhere in St-Béat, the **Maison Consulaire** in Rue Galliéni dates from 1553; it inspired the balcony scene in Rostand's *Cyrano de Bergerac*. The street is named after Maréchal Joseph-Simon Galliéni, who was born here in 1849 and went on to serve the Third Republic's colonial ambitions in Indochina, Madagascar and Senegal, and who, as his last great act for the *patrie*, was instrumental in 1914 in rounding up Paris taxis to transport troops to the front in the Battle of the Marne; his statue stands on the right bank.

East of St-Béat, the **Col de Mente** sounds like a green drink but is actually a lovely pass (1,349m/4,425ft), reached by enough hairpin bends to make a ringlet. It is the perfect place to begin a walk for people who like easy strolls in the mountains; a sweet and easy shepherds' path begins by the refuge and leads up in an hour to a second shepherds' hut with superb views down to St-Béat, the Garonne valley and the peaks rimming the frontier around Luchon, including Maladetta, the highest of them all (3,404m/11,168ft). Rather than backtrack, you can make a scenic loop by taking the D618 back around over the Col des Ares.

The Upper Comminges: Bagnères-de-Luchon and its Valleys

The 'Queen of the Pyrenees', Bagnères-de-Luchon, or just Luchon as everyone calls it, wears two different hats: as France's fourth (some say fifth) largest spa and as a favourite base for walking, canoeing, skiing, paragliding and a host of other sports in the mountains. Set in a sunny amphitheatre on the river One, surrounded by the highest peaks of the Pyrenees and a web of luscious emerald valleys, Luchon began its career under Tiberius in 25 AD as the Baths of Ilixo, named after the Celtic god of hot springs. It was not only the local spa for *Lugdunum Convenarum* (St-Bertrand-de-Comminges), but one whose hot springs, rich in sulphur and sodium, attracted rheumatic Romans from across the Empire. After the various invaders literally wiped it off the map, Luchon's hot waters went to waste for over 1,000 years until 1759, when Antoine Mégret, Baron d'Etigny and *Intendant* of Gascony, Béarn and Navarre,

Getting There and Around

Both **trains** and **buses** pull in at the *gare*, just over the river from the centre. All come by way of Montréjeau, with connections to Lourdes, Tarbes and Toulouse. For information, call **t** 05 61 79 03 36.

Tourist Information

Bagnères-de-Luchon: 18 Allée d'Etigny, **t** 05 61 79 21 21, **f** 05 61 79 11 23, *www.luchon.com. Open daily 9–12 and 2–7; July–Aug open daily 9–7; closed weekends in Nov.*

Market Days

Bagnères-de-Luchon: Wednesday and Saturday mornings, daily in July and August.

Where to Stay and Eat

Bagnères-de-Luchon ✉ 31110

Luchon claims a pair of powerful specialities you may want to watch out for if you eat out here: *pétéram*, a stew made of ham and sheep's tripe and trotters, and *pistache*, mutton braised in wine and vegetables and 50 cloves of garlic.

******Corneille**, 5 Av A. Dumas, **t** 05 61 79 36 22, **f** 05 61 79 81 11, *www.hotel-corneille.com* (*expensive–moderate*). At this handsome 19th-century hotel set in a lovely garden on the edge of Luchon, you'll find tranquil rooms and a restaurant. Has been taken over by Best Western chain. *Menus €19–33.*

****Hotel d'Etigny**, 3 Av Paul Bonnemasion, **t** 05 61 79 01 42, **f** 05 61 79 80 64 (*expensive–moderate*). Opposite the baths, this is a solid, atmospheric, old-fashioned place with a restaurant. *Menus €15–20. Open May–Oct.*

Jardin des Cascades, near the church of Montauban-de-Luchon, east of Luchon, **t** 05 61 79 83 09 (*inexpensive*). Here you'll find a few double rooms, enchanting views from the dining terrace and excellent preparations of traditional dishes, although they don't come cheap. The restaurant's always packed, so book. *Menus lunch €19 and about €38 for à la carte. Closed mid-Oct–mid-Mar.*

***Des Deux Nations**, 5 Rue Victor-Hugo, **t** 05 61 79 01 71, **f** 05 61 79 27 89 (*inexpensive–cheap*). Quiet, yet central and an old favourite, this hotel-restaurant is run by a friendly family, who are also more than competent in the kitchen. *Menus €14–29, huge portions. Restaurant closed Sun eves, and all day Mon in Nov, Dec, Jan and Mar.*

Hôtel des Neiges, 27 Rue Victor Hugo, **t** 05 61 79 00 02 (*inexpensive–cheap*). This well-priced option has a garden. *Closed Nov.*

François Ier, 1 Allée d'Etigny, **t** 05 61 94 89 89, **f** 05 61 94 89 90 (*inexpensive–cheap*). This is also a low-priced option and is open all year. Part of *brasserie* on the main boulevard. *Closed 1 week in Oct and 1 week in April.*

***La Petite Auberge**, 15 Rue Lamartine, **t** 05 61 79 02 88 (*inexpensive–cheap*). Also has a very reasonably priced restaurant. Rooms are bright, clean and comfortable with new bathrooms. *Menus €14. Closed Nov–mid-Dec.*

La Lanette, just east of Luchon at Montauban-de-Luchon. This camp site is one of the best of the many in the area, with trees and lovely views.

Around Luchon ✉ 31110

Hostellerie des Spijeolles, Oô, **t** 05 61 79 06 05 (*inexpensive*). Situated in this quiet village, the hotel has a handful of rooms and a restaurant. Very simple. *Menu €15. Closed the end of June and 1–15 Nov.*

Auberge d'Astau, 4km from Oô, **t** 05 61 79 19 34, *www.astaupyrenees.com* (*inexpensive*). Very simple auberge in a beautiful setting, ideally placed for the trek up to the Lac d'Oô. Bedrooms are in a modern annexe.

****L'Esquerade**, Castillon-de-Larboust, **t** 05 61 79 19 64, **f** 05 61 79 26 29, *www.esquarade.com* (*inexpensive*). A handsome old mountain inn, set in the lush green valley. Opt for the *demi-pension* scheme, or just stop by to eat. *Menus €15–58. Restaurant closed Mon, Wed and Tues lunch plus Fri in winter. Hotel closed April and mid-Nov–mid-Dec.*

****Le Sapin Fleuri**, Bourg d'Ouell, **t** 05 61 79 21 90, **f** 05 61 79 85 87, *www.hotelsapin-fleuri.com* (*inexpensive*). At 1,400m/4,620ft, this comfortable little Logis de France chalet hotel is in a magnificent setting. *Menus €15–35. Closed 10 Oct–26 Dec.*

decided it was time to do as the Romans did and revive the genteel custom of taking the waters. He built the road down from Montréjeau and persuaded the governor of Languedoc, the influential Duke of Richelieu (great-nephew of the famous Cardinal) to take a cure. The duke found it simply marvellous, and especially liked picking out Roman artefacts that were then scattered about everywhere. He did the baron the supreme favour of telling everyone at Versailles what a good time he had in Luchon, and before long an entire *Who's Who* of Europe had descended upon Luchon, from Flaubert and Louis Napoléon to Bismarck and Mata Hari.

Luchon

Luchon (locally pronounced Lootch-ON) is a bustling modern town, but the gilded days when its spa hosted princes, politicians, literati and spies have left a burnished glow, especially along the elegant Allée d'Etigny, laid out in 1759 by the baron whose name it bears. Lined with lime trees, grand old hotels, restaurants and cafés, it culminates in the lovely **Parc des Quinconces**, with its catalpas and tulip trees planted in quincunxes (like fives on a dice) and Luchon's **Thermes** (1849). In 1973, a natural cave sauna and hot pool called the **Vaporarium** was added to the baths complex; the vapours are apparently good for respiratory ailments, and singers, preachers and lawyers form a large part of the clientele. The sauna attracts thousands of *curistes* a day in the summer (as in Dax, French national health reimbursements have something to do with this). One of Baron d'Etigny's innovations at Luchon was having doctors on duty at the spa, but the first pioneering patients could hardly have felt like up-to-date Romans. In 1787 Arthur Young visited and wrote: 'The present baths are horrible holes; the patients lie up to their chins in hot sulphurous water, which, with the beastly dens they are placed in, one would think sufficent to cause as many distempers as they cure.' A French writer from the same period mentioned that the hot waters attracted hundreds of snakes, which were a bit of a nuisance slithering about when one was naked in the bath.

Luchon has a second public garden, the **Parc du Casino**, with exotic trees and shrubs and a lake; both of Luchon's gardens are famous for their large population of marble ladies and gents. When wallowing in pungent water, strolling past the statues and lounging around in the cafés begins to pale, you can take in the atmospheric municipal attic called the **Musée du Vieux Luchon** (*18 Allée d'Etigny,* **t** *05 61 79 29 87; open daily all year except bank hols 9–12 and 2–6*) and learn about the early days of mountaineering, speleology and *thermalisme* through old photos, memorabilia of celebrity visitors (including the flamboyant Count Henry Russell and Edmond Rostand, author of *Cyrano de Bergerac,* who spent much of his youth here), traditional rural gear, a few Roman bits and bobs, a small hermaphrodite Celtic god, a display of the Romanesque churches in the surrounding valleys (the photos from the Vall d'Aran in Spain may well tempt you over the border for a closer look), stuffed animals and birds, and some of the tools used by the legendary Pyrenean explorer and speleologist, Norbert Casteret.

The Valleys Around Luchon

Exploring the majestic high-altitude scenery that surrounds Luchon can take up an entire holiday. Of the classic excursions, perhaps the most classic is to the Port de Venasque, beginning at the top of the superb Vallée de la Pique, lined with forests of silver firs and beech trees – unfortunately, many ill from the worst acid rain problem in the Pyrenees. From the end of the D125 it's a 30-min walk up to the **Hospice de France** (1,385m/4,570ft), founded by the Knights Hospitallers in the Middle Ages to shelter wayfarers or the occasional pilgrim who passed this way; these days it's a popular family picnic destination. To make it to the 2,448m/8,078ft **Port de Venasque** on the Spanish border and back, get to the Hospice early in the morning and count on at least a 6-hr march past forests, waterfalls and pastures. The reward: the unforgettable view from Port de Venasque of the looming rock-bound massif called **Maladetta**, the 'accursed mountains', a jagged, 6km-long, glacier-crowned spine, reaching 3,404m/11,168ft at Aneto, the highest peak in the Pyrenees. In the 19th century, visitors to Luchon thrilled to the dark legends surrounding Maladetta, said to be responsible for more deaths than any other mountain in the Pyrenees. One story relates how shepherds on Maladetta refused to help two poor pilgrims (Jesus and St Peter, in disguise) and were turned into stone with all their sheep – a story believed into the 18th century, the mayor of one village counting 7,000 'petrified people and sheep'. Others tell how countless other shepherds, working men and mountain guides have been entombed in its rocky embrace, under avalanches, or at the bottom of its lakes, lured there by *fadas* or sirens. The locals held the peaks of Maladetta in such awe that it fell to foreigners with piquant names (Wilhelm von Parrot and Platon de Tcihatcheff) to be the first to scale their highest peaks. Linguists, for their part, say the whole thing is baloney, that the *Mala* in its name is simply an old word for 'mountain'.

The Spanish village of **Venasque** (by road the easiest way to get there is by way of St-Béat) is so remote from the rest of Spain that through the Franco years it was the only place where you could hear the *Marcha de Riego*, the national anthem of Republican Spain.

Branching off from the Vallée de la Pique, the D46 follows the Vallée du Lys (or more properly, the Bat de Lys, the 'valley of avalanches'), carved by glaciers with a rare symmetry; both sides of the valley are nearly equal in shape and size. Along the way you can peer down an abyss, the **Gouffre Richard**, then take the road up to the ski resort, **Superbagnères**, 18km from Luchon (take the D125 and D46), with superb views; there's an orientation table by the Grand Hotel. Best of all, continue up the main road past the hydroelectric plant to the **Cirque de Lys** and its **Cascade d'Enfer**, a waterfall splashing through a narrow cleft in the rocks that could pass for the gate of hell. The gentler, more pastoral Vallée d'Oueil northwest of Luchon (take the D618 and D51) has a church with colourful 15th-century murals at **Benque-Dessous-et-Dessus** (they're in the upper church). Further up the road, a belvedere called the Kiosque de Mayrègne offers a panoramic view and a chance for refreshments; **Cirès**, a charming mountain village, lies below **Bourg d'Oueil**, a resort popular with cross-country skiers.

One of the most popular excursions is up the Vallée d'Oô (take the D618 and turn on the D76), passing by way of St-Aventin, 5km from Luchon. Perched high on its promontory, and a good 100-yard walk up a steep slope from the road, **St-Aventin** is a 12th-century gem with two beautiful bell towers and a tympanum carved with a *Christ in Majesty* and an excellent *Virgin and Child*. The capitals are finely carved as well, with the *Massacre of the Innocents*, the *Washing of the Feet* and, curiously, a bear; according to the story, Aventin, an 8th-century hermit, was a protector of bears, to the extent that they would come to him to have thorns removed from their paws. A number of Gallo-Roman blocks were reused to build the church, most strikingly the three monuments embedded in the south wall. Inside, the stoup is a remarkable pre-Romanesque work, decorated with the lamb of Christ, little fish (the newly baptized) and doves (the souls of the blessed). The lacy choir screen is a fine example of Pyrenean iron work, and around Aventin's tomb are more sculpted capitals, one showing the saint helping a bear, the other showing him holding his head after the Moors lopped it off. The murals from the 12th century found under the plaster show St Sernin, patron of Toulouse, with St Aventin.

At Castillon, the road forks; take the left along the Neste (another word for 'river') d'Oô, which is drivable as far as the **Granges d'Astau** (1,139m/3,736ft). There you can pick up the GR 10, passing the silvery waterfall known as the Chevelure de Madeleine, for its resemblance to the Magdalen's flowing hair. The track continues up, taking about an hour in all, to the stunningly azure **Lac d'Oô**, the loveliest of a pocket of glacier lakes, set in nearly lunar surroundings. In the background, a 900ft waterfall from the lake of Espingo adds to the setting, and if you're feeling energetic, you can walk up to Espingo, or continue even further up to the spectacular Lac du Portillon; there are *refuges* at both lakes.

The Larboust and West Towards the Vallée de Louron

West of Luchon, the **Vallée de Larboust** leads up to the Col de Peyresourde, one of the highest passes in the Pyrenees, linking the Comminges to the Vallée de Louron (*see* p.280). Larboust is still relatively densely populated for a high valley in the Pyrenees, and it was one of the final valleys to be inhabited by Cagots, the last of whom died in the early 20th century (*see* **Culture**, pp.52–4). Just after the turn-off for the Vallée d'Oô, on the D618, **Cazaux** has a church with a remarkable late medieval mural of the *Last Judgement*, discovered in the last century under the plaster by a local painter. The iconography is unique: the Christ is shown sitting atop a solid rainbow, not in stern triumph or majesty, but with the bleeding wounds of the Passion. On his right, the Virgin Mary pleads for mercy, but intercedes in a most unusual way: she bares her breasts and squirts milk on her son's wounds. Another scene shows Adam dozing away during the Creation of Woman, and the Temptation of St Anthony. Unfortunately, the church is usually locked because of a theft, but the Luchon tourist office may help you locate the key. A bit further on, high on the left-hand side of the road, there's another fine Romanesque chapel, **St-Pé**, made out of Roman tombstones. At the top of the Col de Peyresourde are two fairly ugly but excellent ski resorts, **Peyragudes** and **Les Agudes**.

St-Gaudens and North of the Garonne: the Petites Pyrénées

For 90 per cent of people travelling in the region, bedazzled by the beauty of the Pyrenees, the area north and west of the Garonne of the baby mountains, or 'Petites Pyrénées', is *terra incognita*. Yet these rolling hills of the Comminges were beloved in antiquity and have seemingly changed little since: remarkably intact landscapes, unspoiled by billboards, subdivisions, and all the other detritus of our times. The departmental roads are still lined on either side with ancient plane trees, rare in the rest of France, where one or both sides are sacrificed to road-widening schemes. Here there's not enough traffic to bother.

St-Gaudens

Busy St-Gaudens, with a population of 13,000 and the big factory of Cellulose d'Aquitaine, is the metropolis in these parts. It offers a striking contrast to the Petites Pyrénées and would be a perfect point of departure for visiting them, if you can manage to escape the infernal circle of its road system, which has been designed with inscrutable Gallic logic.

St-Gaudens is named after a 12-year-old shepherd boy, who (the pious story says) met a band of Moorish cavalrymen who demanded that he convert to Islam. Like a good boy, young Gaudens asked his mother if it was all right, but she said no. The Moors then chopped off his head, but like so many regional saints his body still had the panache to pick it up, and with the wicked Moors in hot pursuit, he ran with it all the way to the safety of the nearest church. No wonder Gascons make such good rugby players.

The most important church, however, is the **Collégiale St-Pierre-de-St-Gaudens**, in Place Jean-Jaurès, with a great square bell tower (containing the biggest carillon in the Midi-Pyrénées) and a flamboyant Gothic portal from the 17th century. Walk around the sides to see the modillons, the capitals from the cloister on the south end, and various Roman bits embedded in the walls. Along the nave, 18th-century tapestries from Aubusson illustrate the *Martyrdom of St Gaudens*, the *Transfiguration* and the *Triumph of Faith*, and the 17th-century choir stalls and organ are worth a glance. Best of all are the unusual sculpted capitals around the choir, carved by sculptors from Navarre or Aragon: bears fight, monkeys make faces, Adam seems to gag on the forbidden fruit, King Nebuchadnezzar is turned into a beast, and people queue up under the palms, perhaps to be baptized.

Just east of the Collégiale, the **Musée du Comminges** (***t*** *05 61 89 05 42; open all year Tues–Sat 9–12 and 2–6*) has an interesting ensemble of traditional tools, costumes and domestic items, local minerals, medieval manuscripts, and memorabilia related to the three great military men from the Pyrenees: Foch (from Tarbes), Joffre (from Rivesaltes, in the eastern Pyrenees) and Galliéni (from St-Béat). The three are also the

Getting There and Around

St-Gaudens is the transport centre for the region, with **train** connections (**t** 05 62 00 78 73) to Toulouse and Luchon, and TER **bus** connections to Montréjeau, Lannemezan, Tarbes and Lourdes, as well as to Luchon and Martres-Tolosane.

Tourist Information

St-Gaudens: 2 Rue Thiers, **t** 05 61 94 77 61, **f** 05 61 94 77 50. *Open 1 July–15 Sept Mon–Sat 9–7; the rest of the year 9–12 and 1.30–6.*

Boulogne-sur-Gesse: Place de l'Hôtel de Ville, **t** 05 61 88 13 19, *www.citaenet.com/boulogne-sur-gesse. Open daily in the summer except Sun; winter open Tues–Sat 9–12.*

L'Isle-en-Dodon: **t** 05 61 94 53 56. *Open all year Mon–Sat 9–12 and 2–6.*

Aurignac: Rue des Nobles, **t** 05 61 98 70 06, **f** 05 61 98 71 33. *Open July and Aug daily 9.30–12.30 and 2–6; the rest of the year Mon–Fri 9–12 and 1.30–6.* Ask at the *Mairie* **t** 05 61 98 90 08.

St-Martory: *mairie*, Place de la Poste, **t** 05 61 97 40 48, **f** 05 61 90 23 03. *Open Tues–Sat, 2–6.*

Salies-du-Salat: Boulevard Jean-Jaurès, **t** 05 61 90 53 93, **f** 05 61 90 47 43, *www.salinea.free.fr/salies-salat. Open Oct–April Mon–Thurs 10–12 and 2–6, Fri until 5; May, June and Sept Mon–Fri 10–12 and 3–6 plus Sat 10–12 and 3–5; July and Aug Mon–Fri 10–1 and 2.30–6.30 plus Sat 10–1 and 2.30–5.30.*

Martres-Tolosane: *mairie*, **t** 05 61 98 66 41. *Open all year Mon–Fri 9.30–12.30 and 1.30–5.30, Sat and Sun from 10.*

Market Days

St-Gaudens: Thursdays veal market.
Boulogne-sur-Gesse: Wednesdays.
L'Isle-en-Dodon: Saturdays.
Aurignac: Tuesdays.
Salies-du-Salat: Mondays.

Where to Stay and Eat

St-Gaudens ✉ 31800

★★★**Hostellerie des Cèdres**, just outside St-Gaudens in Villeneuve de Rivière, **t** 05 61 89 36 00, **f** 05 61 88 31 04, *www.hotel-descedres.com* (*moderate*). Set in a large park, the building formerly belonged to the Marquise de Montespan, Louis XIV's mistress. Rooms are elegantly furnished with antiques, and there is a pool, tennis courts and a fitness room. The restaurant specializes in various veal dishes of which the marquise would have approved. *Menus €22–37. Open all year. Closed Mon lunch out of season.*

★★**Pedussaut**, 9 Av de Boulogne, **t** 05 61 89 15 70, **f** 05 61 89 11 26 (*inexpensive–cheap*). Recently renovated, this hotel has an excellent restaurant, serving good-value menus

subject of the **Monument des Trois Maréchaux**, near St-Gaudens' belvedere, located just across Boulevard Bepmale from the museum. Near here, in the Jardin Publique, the elegant twin-columned gallery once adorned the cloister of the abbey of Bonnefont (*see* below).

Montmaurin: Roman Indolence North of St-Gaudens

It's 16km on the D9 north of St-Gaudens to the banks of the river Save and Montmaurin, where the well-preserved **Gallo-Roman Villa** (**t** *05 61 88 74 73; open daily May–Sept 9.30–12 and 2–6, Oct–April closes at 5 plus Tues; adm*) stands in bucolic splendour on the crest of a hill – a setting little changed since Roman times. In the 1st century a rich man named Nepotianus, owner of the surrounding 7,000 hectares (*see* p.146 for an idea of how the other half lived in Roman Gaul) built himself a typical country estate, with all the farm outbuildings. At some point the Save flooded and covered it irredeemably in muck, but by the 4th century Nepotianus' heirs were ready chock full of regional ingredients. *Menus €12–32. Restaurant closed Sun in winter. Closed one week at the end of Dec beginning of Jan.*

Restaurant de l'Abattoir, Bd Leconte de l'Isle, **t** 05 61 89 70 29. St-Gaudens is famous throughout France for its white veal, and it and any number of high-quality meats are prepared here at a genuine carnivore's oasis, located just opposite you know what. *Menus €12–21. Closed Sun and bank hols.*

Montmaurin ✉ 31350

Caso Nuosto, in the woods not far from the Roman villa, **t** 05 61 88 25 50 (*inexpensive*). This place offers three *chambres d'hôte* in a restored old farmhouse, with a pool and garden. Table d'hôte also available specializing in regional cuisine using the farm's produce. *Menus €14 and €16. Open all year.*

Boulogne-sur-Gesse ✉ 31350

Ferme–Auberge du Péguilhan, Péguilhan, **t** 05 61 88 75 78 (*inexpensive*). Located in an old half-timbered farmhouse, this hotel-restaurant serves delicious stuffed lamb shoulder, *poule au pot* and other tasty home-grown fare, and is one of the very few *ferme-auberges* to offer a vegetarian menu if you order ahead. *Menus €11–23. Open daily all year by reservation only.*

Restaurant La Ferme de Préville, on the road to Auch, **t** 05 61 88 23 12 (*cheap*). Pleasant restaurant offering traditional, hearty menus at €14 for lunch and €23–35 in the evening. *Closed Tues and Sat lunch all year, from Oct–April also closed Mon, Thurs and Sun eves.*

Aurignac/Alan ✉ 31420

Notre-Dame de Lorette, Alan, **t** 05 61 98 98 84, *www.notredamedelorette.com* (*inexpensive*). For something different, two magnificent *chambres d'hôte* have been installed in this 18th-century hospital, one in the old pharmacy, the other next to a fireplace large enough to roast a camel. Gîtes only.

****Le Cerf Blanc**, Aurignac, **t** 05 61 98 95 76, **f** 05 61 89 76 80 (*inexpensive–cheap*). The hotel is well-equipped and open year round, and also has a good restaurant featuring regional cooking. *Menus €24–50. Restaurant closed Sun eves and Mon except July–Sept.*

Salies-de-Salat ✉ 31260

***Hotel Central**, 1 Av de la Gare, **t** 05 61 90 50 01 (*inexpensive–cheap*). This may be the only hotel-restaurant in town, but it's a pleasant little place. *Menus €11–28. Closed Fri eve and Sat lunch Nov–Mar, plus 1–15 Sept.*

St-Martory ✉ 31360

Ferme-Auberge Auzas, near the centre of the village, **t** 05 61 90 23 61. This restaurant is open all year, but by reservation only. It serves its own farm lamb, foie gras, *confits* and delicious home-made bread. *Menu €14. Can also provide simple chambres d'hôte for €38.*

to rebuild. Their pretensions had outgrown a mere agricultural manor: nothing would do but a white marble palace fit for a prince, or at least a Hollywood mogul, with 200 rooms, complete with its own private baths, shady porticoes, gardens, fountains, temple, swimming pool, heated dining rooms, summer and winter apartments with terraces and views – a self-contained *villa urbana*, a pleasure dome isolated not only from the city but from its own agricultural domains. It's the largest and most luxurious Gallo-Roman villa ever discovered in France; the mountains of oyster shells the archaeologists turned up confirmed the *dolce vita* led by its residents. In the 5th century the villa burned down and was abandoned and buried in the mud. In the centre of Montmaurin village, a **museum** (*same hours and tickets*) in the *mairie* contains a scale model of the villa and a collection of Roman and prehistoric finds from the area, including a cast of the celebrated fat lady from the Aurignacian period, the Vénus de Lespugue, found in the nearby Grotte des Rideaux by the Countess of St-Périer in 1922, and now in the Musée de l'Homme in Paris.

Around Montmaurin: along the Save and Gesse Rivers

Anyone who has been along the river Vézère in the Dordogne will recognize the nearby **Gorges du Save** along the D69c as just the kind of place to warm the cockles of prehistoric hearts, pocked with caves and natural rock shelters; a number of grottoes here have yielded not only the Venus but other interesting finds. At **La Hillère**, just outside Montmaurin, the cemetery chapel has a beautiful mosaic with a swastika – an ancient sun symbol – left over from a 4th-century sanctuary by a spring. **Lespugue** further down-river controlled much of this area; you can explore the striking ruins of its 13th-century castle, dramatically balanced on the lip of a ravine. In 1913 an experimental botanical forest, the **Forêt de Cardeilhac**, was planted east of Larroque, to see what sort of trees from around the world would adjust to the climate; part of it's now a public arboretum and a pretty place for a stroll.

Hill Towns of the Petites Pyrénées

North of Montmaurin, **Boulogne-sur-Gesse** began its career as a *bastide* in 1282, founded by the king and abbot of the nearby Cistercian abbey of Nizors, who named the new town after his university, Bologna. The main square is closed in by arcades and old houses, and the old *halles* in the centre is now the *mairie*.

Boulogne-sur-Gesse is only the largest of a fine set of *villages perchés* in this corner of the Petites Pyrénées, touching on the western confines of the Lannemezan Plateau. The most spectacular, **Mondilhan**, 9km to the northeast, sits on the highest hill around and enjoys an extraordinary, magical view of the big Pyrenees that on a clear day ranges 250 kilometres; the view from nearby **Péguilhan** is almost as good. Southeast of Boulogne and back over the Save, Ciadoux and Escanecrabe also crown the hills; **Ciadoux** has an excellent life-size 16th-century *mise au tombeau* in its church, the figures carved in stone (*pick up the key at the café*), while **Escanecrabe** (it sounds like 'Is can of crab?' but apparently means Goat Hill after the steepness of its slopes) offers a fortified 14th-century **church** with an octagonal tower typical of the Toulouse region, and has another lovely panorama of the Pyrenees, with the river Save in the foreground. Lastly, follow the tree-lined D17 north along the Save to **L'Isle-en-Dodon**, another *bastide* town with an arcaded square, well worth a halt for its fortified red brick **church** and handsome octagonal bell tower, both from the 14th century, and gorgeous Renaissance stained-glass windows in the choir made by the school of Arnaud de Moles.

Northeast of St-Gaudens and into the Aurignacian Era

The St-Marcet natural gas field north of St-Gaudens, discovered back in 1939, was responsible for many of the jobs in the area. The gas has been sucked nearly dry now, but the pleasant village of **St-Marcet**, 10 kilometres north of St-Gaudens, carries on regardless, with one of the oldest *halles* in the region and ruins of the 12th-century castle of the Counts of Comminges sitting on a nearby hill.

When the counts were bored there they could hop over to the pretty medieval village of **Aurignac**, gathered around the skirts of another castle of theirs, built in 1240; you can climb up the surviving donjon for the view of the Pyrenees. The church has a flamboyant Gothic portal and porch, framed by twisted barley-sugar columns left over from a previous church; above are figures of the Virgin and Child from the 17th century, and one of Christ awaiting death from the 15th.

In 1852, a labourer digging along the road to Boulogne-sur-Gesse came upon a cache of skeletons tucked under a rock shelter. No one was too surprised; the locals had often found skeletons in their fields from the murderous Wars of Religion and the bones were dutifully gathered and reburied in the local cemetery. In 1870, a palaeontologist in the Gers, named Edouard Lartet, heard of the discovery and came over to investigate, and found enough bones and ancient tools to theorize that perhaps the traditional, biblical chronologies of the creation of man then current were not quite accurate. His hunch was confirmed in 1888, when railworkers at Cro-Magnon (near Les Eyzies) found similar skeletons, and since 1906, the first ten millennia of the Upper Palaeolithic era (30,000–20,000 BC) have been known as the Aurignacian era. Although Aurignac's most important finds are in the National Museum at St-Germain-en-Laye near Paris, the local **Musée de la Préhistoire** (*Rue Fernand-Lacorre,* ***t*** *05 61 98 70 06; open July–Aug daily 10–12 and 2–6, the rest of the year open Mon–Fri 9–12 and 2–6*) contains local finds, including animal bones and tools – the interesting personal collection of prehistorian Fernand Lacorre, who studied the shelter at Aurignac in the 1930s.

Just because their cathedral was down in St-Bertrand-de-Comminges, it didn't mean the bishops of Comminges had to spend all their time there. In 1270, they petitioned the Counts of Toulouse to let them build a winter palace halfway between St-Bertrand and Toulouse, at the old *bastide* hilltown of **Alan**, 5 kilometres east of Aurignac. The **Palais des Evêques de Comminges** (***t*** *05 61 98 90 72; open end of June–end of Sept Sat 3–6 and Sun, 10–12 and 3–6; rest of the year, by appointment only; adm*) remained a favourite residence over the next five centuries, although the building is marked most by the taste of Bishop De Foix-Grailly who, in 1470, converted a feudal castle into a flamboyant Gothic palace. The magnificent portal has a striking cow carved on the tympanum – the cow of Béarn from the bishop's own coat of arms, although it has always been known as the cow of Alan. Inside the portal, much of the palace has been carried off bit by bit by 20th-century antique collectors, but it's still impressive to see the scale to which a medieval bishop could aspire, and there are fine views from the top floor. In 1784, just before the Revolution and the end of the bishopric of the Comminges, Bishop du Bouchet built the handsome **Hôpital Notre-Dame-de-Lorette** (a kilometre away) to care for the people of the local parish. It's one of the rare French classical buildings in these parts, and usually open on Sundays if you want a look at its monumental stair, pharmacy, chapel and courtyard.

Down the Garonne from St-Gaudens Towards Toulouse

Few towns in France have been inhabited as long as **St-Martory**, where human bones found in the caves and shelters go back 240,000 years. Although not the most exciting of towns, it produced Norbert Casteret (*see* p.294) and has a 12th-century medieval castle and **church** with a menhir and Gallo-Roman stele by its side, and a Romanesque door from the nearby Cistercian **abbey of Bonnefont**. This once-proud

12th-century abbey founded priories and *bastides* in France and Spain, and served as the burial place of all the Counts of Comminges. Nevertheless, after the Revolution Bonnefont was broken to bits and auctioned off, its cloister divided between St-Gaudens, Nice and New York, while its chapterhouse was moved to the west end of St-Martory to be used as a *gendarmerie*, of all things. Now even the cops have vanished.

St-Martory has a an attractive **18th-century bridge** over the Garonne, which you should take for **Montsaunes**, once the site of the most important commandery of the Knights Templars in southwest France. Nothing remains, although the fortified 12th-century brick Romanesque **church** they built has some excellent carvings over its north and west portals of scenes from the childhood of Christ, including one referring to an apocryphal story of the blind wife who miraculously regains her sight on washing the newborn Infant – a common theme in Eastern church art, but one rarely seen in the West. There are paintings of holy and not-so-holy scenes, and symbols inside include six-pointed stars, wheels and crisscrossed circles. A bit further on, **Salies-du-Salat** is a little spa village in the Salat valley that enjoys an exceptionally sunny microclimate. Romans came to bathe in its salty waters, '*la plus minéralisée d'Europe!*', now installed in a curious Neo-Egyptian Art Deco spa building, built in 1898 and remodelled in 1924. A ruined donjon, all that survives of the 12th-century castle of the counts of Comminges, stands over the town like a big stone thumb.

There are famous views over the Pyrenees due north of **Belbèze-en-Comminges** and the hamlet of **Ausseing**; take the panoramic D83, which noodles back down to the Garonne and **Martres-Tolosane**, where the Petites Pyrénées give way to the great plain of the Garonne. In the old centre, the **Musée Archéologique Municipal** (*Rue du Donjon, **t** 05 61 98 66 41; open July and Aug daily 9.30–12.30 and 1.30–5.30, the rest of the year see tourist office*) contains a large assortment of busts and sculptures found in the Gallo-Roman villas that once surrounded Martres-Tolosane, most notably at Chiragan (many are copies of the originals in the Musée St-Raymond in Toulouse). The 14th-century brick **church**, dedicated to the town's patron, St Vidan, has an octagonal bell tower, and among the marble sarcophagi inside is one belonging to the saint who was killed in combat against the Moors in the 8th century; the battle is annually reproduced with considerably pageantry on the first Sunday after Pentecost. Since the 16th century, **Martres** has been synonymous with ceramics, although the unique local style of decoration, known as 'meadow flowers', dates only from the 19th century. Two potteries still make it in Martres and welcome visitors during working hours; the tourist office has details.

Toulouse

11

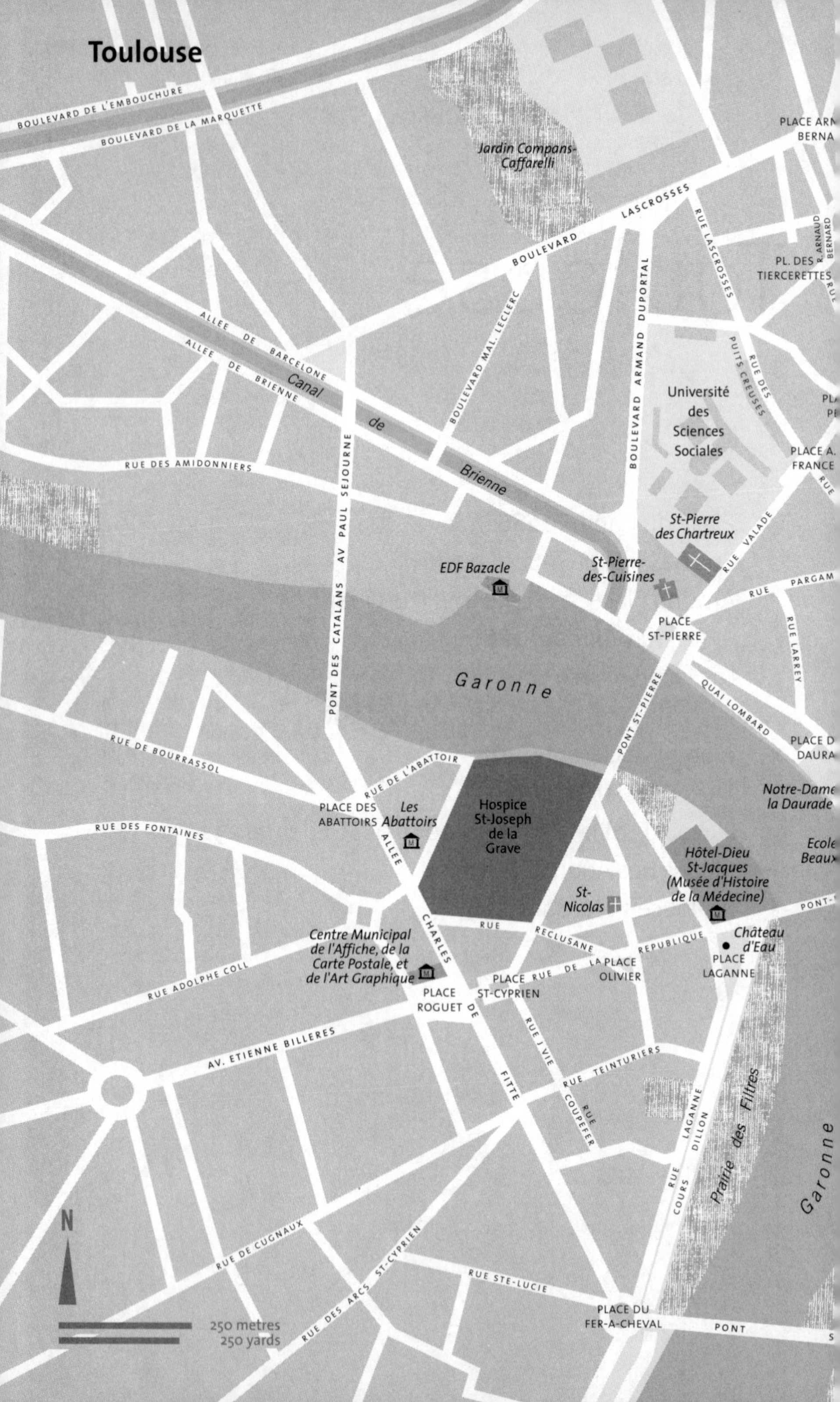
Toulouse
BOULEVARD DE L'EMBOUCHURE
BOULEVARD DE LA MARQUETTE
Jardin Compans-Caffarelli
BOULEVARD LASCROSSES
RUE LASCROSSES
PL. DES TIERCERETTES
ALLEE DE BARCELONE
ALLEE DE BRIENNE
Canal de Brienne
BOULEVARD MAL. LECLERC
BOULEVARD ARMAND DUPORTAL
Université des Sciences Sociales
RUE DES PUITS CREUSES
PLACE A. FRANCE
RUE DES AMIDONNIERS
PONT DES CATALANS AV PAUL SEJOURNE
St-Pierre des Chartreux
RUE VALADE
EDF Bazacle
St-Pierre-des-Cuisines
PLACE ST-PIERRE
RUE LARREY
Garonne
PONT ST-PIERRE
QUAI LOMBARD
RUE DE BOURRASSOL
RUE DE L'ABATTOIR
PLACE DES ABATTOIRS
Les Abattoirs
Hospice St-Joseph de la Grave
Notre-Dame la Daurade
RUE DES FONTAINES
ALLEE CHARLES DE FITTE
St-Nicolas
Hôtel-Dieu St-Jacques (Musée d'Histoire de la Médecine)
RUE RECLUSANE
RUE DE LA REPUBLIQUE
Château d'Eau
Centre Municipal de l'Affiche, de la Carte Postale, et de l'Art Graphique
PLACE OLIVIER
PLACE LAGANNE
RUE ADOLPHE COLL
PLACE ST-CYPRIEN
PLACE ROGUET
AV. ETIENNE BILLERES
RUE J VIE
RUE TEINTURIERS
RUE COUPEFER
RUE LAGANNE
COURS DILLON
Prairie des Filtres
Garonne
N
RUE DE CUGNAUX
RUE DES ARCS ST-CYPRIEN
RUE STE-LUCIE
PLACE DU FER-A-CHEVAL
PONT
250 metres
250 yards

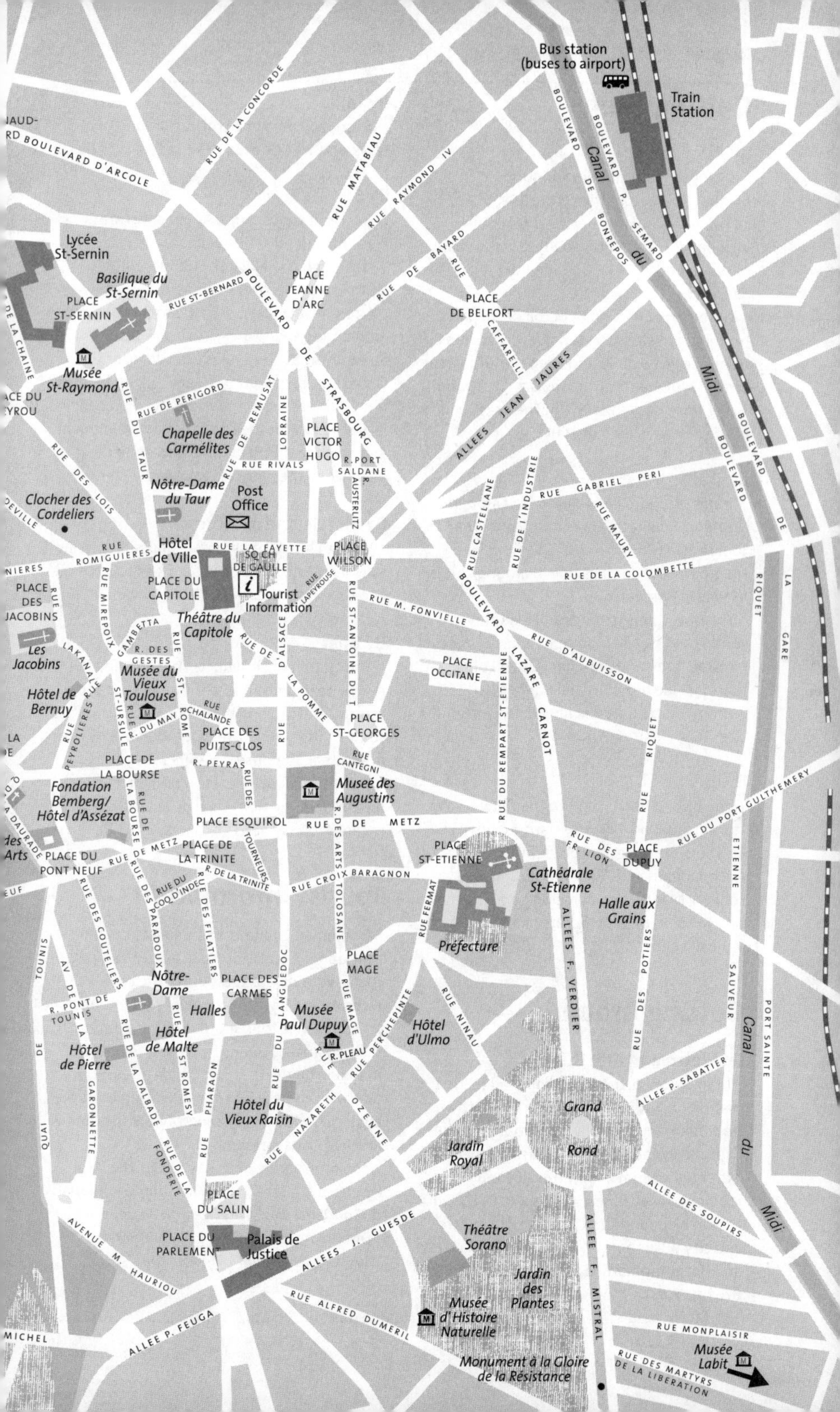

Bus station
(buses to airport)
Train Station
Lycée St-Sernin
Basilique du St-Sernin
Place St-Sernin
Musée St-Raymond
Place Jeanne d'Arc
Place de Belfort
Chapelle des Carmélites
Place Victor Hugo
Nôtre-Dame du Taur
Post Office
Clocher des Cordeliers
Hôtel de Ville
Sq Ch de Gaulle
Place Wilson
Place du Capitole
Tourist Information
Théâtre du Capitole
Place des Jacobins
Les Jacobins
Musée du Vieux Toulouse
Hôtel de Bernuy
Place Occitane
Place des Puits-Clos
Place St-Georges
Place de la Bourse
Fondation Bemberg/ Hôtel d'Assézat
Museé des Augustins
Place Esquirol
Place de la Trinite
Place du Pont Neuf
Place St-Etienne
Cathédrale St-Etienne
Place Dupuy
Halle aux Grains
Préfecture
Place Mage
Nôtre-Dame
Place des Carmes
Halles
Musée Paul Dupuy
Hôtel d'Ulmo
Hôtel de Malte
Hôtel de Pierre
Hôtel du Vieux Raisin
Grand Rond
Jardin Royal
Place du Salin
Place du Parlement
Palais de Justice
Théâtre Sorano
Jardin des Plantes
Musée d'Histoire Naturelle
Monument à la Gloire de la Résistance
Musée Labit
Canal du Midi
Boulevard d'Arcole
Rue de la Concorde
Rue Matabiau
Rue Raymond IV
Rue de Bayard
Boulevard de Bonrepos
Boulevard P. Semard
Boulevard de Strasbourg
Rue St-Bernard
Rue Caffarelli
Allees Jean Jaures
Rue de Perigord
Rue de Remusat
Rue Lorraine
Rue Rivals
R. Port Saldane
R. Austerlitz
Rue Gabriel Peri
Rue Castellane
Rue de l'Industrie
Rue Maury
Rue de la Colombette
Rue La Fayette
Rue Romiguieres
Rue du Taur
Rue des Lois
Rue Mirepoix
Rue Lapeyrouse
Rue M. Fonvielle
Rue St-Antoine du T
Boulevard Lazare Carnot
Rue du Rempart St-Etienne
Rue d'Aubuisson
Rue Gambetta
R. des Gestes
Rue St-Rome
Rue de la Pomme
Rue d'Alsace
Rue Lakanal
Rue Peyrolieres
Rue St-Ursule
R. du May
Rue Chalande
R. Peyras
Rue Cantegni
Rue Riquet
Boulevard Riquet
Boulevard de la Gare
Rue du Port Guilthemery
Rue de Metz
Rue des Fr. Lion
Rue de la Bourse
Rue des Tourneurs
R. de la Trinite
Rue Croix Baragnon
R. des Arts
Rue Tolosane
Rue Fermat
Rue du Coq d'Inde
Rue des Paradoux
Rue des Filatiers
Rue des Couteliers
Allees F. Verdier
Rue des Potiers
Rue Ninau
Rue Perchepinte
Rue Mage
Rue du Languedoc
R. Pleau
Rue Ozenne
Rue Nazareth
Rue Pharaon
Rue St Romesy
Rue de la Dalbade
Rue de la Fonderie
R. Pont de Tounis
Av de la Garonnette
Quai de Tounis
Allee P. Sabatier
Port Sainte Sauveur
Allee des Soupirs
Allee F. Mistral
Allees J. Guesde
Avenue M. Hauriou
Rue Alfred Dumeril
Allee P. Feuga
Rue Monplaisir
Rue des Martyrs de la Liberation

Getting There

By Air

Toulouse's international **airport** is at Blagnac, 10km from the centre, **t** 05 61 42 44 00, *www.toulouse.aeroport.fr*. Airlines include Air France (**t** 08 20 82 08 20), British Airways (**t** 08 25 82 54 00) and Buzz (**t** 01 55 17 42 42, *www.buzzaway.fr*).

The **airport bus**, t 05 34 60 64 00, departs from Toulouse's SNCF station every 20 mins from 5.20–8.20 daily, and from the airport to central Toulouse every 20 mins 7.30–11.30pm. Ticket price is €3.70 one way. The ticket booth at the airport is outside Hall 1.

By Train

Trains run from Paris-Austerlitz through Gourdon, Souillac, Cahors and Montauban to Toulouse in 6 hrs 30 mins; TGVs from Paris-Montparnasse do the same in around 5hrs – by way of Bordeaux.

The slow trains to Bordeaux take 2hrs 30mins and stop in Montauban, Castelsarrasin, Moissac, Agen and Aiguillon. Other connections include Albi (1hr) and Castres (1 hr 30 mins), Auch, Carcassonne, Nice, Lyon and Lille (TGV, 7 hrs).

By Bus

The **bus station** is next to the railway station at 68 Bd Pierre Semard, **t** 05 61 61 67 67; there are buses to Foix, Albi, Gaillac, Auch, Nogaro and Montauban, and also to London, Madrid and Barcelona on Eurolines, **t** 05 61 26 40 04 (buy tickets in advance from a travel agent).

Getting Around

By Métro and City Bus

In 1993 Toulouse proudly opened its first métro line, running northeast to southwest from Joliment, the railway station and the Capitole to the Mirail; this has now been extended several kilometres beyond Joliment. A new line, running north to south, should be operational by 2007. The métro and city buses are run by SEMVAT, which has an **information office** at 7 Place Esquirol, **t** 05 61 41 70 70.

By Taxi

If you can't find one cruising around or at a taxi stand, try **t** 05 61 42 38 38, or **t** 05 34 25 02 50.

By Car

The most convenient pay **car parks** are at Place du Capitole, Allée Jean Jaurès, Place Victor Hugo and Place St-Etienne; but it is quite expensive, over €1 an hour.

Alternatively, you can battle to find a space in the free parking areas such as Place St-Sernin and Allées Jules Guesde (near the Grand Rond), trawl the streets looking for a free spot (easiest in the summer when people leave the city for the coast) or park at Joliment and take the métro in – the price of parking is included in the métro ticket price.

By Bicycle and Motorcycle

You can hire bikes, scooters and motorcycles from **Rev Moto**, 14 Bd de la Gare, **t** 05 62 47 07 08, and they organize tours. Phone for details.

By Boat

The system of aqueducts that enabled the people to paddle around the city in the 6th century is sadly long gone, but you can still see some of the nicest corners of Toulouse by river. In summer, **Toulouse Croisières** (**t** 05 61 25 72 57, *www.toulouse-croisieres.com*) offers trips on the Garonne from Quai de la Daurade, daily except Monday, at 10.30, 4.30 and 6 (€8).

Tourist Information

Donjon du Capitole, Rue Lafayette, behind the Capitole, **t** 05 61 11 02 22, **f** 05 61 22 03 63; or check *www.mairie-toulouse.fr*, the city's website, and *www.ot-toulouse.fr*, the tourist office site. The tourist office offers a range of themed **guided tours**; if you plan to do more than one buy a *passeport* which gives reductions on the price (at time of writing tours are about €8, with the *passeport* two visits for €14 and five visits for €32).

For information on the whole of the Midi-Pyrénées region, stop by the **Comité Régional du Tourisme Midi-Pyrénées**, 54 Bd de l'Embouchure, **t** 05 61 13 55 55 (ring first), *www.tourisme-midi-pyrenees.com*.

Markets and Shopping

There are regular **markets** at Place des Carmes (*daily exc Mon*) and at Les Halles in **Bd Victor Hugo** (*Tues–Sun 6am–1pm*). On Wed mornings, **Place du Capitole** has a lively food and flea market. There is a good fruit and veg market (*daily exc Mon*) along **Boulevard de Strasbourg**, starting near Place Jeanne d'Arc, and Sun (and to a lesser extent Sat) morning sees a huge flea market around **St-Sernin** and along the length of the boulevards, the 'relics' of modern Toulouse that draw thousands of 'pilgrims'.

With all the major French department stores, the Pink City is the shopping mecca of the southwest. You can obtain superb chocolates at Olivier, 20 Rue Lafayette; Maison Pillon, at 2 Rue Ozenne, also produces delicious handmade **chocolates** which won the prize for the best in France in 1996.

The Bookshop, 17 Rue Lakanal, **t** 05 61 22 99 92, has books in English. For **posters** and reprints, try the shop in the Centre Municipal de l'Affiche.

If you fancy tasting some of the best **cheese** that France has to offer, head for Betty, 2 Place Victor Hugo; you smell it from fifty paces. There are 200 different types from all over the country, some of them quite special, such as the Vieux Salers, made in just one village in the Cantal and given a minimum of one year to mature.For fine **preserves** and French classics such as **olive oil** and very dark chocolate, go to La Boutique des Saveurs at 1 Rue Ozenne, **t** 05 61 53 75 21, a delightful shop that bombards you with tantalizing smells.

Sports and Activities

At the time of writing, the **Toulouse Football Club** (T.F.C., pronounced 'tayfessay') plays in France's second division. The city hosted matches in the 1998 World Cup, but the city's heart lies with its **rugby** team, the Stade (*www.stadetoulousain.fr*), over a hundred years old, and frequent champion of France (and champion of Europe in 1996). They play on Sun afternoons at the stadium.

You can swish out a figure eight at the Patinoire Olympique de Blagnac, an **ice rink** at 10 Av du Général de Gaulle, **t** 05 62 74 71 40 (buses 66 or 70). *Open Wed–Fri afternoons and evenings, all day Sat and Sun.*

Where to Stay

Toulouse ✉ 31000

Toulouse has chain hotels galore for its numerous business visitors as well as a short list of reliable independent establishments in the historic centre. Try to avoid the cheap fleabags near the station.

★★★★**Grand Hôtel de l'Opéra**, 1 Place du Capitole, **t** 05 61 21 82 66, **f** 05 61 23 41 04, *www.grand-hotel-opera.com* (*luxury–expensive*). This, the most beautiful hotel in Toulouse, has 50 luxurious rooms and three suites set in a former convent, with sumptuous Italianate rooms, indoor pool, fitness room and a magnificent restaurant.

★★★**Hôtel des Beaux Arts**, 1 Place Pont-Neuf, **t** 05 34 45 42 42, **f** 05 34 45 42 43 (*very expensive–moderate*). Set in an 18th-century *hôtel*, this is charming with pleasant, soundproofed rooms overlooking the Garonne.

★★★**Grand Hôtel Capoul**, 13 Place Wilson, **t** 05 61 10 70 70, **f** 05 61 21 96 70, *www.hotel-capoul.com* (*expensive–moderate*). Large, light, air-conditioned rooms, a Jacuzzi and an excellent *bistro*, now part of Holiday Inn.

★★★**Mermoz**, 50 Rue Matabiau, **t** 05 61 63 04 04, **f** 05 61 63 15 64, *www.hotel-mermoz.com* (*expensive–moderate*). Delighful air-conditioned rooms overlooking inner courtyards and one of the best breakfasts to be found in Toulouse.

★★★**Hôtel de Diane**, 3 Route de St-Simon, **t** 05 61 07 59 52, **f** 05 61 86 38 94 (*moderate*). In a country setting, yet reasonably close to the centre; there's a pool, and an excellent restaurant serving southwest favourites.

★★**Arnaud-Bernard**, 33 Rue de la Chaîne, **t** 05 61 21 37 64, **f** 05 61 29 86 91 (*moderate*). In the centre of Toulouse's lively popular quarter near St-Sernin; has renovated rooms.

★★**Grand Hôtel d'Orléans**, 72 Rue de Bayard, **t** 05 61 62 98 47, **f** 05 61 62 78 24 (*moderate–inexpensive*). Near the station. Plenty of character, with its interior galleries, garden, and satellite TV too.

★★**Park Hôtel**, 2 Rue Porte-Sardane, **t** 05 61 21 25 97, **f** 05 61 23 96 27, *www.au-park-hotel.com* (*inexpensive*). Within easy walking distance of the Capitole; modern rooms with most creature comforts, including a sauna and Jacuzzi.

★★Relais Blanhac, 200m from the airport, **t** 05 61 71 93 93. Good bet for those early flights; motel-like rooms sleep up to four. Ok restaurant. Luggage trolleys available, but make sure to book for a weekday stay.

★Anatole France, 46 Place Anatole France, **t** 05 61 23 19 96 (*inexpensive*). Near the Capitole, with some of the nicest cheap rooms in Toulouse, all with showers and phones.

★Hôtel des Arts, 1 bis Rue Cantegril, **t** 05 61 23 36 21, **f** 05 61 12 22 37 (*inexpensive*). A friendly place near lively Place St-Georges: good rooms with showers.

Eating Out

Toulouse, one of the boom towns of France, has enjoyed a restaurant revolution that has trickled down from *les grandes tables* to the corner *bistro*. Yet along with this leap in the quality of food, the city hasn't quite forgotten its key place in the southwest bean belt, and claims to make a *cassoulet* that walks all over the cassoulets of rivals Carcassonne and Castelnaudry.

Very Expensive–Expensive

Les Jardins de l'Opéra, 1 Place du Capitole, **t** 05 61 23 07 76. Toulouse's finest gastronomic experience is also one of the most beautiful restaurants in the southwest, a cool and refreshing glass-covered oasis overlooking a garden pool. The food matches the setting, orchestrated by the excellent Dominique Toulousy. *Closed Sun, Mon, end of July and most of Aug.*

Le Pastel, 237 Rue de St-Simon, in a villa at Mirail, **t** 05 62 87 84 30. Make the extra effort to book lunch for some of the finest, most imaginative gourmet food in Toulouse at some of the kindest prices. *Closed Sun and some of Aug.*

Expensive–Moderate

Le Bibent, 5 Place du Capitole, **t** 05 61 23 89 03. One of the most beautiful *brasseries* in Toulouse, strategically located, with a grand dining room last remodelled in the Roaring Twenties, and a terrace; excellent shellfish selection and southwest favourites.

Au Pois Gourmand, 3 Rue Emile Heybrard, **t** 05 61 31 95 95, *www.pois-gourmand.fr*. In a handsome old manor house with wooden galleries in Casselardit (just off the *rocade*, or ring road around the city). The perfect atmosphere for the refined and original cuisine that comes out of the kitchen. *Closed Sat lunch, Sun and Mon, and several weeks in Aug.*

Chez Emile, 13 Place St-Georges, **t** 05 61 21 05 56. Something of a city institution, preparing some of the very finest seafood in Toulouse or a *confit de canard*, or other meat; in warm weather, there are worse things to do than sit out on the terrace. *Closed Sun and Mon, just Sun and Mon lunch in summer.*

Grand Café de l'Opéra, 1 Place du Capitole, **t** 05 61 21 37 03. Excellent versions of the classics with a particular emphasis on seafood, in a cosy *brasserie* atmosphere – the original was burnt to the ground before being rebuilt exactly as it was. *Closed most of Aug.*

Les Ombrages, 48 bis Route de St-Simon, **t** 05 61 07 61 28. A bit hard to find (taking a taxi is recommended) but worth the effort for its fresh, sunny cuisine, immaculately prepared (*excellent lunch menu, prices up to €36*). *Closed Mon.*

Sept Place St-Sernin, 7 Place St-Sernin, **t** 05 62 30 05 30. A large ivy-covered house in a perfect spot opposite the cathedral. The menus are delightful and varied: try *foie gras de canard aux figues et salade d'herbes*. *Closed Sat and Sun.*

Moderate

La Bascule, 14 Av Maurice-Hauriou, **t** 05 61 52 09 51. A popular *brasserie* a bit out from the centre and on a busy corner, but set back enough that you can eat on the terrace lined with bamboo. Good selection of fish including oysters, and traditional meat dishes plus some a bit different such as *gigot d'agneau des Pyrénées en croûte avec jus d'estragon*. *Closed Sat lunch, Sun and Mon.*

Les Beaux-Arts-Flo, 1 Quai Daurade, **t** 05 61 21 12 12. On the Garonne, this handsome *belle époque brasserie* offers well-prepared favourites: seafood platters, salmon and sorrel, *cassoulet*, good desserts.

Le Belvédère, 11 Bd des Récollets, **t** 05 61 52 63 73. Southwest classics in a modern setting south of the centre, to accompany its grand panoramic views over Toulouse. *Closed Sun and Aug.*

Le Bon Vivre, 15 Place Wilson, **t** 05 61 23 07 17. This place packs them in with its authentic southwestern cooking: *confits, magrets, et al.*

Moderate–Cheap

Benjamin, 7 Rue des Gestes (off Rue St-Rome), **t** 05 61 22 92 66. Positioned right in the centre of old Toulouse, here you will find the likes of fennel and courgette terrine and steak with *cèpes* – and all for some of the friendliest prices in town.

Caves de la Maréchale, 3 Rue Jules-Chalande, **t** 05 61 23 89 88. Set in the immense cellar of a 13th-century Dominican priory off Rue St-Rome, and populated with copies of classical statues. *Closed Sun and Mon lunch.*

Cheap

The first floor of the **Marché Victor Hugo** is chock-a-block with cheap little beaneries that daily attract Toulousains of every ilk for lunch (*exc Mon*). *Open Tues–Sun.*

A la Truffe du Quercy, 17 Rue Croix-Baragnon, **t** 05 61 53 34 24. The same family has been dishing out southwestern home-cooking for three generations. Spanish options too (*formule menu €8.50, delicious regular menu for a bit more*). *Closed Sun and hols.*

Cafés, Bars and Wine Bars

Le Père Louis, 45 Place des Tourneurs, between Rue Peyras and Rue de Metz, **t** 05 61 21 33 45. The most resolutely traditional bar in Toulouse has drawn Toulouse's *quinquina* drinkers for over a century (*open 9.30am–10pm, closed Sun and Aug*).

Bar Florida, Place du Capitole, **t** 05 61 23 94 61. The place in central Toulouse to sit outside on a warm day with a drink in hand and watch the world go by. Some tourists, but plenty of Toulousains too. Champagne, cocktails, spirits, beer or coffee on offer.

L'Ancienne Belgique, 16 Rue de la Trinité. Try a pint or two from their big selection.

Gay bars are clustered around Rue de la Colombette, east of Place Wilson.

Entertainment and Nightlife

The weekly ***Flash***, available at any newsstand, will tell you what's on in Toulouse.

From October to June, the Théâtre du Capitole, Place du Capitole, **t** 05 61 22 31 31, presents a series of **opera** and **dance**.

The LSorano Théâtre National de Toulouse Midi-Pyrénées, 35 Allées Jules-Guesde, **t** 05 34 31 67 87, probably puts on the finest **plays** in Toulouse.

For a listen to the current state of French **poetry**, ***chanson*** and **theatre**, there's La Cave Poésie, 71 Rue du Taur, **t** 05 61 23 62 00. **Concerts** and exhibitions of dance are also given in the renovated auditorium of the old church of St-Pierre-des-Cuisines, Place St-Pierre, **t** 05 34 45 05 61.

Zénith, Av Raymond Badiou, **t** 05 62 74 49 49, is the biggest **stage and performance** venue in the area and hosts a range of events from displays of Basque sport to pop concerts, and more besides. At the time of writing, it is still closed following the chemical factory explosion in September 2001, but should be open when you read this.

Toulouse likes its **movies** as well; the Cinémathèque, 69 Rue du Taur, **t** 05 62 30 30 10, is the second most important in France, and often shows films in V.O. (*version originale*), as does ABC, 13 Rue St-Bernard, **t** 05 61 29 81 00.

Favourite **clubs** include:

Shanghaï Club, 12 Rue de la Pomme, **t** 05 61 23 37 80. Central and one of the oldest discos in Toulouse, something of an institution.

L'Aposia, 9 bit Rue Jean Rodier, **t** 05 05 71 84 11. Huge club with several different rooms.

Puerto Habana, 12 Port St-Etienne, **t** 05 61 54 45 61. Good venue for a lively night out. *Closed Sun.*

El Barrio Latino, 144 Av de Muret, **t** 05 61 59 00 58. Good Latin music venue. *Closed Sun to Wed.*

Toulouse, called La Ville Rose for its millions of pink bricks, has 750,000 lively inhabitants, counting over 110,000 university students and 70 per cent of the industry in the Midi-Pyrénées region, much of it high-tech and related to aeronautics and space.

Toulouse should have been the rosy capital of a nation called Languedoc, but it was knocked out of the big leagues in the 1220s by the popes and kings of France. Spain, and in particular Barcelona, extends her cape here, distilling enough passion to give the heirs of medieval Toulouse's fat merchants a dose of madness. Toulouse is above all *une ville d'émotion*; listen to the Toulousains chant their national anthem, which they do at every possible occasion: '*O moun paiës, Toulouse, Toulouse! O moun paiës, Toulouse, Toulouse!*' over and over again. There aren't any other verses; according to the natives, there's nothing else to say.

History

Toulouse grew up at a ford in the Garonne, a natural strategic crossroads at the centre of what the ancient Greek geographer Strabo called the 'Gallic isthmus' between the Mediterranean and the Atlantic. When the Romans found it, its inhabitants were the Tectosage Gauls, a tribe that had grown rich from mining and the wine trade. After first forcing them into an alliance, the Romans crushed them in 107 BC, gobbling up the Tectosages' fabulous treasure – 100 tons of gold and silver hidden at the bottom of a swamp. As a refounded Roman colony, *Palladia Tolosa* enjoyed five centuries of peace and quiet, developing into a modest provincial city of some 20,000. The Visigoths took over in 420 AD, but instead of a sacking and burning Tolosa got a surprising new role to play – as capital of a new Visigothic Kingdom, under the warrior King Ataulf and his loving bride, the Roman imperial princess Galla Placidia.

That kingdom lasted only until 507, when Clovis's Franks decisively defeated the Visigoths. They moved over the Pyrenees to found a new kingdom in Spain, while under Clovis's 'do-nothing' Merovingian successors, Toulouse and the rest of the southwest was largely left to itself. And by its own efforts, the city repelled an attack by the Arabs in 721, a decade before Charles Martel chased them out of Gaul for good. After that, the new Carolingian dynasty enjoyed a nominal rule over the southwest, and to hold on to it they set up a branch of the family as Counts of Toulouse, governing a vast territory extending from the Rhône to the Garonne and from the Pyrenees to the Dordogne.

Most of these counts were named Raymond, and over the next two centuries they would become a powerful dynasty, retaining most of these lands and ruling them more as independent princes than vassals of the French king. Toulouse's golden age began in the 11th century, under such mighty counts as Raymond IV, who built the great basilica of St-Sernin and led the Christian armies in the First Crusade in 1095. Raymond V, a princely troubadour, granted the city of Toulouse a large degree of self-rule, and did his best to fight off that eternal troublemaker Richard the Lion-Heart, who invaded his domains in the 1190's.

Under its governing *capitouls*, Toulouse grew wealthy and fat, with one of the biggest grain-milling industries in Europe. But more troubles would soon be coming from outside. Raymond VI, who became count in 1195, was a modern, tolerant soul; the new religion of the Cathars was making great advances in his lands, and

Raymond defended them against the powers of the Church. That resulted in a powerful coalition against him, led by Innocent III, strongest of all the medieval popes, and the King of France. The 'Albigensian Crusade', as the attack on the Cathars came to be known, was in reality a massive grab for land and power at Toulouse's expense. A northern army under Simon de Montfort invaded the county in 1209.

In 1213, the crushing defeat of Raymond and his Aragonese allies at Muret, just outside Toulouse, ensured the end of Languedoc's independence, and also of southern culture and prosperity. Simon de Montfort entered Toulouse as its new count two years later, while Bishop Folquet de Marseille, a former troubadour who became the most rabid bigot of them all, presided over a grisly Inquisition. Toulouse revolted successfully two years later, and de Montfort died besieging it, but the last two Raymonds of the line were only able to hold out a little longer. King Louis VIII himself led another bloody invasion in 1229, and the county reverted to the French crown when the last count, royal appointee Alphonse de Poitiers, died childless in 1271.

Under French rule, Toulouse gradually lost its rights and privileges, and over the next three centuries it would decline to an economic and cultural backwater. The city was lucky to avoid the calamities of the Hundred Years' War, and it even enjoyed a period of prosperity after 1560 thanks to *pastel*, a locally-grown crop much in demand across Europe for dyeing. Indigo from the Carolinas put an end to pastel's prominence in the 1660's, but at the same time, a new engine of prosperity was taking shape – the Canal du Midi (1666–81), a locally-planned and financed effort that linked the Atlantic and the Mediterranean by way of the Garonne, and brought Toulouse a considerable amount of new wealth and trade.

Still, compared to its medieval heyday Toulouse remained little more than a sleepy provincial city; even with the coming of the railroad in 1856. What proved to be the turning point for modern Toulouse literally fell from the sky. The city's surprising aerial adventures began with pioneer aviator Clément Ader, who managed to get a steam-powered plane off the ground in the 1890's. By World War I Toulouse had an aircraft factory, and afterwards it served as the hub of France's first big air mail service. Another local firm, nationalized in the 1930's, has grown to become Aérospatiale. In the 50s the government decided to concentrate all its air and space efforts here, and the last few giddy decades have seen France's City of the Air give birth to the Ariane rockets and Hermès, the European space shuttle, as well as Caravelle, Concorde and Airbus jets. Today, many visitors' startling introduction to the city will be the vast complex of factories, research centres and industrial parks that surrounds the airport at Blagnac.

The new Toulouse has become the fourth-largest city in France, and the capital of the Midi-Pyrenees region, giving it a political role, albeit a limited one, for the first time since the Middle Ages. New building and improvements are everywhere, including a shiny new metro. At times Toulouse may seem all business, but a lively population that includes the descendants of the wave of refugees from the Spanish Civil War and *pieds noirs* from Algeria, along with hordes of students at the bustling University, keeps it one of the most engaging cities of the Midi.

Place du Capitole

This dignified front parlour of Toulouse dates from 1850, when the 200-year-long tidying away of excess buildings was completed and the edges rimmed with neoclassical brick façades. As a permanent memorial to the southern kingdom of nevermore, the centre of the pavement is marked by an enormous **Cross of Languedoc**. This same golden cross on a red background hangs proudly from Toulouse's city hall, the **Capitole**, or CAPITOLIUM as it reads, bowing to a 16th-century story claiming that ancient Rome got its Capitol idea from Toulouse's temple of Capitoline Jupiter.

The portal on the right belongs to the **Théâtre du Capitole**, while over the central door eight pink marble columns represent the eight *capitouls*; the pompous historical rooms upstairs (***t** 05 61 22 29 22; open Mon–Fri 9–5*) were decorated in the 1800s with busts of famous Toulousains and a painting by Henri Martin of *Jean Jaurès on the banks of the Garonne*. Behind the great façade, the Cour Henri IV gives on to Square Charles de Gaulle, defended by the **Donjon** of 1525, where the *capitouls* kept the city archives. The building, well restored by Viollet-le-Duc, now houses the city tourist office.

The Basilica of St-Sernin

Running north from Place du Capitole, narrow **Rue du Taur** was the road to Cahors in Roman times. The Taur in its name means 'bull', which features in the life of the city's first saint, Sernin, who died here in the 240s. Sernin (a corruption of Saturnin) was a missionary from Rome who preached in Pamplona and Toulouse. One day, runs the legend, he happened by the temple of Capitoline Jupiter, where preparations were under way for the sacrifice of a bull to Mithras. The priests ordered him to kneel before the pagan idol, and, when Sernin refused, a sudden gust of wind blew over the statue of Mithras, breaking it to bits. In fury the crowd demanded the sacrifice of Sernin instead, and he was tied under the bull, which, maddened by the extra weight, dragged his body through the city streets.

After turning Sernin to pulp, the bull left his body where the 14th-century **Notre-Dame-du-Taur** now stands, replacing an oratory built over Sernin's tomb in 360. Its 135ft *clocher-mur* looks like a false front in a Wild West town; the nave is surprisingly wide, and has a faded fresco of the Tree of Jesse along the right wall. Sernin's tomb attracted so many pilgrims and Christians who desired to be buried near him that in 403 a *martyrium* was built 300 yards to the north. An imperial decree permitted the removal of the saint's relics to this spot, and over the centuries tombs lined the length of Rue de Taur, as in the Alyschamps in Arles. In 1075, just as the pilgrimage to Compostela was getting under way, Count Guilhem decided Sernin deserved something more grand. The construction of the **Basilique de St-Sernin** (***t** 05 61 21 80 45; open Oct–June 8.30–11.45 and 2–5.45, Sun 8.30–12.30 and 2–7.30; July–Sept 10–6, Sun 12.30–6*) was continued by his famous brother Raymond IV, and of such import that in 1096 Pope Urban II, on tour that year preaching the First Crusade, came to consecrate its marble altar.

In 1220 St-Sernin was finished – at 380ft the largest surviving Romanesque church in the world (only the great abbey church of Cluny, destroyed in the Revolution, was bigger). It was begun at the same time, and has the exact same plan as the basilica of St James at Compostela: a cross, ending in a semi-circular apse with five radiating chapels. In the 19th century the abbey and cloister were demolished, and in 1860 Viollet-le-Duc was summoned to restore the basilica. He spent 20 years on the project – and botched the roof so badly that rainwater seeped directly into the stone and brick. A century later the church was found to be in danger of collapse – hence a 22 million-franc 'de-restoration' project to undo Viollet-le-Duc's mischief. Off came all his neo-Gothic ornamentation and heavy stone, to be replaced with tiles handcrafted in the 13th-century manner.

The Exterior

The apse of St-Sernin (seen from Rue St-Bernard) is a fascinating play of white stone and red brick, a crescendo culminating in the octagonal bell tower that is Toulouse's most striking landmark. New York had its war of skyscrapers in the 1930s; 13th-century Toulouse had its war of bell towers: St-Sernin's original three storeys of arcades were increased to five for the sole purpose of upstaging the bell tower of the Jacobins. The most elaborately decorated of the basilica's portals is an odd, asymmetrical one on the south side, the **Porte Miège-ville**. It faces Rue du Taur; apparently this street, called Miège-ville or 'mid-city' in medieval times, ran right through the spot before the basilica was built. Devotees of medieval Toulousain arcana – a bottomless subject – say that this portal is the real cornerstone of the kingdom of Languedoc that the 11th-century counts were trying to create; books have been written about its proportions and the symbolism of its decoration, even claiming that it is the centre of a geomantic construction, with 12 lines radiating from here across the counts' territories, connecting various chapels and villages and forming Raymond IV's twelve-pointed Cross of Languedoc. The tympanum was carved by the 11th-century master Bernard Gilduin, showing the *Ascension of Christ*, a rare scene in medieval art, and one of the most choreographic: Christ surrounded by dancing angels, watched by the Apostles on the lintel. On the brackets are figures of David and others riding on lions; the magnificent capitals tell the story of the Redemption (*Original Sin, Massacre of the Innocents, Annunciation*), all from the expressive chisel of Gilduin. The north transept door, now walled up, was the royal door; the south transept door, the **Porte des Comtes**, is named after the several 11th-century counts of Toulouse who are buried in palaeo-Christian sarcophagi in the deep *enfeu* nearby. The eight capitals here, also by Gilduin (*c.* 1080), show the torments of hell, most alarmingly a man having his testicles crushed and a woman whose breasts are being devoured by serpents, both paying the price for Lust.

The Interior

Begun in 1969, the 'de-restoration' of the barrel-vaulted interior stripped the majestic brick and stone of Viollet-le-Duc's ham-handed murals and fiddly neo-Gothic bits. In the process, some fine 12th-century frescoes have been found, especially the serene angel of the Resurrection in the third bay of the north transept, which also has some of the best capitals. In the south transept, the shrine of St Jude, the patron saint of lost causes, blazes with candlelight in July – when French students take their exams.

For a small fee you can enter the **ambulatory** (*open daily 10–11.30 and 2–5.30; afternoons only on Sun; July–Sept 10–6, closed Sun morning*) and make what the Middle Agers called 'the Circuit of Holy Bodies', for the wide array of saintly anatomies stashed in the five radiating chapels. In the 17th century, bas-reliefs and wood panels on the lives of the saints were added to bring the relics to life, and although these were removed in the 1800s they were restored and replaced in 1980. Opposite the central chapel are seven magnificent marble bas-reliefs of 1096, carved and signed by Bernard Gilduin.

The Holy Bodies circuit continues down into the upper crypt, with the silver shrine of St Honoratus (1517) and the 13th-century reliquaries of the Holy Cross and of St Sernin, the latter showing the saint under the hooves of the bull. The lower crypt contains, more bodily, two Holy Thorns (a present from St Louis), 13th-century gloves and mitres, and a set of six 16th-century painted wooden statues of apostles. In the choir an 18th-century baldachin shelters St Sernin's tomb, remade in 1746 and supported by a pair of bronze bulls. In the south transept, note the big feet sticking out of a pillar, all that remains of a shallow relief of St Christopher effaced by the hands of centuries of pilgrims.

Around Place St-Sernin and the Quartier Arnaud-Bernard

At No.3, the Lycée St-Sernin occupies the **Hôtel du Barry**, built by Louis XV's pimp, the Roué du Barry. Du Barry married his charming lover, Jeanne de Bécu, to his brother and then in 1759 introduced her to the king. His pandering earned him the money to build this mansion in 1777; it would later earn the Comtesse du Barry the guillotine in the Terror. (The word *roué*, incidentally, was first used in the 1720s, to describe the bawdy companions of the regent, the Duke of Orléans; it was invented by some disapproving soul who thought they should have been broken on the wheel.)

On the south side of the square stood a pilgrims' hostel, founded in the 1070s by a chanter of St Sernin named Raymond Gayard, who was canonized for his charity to the poor. His hostel was succeeded by the *collège* of St Raymond (1505) for poor university students, and now by the rich archaeological collections of the **Musée St-Raymond** (*t 05 61 22 31 44; open daily 10–6; June–Aug 10–7*). This is the antiquities museum of Toulouse, with some exceptional pieces. The top floors concentrate on finds from the Roman region of Narbonnaise and one of its biggest towns, Tolosa, ancient Toulouse. One of the most interesting exhibits is the section of a relief depicting two Amazons in combat, one clearly with the upper hand over a man: this would have formed part of a temple or major monument. The collection of outstanding busts is small compared to the avenue of heads of emperors, men, women and children on the floor below: all found, with the other exhibits here, at Chiragan in Martres-Tolosane, 60 kilometres to the south of Toulouse. Don't miss the splendid marbles depicting the *Labours of Hercules*. Digs carried out in the basement of the museum have revealed the presence of a Christian necropolis dating from the 4th century which grew up around the tomb of St Sernin. Several of the tombs have been left not far from where they were found, close to a large, circular 5th-century lime kiln. Ornate sarcophagi from southwest France and other funerary objects are also on display. There are also vestiges of walls from an 11th-century hospital and 13th-century college. Temporary exhibitions allow the public to see other museum artefacts, principally from the Iron Age through the Middle Ages.

Just south of St-Sernin in Rue du Périgord, the southern Gothic **Chapelle des Carmélites** (1643) owes its existence to Anne of Austria, wife of Louis XIII. The walls are covered with paintings, and vaulting has been restored to bring out its lavish ceiling, with an unusual allegory on the *Glory of Carmel* by Jean-Baptiste Despax.

This northernmost medieval neighbourhood, the lively **Quartier Arnaud-Bernard**, has been the city's Latin Quarter ever since 1229, when the **University of Toulouse** was founded in Rue des Lois (part of it now occupies the old seminary of St-Pierre-des-Chartreaux to the west). Although forced down Toulouse's throat by Paris (*see* 'History', above), the university enjoyed a certain prestige in the Middle Ages; among its alumni were three popes, Montaigne, and Rabelais.

The three principal squares of the quarter – Place du Peyrou, Place des Tiercerettes and Place Arnaud Bernard – became the centre of immigrant life in the last century; today they are quickly being gentrified, but are still quite lively after dark. North of the boulevard, the neighbourhood's 'lung', the **Jardin Compans-Caffarelli**, was laid out in 1982 with exotic plants, a Japanese garden and tearoom.

Les Jacobins

***t** 05 61 22 21 92; open 9–7 daily; adm for the cloister.*

Just west of Place du Capitole stands the great Dominican mother church, Les Jacobins, the prototype for Dominican foundations across Europe and one of the masterpieces of southern French Gothic. The Spanish priest Domingo de Guzmán had tried hard to convert the Cathars before the Albigensian Crusade; by 1206 he had reconverted enough women to found a convent, which became the germ of his Order of Preaching Friars, established in Toulouse in 1215. Confirmed by the pope in 1216, the new Dominican order quickly found adherents across Europe. In 1230, the Dominicans erected this, their third convent in Toulouse, which took the name of the Jacobins from the Dominicans' Paris address, in Rue St-Jacques (the very same convent where the fanatical party of Robespierre would later meet, hence the *Jacobins* of the French Revolution – a fitting name in light of the Dominicans' role as Inquisitors). The magnificent Jacobins in Toulouse so impressed the popes that they made it the last resting place of the greatest Dominican of them all, St Thomas Aquinas (*d*. 1274). Confiscated in the Revolution, Napoleon requisitioned the church and convent as a barracks for his artillery, which built an upper floor in the nave. When Prosper Mérimée, inspector of historic monuments, visited Toulouse in 1845, he found the mutilated complex occupied by 500 horses and cannoneers. In 1865 the military was finally convinced to leave the Jacobins to the city, and Toulouse spent a hundred years on its restoration.

The church is the perfect expression of the 13th-century reaction to Rome's love of luxury, which made the great preaching orders, the Dominicans and Franciscans, so popular in their day. Gargoyles are the only exterior sculpture in this immense but harmonious brick pile of buttresses, alternating with flamboyant windows; its octagonal bell tower of brick and stone crowned with baby towers is one of the landmarks of the city skyline. The interior is breathtakingly light and spacious, consisting of twin naves divided by seven huge columns, crisscrossed by a fantastic interweaving of ribs in the vault, reaching an epiphany in the massive flamboyant *palmier* in the apse. The painted decoration dates from the 13th to the 16th century, but only the glass of the rose windows on the west side is original.

A small door leads out into the lovely garden **cloister** (1309), with brick arcades and twinned columns in grey marble. The east gallery gives on to the large **chapter house**, supported by a pair of slender marble columns. The walls of the adjacent **Chapelle St-Antonin**, the funerary chapel, were painted in the early 1300s with scenes from the life of St Antonin, while the ceiling is decorated with southwest France's favourite vision from the Apocalypse: the 24 Elders and angels glorifying Christ. In Rue Pargaminières, the **Refectory** (*same hours*), nearly 200ft long, houses temporary exhibitions, often on historical and cultural themes.

West of Les Jacobins, near the Garonne's hog-backed bridge, Pont St-Pierre, are Toulouse's two churches dedicated to St Peter. **St-Pierre-des-Cuisines** (***t*** *05 61 22 31 44; open Sept–July 9–12.30; Aug 2–7*), a little Romanesque priory associated with Moissac, is named after its kitchens, where a person's bread could be baked at cheaper rates than at the counts' ovens. **St-Pierre-des-Chartreux**, to the north in Rue Valade, was founded in the 17th century and, if open, has some fine works from the 17th and 18th centuries.

Pastel Palaces and Violets of Gold

Just south of Les Jacobins, to the south end of Rue Gambetta, is one of the city's most splendid residences, the **Hôtel de Bernuy**, built in 1504 by a *pastel* merchant from Burgos, Don Juan de Bernuy, a Spanish Jew who fled Ferdinand and Isabella's Inquisition and became a citizen – and *capitoul* – of Toulouse. Although Gothic on the outside, inside his master mason Loys Privat designed an eclectic fantasy courtyard, a mix of Gothic, Plateresque and Loire château, topped by a lofty tower rivalling those of all the other *pastel* nabobs. De Bernuy had a chance to repay France for the fortune he made by paying the ransom for King François I when he was captured at the battle of Pavia by Emperor Charles V. In his distress the king had promised an *ex voto* to St Sernin if he survived, and in the ambulatory you can still see the black marble statue he donated when he came in 1533 to thank the saint and de Bernuy for his generosity.

Not long after de Bernuy's time the Jesuits converted his *hôtel particulier* into a college, now the prestigious **Lycée Pierre de Fermat**, named after its star pupil, the brilliant mathematician (1595–1665) who left his last theorem as a challenge to subsequent generations of mathematicians. Just to the east, a 16th-century *hôtel particulier* houses the **Musée du Vieux Toulouse** (*7 Rue du May,* **t** *05 61 13 97 24; open June–Sept Mon–Sat 3–6*) with a fascinating collection from the city's history and its former porcelain industry, as well as paintings and etchings. Rue du May gives on to Rue St-Rome, decorated with 16th-century mansions built by the *capitouls* and wealthy merchants. At its south end don't miss the triangular **Place de la Trinité**, with a 19th-century fountain supported by bronze mermaids. Near here, you can examine the popular artistic pulse of Toulouse in the ever-changing murals along Rue Coq-d'Inde.

One of the finest private residences built in Toulouse, the **Hôtel d'Assézat** is just west, off Rue de Metz. The *hôtel* was begun in 1555 by another *pastel* magnate, Pierre d'Assézat, who had a near monopoly on the dye in northern Europe. Designed by Nicolas Bachelier, Toulouse's master architect-sculptor-engineer, it consists of two buildings around a large square court, and a curious tower crowned with an octagonal lantern and dome that served the merchant as an observation post over the Garonne, enabling him to keep an eye on his fleet. Facing the street, an Italianate loggia has seven brackets decorated with *pastel* pods. Inside, the **Fondation Bemberg** (**t** *05 61 12 06 89; open Tues–Sun 10–12.30 and 1.30–6; nocturnal visits Thurs 9pm, themed visits Thurs 7pm; courses on the history of art Sat 10.30; adm*) has a collection of art, specializing in Renaissance and modern French paintings.

Along the Garonne

Rue de Metz continues to Toulouse's oldest bridge, which, as in Paris, is rather confusingly known as the new, or **Pont Neuf**. This Pont Neuf, with its seven unequal arches of brick and stone and curious holes (*oculi*), took from 1544 to 1632 to build, and links Gascony – the Left Bank – with the medieval province of Languedoc. Just down the quay stands the **Ecole des Beaux-Arts**, its façade larded with allegorical figures (1895). Hidden under the icing is a 17th-century U-shaped monastery connected to **Notre-Dame-la-Daurade**. Only the name recalls what was for centuries one of the wonders of Toulouse, the 10-sided, domed, 5th-century palatine chapel of the Visigothic kings, known as the Daurade ('the golden one') after its shimmering mosaics. Similar to the churches of Ravenna, it was destroyed in 1761, when the nitwitted monks who owned it decided to replace it with a reproduction of the Vatican, completed in the mid-19th century. The paintings in the choir are by Ingres's master, Roques.

One of the finest views of the Pont Neuf and river front is to the south along the **Quai de Tounis**. Rue du Pont de Tounis, built in 1515 as a bridge over the Garonnette (a now covered tributary of the Garonne), leads back to the original riverbank and **Notre-Dame-la-Dalbade** (Our Lady the Whitened, after its medieval whitewash, in contrast to the Golden One). This church too has taken some hard knocks. It was rebuilt in the Renaissance with a 280ft spire, to show up St-Sernin's bell tower.

The Quartier du Jardin

At the south end of Rue de la Dalbade/Rue de la Fonderie in Place du Salin stood the fortified residence of the counts of Toulouse, the celebrated Château Narbonnais; it was also the site of the *parlement*, established in Toulouse in 1443. The whole complex was demolished in the 19th century for the **Palais de Justice**, with only the square brick tower, the 14th-century royal treasury (converted into a Protestant church), as a memory. In the adjacent Place du Parlement is an old house built on the Roman wall, donated to Domingo Guzmán for his new preaching order, and later converted to the use inscribed over the door: 'Maison de l'Inquisition'.

South of the Place du Parlement, Allées Jules Guesde replaces the walls torn down in 1752. At No.35 is Toulouse's fascinating, fusty old **Musée d'Histoire Naturelle** (*closed for renovations; contact the tourist office for details*). The **Jardin Royal** was planted outside the walls and, in the 19th century, Toulouse's prettiest park, the **Jardin des Plantes**, was added. The garden's grand 16th–17th-century portal on Allée Frédéric-Mistral was salvaged from the original Capitole; just south of this is the **Monument à la Gloire de la Résistance**, with a crypt aligned to be illuminated by the sun's rays on 19 August, the anniversary of the Liberation of Toulouse (*open Mon–Fri 10–12 and 2–5, closed weekends and hols*).

There is one last museum in this quarter, and one not to be missed if you're fond of Egyptian, Coptic, Indian and Far Eastern Art. This is the **Musée Georges Labit**, in a neo-Moorish villa (*43 Rue des Martyrs-de-la-Libération, off Allée Frédéric-Mistral, **t** 05 61 22 21 84; open 10–5, till 6 in summer; closed Tues and hols*). Labit was a 19th-century traveller with plenty of money and a good eye who accumulated a choice Oriental collection, considered the best in France after the Guimet Museum in Paris.

Place du Salin to the Cathedral of St-Etienne

The parliamentarians liked to build themselves distingished houses in the homogenous quarter between the old *parlement* and the cathedral: all uniform pink brick, with light grey shutters and black wrought-iron balconies. In this mesh of quiet lanes, there are a few to pick out during a stroll, such as the sumptuously ornate **Hôtel du Vieux Raisin** (1515), 36 Rue du Languedoc, built by another *capitoul* in love with Italy. Another *hôtel* houses the **Musée Paul Dupuy** (*13 Rue de la Pleau, **t** 05 61 14 65 56; open 10–5, until 6 in summer, closed Tues and hols*), named after the obsessed collector who left to Toulouse his hoard of watches, automata, guns, coins, fans, faïence, pharmaceutical jars and gems.

Rue Perchepinte and Rue Fermat, lined with antique shops, lead up to Place St-Etienne, with Toulouse's oldest fountain (1546) and the massive archbishop's palace (1713), now used as the Préfecture. All are overpowered by the **cathedral of St-Etienne** (***t** 05 61 52 03 82*) begun in the 11th century by Raymond IV, but completed only in the 17th century. Fashions and finances rose and fell in the three major building campaigns, resulting in a church that seems a bit drunk. Have a good look at the façade: in the centre rises a massive brick bell tower with a clock, over the

Romanesque base. To the right is a worn, asymmetrical stone Gothic façade, where the portal and rose window are off-centre; to the left extends the bulge of the chapel of Notre-Dame, a small church in itself stuck onto the north end. It's even tipsier inside. In 1211, Raymond VI inserted the oldest known representation of the Cross of Languedoc as the key in one of the vaults, just before 1215, when Bishop Folquet rebuilt most of Raymond IV's church in the form of a single nave 62ft high and 62ft wide, with ogival crossings, a style that went on to become the model for southern Gothic. In 1275, Bishop Bertrand de l'Isle-Jourdaine decided Bishop Folquet's bit of the cathedral was hardly grandiose enough for Toulouse's dignity and came up with a plan based on northern French Gothic that involved realigning the axis of the church. The choir was built, a fine example of flamboyant Gothic, with beautiful 14th-century glass on the west side, but the vaults, designed to be 132ft high, were cut short at 90ft due to limited funds. Money and energy ran out completely when Bishop Bertrand died, leaving a curious dogleg where his choir meets Raymond IV and Bishop Folquet's nave, marked by the massive Pilier d'Orléans, one of four intended to support the transept; it bears a plaque marking the tomb of Pierre-Paul Riquet, father of the Canal du Midi. Although many of the cathedral's best decorations are now stowed away in the Musée des Augustins, there are tapestries, faded into negatives of themselves, from the 15th and 16th centuries, and some interesting grotesques in the choir.

Musée des Augustins

t 05 61 22 21 82; open 10–6, till 9 on Wed; closed Tues and hols.

Rue Croix Baragnon, opposite the cathedral, has two beautiful Gothic houses, especially No.15, decorated with a band of stone carvings. But the greatest medieval art in this part of town is in the Musée des Augustins, a block north at the corner of Rue de Metz and Rue d'Alsace-Lorraine. The museum, one of the oldest in France, is housed in a 14th-century Augustinian convent, beautifully restored in 1950.

The nave of the convent church is devoted to religious paintings (Van Dyck's *Christ aux anges* and *Miracle de la mule*, Rubens's *Christ entre deux larrons* and *San Diego en extase* by Murillo) and reliefs by Nicolas Bachelier. Best of all are the Romanesque works, most of them rescued from demolished cloisters: from St-Sernin, there's a capital sculpted with the *War of Angels* and an enigmatic bas-relief from the Porte des Comtes showing two women looking at one another, one holding a lion in her arms, the other a ram, an image that also appears on the main portal at Compostela. Other capitals stylistically related to those of Moissac come from the Romanesque cloister of the Daurade; the most beautiful of all are from Raymond IV's 11th-century cloister of St-Etienne – note especially the delicate, almost fluid scene of the dance of Salome and the beheading of John the Baptist.

The first floor of the convent is devoted to paintings, including two portraits of *capitouls*; one of their oldest prerogatives was the *droit d'image* – the right to have their portraits painted. In the 13th and 14th centuries this was exceptional: kings, emperors, the doge of Venice and the pope were among the few allowed to leave their likenesses for posterity. Other paintings include a 15th-century Florentine hunt scene, an extremely unpleasant *Apollo flaying Marsyas* by the 'Divine' Guido Reni and works by Simon Vouet, Philippe de Champaigne, Van Dyck, Rubens (in the Augustins' church), the two Guardis, Delacroix, Ingres, Manet, Morisot, Vuillard, Maurice Denis and Count Henri de Toulouse-Lautrec.

Toulouse's Left Bank

Although the Left, or Gascon, bank of the Garonne has been settled since the early Middle Ages, the periodic rampages of the river dampened property values until the end of the 19th century, when flood control projects were completed. The main reason for visiting is just over the Pont Neuf: the round brick lighthouse-shaped tower of a pumping and filtering station, built in 1817 to provide pure drinking water to the city. In 1974 this found a new use as the **Galerie Municipale du Château-d'Eau** (***t*** *05 61 77 09 40; open Wed–Mon 1–7, closed hols; adm*). The hydraulic machinery is still intact on the bottom level, while upstairs you can visit one of Europe's top photographic galleries; exhibits change 15 times a year. An annexe has been installed in a dry arch of the Pont Neuf. There is also a reference library on the history of photography (*open to the public Mon–Fri 1.30–6 and the 1st Sat of each month*).

Opposite the water tower is the **Hôtel-Dieu St-Jacques**, a medieval pilgrimage hospital rebuilt in the 17th century. The grand Salle St-Jacques and Salle St-Lazare have magnificent ceilings, while down on floor level the hospital now houses a **Musée d'Histoire de la Médecine** (***t*** *05 61 77 84 25; open Wed–Sun 2–6*). Each of France's four great rivers has a nickname, and the Garonne is 'the Laughing'. Often enough, the joke has been on Toulouse. St Cyprien, the original dedicatee of the Left Bank's parish church (behind the Hôtel-Dieu), proved to wield so little celestial influence over the water that when his church was rebuilt in 1300 he was sacked in favour of **St Nicolas**, patron of sailors and protector of the flooded. The church is a small southern Gothic version of the Jacobins and boasts a grand 18th-century altar painted by Despax.

More visual arts, this time in the form of graphics, posters, ads and postcards from the 17th century to the present, are the subject of the changing exhibits at the **Centre Municipal de l'Affiche, de la Carte Postale et de l'Art Graphique** (*58 Allées Charles de Fitte,* ***t*** *05 61 59 24 64, St-Cyprien métro; open Mon–Fri 9–12 and 2–6; adm*); there's an extensive book, film and record library, and, most popular of all, French commercials – those that used to be shown in the cinemas – from 1904 to 1968, on video cassettes (*open to the public by appointment*). Just up the road is Toulouse's newest museum, **Les Abattoirs** (*76 Allée Charles de Fitte,* ***t*** *05 62 48 58 01; open Tues–Sun 12–8, 11–7 in winter*), dedicated to modern art. The prize exhibit, displayed on and off throughout the year, was created just outside the timeframe for most of the work: a stage curtain for the play *14 Juillet* by Romain Rolland, painted by Luis Fernandez in 1936 on the request of Pablo Picasso, and copied from the great man's gouache of the corpse of a Minotaur in the costume of a Harlequin.

The Ariège, Andorra and the Eastern Pyrenees

12

Highlights

1 Sensational underground river-boating at Labouiche, near Foix

2 The Château de Montségur, the Alamo of the Cathars

3 An intriguing multi-layered church at Vals

4 Fabulous caves around Tarascon-sur-Ariège

5 Upper Palaeolithic artistry in the Grotte de Niaux

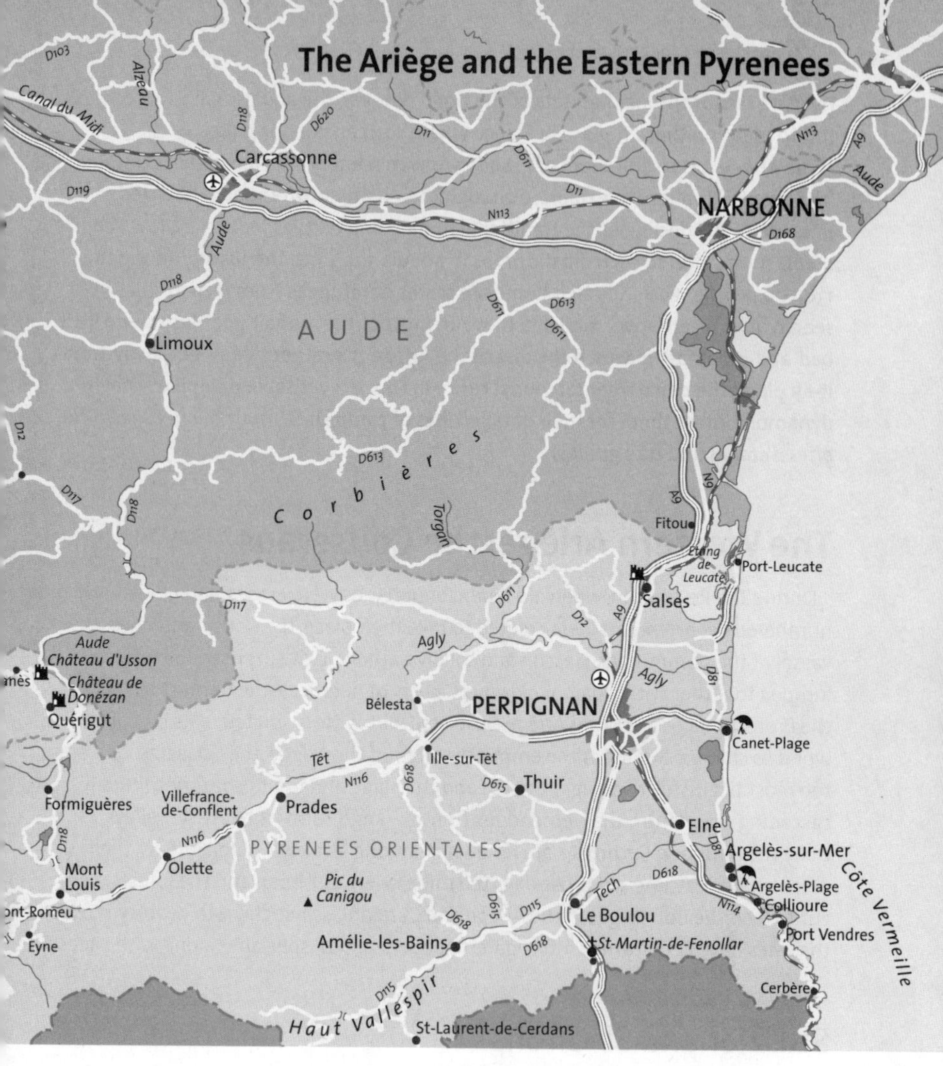

Once the proud, remote and independent Comté de Foix, the Ariège occupies several frontiers: obviously Spain and Andorra over the Pyrenees, but also the more subtle division between Gascony (west of the river Ariège) and the Mediterranean-facing region of Languedoc. The difference was most acute between the 12th and 14th centuries, when the Cathar heresy thrived on the Languedoc side and Montségur, the Cathars' famous temple-cum-fortress, defied the Albigensian Crusaders from the north. The Ariège has another distinction, magnificent on at least one level, even if it's subterranean: it has more caves than any *département* in France, including 13 that were decorated in prehistoric times (one, Niaux, has the best art of any cave that's readily open to the public). Just as prehistoric are the *mérens* of the Ariège, a sturdy breed of black horses with a pedigree as old as Magdalenian times – now stables hire them out for mountain treks. The wilder tributaries of the Ariège

river are one of the last habitats of the timid *desman*, the aquatic web-footed mole, not to mention the last place in France where you can pan for gold.

The Ariège has its full share of grand Pyrenean scenery to offer: high mountains and beautiful valleys to explore, although their hamlets often seem haunted. Because of the decline of the traditional mining and textiles industries, few *départements* have suffered such drastic drops in population since the 1850s. Among the 136,500 people who still call it home are scores of refugees from French cities in search of an alternative, rural life; they run most of the mohair goat farms and little bed-and-breakfast places. If the rest of the Ariège is a rather sleepy, get-away-from-it-all place, the departmental tourist office in Foix is a veritable pamphlet-spewing dynamo: contact them for their detailed lists of camp sites, mountain *refuges*, *gîtes*, *gîtes d'étapes* and trail guides.

The Western Ariège: the Couserans

During the Revolution, when old feudal boundaries were erased and new, neatly numbered *départements* were created to take their place, the Couserans, once a vassal of the Comminges, Gascon and solidly Catholic, was surprised to find itself lumped together with a pair of old vipers' nests of heretics – the Cathars of Foix and the Protestants of the lower Ariège. Surprised, but far too isolated in its own little world to change. But if it is the emptiest corner of the Ariège, the Couserans is also the most beautiful: two rivers, the Lez and the Salat, and their tributaries, literally cascading down from the tremendous frontier range, form its heart. Its valleys, especially the Biros and Bethmale, are renowned among students of folklore for their astonishing costumes. In those days the mines were still open and the forests were cut to feed the iron forges in the Ariège and Catalonia; since the 18th century, most of the trees have been turned into cigarette papers, a local speciality, along with cheese.

St-Lizier and St-Girons

Prettily piled on its hill like a Tuscan hill town, St-Lizier is the age-old capital of the Couserans, one of the chief cities of Gallo-Roman *Novempopulanie*. Its founding father, Pompey, called it *Lugdunum Consoranum*, a mouthful the inhabitants soon changed to *Austria*, and then to St-Lizier, after a 7th-century Portuguese priest who defended the town against the Visigoths. After being thoroughly sacked in 1130 by Count Bertrand III of Comminges, the population trickled down to a new town, St-Girons, located at the confluence of the Salat and the Lez, leaving lofty St-Lizier alone with its bishop. The Revolution not only gave him his walking papers, but forced St-Lizier and St-Girons to join together as one *commune*.

There's no reason to loiter in St-Girons; instead make your way up to St-Lizier by way of the D117, passing a 13th-century **bridge** built from cannibalized Roman stones, including an altar to Belisama, the Gallo-Roman goddess of wisdom. Roman stone also went into the quirky **Cathédrale St-Lizier**, begun in the 11th century; the name of

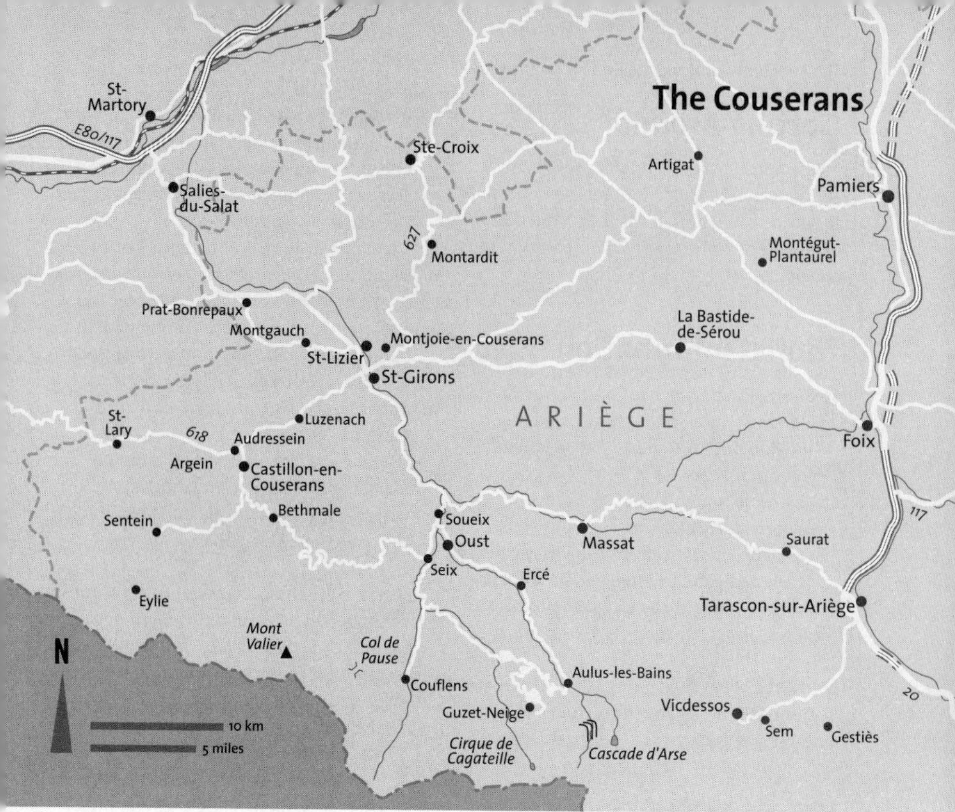

the architect is unknown, but anyone who knows their nursery rhymes will recognize the hand of the crooked man who built the crooked house. From the outside it looks fairly normal, sporting a stout, straight octagonal bell tower, good modillons around the apse and a Gothic brick portal. Cross this threshold and everything's a bit fishy: the nave and choir are built on different axes, the left wall is at a tilted angle, the columns with little faces and carvings peering out from the bases don't match up and the transepts are of uneven length. The walls of the apses are 6ft thick, and may have originally been defensive towers. Rare, faded 12th-century frescoes of the *apostles*, the *Annunciation* and the *Epiphany* decorate the arches, while in the apse there's a 14th-century po-faced *Christ Pantocrator*, with rosy cheeks and a stern, startled expression (doubtless a comment on the architecture). The oak choir stalls and gilded *Pietà* date from the 17th century; don't miss the richly coloured 15th-century stained glass near the entrance.

The very pretty yet simple two-storey 12th-century **cloister** is to the right, its arcades of twinned marble columns crowned with carved capitals, some with interlacings, others with figures of imaginary beasts and demons. St-Lizier's **trésor** (*open only with the guided tour, see box overleaf*) is full of precious things that somehow escaped the usual robbers, Protestants and anti-clerical *sans-culottes*: a 14th-century reliquary bust of St Lizier, made of silver and semi-precious stones, a 12th-century bishop's mitre of white silk, a 13th-century painted wooden chest, and much more. The tour also includes a visit to the perfectly intact 18th-century hospital **pharmacy** in the

Getting Around

Buses link St-Girons to Toulouse, Martres-Tolosane and St-Martory; others descend daily to Seix and Aulus-les-Bains (**t** 05 61 66 08 87), while one or two go to Castillon-en-Couserans and Sentein (**t** 05 61 66 26 56).

Tourist Information

St-Girons: Place Alphonse-Sentein, **t** 05 61 96 26 60, *www.ville-st-girons.fr. Open July and Aug Mon–Sat 10–6.30 plus Sun 10–1; winter Mon–Sat 10–12 and 2–6.*

St-Lizier: Rue Neuve, **t** 05 61 96 77 77, *www.ariege.com/st-lizier.* Has daily tours in season (*10–12 and 2–6*), the only way you can see the cathedral treasure and hospital pharmacy. Book ahead for guided tours in winter. *Open daily June–Sept 10–12 and 2–6.*

Market Days

St-Girons: Saturday and the second and fourth Monday of each month.

Where to Stay and Eat

St-Girons ✉ 09200

******Eychenne***, 8 Av Paul-Laffont, **t** 05 61 04 04 50, **f** 05 61 96 07 20, *www.ariege.com/hotel-eychenne* (*moderate*). Built as St-Girons' post house, it has been in the same family for six generations. Over the decades they have made it into a wonderfully comfortable inn with a heated pool and garden. The vast old-fashioned dining room has a menu of classic French specialities and one of the Ariège's best wine lists. *Closed Sun eve and Mon from Nov–Mar; also closed Dec and Jan. Menus €23–50.*

****La Clairiere**, Av de la Résistance, **t** 05 61 66 66 66, *www.ariege.com/la-clairiere* (*inexpensive*) A modern, wood-shingled hotel and restaurant just outside St-Girons, with a garden, swimming pool and a pretty good restaurant. *Hotel open all year. Restaurant closed Sun eve and Mon and Nov. Menus €14–34.*

****Hôtel de l'Union**, 1 Place du Champ-de-Mars, **t** 05 61 66 09 12 (*inexpensive*). A reasonable hotel in an old building beside the river. There's a jazz bar and brasserie. *Open all year.*

Le Relais d'Encausse, 1.5km outside St-Girons, at Saudech, **t** 05 61 66 05 80, mornings **t** 05 61 96 21 03 (*inexpensive*). A beautifully restored old country inn with four rooms, and a salon with a fireplace. *Open all year.*

La Maison Blanche, **t** 05 61 66 48 33, **t** 06 12 52 36 00 (*inexpensive*). In Lorp, west of St-Lizier. Three bed-and-breakfast rooms for non-smokers only. There is also a restaurant (*cheap*). *Open all year.*

Restaurant Le Pâtre Gourmand, 14B Av A. Berges, 09190 Lorp, Senteraille. On D117, direction Salies. 5.5km from St. Girons, **t** 05 61 66 54 49. Excellent food, good value, friendly and efficient service. The management also runs the Château de Beauregard (same phone and web). *Menus €11–26. Closed Mon and Tues from Oct–May.*

former Hôtel Dieu (now a retirement home), with its lovely woodwork, shelves of pharmaceutical jars made in Martres-Tolosane and an armillary sphere the doctors would consult to calculate the most auspicious time for an operation.

While strolling the narrow streets of St-Lizier, look out for traces of ancient Austria's 3rd-century **walls** and dozen **towers**, some of which have melded with later buildings. The road from the cathedral square leads up to the garden terrace and the massive 1660 **Palais des Evêques** (*t 05 61 04 81 86; open April, May and Oct 2–6; June and Sept 10–12 and 2–6; July and Aug 10–7; closed Monday except in school hols*) that dominates the skyline; it incorporates three semi-circular Roman towers and the Gothic cathedral of Notre-Dame-de-la Sède (12th–15th centuries; *under restoration at the time of writing*), and has excellent views over the Couserans. Housed in the palace is the Musée Départemental de l'Ariège, with the anthropological collections of Jacques Bégouen and Chaubert Mader, focused particularly on the Valley of Bethmale.

Around St-Lizier

Just east of St-Lizier, a narrow road climbs up to 14th-century **Montjoie-en-Couserans**, a tiny fortified town with a massive warlike church, built on the site of a temple dedicated to Jupiter. North, the pretty D627 leads to **Montardit**, where the charming little **chapel** of Notre-Dame-de-la Goutte was built by the local abbé using only pebbles and stones from the river Volp. Further north, the luxuriant fir **Fôret de Ste-Croix** is a botanical oddity, at only 350m altitude instead of the cool 1,400 or so metres that the species usually prefers – an odd pocket of trees that found the micro-climate convivial after the retreat of the glaciers in the last Ice Age, 15,000 years ago.

The little D33 leads west of St-Lizier to the charming Romanesque church of **Montgauch**, containing medieval frescoes by an itinerant Catalan artist. The road continues around to **Prat-et-Bonrepaux**, a largish town under a 13th-century castle belonging to the Counts of Comminges. Its Renaissance decoration dates from its occupation by Jean de Mauléon, the art-loving bishop of Comminges.

The Valleys of the Couserans

For centuries cut off from the mainstream, the magnificent high valleys of the Couserans are now almost deserted. But life, if very colourful, was always hard here. The women hired themselves out as wet nurses, the men as miners, woodcutters or shepherds; they brought ice down the mountains to Toulouse, or trained dancing bears. While travelling in the region, you may want to consider a Couserans cheese-tasting tour; four *fromageries* with their ripening caves welcome visitors: Du Château, at Moulis, ***t** 05 61 66 09 64*; Le Moulin Gourmande at Engomer, ***t** 05 61 96 83 38*; Le Bamalou, at Castillon, ***t** 05 61 96 76 19*; and Fromagerie Jean Faup ***t** 05 61 66 01 63*. (*Visits in July and Aug, Mon–Sat at 10am; phone ahead for rest of year.*)

Up the Vallée du Lez

South of St-Girons, the D618 follows the torrential river Lez to **Aubert**, an otherwise nondescript hamlet with marble quarries that produced stone used for Napoleon's tomb in the Invalides (he's boxed in seven sarcophagi, all of different materials, to make sure he never gets out again). The next hamlet, **Luzenac**, has a pretty Romanesque church, with mullioned windows in its bell tower and a unique undulating façade. **Audressein** is one of many villages in the Couserans with a very nasal 'ein' ending, believed to go back to the Iron Age language of the Pyrenees. It has a remarkable pilgrimage church, the Gothic **Notre-Dame-de-Tramezaygues** (from the Latin *inter-amabas-aquas*, 'between two waters'), built in the 13th century. Murals cover its porch: SS. James and John the Baptist, pilgrims with candles and a whole series of vivid *ex votos* from the 1400s and 1500s thanking the Virgin for assistance rendered in all aspects of life, from stopping nosebleeds to cushioning falls out of trees (note the flagrant lack of underwear!). One man in his *ex voto* seems to be thanking the Mother of God for a successful murder.

If all this is too cosmopolitan, there's the **Vallée de la Bellongue** west of Audressein, lined with beech and fir forests and twelve tiny hamlets, including **Argein**, which are

Tourist Information

Castillon-en-Couserans: t 05 61 96 72 64, *www.ot-castillon-en-couserans.fr. Open Mon–Sat 9–12 and 2–6.*

Sentein: t 05 61 96 10 90. For information on *gîtes*, call t 05 61 02 30 80; they have a list of *gîtes* which can accommodate between 3 and 10 people in restored houses in a dozen hamlets. *Open July and Aug Mon–Fri 10–7 plus Sat 8–12 and 3–8, Sun 11–1; winter Mon–Sat 9–12 and 2–6.*

Seix: t 05 61 96 00 01, *www.haut-couserans.com. Open July and Aug daily 9.30–12.30 and 2.30–6.30; winter Mon– Fri same hours as above.*

Aulus-les-Bains: t 05 61 96 02 22.

Massat: t 05 61 96 92 76, *www.ariege.com/massat. Open July and Aug Mon–Fri 10–1 and 2–7, Sat 9–1 and 2–7, Sun 10–1; winter Tues–Fri 9.30–1 and 2–6, Sat 9–1 and 2–7.*

Market Days

Seix: first and third Thursday Sept–Oct, and second and fourth Wednesday only during the rest of the year.

Where to Stay and Eat

Accommodation is a bit scarce on the ground in the Couserans. Even so, it is not the most frequented of areas and you may have it all to yourself, except in July and August when it is wise to book in advance.

Argein ✉ 09800

****La Terrasse,** t 05 61 96 70 11 (*inexpensive*). Charming, with 10 comfortable rooms. The restaurant has good local specialities on the menu, including fresh trout and wild boar with chestnuts. *Closed from 15 Nov–1 Mar. Closed for lunch, except Sun. Menu €15.*

***L'Auberge d'Audressein,** 3km from Argein, t 05 61 96 11 80, *www.visitorama.com* (*cheap*). An old stone house beside a stream; a good place to book a table for a special meal. Some of the most delicately prepared dishes in the whole *département* are served in the cosy dining room; try *Quartier d'agneau ariégeois, rôti au jus clair de morille.* There is also a handful of cheap rooms available. *Closed mid-Nov to mid-Feb. Closed Sun eve and all Mon except July and Aug. Closed Jan. Menus €14–44.*

Oust ✉ 09140

****Hostellerie de la Poste,** Rue Principale, t 05 61 66 86 33, *www.ariege.com/hoteldelaposte* (*inexpensive*). In an old village house with a garden, pool and rooms with their own terraces. The restaurant is a local favourite for Sunday lunch, especially for the stuffed pigeon with garlic cream. *Closed Mon and Tues plus 11 Nov–Easter. Menus €18–39.*

Seix ✉ 09140

Auberge des Ormeaux, Trein d Ustou, 09140 Seix (on D8), t 05 61 96 53 22, *www.ariege.com/aubergedesormeaux.* Pleasant auberge with pretty bedrooms and

the best places to stay and eat in the Couserans. Further up the valley, **Castillon-en-Couserans** was the local seat of the Counts of Commminges, although the castle was demolished by Cardinal Richelieu, leaving only the **Chapelle de St-Pierre**, with a large wooden porch and a pretty door with marble columns, sculpted capitals and a very old statue of St Peter. There's a big hydroelectric plant at **Bordes-sur-Lez**, standing at the confluences of the Biros and Bethmale valleys; nearby, the teeny tiny hamlet of **Ourjout** has a quaint old bridge and a quaint old church from the 11th century.

The Vallées de Biros and Mont Valier

Francis Bacon's 'One triumphs over nature only by obeying its rules' is the slogan of the enchanting Biros valley, with its peaceful, rural landscapes frozen in time, lush green in the spring and shimmering with a golden patina in early autumn. It is one of a jolly host. Restaurant serves regional cuisine. *Menus: €13, 15. Closed Wed except July and Aug plus 2 weeks in Nov.*

*__Auberge des Deux Rivières__, **t** 05 61 66 83 57, *www.ariege.com/auberge2riviere*. In a pretty former post house, with a terrace overlooking the river and good local cooking. *Menus €15–30. Closed Sun eve and Mon exc July and Aug, plus mid-Nov–Feb.*

Le Moulin Gourmand: **t** 05 61 96 83 38. A *fromagerie* that includes a restaurant (meals served in July and August only.). Mr. Gimbrede uses methods that date all the way back to the 18th century. You can visit the *fromagerie* daily at 10am, or, rather than the usual tasting, enjoy his wonderful cheeses accompanying local cooking. Try the cheesecake with honey, or with coffee and rum. *Menus €20 and €24. Closed Mon and Tues.*

*__Auberge du Haut Salat__, **t** 05 61 66 88 03 (*cheap*). A simple but comfortable hotel. *Closed Nov.*

Aulus-les-Bains ✉ 09140

***__Hostellerie La Terrasse__, in the main street, **t** 05 61 96 00 98 (*moderate*). The most delightful place to stay and eat in Aulus, with a terrace over the Garbet and an interior furnished with antiques. Try one of the delicious specialities of the house, *capeline de veau mijotée aux herbes* or salmon with *foie gras en papillotes*. *Closed Dec–mid-May. Menus €16–31.*

__Les Oussaillès__, **t 05 61 96 03 68, *www.ariege.com/les-oussailles* (*inexpensive*). Mock-Gothic turrets and balconied rooms. You can feast on delicious salads, trout or veal, or ask for a picnic basket to take away. Even vegetarians are catered for. *Menus €14–31. Open all year.*

__Le France__, **t 05 61 96 00 90 (*cheap*). Unbeatable in price. The *half-pension* is a bargain, and the food is good too. Look out for the old wild cat that was rescued from the forest that holds court over the dining room. *Menus €11–25. Closed end Oct to end Dec.*

Massat ✉ 09320

__Hostellerie des Trois Seigneurs__, **t 05 61 96 95 89, **f** 05 61 04 90 52 (*inexpensive*). A chalet-style *auberge* with a terraced restaurant (*moderate–cheap*), comfortable salon and garden. Good country cooking includes delicious *coq au vin* and river perch with sorrel. *Menus. €15–20. Open mid-April–mid-Nov.*

__Le Globe__, in the centre, **t 05 61 96 96 66, **f** 05 61 04 91 63 (*inexpensive*). A comfortable old inn with a garden. There's a café serving breakfast and sandwiches. *Open all year.*

Ferme-Auberge Las Trinquades, Boussenac, **t** 05 61 96 95 39 (*inexpensive*). In a peaceful village in the middle of nowhere, 6km east of Massat. Superb location, isolated in the mountains. Very comfortable lodging is available in three chalets during July and August, and at weekends only the rest of the year. *Chambre d'hôte* accommodation is available year round. For a meal based on lamb, book a table here. *Menus €13–17.*

the finest places for walks in the Pyrenees, with the majestic backdrop of **Mont Valier** (2,839m/9,369ft), which is also a popular and easy ascent if you think you may be up to a bit of mountain climbing. Named after the first man to scale it, the 5th-century bishop of the Couserans, St Valerus, the mountain was long thought to be the highest of the Pyrenees; its abrupt east flank, rising 1,700m/5,577ft (including 800m of sheer rock wall), holds the record for the highest rock face in the range, and Valier's glacier is the easternmost in the Pyrenees. In St Valerus' day, the forests were full of wolves and bears; these days the mountain is a *Réserve de Chasse*, where you're quite likely to see izards springing from rock to rock. The classic route up Valier is to drive up the Riberot valley (south of Bordes-sur-Lez) to the car park, then make the four-hour walk up to the **Refuge des Estagnous** (***t*** *05 61 96 76 22; open June–Sept daily plus May and Oct weekends only*), leaving the remaining two-hour ascent until the next morning.

The capital of the Biros valley, **Sentein**, has a very old church built in the 15th century, once fortified and still defended by three square towers (a fourth was lopped off). One forms the base for an octagonal bell tower with a jauntily tilted weathervane; frescoes inside depict the *Tree of Jesse* and the *Last Judgement*. A fairly easy one-day's walk from Sentein leads up to the **chapelle d'Isard**, where until recently pilgrim shepherds would spill sheep's milk offerings over the rocks; the beautiful setting is enough to make you religious.

Serious walkers can continue on the same route for the two-day hike up the GR 10 to the **Pic de Crabère** (2,629m/8,676ft). If you make it to the top you are rewarded by some wonderful views west over Maladetta. South of Eylie, at the end of the Biros valley road, you can take an even more difficult path right up to the frontier at the **Port d'Urets** (2,512m/ 8,290ft), which is at the foot of the local landmark, the rounded **Pic de Maubermé**, a two-day trek; contact the Sentein tourist office, which has all the details and maps.

The Vallée de Bethmale

Bordes-sur-Lez stands at the entrance to the most famous valley of the Couserans, the Vallée de Bethmale, celebrated for both its natural beauty and its delightful red and black costumes. The men's costumes are remarkably similar to those once worn in the Peloponnese (these days they're only taken out of the closets for holidays; 15 August is a good time to see them). The striking physical differences between the natives of the Biros and Bethmale valleys has often been commented on. While the people of Biros are short, those in Bethmale are tall and famous for their exceptional good looks. Local stories account for the difference and the costumes: one, that a Bethmale man named Soulan led a colony of Irish to Greece, but they were eventually evicted and ended up back here; another, perhaps slightly less outlandish, tells how a 17th-century merchant made his fortune in Greece, came back with a harem of a dozen wives and repopulated the valley with his progeny. The most extraordinary part of the Bethmale costume is the pointy, scimitar-shaped clogs decorated with copper nails and hearts. Wonderfully bizarre, they are remarkably similar to the footwear featured in that 1989 Finnish film classic, Aki Kaurismäki's *Leningrad Cowboys Go America*. In the old days, the clogs would be carved out of walnut wood by a man for his fiancée; the points are said to have shielded tender toes from the mountain rocks. If seeing is believing, go to **Samortein-en-Bethmale** (*t 05 61 96 78 84; open all year 3–7*) where they're still made, displayed and sold by one of the two last clog-makers in the Ariège (there are only 10 left in the whole of France), or *sabotiers* (the word 'sabotage' comes from disgruntled French workers hurling their *sabots* into factory machinery; a Bethmale *sabot* could stop a tank).

Other sights in the valley are slightly less pointed, including a 7ft menhir, **Peyro-Quillado**, near Ayet. The most traditional village, **Ayet-en-Bethmale**, is also the starting point for the valley's prettiest walk, to the romantic **Lac de Bethmale** (about two hours, there and back). At the top of the valley, the D17 continues east over the beautiful Col de la Core to Seix and the Vallée de Salat (*see* below).

The Valleys of the Salat

If you're not riding over the Col de la Core, the main approach to the Couserans' eastern river from St-Girons is on the D3, through the Gorges of Ribaouto and the Kercabannac tunnel. Following this and the Salat to the south, the first village is **Soueix**, where the Romanesque chapel of St-Sernin has some pretty capitals. The main centre is **Seix**, a convivial old cheese-making village, with houses overlooking the Salat and places to hire canoes or kayaks for thrills and spills. By car you can continue straight up the Salat river gorge to **Couflens**: if your brakes are in perfect working order, you can twist and turn up the zigzagging D703 to the **Col de Pause** (1,527m/5,039ft) for the breathtaking view of Mont Valier just to the west. If you're very adventurous, you can continue up the even more hair-raising and hairpin extension to the **Port d'Aula** (3,360m/7,458ft) for a look into the wildest corner of Spain. The much more sedate D8 south of Seix runs up the bucolic, pastoral **Vallée d'Ustou** and over to Aulus-les-Bains.

From the north, the approach to Aulus is down the equally beautiful **Vallée du Garbet** (take the D32 between Soueix and Seix). **Vic d'Oust**, the first hamlet, is a pretty little place, built around a Romanesque church with a charmingly painted ceiling and a 16th-century manor house. In the 19th century the next hamlet, **Ercé**, was famous for its **Bear School**. As far as anyone knows the first bears were trained to dance, perform tricks and simulate mock fights in the 12th century. If a cub was captured young (the fiercely protective mother bear invariably had to be killed first), it could be as easily domesticated as a dog, raised to play with the children and fed with milk. The rest of the dancing bear's life was tough, beginning with rigorous training, with far more stick than carrot. When the year's graduating class of bears was ready, they would be brought into Ercé's main square and bound tightly to the trees, soon to be roaring with agony as white-hot irons were driven through their muzzles for the nose rings they would wear for the rest of their lives. By the 1850s, bears were so rare that the Ariégeois trainers had to import them from Russia or Hungary; they were so prized that a local bride could have a bear as her dowry (which is a bit more exciting than the typical dowry of a country maiden in the Gers: a bag of pigeon droppings).

Aulus-les-Bains

At the top of the narrow, forested valley of the Garbet, surrounded by a *cirque* of wild rocky walls and waterfalls, Aulus-les-Bains, the spa of the Couserans, enjoys one of the most spectacular settings of any town in the Pyrenees. Until recently dismissed as a rather fuddy-duddy old place for people with digestive and urinary ailments, Aulus has built itself a brand-new glass and wood **Thermes** worthy of its lovely suroundings, with a pool open to the general public. The most popular day excursion from Aulus is on the GR 10 to the absolutely gorgeous triple waterfall with an irresistible name, the **Cascade d'Arse**; from there circle back to Aulus by way of the Etang de Guzet. Other beauty spots are the **Col d'Escot**, along the D68 above Aulus, and the ski resort of **Guzet-Neige** (there are buses in the winter from Aulus); both overlook the bewitching **Cirque de Cagateille**, one of the most beautiful in the Pyrenees.

The Green Valleys

The drive east of Aulus to the **Vallée de Vicdessos** on the D18 is just as spectacular, passing by way of the **Col d'Agnes** (1,570m/5,181ft), with its excellent views of the Andorran frontier chain, and the lake and waterfalls of **Lers** (or Lhers). Lers sits in luscious emerald scenery; the lake lent its name to Lherzolite, the curious green volcanic rock formations you see along its banks. At the lake, a secondary road leads north to **Massat**, former capital of the viscounts of the Couserans and today the centre of the Vallées Vertes, a region if anything even quieter and more forgotten than the rest of the Couserans. Massat itself is a handsome old village, with plenty of room to spare, surrounded by chestnuts, beech and pine forests; there's a stable of *mérens* for riding tours, and good cross-country skiing in the winter. East of Massat the scenic D618 leads eventually down to Tarascon, or you can cut across the mountains at Caougnous (a short but very steep road) for the D17, the beautiful 'Route Verte' where one enchanting view follows another all the way down to Foix.

East of St-Girons and the Lower Ariège

The northeast corner of the Ariège has for its centrepiece the Grotte du Mas-d'Azil, a cave with a record-breaking occupancy rate for more millennia than tongue can tell. It occupies the green hilly *piedmont* area where the mountains meet the plain, but where far too often the traditional free spirit of the mountains collided head on with less tolerant central powers, especially in the Wars of Religion, when most of the Basse Ariège belonged to the Protestant camp.

Le Mas-d'Azil: the Cave and the Village

It sounds like something you'd expect in California: a drive-through prehistoric cave. But there it is – the D119 winds right through the yawning 214ft mouth of the **Grotte de Mas d'Azil**, running alongside the cave-tunnel's architect, the River Arize. The first human inhabitants settled here in the Aurignacian era (30,000 BC) and stayed on through the Solutrean (18,000 BC) and the Magdalenian (12,000 BC). At the end of the Ice Age (8000 BC), the cave still had its inhabitants, and gave its name (Azilian) to their culture, one of the chief links between Upper Palaeolithic and Neolithic civilizations. In the Azilian era, the glaciers slowly retreated, along with the reindeer that Palaeolithic hunters had depended on, forcing them to make the change from hunting to pastoral and agricultural pursuits. The first persecuted Christians in the region, in the 3rd century, worshipped in the cave; in the 9th century the Benedictines built an abbey here. Every possible band of Pyrenean fugitives – Moors, Cathars and Protestants – took refuge at Le Mas-d'Azil at some point.

Some of the galleries on the right bank may be visited (*Closed Mon except for school hols. Open April–Sept 10–6; closed Dec–Mar. In Oct and Nov call* **t** *05 61 69 97 71 or mairie* **t** *05 61 69 99 90*). There are three upper floors; the lowest one, unfortunately not open, is named after the great prehistorian Henri Breuil, who discovered its

Magdalenian-era **etchings** (one, unusually, of Atlantic fish). The next level has the **Salle du Temple**, where the Protestants worshipped in 1625 while holding out against the Catholic army (*see* below), and on top is the **Galerie des Ours**, full of bones and teeth left behind by the enormous but now extinct cave bears. A discovery made here in 1961, of the skull of a girl with carved bones simulating eyes stuck in the sockets, is remarkable as the only known example of a Palaeolithic skull prepared in any ritual way; some scholars see it as proof of a Stone Age belief in the afterlife. Tools from the Azilian technological revolution and other finds are exhibited here, while others have been deposited in the **Musée de la Préhistoire** (***t*** *05 61 69 97 22; open for Easter hols and June–Sept daily 10–1 and 2–7; winter 2–6; call ahead for confirmation*), in the village of **Le Mas-d'Azil**, just opposite the 17th-century church with a bulbous dome.

Tourist Information

Le Mas-d'Azil: opposite the church, **t** 05 61 69 99 90. *Open all year Mon–Fri 9–12 and 2–6 plus Sat 9–12.*

La Bastide-de-Sérou: **t** 05 61 64 53 53. *Open all year Mon–Fri 9–12 and 2–6 plus Sat 9–12.*

Pamiers: Bd Delcassé, **t** 05 61 67 52 52, *www.pamierstourisme.com. Open all year Mon–Fri 9–12 and 2–6 plus Sat 9–12.*

Market Days

Le Mas-d'Azil: Saturday farmer's market. Fair on Wednesday.

Pamiers: Tuesday, Thursday and Saturday.

Mazères: Friday and Monday.

Saverdun: Friday and Sunday.

Where to Stay and Eat

Le Mas-d'Azil ✉ 09290

★★**Hôtel Gardel**, on the main square, **t** 05 61 69 90 05 (*inexpensive*). Pleasantly old-fashioned. The restaurant features freshwater fish and Ariègeois cheeses. *Menus €11–25. Closed mid Nov–mid-Mar. Restaurant closed Sun eves (Sept–May).*

Le Jardin de Cadettou, St-Ferréol, **t** 05 61 69 95 23, *www.cadettou.fr* (*inexpensive*). Just outside the centre, serving the best food in Le Mas-d'Azil in its cosy dining room. The top-notch restaurant specializes in an unusual variety of *confits* – potted duck, pork, lamb, rabbit and pigeon; the pork served with an onion confiture is especially good. Also try their famous *omelette aux pommes du Mas d'Azil. Menus €14–32. Closed Jan plus all Mon, Sat lunch and Sun eves exc July and Aug.*

Auberge des Traouques, Montfa, **t** 05 61 69 85 79 (get there by way of Sabarat and Les Bordes-sur-Arize, then take the D114 west). The local favourite for a long, laid-back afternoon outing. There is no accommodation but the cuisine is cheap and copious, and there's a pool for a dip, before or after the meal (make sure you leave enough time to digest the meal). You'll need to reserve a table if you want to eat on the terrace.

La Bastide-de-Sérou ✉ 09240

Le Cent-Dix-Sept, **t** 05 61 64 50 26 (*inexpensive*). Convenient for the golf course and Le Mas-d'Azil. *Menus from €12. Open all year.*

Château Rhodes, 3.5km from Bastide, on D117, **t** 05 61 03 24 50, *www.chateaurhodes.com*. This is a truly lovely place set majestically in its own park. It has been renovated and

Artistically, the Azilian era was marked by abstract designs in pebbles painted red with iron pyroxide. These aren't nearly as arresting as earlier Magdalenian-era pieces: the ivory carved animals and casts of two masterpieces from Le Mas-d'Azil (both now in the National Prehistory Museum in St-Germain-en-Laye), the expressive *Protome de Cheval*, carved from a reindeer's antler, and the *Faon aux Oiseaux*, a throwing stick topped with a remarkable carving of a fawn bent over to unburden itself of a large turd, which has two birds sitting and pecking on it. As other items decorated with the same motif have been found around the Pyrenees, the fawn and birds may have had a secret meaning, or it could just be that French cavemen had the same scatalogical sense of humour as their descendants. On the museum's top floor there's an exhibition on the Ariège's **glass industry** – now as extinct as its bears.

Le Mas-d'Azil itself is a pleasant *bastide* town founded in 1286. It was the main Protestant centre in the area in the 16th century; legends say Calvin himself preached here. The ubiquitous Jeanne d'Albret sent money for the town to turn its remarkable cave into a remarkable fortress, and, defended by only a thousand Protestants, it stood up in 1625 to a royal army of 14,000 troops for five weeks before they retreated. Not surprisingly, Cardinal Richelieu put it at the top of his castle decorated beautifully throughout, crammed with antiques but with the additional benefit of all mod-cons. There is a pool, Jacuzzi, billiards, and tennis, and all bedrooms have internet access and cable TV. The young chef offers a gastronomic menu with a hint of the orient. Try the *salade thaïlandaise aux gambas grillées*, fishcakes *et noix St-Jacques sautées au gingembre*, followed by *filet mignon de veau au pancetta garnie de foie gras, pommes caramelisées et jus de veau au poivre*. (€38) There is also a good vegetarian menu for €23. *Meals are served Wed–Sat, eves only plus Sun lunch. Closed Nov–Mar.*

Lanoux/Artigat ✉ 09130

Thibaut, 1km from Artigat, **t** 05 61 68 58 45 (*inexpensive*). Handy if you want to spend time in the *pays de Martin Guerre. Table d'hote menu €15. Closed Dec–Mar.*

Pamiers ✉ 09100

****Hôtel de France**, 5 Cours J. Rambaud (near the Hospital Loumet), **t** 05 61 60 20 88, **f** 05 61 67 29 48 (*inexpensive*). A bit too cute for its own good but has comfortable rooms and good meals. *Menus €12–35. Restaurant closed Sun eve, Oct–June.*

****Hotel de la Paix**, 4 Place Albert Tournier, **t** 05 61 67 12 71, **f** 05 61 60 61 02 (*inexpensive*). An old post house with original Empire decoration. It serves hearty traditional cuisine featuring plenty of foie gras, and also good fish dishes. *Menus €12–30. Open all year.*

Le Roi Gourmand, 21 Rue Pierre Sémard, Hotel-restaurant **t** 05 61 60 12 12. A promising new restaurant serving local delicacies with a twist, including *magret de canard* with *vin d'orange*, and fish roasted with Banyuls. *Menus €12–30. Open all year.*

Carla-Bayle ✉ 09130

Auberge Pierre Bayle, Rue Principale, **t** 05 61 60 63 95. Bar and restaurant with views of the Pyrenees. It serves simple local cuisine such as warm *chèvre* salad with honey, and *confit de canard* with *cèpes. Menus €18–33. Closed Mon plus Wed mid-Sept–mid-April.*

Mazères ✉ 09270

Auberge de l'Hers, Faubourg St-Louis, **t** 05 61 69 45 22. Terrace restaurant beside the river , serving local delights such as duck stuffed with foie gras, *cassoulet* and *azinat* (Ariègeois cabbage soup). *Menus €18–22. Closed Mon and Tues eves plus end Oct–mid-Nov.*

demolition list. The Neolithic salt road passed by here, and there are several dolmens close by: the best one, **Cap del Pouech**, is some 2km up a narrow country road. It's in better shape than the weird abandoned hillside calvary a few kilometres down the D119, in Raynaude.

Around Le Mas-d'Azil

The region around Le Mas-d'Azil is known as the **Montagnes du Plantaurel** – mountains that are hardly mountains at all, but gentle green hills, real golf-course and horse country. **La Bastide-de-Sérou**, along the main D117 between St-Girons and Foix, supplies both: the 18-hole Golf Club de l'Ariège and the Centre National du Chevel des Mérens, where the black horses of the Ariège are bred. Note the *halles* in the centre of the village, with its original grain measure intact. Northeast, at **Montégut-Plantaurel**, you can visit the *Sculpture Monumentale d'Amnesty International*, designed by Christian Lovis. Plaques with the names of political prisoners cover the walls, and are removed whenever the prisoner is freed – and replaced by the name of another prisoner of conscience. The sphere in the centre of the sculpture is to be rebuilt on the day (don't hold your breath) when there are no more plaques to put up.

North of Le Mas-d'Azil, **Carla-Bayle** is a pretty village on a hillcrest with a fine panoramic view of the Pyrenees and a beautiful man-made **lake**, where you can swim. It was called Carla-le-Comte until the Revolution, when it chopped the Comte off and replaced him with Carla-le-Peuple; in 1879 it decided to change once more, dismissing the people and adding Bayle in honour of its most famous son, philosopher-writer Pierre Bayle, a brave soul who fought his own battles against intolerance. Born in 1647, Bayle, a Protestant, lived and died in exile in Rotterdam; his most famous works, an analysis of superstitions (*Pensées sur la comète*) and his *Dictionnaire historique et critique*, were among the main precursors of the 18th-century encyclopedists. You can learn more in the **Musée Pierre-Bayle** (***t*** *05 61 68 51 32; open winter Mon, Wed, Sat and Sun 10–12 and 2–6; summer open daily 10–12 and 3–7*).

East of Carla-Bayle, **Artigat** was the scene of one of the most haunting stories to come out of the 16th century, when a man returning from war convinced most of the village and his 'wife' that he was really who he said he was, even if he bore only a faint resemblance to Martin Guerre. When the real Martin Guerre returned, there was big trouble. The impostor's trial in Toulouse was diligently recorded by Jean de Coras, whose account was used as the basis for *The Return of Martin Guerre* – the book by Natalie Zemon Davis and the movie with Gérard Depardieu, filmed in lushest Ariège.

Le Fossat, further north, has a row of old houses and a powerful fortified church, but more geometrically memorable is **St-Martin-d'Oydes**, to the east, its houses built as a solid circle wall around the fortified church; until 1880, the only entry into the round central square was through a corridor 'for the living and the dead' in one of the houses. The **church**, quirkily modified in the 19th century, still has four baby crenellated towers sprouting out from the bell tower and a few frescoes about a local saint, Anasthase, who was tending plague victims when he collapsed in exhaustion outside the round walls of St-Martin. Satan, who just happened to be passing by, offered to cure Anasthase in exchange for a bowlful of his blood. But the bowl had a leak, and as the saint grew even weaker, he seized his stick and threatened Satan, who beat a hasty retreat; the stick fell in the spilled blood and at once a miraculous spring gurgled up. Washing himself with the water, Anasthase was cured and entered St-Martin, healed a number of people, died on 16 October 1085, and was buried in the church. In May there's a popular pilgrimage to the spring.

Lastly, **Lézat-sur-Lèze**, the northernmost village of the Ariège, is worth a stop for its church of **St-Jean**, with an octagonal bell tower and steeple and a Romanesque portal; inside are a few frescoes and a beautiful 16th-century *Mise au tombeau*.

Pamiers

Pamiers, 'Gateway to the Pyrenees' (if you're coming from Toulouse) and home of flat green beans called *haricots cocos*, is a square peg in the round Ariège, but a successful square peg that has long outgrown Foix and was most upset in the 18th century when the backward old seat of the counts got to be departmental capital. Originally known as Frédèlas after a 5th-century prince of Toulouse, the town and its *pays* were annexed to the Comté de Foix in 1111; when the count returned from the First Crusade, he renamed it *Castrum Apamée* (after Apamea in Syria), hence 'Pamiers'.

If the rest of the *comté* was tempted by Catharism, Pamiers stayed orthodox Catholic; its bishop-inquisitor, Jacques Fournier, became Pope Benedict XII (*see* p.329). The Protestants savaged the town so thoroughly in the Wars of Religion that there's little left to see outside of the central Place du Mercadel and the **St-Antonin Cathedral** (the Romanesque door and carved capitals, and the octagonal brick bell tower with a carillon that plays songs every Sunday morning at 9.45). A second church, **Notre-Dame du Camp**, has a high, austere windowless façade and twin watchtowers; like the cathedral it was mostly rebuilt after the Wars of Religion.

The low rolling agricultural lands of the Basse Ariège around Pamiers offer a few attractions if you're passing through. In the spirit of intolerance that has scarred this region, it was a choice area for concentration camps: there was one at Mazères, another at Villeneuve du Paréage, but the biggest and longest-lasting (1939–44) was just north of Pamiers at **Le Vernet**; the second floor of the *mairie* houses the **Musée du camp de concentration du Vernet** (*t 05 61 68 36 43; open all year Mon–Fri 9–12 and 2–5; closed Wed pm*). Prisoners from many countries were locked up at Le Vernet, including a number of important figures in Resistance movements across Europe. Those who never left are buried in Le Vernet's international cemetery.

North of Le Vernet, **Saverdun**, in spite of being the birthplace of Benedict XII (there are 17th-century frescoes of his life in the church), was and still is the main Protestant stronghold in the Ariège. The troops of the Duke of Wellington used the bell tower of the Romanesque church in nearby **Canté** as target practice, so only half of it stands; if it's open, don't miss the Gallo-Roman **statue** disguised as a holy water stoup. Just west, **Mazères** is an interesting *bastide* founded in 1252, with a beautiful *halles*. It was once one of the most important towns in the Ariège: in 1390, Gaston Fébus entertained Charles VI of France in the Palace of Mazères; part of the welcoming committee was a huge herd of Béarn cows with blue painted horns. Mazères was also the land of the powerful **abbey of Boulbonne**, founded in 1129 by Roger IV of Foix and used for generations as the pantheon of the Counts; both palace and abbey were razed to the ground by the Huguenots. The abbey was rebuilt massively in brick in 1652 and still stands rather forlornly near Calmont.

Foix

Foix may be among the tiniest departmental capitals in France, but it's one of the most striking, a wing of a town tucked between the Arget and Ariège rivers, crowned with a triple tiara of towers on top of its immense rock. This was once the base of the Counts of Foix, who made Foix famous throughout France and Italy, especially when they were named Gaston.

The first Fuxéens, as they're called, lived in the Magdalenian era around the big rock. The Romans planted a military camp here, although the first reference to the town's name (*Castro Fuxi*) only appears on a Merovingian coin. Not long after, a Carolingian abbey was founded here, joined in the 11th century by a castle when the lord of Foix was made a count. Together with the great lords of Languedoc – the Counts of

Getting There and Around

Foix is on the Toulouse–Barcelona rail line, with connections to Pamiers, Tarascon-sur-Ariège, Ax-les-Thermes and L'Hospitalet (with bus connections to Pas de la Casa and Andorra). The station is on Av Pierre Semard, **t** 05 61 02 03 60; information and tickets **t** 08 36 35 35 35.

Several of the runs are taken by SNCF **buses**; all depart from the station at the north end of town off Cours Irenée-Cros. SALT buses, **t** 05 61 65 08 40, link Pas de la Casa and Toulouse; Denamiel buses, **t** 05 61 65 06 06, run from Foix to St-Girons; and Sovitours, **t** 05 61 01 02 35, link Pamiers, Foix, Lavelanet, Mirepoix and Perpignan.

Tourist Information

45 Cours Gabriel-Fauré, next to the *mairie*, **t** 05 61 65 12 12, *www.mairie-foix.fr*. For the whole of the Ariège, contact the Comité Départemental du Tourisme Ariège, Hôtel du Département, B.P. 143, 31 bis Av Charles de Gaulle, **t** 05 61 02 09 70. *Open daily Jul and Aug 9–7. Sept–June Mon–Sat 9–12 and2–6.*

Market Days

Place St-Volusien, Wednesday and Friday. Fair on the 1st, 3rd and 5th Monday.

Where to Stay and Eat

Foix ✉ 09000

*****Audoye-Lons**, Place Duthil, **t** 05 61 65 52 44, **f** 05 61 02 68 18 (*moderate–inexpensive*). Former post house near the Ariège river. A comfortable place to stay, with a terrace restaurant. *Menus €12–30. Closed Fri eve and Sat lunch in winter, plus mid-Dec– mid-Jan.*

*****Hôtel Pyrène**, Rue Serge-Denis, Le Vignoble (2km north on the N20), **t** 05 61 65 48 66, **t** 05 61 65 51 12, **f** 05 61 65 46 69, *www.hotelpyrene.com* (*moderate*). Up-to-date furnishings, a pool and garden. *Closed mid-Dec–mid-Jan.*

****Barbacane**, Av de Lérida, **t** 05 61 65 50 44 (*inexpensive*). One of the nicer places to stay in the centre of town, in a grand bourgeois mansion. *Closed Nov–Mar.*

Gaec de Caussou, 2km from Foix at Cos, **t** 05 61 65 34 42 (*inexpensive*). A renovated old farm with rooms with views over the château and the Pyrenees. *Menus from €15. Open all year.*

Sud Asie, 36 Cours Irenée Cros, just up the Toulouse road, **t** 05 61 02 82 61. A sensation in Foix; a rather austere-looking Vietnamese restaurant (*moderate*) with a large selection of delicious soups, starters and main courses (get there early if you want a table). *Menus €10–30. Closed Mon, Sat and Sun lunch.*

L'Orientale, Rue du Four d'Amont, in the medieval centre, is also okay. *Menus €14–20. Closed Wed.*

Le Phoebus, 3 Cours Irenée-Cros, **t** 05 61 65 10 42. Popular local restaurant with a balcony facing the château. They serve local produce with a rich twist; try duck liver with caramelised apples. There's a good wine list. *Menus €19–36. Closed Sat lunch and Mon from mid July–mid Aug.*

Le Ste-Marthe, 21 Rue Noel Peyrévidal, **t** 05 61 02 87 87. A restaurant serving classics such as *cassoulet*, but also inventive dishes such as a tart of *boudin noir* with *champignons* and salmon with vanilla. *Menus €24–44. Closed Tues and Wed exc July and Aug.*

Around Foix

Le Château de Bénac, Bénac, **t** 05 61 02 65 20 (*inexpensive*), 6km west of Foix. Nine tranquil rooms overlooking the lawn, with good views over the Vallée de la Barguillère. *Menu €16. Closed mid-Nov– 1st Feb.*

****La Barguillère**, St-Pierre-de-Rivière, on the D17, **t** 05 61 65 14 02 (*expensive–moderate*), is a fine little Logis de France hotel with an excellent restaurant. There are a number of fish dishes on the menu, which is rare in the heart of the mountains. *Menus €12–35. Closed Wed and Nov–Mar.*

Auberge des Myrtilles, on the D17 (head west of Foix up to the Col de Marrous), **t** 05 61 65 16 46 (*inexpensive*). Little timbered mountain *auberge*, tucked away in the forest. Comfortable rooms with full bathrooms plus indoor pool, sauna and Jacuzzi. The restaurant specializes in grills, local trout, duck sausage and, naturally, *tarte aux myrtilles* (mountain bilberries). *Menus €15–22. Closed Mon and Tues out of season and Nov until Feb.*

Toulouse and Carcassonne – the Counts of Foix protected the Cathars and fought for their independence against the northern French invaders in the Albigensian Crusade (*see* 'Montségur', below). Their defeat discouraged the Counts for about five minutes. Throughout the 13th century their power and influence spread over the Pyrenees; in 1278 they were made co-princes of Andorra; in 1290 Count Roger Bernard III inherited the country of Béarn through his wife. This juicy prize made the dynasty's fortune, especially under the leadership of Gaston de Foix, better known as Gaston Fébus (d. 1391) who made himself one of the most powerful lords in the 14th century and came close to creating a new Pyrenean state (*see* pp.200–201). His descendant, Catherine de Foix, Queen of Navarre, married Jean d'Albret, and their son, another Gaston de Foix, made his reputation in Flanders and the wars of Italy, as the Renaissance's 'perfect knight', before he was killed in the Battle of Ravenna.

Foix had already lost much of its importance in the 14th century, when its counts abandoned it to reside in Béarn. In 1663 it lost its bishopric and administrative roles to Pamiers, and was well along the way to sinking into even greater obscurity when the deputies of the Revolution gave it a new lease of life as the capital of the new *département* number 09 – the Ariège.

A Walk Around Medieval Foix

Although ringed by 19th-century development, the narrow winding street plan of old Foix is still intact, closed in by its rivers and the mighty rock of the castle. The town wall has been replaced by busy Cours Gabriel Fauré, named after the musician and composer (1845–1924) who was born in Pamiers but spent much of his early life in Foix; it's the easiest place to park as well. Behind the Hôtel de Ville, half-timbered houses from the 14th to 16th centuries lean out, especially over Place Parmentier, Place Lazema, Rue des Chapeliers (note No.30, the house of De Téville, captain of the Mousquetiers under Louis XII) and Rue de la Faurie, the street of the blacksmiths. Where Rue de la Faurie meets Rue des Marchandes, a bronze relief of a swan decorates the lovely if misnamed 19th-century **Fontaine de l'Oie**.

Down at the bottom of Rue des Marchandes you'll find Foix's cosy **market square** and its church, **St-Volusien**, begun in the 11th century by the counts, and mostly rebuilt in the 17th century. St Volusien, who lived in the 5th century, doesn't exactly get a lot of churches. A senator of Tours, married to a famous nagging shrew, Volusien managed to stay out of his wife's way by becoming one of the most powerful, high-ranking supporters of Clovis, King of the Franks. He was made bishop of Tours in 488, but was exiled to Toulouse by the Visigoth King Alaric II for his refusal to support the Arian heresy. When Clovis killed Alaric II in 507 and besieged Toulouse, the Visigoths under their new king Amalric made a run for Spain with their hostages, including Volusien, who died of exhaustion along the road, somewhere between Pamiers and Foix. After thumping the Visigoths, Clovis brought the remains of his regretted supporter here, where the monks of the abbey that sheltered his reliquary invented a more exciting decapitation-martyrdom and plenty of miracles to make Volusien a bit more interesting to the parish. Only the portal and part of the transept survived destruction in the Wars of Religion, while the rebuilt interior is reminiscent of Catalan

Gothic churches, with a spacious, wide and lofty nave unhindered by aisles. The painted capitals and frieze around the choir apses are imitation Gothic, but the excellent 16th-century terracotta painted *Mise au tombeau* in the easternmost chapel is the real McCoy. The 17th-century choir stalls were originally in Toulouse's St-Sernin. The Romanesque crypt, rebuilt in the 16th century, no longer houses either the relics or the casket of the unfortunate Volusien; the Huguenots chucked them from the castle rock into the River Arget.

The **Château des Comtes de Foix** (*open May, June and Sept daily 9.45–12 and 2–6; July and Aug 9.45–6.30; Oct–April 10.30–12 and 2–5.30; closed Mon and Tues from Nov–Mar plus Jan; adm*) has seen its share of action, especially under Count Raymond Roger, the arch-enemy of the Albigensian Crusaders from the north. After the disastrous defeat of the southern cause at the Battle of Muret near Toulouse (1213), Simon de Montfort, the fiendishly efficient leader of the Crusaders, came down to Foix, vowing to 'make the Rock of Foix melt like fat and grill its master in it'. When he couldn't capture the castle or its count even after four tries, Montfort burned the rest of Foix to the ground, and in 1215 Raymond Roger gave in and surrendered the castle to the Papal Legate. Still unbowed, he made the obligatory journey to Rome, where he boasted to the Lateran Council: 'No Catholic who fell into my hands or those of my followers failed to have his eyes, hands or feet chopped off.' Yet as soon as Simon de Montfort was killed trying to recapture Toulouse in 1219, the castle was returned to the count.

Although the Counts of Foix, along with all the other barons of the south, were officially reconciled with the Church in Montpellier in 1223, they were not too chastened; the pride and independence of Roger Bernard 'the Great' brought King Philip the Fair down to Foix in person in 1272. Rather than smoke out the Count, the king set his men to dig the rock out from under him, before he surrendered and swore to be a good vassal.

The castle isn't all quite as old as it seems. The square tower on the end is from the 11th century, but the most feudal-looking tower, in the middle, was reconstructed in the 19th century; the great round tower, generally attributed to Gaston de Foix, actually dates from the 15th century. The lower, lightless floor served as a royal prison from the 17th century until 1864; the walls are scratched with pathetic graffiti in several languages. In the old days the prison guards had an easy time of it, thanks to the fierce and reliable Pyrenean sheepdogs who patrolled the enclosure between the towers, ready to rip the throat out of anything that moved. These days instead of prisoners, the Château de Foix houses the **Musée Départemental du Château de Foix**. The palaeontology section has finds from the Ariège's caves – prehistoric reindeer and bears and the most complete mammoth skeleton found in southern France. There's a reconstruction of an *oustal*, the one-room dwelling typical of the Vallée de Vicdessos; a Neolithic sepulchre from Bédeilhac; pre-Roman and Roman altars (among them, two dedicated to Nero and Hadrian) and votive offerings; a cast of the sarcophagus of Mas St-Antonin (the original is in the Louvre); weapons; and Romanesque capitals from the medieval abbey of St-Volusien, one showing the siege of Toulouse in 507 and the other the saint's supposed martyrdom.

For the best view the other way, towards Foix and the surrounding Pyrenees, climb up the steep and rocky path to the **Croix-de-St-Sauveur**, beginning in the Rue St-Sauveur. The few ruins on top belonged to a hermit who used to enjoy the same fabulous view; now it's lorded over by a giant cement cross, put up there as some kind of heretic-detector.

Around Foix

Just outside Foix, at Montgailhard, is **Les Forges de Pyrène** (***t*** *05 34 09 30 60; open June and Sept daily 10–6; July and Aug until 7; Oct–May Mon–Fri 1.30–6 plus weekends 10–6*), a new museum based on one of the great iron forges of the region. You can see the restored forge in operation, a collection of old tools and equipment, and artisans demonstrating crafts and techniques from the past, from bread-making to panning for gold.

Six kilometres northwest of Foix on the D1 is the entrance to the chief curiosity around Foix, the **Rivière Souterraine de Labouiche**, nothing less than 'Europe's Longest Subterranean River Open to the Public' (***t*** *05 61 65 04 11; open either 1 April or Easter, whichever comes first, to Pentecost, 2–6 and Sun and school holidays 10–12 and 2–6; Pentecost–Sept, daily 10–12 and 2–6; July–Aug, continuous 9.30–6; Oct to 11 Nov Sun only 10–12 and 2–6; adm; the boat journey lasts about 75 mins*). There are two waterfalls, several levels of galleries, streams and sinkholes; Norbert Casteret said it was 'the most sensational of all underground excursions', and having done nearly every possible one himself, it must be true.

Down the Ariège, just north of Foix, **St-Jean-de-Verges** is a striking, harmonious Romanesque church, once part of a priory founded by Foix's abbey of St-Volusien. In 1229 Count Roger Bernard came here to make his submission to the Church and king. It has a pretty apse, with windows and capitals decorated with carvings.

East of Foix: Montségur and Mirepoix

The haunting memories evoked by Montségur attract thousands of pilgrims each year. If you're approaching from Foix and have a little extra time, don't take the main Lavelanet road, the D117, but rather climb the scenic D9, passing by way of another Cathar citadel, built in the 13th century high on an eyrie above the village of **Roquefixade**, its walls blending in with rocky outcroppings around it. Simon de Montfort didn't even try to bag it, but after the Comté de Foix was subdued by Philip the Bold, it was annexed by the Crown.

Montségur: the Cathars' Last Stand

The castle of Montségur, hovering spectacularly high on a rocky outcrop (or *pog* in Occitan) at the edge of the St-Barthélemy massif, is the special shrine and Alamo of the Cathars, a magnet for anyone fascinated by the virtuous heretics, or 'goodmen' as they called themselves. But for both sentimental and activist southerners, Montségur symbolizes more than religion, something like the lost soul of an aborted nation: the tolerant, sophisticated nation of southern France, or Occitania, where Cathars and

The Good, the Bad and the Inquisition

For years now I have brought you words of peace. I have preached, I have implored, I have wept. But as the common people say in Spain: if a blessing will not work, then it must be the stick. Now we shall stir up princes and bishops against you, and they, alas, will call together nations and peoples, and many will perish by the sword. Towers will be destroyed, walls overturned, and you will be reduced to slavery. Thus force will prevail where gentleness has failed.

Domingo Guzman (later St Dominic), to the Cathars

Few beliefs have had the staying power of dualism, a doctine first expounded by the Greek Gnostics in the first three centuries of the Christian era. Good and Evil were explained as eternal opposing forces, Good residing somewhere beyond the stars, while Evil was here and now – in fact all of creation was Evil, the work not of the God of the Old Testament but of a fallen spirit, identifiable with Satan. Our task on earth was to seek purity by having as little to do with creation as possible.

In the 3rd century, a Persian holy man named Mani came up with a popular revision of the Gnostic dualism that spread like wildfire as far as southern Gaul. Although the Church in Rome condemned his doctrines as the 'Manichaean heresy' and stomped them out along with many other alternative beliefs in those early years, dualism continued to attract adherents in the East, making an organized revival in the 9th century with the 'Bogomils' in the Balkans. By the 11th century it had spread through much of Europe, its adherents known as Bulgars or Paterenes, Cathars or Albigensians. The Church in Italy and northern France massacred and burned as many of the heretics as it could catch, but in southern France, the faith attracted many merchants, craftsmen, poor people and members of the nobility. In 1167, Occitan Catharism was organized into a proper church at a council at St-Félic-de-Caraman.

The Cathars believed that their faith was a return to the heroic virtue and simplicity of the early Church. Their teaching encouraged complete separation from the Devil's world; feudal oaths were forbidden, and believers solved differences between themselves by arbitration rather than going to the law. Some features were quite modern: Cathars promoted vegetarianism and non-violence; marriages were by simple agreement, not a sacrament – enhancing the freedom of women by doing away with the

Catholics had lived side by side as neighbours until the king of France and the pope made its demise and annexation the goal of a war of northern conquest officially known as the Albigensian Crusade. Human beings are easier to kill than ideas: *Occitania Indépendente!*, scrawled on the big rock under Montségur castle, is a sentiment shared by many these days, when the Occitan/Provençal language of the troubadours is being revived across the south (if mostly on a literary level) and contacts between nationalistic Occitans and Catalans have already begun to create a cross-border cultural union – an eastern counterpart to the relationship between French and Spanish Basques. One last attraction of Montségur, especially for lovers of the occult and esoteric, are the persistent legends that identify it as the Castle of Montsalvage, the home of the Holy Grail.

old Roman paternalist traditions and laws. Two other points made Catharism especially attractive to an increasingly modern society. It had a much more mature attitude towards money and capitalism than the Roman Church, with no condemnation of loans as usury, and no church tithes. This earned it support in the growing cities; like the later Protestants, many Cathars were involved in the textile trades. And Cathar simplicity, and its lack of a big Church organization, made a very favourable contrast with the bloated, bullying and thoroughly corrupt machinery of the Church of Rome.

Best of all, Catharism had a very forgiving attitude towards sinners. If creation itself was the Devil's work, how could we not err? Cathars were divided into two levels: the mass of simple believers, upon whom the religion was a light yoke indeed – no Mass and few ceremonies, no money-grubbing, easy absolution – and the few *perfecti*, those who had received a sacrament called the *consolament* and were thenceforth required to lead a totally ascetic life devoted to faith and prayer. Most Cathars conveniently took the *consolament* on their deathbeds.

In 1203, a Spanish monk named Domingo Guzman embarked on a mission to save the souls of the heretics of Occitania, founding along the way a preaching Order that would become the Dominicans. The Order was more successful than its founder's attempts to herd the Cathars back to the fold; by 1209, the papacy, the behaviour of which has always been a strong argument for the basic tenet of dualism, saw enough of a threat to its power to require a policy of genocide. The terror, enforced by French arms (and fuelled by the promise that all the lands of lords who tolerated the Cathars would be given to good Catholics), was overseen at first by local bishops. When many of these failed to kill enough Cathars, the Church decided to entrust the task to specialists – the followers of Dominic. The first group of Inquisitors, led by Guillaume Arnaud, was based in Toulouse and torched so many people in mass *auto-da-fés* that the Toulousains rioted and expelled them in 1235. But they were back the next year, worse than before, leaving a swathe of blood across the south. In May 1242, knights from Montségur murdered Guillaume Arnaud and his court of 11 Inquisitors. The Inquisitors were quickly beatified by the pope and the next year 6,000 men under Hugues des Arcis, seneschal of Carcassonne, began their siege of Monségur, where some 350 Cathars lived, protected by a garrison of 150 men.

The Castle and Siege of Montségur

***t** 05 61 01 06 94, www.citaenet.com/montsegur; Château open Feb, Mar, Nov and Dec daily 10–5 (depending on the weather); April, Sept and Oct 9.30–6; May–Aug 9–7.30. Museum open Feb–April and Nov and Dec daily 2–4.30; May–Sept 10–12 and 2–7.*

In 1204, just as St Dominic began his preaching mission, the Cathars asked Raymond de Péreille, one of their supporters, to rebuild his castle at Montségur ('Mount Safety' in French, for the site is nearly impregnable). It became their chief stronghold, the seat of their church and their bishop Bertrand Marty. While the Cathars' other castles fell easily, the besiegers found Montségur impossible to seal up

Getting Around

Public transport is pretty thin on the ground here, although there are **bus** connections from Toulouse to Lavelanet and Mirepoix (Pouplain **t** 05 61 01 54 00; SALT buses **t** 05 61 65 08 40), and from Foix to Lavelanet on Sovitour buses, **t** 05 61 01 02 35.

Tourist Information

Montségur: **t** 05 61 03 03 03, *www.montsegur.org. Open July and Aug daily 10.30–1 and 2–7; rest of the year same hours, closed Mon and Tues and Dec–Feb.*

Lavelanet: Foyer Municipal, BP 89, **t** 05 61 01 22 20, *www.paysdolmes.org. Open all year Mon–Sat 9–12 and 2–6 plus Sun 9–12 (July and Aug).*

Mirepoix: **t** 05 61 68 83 76, *www.ot-mirepoix.fr. Open Mon–Fri 10–12 and 3–7.*

Montferrier: **t** 05 61 01 14 14. *Open all year Mon–Sat 9–12 and 2–6.*

Market days

Lavelanet: Wednesday and Friday.
Mirepoix: Thursday and Monday.
Laroque d'Olme: Thursday and Saturday.

Where to Stay and Eat

Montségur and Environs ✉ 09300

****Costes**, **t** 05 61 01 10 24, **f** 05 61 03 06 28 (*inexpensive*). A pleasant creeper-covered old hotel with a garden in the middle of town. It has an excellent restaurant serving omelettes with *cèpes* and other south-western delicacies. *Menus €14–28. Closed mid-Nov–end Mar.*

Hôtel Couquet, 81 Rue Principal, **t** 05 61 01 10 28. This is an old place; some of the plumbing is out of the ark, but it's well kept and cheap.

L'Occitadelle, **t** 05 61 01 21 77. Well-prepared dishes such as perch in sorrel sauce. *Menus €15–20. Closed Fri exc July and Aug plus mid-Nov–end Jan.*

tightly and starve out, even with 6,000 men. It held out for ten months, into the difficult winter; impatiently, Hugues des Arcis hired mercenaries from the surrounding villages, who in the dead of night led the Crusaders up to the east end of the *pog*, where they killed the defenders and captured a tower within catapult range of the castle. The Cathars held out another two months in the snow, but on 2 March, as food ran low and all chances of relief were eliminated, the commander of the Montségur garrison, Pierre Roger de Mirepoix, opened talks with Hugues des Arcis. The Cathars were given two weeks' respite: they would then be freed if they became Catholics, and burnt at the stake if not. The soldiers who defended them would also be freed, once they had appeared before the Inquisition. The Cathars spent the two weeks receiving the sacrament of the *consolament* and giving away their worldly goods to the soldiers. A number of the soldiers themselves decided to become Cathars, even though they knew what awaited them.

At the beginning of the path up to the fortress, a stone memorial erected by the Society for Cathar Studies marks the **Camp des Crémats**, the burning field, where a stockade full of firewood was set alight as the archbishop of Narbonne arrived to take possession of Montségur and all the souls who converted to Catholicism. Not a single one took up the offer; all 225 *perfecti* and *perfectae* climbed the ladders and jumped into the flames rather than abjure their religion. The inscription reads: ALS CATARS/ALS MARTIRS DEL PUR AMOR CRESTIAN 16 MARS 1244. The castle itself has been partially rebuilt: after the Cathars' hecatomb, the present village of Montségur reused much of the castle's stone for its houses. A curious feature of the castle are two lateral openings in its triangular walls, perfectly aligned to the rising of the sun

Les Sapins, Conte, 09300 Nalzen. On the D117, direction Lavelanet, **t** 05 61 03 03 85. Cuisine of the Ariège served with care. *Menus €12–25. Closed Sun & Wed eves plus all Mon.*

Léran ✉ 09600

Bon Repos, **t** 05 61 01 27 83 (*inexpensive*). An isolated country farm 3km from the lake of Léran-Montbel. You can sleep peacefully in the comfortable rooms here. Home-cooked meals are available on demand. *Menu €16. Open all year.*

Camon ✉ 09500

Bergerie, **t** 05 61 68 81 96 (*expensive*). Hotel that serves a famous *agneau en croûte*. *Menus €12–31. Closed Wed exc July and Aug plus Jan.*

Domaine du Couchet, Peyrefitte-du-Razès. On the road from Mirepoix to Limoux, **t** 04 68 69 55 06. A lovely 18th-century *maison particulier* with grand bedrooms, individually decorated. *Open all year by reservation only.*

Mirepoix ✉ 09500

***La Maison des Consuls**, 6 Place Couvert, **t** 05 61 68 81 81, **f** 05 61 68 81 15, *www.maisondesconsuls.com* (*moderate*). Stylishly decorated hotel in the Maison des Consuls, an arcaded building with wonderful carved beams. Rooms overlook the medieval streets. *Open daily all year.*

Commerce, Cours Docteur-Chabaud, **t** 05 61 68 10 29, **f** 05 61 68 20 99, *www.chez.com/lecommerce* (*inexpensive*). The nicest place in town, with a welcome shady garden and good restaurant. *Menus €12–24. Closed Sat, exc July and Aug, plus 12–21 Nov and Jan.*

Roquefixade ✉ 09300

Le Relais des Trois Châteaux, Palot, **t** 05 61 01 33 99, *www.troischateaux.com* (*inexpensive*). A prettily decorated hotel and restaurant, which offers a changing menu according to season; try combinations such as eel with shrimps, kidneys with *cèpes*, or frog's legs with grapes. *Menus €23–44. Closed Fri and Sun eve plus Tues and 3 weeks Jan–Feb.*

on the summer solstice, fuelling considerable speculation about the castle as a solar temple, if not for the benefit of the Cathars, for the masons who originally built it; special celebrations are held every 21 June. Recent archaeological excavations around the castle have uncovered wells, cellars, and stairways from the Cathar village.

The 'Treasure' of the Cathars and Parzifal

An incident that happened in the last two weeks before the final surrender of Montségur has intrigued people for centuries. As the Crusaders knew that the Cathars had a spotless record for honesty and integrity, they didn't stand a very close guard over the castle once Pierre Roger de Mirepoix brokered the surrender agreement. Yet by a special request of Bishop Marty, four Cathars were secretly lowered by ropes over the cliffs on the night of 15 March. They made their way over La Peyre pass to a cave, where they picked up a treasure hidden three months earlier by two other *perfecti*. From there they travelled east to the Castle of Usson, where they met one of the *perfecti* who hid the treasure, and then disappeared from history.

What the Cathars' 'Treasure' might have been, according to a number of writers, was the Holy Grail, as in Wolfram Von Eschenbach's great Arthurian romance, *Parzifal*, a poem completed around 1212. The Grail – a precious jewelled cup with divine powers – had already neatly made the voyage from Celtic mythology to Christian thanks to the 12th-century Welsh stories of Parsifal brought to France through the court of Eleanor of Aquitaine and the Plantagenets. According to the various versions of the legend, the Grail is either the cup used by Christ in the Last Supper or the cup in which Joseph of Arimathea collected the blood of Christ on the cross (hence the presumed etymology of Holy Grail from San Graal or Sang Real – 'Holy Blood'). Wolfram always claimed he got the story of his masterpiece from a certain Kyot, a singer or magician from Provence, and there is certainly an uncanny resemblance between some of the places and names in *Parzifal* and those of the Cathars, suggesting that the romance could be read as an allegory of the Albigensian Crusade: Montségur means the same thing as Wolfram's Munsalvaesche, where the Grail ceremony takes place; the mother of Parsifal, Herzeloyde, who was first married to Castis, could be Adélaïde, wife of King Alphone the Chaste, who was alive at the time; the Vicomte Raymond Trencavel of Carcassonne, a knight errant and protector of the Cathars, has in a number of aspects been identified with Parzifal (his contemporaries certainly didn't shy from comparing him to Christ himself, especially after his betrayal and death at the hands of Simon de Montfort). Perhaps another argument in favour of the Cathar interpretation is the fact that Wolfram's only other surviving epic, *Willehalm*, concerns the same geographical era, dealing with the 8th-century knight, Count William of Toulouse, who fought the Saracens with Charlemagne's son, Louis the Pious.

Legends of treasure in the Pyrenees are certainly old hat. One was discovered by the Visigoths in the Grotte de Pyrène, that included a fabulous chalice and an emerald table. This was taken to Spain when the Franks invaded Aquitaine; with the conquest of Spain by the Moors, the Visigoths' treasure was taken by the Omayyads to Syria, whence during the Crusades the Genoese brought it back to Genoa, where you can see it to this day in the Cathedral Treasury, labelled the 'Chalice of the Last Supper'.

This hardly satisfies some people. The weirdest of all modern Europe's occultist sects, the Nazis, were obsessed with the Cathars. After their occupation of the south in 1942, they sealed off all the important Cathar sites and cave refuges in the Pyrenees, and Nazi high priest Alfred Rosenberg sent teams of archaeologists to dig them up amidst the utmost secrecy. In 1944, not long before liberation, a group of local Cathars sneaked up to Montségur for an observance to commemorate the 700th anniversary of their forebears' last stand. A small German plane with a pilot and a passenger appeared and circled the castle. The Cathars, expecting the police, watched in amazement as the plane, using skywriting equipment, traced a strange eight-branched cross over their heads, and then disappeared beyond the horizon.

A steep road winds down to the small village of Montségur, a cute little place built in tiers on the hillside with more footpaths than streets. Here **L'Occitadelle** offers an audio-visual on the history of the Cathars and the Albigensian Crusade. Montségur's little **Musée Archéologique** (***t** 05 61 01 06 94; opening times vary every month, see p.323 for guidelines; calling ahead is recommended*) has finds from excavations and a model of the château.

Around Montségur: The Pays d'Olms

This region east of Foix has its full share of minor curiosities and enough altitude to support a ski resort, **Les Monts d'Olmes**, south of Montségur. If, however, you continue east of Montségur village, the D9 leads to the Hers, the most important river in these parts, where an 18th-century **mill** at **L'Espine** (near Fougax-et-Barrineuf) has been restored to working order (***t** 05 61 67 54 18; guided tours in the summer, on Tues and*

Thurs afternoons; by reservation only). A narrow road follows the Hers up as far as the savage **Gorges de la Frau** (the Gorge of Fear), where you can pick up the trail to Montaillou. Along the road from Fougax-et-Barrineuf to **Bélesta** and its lovely forest, stop to see the 'mad fountain', the **Fontaine Intermittente de Fontestorbes**, famous since Roman times; a subterreanean river comes flowing out of a cave – at variable intervals (from mid-July to August, it flows for a few minutes every half-hour or so). This is because the fairies, or *Encantadas*, who live in a subterranean palace, are washing and rinsing their laundry – at least that's as good an explanation as any.

Lavelanet is the industrial power of the Pays d'Olms, an important manufacturer of carded wool and textiles. Until the invention of plastic, it had another more unusual, specialized craft – the manufacture of combs from horn and boxwood. Established all along the Hers valley by Protestants after Henry IV's Edict of Nantes (1598), the horn comb industry once employed over a thousand workers. You can learn about them in the **Musée du Textile et du Peigne en Corne** (*65 Rue Jean-Jaurès;* ***t*** *05 61 03 01 34; open mid-June–mid-Sept Mon–Sat 2–7, last visit at 6*) or watch how it's done at **Art Mony**, the last horn comb factory in the region, at Lesparrou, 7 kilometres to the east (***t*** *05 61 01 11 09; open Mon–Fri 9–11 and 2–6*).

West of Lavelanet, **Montferrier** has a curious Neolithic monument known as the **sacrificial rock of Peyregade** (up the Touyre stream) and complements Lavelanet's museum with its own **Musée des Traditions Populaires et Petits Métiers**, containing costumes and traditional arts and crafts, and a unique collection of jet pearls (***t*** *05 61 01 91 47; open June–Nov daily 2–6; at other times phone for an appointment*).

Mirepoix

Mirepoix, centre of the little sister *pays* north of the Pays d'Olme, is one of the prettiest villages in the Ariège. A few detours may tempt you off the main D625 from Lavelanet: the *bastide* village of **Léran**, for instance, has a well-preserved castle of the dukes of Lévis-Mirepoix, the descendants of Gui de Lévis, right-hand man of Simon de Montfort. The vast artificial **lake of Léran-Montbel** has become a focus of summer leisure activities and bird-watching in the area. Further north along the Hers, picture-postcard **Camon** is a little fortified village that grew up under the protection of its 10th-century abbey; its cloister, church and frescoed oratory are open for guided tours (*daily from 10am*).

An inventory showed 600 Cathars living in Mirepoix in 1209, when Simon de Montfort deposed its lord, Pierre-Roger de Mirepoix, and replaced him with Gui de Lévis. In 1279, a dam holding the waters of the Hers burst and flooded Mirepoix so badly it had to be abandoned. Jean de Lévis rebuilt it as a regular *bastide* on higher ground; in 1355, during the Hundred Years' War, the Black Prince sacked and pillaged it, and a band of *routiers* burned it down again a decade later. But little has happened since; Mirepoix looks very much as it did at the end of the 14th century, with its half-timber houses, its arcaded square on wooden pillars and 13th-century **Maison des Consuls**, the ends of its beams carved with heads of people and monsters. The Maison des Consuls is now a stylish hotel. One of its fortified **gates**, the Porte d'Aval, survives at the west end of town.

In 1317, the Avignon Pope John XXII elevated Mirepoix to a bishropic as part of his scheme to bring danger zones of heresy back into the fold. The Lévis, who had already paid to build a new church in Mirepoix, began its enlargement into the **Cathédrale St-Maurice**, work was more or less completed when Philippe de Lévis was bishop in the 15th century. Southern Gothic in style, the cathedral seems designed for a much larger town than Mirepoix; its octagonal bell tower stands 190ft high, and behind its handsome Gothic portal the church stands 79ft high and measures 158ft long and 73ft across, making it the second widest single nave in Europe.

The Vertical Church of Vals

Lastly, towards Pamiers are a pair of Romanesque **churches** well worth a detour, but do check at the Mirepoix tourist office before setting out to make sure the one at Vals is open. The church at **Teilhet** is fortified with a *clocher-mur*, sculpted with a knight on his horse (just under the bell); the portal has beautifully carved capitals and a frieze of grotesques. Two kilometres further on, the unique church at **Vals** is a local version of Rome's San Clemente. The huge rock it stands on had a sacred spring and was first inhabited in the Bronze Age; in Gallo-Roman times it supported a temple to the Celtic god Rahus. The entrance itself is uncanny, a tunnel and stair that follows a natural fault in the rock. It leads to the original 8th-century church: a nave measuring 35ft, excavated from the living rock. To this, a vaguely Mozarab apse was added in the 11th century; in the 12th century it was beautifully frescoed by Catalan artists with the *Life of Christ*, the paintings rediscovered under the plaster in 1956. The original nave came to resemble a crypt when a second, upper nave was added, dedicated to the Virgin Mary (restored in 1887); above that, orientated sideways, there's a 12th-century chapel of St-Michel, built into a *clocher-mur* that looks just like a castle keep. The idea was that the archangel would act as the protector of the gentle Virgin.

Tarascon-sur-Ariège and its Caves

Up the river Ariège from Foix, the main N20 passes the twin-towered '**Devil's Bridge**' at Mercus-Garrabet (famous for tele-waterskiing if you like being dragged across the water) and the river rafting centre at **Bompas** before reaching Tarascon-sur-Ariège, one of the main crossroads of the *département*. Tarascon held a similar status in the dawn of time: today it's the proud capital of prehistory in the Pyrenees.

Tarascon-sur-Ariège

Tarascon-sur-Ariège (like the Tarascon in Provence) was first settled by the Tarusques, a Ligurian tribe mentioned in Pliny's *Natural History*. It has an isolated baby mountain for its landmark, crowned by a round clock tower, the **Tour du Castella** – all that remains of the castle that once stood here. In 1702, Tarascon was consumed by a huge fire, and never really recovered its former importance. Recently, however, a group of historically minded gourmets in Tarascon has revived the distillation of *Hypocras*, the favourite chugalug of Gaston Fébus himself. Named after Hippocrates, the Father of Medicine, it was regarded in the Middle Ages as a panacea and aphrodisiac; Gaston Fébus attributed all his prowess to drinking the elixir every day. Based on an infusion of mountain herbs, Malvasy wine, cinnamon, ginger, cloves and cardamon, the recipe of 'sweet and savage Hypocras' has been the subject of long research. Elyane and Michel Séguélas at Tarascon's **Caves du Castella** are the official producers; if you don't see it in the shop, ring them up on **t** 05 61 05 60 38. It's strong stuff – 16° – and best drunk well chilled as an apéritif.

Also new and old at the same time, Tarascon's **Parc Pyrénéen de l'Art Préhistorique** (*on the route to Banat;* **t** *05 61 05 10 10; open April–mid-Nov daily 10–6 (7 at weekends and 8 in July and Aug); adm*) opened in August 1994 to console the many hopeful visitors turned away from the Grotte de Niaux; among its attractions are perfect replicas of the paintings of Niaux, 'the biggest facsimile in the world', a 'sonar labyrinth', a circular diorama of a Magdalenian-era hunt, a meadow planted with Pyrenean plants and flowers, and a picnic area.

Really Big Caves: Bédeilhac and Lombrives

From Tarascon it's 5km up the D618 to Mt Soudour and its **Grotte de Bédeilhac**, marked by a huge porch (**t** *05 61 05 95 06, www.grotte-de-bedeilhac.org; open July and Aug daily 10.30–5.30, rest of year open afternoons only. Book in advance and bring something warm*). The first scientists in the Pyrenees in the 18th century remarked that Bédeilhac was a typical large Pyrenean stalactite cave with a kilometre-long

Tourist Information

Tarascon-sur-Ariège: BP 33, Centre Multimedia, Av des Pyrénées, **t** 05 61 05 94 94. *Open summer Mon–Sat 9–1 and 2–6; winter mornings only.*

Auzat: Maison du Tourisme, **t** 05 61 64 87 53. *Open all year Mon–Sat 9–12 and 2–6 plus Sun in July and Aug.*

Market Days

Tarascon-sur-Ariège: Wednesday and Saturday.

Vicdessos: Thursday. Fair, first Thursday of each month.

Where to Stay and Eat

Tarascon-sur-Ariège ✉ 09400

****Hostellerie de la Poste**, 16 Av V. Pilhes, **t** 05 61 05 60 41, *www.hostellerieposte.com* (*inexpensive*). A terrace over the river and a restaurant. *Menus €11–30. Open all year.*

****Le Confort**, 3 Quai A. Sylvestre, **t** 05 61 05 61 90, *www.paysdetarascon.com* (*inexpensive*). Small and nice, overlooking the Ariège. *Closed 6–24 Jan.*

Hôtel-Restaurant Le Bellevue, 7 Place Jean-Jaurès, **t** 05 61 05 52 06 (*cheap*). An adequate small hotel with a decent restaurant, serving local specialities such as *azinat*, Ariège's famous filling cabbage soup. *Menus €14–27.*

Ornolac/Ussat-les-Bains ✉ 09400

****Hôtel Thermal du Parc**, **t** 05 61 02 20 20, *www.thermes-ussat.com* (*moderate*). The biggest hotel in Ussat, with a pool. *Menus €14–25. Closed end Nov–6th Jan.*

****Villa des Roses**, **t** 05 61 05 63 39 (*inexpensive*). Quiet and comfortable. *Closed 20 Oct–20 Dec.*

Up the Vicdessos ✉ 09220

Hivert, **t** 05 61 64 88 17, *www.hotelhivert.com.* The only hotel in Vicdessos, but it's *open all year* and has a restaurant. *Menus €11–14. Closed Oct.*

Relais d'Endron, Goulier (5km from Vicdessos), **t** 05 61 03 87 72. In an old school building, now part inn, part dormitory. They also serve filling home-cooked meals (*moderate–cheap*), perfect for tired cross-country skiers. *Closed mid-Oct–mid-Nov.*

gallery, famous for its formations (among them the 'tomb of Roland', a fallen stalagmite the size of a sequoia), but it was the Abbé Henri Breuil, the indefatigable 'father of prehistory', who discovered the Palaeolithic art inside in 1906: deer, horses, bison, mountain goats and mysterious symbols painted on the wall, and four bison modelled out of clay with a pubic triangle inscribed above them, very similar to those found by Norbert Casteret in the cave of Montespan in the Haute-Garonne, and perhaps moulded by the same 'sorcerers' college'. After the Magdalenian artists departed, the cave was inhabited until the Iron Age. The Neolithic skeleton of a man aged between 30 and 40 years, but only 4ft 6in tall, was found near the entrance of the cave, before it was spoiled by the Germans, who installed an aircraft factory here during the last war.

Saurat, just up the valley from Bédeilhac, is the last place in France where whetstones are mined and polished, by Sylvain Cuminetti (*39 Chemin des Planèzes;* ***t*** *05 61 05 92 54; visitors must ring ahead throughout the year*). The D618 continues over the spectacular Col de Port with splendid scenery to Massat (*see* p.306). The next valley south, the beech-wooded **Vallée de la Courbière**, is especially fine walking country, especially beyond **Rabat-les-Trois-Seigneurs**, a magnificently set village where the Cathars took refuge in the castle Roche des Irretches.

If you think Bédeilhac is a monster of a cave, a few kilometres south of Tarascon on the N20 is the **Grotte de Lombrives**, the biggest cave in Europe open to the public, so vast that even though visits are by a little train, you'll still only see a fraction of the whole (***t*** *05 61 05 98 40; July and Aug visits every 20 mins 10–7; Spring hols, June and Sept 10, 11, 3.30 and 5; May 2, 3.30 and 5; Winter 2 and 3.30*). Among the stalactite and stalagmite formations is the remarkable *Mammoth*, the *throne of King Bébrix*, and the *sepulchre of Pyrène*, his daughter, the lover of Hercules and namesake of the mountains that became her funerary monument. Lombrives goes on and on – it's said to have subterranean links to Niaux – and has upper galleries, 150ft up, accessible only by ladders. Numerous skeletons, nearly all women and children, were found up there; in his Gallic Wars, Caesar wrote how the Romans snuffed out many Pyrenean tribes by walling them up in their cave refuges, but in Lombrives all the legionnaires had to do was take away the ladders. Another cave nearby, the **Grotte de Bethléem**, was apparently used by the Cathars for initiation ceremonies of the *consolament*; no one knows what kind of mumbo-jumbo they got up to, but there's a very Pythagorean pentangle deeply engraved in the wall.

Lombrives is in the small spa town of **Ussat-les-Bains**. Ussat became fashionable after 1807 when Napoleon's brother Louis Bonaparte, king of Holland, came here to soak in the relaxing tepid, sulphuric (but not smelly) waters, recommended for nervous disorders. The pretty arcaded thermal establishment was built in 1850, and in 1982 reopened for patients stressed out by modern life. Above Ussat, the **church of Ornolac** is a model of Romanesque simplicity, but has two curious bends in the axis of its nave, commonly interpreted as an attempt by the architect to represent the contortions of Christ on the Cross. Not a few people come to see the grave of the famous 19th-century poisoner, Madame Lafarge, who was pardoned by Napoleon III and came to Ussat to recover her health, but died anyway in 1852.

The Grotte de Niaux and up the Vallée de Vicdessos

In the old days the region around Tarascon was called the **Sarbates**, a name that lives on in the Pechiney-Sabart aluminum factory and the tiny 11th- and 12th-century church of **Notre-Dame de Sarbates** at the entrance of the Vicdessos valley (take the D8 just southwest of Tarascon). According to legend, the first church on this site was founded by Charlemagne after he defeated the Saracens. A brief apparition of Mary in a halo of light had accompanied the victory; the day after, Charlemagne brought his army to the spot, where a bronze statue of the Virgin on a stone altar was found. Charlemagne tried to send the precious statue to the abbey of St-Volusien in Foix, but the statue kept mysteriously disappearing and reappearing on this site, so a church was built here. It was burnt by the Huguenots in 1568 and rebuilt from the ruins; the statue of the black Virgin draws her share of pilgrims on 8 September.

Niaux is one of Abbé Breuil's 'six giants' of prehistoric mural art and justly attracts most of the attention around Tarascon. But do slot in a little extra time to see the fascinating **Musée Paysan de Niaux**, just below the cave (***t** 05 61 05 88 36; open daily July and Aug 9–8, other times 10–12 and 2–6; adm*), housing a private collection of over 2,000 artefacts assembled by Max and Denise Déjean, experts on rural life and traditions in the Pyrenees. There are unique pieces among the ingenious tools and widgets that made the harsh life in the mountains a bit easier and sometimes just a little more fun.

The Grotte de Niaux

*Open July and Aug 9.15–5.30, Sept 10–5.30, Oct–June visits at 11, 2.30 and 4 (closed Mon Nov–April; only 20 people (including babies and children) admitted at a time; reservations essential, **t** 05 61 05 88 37. Arrive 15mins before your departure time. The walk in the cave is nearly 2km and somewhat hard, and not advised for anyone who has difficulty walking. Bring something warm; the cave temperature is a fairly chilly 12°C/54°F.*

The most beautiful prehistoric art in all the Pyrenees and, according to many, the best after Lascaux and Spain's Altamira, is in Niaux, discovered in 1906 in the cliffs of the Cap de la Lesse. A winding road leads up to its spectacular gaping mouth, marked by a 'porch' – a modern metal prow-like structure extending into space over the cliff. Mysterious signs are painted in red and black on the walls near the entrance, reminiscent of the private symbols of Joan Miró, and reach a remarkable intensity and complexity at the cave's natural crossroads; they appear to bear some hidden message about the topography, perhaps directing Magdalenian-era visitors to the superb **Salle Noir**, an immensely powerful and poetic composition of charcoal line-drawings, dated at around 10,500 BC. Bison, horses (both *mérens* and furry Basque *pottok* ponies) and lively mountain goats are beautifully rendered, a few superimposed over one another but all wonderfully clear, making expert use of the natural contours and formations of the walls. Here is Niaux's famous stag, exquisitely posed,

Prehistoric postmodernism

Part of the wonder and magic of Niaux and the other decorated prehistoric caves (nearly all are in southwest France or northwest Spain) is that they uncannily achieve many of the aims of art in the late 20th century – they suggest far more than they actually show and invite the viewer to participate actively in their meaning; they admirably make use of their environment and the palette presented by nature; they are not bound as compositions into the artificial rigours of a canvas, or limited by ideas of up and down or north and south – a cave is a perfect three-dimensional installation. Most of all, the painted caves beautifully combine form, function and meaning, so that even if their exact nature may never be discovered, their art leaves a strong and poignant impression even after thousands of years.

graceful and noble, and a spontaneous finger engraving of a salmon, preserved in the mud. Whether you believe in the traditional school of prehistoric art historians that the Magdalenian artists were motivated by hunting magic, or in Leroi-Gourhan's more recent theories that another kind of ritual language and meaning was communicated through the drawings, the Salle Noir was certainly a sanctuary, where a lost and unfathomable civilization kept its secrets.

The people who painted caves such as Niaux never lived in them, whereas just opposite the valley, in the **Grotte de la Vache**, in Alliat, palaeontologists have unearthed a regular Magdalenian hunters' camp – but no paintings (***t** 05 61 05 95 06; booking is obligatory all year; July and Aug 10–5.30, rest of year open afternoons in school hols*). Here the **Salle Monique** stands out, where, 13,000 years ago, pebble walls were built to divide the households, and flint tools and bones from their meals were found. The cave yielded engraved bones, ivory and antlers – movable art, or *art mobilier*, as it's called. Some of it looks like idle scratching while sitting around a fire; other works seem to have a deeper meaning.

Up the Vallée de Vicdessos

Beyond Niaux and Alliat, the D608 continues up the Vicdessos valley; there are turn-offs for **Miglos**, crowned with a ruined castle, and for **Siguer**, site of a delightful Renaissance house said to have been a hunting lodge of Gaston Fébus. Some fine Romanesque paintings decorate the chapel of **St-Nicolas**, just outside the nearby hamlet of **Gestiès**.

Further up, **Vicdessos** is the biggest village in the valley with all of 700 people. Nearby **Sem** has a massive dolmen known as the **Palet de Samson**. It differs from most megalithic monuments; this one was made by Mother Nature, the giant table-top stone deposited atop two other rocks by an ancient glacier. **Auzat**, at the top of the valley, looks over the 'roof of the Ariège', the Pic de Montcalm (3,077m/10,154ft). The upper valleys of Vicdessos and Auzat are dotted with dry-stone *orrys*, built by shepherds since Neolithic times and used for shelter, cheese-making, storage or even dog houses. The GR 10 weaves between them and a string of lakes that Montcalm and the Andorran range wear like blue brooches across their stony bosoms.

Up the Ariège: Ax-les-Thermes and Around

There are two ways to continue southeast of Tarascon to Ax-les-Thermes. The main valley road, the N20 is often saturated with all the extra traffic trundling to and from Spain by way of the duty-free republic of Andorra (*see* p.337). The alternative, the longer, twisting and far more scenic D20/D2 or **Route des Corniches**, follows the upper rim of the valley, beginning 3km north of Tarascon at Bompas.

Tarascon to Ax-les-Thermes

If you do opt for the longer, slower Route des Corniches, the views over the Ariège valley are complemented by the discreet charm of the little Romanesque churches along the way. The first one is in **Verdun** above Les Cabannes, and the next one, at **Axiat**, once belonged to Cluny. Just beyond, the ruined 11th-century **castle** at **Lordat** towers 1,300ft over the river below; it was one of the largest owned by the Counts of Foix, and after the fall of Montségur the last die-hard Cathars took refuge here. In 1582 Henry IV ordered the castle knocked down, but received the plaintive message from his governor: 'the castle of Lordat is too big to be destroyed', which Henry must have found amusing enough to let the issue slide. Time has since accomplished much of the governor's task. A path leads up from the village to the top of the hill for a huge view. These days Lordat makes its living from its mountain of baby powder, excavated from the **Carrière de Talc de Trimouns**, a huge blinding white scar carved from the Montagne de Tabe, that yields 8 per cent of the world's supply (***t*** *05 61 64 60 60. Open Mon–Fri May, June, Sept and Oct; site closed during bad weather; sunglasses essential*).

One of the best Romanesque churches in the whole of the Ariège is at **Unac**, another gift from the Counts of Foix to Cluny, with a lovely bell tower, exquisitely chiselled windows in the apse, and fine capitals and friezes inside. Unac also has a donkey farm, **La Ferme aux Ans** (***t*** *05 61 64 44 22*), with sweet little beasts ready to carry your children or up to 40kg of supplies on treks of one or several days; they also hire out donkeys at **Marc** for treks in the Vicdessos and at Pont de Caralp for walks in the Réserve Nationale d'Orlu. Along the main N20, Les Cabannes marks the crossroads to the **Plateau de Beille**, excellent cross-country skiing territory.

Ax-les-Thermes

Nestled in green mountains, Ax has a long history, but unfortunately a long record of fires to go with it. Although commonly presumed to be named for its waters (*aquae*) like Aix-en-Provence and Aix-la-Chapelle, another school of thought derives its name from the Iberian word *ats*, meaning 'stinker', after the pungent smell of its highly sulphurous waters that gush out of the earth at 77°C. One of the first people since the Romans to exploit Stinker-les-Thermes' medicinal possibilities was St Louis, who in 1260 built a hospital here for his Crusaders who caught leprosy in the Holy Lands. All that survives is the Bassin des Ladres, in Place du Teich; if the waters didn't heal leprosy, they proved handy for melting the ice off the streets in the winter. As elsewhere in the Pyrenees, the spa is undergoing a revival, specializing in rheumatism and respiratory diseases.

Ax is the best base for exploring the highest mountains of the Ariège; the tourist office has a detailed list of all the walks and *refuges* in the environs, many taking less than a day. There is excellent, exciting skiing up at **Ax-Bonascre**, 8km south on the D820, 2,305m/7,562ft up – some of the pistes are over 3km long – and at the smaller **Ascou-Pailhères**, 13 kilometres east.

Around Ax

Northeast of Ax on the D613, **Montaillou** is synonymous with Emmanuel LeRoy Ladurie's now classic study of a 14th-century village. Even after the fall of Montségur (*see* pp.323–8), Catharism continued to exist in pockets, especially in the mountains of the Ariège and Catalunya; in spite of the threat of the Inquisition, there was even a heresy revival in 1300 until 1326, when the last Cathars were all rounded up, burned at the stake, imprisoned, or made to wear a big yellow cross sewn on their backs. Ladurie owed the amazing detail in his *Montaillou: The Promised Land of Error* to the zeal of the head Inquisitor, Jacques Fournier, Bishop of Pamiers, who painstakingly had every

Getting Around

The **railway** between Tarascon-sur-Ariège, Ax-les-Thermes and L'Hospitalet is the highest in Europe and was a great engineering feat when it opened in 1888. For train information in Ax, ring **t** 05 61 64 20 72.

Tourist Information

Ax-les-Thermes:La Résidence, 6 Av Théophile Délcassé, **t** 05 61 64 60 60. *Open daily June–Sept 9–12 and 2–7; rest of year until 6, closed Sun.*

Luzenac: office for the Vallées d'Ax, **t** 05 61 64 60 60. *Open all year Mon–Sat 9–12 and 2–6.*

Where to Stay and Eat

Unac ✉ 09250

Oustal, **t** 05 61 64 48 44 (*inexpensive*). A warm and welcoming authentic old mountain Chambre d'hôtes with 2 bedrooms at €69 each. Both of the rooms have breathtaking mountain views. *Evening meals on demand by reservation. Open all year, must book ahead.*

Jean-Claude Berde, **t** 05 61 64 45 51 (*inexpensive*) runs a bed-and-breakfast in his typical Ariègeois house. *Meals €14. Closed mid-Nov–31 Dec.*

Ax-les-Thermes ✉ 09110

★★Le Grillon, Rue St-Udaut, **t** 05 61 64 31 64, **f** 05 61 64 25 48, *www.hotel-le-grillon.com* (*inexpensive*). Lovely views, a garden and pretty panelled rooms, making it the nicest place to stay in Ax. The restaurant is excellent. *Menus €16–26. Closed mid-April–May and 24 Oct–7 Nov.*

★★L'Orry Le Saquet, **t** 05 61 64 31 30, **f** 05 61 64 00 31, *www.auberge-lorry.com* (*inexpensive*), just south of Ax. Nice rooms, a garden, a terrace, and a fireplace in winter. They also have a refined kitchen that keeps travellers coming back year after year. Inventive cuisine. *Menus €18–34. Restaurant closed Wed in July and Aug and Mon and Wed lunch rest of year.*

L'Auzeraie, Av Delcassé, **t** 05 61 64 20 70, *www.auzeraie.com* (*inexpensive*). Central and also good, with a decent restaurant. *Menus €14–30. Closed mid-Nov–mid-Dec.*

La Terrasse, **t** 05 61 64 20 33 (*cheap*). An adequate place to stay. Chambre d'hôtes.

L'Hospitalet ✉ 09390

★Puymurens, **t** 05 61 05 20 03 (*cheap*). A simple choice (*open all year*).

Le Chalet, Av Turrel, Ax, **t** 05 61 64 24 31, *www.le-chalet.fr*. Clean, bright bedrooms and a very good restaurant. *Menus €16–38. Closed Sun eve and Mon, exc school hols and 5 Nov–7 Dec.*

word of his inquiries recorded and translated into Latin. Born in 1280 in Saverdun, the incorruptable, ascetic Fournier so distinguished himself for his diligence in catching heretics (and enforcing the new, much resented decrees of tithes paid to the Church), that he was made cardinal and, in 1334, elected Pope Benedict XII. (During his pontificate, Benedict XII amassed so much loot for the papacy that he was believed to have found the priceless 'treasure of the Jews'; he began the building of the great papal palace at Avignon, imported the best Italian painters to decorate it, and still died with a full till.) Only a handful of souls live in Montaillou now, but in the 1970s Ladurie looked through the telephone directory and found the same surnames common 650 years ago.

Southeast of Ax, the forests of the **Réserve Naturelle d'Orlu** once fed the big iron forge at Orlu, still rusting under the sharp shadow of the Dent d'Orlu. In 1975 the valley was set aside to increase its herd of izards, until 2010 at least, when it's supposed to reopen to hunters. The best place to see them, as well as marmots, boar and golden eagles, is by the **Etang de Beys**, a lovely mountain lake with a *refuge*; you can make a circuit beginning at the end of the Orlu valley, then return by way of the Etang de Naguilles.

There is also a wolf reserve, **La Maison des Loups**, at Les Forges d'Orlu (***t** 05 61 64 02 66, www.maisondesloups.com; open April–June daily 10–5.30, Sept–Oct Wed–Sun 11–5, July–Aug daily 10–7*), with wolves from Europe and Canada, part of the European programme for breeding and the preservation of endangered species. You can observe the wolves in the wild from specially constructed observatories.

Further east, the D25 from Ax gives you access to the thrilling 15km drive up the D22 to the **Col du Pradel** for a tremendous eagle-eye view (1,680m/5,544ft); meanwhile the D25 continues east over the Port de Pailhères pass (2,001m/6,603ft; closed in winter) to the remotest region of the Ariège, the wild and rugged **Donézan**. On the map it looks like a big toe stuck in the *départements* of the Aude and Pyrénées Orientales; in the 19th century, because of its isolation, it tried to secede from the Ariège and join up with Perpignan. **Mijanès** is the prettiest village, and opens up its handful of drag lifts whenever there's enough snow. **Quérigut** is the main village, with its stumpy ruined **castle of Donézan**, where Cathars held out for a decade after Montségur.

The nearby fierce if crumbling **château at Usson** (***t** 04 68 20 41 37; open July–mid-Sept daily 10–1 and 3–7; mid-Sept–Oct Sat–Sun 2–5, school holidays daily 2–5; closed 25 Dec and 1 Jan*) was built by the Counts of Foix to defend their lands from the king of France; it was the place where the four Cathars from Montségur brought their treasure before vanishing from history.

On the road to Andorra, **Mérens-les-Vals** is named after the small, amiable, sure-footed black horses believed to be the direct descendants of the horses painted at Niaux. Kevin Henshall, an Englishman who loves them, runs a stud farm. For horse-riding (*call **t** 06 08 52 32 29*). Further south, **L'Hospitalet**, once the site of a pilgrims' hostel, stands at the southernmost end of the Ariège, at the entrance into Andorra and Spain; the latter has been made much easier to access since the opening of the tunnel of Puymorens in 1994.

Andorra

The little **Principat de les Valles de Andorra**, as it's officially known, is an independent historical oddity in the style of Grand Fenwick and the Marx Brothers' Fredonia, a little Catalan-speaking island of mountains measuring 468 square kilometres that has managed to steer clear of the French and Spanish since its foundation by Charlemagne. Its name is apparently a legacy of the Moors, derived from the Arabic *Al-gandûra* – 'the wanton woman' – though unfortunately the story behind the name has been forgotten. Andorra has two 'co-princes', the President of France (as the heir of the Count of Foix) and the Bishop of La Seu d'Urgell in Catalunya. According to an agreement spelled out in 1278, in odd-numbered years the French co-prince is sent 1,920 francs in tribute, while in even-numbered years the Spanish co-prince receives 900 pesetas, twelve chickens, six hams and twelve cheeses. Napoleon thought it was quaint and left it alone, he said, as a living museum of feudalism.

Being Catalan, the Andorrans were always most adamant about preserving their local privileges, which they did through the **Consell de la Terra**, founded in 1419, one of Europe's oldest continuous parliaments. The citizens also claim to be the only people in the world who have avoided warfare for 800 years (surely a claim for 'small is beau-

Getting There

By air: There's a small airport near La Seu d'Urgell, 23km from Andorra la Vella, especially used by ski charters. The weather, however, is unpredictable, and there are plans for regular helicopter services from Toulouse.

By train and bus: SNCF **trains** on the Toulouse–Perpignan–Barcelona line (**t** 05 62 15 18 09/03 76 82 11 38) get as close as L'Hospitalet, with bus connections the rest of the way. Other **buses** to Andorra depart from Toulouse every morning (**t** 05 61 61 67 67 or (376) 80 51 51) and also from Ax-les-Thermes. From Perpignan you can catch the Villefranche train at 7.58am, which links up with the narrow-gauge ***Petit Train Jaune*** ('little yellow train') which passes through some awesome mountain scenery on its way to La-Tour-de-Carol, where a Pujol Huguet bus meets it at 1.35pm to go to Andorra, through the Port d'Envalira, at 2,407m the highest pass in the Pyrenees.

Tourist Information

Andorra la Vella: C/ Dr. Vilanova, **t** (376) 82 02 14, **f** (376) 82 58 23, *www.andorra.ad and www.tourisme-andorra.net. Open summer 9–1 and 3–7, winter 10–1 and 3–7, Sun and hols 10–1 only.*

Andorra Delegation Tourist Office: 63 Westover Rd, London SW18, **t** (020) 8874 4806.

The Syndicat d'Initiative sells a map of Andorra's camp sites and mountain refuges (*refugios* and *cabanas*). Two trails (*sentiers de grande randonnée*) pass through Andorra: GR 7 and GR 75.

Currency and shopping regulations

Although **Catalan** is the official language of Andorra, **French** and **Spanish** are well understood. Local currency is the euro. **Credit cards** are widely accepted in this region. Andorra's recent agreement with the EU on **customs allowances** has considerably increased the permitted value of goods bought in Andorra and taken back to EU countries; check *www.turisme.ad/angles/compres.htm* for a simple table of allowances.

Entrance formalities are a breeze, though there are checks at both French and Spanish customs and you may well be stopped twice.

Telephones

If you're dialling an Andorran number from France, dial 00, wait for the tone, and then dial the prefix **t** 376 and the number.

tiful'), though there was a close call in 1934, when a White Russian count proclaimed himself King Boris I of Andorra and declared war on the bishop at Seu – a war the bishop ended after two weeks by sending four Guardias Civils, who escorted King Boris to Barcelona and thence out of Spain.

Until the 1940s Andorra remained isolated from the world, relying on dairy-farming, tobacco-growing, printing stamps for collectors, and more than a little smuggling. This peaceful Ruritania began to change with the Spanish Civil War, with an influx of refugees and a new popular sport called 'downhill skiing'. And then came the great revelation: why bother smuggling when you can get the consumer to come to you? For many Andorrans, it was simply too much of a good thing; their traditional society, already swamped by emigrants (32,000 Spaniards, 4,000 French; only 12,000 native Andorrans) all but disappeared under a wave of over 6 million visitors a year, most of whom were only passing through to purchase tax-free petrol, electronics, booze and American smokes, imported tax-free by Philip Morris and Reynolds, who ran the native tobacco-growers out of business. In 1993, Andorra even gave up feudalism and voted for a constitution – although the co-princes still get their cash and cheese.

Outside the summer and peak ski seasons, however, Andorra slows down considerably; even in the summer a stout pair of walking shoes and a reasonable amount of energy can take you far away from the congestion, sophisticated sport complexes, high-rise hotels and discos to some breathtaking scenery, a storybook land of green meadows and azure lakes, waterfalls and minute hamlets with stone houses drying tobacco on their south walls, clustered below Romanesque churches, with mountains towering in grandeur overhead, the silence broken only by the tinkling of cowbells.

Andorra la Vella

Andorra la Vella ('Europe's Highest Capital') and the former villages of **Les Escaldes-Engordany** have melded into a vast arena of conspicuous consuming. Worth a visit, however, is the old stone **Casa de la Vall** (*Calle de la Valle,* **t** *(376) 829 129,* ***f*** *(376) 869 863; free guided tours by appointment Mon–Sat 9–1 and 3–7, Sun 10–2, closed Sun Nov–May*), the seat of the Counsell de la Terra since 1580, and home of the famous **Cabinet of the Seven Keys**, containing Andorra's most precious documents, accessible only when representatives from each of the country's seven parishes are present. A folklore museum (*not open to the public*) has been installed on the top floor. You can visit the main hall and kitchen. The latter is where the parish meetings used to take place – the councillors would walk long distances in the cold to come here, and then would warm up by the stove and eat at the table there, discussing parish business. There is also a dovecote, a fountain, ornamental gardens and a monument by Pujol. If there is a session going on you won't be allowed to visit.

Around Andorra

Andorra is famous for its Romanesque churches and bell towers: a 40-minute walk south of Andorra la Vella will take you to the best one, the 11th-century **Santa Coloma**, with a unique, round bell tower and Visigothic arches. A winding road from Escaldes (or ride on the *telecabina* from Encamp to the north) ascends to the isolated 11th-

Skiing

Andorra has abundant snow from December to April, combined with clear, sunny skies – a skier's heaven. It has six major installations. *See www.skiandorra.ad.*

High season, when everywhere is extra busy, includes the following religious holidays: 4–10 December (4–12 in Ordino), 23–7 Jan, 3 Feb–4 Mar, 12–16 April, and weekends.

Pas de la Casa-Grau Roig (2,050–2,600m), just within the border with France, **t** 80 10 60, **f** 80 10 70, *www.pasgrau.com.* The oldest (1952), with 55 pistes, 33 ski lifts, 360 snow cannons, a slalom course, and several slopes for beginners as well as the advanced, night skiing (floodlit, on the Font Negre run), two medical centres; 31 lifts, six cafés and restaurants and 40 hotels.

Ordino Arcalís (1,940–2,600m), 17km from town and 4km from El Serrat, **t** 73 70 80 *www.vallordino.com.* Served by half-hourly buses from Andorra la Vella. Perhaps the most dramatically beautiful and the best place to ski in Andorra. It has 27 pistes and 14 lifts, a medical centre, eight cafés, restaurants and hotels in Ordino itself.

Soldeu-El Tartar (1,710–2,560m), near Canillo, **t** 89 05 00 or 89 05 01, *www.sodeu.ad,* for piste condition. The biggest and most popular complex, 850 hectares, with 88km of slopes including 52 runs (some especially for children), 29 lifts, 380 snow cannons, a 2km cross-country course, a surf park, a new snowboard school and snowpark, three medical centres, four cafés and restaurants, 25 hotels and five self-catering apartment blocks. (Soldeu and Pas de la Casa have also joined forces but as they are from two different parishes the join is not as complete as Arinsal-Pal).

Arinsal-Pal, t 73 70 00 or 70 70 20, *www.palarinsal.com.* The Arinsal and Pal resorts linked up in the 2000/2001 winter season for the first time. They have joint services and share lift connections, and you can get a combined pass. There's a snow park for snowboarders, 28km of runs, monoskiing, big foot, alpine, snowboarding, heliskiing, 78 snow cannons and 60 instructors.

La Rabassa (2,050m), near Sant Julià de Lòria, **t** 84 34 52, **t** 32 38 68, *www.campdeneudelarabassa.ad.* A cross-country skiing station and features 15km of pistes through meadows and forests, separate pistes for snowmobiles, 2.6km of runs, 17 snow cannons, 13 lifts, a children's snow park complete with snow slides, sleds and the like, a sports centre with pool, gym, sauna, etc, and horse-riding and guided ecology tours. There are rooms, and a café and restaurant at the refuge which is approached by a good road.

Note that Andorra's high altitude and even terrain make it especially good for ski trekking, or *ski randonnée*, with overnight accommodation in refuges around the rim of Andorra.

Other Sports

There are a number of sports complexes and facilities all over Andorra, providing an inescapable chance for holiday-fitness.

century **Chapel of Sant Miquel d'Engolasters**. Its fine frescoes, now in the Museu Nacional d'Art de Catalunya in Barcelona, have been replaced by copies, and its three-storey *campanile*, as often in Andorra, totally dwarfs the church. Beyond the chapel lies a forest and the pretty **Lago d'Engolasters** ('lake swallow-stars') where an old tradition states that all the stars in the universe will one day fall. It's a good place for walking or fishing.

Exploring the hidden corners of old Andorra can be difficult if you're not walking or don't have a car to zigzag up the narrow mountain roads. Buses ply the two main roads through Andorra every couple of hours towards El Serrat, and more frequently towards Soldeu. **La Cortinada**, en route to Soldeu, is a good tranquil base, with only

Andorra la Vella

Andorra's **sports complex**, **t** 80 45 60 is used for indoor sporting events and has a shiny multi-purpose court with stands for over 5,000 people.

Mercure health centre, Ctra la Roda, **t** 87 36 02, **f** 87 36 52, *mercureandorra@riberpueg.ad*, *www.andorraeskviagratis.com*, is part of the Mercure hotel but is open to non-residents and offers saunas, swimming pool, gym, solarium, mini-golf, Jacuzzi and, most usefully, pre-ski warm-up programmes and après-ski relaxation.

Serradells swimming pool, Ctra de la Comella, **t** 87 41 00. An Olympic-size pool. *Open all year, Mon–Fri 7–10.45, Sat and Sun 10–9*. This complex has both indoor and outdoor pools, a shallow learning pool, gym, sauna, tennis courts, squash court and a snack bar.

Canillo

Palau de Gel, Ctra General, **t** 80 08 40, **f** 80 08 41, *wwww.palaudegel.ad* is a giant skating-rink (*patinaje*): in addition there is a 25m swimming pool, gym, sauna, games room and much more. Would-be skaters can book up for lessons for both ice-hockey and normal/'artistic' skating. There is even accommodation, but that's aimed at teams and pros.

Encamp

Encamp's **sports centre**, **t** 83 28 30, **f** 83 20 04, has the usual facilities (squash, tennis, swimming, gym, etc), plus some surprising ones, such as a library, exhibition hall, table-tennis, billiards, martial arts and dancehall. *Open weekdays 7.30–11pm plus Sat and Sun 9–8.*

La Massana

In nearby Anyós the **sports centre**, **t** 73 75 73, *www.anyospark.com* includes a shooting gallery, solarium, massage rooms, sunbeds, jacuzzis, Turkish baths and saunas as well as swimming pools, squash and tennis courts. *Open 8am–11pm.*

A few kilometres north in L'Aldosa, the **sports complex**, **t** 83 72 75, **f** 83 63 24, has both indoor and outdoor facilities along with its saunas, jacuzzis, vertical sunbed. *Open 10am–10pm. Open school hols only.*

Sant Julià de Lòria

La Rabassa Shooting Range, **t** 84 37 47, **f** 84 36 73, is a nice, new outfit with six semi-automatic posts, Olympic and universal pits, an armoured gun room and, comfortingly, a first-aid room. *Open all year.*

Escaldes-Engordany

Caldea, an impressive hydrotherapy centre and spa near the centre of town at Parc de la Mola 10, **t** 80 09 99, **f** 86 56 56, *www.caldea.ad*. This is the largest spa centre in southern Europe and perfect for après-ski. A modern, mirrored, pyramidal structure with thermal water facilities (60°C), air baths, indoor and outdoor jacuzzis, hydro-massage and many, many more watery things all within luxurious, aquatic surroundings. You'll need to book the inexpensive treatments. There's a shopping centre, restaurant and bars.

one very reasonably priced hotel, excellent scenery, and some of Andorra's oldest houses. In a 1967 restoration of its parish church, **Sant Martí**, some of the original Romanesque frescoes were uncovered. **El Serrat** is more touristy but worth a visit in the summer for the gorgeous panorama of snow-clad peaks from the **Abarstar de Arcalís** (via the ski resort). Another branch of the road from El Serrat leads to the three stunning mountain lakes of **Tristaina** in Andorra's loveliest and least developed northwestern corner, and site of its finest ski resort, Ordino-Arcalis. There's also a museum of note in Ordino town, the **Areny-Plandolit Museum** (*visits by appointment*, ***t** (376) 836 908; open Tues–Sat 9.30–1.30, 3–6.30, Sun 10–2; closed Mon*). It is the ancestral home of a long line of local nobility and has three floors; the oldest part of the building dates from 1613.

Where to Stay

Andorra ✉ 61699

Andorra now has some 300 hotels, the vast majority of them spanking new. The Association of Hoteliers, *www.turismeandorra.com* can help.

********Roc Blanc****, Plaça de Co-Prínceps 5, Escaldes, **t** 87 14 00, **f** 86 02 44, *www.grouperocblanc.com* (*luxury*). In terms of glamour, this takes the cake, with a five-storey atrium lobby and a glass elevator, sauna and a thermal spa with a number of treatment programmes offered, including two weeks of magnetotherapy to realign your electrons. The Roc Blanc's two restaurants, **El Pi** and **El Entrecôt**, features a very good selection of French, Spanish and Catalan dishes. *Menus €14–35.*

********Andorra Park****, 24 C/ de les Canals, Andorra la Vella, **t** 87 77 77, *www.hotansa.com* (*luxury*). A charming little palace set in a park with a beautiful rock-cut pool, croquet lawn, driving range and tennis court. Its restaurant is one of the best in Andorra, with fresh pasta dishes and excellent Spanish and Chilean wines.

*********Plaza****, María Pla 19, Andorra la Vella, **t** 87 94 44, *www.hotels.andorra.com* (*expensive*). Ultra-contemporary, elegant and classy, if right in the centre of the hubbub. The C˙pula restaurant has a reasonably priced set menu, with *à la carte* around €50.

*******Pitiusa****, C/ d'Emprivat 4, Andorra la Vella, **t** 86 18 16, **f** 86 19 88, *www.hotelpitiusa.com* (*moderate*), which is modern and quiet, on the edge of town.

*******Xalet Sasplugas****, C/ La Creu Grossa 15, Andorra la Vella, **t** 82 03 11, **f** 82 86 98, *www.hotelsasplugas.com* (*moderate*), is even quieter and more traditional.

Holiday Inn, Prat de la Creu 88, **t** 87 44 44, **f** 87 44 45 (*expensive*). Well-equipped, with two restaurants and a cafeteria.

******Marfany****, Avda Carlemany 99, Escaldes, **t** 82 59 57 (*inexpensive*). Long-established and comfortable, though only 24 rooms have baths; the rest come with a shower.

Hostal del Sol, Plaça Guillemó, Andorra la Vella, **t** 82 37 01 (*cheap*). Outside the capital hub there are numerous alternatives, which are especially convenient for skiers.

Eating Out

La Bohême, Av Meritxell 1, 3rd floor, Andorra la Vella, **t** 88 12 73. The better restaurants in Andorra tend to be French; this serves fine fish and fowl dishes. *Menus €15–25.*

Versailles, Cap. del Carrer 1, Andorra la Vella, **t** 82 13 31. *A la carte only for about €30. Closed Sun and Mon plus 3 weeks in July.*

La Borda de l'Avi, on the Arinsal road, **t** 83 51 54. Typical Andorran meals roasted in front of you on a wood fire, as well as fresh fish, foie gras, *magrets* or snails . Menus €30–50.

Topic, on the main road in Ordino, **t** 73 61 02, serves Belgian beer and a selection of fondues alongside. *Pizzas. €10–31.*

La Guingueta, on the Rabassa road, in Sant Julià de Lòria, **t** 84 29 41. Restaurant offers dishes like roast dove with foie gras and charcoal-grilled sea bass with cured ham in its rustic interior. *French and Mediterranean cuisine. Menu €50. Closed Sun eve and Mon.*

Another destination reached by bus (on the Soldeu road) is **Meritxell**, the holy shrine of Andorra – an old Romanesque church standing in ruins since a devastating fire in 1972, and next to it, a new sanctuary housing a copy of the 11th-century *Virgen de Meritxell*, designed in 1976 by Barcelona's overrated superstar architect Ricardo Bofill. The Andorrans have their doubts about this gruesome hybrid of their traditional architecture with the modern, which may explain why the principality decided a few years ago against going ahead with a Bofill-designed ski resort near Andorra la Vella. The lovely 12th-century church **Sant Joan de Caselles** is located on a hillside on the north edge of Canillo (the big village in these parts), its interior adorned with a Gothic *retablo*, painted wooden ceiling, and Romanesque paintings; the bell tower has fine mullioned windows in the Lombard style.

The Pyrénées Orientales

The southeastern corner of the Pyrenees, or the Pyrénées Orientales, belong to the old province of Roussillon. You'll notice that some malcontents have decorated the yellow diamond 'priority road' signs with four red stripes, making them into little escutcheons of the long-ago Kingdom of Aragon. On your restaurant table, sweet wines and peculiar desserts will appear, and you may begin to suspect that you are not entirely in France any more.

As in Andorra, you are in fact among the Catalans, in the corner of Catalunya that, for military considerations in the 17th century, was destined to become part of France. Like the other captive nations of the Hexagon – the Bretons and Corsicans, for example – most of Roussillon's people have rationally decided that being French isn't such a terrible fate after all. Catalan is spoken by relatively few (though numbers are growing), and this culturally passionate people stays in close touch with the rest of Catalunya, over Barcelona way, and in the squares of many villages they still do a weekly *sardana*, the national dance and symbol of Catalan solidarity.

Perpignan is the capital; around it stretches the broad Roussillon plain, crowded with the dusty, introverted villages that make all that sweet wine. The city is the best base for trips into the valleys that climb up into the eastern Pyrenees.

Perpignan

'PERPIGNAN DEAD CITY' is the slogan the local anarchists write on the walls, and if that's slightly premature, you can't help wondering about a town named after a reactionary murderer, one that has let its most beautiful Gothic monument become a hamburger franchise, and which highlights its tourist brochure with a photo of its trucking terminal.

There's a little craziness in every Catalan soul. In *Perpinyà* (as its residents call it), this natural exuberance is rather suppressed by French centralization. While grateful for the croissants, this former capital of the Kings of Majorca and the Counts of

Getting Around

The **coach and train service** is probably better here than in any other rural region in this book – only it won't help you see rural monuments like St-Michel or Serrabone. Using Perpignan as a base, it's possible to see quite a bit of the Conflent and Vallespir; from the *gare routière* there are 10 or 12 **buses** a day to Prades and Villefranche-de-Conflent, and a few of these continue on to Font-Romeu and Latour-de-Carol. At Villefranche you can pick up ***Le Petit Train Jaune***, a scenic narrow-gauge train that runs twice a day into the Cerdagne, practically unchanged since 1910. One of the most unlikely railways in France, it was entirely a political project, meant to bring some new life into the mountain valleys. It has kept puffing ever since – only tourism has saved it from closing: while checking the schedule make sure you don't choose one of the departures taken over by buses. The last station is Latour-de-Carol, where you can pick up a bus to Andorra and Spain, or a train to Toulouse. For the Vallespir, there are frequent, convenient daily **buses** to Arles-sur-Tech and Amélie-les-Bains-Palada, with a few pressing on further up the valley to Prats-de-Mollo.

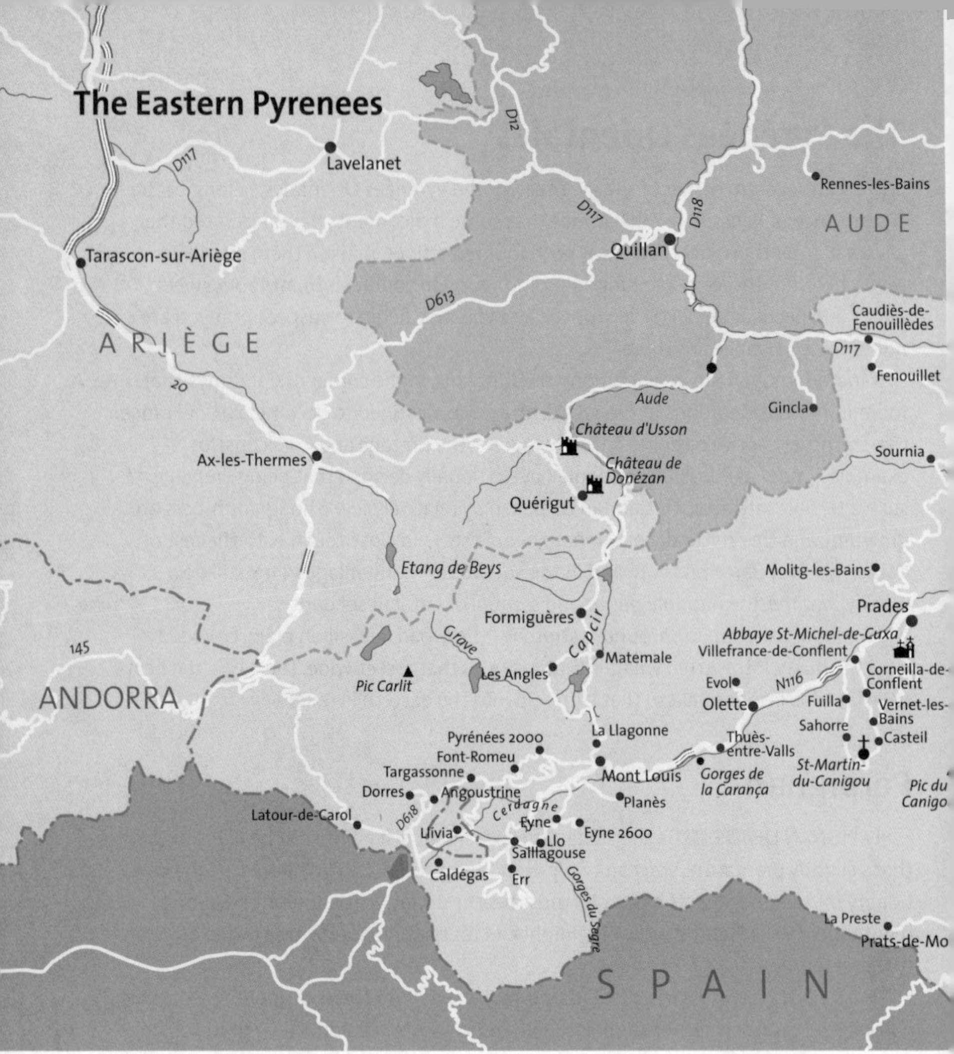

Roussillon is obviously a bit bored, and not a few Perpignanais hope that as Europe's frontiers melt away, the electricity of Barcelona may once again galvanize it along with the rest of greater Catalunya. The king of kookiness himself, Salvador Dalí, set off the first sparks when he passed Perpignan's train station in a taxi, and 'it all became clear in a flash: there, right before me, was the centre of the universe!' The otherwise ordinary Gare SNCF has been a hot destination for surrealist pilgrims ever since; at the time of writing, the street leading to the station, Av du Général de Gaulle, is undergoing a *traitement dalinien*, which includes the installation of benches shaped like Mae West's lips and a Dalínien railway carriage suspended in front of the station.

History

Perpignan is named after Perperna, a lieutenant of the great 1st-century BC populist general, Quintus Sertorius. While Rome was suffering under the dictatorship of

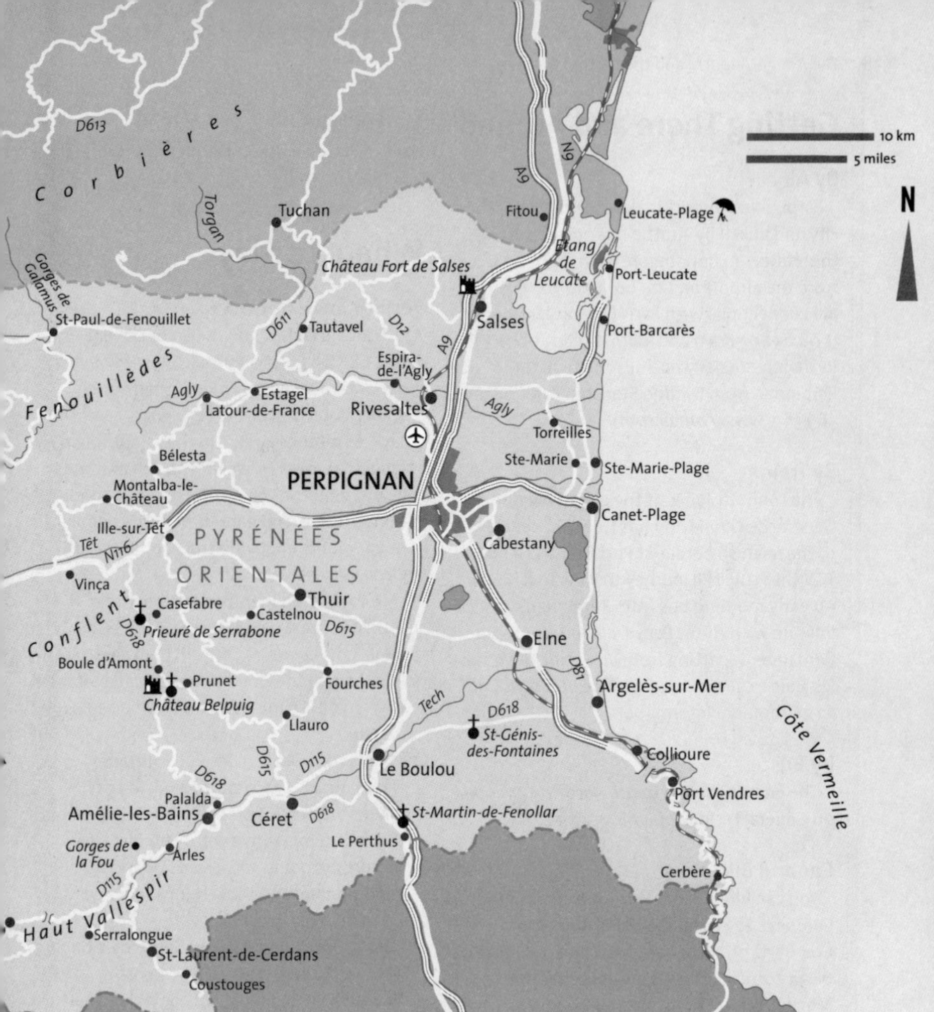

Pompey, Sertorius governed most of Spain in accordance with his astonishing principle that one should treat Rome's provinces decently. The enraged Senate sent out five legions to destroy him, but his army, who all swore to die if he were killed, defeated each one until the villainous Perperna invited his boss to a banquet in the Pyrenees and murdered him.

In 1197, Perpignan became the first Catalan city granted a municipal charter, and governed itself by a council elected by the three estates or 'arms'. Its merchants traded as far abroad as Constantinople, and the city enjoyed its most brilliant period in the 13th century when Jaime I, king of Aragon and conqueror of Majorca, created the Kingdom of Majorca and County of Roussillon for his younger son Jaime II. This little kingdom was absorbed by the Catalan kings of Aragon in the 14th century, but continued to prosper until 1463, when Louis XI's army came to claim Perpignan and Roussillon as payment for mercenaries sent to Aragon. Besieged, the Perpignanais ate

Getting There and Around

By Air

Perpignan's airport is 7km northwest of the city and linked by shuttle bus *navettes* from the station an hour before each flight (info from the airport on **t** 04 68 52 60 70). There are connections with Paris Orly on Air Liberté (**t** 08 03 80 58 05) and AOM (**t** 08 03 00 12 34). Ryanair has a daily no-frills cheap flight to Perpignan from London Stansted (UK **t** 08701 569 569, *www.ryanair.com*).

By Train

The train station is at the end of Avenue du Général de Gaulle and has frequent services to the Spanish border at Port Bou and a new TGV that cuts the journey to Paris to 6 hours. An early morning bus from Perpignan's station links up with the *Le Petit Train Jaune* into the Cerdagne, departing from Villefranche-Vernet-les-Bains; call the tourist office on **t** 04 68 96 22 96 for more information.

By Bus

The *gare routière* is to the north, on Avenue du Général Leclerc, **t** 04 68 35 29 02.

Car and Bike Hire

You can hire a **car** at the airport, or from Europcar, 203 rue Bobo, ZI Polygone Nord **t** 04 68 52 95 29, or Avis, 13 Bd du Conflent, **t** 04 68 34 26 71. **Bike** hire is available at Cycles Mercier, 20 Av Gilbert-Brutus, **t** 04 68 85 02 71.

Tourist Information

Tourist office: Palais des Congrès, Place Armand-Lanoux, **t** 04 68 66 30 30, **f** 04 68 66 30 26, *www.perpignantourisme.com. Open mid-June–mid-Sept Mon–Sat 9–7 plus Sun 10–4; rest of the year Mon–Sat 9–6 plus Sun 9–12.*

Market Days

Daily in Place de la République; Saturday and Sunday mornings in Place Cassanyes.

Where to Stay

Perpignan ✉ 66000

★★★★**La Villa Duflot**, 109 Av Victor Dalbiez, **t** 04 68 56 67 67, **f** 04 68 56 54 05, *www.villa-duflot.com* (*expensive*). Perpignan's only luxury hotel is near the Perpignan-Sud-Argelès motorway exit, in the middle of an industrial zone! However, you can pretend to be elsewhere in the comfortable air-conditioned rooms and garden, or in the popular restaurant overlooking the pool. *Menus €31. Open daily all year.*

★★★**Le Park**, 18 Bd Jean-Bourrat, near the tourist office, **t** 04 68 35 14 14, **f** 04 68 35 48 18, *www.parkhotel-fr.com* (*inexpensive*). Plush, air-conditioned, soundproofed rooms with an old Spanish feel and flair. *Open daily all year.*

★★★**Hôtel de la Loge**, 1 des Rue Fabriques-Nabot, **t** 04 68 34 41 02, **f** 04 68 34 25 13, *www.hoteldelaloge.fr* (*inexpensive*). Nicest in the centre, in a 16th-century building, this has pretty rooms, some with TV and air conditioning, and a lovely inner courtyard. *Open all year.*

★★**Le Maillol**, 14 Impasse des Cardeurs, **t** 04 68 51 10 20, **f** 04 68 51 20 29 (*inexpensive*). In a 17th-century building: not too noisy, and convenient for the sights. *Open all year.*

★★**La Poste et Perdix**, 6 Rue des Fabriques-Nabot, **t** 04 68 34 42 53, **f** 04 68 34 58 20 (*inexpensive*). This charming place has kept much of its original 1832 décor; the restaurant has menus. *Menus €11–19. Closed Feb; restaurant closed Mon.*

★★**Le Helder**, Av du Général de Gaulle, **t** 04 68 34 38 05 (*cheap*). *Open all year.*

rats rather than become French, until the King of Aragon himself ordered them to surrender. In 1493 Charles VIII, more interested in Italian conquests, gave Perpignan back to Spain. But in the 1640s Richelieu pounced on the first available chance to grab back this corner of the mystic Hexagon, and French possession of Roussillon and the Haute Cerdagne was cemented in the 1659 Treaty of the Pyrenees.

***Le Berry**, 6 Av du Général de Gaulle, **t** 04 68 34 59 02 (*cheap*). *Closed Jan and Feb.*

Auberge de la Jeunesse, Av de Grande-Bretagne, **t** 04 68 34 63 32. A small youth hostel; bed and breakfast €10 (*book in summer*). *Closed 20 Dec–20 Jan.*

Eating Out

Expensive

Le Chapon Fin, Park Hôtel (*see* above). This has been Perpignan's finest restaurant for years, as well as one of the prettiest in the area with its Catalan ceramics. But it's the *tartare de saumon* and ravioli stuffed with scallops that keep its clients coming back for more, even all the way from Spain. *Menus €25–100, A la carte €25–45. Closed Sun 1–15 Jan and last 2 weeks in Aug.*

Moderate

Casa Sansa, 3 Rue Fabriques Couvertes, near Le Castillet, **t** 04 68 34 21 84. Lively, with excellent food in a 14th-century cellar – from Catalan *escargots* to rabbit with *aïoli* – occasional live music and wine-tasting, and more than its share of Catalan flair (*book Fri and Sat nights*). *Menus €25–39. Closed Sun and Mon lunch.*

Le Vauban, 29 Quai Vauban, **t** 04 68 51 05 10. This restaurant is well situated in the centre of town with a flowery summer terrace. It's a sure bet, and has well-prepared *plats du jour. Menus €14–26. Closed Sun.*

Les Antiquaires, Pl Desprès, **t** 04 68 34 06 58. Les Antiquaires is a local favourite for reliable classic French cooking. *Menus €20–38. Closed Sun eve and Mon plus 1–20 July.*

Les Trois Sœurs, 2 Rue Fontfroide, **t** 04 68 51 22 33. Fashionable new restaurant with stylish modern bar and terrace tables on cathedral square. Fine Catalan cooking with an extra dash of invention, like monkfish with *mousserons* (tiny wild mushrooms), sea bass with sesame seeds, lamb with honey and spiced pears. *Menus €24. Closed Sun and Mon eve, plus 1 week Oct–Nov and 1 week Feb–Mar.*

Cheap

Brasserie l'Arago, Place Arago, **t** 04 68 51 81 96. Packed day and night; good food and pizza – not always a strong point with the Catalans. *Menus from €10.*

Les Expéditeurs, 19 Av du Général Leclerc, **t** 04 68 35 15 80. The classic €12 lunch with wine; Catalan cooking and paella on Wed. *Menus €12. Closed Sat and Mon eve plus Sun and all Aug.*

Entertainment and Nightlife

On evenings from June to September in Place de la Castillet, the Perpignanais come to dance *sardanas*, the national Catalan circle dance. Nightlife is mostly concentrated on students.

Le Zinc, 8 Rue Grand-des-Fabriques, **t** 04 68 35 08 80. Jazz and cocktails; specially animated during the Perpignan Jazz Festival in Oct.

Every year in September, Perpignan is host to ***Visa pour Image***, the annual world festival of photojournalism, with exhibitions from top photographers in venues from churches to shops, all over the city.

Cinemas

Cinema Castillet, 1 Bd Wilson, **t** 04 68 51 25 47.

Le Drive-In-Ciné, Mas Sabole, 11km south. An American-style drive-in cinema (*first show at 9.45pm*).

Le Castillet

When most of Perpignan's walls were destroyed in 1904, its easy-going river-cum-moat, La Basse, was planted with lawns, flowerbeds, mimosas and Art Nouveau cafés. The fat brick towers and crenellated gate of **Le Castillet** in Place Verdun were left upright, for memories' sake; built in 1368 by Aragon to keep out the French, it became a prison once the French got in, especially during the Revolution. In 1946, a mason broke through a sealed wall in Le Castillet and found the body of a child, which on contact with the air dissolved into dust; from the surviving clothing fragments the corpse was dated to the end of the 18th century. And ever since, people have wondered: could it have been Marie-Antoinette's son, the dauphin Louis XVII? After all, the child buried in the Temple in Paris was known to be a substitute, and there have always been rumours that the Revolutionaries used the Dauphin as a secret bargaining chip in dealing with his Bourbon relatives in Spain.

Along with this mysterious ghost, Le Castillet houses a cosy museum of Catalan art and traditions, the **Musée Pairal** (***t*** *04 68 35 42 05; open May–Sept 10–7; rest of year 11–5.30; closed Tues*), with items ranging from casts of Pau (Pablo) Casals' hands to a kitchen from a Catalan *mas*, complete with a hole in the door for the Catalan cat. **Place du Verdun**, by Le Castillet, is one of Perpignan's liveliest squares, while just outside the gate, the **Promenade des Platanes** is lined with rows of magnificent plane trees.

Loge de Mer to the Musée Rigaud

From Le Castillet, Rue Louis Blanc leads back to Place de la Loge, where the cafés provide a grandstand for contemplating Aristide Maillol's voluptuous bronze *Venus* and Perpignan's most beautiful building, the Gothic **Loge de Mer**, or **Llotja**, built in 1397 by the king of Aragon to house the exchange and the Consolat de Mar, a branch of the Barcelona council founded by Jaime I to resolve trade and maritime disputes. This proud and noble building of ochre stone, with its Venetian arches and loggia and ship-shaped weathercock, fell on hard times – but Perpignan takes good care of its monuments. The city rented the Llotja to a fast food chain, and now it looks very much the beggared pasha, flipping out quick burgers.

The neighbouring 13th-century **Hôtel de Ville** has been spared the Llotja's humiliation, probably because it still serves its original purpose: on Saturday mornings, its courtyard fills with blushing brides posing for photos by Maillol's allegory of the Mediterranean (as a naked woman, of course). The Hôtel is built of rounded river pebbles and bricks in the curious layer-cake style of medieval Perpignan; three bronze arms sticking out of the façade are said to symbolize Perpignan's three estates, or *bras*.

To the right, the **Palais de la Députation Provinciale** (1447) is a masterpiece of Catalan Renaissance, formerly the seat of Roussillon's parliament and now housing dismal municipal offices. Rue Fabrique d'en Nabot, opposite the palace, was once the street of drapers: note the **Hôtel Julia** (No.2), a rare survival of a 1400s town house, with a Gothic courtyard.

South of the Députation, in Rue de l'Ange the **Musée Rigaud**, (***t*** *04 68 35 43 40; open May–Sept 12–7; winter 10–5; closed Tues; adm*), is named after Perpignan native Hyacinthe Rigaud (1659–1743), portrait painter to Louis XIV. Hyacinthe, master of raising the mediocre and unworthy to virtuoso heights of rosy-cheeked, debonair charm and sophistication, is well represented, but all the hyper-sensitive alarms, however, are around the *Retable de la Trinité* (1489) by the Master of Canapost, painted for the 100th anniversary of the Consolat de Mar and showing, underneath, a fanciful scene of the sea lapping at the base of the pre-Quick Burger Llotja. Works by Picasso, Dufy, Maillol, Miró and a score of others, are upstairs.

Cathédrale de St-Jean and the Dévôt Christ

Just east of Place de la Loge unfolds Place Gambetta, site of Perpignan's pebble-and-brick cathedral, topped by a lacy 19th-century wrought-iron campanile. Begun in 1324 but not ready for use until 1509, the interior is a success because the builders stuck to the design provided in the 1400s by Guillem Sagrera, architect of the great cathedral of Palma de Majorca. Typical of Catalan Gothic, it has a single nave, 157ft long, striking for its spacious width rather than its soaring height.

The chapels, wedged between the huge piers, hold some unique treasures, the oldest of which is a mysterious marble **baptismal font** (first chapel on the left). Pre-Romanesque, perhaps even Visigothic in origin, and carved from the drum of a Roman column to look like a tub bound with a cable, it bears a primitive face of Christ over an open book. Further up the left aisle, the massive organ was decorated in the 15th century with painted shutters and sumptuous carvings. On the pendentive under the organ note the **Moor's head** – a common Catalan conceit symbolizing wisdom, taken from the Templars, who exerted a powerful influence over the kings of Aragon. The jaw was originally articulated, to vomit sweetmeats on holidays; now it's stuck, gaping open.

The cathedral is proudest of its exquisite **retables**: on the high altar, the marble *Retable de St-Jean*, carved in a late Renaissance style in 1621 by Claude Perret; at the end of the left crossing, the *Retable des Stes Eulalie et Julie* (1670s); in the apsidal chapels, the painted wood *Retable de St-Pierre* (mid-1500s) and to the right, the lovely, luminous *Notre-Dame de la Mangrana* (1500) – its name 'of the pomegranate' comes from an earlier statue of the Virgin, which held a pomegranate, symbolic of fertility.

A door in the right aisle leads out to a 16th-century chapel constructed especially to house an extraordinary wooden sculpture known as the ***Dévôt Christ***. Carved in the Cologne region in 1307, this wasted Christ, whose contorted bones, sinews and torn flesh are carved with a rare anatomical realism, is stretched to the limits of agony on the Cross. Almost too painful to behold, it comes straight from the gloomy age when Christendom believed that pain, contemplated or self-inflicted, brought one closer to God.

Nearby in Place Gambetta is the entrance to the cathedral's **Campo Santo** (1302) (*Open Oct–Mar 11–5; April–Sept 12–7; closed Mon plus July and Aug*), the only cloister-cemetery of its kind of France, the tombs decorated with fine bas-reliefs; this being Perpignan, until the late 1980s it was used as offices by the local Gendarmerie. A door from the cloister leads into the striking 15th-century **Salle Capitulaire**, its complex ogival vaulting attributed to Guillem Sagrera. To the left of the cathedral's façade is Perpignan's oldest church, **St-Jean-le-Vieux** (1025), converted into an electrical generating station in 1890. Its Romanesque portal offers a very different view of Jesus from the German *Dévôt Christ*: the imperious and typically Catalan *Majestat* (Christ in Majesty).

Quartier St-Jacques

The piquant neighbourhood south of the cathedral, built on the slopes of Puig des Lépreux (Lepers' Hill) was once the *aljama*, or Jewish quarter of Perpignan. In its happiest days, in the 13th century, it produced a remarkable body of literature – especially from the pen of the mathematician and Talmudic scholar Gerson ben Salomon (author of the philosophical *Gate of Heaven*), as well as rare manuscripts and calligraphy, all now in Paris.

After the Jews were exiled, the quarter was renamed St-Jacques, and inhabited by working men's families and gypsies, and most recently by Algerians. The 12th- to 14th-century church of **St-Jacques** is opulent and rich inside: there's a 'Cross of Insults' as in Elne, a statue of St James in Compostela pilgrimage gear (1450) and more fine retables, especially the 15th-century *Notre-Dame de l'Espérance*, featuring a rare view of the pregnant Virgin. In the early 1400s, while the fire-eating Dominican preacher St Vincent Ferrer was in Perpignan to advise in the dispute between Antipope Benedict XIII and Rome, he founded in this church the confraternity of the Holy Blood (*de la Sanch*) to bring religious comfort to prisoners condemned to death. As in Seville, the confraternity reaches a wider audience during Holy Week, when it dons spooky Ku Klux Klan-like hoods and bears a procession of holy floats (the *misteri*) while singers wail dirges from the crowd.

The Palace of the Kings of Majorca

Enclosed in a vast extent of walls, originally medieval and later enlarged by Vauban, the **Palais des Rois de Majorque** (*entrance in Rue des Archers,* **t** *04 68 34 48 29; open daily June–Sept 10–6; Oct–May 9–5; adm*) is the oldest royal palace in France, begun in the 1270s by Jaime the Conqueror and occupied by his son Jaime II after 1283. Yet for all its grandeur, only three kings of Majorca were to reign here before Roussillon, Montpellier, the Cerdagne and the Balearic islands were reabsorbed by Aragon in 1349. The scale of magnificence that they intended to become accustomed to survives, but not much else.

A rectangle built around a mastodonic but elegant Romanesque-Gothic courtyard, the palace is now a favourite venue for events, exhibitions and dancing the *sardana*, the Catalan national dance. The **Salle de Majorque**, or throne room, with its three vast fireplaces, and the double-decker chapels in the **donjon**, with the queen's chapel on the bottom and the king's on top, both offer hints at the exotic splendour of the Majorcan court.

The sacristy was the entrance to a network of underground passageways that connected the palace to its enormous 147ft-deep wells, which also afforded Jaime II an escape from his fierce and unwelcome older brother, Pedro III of Aragon. The palace once stood in the midst of what the archives call 'Paradise' – partly enclosed terraced gardens, inspired by Moorish gardens on Majorca.

A few traces remain to the right of the mightiest tower, the **Tour de Homage**. The narrow grid of streets under the palace, around the church of St-Mathieu, were designed by the Templar tutors of Jaime the Conqueror, although most of the buildings date from the 18th century.

Cabestany

Of all the villages ingested by Greater Perpignan, none is as celebrated as **Cabestany** (*Cabestanh*), 4 kilometres to the southeast. It produced a highly original Romanesque sculptor known as the Master of Cabestany who worked as far afield as Tuscany, and left his hometown church a tympanum of the *Dormition and Assumption of the Virgin*, and a scene of the Virgin in heaven, handing her girdle (definitely not Playtex) down to St Thomas. Cabestany was also the home of the troubadour Guilhem de Cabestanh, who wrote some of the most popular love poems of the Middle Ages.

West of Perpignan: Pyrenean Valleys

There are two important valleys: the **Conflent** (the valley of the river Têt) and the **Vallespir** (of the river Tech), sloping in parallel lines toward the Spanish border. Don't think that this butt end of the Pyrenees consists of mere foothills; in between the two valleys stands snow-capped **Canigou**, not the highest (a mere 9,134ft) but certainly one of the most imposing peaks of the chain, jauntily wearing a Phrygian cap of snow until late spring. The *muntanya regalada*, 'fortunate mountain' of the Catalans, is one of the symbols of the nation, the subject of one of the best-known Catalan folksongs. Every summer solstice Catalans from both sides of the frontier ceremoniously light a huge bonfire on its summit, the signal for surrounding villages to light their own, all at the exact moment. Legends and apparitions abound on Canigou. Fairies and 'ladies of the waters' are said to frequent its forested slopes, and King Pedro of Aragon climbed it in 1285, and met a dragon near the top.

The Conflent

From Perpignan to Ille-sur-Têt

The fish-filled Têt, before passing through Perpignan, washes a wide plain packed full of vineyards and fat villages. The fattest, **Thuir**, puts up signs all over Roussillon inviting us over to see the World's Biggest Barrel, in the cellars of the famous apéritifs Byrrh and Dubonnet – wine mixed with quinine, invented here a little over a century ago (***t*** *04 68 53 05 42, www.byrrh.com; tours April–Sept 9–11.45 and 2.30–5.45, July and Aug 10–11.45 and 2–6.45; adm*). After a few apéritifs, head 6 kilometres west for golden-hued **Castelnou**, a perfectly preserved medieval village on winding, pebble-paved lanes and steps under the 10th-century **castle** of the Counts of Cerdagne (***t*** *04 68 53 22 91; open 21 Mar–20 June and 23 Sept–21 Dec 11–6; 22 June–22 Sept 10–8; 22 Dec–20 Mar 11–5. Open weekends only in Jan; adm*).

The narrow D48 wiggling west of Castelnou is unabashedly beautiful: if you have a couple of hours to spare, you can circle around to the Prieuré de Serrabonne (*see* below) by way of the D2 to Caixas, Fourques, then on to the D13 for Llauro, and **Prunet-et-Belpuig**, where the ruins of the Château de Belpuig offer a superb view and the 11th-century Chapelle de la Trinité has sculpture by the same school as Serrabonne; in Boule d'Amont just up the road, there's another church from the same century.

At **Ille-sur-Têt**, an attractive old village at the gateway to the mountains, neglected art from the 11th to 19th centuries from churches all over Roussillon has been assembled in a 16th-century hospital, the **Centre d'Art Sacré**, with exhibitions on various themes and periods, changing every six months or so (***t** 04 68 84 83 96; open mid-May–30 Sept 10–12 and 2–7, closed Sat morning and Sun; the rest of the year 2–6, closed Tues; closed Dec and Jan*).

The D2 northwest of Ille to Montalba-le-Château takes you very quickly to some surprising scenery: orange eroded 'fairy chimneys' called the **Orgues** (***t** 04 68 84 13 13; open Nov–Jan 2–5; Feb and Mar 10–12 and 2–5.30; April, June and Sept 10–6.30. July and Aug 9.30–8; Oct 10–12.30 and 2–6; adm*), with a forgotten ruin of the 12th century **tower** perched on top, with the Pyrenees forming a magnificent backdrop.

The fortified church of **Régleille** (from Ille, take the D2 over the river, and after one kilometre turn right on a little road) looks like a castle at first sight – a typical example of a monastic church, in an area without any castles, that grew into a

Tourist Information

Ille-sur-Têt ✉ 66130: Av Pasteur, **t** 04 68 84 02 62, **f** 04 68 84 02 62, *www.ille-sur-tet.com. Open Sept–June, Mon–Fri 9–12 and 2–6 (5 on Fri), closed Wed; summer open Mon–Sat 9–12 and 2–6 plus Sun morning.*

Prades ✉ 66500: 4 Rue Victor Hugo, **t** 04 68 05 41 02, **f** 04 68 05 21 79, *www.prades-tourisme.com. Open May, June, Sept and Oct Mon–Fri 9–12, 2–6; July and Aug Mon–Sat same times plus Sun, 10–12; Nov–April Mon–Fri 9–12, 2–5.*

Vernet-les-Bains ✉ 66820: 6 Pl de la Mairie, **t** 04 68 05 55 35, **f** 04 68 05 60 33, *www.ot-vernet-les-bains.fr. Open June–Sept Mon–Sat 9–12.30 and 3–6.30 plus Sun 10–12.30; winter Mon–Fri 9–12 and 2–6.*

Villefranche-de-Conflent ✉ 66500: 38 Rue St-Jacques, **t** 04 68 92 22 96, **f** 04 68 96 23 93. *Open daily July and Aug 10–7.30; June and Sept 10–6.30; Oct–May 2–5 plus school hols 10–12 and 2–5; closed Jan.*

Market Days

Ille-sur-Têt: Wed and Fri; flea market Sun.

Prades: Tues.

Where to Stay and Eat

Although until recently this area has been a gastronomic desert, prospects are improving, with imaginative treatment of Catalan cuisine and excellent fish and seafood.

Prades ✉ 66500

Les Glycines, 12 Rue Général De Gaulle, **t** 04 68 96 51 65, **f** 04 68 96 45 57, *www.glycines.com* (*inexpensive*). Tucked away in a quiet courtyard, with comfortable rooms and a restaurant. *Restaurant closed Sat lunch, Sun except July and Aug and first half of Jan. Menus €13–30.*

***Hostalrich**, 156 Rue Général De Gaulle, **t** 04 68 96 05 38 (*cheap*). A big neon sign makes it easy to find the Hostalrich, where all rooms have TV and showers and some have balconies from which to observe the throbbing street life below. Avoid the restaurant if you can; the food served is simple to the point of dullness (although there is a wonderful chestnut-shaded garden).

Jardin de L'Aymeric, 3 Av du General de Gaulle, **t** 04 68 96 53 38. The best bet for stylish regional cooking, though the excess of neon detracts from the atmosphere. *Menus €13–29. Closed Sun eve and Mon plus 2 weeks Jun–July.*

L'Hostal de Nogarols, Chem Nogarols, on the way to St-Michel-de-Cuxa, **t** 04 68 96 24 57. A good stop before music concerts, serving excellent wood-fired pizzas, as well as Catalan classics like *petit gris* snails and rabbit, in an airy dining room or pretty shady garden. *Menus €16–30. Closed Wed eve and Thurs in summer; winter lunch plus Fri and Sat eve only.*

fortress to protect not only the monks, but the population of the village; Ille was located here before its population drifted to the present site.

Six kilometres north on the D21, in little **Bélesta**, is the **Château-Musée** (**t** *04 68 84 55 55*), which holds the treasure found in a Neolithic tomb in 1983 and the superbly restored **castle**, itself a 13th-century work built by St Louis (*open daily mid-June–mid-Sept 2–7; 1 Jan–14 June 2–5.30, closed Tues and Sat; closed Feb*).

Prieuré de Serrabonne

Seeing the finest medieval sculpture in Roussillon requires dedication: even the most direct route (for others, *see* above) requires 13km of hairpin turns on a road where you dread oncoming traffic, starting from the D618 at Bouleternère, just west of Ille, and ending in a lofty, remote, barren spot on the slopes of a mountain called Roque Rouge. The solemn, spare shape and dark schist of Serrabonne's church (**t** *04 68 84 09 30; open daily 10–6; adm*) are not promising, making the surprise

Molitg-les-Bains ✉ 66500

★★★★**Château de Riell**, **t** 04 68 05 04 40, **f** 04 68 05 04 37, *www.relaischateaux/riell* (*expensive*). Molitg may have only 180 inhabitants, but it can claim Roussillon's top luxury hotel, the sumptuous Relais et Châteaux Château de Riell. This Baroque folly from the turn of the century is in a theatrically Baroque setting, perched on a rock with exquisite views of Canigou; it has elegant, luxurious Hollywoodian rooms – a contrast with the medieval *oubliettes*, which you can visit – and two pools, including one on top of the tower, perhaps the best place in the world to watch the Catalan bonfires go up on the equinox. Lots of extras, and a restaurant worthy of the décor. *Menus €33–64. Closed Nov–Mar.*

Grand Hotel Thermal, **t** 04 68 05 00 50 (*moderate*). Less pricey, but almost as splendid, with marble spa rooms, swimming pool and marble terrace, glorious views and also a very good-value restaurant. *Menus €21. Closed Dec–Mar.*

Mas Lluganas, just outside Mosset, **t** 04 68 05 00 37, **f** 04 68 05 04 08, *www.maslluganas.com* (*inexpensive*). Offers rooms and chambre d'hôte meals based on its own produce of ducks, guinea fowl, veal and foie gras. The same family also offers inexpensive *chambre d'hôte* accommodation at La Forge, a peaceful retreat by the river (**t** 04 68 05 04 84, **f** 04 68 05 04 08).

Vernet-les-Bains ✉ 66820

★★★**Le Mas Fleuri**, 25 Bd Clemenceau (the road up to St Martin), **t** 04 68 05 51 94, **f** 04 68 05 50 77, *www.hotelmasfleuri.fr* (*moderate*). At the top of the list, this century-old hotel is set in a pretty park, with a pool; rooms are air-conditioned. A modern annexe for bedrooms has recently been added. (*No restaurant*). *Closed Nov–mid-April.*

★★**Princess**, Rue Lavandières, **t** 04 68 05 56 22, **f** 04 68 05 62 45, *www.hotel-princess.com* (*inexpensive*). A pleasant Logis de France with a better-than-average restaurant. *Menus €16–32. Closed Dec–mid-Mar.*

Villefranche-de-Conflent ✉ 66500

★★**Auberge du Cèdre**, Domaine Ste-Eulalie, outside the walls, **t** 04 68 96 05 05 (*inexpensive*). Nine comfortable rooms, an adequate restaurant and two fat, friendly ginger cats in the garden. *Dinner and breakfast €20 p/p. Open all year.*

Auberge St-Paul, Place de l'Eglise, **t** 04 68 96 30 95, *www.auberge.stpaul.free.fr*. The chef at this lovely restaurant fetches from Canigou the basic ingredients for mountain surprises like *filet mignon de sanglier* (boar) and beef with morel mushrooms. *Menus €23–75. Closed Mon plus Sun eve and Tues Oct–mid-April. Closed 1 week mid-June.*

Au Grill, 81 Rue St-Jean, **t** 04 68 96 17 65. Solid traditional cuisine. *Menus €9–22. Closed Tues eve and Wed.*

inside that much the greater. The best efforts of the 12th-century Catalan sculptors were concentrated in the single gallery of the cloister and especially in the **tribune**, in rose marble from Canigou. Perfectly preserved in its isolated setting, this includes a fantastical bestiary, centaurs, a grimacing St Michael, reliefs of the four evangelists and more.

Prades, St-Michel-de-Cuxa, and Canigou

Prades is known around the world in connection with the music festival founded in 1951 by Pablo Casals, but few people could place it on a map. Casals, in exile after the Spanish Civil War, spent much of the 1940s and 50s here, in the one safe corner of his beloved Catalunya. From the beginning his festival (late July–early August) attracted many of the world's greatest musicians. Otherwise Prades is a rather typical, stolid Catalan town. There are a couple of things to see: the **Musée Pablo Casalo** (*4 Av Victor Hugo;* ***t*** *04 68 05 41 02; open Mon–Sat 9–12 and 2–6 in summer, Mon–Fri 9–12 and 2–5 in winter*) has a section dedicated to Casals – photos, his piano and pipes, records, letters, etc. In the heart of Prades, the church of St-Pierre has a fine Romanesque bell tower with a pyramid crown and inside, an operatic Baroque retable in full 17th-century fig by Catalan chisel virtuoso Joseph Sunyer and an exhibition of church treasures.

Best of all, it's only a few kilometres from Prades up through orchards to **St-Michel-de-Cuxa**, one of the most important monasteries of medieval Catalunya (***t*** *04 68 96 15 35; open 9.30–11.50 and 2–6, to 5pm in winter, closed Sun am; adm*). Even in its reduced, semi-ruined state, the scale is impressive; this was one of the great monastic centres from which medieval Europe was planned and built.

The coming of the French Revolution found St-Michel already in a state of serious decay. Looted and abandoned, the abbey suffered greatly in the last century. One of the two bell towers collapsed, and much of the best sculptural work went 'in exile' as the Catalans put it, carted off to the Cloisters Museum in New York. Now restored, St-Michel is occupied once again by a small community of Benedictine monks from Montserrat, the centre of Catalan spiritualism and nationalism.

While much of the inspiration for early medieval architecture in Languedoc came from north Italy or France, Roussillon was heavily influenced by nearby Spain. Here the obvious Spanish feature is the more-than-semicircular 'Visigothic' arches in the nave. This style, which goes back almost to Roman times, never became too popular in Christian Europe, though the Muslims of Spain adopted it to create the architectural fantasies of Seville and Granada. Other notable features of St-Michel include the massive and extremely elegant **bell tower**, and an unusual circular **crypt**, built in the 11th century under a building that was later demolished. The crypt is covered by toroid barrel-vaulting, with a mushroom-like central column almost unique in medieval architecture. Antonio Gaudí used similar columns in his work in Barcelona – a fascinating piece of Catalan cultural continuity; Gaudí could not have got the idea here, since the crypt was discovered and excavated only in 1937. In the **cloister**, you can see the galleries and capitals that didn't go to Manhattan.

If **Canigou's** magnetism is working its juju on you, don't resist the call. You can make two thirds of the climb – 7,053ft – by car, on a forest road that begins on the east end of Prades. This leaves you at the Chalet-Hôtel des Cortalets *refuge* (*open May–Sept; call* ***t*** *04 68 96 36 19 to book a bed; bed €14, meals €15*). From here it's a fairly easy three- to four-hour walk to the summit, requiring only a decent pair of walking shoes and windbreaker. There's a second, even more hair-raising forest road up to the *refuge* from the D27, practical only in a four-wheel drive. The Prades tourist office has a list of operators; leave the driving to them.

Vernet-les-Bains and St-Martin-du-Canigou

The D27, the narrow road that snakes around the lower slopes of Canigou, is an exceptional drive through the mountain forests, with grand views of the big mountain itself; after St-Michel-de-Cuxa, it meets **Vernet-les-Bains**, a bustling modern spa with most of the accommodation in the area, and hot sulphuric waters that are good for your rheumatism and respiratory problems. Three kilometres further up, **Casteil**, a little wooded resort with a small museum of mountain life and plenty of picnic grounds, is the base for visiting Canigou's other great medieval monument, the abbey of **St-Martin-du-Canigou** – a taxing though lovely 40-minute walk up from the town (***t*** *04 68 05 50 03; open daily in summer, closed Tues in winter, tours at 10, 11.45 (12 on Sun), 2, 3, 4 and 5 in summer, 10, 11.45, 2.30, 3.30 and 4.30 in winter; adm*).

A monkish architect named Sclua designed this complex, begun in the early 11th century by a count of the Cerdagne named Guifred Cabreta. Sclua was a designer ahead of his time; he made his monastery a rustic acropolis, spectacularly sited with views around Canigou and the surrounding peaks, and arranged as a series of courtyards and terraces on different levels. The church, with its immense, fortress-like bell tower, has two levels, an upper church dedicated to St-Martin and a lower crypt for a certain obscure subterranean Virgin Mary: Notre-Dame-sous-Terre. Some good white marble capitals can be seen in the cloister, heavily restored in the early 1900s, and medieval tombs, including Count Guifred's, survive in the upper church. But on the whole St-Martin, damaged by an earthquake in 1428, abandoned after the Revolution, restored between 1952–71 and reinhabited, retains relatively few of its former glories.

To complete the tour of Romanesque Canigou, there is another 11th- to 12th-century **church** in the village of **Corneilla-de-Conflent**, a former Benedictine priory full of good sculpture. Side roads to the west, in the valley of the Rotja, can take you to several more, including rare 10th-century churches in the tiny villages of **Fuilla** and **Sahorre**. Not all the area's attractions are on Canigou. Five kilometres northeast of Prades, in the empty, largely forested Pyrenean foothills, **Eus**, 'One of the most beautiful villages in France', is an ambitious place; it also claims to have 'the most sunshine of any *commune* in France'. Spilling down its steep hillside, as you see it from the Têt valley, it makes an elegant composition. The parish church has some elaborate 17th-century polychrome retables. Heading up from Prades in the Castellare valley, on the D14, **Molitg-les-Bains**, on a hill in the forest, has been a spa (specializing in skin disorders) since the *belle époque*, with a suitably grand hotel with a lake, river and lovely gardens open to the public. Beyond Molitg the road climbs up to the Col de Jau, a pass with stunning views, once the border between France and Spain, and a route to the Aude valley. On the way you pass the fortifed village of Mosset, a little haven of artists and potters, where there is a beautifully restored Romanesque chapel, the *capelletta*, in the old village.

Villefranche-de-Conflent

Some villages have their own ideas for welcoming visitors. This one casually points cannons down at you as you pass along the N116, by way of an invitation to drop in. Villefranche, the most logical place from which to defend the Têt valley, has had a **castle** at least since 1092. In the 17th century it took its present form, as a model Baroque fortress-town, rebuilt and re-fortified by Vauban. Almost nothing has changed since, and Villefranche remains as a fascinating historical record, a sort of stage set of that era. Tours of Vauban's **ramparts** with their walkway built through in the wall are offered (***t** 04 68 96 22 96; open July and Aug daily 10–8.; June and Sept 10–7; Feb and Nov 10.30–12.30 and 2–5; Mar–May and Oct 10.30–12.30 and 2–6; Dec 2–5; closed Jan*) and if you have sufficient puff and military curiosity, there's a steep climb up the remarkable 1,000 subterranean rock hewn steps (at the end of Rue St-Pierre) to **Fort Liberia** (***t** 04 68 96 34 01; open daily 9–8 in summer, 10–6 in winter; adm*), another Vauban opus, further fortified by Napoleon III, dominating the valley and long used as a prison where you can 'meet the villainous female prisoners' (don't be alarmed – they're made of wax). There's a bus up from Villefranche's Café Canigou if you're feeling lazy.

A survivor from the pre-Vauban Villefranche, the church of **St-Jacques** is a fine 12th-century building with the familiar capitals from the workshop of St-Michel-de-Cuxa; inside there's another retable by Sunyer and, by the door, note the measures engraved in the stone, used by drapers who had market stalls in the square. Vauban built its walls and tower into his wall to help with the defence. For all its grim purpose, Villefranche is a lovely town. A kilometre up the Vernet road, some of the Pyrenees' most peculiar stalactites await your inspection at the **Grotte des Canalettes** (***t** 04 68 96 23 11; open Palm Sunday–mid-Nov 10–6; adm*) and the **Grotte des Grandes Canalettes** (*open Easter–Oct 10–12 and 2–6.30, July and Aug 10–6.30, the rest of the year Sun only 2–5; adm*).

The Cerdagne

The lofty plateau of the Cerdagne (*Cerdanya* in Catalan) was an isolated and effectively independent county in the Middle Ages; from the 10th century its counts gradually extended their power, becoming eventually Counts of Barcelona – the founders of the Catalan nation. In spite of this heritage, the Cerdagne was split between Spain and France in the 1659 Treaty of the Pyrenees. The building of the Little Yellow Train, in 1911, brought the French Cerdagne into the modern world (*see* p.343); skiing has made it rather opulent today. And besides skiing, you can see some good Romanesque churches, warm up at the world's largest solar furnace, visit the highest railway station in France – and circumnavigate Spain in less than an hour.

To Mont-Louis and the Capcir

After Villefranche, the main N116 climbs dramatically into the mountains. There are a few possible stop-offs on the way: at **Olette**, you can turn off to explore nearly abandoned old mountain villages like **Nyer** and **Evols**. A bit further up, at **Thuès-entre-Valls**, you can stretch your legs in the beautiful **Gorges de la Carança**, then soak your weary bones in the natural hot-springs jacuzzi at **St-Thomas-les-Bains** at Fontpedrouse, where no matter the weather you can take a dip outside (***t** 04 68 97 03 13; open daily 10–7, till 9 in the summer; adm*).

Climb, climb, climb and at last you'll reach the gateway to the Cerdagne, **Mont-Louis**, another work of Vauban's and the highest fortress in France (5,250ft), named after Louis XIV. The army still resides here, though only to look after a pioneer **solar furnace** (***t** 04 68 04 14 89; open 10–12.30 and 2–6 and until 7 in summer; adm*), built in 1953 and used, not for generating power, but for melting substances for scientific experiments. A 7 kilometre detour up into the mountains will take you to tiny **Planès** and its equally tiny and unique triangular 11th-century church. Like the seven-sided model at Rieux-Minervois, this one has occasioned much speculation; some have claimed it as the centre of a network of ley-lines.

The road to Planès is a dead end, but there are better choices from the big crossroads at Mont-Louis. To the north, D118 carries you to the isolated **plateau of the Capcir**. It's a perfect place to get away from it all – after a road was built into the Capcir in the last century, almost the entire population deserted it, tired of scratching a living from land that would only support a few cows. They left behind beautiful pine forests, and a score of little lakes carved out long ago by Pyrenean glaciers. Skiing has brought the Capcir back to life since the 1960s, and the government has transformed the landscape with a number of dams and artificial lakes.

On your way into the Capcir, don't miss the church of **St-Vincent** in **La Llagonne**, only 3 kilometres from Mont-Louis. The centuries have left it in peace, with a remarkable collection of medieval art, including an altarpiece and painted baldachin (12th- and 13th-century) and an excellent polychrome *Majestat*. Further north, Les Angles, Matemale and Formiguères are the main ski centres. **Les Angles** has, as well as some 30 ski pistes, a **Parc Animalier** (***t** 04 68 04 17 20, www.faune-pyreneenne.com; open daily summer 9–6 and winter 9–5*), a free-range zoo with native fauna of the Pyrenees, both current and past residents, including bears, reindeer, wolves and bison. **Formiguères** (not the ski station, but the village, 4 kilometres away) is one of the prettiest and best preserved in the region, hardly changed since the days when the kings of Majorca sojourned here to relieve their asthma. This region is great for hiking. The best parts lie to the west, on the slopes of the 2,921m **Pic Carlit**; there you will find the sources of the Têt and Aude (above the D60, in the Forêt de Barrès).

Font-Romeu

The western road (D618) will take you through more pine forests to Font-Romeu; along with its new satellite towns, **Super-Bolquère** and **Pyrénées 2000**, this is one of the biggest ski resorts in France. Font-Romeu grew up after 1910, around a now-closed 'Grand Hôtel'; it prospers today partly by its excellent sports facilities, often used for

Tourist Information

Mont-Louis ✉ 66210: Rue du Marché, **t** 04 68 04 21 97, *www.mont-louis.net. Open daily July and Aug 9.30–12 and 2–6; rest of year 10–12 and 2–6, closed Sun and Mon.*

Les Angles ✉ 66210: 2 Av de l'Aude, **t** 04 68 04 32 76, **f** 04 68 30 93 09, *www.lesangles.com. Open daily all year 9–7.*

Font-Romeu ✉ 66120: 33 Av E.-Brousse, **t** 04 68 30 68 30, **f** 04 68 30 29 70, *www.font-romeu.fr. Open daily 9–12 and 2–6; summer and school hols 8.30–7.*

Bourg-Madame ✉ 66760: Place de la Mairie, **t** 04 68 04 55 35, **f** 04 68 04 66 55, *Open July and Aug daily 9–8; winter 9–12 and 2–6.*

Market Day

Puigcerdà: Sunday morning, the best market in the area.

Where to Stay and Eat

Olette ✉ 66360

La Fontaine, 3 Rue de la Fusterie, **t** 04 68 97 03 67, **f** 04 68 97 03 67 (*inexpensive*). Sweet little hotel in a mountain village on the route to Font Romeu, with several pleasant rooms and hearty meals. *Menus €13–28. Closed Wed lunch and Jan.*

Mont-Louis ✉ 66210

****Le Clos Cerdan**, **t** 04 68 04 23 29, **f** 04 68 04 23 79, *www.lecloscerdan.com* (*inexpensive*). Get a room with a view at this grey stone hotel on a cliff overlooking the valley; modern but comfortable. There's a restaurant. *Menu €15–30. Closed 3 weeks Nov.*

Lou Rouballou, Rue des Ecoles-Laïques, **t** 04 68 04 23 26, **f** 04 68 04 14 09 (*cheap*). In the village, by the ramparts, the family-run Lou Rouballou is pleasant and serves delicious food specializing in mushrooms (including one called the *rouballou*) in various guises. *Menus €20–30. Closed Wed plus May and Nov–15 Dec.*

Font-Romeu ✉ 66120

****Clair Soleil**, Rte Odeillo, **t** 04 68 30 13 65, **f** 04 68 30 08 27, *www.la-rando.com/clairsoleil* (*inexpensive*). With a view, a swimming pool and a restaurant. *Menus €16–32. Closed Nov and Dec and mid-April–mid-May.*

Cal Xandera, Angoustrine, 8km away, **t** 04 68 04 61 67, *www.calxandera.com* (*cheap*). Completely different – a beautifully restored 18th-century farmhouse serving flavour-packed traditional mountain cuisine, with *gîtes d'étape* (dormitory accommodation). *€33 pp with half board. Jazz and dinner €25 on Thurs eve. Menus €13. Open all year if booked ahead.*

Llo and Saillagouse ✉ 66800

*****Auberge l'Atalaya**, Llo, **t** 04 68 04 70 04, **f** 04 68 04 01 29, *www.chez.com/atalaya* (*expensive*). A rare example of a country inn unconcerned with the skiing business; tranquillity is assured in this setting, close to the wild flowers of the Vallée d'Eyne, with a pool and an excellent restaurant. *Menus €25–42. Closed Nov–20 Dec and mid-Jan–Mar.*

****La Vieille Maison Cerdane**. Place des Comtes-de-Cerdagne, Saillagouse, **t** 04 68 04 72 08, **f** 04 68 04 75 93, *www.planotel.fr* (*inexpensive*). This restaurant has been going 1895; the dining room, with its huge fireplace, is a great place to settle down to a plate of Catalan anchovies. *Menus €16–40. Closed mid-Oct–mid-Dec.*

Planotel, Rue de la Poste, **t** 04 68 04 72 08, *www.planotel.fr* (*inexpensive*). Modern, with a heated pool; run by the same family that runs La Vielle Maison Cerdane. The restaurant has menus for *€11–30. Closed Oct–May.*

Valcebollère ✉ 66340

Les Ecureuils, **t** 04 68 04 52 03, **f** 04 68 04 52 34 (*moderate*). Friendly mountain *auberge* in the Cevennes, offering charming rooms and well-cooked local produce. The proprietor will take you on guided mountain walks. *Menus €15–40. Restaurant closed Mon or Tues. Plus Nov–mid-Dec and mid-April–mid-May.*

training France's Olympic teams. Stamped from the same mould as every other continental ski resort, it has plenty of fake Alpine chalets, innumerable pizzerias, and 260 snow machines to help out when the weather isn't co-operating. But no other resort has the **World's Largest Solar Furnace**, 'stronger than 10,000 suns!' the successor to the one in Mont-Louis. With its curved mirror, covering an entire side of the nine-storey laboratory building, it reflects the Pyrenees beautifully while helping scientists work out all sorts of high-temperature puzzles (*t 04 68 30 77 86; open daily 10–6 in summer, 10–12.30 and 2–6 in winter; adm*). Above the town, the pilgrimage chapel of **Notre-Dame-de-Font-Romeu** has an exuberant altarpiece by Joseph Sunyer and a 12th-century statue of the Virgin.

Another solar experiment can be seen at **Targasonne** west of Font-Romeu on the D618; this big mirror was built to generate electricity, but hasn't quite worked as well as intended. The glaciers that reshaped the Capcir were busy here too, leaving a strange expanse of granite boulders called the **Chaos**. The Cerdagne is famous for its Romanesque churches and chapels, testimony to the mountain Catalans' prosperity and level of culture even in the very early Middle Ages. One of the best of the churches is **St-André**, at **Angoustrine**, west of Targasonne, with fragments of 13th-century frescoes representing the months of the year. To the west, **Dorres** is a lofty *village perché* with another church, this one from the 11th century, with another Romanesque Virgin inside and a chance to soak in a granite hot tub with a sulphurous pong (**t** 04 68 04 66 87; *open daily 9–7*).

The Vallée du Carol

From the village of **Ur** (with yet another richly decorated Romanesque **church**), you can make a northern detour into the Vallée du Carol, the western edge of Roussillon. **Latour-de-Carol** is a romantic name for another great border rail-crossing most of us have blinked at in the dark; the name does not come from Charlemagne, as most people think, but the Carol river. Latour's church has more work by Joseph Sunyer. The best church in the area, however, is the Chapelle St-Fructueux in the minuscule village of **Yravals**, above Latour-de-Carol – with a wealth of medieval art inside, and a magnificent mid-14th-century altarpiece of St Martha. Further up this scenic valley, you'll pass the tower of the ruined 14th-century castle that gives Latour its name. The trees give out as the tortuous road climbs to the pass of Puymorens. From here, if you have a sudden hankering for some tax-free Havanas, or a new phonograph, it's only 40km to the Pyrenean Ruritania, the Principality of Andorra (*see* p.330).

Llivia, Llo and Eyne

Bourg-Madame, 'the same latitude as Rome, but sunnier' as its brochure claims, is the crossing point for Spain; just across the border lies **Puigcerdà**, with a 14th-century church and the best ice-hockey squad on the Iberian peninsula. The N116 will take you northeast from here, back to Mont-Louis, completing your circumnavigation of Spain – or at least the tiny Spanish enclave of **Llivia**, left marooned by accident in the Treaty of 1659. The treaty stipulated that Spain must give up the villages of the Cerdagne, and everyone had forgotten that Llivia had the legal status of a *ville*; it had been a Roman *municipium*, the capital of the Cerdagne in ancient times. Llivia's historic centre is clustered around a 15th-century fortified **church**; opposite, in the **Musée Municipal** (*open Tues–Sat 10–1 and 4–7, Sun 10–2, closed Mon*), the unlikely attraction is a 16th-century pharmacy, one of the oldest and best-preserved in Europe.

East of Bourg-Madame, more Catalan Romanesque churches can be visited: at **Hix**, an impressive edifice of 1177, built when the town was the residence of the counts of the Cerdagne, and containing a majestic Romanesque Virgin, with a little kingly Christ child on her lap, and at **Caldégas**, where the frescoes include a hunting scene with falcons. Further east, along the N116, road signs will startle you with town names like Llo and Err; linguists say they're Basque, evidence that the Basques lived here in remote times. **Llo** has a church with a lovely sculptured portal and an exceptionally sweet cemetery in nearby **Ste-Léocadie** (home of the highest vineyard in Europe). You can visit the **Musée de Cerdagne** (*t 04 68 04 08 05; open July–Sept 11–5; closed Wed*) in a 17th-century farm, dedicated to the pre-ski trades of the great plateau – shepherding and farming. There are opportunities for hiking, southwards into the narrow **Gorges du Sègre**. Even better, come to nearby **Eyne** in May, late enough to avoid the skiers from the resort called Eyne 2600, and just in time for a spectacular display of wildflowers and medicinal herbs in the Vallée d'Eyne, climbing up to the Spanish border. The aforementioned Musée de Cerdagne offers day or half-day guided tours in July and August through the **Réserve Naturelle d'Eyne** (*t 04 68 04 77 07*) as well and a three-hour **Balade Archéologique** to the village's menhirs and dolmens (*the last two weeks of July–Aug Wed–Sat, departing from the village; **t** 04 68 04 08 05 for more information*).

The Vallespir

The valley of the Tech, the southernmost valley of Roussillon, and of France, winds a lonesome trail around the southern slopes of Canigou. Known for its mineral waters since Roman times, it traditionally made its living from these and from ironworking, the basis of Catalan prosperity in the Middle Ages. When the iron gave out, there was smuggling. Today, as smugglers have become superfluous, the Vallespir lives by tourism, with some francs on the side from cherries and cork oak.

Le Boulou and St-Martin-de-Fenollar

From Perpignan, you reach the Vallespir by the A9, getting off at **Le Boulou**, a truck-stop known to every European TIR jockey. The ancient Roman teamsters knew it too. Le Boulou has been fated by geography as an eternal transit point; just coincidentally it has a fine Romanesque church with a superb white marble tympanum sculpted by the Master of Cabestany, portraying the *Resurrection of the Virgin*. The cornice shows scenes of the Nativity, the Christ Child's first bath (also rarely depicted in art), the *Shepherds*, *Magi* and *Flight into Egypt*. East of Le Boulou, **St-Génis-des-Fontaines** was one of the important early medieval monasteries of Roussillon. Its church has a remarkable carved lintel dated 1020, with a *Majestat* and stylized apostles shaped like bowling-pins; the cloister was dismantled and sold off in 1924, one of the final scandals of France's traditional lack of concern for its medieval heritage. In 1988 it was rebuilt as it was, with originals and copies (***t** 04 68 89 84 33; open May–Sept daily 10-12 and 3–7, Oct–May Mon–Fri 9.30–12 and 2–5*).

The A9 and N9 continue south into Spain, passing **St-Martin-de-Fenollar** and its 9th-century church (**t** *04 68 87 73 82; open mid-June–mid-Sept 10.30–12 and 3.30–7; the rest of the year 2–5, closed Tues; adm*), with some of the most unusual and best-preserved 12th-century frescoes in the Midi. Nine-tenths of all early medieval painting is lost to us, and this is a rare example of the best of what is left: brilliant colours and a confident stylization, with an imagery untroubled by the dogma of later religious painting, as in the *Nativity*, where Mary lies not in a stable but in a comfortable bed under a chequered baldachin.

Tourist Information

Céret ✉ 66400: Av Clemenceau (opposite Funetech, a pseudo-Egyptian funeral parlour), **t** 04 68 87 00 53, **f** 04 68 87 00 56, *www.ceret.fr. Open all year Mon–Sat 9–12 and 2–6.*

Arles-sur-Tech ✉ 66150: Rue Barjau, **t** 04 68 39 11 99, **f** 04 68 39 11 99, *www.tourisme-haut-vallespir.com. Open July and Aug Mon–Sat 9–7 plus Sun 2–5; rest of year Mon–Sat 9–12 and 2–6, Sun 2–5.*

Prats-de-Mollo ✉ 66230: Place le Foiral, **t** 04 68 39 70 83, **f** 04 68 39 74 51, *www.pratsdemollolapreste.com. Open daily July and Aug 9–12 and 1.30–6.30; rest of year Mon–Sat 9–12 and 2–6.*

Market Days

Céret: Saturday.

Arles-sur-Tech: Wednesday.

Where to Stay and Eat

Céret ✉ 66400

★★★★**Terrasse au Soleil**, Route Fontfrède, **t** 04 68 87 01 94, **f** 04 68 87 39 24, *www.la-terrace-au-soleil.fr* (*expensive*). A restored, modernized *mas* on a hill above Céret, with a view, a heated pool and tennis court (a bit dear, especially on full board). Restaurant Cerisaie has menus for *€43–98. Restaurant closed for lunch exc Sat and Sun.*

Le Mas Trilles, Pont de Reynes, on the Céret–Amélie-les-Bains road, **t** 04 68 87 38 37, **f** 04 68 87 42 62, *www.romantikhotels.com/ceret* (*expensive*). A tastefully renovated *mas* with a heated pool and a charming garden overlooking a trout stream. The restaurant does dinner for residents only. *Menus from €28. Closed Oct–April.*

★★**Les Arcades**, 1 Place Picasso, **t** 04 68 87 12 30, **f** 04 68 87 49 44 (*inexpensive*). Artistically decorated, with balconies overlooking the market square. *Open all year.*

★**Vidal**, 4 Place du 4 Septembre, **t** 04 68 87 00 85, **f** 04 68 87 62 33 (*cheap*). In a charming, if quirky, listed building. There's a restaurant. *Menus €14–25. Open all year.*

Les Feuillants, 1 Bd Lafayette, **t** 04 68 87 37 88. Catalan cooking with *haute cuisine* ambitions, in startling 1930s décor. *Menus €30–45. Closed Sun eve and Mon.*

Le Pied dans le Plat, Plaça dels Nou Raigs, **t** 04 68 87 17 65. For something a tad simpler, with tables out in the pretty square. *Menus €10–16. Closed Sun.*

Amélie-les-Bains ✉ 66110

★★**Castel Emeraude**, Route de la Corniche, **t** 04 68 39 02 83, **f** 04 68 39 03 09, *www.lecastelemeraude.com* (*inexpensive*). This is the place to get away from it all: a big white manor on the banks of the river, with a good restaurant. *Menus €17–34. Closed mid-Nov–mid-Mar.*

Arles-sur-Tech ✉ 66150

★★**Les Glycines**, Rue Joc de Paume, **t** 04 68 39 10 09, **f** 04 68 39 83 02 (*inexpensive*). Named for the ancient wisteria that shades the garden terrace, Les Glycines has modernized rooms, all with bath, and a wonderful restaurant where chef Thierry Pineda defies every snide remark we've made about Catalan cuisine with the best menu for miles: try his aubergine *tian* and delectable *panaché* of Mediterranean fish; lunch is cheaper. *Menus €14–29. Closed mid-Nov–mid-Feb.*

Hannibal entered Gaul through **Le Perthus**, the last, or first stop in France. As a fitting book end to this long volume, archaeologists have recently uncovered, at Panisars, a monumental pedestal, identified as belonging to the **Trophée de Pompée**. This monument was erected by a victorious Pompey in 71 BC on the Gallo-Hispanic frontier. Part of the stone was used to build a priory in 1011 (the ruins are nearby); the rest was quarried by Vauban in the 17th century to build the **Fort de Bellegarde** (***t*** *04 68 83 60 15; open July and Aug 10–6, open end June–end Sept 10.30–12.30 and 2.30–6.30; adm*).

Céret: the 'Mecca of Cubism'

Back in the valley of the Tech, the D115 streaks from Le Boulou to Céret, centre of the optimal cherry-growing region suspended between the Pyrenees and the sea. Amid the orchards, Céret is a laid-back town under enormous plane trees, with perfect little squares (especially the **Plaça dels Nou Raigs**), medieval gates, the biggest Baroque church in Roussillon, **St-Pierre**, a war memorial by Maillol and an elegant 14th-century **bridge** over the Tech.

Have a look around Céret before visiting the **Musée d'Art Moderne** (*8 Bd du Maréchal Joffre,* ***t*** *04 68 87 27 76; www.musee-ceret.com; open July–mid-Sept daily 10–7, rest of year until 6; closed Tues from Oct–April; adm*) and you'll be surprised at how many scenes you'll recognize. Céret found its artistic destiny at the turn of the century, thanks to Picasso, Braque, Gris, Manolo, Matisse, Soutine, Kisling, Masson, Tzara, Lhote, Marquet and others who spent time here up until 1940, and whose works fill the rooms. Best of all are the works donated by Picasso in 1953, among them 28 little plates painted in a five-day spurt of energy, all with variations on the *corrida* under a blasting sun. Although not as dazzling, the **Maison de l'Archéologie** in the Tour Port d'Espagne (***t*** *04 68 87 31 59; open daily July and Aug 10–12 and 1–6, rest of the year Mon–Fri 10–12 and 2–5*) has well arranged Neolithic, classical and medieval finds from the Vallespir.

Amélie-les-Bains and Arles-sur-Tech

Sulphurous waters, good for your rheumatism, have been the fortune of **Amélie-les-Bains** since ancient times; a Roman swimming pool with a vaulted roof has been uncovered, and the spa, rising on either side of the river Tech, still does a grandstand business. Amélie's pretty medieval ancestor, **Palalda**, is piled on a nearby hill, and offers a small **Musée de la Poste** (***t*** *04 68 39 34 90; open summer Mon–Fri 10–12 and 2–5; adm*) for snail-mail nostalgia from the days of Louis XI to 1900; there's a collection of stamps, and telephones, too.

Just west, **Arles-sur-Tech**, the ancient capital of the Vallespir, is a curious old village built on a narrow maze of lanes and offers some even curiouser hagiography in its 11th- and 12th-century church of Ste-Marie, originally the centre of an important monastery. Dark Age Arles-sur-Tech got by with an anonymous saint – an empty 4th-century sarcophagus known as *Sainte-Tombe* – until the dreaded *simiots* came to town, ape-like monsters that trampled the crops and violated the women. In despair, the abbot of Ste-Marie went to the pope asking for some holy relics. This was in 957, when demand for saints' bones was at its historic high, and the best the pope could offer was a pair of Persian martyrs named Abdon and Sennen. The abbot brought them back in a false-bottomed water-barrel, to fool the Venetians and Germans and any other relic thieves, and they dealt with the *simiots* as efficiently as if they had been the bones of St Peter himself. The story is portrayed in a 17th-century retable, in the chapel where Abdon and Sennen's relics are kept. The *Sainte-Tombe* itself, once a major pilgrimage attraction, is kept in a little enclosure outside the front door. It fills continually with perfectly pure water – some 500 to 600 litres a year, ceremoniously pumped every 30 July.

Arles-sur-Tech is the home of Tissages Catalans, where they've been making cloth since 1900 (there's a little museum on Rue des Usines; ***t*** *04 68 39 10 07; open Mon–Sat 9–12 and 3.30–5.30*), and it was the last redoubt of the valley's famous medieval iron industry; the last working mine in Roussillon, up at Batère, closed down in the early 1990s. Two kilometres northwest along the D44 you can go through the World's Narrowest Gorge, the **Gorges de la Fou** (***t*** *04 68 39 16 21; open April–Nov daily 10–6*), a giant crack in the rock with sides towering 650ft, with waterfalls and caves along the mile-long walkway. Legend made it the lair of witches, bogeymen and *traboucayres*, robbers who pounced on passing diligences.

Continuing up the valley, just south of the D115, the hill-top village of **Serralongue** has a church dating from 1018, with a fine portal and one of the only surviving examples of a Catalan *conjurador*; this is a small, square pavilion with a slate roof and statues of the four Evangelists facing the four cardinal directions. When a storm threatened, the priest would go up to the *conjurador* and perform certain rites facing the direction of the storm to avert its wrath.

A detour further south, on the D3, will uncover **St-Laurent-de-Cerdans**, famous for making espadrilles, and **Coustouges**, which has a lovely early 12th-century fortified church with a slate roof and two carved portals, one inside the other.

Some towns just ask for it. As if having a name like **Prats-de-Mollo** wasn't enough, this tiny spa advertises itself as the 'European Capital of Urinary Infections'. The baths are really at **La Preste**, 8 kilometres up in the mountains; Prats-de-Mollo itself is an attractive old village. Don't miss the whale bone stuck in the church wall. This is as far as we go; the Spanish border is 14 kilometres away.

Index

Main page references are in **bold**. Page references to maps are in *italics*.

Gascony touring atlas

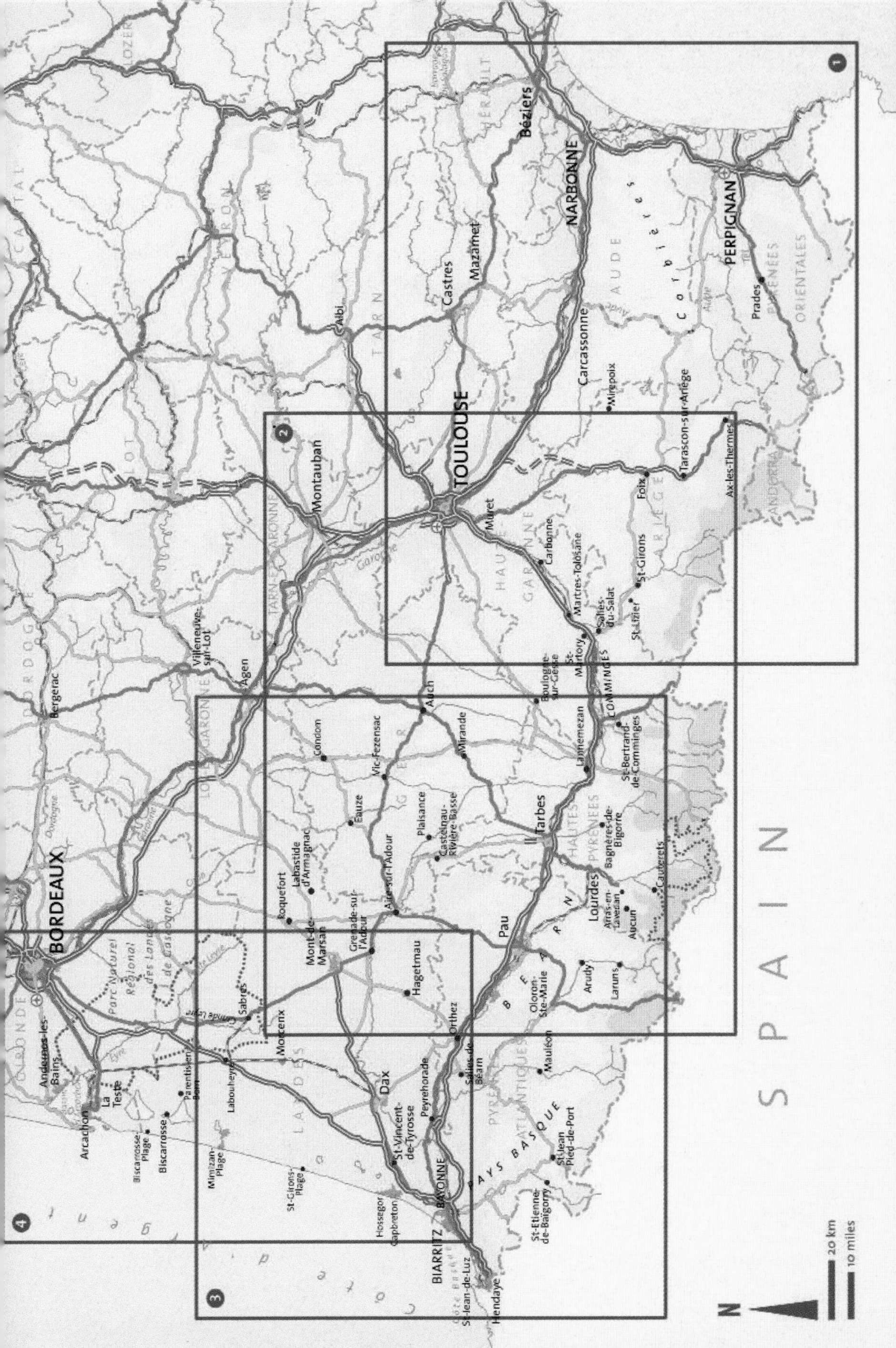

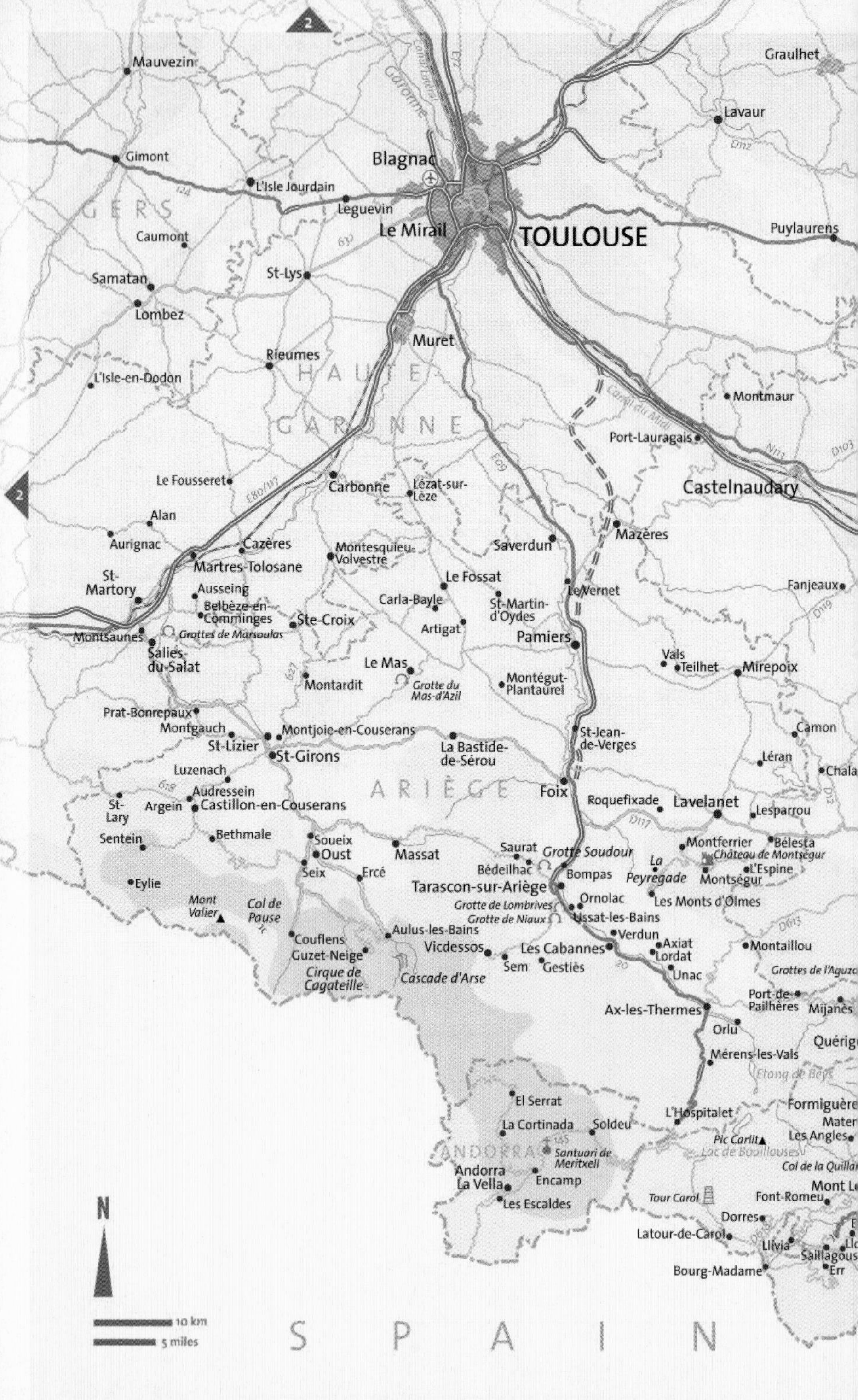

TOULOUSE
Blagnac
Le Mirail
Mauvezin
Gimont
L'Isle Jourdain
Leguevin
GERS
Caumont
Samatan
Lombez
St-Lys
Muret
Rieumes
L'Isle-en-Dodon
HAUTE-GARONNE
Graulhet
Lavaur
Puylaurens
Montmaur
Port-Lauragais
Castelnaudary
Canal du Midi
Le Fousseret
Carbonne
Lèzat-sur-Lèze
Alan
Aurignac
Cazères
Martres-Tolosane
Montesquieu-Volvestre
Saverdun
Mazères
St-Martory
Ausseing
Belbèze-en-Comminges
Ste-Croix
Le Fossat
Carla-Bayle
St-Martin-d'Oydes
Le Vernet
Fanjeaux
Montsaunes
Grottes de Marsoulas
Salies-du-Salat
Artigat
Pamiers
Le Mas
Grotte du Mas-d'Azil
Montardit
Montégut-Plantaurel
Vals
Teilhet
Mirepoix
Prat-Bonrepaux
Montgauch
St-Lizier
Montjoie-en-Couserans
St-Girons
La Bastide-de-Sérou
St-Jean-de-Verges
Camon
Léran
Luzenach
Audressein
Argein
Castillon-en-Couserans
St-Lary
ARIÈGE
Foix
Roquefixade
Lavelanet
Lesparrou
Sentein
Bethmale
Soueix
Oust
Seix
Massat
Ercé
Saurat
Grotte Soudour
Bédeilhac
Bompas
Tarascon-sur-Ariège
Montferrier
Bélesta
Château de Montségur
La Peyregade
Montségur
L'Espine
Les Monts d'Olmes
Eylie
Mont Valier
Col de Pause
Grotte de Lombrives
Grotte de Niaux
Ornolac
Ussat-les-Bains
Verdun
Couflens
Guzet-Neige
Aulus-les-Bains
Cirque de Cagateille
Cascade d'Arse
Vicdessos
Sem
Les Cabannes
Gestiès
Axiat
Lordat
Unac
Montaillou
Grottes de l'Aguzo
Port-de-Pailhères
Mijanès
Ax-les-Thermes
Orlu
Mérens-les-Vals
Étang de Beys
El Serrat
La Cortinada
Soldeu
ANDORRA
Santuari de Meritxell
Andorra La Vella
Encamp
Les Escaldes
L'Hospitalet
Pic Carlit
Lac de Bouillouses
Formiguère
Les Angles
Col de la Quillan
Tour Carol
Font-Romeu
Dorres
Latour-de-Carol
Llívia
Saillagous
Err
Bourg-Madame
SPAIN
N
10 km
5 miles

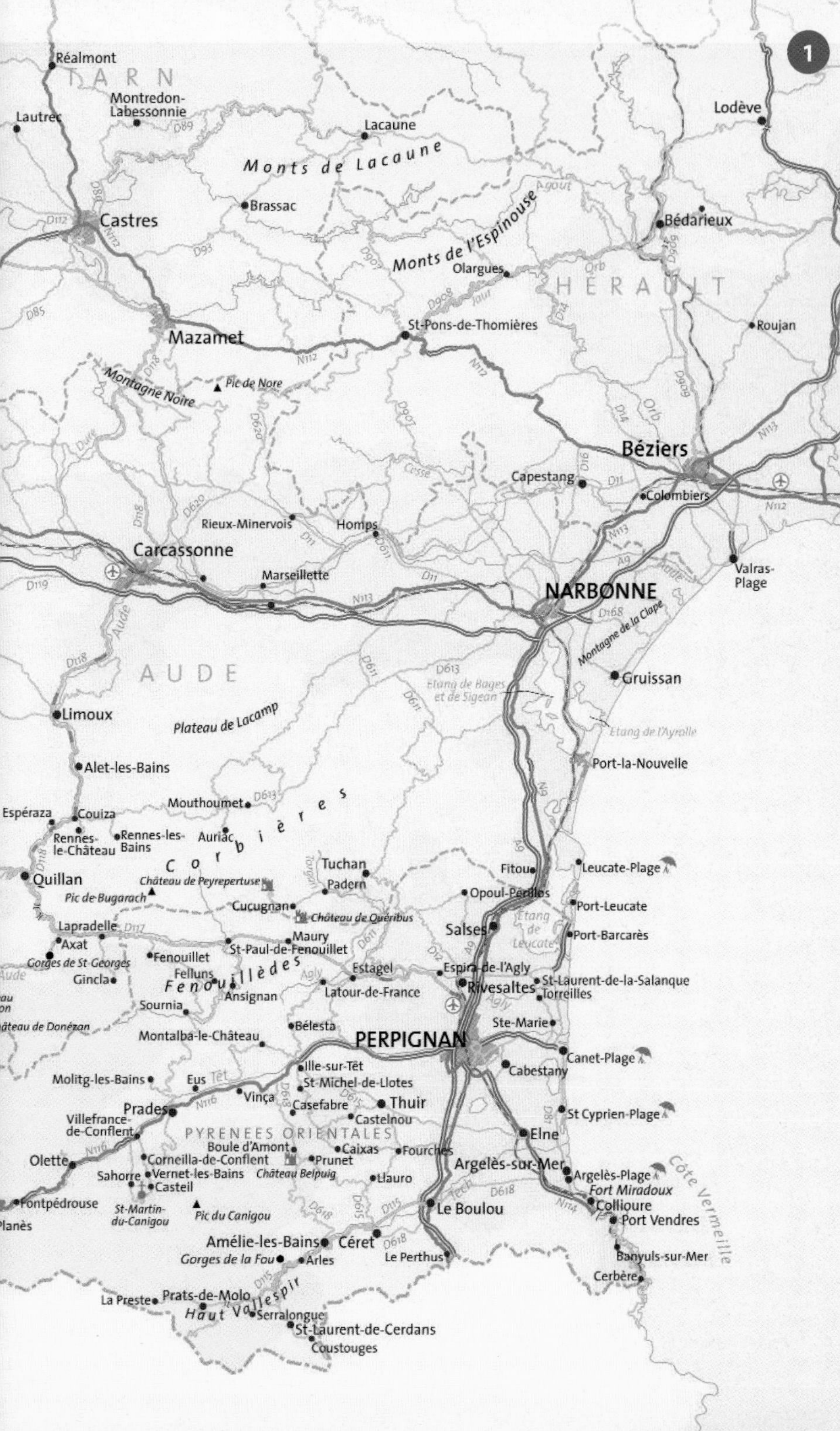
1
Réalmont
TARN
Montredon-Labessonnie
Lautrec
Lacaune
Monts de Lacaune
Brassac
Castres
Monts de l'Espinouse
Olargues
Lodève
Bédarieux
HÉRAULT
Mazamet
St-Pons-de-Thomières
Roujan
Montagne Noire
Pic de Nore
Béziers
Capestang
Colombiers
Rieux-Minervois
Homps
Carcassonne
Marseillette
NARBONNE
Valras-Plage
Montagne de la Clape
AUDE
Gruissan
Etang de Bages et de Sigean
Etang de l'Ayrolle
Limoux
Plateau de Lacamp
Alet-les-Bains
Port-la-Nouvelle
Mouthoumet
Corbières
Espéraza
Couiza
Rennes-le-Château
Rennes-les-Bains
Auriac
Quillan
Château de Peyrepertuse
Tuchan
Padern
Fitou
Leucate-Plage
Pic de Bugarach
Cucugnan
Château de Quéribus
Opoul-Périllos
Port-Leucate
Lapradelle
Axat
Maury
Salses
Etang de Leucate
Port-Barcarès
Gorges de St-Georges
Fenouillet
St-Paul-de-Fenouillet
Fenouillèdes
Felluns
Ansignan
Gincla
Estagel
Espira-de-l'Agly
Rivesaltes
St-Laurent-de-la-Salanque
Torreilles
Latour-de-France
Sournia
Bélesta
Ste-Marie
Château de Donézan
Montalba-le-Château
PERPIGNAN
Canet-Plage
Ille-sur-Têt
Cabestany
Molitg-les-Bains
Eus
St-Michel-de-Llotes
Vinça
Thuir
Prades
Casefabre
Castelnou
St Cyprien-Plage
Villefranche-de-Conflent
PYRENEES ORIENTALES
Elne
Boule d'Amont
Caixas
Fourches
Olette
Corneilla-de-Conflent
Prunet
Argelès-sur-Mer
Argelès-Plage
Sahorre
Vernet-les-Bains
Château Belpuig
Llauro
Côte Vermeille
Casteil
Fort Miradoux
Fontpédrouse
St-Martin-du-Canigou
Pic du Canigou
Le Boulou
Collioure
Planès
Port Vendres
Amélie-les-Bains
Céret
Gorges de la Fou
Arles
Le Perthus
Banyuls-sur-Mer
Cerbère
La Preste
Prats-de-Molo
Haut Vallespir
Serralongue
St-Laurent-de-Cerdans
Coustouges

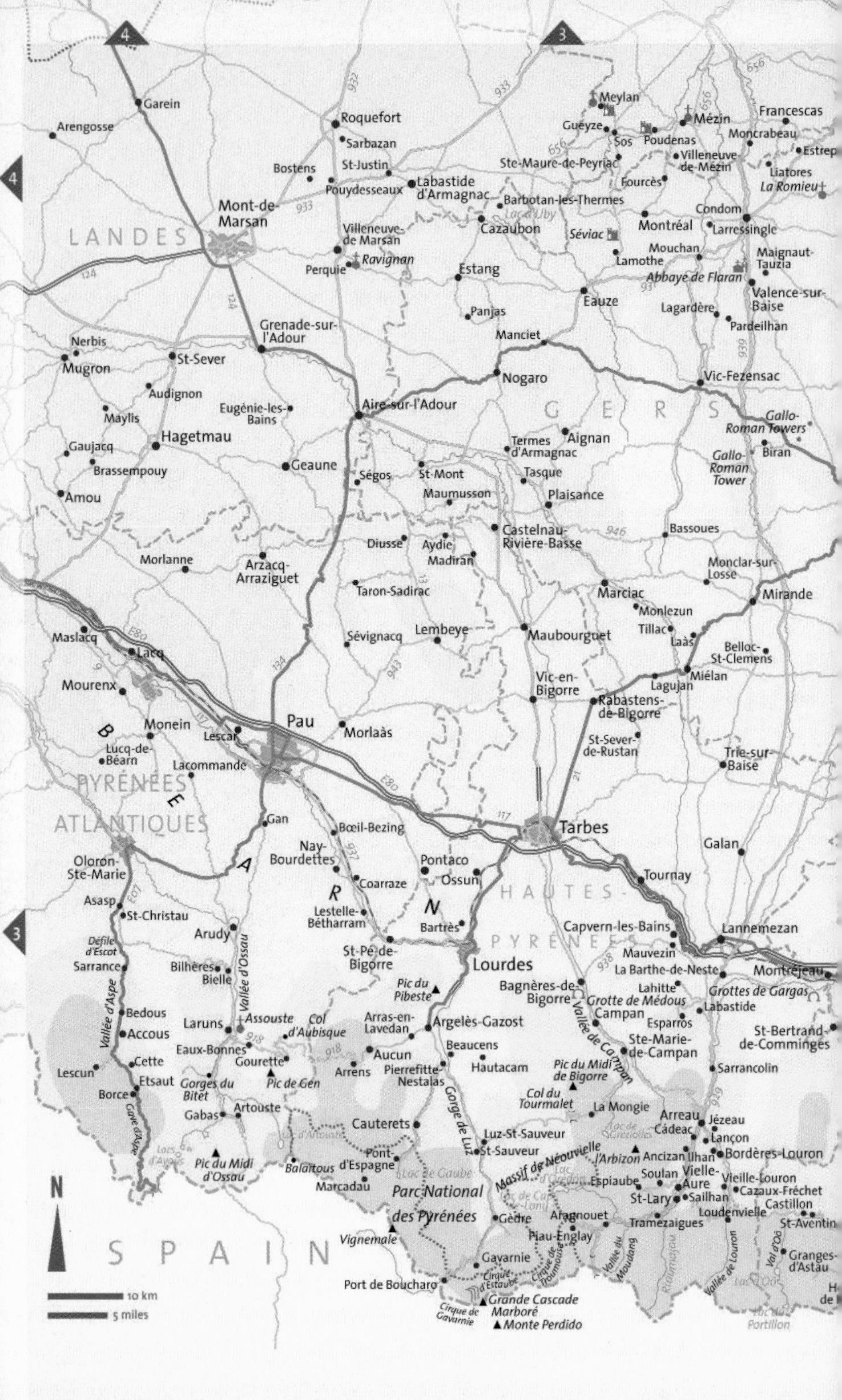

4
3
Garein
Arengosse
Roquefort
Sarbazan
Meylan
Gueyze
Sos
Poudenas
Mézin
Francescas
Moncrabeau
Estrep
Bostens
St-Justin
Pouydesseaux
Labastide d'Armagnac
Ste-Maure-de-Peyriac
Villeneuve-de-Mézin
Fourcès
Liatores
La Romieu
Mont-de-Marsan
Barbotan-les-Thermes
Lac d'Uby
LANDES
Villeneuve-de Marsan
Cazaubon
Séviac
Montréal
Condom
Larressingle
Perquie
Ravignan
Mouchan
Lamothe
Maignaut-Tauzia
Estang
Abbaye de Flaran
Valence-sur-Baise
Eauze
Panjas
Lagardère
Pardeilhan
Grenade-sur-l'Adour
Manciet
Nerbis
Mugron
St-Sever
Nogaro
Vic-Fezensac
Audignon
Aire-sur-l'Adour
Eugénie-les-Bains
Maylis
G E R S
Gallo-Roman Towers
Hagetmau
Termes d'Armagnac
Aignan
Gaujacq
Biran
Brassempouy
Geaune
Gallo-Roman Tower
Ségos
St-Mont
Tasque
Amou
Maumusson
Plaisance
Castelnau-Rivière-Basse
Bassoues
Diusse
Aydie
Madiran
Morlanne
Arzacq-Arraziguet
Monclar-sur-Losse
Taron-Sadirac
Marciac
Mirande
Monlezun
Maslacq
Tillac
Lembeye
Maubourguet
Sévignacq
Laàs
Belloc-St-Clemens
Lacq
Miélan
Mourenx
Lagujan
Vic-en-Bigorre
Rabastens-de-Bigorre
Pau
Monein
Morlaàs
B
Lescar
St-Sever-de-Rustan
Lucq-de-Béarn
Lacommande
Trie-sur-Baise
PYRÉNÉES
E
ATLANTIQUES
Gan
Bœil-Bezing
Tarbes
Galan
Oloron-Ste-Marie
Nay-Bourdettes
Pontacq
A
Ossun
Tournay
HAUTES-
Asasp
Coarraze
St-Christau
R
Lestelle-Bétharram
N
Bartrès
Capvern-les-Bains
Lannemezan
Arudy
Défilé d'Escot
PYRÉNÉES
Mauvezin
Sarrance
St-Pé-de-Bigorre
Lourdes
La Barthe-de-Neste
Montréjeau
Bilhères
Bielle
Vallée d'Ossau
Pic du Pibeste
Bagnères-de-Bigorre
Lahitte
Grottes de Gargas
Vallée d'Aspe
Grotte de Médous
Campan
Labastide
Bedous
Assouste
Col d'Aubisque
Arras-en-Lavedan
Argelès-Gazost
Esparros
Accous
Laruns
St-Bertrand-de-Comminges
Vallée de Campan
Eaux-Bonnes
Beaucens
Ste-Marie-de-Campan
Cette
Gourette
Aucun
Lescun
Arrens
Pierrefitte-Nestalas
Hautacam
Pic du Midi de Bigorre
Sarrancolin
Etsaut
Gorges du Bitet
Pic de Gen
Borce
Gorge de Luz
Col du Tourmalet
Gave d'Aspe
La Mongie
Arreau
Jézeau
Gabas
Artouste
Cadeac
Cauterets
Lac d'Artouste
Luz-St-Sauveur
Lac de Greziolles
Lançon
Lacs d'Ayous
Pic du Midi d'Ossau
Pont-d'Espagne
St-Sauveur
Massif de Néouvielle
l'Arbizon
Ancizan
Ilhan
Bordères-Louron
Balaïtous
Lac de Gaube
Soulan
Vielle-Aure
Vieille-Louron
Marcadau
Parc National des Pyrénées
Espiaube
Cazaux-Fréchet
St-Lary
Sailhan
Castillon
N
Gèdre
Aragnouet
Loudenvielle
Tramezaigues
St-Aventin
Vignemale
Piau-Engaly
S P A I N
Gavarnie
Cirque de Troumouse
Vallée du Moudang
Vallée de Louron
Val d'Oô
Granges-d'Astau
Cirque d'Estaubé
Lac d'Oô
Port de Boucharo
10 km
5 miles
Grande Cascade
Marboré
Cirque de Gavarnie
Monte Perdido
Lac du Portillon
E80
E07
124
933
932
656
939
946
943
937
918
938
929
117
21

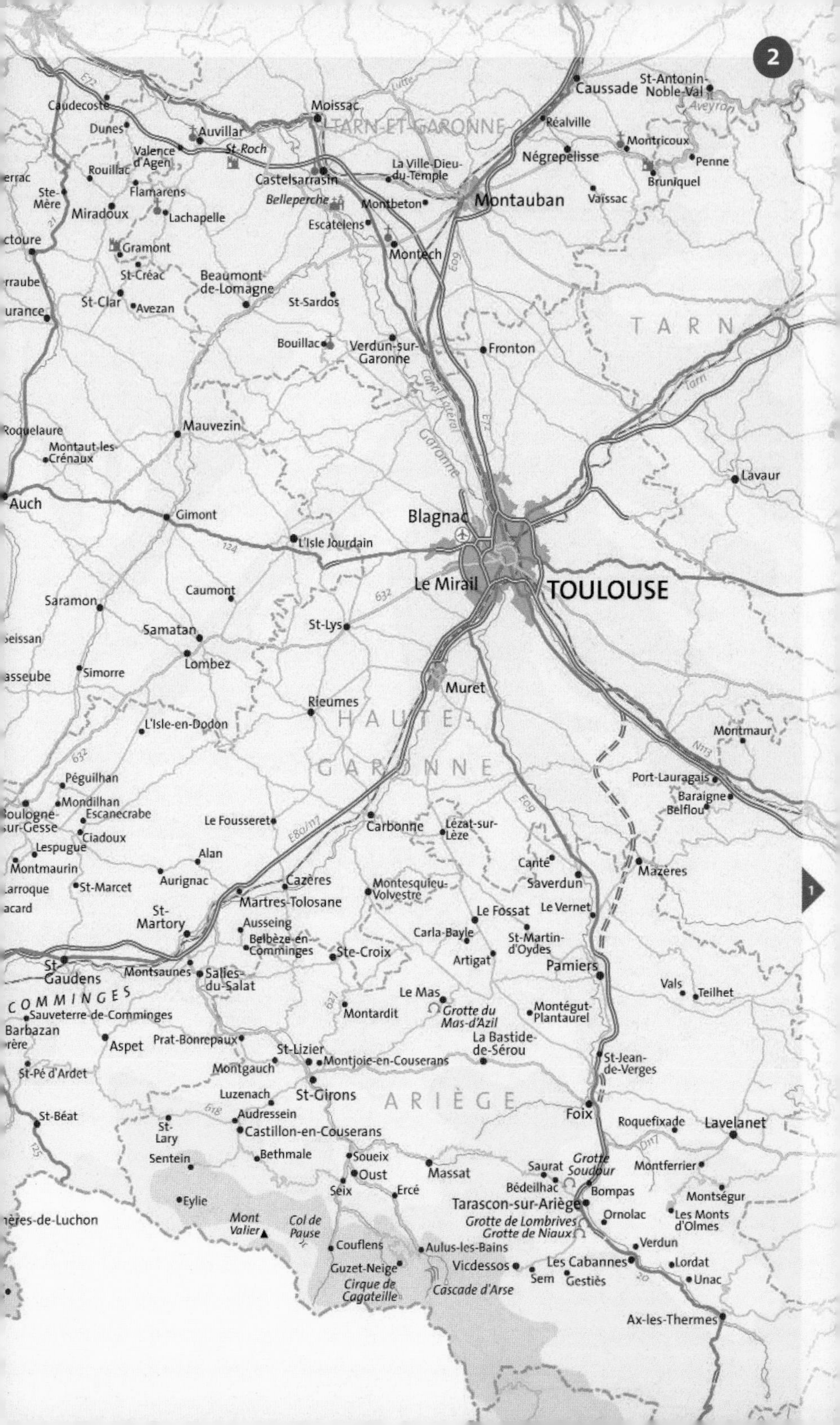

2

Caussade
St-Antonin-Noble-Val
Aveyron
Caudecoste
Moissac
TARN-ET-GARONNE
Réalville
Dunes
Auvillar
St-Roch
Montricoux
Valence d'Agen
Négrepelisse
Penne
Rouillac
La Ville-Dieu-du-Temple
Bruniquel
Flamarens
Castelsarrasin
Ste-Mère
Belleperche
Montbeton
Montauban
Vaïssac
Miradoux
Lachapelle
Escatelens
Lectoure
Gramont
Montech
St-Créac
Beaumont-de-Lomagne
St-Clar
Avezan
St-Sardos
Fleurance
TARN
Bouillac
Verdun-sur-Garonne
Fronton
Canal Latéral
Garonne
Tarn
Roquelaure
Mauvezin
Montaut-les-Crénaux
Lavaur
Auch
Gimont
Blagnac
L'Isle Jourdain
Le Mirail
TOULOUSE
Saramon
Caumont
Samatan
St-Lys
Seissan
Lombez
Simorre
Pavie
Rieumes
Muret
HAUTE-GARONNE
L'Isle-en-Dodon
Montmaur
Péguilhan
Port-Lauragais
Mondilhan
Baraigne
Boulogne-sur-Gesse
Escanecrabe
Belflou
Ciadoux
Le Fousseret
Carbonne
Lézat-sur-Lèze
Lespugue
Alan
Canté
Mazères
Montmaurin
Aurignac
Saverdun
Larroque
St-Marcet
Cazères
Montesquieu-Volvestre
Martres-Tolosane
Le Vernet
Le Fossat
St-Martory
Ausseing
Carla-Bayle
St-Martin-d'Oydes
Belbèze-en-Comminges
Ste-Croix
Artigat
St-Gaudens
Montsaunès
Salies-du-Salat
Pamiers
Le Mas
Vals
Teilhet
COMMINGES
Sauveterre-de-Comminges
Montardit
Grotte du Mas-d'Azil
Montégut-Plantaurel
Barbazan
Aspet
Prat-Bonrepaux
La Bastide-de-Sérou
St-Lizier
Montjoie-en-Couserans
St-Jean-de-Verges
St-Pé d'Ardet
Montgauch
Luzenach
St-Girons
ARIÈGE
Foix
St-Béat
St-Lary
Audressein
Roquefixade
Lavelanet
Castillon-en-Couserans
Sentein
Bethmale
Soueix
Oust
Massat
Saurat
Grotte Soudour
Montferrier
Bédeilhac
Bompas
Eylie
Seix
Ercé
Tarascon-sur-Ariège
Montségur
Bagnères-de-Luchon
Mont Valier
Col de Pause
Grotte de Lombrives
Grotte de Niaux
Ornolac
Les Monts d'Olmes
Couflens
Aulus-les-Bains
Verdun
Guzet-Neige
Vicdessos
Les Cabannes
Lordat
Cirque de Cagateille
Cascade d'Arse
Sem
Gestiès
Unac
Ax-les-Thermes

1

4
10 km
5 miles
N
Côte d'Argent
Ste-Eulálie-en-Born
Mimizan-Plage
Labouheyre
Trensacq
Ecomusée de Marquèze
Chemin de Fer Touristique
Sabres
Bias
Solférino
Contis-Plage
St-Julien-en-Born
Mézos
Cap-de-l'Homy Plage
Lit-et-Mixe
Lévignacq
Morcenx
Arengosse
St-Girons-Plage
St-Girons
LANDES
Léon
Castets
Moliets-Plage
Messanges-Plage
Messanges
Vieux-Boucau-les-Bains
Etang de Soustons
Tartas
N. D. de Buglose
Soustons
St Paul les Dax
Etang Blanc
Berceau-de-St Vincent-de-Paul
Laurède
Nerbis
Mugron
Seignosse
Tosse
Hossegor
Montfort-en-Chalosse
Dax
Saubusse
Capbreton
St-Vincent-de-Tyrosse
Œreluy
Maylis
Labenne-Océan
Labenne
Orx
Pomarez
Gaujacq
Pouillon
Brassempouy
Ondres-Plage
St-Martin-de-Hinx
Amou
Peyrehorade
Hastingues
BIARRITZ
BAYONNE
Abbaye d'Arthous
Sorde l'Abbaye
Bellocq
Château de Gramont
Orthez
Côte Basque
Bidart
Bidache
Guéthary
Arcangues
Labastide-Clairence
Salies-de-Béarn
St-Jean-de-Luz
Corniche Basque
Ustaritz
Route Impériale des Cimes
Maslacq
Athos
Ciboure
Hasparren
Larressore
Sauveterre-de-Béarn
Urrugne
St-Pée-sur-Nivelle
Cambo-les-Bains
Grottes d'Istaritz et d'Oxocelhaya
Laàs
Hendaye
Ascain
Espelette
Mourenx
St-Esteben
PYRÉNÉES
Sare
Ainhoa
St-Palais
Navarrenx
Grottes de Sare
Artxamendi
ATLANTIQUES
Bidarray
Gurs
Lucq-de-Béarn
PAYS BASQUE
Ossès
Larceveau
L'Hôpital-Saint-Blais
Mauléon
St-Jean Pied-de-Port
Ordiarp
St-Etienne-de-Baïgorry
St-Jean-de-Vieux
Forêt des Arbailles
Aussurucq
Tardets
Asasp
Ahusquy
Alçay
Etchebar
Défilé d'Escot
Larrau
Ste-Engrâce
Gorges d'Holzarté
Forêt d'Iraty
Gorges de Kakouetta
Vallée d'Aspe
SPAIN
Pic d'Anie
Lescun
E05
E80
A64
A63
117
124

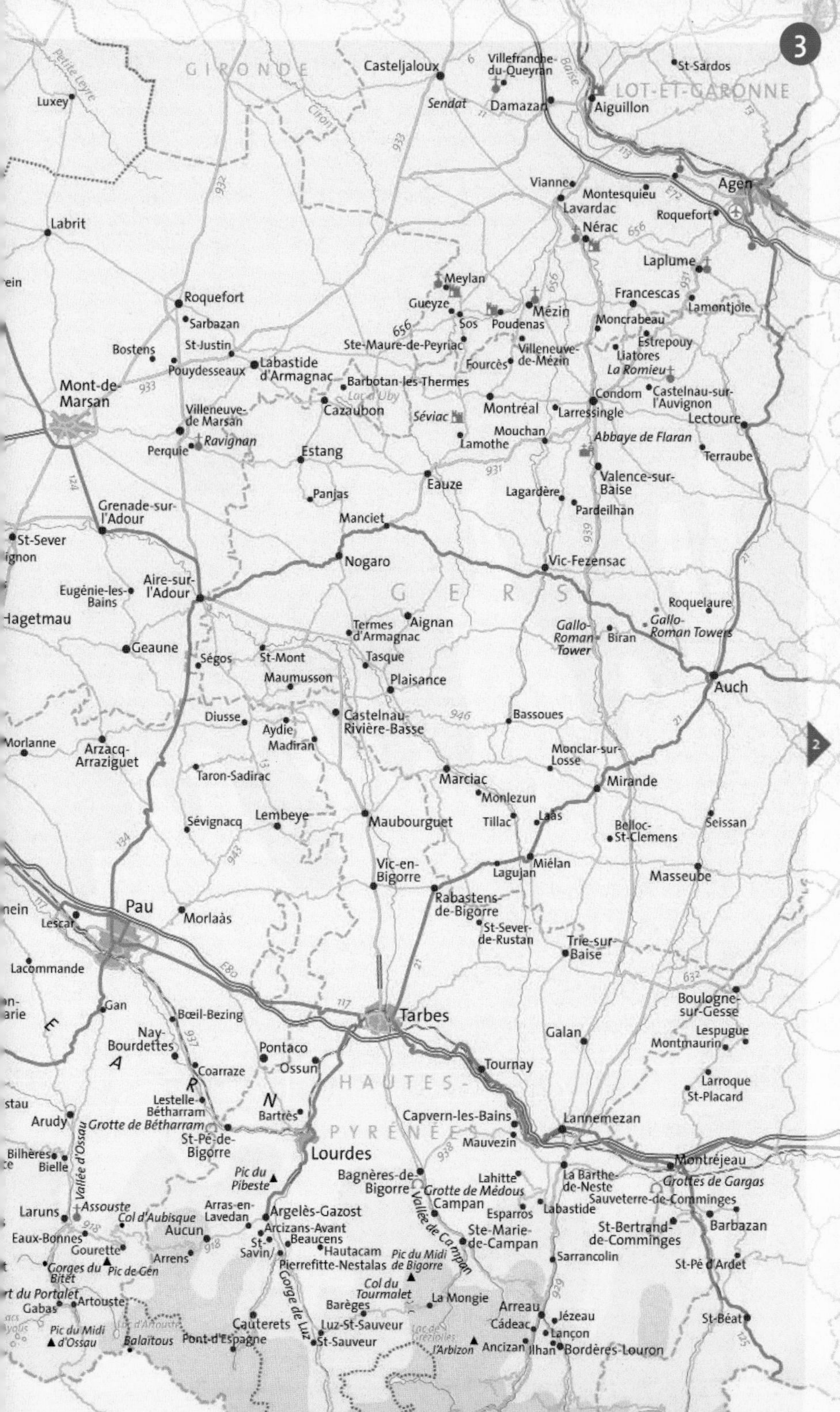

3
GIRONDE
LOT-ET-GARONNE
GERS
HAUTES-PYRÉNÉES
BEARN
Casteljaloux
Villefranche-du-Queyran
Damazan
Aiguillon
St-Sardos
Sendat
Agen
Vianne
Montesquieu
Lavardac
Roquefort
Nérac
Laplume
Luxey
Labrit
Roquefort
Sarbazan
St-Justin
Bostens
Pouydesseaux
Labastide d'Armagnac
Barbotan-les-Thermes
Mont-de-Marsan
Villeneuve-de Marsan
Ravignan
Perquie
Cazaubon
Estang
Panjas
Meylan
Gueyze
Sos
Poudenas
Mézin
Ste-Maure-de-Peyriac
Villeneuve-de-Mézin
Fourcès
Séviac
Montréal
Lamothe
Mouchan
Francescas
Lamontjoie
Moncrabeau
Estrepouy
Liatores
La Romieu
Condom
Castelnau-sur-l'Auvignon
Larressingle
Abbaye de Flaran
Lectoure
Terraube
Valence-sur-Baise
Lagardère
Pardeilhan
Eauze
Manciet
Nogaro
Grenade-sur-l'Adour
St-Sever
Aire-sur-l'Adour
Eugénie-les-Bains
Hagetmau
Geaune
Ségos
St-Mont
Maumusson
Termes d'Armagnac
Aignan
Tasque
Plaisance
Vic-Fezensac
Roquelaure
Gallo-Roman Tower
Biran
Gallo-Roman Towers
Auch
Diusse
Aydie
Madiran
Castelnau-Rivière-Basse
Bassoues
Morlanne
Arzacq-Arraziguet
Taron-Sadirac
Marciac
Monclar-sur-Losse
Mirande
Monlezun
Tillac
Laas
Sévignacq
Lembeye
Maubourguet
Belloc-St-Clemens
Seissan
Vic-en-Bigorre
Lagujan
Miélan
Masseube
Pau
Lescar
Morlaàs
Rabastens-de-Bigorre
St-Sever-de-Rustan
Trie-sur-Baise
Lacommande
Gan
Bœil-Bezing
Nay-Bourdettes
Coarraze
Pontaco
Ossun
Tarbes
Tournay
Galan
Boulogne-sur-Gesse
Lespugue
Montmaurin
Larroque
St-Placard
Lestelle-Bétharram
Grotte de Bétharram
St-Pé-de-Bigorre
Bartrès
Lourdes
Arudy
Capvern-les-Bains
Mauvezin
Lannemezan
Montréjeau
Grottes de Gargas
Bilhères
Bielle
Vallée d'Ossau
Pic du Pibeste
Bagnères-de-Bigorre
Grotte de Médous
Campan
Lahitte
La Barthe-de-Neste
Sauveterre-de-Comminges
Laruns
Assouste
Col d'Aubisque
Aucun
Arras-en-Lavedan
Argelès-Gazost
Esparros
Labastide
St-Bertrand-de-Comminges
Barbazan
Eaux-Bonnes
Gourette
Arrens
St-Savin
Arcizans-Avant
Beaucens
Hautacam
Ste-Marie-de-Campan
Vallée de Campan
Sarrancolin
Gorges du Bitet
Pic de Gen
Pierrefitte-Nestalas
Pic du Midi de Bigorre
St-Pé d'Ardet
Col du Tourmalet
La Mongie
Gabas
Artouste
Barèges
Gorge de Luz
Arreau
Jézeau
St-Béat
Pic du Midi d'Ossau
Balaïtous
Pont d'Espagne
Cauterets
Luz-St-Sauveur
St-Sauveur
Cadéac
Lançon
Ancizan
Ilhan
Bordères-Louron
Lac de Grézioles
l'Arbizon
Petite Leyre
Ciron
Baïse
Lac d'Uby
2

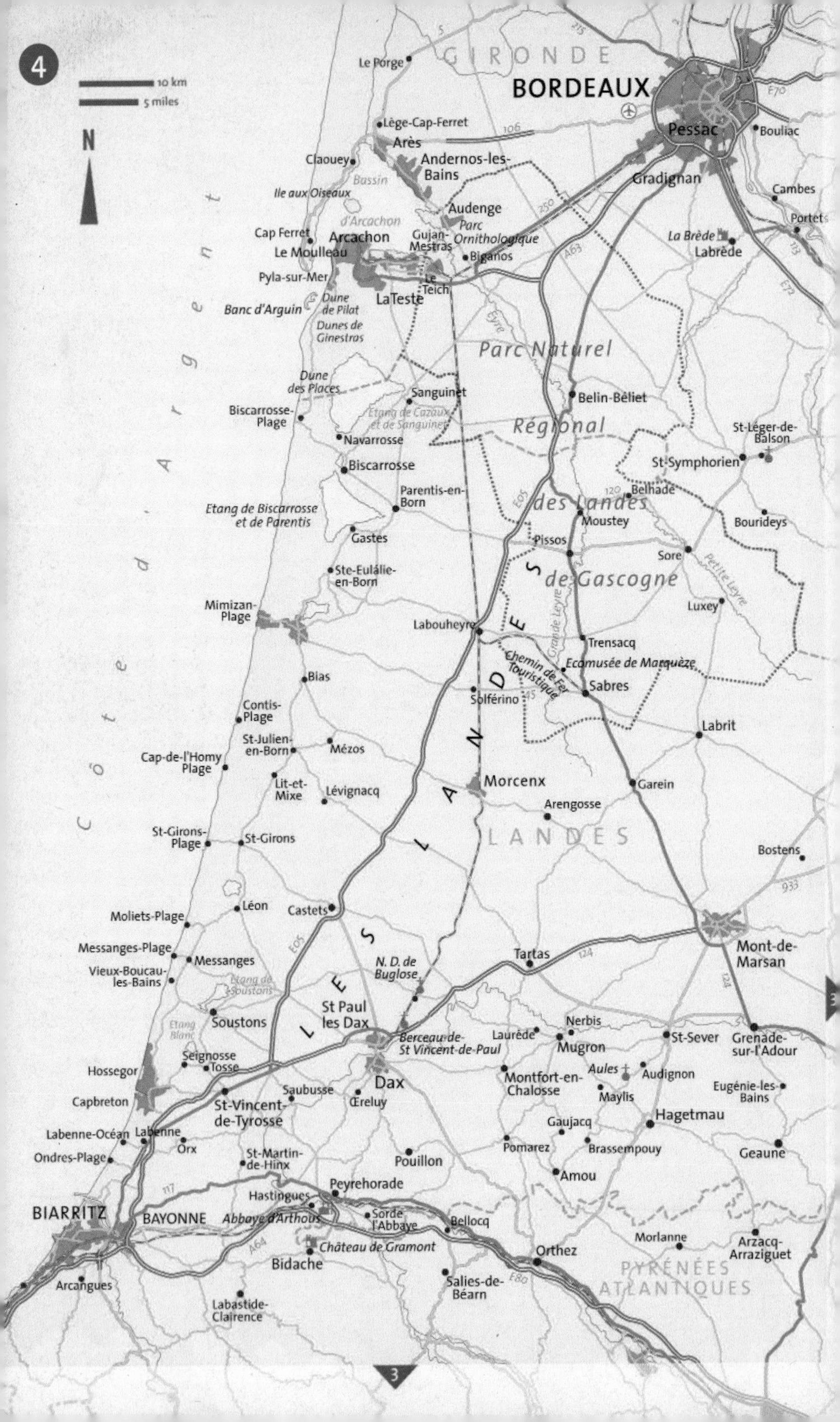

4

10 km
5 miles

N

GIRONDE
Le Porge
BORDEAUX
Pessac
Bouliac
Lège-Cap-Ferret
Arès
Claouey
Andernos-les-Bains
Bassin d'Arcachon
Ile aux Oiseaux
Gradignan
Cambes
Audenge
Parc Ornithologique
Portets
Cap Ferret
Arcachon
Le Moulleau
Gujan-Mestras
Biganos
La Brède
Labrède
Pyla-sur-Mer
Le Teich
LaTeste
Dune de Pilat
Banc d'Arguin
Dunes de Ginestras
Parc Naturel Régional des Landes de Gascogne
Dune des Places
Sanguinet
Etang de Cazaux et de Sanguinet
Belin-Béliet
Biscarrosse-Plage
Navarrosse
St-Léger-de-Balson
St-Symphorien
Biscarrosse
Parentis-en-Born
Belhade
Etang de Biscarrosse et de Parentis
Moustey
Bourideys
Gastes
Pissos
Sore
Ste-Eulalie-en-Born
Petite Leyre
Grande Leyre
Luxey
Mimizan-Plage
Labouheyre
Trensacq
Chemin de Fer Touristique
Ecomusée de Marquèze
Bias
Sabres
Solférino
Contis-Plage
Labrit
St-Julien-en-Born
Mézos
Cap-de-l'Homy Plage
Lit-et-Mixe
Lévignacq
Morcenx
Garein
Arengosse
LES LANDES
LANDES
St-Girons-Plage
St-Girons
Bostens
Côte d'Argent
Léon
Castets
Moliets-Plage
Mont-de-Marsan
Messanges-Plage
Messanges
Tartas
Vieux-Boucau-les-Bains
N. D. de Buglose
Etang de Soustons
Soustons
Etang Blanc
St Paul les Dax
Berceau-de-St Vincent-de-Paul
Laurède
Nerbis
Mugron
St-Sever
Grenade-sur-l'Adour
Seignosse
Tosse
Hossegor
Dax
Montfort-en-Chalosse
Aules
Audignon
Capbreton
Saubusse
Œreluy
Maylis
Eugénie-les-Bains
St-Vincent-de-Tyrosse
Hagetmau
Labenne-Océan
Labenne
Orx
Gaujacq
Ondres-Plage
St-Martin-de-Hinx
Pouillon
Pomarez
Brassempouy
Geaune
Amou
Peyrehorade
Hastingues
BIARRITZ
BAYONNE
Abbaye d'Arthous
Sorde l'Abbaye
Bellocq
Morlanne
Arzacq-Arraziguet
Château de Gramont
Orthez
Bidache
PYRÉNÉES ATLANTIQUES
Arcangues
Salies-de-Béarn
Labastide-Clairence